A Roving Commission

High Flight

Oh, I have slipped the surly bonds of earth,
And danced the skies on laughter-silvered wings;
Sunward I've climbed, and joined the tumbling mirth
Of sun split clouds-and done a hundred things
You have not dreamed of.

I've wheeled and soared and swung high in
The sunlit silence and, hovering there, chased
The shouting wind along and flung my eager
Craft through footless halls of air.

Up, up, the long delirious blue, I've
Topped the windswept heights with easy grace
Where lark, nor even eagle flew.
And while, with silent lifting mind I've trod
The high untrespassed sanctity of space,
Put out my hand—and touched the face of God.

John Gillespie Magee, jnr

A Roving Commission

Kel Palmer

iUniverse, Inc.
New York Lincoln Shanghai

A Roving Commission

Copyright © 2006 by Kel Palmer

iUniverse books may be ordered through booksellers or by contacting:

iUniverse
2021 Pine Lake Road, Suite 100
Lincoln, NE 68512
www.iuniverse.com
1-800-Authors (1-800-288-4677)

ISBN-13: 978-0-595-39189-9 (pbk)
ISBN-13: 978-0-595-83578-2 (ebk)
ISBN-10: 0-595-39189-3 (pbk)
ISBN-10: 0-595-83578-3 (ebk)

Printed in the United States of America

FOR ROSEMARIE with love—for her encouragement and persistence, and for my children and hers so that they might better understand me.

Contents

I lose friends but retain integrity as I scupper an ill advised AEW export programme, I move to a 17 century cottage with a presence, renew my love/hate relationship with India, concentrate on Maritime Patrol aircraft and start commuting to South America, Australia and the Far East. I frighten myself up Everest, see a dance to end all dances, spare a tiger, taste the wonders of the Amazon, and explore Australia looking for an elusive magic. Trouble looms large on the home front.

THORN EMI buys MEL and take me and my lightweight systems to partner Nimrod MPA. I help win a key RAF contract, modernise Searchwater for the Nimrod replacement and initiate Feasibility Studies for ASTOR. I get critical over after sales support, bombard airframe manufacturers with system options, and expand my travel to South Africa, North America, Korea and Japan, now with Rosemarie along. I fall foul of my church, question Christian ethics, and spend a lot of time in London's finest restaurants. As THORN sells out to RACAL, my domestic problems threaten to end my second career at 65.

A special friend risks his neck to keep me on board and I reward him with success on Nimrod MPA and winning the lucrative ASTOR Feasibility Study. Total darkness on the home front with divorce delays, I develop diabetes and finish up with a triple heart bypass operation. I'm back at work in 10 days, get my divorce and marry Rosemarie a month later. We honeymoon in the USA and enjoy my last three years in industry as we travel the world. I sell the Old Forge, we lose ASTOR by default and sheer stupidity, I sample life in "digs" before retiring at 70 on the last day of the 20 century, having been in non-stop employment for 54 years.

In which I fondly express what music and dancing have meant to me throughout my life and relate those pleasures to people, times and places, the names of which you will find engraved indelibly on my heart. Select my own Desert Island discs.

In which I explain how retirement means merely exchanging a big pay cheque for working like a one armed paperhanger on a voluntary basis for every committee and club known to man in an effort to improve their lot in life. I describe my disappointment with men who are as devious and dishonest as anyone I've ever met. I applaud those who are overcoming the historical difficulties and shackles of Wales to rise above the poor hand that location has dealt them. I begin to lose touch with my children and grandchildren, feel the world turning colder and its values deteriorating, but am determined to continue to say what I feel and believe for those that trust me. Above all, I embrace the ever-increasing love that Rosemarie and I have for each other; she truly is my "Many splendoured thing".

In which I take a candid look at repercussions to my book and voice the odd regret, accepting that if I put my goods in the shopwindow I'm declaring open season on all that I write.

PREFACE

This starts as nothing more than a collection of memories; of things done and not done, of successes and failures, of roads taken and of doors never opened; of places, experiences, lessons learned and discarded—but mainly of people. Whether it will become an autobiography I cannot say, but I am reluctant at the outset even to consider giving it so high and windy a title as I ask myself who on earth would have the slightest interest in what JKP has done in and with his life? The bookshelves are full of ghostwritten autobiographies, but all are about celebrities and luminaries—which I am not.

I'm content therefore to see this as the first step in putting my life on record. Not for anyone else's amusement or enlightenment, but just for me and mine when I've gone. A youngish person reading that will ask—as I would have many years ago—"Why do you need to put on paper something that must be so clearly etched in your mind?" The answer, youngish person, is that you'll find memory isn't like that. With age, you become increasingly aware that whole chunks of your life have dimmed in the memory; and if not actually forgotten, have not been revisited as you've got on with the business of living.

Often I find myself regurgitating a regret that tugs at my conscience, until I realise that I paid my dues long ago. Or I find myself wishing I'd done such and such a thing in my life—only to discover when delving into the old grey matter that I *did* do it, or at least the equivalent of what one would now do. Also, recognising with some surprise, that it wasn't in sepia or black and white, but in vivid Technicolor.

So I shan't be starting with any great master plan. I do have reflections of people and places that were special, of achievements and disappointments, of choosing to turn right when I might have turned left. Memories that are highlights, as opposed to life's trivia that I shall consign to the wastebasket of time. I'm prepared to open a few boxes that have lain closed and dust bound for many decades to re-examine past thoughts and actions. Perhaps as I do I'll get a few blinding glimpses of the obvious, seeing things as they really were. More importantly, being able to understand them in the context of their time and therefore being privileged to realise a few more of my dreams and ambitions.

I've never been an avid reader, but I suppose I've read as much as most and have been immensely impressed and influenced by certain writings—be they novels, speeches, words of wisdom, poetry—whatever. If I choose to quote some of those, I shan't consider it plagiarism because surely we all say or write things to impress, persuade, convince and communicate our thoughts and feelings as best we can? There simply cannot be anything nowadays in anyone's English vocabulary that is truly original; we are all consciously or subconsciously a mixture of all we've heard and said and felt over the years. My fault, I submit, will be one of too good a memory, not of deliberate plagiarism. First problem, then—how to finish the starters and get into the main course? Eyes down, look in!

List of Abbreviations/RAF Slang/Foreign Phrases in text

AEW	Airborne Early Warning
AFN	American Forces Network—WW2 radio
AoC	(AoC in C) Air Officer Commanding in Chief
ASTOR	Airborne stand off radar (RAF Sentinel programme)
ATC	Air Training Corps
AWACS	Airborne Warning and Control System
Ex officio	Accommodation allocated to a given post, no waiting list
Garry	Wheeled transport—derives from Arabic for horse/donkey driven 2 wheel cart
GCA	Ground Controlled Approach (Air traffic radar)
GCI	Ground Controlled Interception
HSC	Higher School Certificate—the final exams at school pre-1960
Jankers	Periods of drill and duties meted out as punishments.
JTIDS	Joint Tactical Information Distribution System (sexy comms!)
Jolly	Something done for fun—excuse for a party
JSTARS	(US) Joint Strike and Reconnaissance System
Kipper fleet	Nickname for RAF Maritime Air (Coastal command)
Klicks	Kilometres
MGS	Manchester Grammar School
MPA	Maritime Patrol Aircraft
Mod (PE)	Ministry of Defence (Procurement Executive)
OCTU	Officer Cadet Training Unit
OCU	Operational Conversion Unit, training on the operational role.

OHMS	On Her/His Majesty's Service
PSO	Personal Staff Officer
R&D	Research and Development
RFC	Royal Flying Corps (before becoming RAF, 1st April 1918)
RSRE	Royal Signals and Radar Establishment (Malvern, Worcs.)
SHAPE	Supreme Headquarters Allied Powers Europe (Mons, Belgium)
Toc H	A mainly wartime Christian social service—"drop in" for tea and buns.
VBS	Vincent Black Shadow—famous motor cycle brand
VSTOL	Vertical/Short take-off lift
WRNS	"Wrens"—Women's Royal Naval Service

Animus non integritatem sed facinus cupit	The mind welcomes evil rather than moral uprightness
Carpe Diem	Seize the day
Cueillez des aujourd hui les roses de la vie	Gather ye rosebuds whilst ye may
Forsan et haec olim meminisse iuvabit	One day it may give pleasure to recall even these things
La grace, plus belle encore que la beaute	Grace, even more beautiful than beauty
Laudator temporis acti	Glory of times gone by
Mens sana incorpore sano	A healthy mind in a healthy body
Non mi Ricardo	No memory of that
Nostalgie de la boue	Yearning for mud
Per ardua ad astra	Through difficulties to the stars
Primus inter pares	First among equals
Quien sabe	Who knows
Si j'ai failli, les peines sont presentes	If I did fail, I have the punishment
Si jeunesse savait, si vieillese pouvait	If youth but knew, and old age only could
Verba volent, scripta manta	The spoken word fades, the written remains
Voir la vie en rose	Life through pink spectacles

Introduction

At 8 a.m. on this beautiful Cyprus morning, I came out on the veranda to launch my writings, and here I am at high noon with my paper still blank. It could be that the local Kokinelli brew is to blame; however, this is not a new experience for me because I've found throughout my life that for me to be able to write anything, for pleasure or for profit, I have to be in the mood with the circumstances favourable. My wife Rosemarie claims it is because I was born in the early hours of the morning. I would not call hers an expert or unbiased opinion since my beloved also blames the time of my birth for my penchant for watching late night films, for being a Manchester United fan, and for snoring. But whatever the reason, there are times I simply cannot write a word or compose a sentence. Other times my head is so full of ideas and dreams that I wish I could write a hundred times faster and get it all down on paper.

Another infuriating habit of mine is to wake up in the wee small hours like a box of birds and have a head full of the right phrases, the most elegant expressions, and the most brilliant of arguments and solutions. If only someone in this dynamic technical age would devise a machine that you plugged into your mind to record all this priceless data as you slept, ready for recovery in the morning!

Not that my inability to make sense can be counted as a disaster on this glorious July day in the eastern Mediterranean. After all, I'm still very much at the stage of writing just for me, rather than for external consumption. I'm still exploring my motives for writing at all, still opening up those hidden matchboxes into which one used to put events and stages in one's life in the fond belief that one day one might slide back the cover and consider the contents at a different time in a different place. My difficulty now is in forecasting whether my little matchbox will turn out to be a real Treasure Chest, Pandora's box—or merely a bag of worms!

I've never been one for ignoring problems. With rare exceptions—notably financial matters—I've tended to face up to things. Nevertheless, there are things in my past of which I should not wish to be reminded and for which I feel remorse. Sometimes, out of the blue and inexplicably, such thoughts will come back to me and I utter an involuntary grunt of disapproval or embarrassment. I'm not talking about committing a crime, or of something nasty or unspeakable, but of statements or actions that I know now—if not at the time—must have caused others pain or disappointment, and still might as they would frustrate explanation. Those are places with too many ghosts; ghosts that tug at my memory with eager claws to drag me into dark uncomfortable spots to taunt me with their tales of woe. Experience has taught me not to let them get the upper hand; I must shut my mind to them or be left in turmoil all night with insoluble fears and unrealisable dreams. Beware, reader, lest you think there are no skeletons in your cupboard; believe me, they are best confronted, then put aside and never again brought to mind.

As I prepare to open my memory matchboxes, I have the problem of bridging a gap of many decades. So much has changed since the events took place; I've changed, the whole environment in which they occurred has changed, and many of the people involved are no longer with us. Doubtless, some of the latter I hold in greater esteem or affection than they deserve—something about time and distance blurring the jagged edges. Others, whom I recall I disliked or disdained, probably did not deserve my condemnation. I can be pretty sure of that as I remember a number of confrontations with "sworn enemies" that ended with us becoming the best of friends. Many in my bad books might well have been "in the black" had the pages of our respective lives been turned differently.

I confess that I'm not all that sure either of being able to trust my own memory as even our own testimonies are suspect. We tend to believe that those people who were present at a particular event will hold the key to what actually happened, but eyewitness accounts of important happenings show this not to be the case. We each can tell our version of what we saw, but in time raw experience becomes moulded into anecdote, perspectives become stretched or are shrunk, fine detail becomes blurred, inconsistencies are tidied up, and the bottom line made to taste more palatable as the bitter and unwanted is filtered out. Perhaps in meaning to write one story, I shall turn over the pages of the final draft in months or years to come to find humbly that I've written another. We shall see.

Doubtless I shall be drawn into my "soapbox" topics, I'll leap onto hobbyhorses that I've ridden over the years and become enmeshed in matters that don't really concern me—but on which I nevertheless hold unshakeably stubborn views. How shall I avoid becoming too intense? Can I be both objective and subjective, and will my inevitable digressions spoil the flow for you? I hope not, but please bear with me as I try to write something that you may not wish to read cover-to-cover all in one sitting, but rather look on as a *cache* of goodies into which you may dip as the mood takes you between TV programmes, read until you fall asleep, or prop up against your coffeepot at the breakfast table, picking up my life willy-nilly, as it were. Erratically—as it has been lived—do I hear someone say?

Perhaps I could be more certain of faithfully recounting my life if I had the luxury of tapes and videos on which to call, or if, like Alan Clarke MP, I'd written copious notes on things as they occurred in his complex political and business world. Certainly, diaries are stronger on spontaneity than sober reflection drawn from memory—on which I must call. Few have the talent and personal wealth and privileged background that give one the combination of confidence and power to say or write what one wants—and not to care much about the consequences. In any event, I admit that I was always too busy doing what I was doing to sit back in a detached way and record who had done what to whom and why. But then again, maybe Alan Clarke wasn't that detached, and maybe his strategic plan for financial gain and fame got in the way of what he was being well paid to do at the time?

It's a fruitless exercise to dwell on, that. Firstly, because he produced a very readable set of diaries. Secondly, because his entire life, lifestyle and circumstances were so different to mine as to make comparisons worthless. I can only comment on the world as seen through my eyes; his world was seen through a different coloured lens, his mind was on a different frequency and in so many ways on a different planet. Not better, not worse, not more exciting or more fulfilling, I suggest—just different. You realise later in life that your own life is unique; you may belong to groups that have many similarities, but the vast majority of folk—including those who live in your neck of the woods and share so much with you—are essentially very different. I have no precedents; I am the first Me that has ever been with a unique mix of forces playing on my life.

So however many pages I rescue from my memory, I don't intend to make it a book about J. K. Palmer *per se*, but more an account of a journey through my life in story mode rather than a report. I expect it to betray most of the defects of autobiographies, all the omissions and many of the sins. I'm not qualified, or perhaps I'm too close to it just now, to say whether it will have many or any of the vital virtues; we shall just have to see. A good sign is that already I feel a spirit of adventure beckoning me to write, and not a little restless curiosity spurring me on.

A final thought that springs to mind, assuming my present enthusiasm is undimmed back in soggy old England or waterlogged Wales, is whether, when I come to write Finis in a year or so, I shall have merely revisited some 70 years or learned something about myself and about Life. As the lovely lyrics go:

> *I've looked at life from both sides now,*
> *From up and down, yet still somehow,*
> *It's life's illusions I recall, I really don't know life at all.*

I can say truthfully, as Charles Dickens said so eloquently, "Constituted to do the work that is in me, I am a man full of passion and energy, and my own wild way that I must go is often—at the best—wild enough." I have been blessed with incredible energy and I have never lacked passion, but I'll pass on the "wild" unless that word in 1858 was closer in meaning to "shy" and "untamed" rather than "angry" or "licentious"!

Some 215 years ago, the Scot, who so many of his countrymen seem anxious to disown, observed, "A chield's amang you takin' notes, and faith he'll prent it." He started his autobiography thus:

> "After you have perused these pages, should you think them trifling and impertinent, I only beg leave to tell you that the poor author wrote them under some twitching qualms of conscience, arising from suspicion that he was doing what he ought not to do—a predicament he has more than once been in before."

Those words of Robbie Burns will do for me.

1

JOHN KELVIE PALMER

(A potted version to whet, or blunt, your appetite)

When I finally stopped writing this story, I thought it might assist the reader if I did what my first form-master preached at Grammar School: "First I tells 'em what I'm going to tell 'em, then I tells 'em, then I tells 'em what I told 'em". So in this chapter I offer you a skeleton map through my 70-odd years; feel free to leave and join the track as you wish.

Beginnings

I can't remember being born anymore than you can, but I'm advised by them that should know that I was born in Wilmslow, Cheshire, at one minute after midnight on 10th June 1930, to Ellen and Jack Palmer, housewife and Market Gardener respectively. My elder brother, Roy, died at 6 a.m. the same morning. I grew up in the so-called "Garden Estate" of Wythenshawe in Manchester where, in spite of WW II, I shared an idyllic childhood with so many children of my own age. Surrounded by beautiful wooded open country with all the delights that a boy could envisage in the 30s/40s, those were the days when the young could play anywhere without danger and without the lure of TV or PCs to detract from living a healthy and full life. There was little money but great fun.

The Forties

Junior school was a bit of a blur, but I somehow won a scholarship to Manchester Grammar at the age of 11 and proceeded to cover myself with glory as a centre forward, fast bowler and speedy wing ¾, whilst my Maths and French teachers became suicidal in their efforts to improve me academically. In 1946, with shaky Higher School Certificates in the bag, University wasn't an option. But I'd had a few experiences that had given me the yen to fly—so I joined the RAF. Being only 16 I first had to learn a trade; I chose Radar (back to the bloody maths!) and

3 years later amazed myself and half of Lincolnshire by graduating and being recommended for flying training and commissioning.

By now a few things in my life had taken shape, some never to change. I had a great liking for most team sports and opened the bowling in the RAF with an old school chum, "Dicky" (Brian) Statham, later of Lancashire and England fame. I signed as an amateur for Matt Busby at Manchester United and am a United nut to this day with a wife, 4 children and 12 grandchildren equally smitten. Rugby too got into my blood at MGS and I later represented the Combined Services, guested for home club Sale and marauded in the Leicester pack as my weight increased and my speed decayed. I was an accomplished boxer until a wise man told me that flying and damage to the eyes don't mix, and I was a dab hand at the sprints and high jump/triple jump either side of twenty before specialising very successfully at the quarter mile distance. For some reason, I was useless in the gym and always hated training for any sport for the sake of training—as opposed to coaching.

When at last I realised girls were different, I developed a passion for dark-haired, long-legged creatures of the opposite sex. So it's not surprising that my teenage heart-throb was a feisty Joan Rowlands from Stockport, my favourite film person (who I know well and still keep in touch with) is dancer Cyd Charisse, and my long-suffering wife Rosemarie is spectacularly attractive. My liking for long legs also extends to dogs, and I have had the honour of having been owned by a succession of Afghan hounds—all grace, power and affection—even when looking down a haughty snout.

The Fifties

Life in the RAF in the '50's for a young Flying Officer was deliciously mad—based in Germany (which then *really was* a foreign country), flying the new jet aircraft just entering service, skiing in Bavaria, and a diet of German beer and wurst. A social life *par excellence* for which, if I had to live it all over again, I wouldn't have the energy! Like most young officers I couldn't afford a car until, in 1956, I acquired the car of my dreams—a 1953 Riley 2½ litre saloon in British Racing Green with a black leather roof and a top speed, downhill with a following wind, of 70 mph (supersonic for those days). My love of sporty cars ended abruptly with the arrival of Palmer Ma' closely followed by Palmer Mi'. There simply wasn't enough cash or time to spend on cars for other than getting from A to B. A journey I made often in hope, always with anticipation.

As one grows older, one's perspective changes, and it's hard to remember why and how you did, what you did, so many years ago. Memory plays strange tricks; indeed, for some, the older they get, the more vivid are their memories of things that never happened at all! One remembers the big events, but sometimes the detail is blurred and it helps to sit on a winter's evening with a dram of malt, room heavy with smoke, Afghan at one's feet, and look long into the roaring fire 'til the embers glow red. A fire is our magic crystal in which we see visions and dream dreams; one may see a face, hear a voice, swim in the deep waters of an old romance, feel a thrill or a chill, and be transported to days long ago in a world beyond return. "Footsteps echo in the memory to a door we never opened." The happiest and most contented of us are surely those who have few doors left unopened.

We all have clear recollections of truly momentous happenings. Most of us know exactly where we were when we heard that JFK had been shot, that Princess Diana had perished and, doubtless from now on, when the terrorists flew into the twin towers. February 6th 1958 was just such a date for Flight Lieutenant Palmer who was flying in his Meteor jet over the wintry hills of the Black Forest. At around 4 p.m. I received an RT call from my CO back in Rutland. He said, "John, you'll want to know that the Manchester United plane has crashed at Munich. Sorry to convey bad news." There was no way of getting more information as I flew back to England with a thousand ifs and maybes running through my mind. Was it a take-off accident from which they'd all walked away, or a collision in which they'd all died?

The answer was written on my boss's grim face as I taxied in and pushed open the canopy. For a non-football fan, it's probably hard to understand why such an accident, however tragic in itself, should affect so many people. But the memory is vivid because, as these pages will reveal, football and Manchester United have played a great part in my life. The whole football world was shocked by Munich and Manchester was, for months, a city in mourning. The ripples still run to this day when low-life from Leeds who call themselves football fans, chant "Munich, Munich!" when they visit Old Trafford.

The 50's were blissfully happy days in the RAF. The flying was exciting and fulfilling, largely unburdened by today's ultra-cautious approach, limitations on flying hours, and restrictions as to where, when, and how low military aircraft can operate. There was also an identifiable and extremely potent enemy that threatened along a border from the Arctic Circle to the Mediterranean. A very different sort of military experience to that faced now by British ground troops trying to find a terrorist needle in an Afghanistan haystack or keep control in the cauldron of Iraq. For a young man, life on an operational Squadron and in an Officer's Mess was a great experience and adventure. It was before the days when air force wives went out to work, everyone lived on base, and there was no talk of mortgages or worrying about what one was going to do in old age. Life was to be lived and enjoyed, whether in the UK or at one of many stations overseas.

An overseas tour in Germany, Singapore, Cyprus or the Gulf meant 3 years in the sun or in an interesting part of the world, with tax-free cars and liquor. A wonderful experience for wives and children. Some of the credit for that must go to The Warsaw Pact. They were the *raison d'etre*, the common cause, the need to have the very best equipment in service, the reason to keep everyone on their toes. That special time only spanned some 35 years; today's air force has changed dramatically and those who served then should count their blessings.

The Sixties

The 60's was probably the most interesting period in my flying career. Folklore has it that they were "the Swingin' Sixties", but at the time one is too busy living, too involved with the *now* to bother unduly about the future. I started that decade living with my family in Texas where I flew the most modern fighters in the USAF. Highlights of that tour included the boast that I'd been to every State in the Union, and my ejection one dark night over the Pacific from an aeroplane that didn't want to fly anymore. I was plucked by helicopter from the sea in a smelly net and dumped unceremoniously like a fish on the deck of an aircraft carrier. Someone had a sense of humour, as 3 months later I converted to fly the superb Phantom off the vast decks of the US carriers whilst criss-crossing the Pacific between San Diego and points west. Life on a US carrier was certainly interesting, though I must admit, not as enjoyable as flying at sea with the Royal Navy. Our Senior Service flies and plays equally as hard as the Americans—but with enviable style and flair.

Nevertheless, my short time with the US Navy was thoroughly rewarding, both professionally and culturally. There was a lot of spare time on board ship, either sitting in a cockpit on stand by (during which I caught up with my reading), or sitting alone above the bow under the flight deck, just sea-watching; looking ahead at "Grey waters, vast as an area of prayer", waiting for something with eyes peeled for the abundant marine life. At my farewell dinner, my Admiral referred to me as "That tall elegant Limey aviator who brought tone to what might otherwise have been a vulgar brawl". Those words spoken in a light-hearted way carried a lot of respect and meant a lot to a British officer serving with a foreign service

The American influence

America has played a huge part in my life. It's foolish to generalise about a nation so big and so diverse, but my view of America and Americans when I lived there in the 60's, was much the same as I found them to be in the 80's and 90's when travelling to the US on business. A land and a people of amazing contrasts and multiple contradictions. Few places on earth can match the incredible beauty and majesty of Monument Valley, the Grand Canyon or the Na Pali coast. Few people are as courteous and generous, few are prepared to work as hard as they, and few remain as loyal to their principles, beliefs and their national flag. They have an education system that gives anyone, of any background, a chance to better themselves; one that even allows them to keep on failing without opprobrium en route to eventual success. They have perfected fast food whilst not abandoning Cordon Bleu, and have a great belief in providing real value for money accommodation and travel, and in making home ownership the affordable norm.

On the downside, there's a disturbing racial problem that, in some States, will not go away. There's an unhealthy emphasis on always having to win which, whilst achieving the desired competitive edge, has the negative impact of cheating, bullying, whistle blowing and pushing the meek into the background. That attitude flourishes in the military and in business. Americans will do almost anything not to be seen as losers; they'll bend the rules, change and disown their representatives, and inject delay and uncertainty into a programme or campaign to ensure that, in the end, the American way and American interests will prevail. To most Americans, what the rest of the world is doing is of no interest. Their regional stations carry little foreign news unless it affects the US or has worldwide impact such as the death of Princess Diana. Whatever Americans *talk* about, they are always *thinking* of themselves.

The Seventies

In the 70's, I travelled between the scores of RAF stations worldwide and lived in Germany, Cyprus, and the UK. I flew mainly fighters, but also the fast low-level strike/attack aircraft with a one-way ticket to Russia while the Cold War became hot. As a Squadron Commander one flies less than a junior officer, and as a Station Commander—if you're lucky to be one—flying is even less available. The higher the rank, the less one flies—with some consolation coming from the interesting and challenging Staff jobs in large HQs like NATO, The Pentagon, and the politically-dominated posts in Whitehall.

The Eighties

In the 80's, as Chief of Nuclear Plans at SHAPE in Belgium, I would have been immersed in the immediate and crucial conduct of nuclear operations in Europe had deterrence failed. What type and yield of nuclear weapon was to be delivered by whom, where and when. It never happened, thank God, and now with the benefit of 20 odd years of hindsight, I am convinced that had it come to a nuclear exchange of blows, it would have resulted in the biggest cock-up in military history. But that's another story. That post in Mons made up my mind to retire early, but the seeds had been sown during my previous tours in Whitehall and as Director of the RAF College at Cranwell. The air force I'd joined and loved was changing, and so was I. The combination of not feeling challenged, and of frustration at the multi-national, US dominated, ineffectual eunuch that was NATO, persuaded me to seek pastures new and take early retirement.

Nulli secundus

Looking for pegs on which to hang one's actions is notoriously unreliable. But without doubt, the fundamental reason for my decision to resign was my wish to spend the rest of my life with one Rosemarie Yvonne Knight (nee Evans). This again is another story, but it is a fact that my life changed forever at around 1 p.m. on Sunday, 6th June 1971. On that typically beautiful June day in Cyprus, I'd taken my family to the Officers Mess for the Sunday ritual of the Band Concert. As I waited in the foyer, a young and exquisitely attractive woman appeared with her daughter at the Buffet. Bells rang and the earth moved, never to stop ringing and moving.

I'd always loved the sun-kissed island of Cyprus. I first went there in the days of Suez and returned many times on exercises or when staging further East. Its charm for me lay in the wonderful mixture of climate, stunning scenery and historical interest. Even today, with its bright lights and tourist traps, one only has to drive a few miles off the main road to be alone in a carob grove, a vineyard, a hillside of waving corn—with only the tinkling of goat bells to disturb the golden silence. A magical island, full of lovely people, a Mecca that calls one back again and again and never fails to satisfy and delight.

When I was posted there in April '71 at the age of 41, I did not expect I should fall so deeply, so contentedly, in love. Strange that I should have had to wait so long for it. It is the illusion of all lovers to think themselves unique and their words immortal. Yet the dream that Rosemarie and I shared was a reality, a wonderful dream of life and love, of laughter and tears, and all the things that those of my generation see as good and equal under Heaven. In the beautiful words of Han Suyin, "We have not missed, you and I, the Many Splendoured thing." (One day I must try to describe a feeling so rare, to make sense of how one can live for so many years in blissful ignorance of what life could be at a different time, a different place and with a different partner. I must make time to do so, because if I don't, she "that has immeasurably enriched my life" will have a few words to say.)

The Defence Industry

In 1983, I left the RAF after 37 years and within days was working in the Defence Industry. I've since wondered why I made a beeline for industry and didn't do something else. All that I can come up with is that it seemed a good idea at the time! We make our big decisions in life based on what we know and what we're doing and experiencing at the time. Years later, we've forgotten most of the ingredients, most of the emotion and pressures that pointed or drove us down a particular path. Perhaps we'll never know what might have happened had we chosen a different route; perhaps, like the fate that awaits us all, it's best that we don't know? "Two roads diverged in a wood, and sorry I could not travel both…"

I found the transition to civilian life painless. I was working on programmes that I'd initiated in the RAF or with which I was familiar. I had regular contact with the RAF and was able to beg, borrow or steal flying on a variety of aircraft in a variety of roles. As always I had a lot to say about everything. I am blessed with boundless energy and a trait of not shutting up even when I've finished, or others think I should have finished. I soon discovered why the British Services seldom got the equipment they wanted, at the time they wanted it, or at the price they'd paid for it. Most of the directors of the four companies for which I eventually worked had little idea of what their company was selling; they were interested only in profit margins or the size of their golden handshake. Few had been to Charm School; even fewer had any idea about Management. To them that was a dirty word.

It's may be unfair to compare the work ethics of RAF and Industry. In the RAF, everyone worked to a common aim. There were few hidden agendas, a clearly defined chain of command and pecking order, and well-proven rules, procedures and regulations to follow. Undoubtedly, too, there was honesty, integrity and a sense of duty, much of which came from good training and excellent career management. Teamwork and mutual trust were endemic. Fulfilment, rather than profit, was the goal.

In industry, such loyalty was rare. People looked after their own interests, tended to be very secretive about what they did, and spent much of their time building an audit-proof trail. Few records were kept, even of key technical matters, because if there were records and anything went wrong, there could always be a witch-hunt; a search for the guilty and persecution of the innocent! One could tell the time to the minute by the arrival over the threshold, or heels disappearing through the door, of a high percentage of staff. It was odd how many times the same people went sick on a Friday or Monday, especially if next to a Bank Holiday or in the summer. However well you got on with those around you, and however much you enjoyed the work, you always felt like the proverbial tap waiting to be screwed. If asked how many people worked at GEC, I was apt to reply, "On a good day-about 25%." I doubt if I exaggerated.

Even so, there was much to be enjoyed and real satisfaction to be gained, especially the opportunity to travel. Travel in the RAF had been extensive, but confined to places where military establishments or Headquarters and Government offices were located. There were countries one could never visit; places over which you flew often but never really saw. With Industry that changed, especially when I controlled market research and was able to decide who travelled where and when. Between 1983 and 2000, I upped my tally of countries visited to 110, on every Continent, with the welcome bonus in the last 8 years of being able to take Rosemarie, often to places not then on the tourist map.

From early days of acute embarrassment at MGS, I had no aptitude for languages. I readily became proficient in ordering another beer and in asking "do you come here often" in everything from Spanish to Swahili, but I survived because the rest of the world (excluding the French, of course) learn English as their first or second language. Rosemarie encountered no such problems; she was capable of spending money and making herself understood anywhere in the world!

They say that things that have greatly concerned and bothered one should never be allowed to recur once settled. They should be left alone, even in thought. Such a period in my life occurred between 1995–97. A combination of a bitter divorce, serious health problems, financial upheaval, family separation, and re-marriage left me shaking my head in disbelief at much of what had happened. I started a new life in Wales with Rosemarie; far different from the life I had been leading. But the key was being with Rosemarie, more in love even than when we met 30 years ago in Cyprus. Against that all else pales.

Those who can face what is actually before them; unburdened by the past, undistracted by the future, and who make the best use of their lives—these are they I submit who have found the secret of contentment. Perhaps for John Kelvie Palmer there are still a few more chapters to be written? Let's see how it goes whilst there's life in the old dog, eh?

Highlights

Identifying highlights over 75 years and a working life of 60 years is difficult, but it might help set the scene for what follows. A man who travels becomes a snapper-up of local customs, dialects, traditions, and history. He sees hundreds of sights that impress him, but relatively few that he can never forget. Those places and associated experiences stay with him and pour out their pleasing memories again and again. I offer you mine:

Most interesting cities:—London, New York, Rome, Rio de Janeiro, Bangkok, Cape Town, San Francisco, Venice; with a qualified mention for Madrid, Cairo, Berlin, Shanghai, Istanbul, Prague, Budapest, Paris, Jerusalem, Washington DC, and Sydney.

"Never again—if I can help it":—Liverpool, Lima, Caracas, Manila, Liverpool, Lagos, Beijing, Karachi, Algiers, Miami, The Gulf States, Jakarta and Liverpool!

Most spectacular scenery:—Monument Valley, Grand Canyon, Guilin, the Himalayas, the Bavarian Alps from Berchestgarden, Victoria Falls, the cliffs of Na Pali, the Peruvian Andes, Cape Town across the Bay, and Western Scotland from 500ft on an autumn evening.

Most rewarding trips: An African Game Park at dawn and dusk, a dugout canoe ride up the Amazon in the rainy season, a cruise off Kauai with the dolphins and whales in December, days under canvas 21,000 ft up Everest, a trawl round southern Tasmania.

Biggest letdowns: Ayer's Rock, Tokyo, Dublin, The Little Mermaid, Great Wall of China, Moscow, Norwegian anything, Aberystwyth, French femmes, Welsh food, Chinese food in China, Italian honesty, Casablanca's nightlife.

Then there are places and sights that linger long in your mind and on which you spend many hours and much money trying to capture on film from different angles, at different times, and with different lighting (only to find they're "saved" forever upstairs):

A tiger aprowl in the bush
    Eilean Donan Castle on a cumulus-cloudy day
        Monument Valley at sundown looking east
            A formation of playful leaping dolphins
                The Taj Mahal at dawn across the swirling river
                    The cobalt flash of a Kingfisher on shimmering waters

A full moon over the Sphinx
    A spectacular elegant Afghan Hound at top speed on green grass
        Neuschwanstein Castle in autumn
            The seventh wave breaking on Luminai beach
                Jets arriving on the heaving deck of a carrier
A golden English hillside of waving wheat
    An angry black cobra awaiting his strike
        A tropical buddleia awash with butterflies
            A busy rushing bubbling gurgling mountain stream
                A Cormorant fisherman on the Lijiang
High on a hill over Hong Kong harbour; the mournful sound of a ship's siren
    A formation of Red Arrows seen from the wing position
        The massed bands of the Highland Regiments in full regalia
            Old Trafford as the teams emerge from the tunnel
                A frisky twitchy Robin in the fresh snow
                    Summer twilight in a Cotswold village

Next, those things that make you scratch your head disbelievingly and question, "Was that really me?" Things you did that make you ask, "How-or why-did I do that?" Was it ignorance, nerve, bravery, arrogance, plain stupidity, or machismo?

- At 14—Climbing into a World War 2 fighter cockpit and flying around Blackpool Tower, crouched behind the pilot's seat.

- At 17—Shinning up a Wembley drainpipe on Cup Final day in my RAF uniform and big boots, 'cos I didn't have a ticket.

- At 19—Being bitten by a King Cobra and running a mile in the pitch dark to find help.

- At 21—Sitting on a wild gusty Irish night in candlelight, waiting for a ghost.

- At 29—Hunting crocodiles from a flat-bottomed boat in Kenya.

- At 31—Punching the star of the Green Bay Packers football team in a San Francisco bar, with the rest of the pack queuing up for English blood.

- At 33—Being teased by Princess Margaret that I was enjoying myself too much as I tried to extricate her heel from a crack in the concrete.

- At 41—Landing on an Omani hilltop to deliver supplies, only to find the Yemenis had occupied it during the night!

- At 50—Telling President Reagan that he was "a bad actor".

- At 64—Paying a Russian pilot $100 for a ride in his SU29.

- At 68—Doing a bungee jump 6 months after a triple heart bypass.

- At 75—Abseiling down the tallest building in Wales.

One of the most intriguing aspects of life is how long the deepest memories stay with us; we never know their true value until they have undergone the test of time. Perhaps we should not trust memory; some say it's a net full of holes through which even the most beautiful prizes can slip. But however many memory gems are lost or temporarily mislaid, a great many have a way of popping up when you least expect them. Some of the most frequent visitors to my vacant brain include:

- Walking into the Great Hall at Manchester Grammar (it still gives me a tingle).

- Crashing on my first solo, standing up to my arse in plywood, saluting and saying, "Sorry Sir."

- Putting on my RAF officer's uniform for the first time.

- Taking my Dad to his first and only Cup Final at Wembley.

- Skiing down the length of the Zugspitz without falling once.

- Sailing on the Queen Mary and seeing the Statue of Liberty emerge from the mist.

- The look on my Mum's face as the Queen pinned a medal on me in Buck. House.

- Watching a shark fin break the water 6 feet in front of me.

- Being a ceremonial night guard for Winston Churchill's lying-in-state.

- My youngest son scoring the winning goal in the Youth Cup Final.

- My youngest daughter jumping her horse Oscar in a Cross Country race.

- Watching my eldest son graduate from Sandhurst.

- A ghostly encounter of the friendly kind.

- The glow of a Canyonland sunset on Rosemarie's face and the wind in her hair.

- Skippering a Rugby team with Gareth Edwards as my number nine.

- That split second transformation when your parachute opens and a deafening silence succeeds noise, confusion, disorientation and fear.

- Rosemarie's face on seeing the Grand Canyon for the first time, again when I awoke from my triple-bypass, and the moment she and I were pronounced man and wife.

- Winning a £1.2B contract for British industry at the eleventh hour.

- The last 3 minutes of the 1999 European Cup Final versus Bayern Munich.

- The sight of Britain being truly Great on the day of the Queen's Jubilee.

- A sporting double over Australia; Wilkinson's last gasp dropped goal in the World Cup and the 2005 Test Match victory.

- A Royal cocktail party in St James's Palace in 2004 for Unsung Heroes.

2

OFF THE BEATEN TRACK

Having given that skeleton of my life, I shall find it tricky as I put flesh on the bones to keep everything in sequence and context as wise editors have told me I must do. But then one gets much conflicting advice and for once in my life I feel justified in doing it my way and not bothering overmuch about the chronology. When I started to write, it was easy to promise that I would root around in the darkest corners of my inner self to relate a story that was interesting, edifying and amusing. I was able to justify my intent since I alone know what has happened in my life and what my feelings have been at the time. Not nearly so clear was the way in which I should couch the tome. Should it be a solemn, "warts and all" account, or a light-hearted relaxed stroll through the years such as one might convey discreetly to a friend? As my thoughts have materialised, I've debated how best I might pass on interesting information in skeletal form, rather than in volumes of overweight turgid prose. How shall I avoid being snared by trivia as my mind latches onto insignificant detail? I squirm with embarrassment when I recall how my Mum in her later years would recount the same story again and again with undiminished enthusiasm. I remind myself not to go down that road.

One surprising bonus that has emerged is the state of my memory. Apart from the odd blank, my memory has improved to the point where not only can I easily recall people, places, and events, but I can remember emotions and my state of mind at the time. The memory bank that I have uncovered is like a huge rambling mansion through which I can wander at will, through countless rooms and corridors each containing different treasures of the past and painted in different colours. I go into the house as often as I choose, turn a different key and always find another little room tucked away up a hidden staircase that contains long forgotten delights and the occasional ghost. There are no cobwebs. Miss Haversham did not live here. All old folk must have such a house at their disposal; how sad they must be if they've lost the key or the appetite to explore it.

This is an appropriate spot to mention a subject of which I know little, and which strangely has begun to affect me only recently. I refer to the state of dream-land, those pillow-time thoughts and reflections in the lap of Morpheus that lovers claim to have and which to experience, or so the songwriters tell us, we merely fall asleep to be whisked away on their magic carpet. Until now, I have hardly ever dreamed a dream that lingered in my mind for more than a few seconds. "They fly forgotten as a dream fades at the opening day." I have only dreamed at all when I've eaten heavy and late; I've never dreamt in colour, never recognised a face or a voice, or experienced pain or smell or any emotion. It has never occurred to me that I might be able to influence what or whom I dream about. So why in old age are my dreams beginning to make sense, dreams that I can recall vividly for hours or days, and in which the people are people I know or recognise? Last night I dreamt I'd been in an accident and my leg was being amputated, but not by doctors or nurses. I actually felt the pain of the saw and recognised some of the people. Last week I took a famous TV personality to a spectacular waterfall and forgot to bring him back. I felt genuine remorse, made all the worse by seeing him brought in by friends in a distressed state and then hearing them make unkind remarks about me (as I am now and in what I do). I awoke with a start, and buried my head in the pillows to get back to sleep and continue the dream. But this time I was in a garden I knew well, with a young lady dressed beautifully in a summer suit and sun hat, the colours of which are imprinted on my mind. I could even tell you that the fragrance she wore was Chanel No 5 and that when she smiled she made my heart jump with joy. When I awoke I could still smell her perfume on my pillow and hear the ring of her laughter.

I had not been drinking, I've never taken a drug in my life, I'm not on any unusual or temporary medicine and for the past three nights I've not eaten anything after 6 p.m. This change in my sleeping habits does not concern me in the least, but I am wondering if my rooting around in my old house and opening up all the matchboxes and other treasure chests might not have disturbed the residue, relics, and odds and ends of my memory. Is that possible, I wonder, and if so, could there be more to come? Once I was a deep sleeper, now I'm a reluctant one that finds his pillow full of worries, of things done and not done, of conundrums, qualms and twinges of guilt.

Nevertheless, my exploration is well underway and I've yet to find anything to dissuade me from digging deep into the past. My bravado I admit is tempered by the certainty that I could embarrass and hurt other people, with the probability that I've misjudged many things. I must also query whether I'm a fit person to record my own life, since any autobiography must include a degree of presumption that, whoever picks up the book tomorrow, or in 50 years, will find the memoirs striking the right chords? If, for instance, I write about the thoughts of a footballer as he prepares to take a decisive penalty kick in a Cup Final, will that engage the readers interest as much as the dismay of the crowd or the financial loss to his club if he misses?

And which of my journeys shall I recount? Everyone has two journeys in life. One an outer journey with it's many incidents and milestones. The other, his or her inner journey with a secret history of its own. I expected there would be some sticky passages; even so, being brutally honest about everything is not as easy as I anticipated when the warm breezes of the Mediterranean were turning the turquoise sea into dancing flecks of sunlight, and Rosemarie and I were in our heaven. Being brutally honest to oneself is even harder when it comes to writing what amounts to a "confession". It's one thing to face up to an error you've made, to castigate yourself in private, to blush with remembered discomfort, and feel genuine regret. It's quite another, I'm finding, to record faithfully the raw experience.

Shooting a Line?

To answer that question, let's start with something fundamental to any autobiographer. An old adage warns, "Lest men believe thy tale untrue, keep probability in view." People have remarked that I appear to have had so many experiences, so many things have happened to me that don't happen to other people, and challenged me to explain why that is so. Well, I certainly plead guilty to being something of a raconteur, often making a good story better with a touch of embellishment here and there. What's the harm in that when most of the things our politicians say should be prefaced "Once upon a time", whilst anything said by a solicitor should be taken with a pinch of salt?

Detractors direct their criticism at experiences that I've recounted, with "A likely story!" type of comment. Well, perhaps my experiences are the richer because I am a pushy, inquisitive, stubborn, and persistent chap in getting involved in situations and with people that interest me. Also, I am sometimes propelled by overwhelming impulses that I know, even as they hit me, I must follow. But then my life experience and my professional and social backgrounds have ensured that I am never overawed or tongue-tied by any personality however famous and important, or by any circumstances however dire. I've felt equally comfortable in Buckingham Palace or a country market; able to converse easily with the Prime Minister or a local Trade Union official, equally at home in a morning suit or a pair of overalls. More to the point, when I have found myself in situations uncomfortable for others, or me, I've recognised the awkwardness and been able to retire gracefully without loss of face. Of course I've had the odd rebuff and red face—but surprisingly few. I've never shirked a direct showdown with a critic, most of whom I've found cease to be articulate or fearsome in face-to-face confrontation.

Being There

Certain people and places that I've seen on film or read about have intrigued me, so I have targeted them and made the opportunity to visit them or talk to them to get closer to my subject. My time in industry, for instance, was a wonderfully convenient passport to the world. Travel to all points of the compass was almost my *raison d'etre*, and without incurring extra expense to the Company, or me, it became relatively simple to make a detour, to follow a routing that took me somewhere I would not normally visit. For instance, a business trip from Sydney, Singapore, Bangkok, Delhi, London might easily route via Bali or Kathmandu. A Beijing, Hong Kong, Cape Town, London itinerary might include Seychelles and Guilin. A return from Sydney to London via Los Angeles could transit Tahiti or Honolulu. It all jots up to experience.

Then it was a matter of how you chose to spend your time. In 1986, eight Brits and Americans toured the Far East on a marketing campaign; seven preferred the bar and swimming pool of the luxury hotels or the expensive city shops. The eighth, JKP, hired a car in Delhi and drove out to an Indian village in the jungle, tracked down a snake charmer and his little friends, and spent all day frightening himself to death and meeting the friendliest folk imaginable.

In Taipei, whilst the rest of his party explored the seedy seamy cellars and finished up with aching heads and a worrying rash, he found his way to a ballroom straight out of the Come Dancing, Victor Sylvester era, with a spacious polished wooden floor and tall elegant Chinese girls who danced the waltz and fox trot in true 40's/50's style. It is a truism that "He travels fastest who travels alone", whilst *off piste* is more exciting than the beaten track. Sometimes you have to *make* life happen or it can easily pass you by.

London Life

As for meeting people, I had the considerable advantage of spending many years living in, working in, or visiting London. Few cities in the world combine the centre of Government and the Military with a mix of attractions, hotels, theatres, sporting venues, restaurants and shops to attract the famous, the notorious and the interesting. Once you know where to go, you are seldom disappointed. New

York, Los Angeles, and possibly Paris and Vegas, are the other main talent-spotting Mecca's. All were on my regular business travel schedule. Mindful of course of their rights to privacy, it is surprising how many famous people will openly and warmly welcome an approach or a cheerful greeting. The haughty "Don't touch me-don't even look at me" attitude of screen stars like Joan Collins or TV personalities like Bruce Forsyth are remarkably rare.

Forgetting to remember

Memory may be a paradise from which we cannot be driven, but it may also be a hell from which we cannot escape. Here again, individually we are what we are, but a blinding glimpse of the obvious that struck me as I delved deep into the past, was the capacity of the human mind to bury those bits of it of which we don't wish to be reminded. Some are able immediately to consign a bad experience to the "never happened" drawer. I have the suspicion that whilst that might be a way of moving through life without taking on too much pain, it may well be a penalty masquerading as a blessing. Something in the line of "without the hurt, the heart is hollow".

My experience here is mixed and confusing. Sometimes, what one day has seemed like a disaster from which recovery would be impossible, has been forgotten the next. Into that category would fall financial crises where a visit to one's old style bank manager would start in the deepest gloom imaginable, only to change to brilliant sunshine as the problem was talked through with the expert. The transformation would be almost immediate as that cold hand of apprehension that gripped one's heart, ruined one's sleep and reached a climax each morning as the dreaded mail fell through the letterbox, was miraculously relieved. I recall a particularly awful Good Friday morning when the contents of a letter that almost burnt a hole in the doormat so upset me that I underwent four days of torture until the bank opened again on the Tuesday. I was incensed that mail should be delivered at all on a Bank Holiday—it hadn't used to be so until the 80's—but the frustration of being unable to tackle the problem for four days was well nigh unbearable. To this day, such agonies have left their mark so that if I receive any sort of financially-related correspondence, I am bound to respond within minutes, irrespective of who is right or wrong or whether or not it's an important issue.

No use crying over spilt milk

I am grateful to my Maker for putting me together so that I have always been able immediately to forget any life-threatening or dangerous incident involving me.

There have been half a dozen or so occasions, mostly in my flying career, when the odds of my surviving were ridiculously low. But the moment of danger passed, and after a quick wipe of the brow and a four-letter exclamation, the matter became at once irrelevant except for its story value across the bar.

People sometimes think of that philosophical attitude as bravery. It is not. Bravery is what my old Dad must have called upon many times in The Great War when, after waiting for hours in a muddy bloody trench, he was obliged to stick his head above the parapet and advance on an enemy—who knew exactly where he was and what he was going to do—because some other poor sod had blown a whistle for the attack to begin. You never know how brave you are until you have to overcome fear. I have little doubt that most men prefer valour to be a chance acquaintance, met in company if at all, but politely avoided whenever possible.

My Dad and his family (1911)

Too painful

As for other hurts, I could not blank out the past and pretend I'd not been hurt; or indeed pretend that something had never happened, so how could one be hurt? For instance, I know I would have been devastated had Rosemarie and I ever been forced apart after we had each discovered how the other felt. But I once had a friend who obliterated his wife's infidelity as if it were merely a bad dream. I never knew whether he had genuinely switched off his mind to the pain, or was able within his make-up to hide his true feelings though inwardly in torment. He was a very bright 30-year-old RAF officer married to a striking 25-year-old Scottish lass. They had been married for 5 years, had one child, and were seemingly happy and contented, when she fell passionately in love with one of his colleagues. The affair was discovered by him coming across love letters that told him most of the story, and he got the rest from her. Tackling his wife's lover "in an adult way", he demanded an undertaking from both that they would never meet again, and pulled down the shutters on his memory to the point that in the next 35 years of marriage he never made reference to her affair. The wife and her lover were to meet occasionally in defiance of their promise and always remained close in heart and spirit. Being in the RAF, their family paths crossed inevitably a number of times over the years, but to the husband, there never had been a lover and his wife had done no wrong. Was there a broken heart amongst his souvenirs I wonder?

Play it as it is

The bottom line is that we all have our own way of doing things. As we become older and hopefully wiser, we realise that each of us is uniquely influenced by the pure chance of our birth, by our environment, by what changes in circumstances do to us, and by the people we meet. An old American Indian saying warns us not to criticise one's fellow man until one has walked a mile in his moccasins. So many times in my younger days I'd be critical of how others acted or lived their lives; either as individuals, families or nationalities—only to realise with experience that they did what was right for them, at the time, and in their environment.

Another challenge for the autobiographer is to avoid the trap whereby the older one gets, the more vivid are the memories of events that never actually took place at all! I suppose that is because memorable things are so often retold, with anecdotes polished and embellished so often that they eventually become the typical "Irish story". Winston Churchill called it "Exaggerating the Truth". Perhaps all memory exaggerates in some way as we readjust our recollections and fall into the trap of comparing like with unlike. But I'm alert to that particular pitfall and therefore plan to write the script just as I saw it at the time; no shooting of lines, nothing contrived, no subterfuge and no deliberate errors of fact.

Finally, one surprising discovery I have made in penning this journey through life is that the deepest memories are not of the steady drip of unnumbered days, the ash of time, the monotone of the lost years, or even the most familiar faces and places. It is a face seen once and lost forever in a crowd, an eye that caught mine and left a message, a face that smiled and vanished on a passing train, the memory of a snowfall in childhood, the laughter of a girl in a summer street long ago, the image of a silver moon on shimmering waters, experiences that fill up all one's senses in an instance. Our lives are written on a canvas of snapshots that return to us painted in our own psychic colours and in a format based on that of our life; some of those memories being better than anything that can ever happen to us again.

What's in a Name?

PALMER (Latin *palmifer*, "palm bearer"). A pilgrim to the Holy Land who was given a consecrated palm branch to carry back, which was usually laid on the alter of his parish church on his return.

> *His sandals were with travel tore*
> *Staff, budget, bottle, scrip he wore;*
> *The faded palm branch in his hand*
> *Showed pilgrim from the Holy Land.*

I once promised myself that I'd research the Family Palmer origins, but having struck rock instead of oil fairly early in the quest, gave up with little more than a whimper. I did unearth data showing that the family lived in Leicester during the 19th century and that there were a few drams of Scottish blood in our veins that led to my Christian name Kelvie—from the Scottish McKelvie. Beyond that I don't have a clue, but I know that my brother Spud went as far as finding or designing a Family crest, so doubtless his autobiography will reveal all.

Kelvie Palmer alias John Palmer

I'm obliged to remind you that this is one person's autobiography—not two. Although christened John Kelvie, I was always known in Manchester and until I arrived in Ireland in 1949 as "Kel". Since retiring in 2000 I have also been called Kel. I became "John" in 1949 at RAF Ballykelly so as not to be confused with three Irish "Kels" already in the radar section, abbreviations of Kelvin. I used John until 2000 although Rosemarie insisted on calling me Kel from the first time we met. I often wanted to revert from John to Kel, but I was too concerned about the opinions of others. The message then is that Kel (vie) and John is one and the same guy in these pages. The moral (which I ignored) is—be yourself and do what you want to do; it's your life.

> *"Voyage upon life's sea, and to yourself be true.*
> *Whatever your lot may be, paddle your own canoe."*

And one more identification; Rosemarie and "Roo" in the text are one and the same; stemming from her granddaughter's mispronunciation of Rosemarie.

3

HERE WE GO

John Kelvie Palmer was born just after midnight on June 10th 1930. His brother Roy, aged two, died of the then killer disease tuberculosis at 6 a.m. the same day. Those were hard times for the Palmer family; shortly afterwards his parents lost their Market Garden Nursery and their home and were forced to live with various relations for a number of years before settling down in 1934 in Wythenshawe, the garden suburb of Manchester. Younger brother Derek was born there in 1936.

My father, Jack Palmer (christened John Kelvie like three previous generations) was born in 1896, the son of a well-known and much respected master tailor. When he was conscripted in 1914 to The Cheshire Regiment, they renamed him "Jack" or "Peddler" and sent him to fight for the whole of WW1 in the mud, blood and confusion of Belgium and France. He had only two short breaks, one to the ill-fated landings in Salonika, the other back to Blighty to recover from a leg wound suffered at the Battle of Ypres.

Dad came back from that war having witnessed such horror and suffered so much physical hardship and mental anguish that, like so many men in so many wars, he effectively closed his mind to what he'd seen and very rarely spoke about it. In later life he'd occasionally joke about lying in the bottom of a wet trench and shooting the big grey rats that infested the body-strewn battlefield—not for sport, but because they looked like the arm of a German soldier in his field grey uniform sliding into the trench. He'd talk of being strapped to the wheels of a gun-carriage for 7 days for calling a young officer a cruel bugger for beating a horse, and he'd shake his head as if to unseat the bitter memories as he spoke of the day when the "poor bloody infantry" saw German tanks lumbering towards them for the first time. He recalled, too, the day when a dense yellow cloud of mustard gas drifted towards the British trenches, before a change of wind shortly after dawn blew it back towards the Germans. I've often thought since that I would have liked to have heard more about that war from him; but in analysing why I didn't ask him when he was here, I realise that at the time I was too busy living—the past didn't seem worth too much thought.

Later, I was to compare my Dad's attitude to his war with the way I heard American soldiers and marines talk about what they'd done to the population of a Nam village, or hear their pilots describe the effects of napalm and bombs on houses and vehicles. If you join the military, you have to see yourself as a hired killer. But to me, there is a world of difference between being a professional soldier, sailor or airman fighting for "King and Country", and being a bloodthirsty bastard who takes great delight in describing how they put so many people, uniformed and civilian alike, to their deaths.

Jack Palmer survived the hell of 1914–18 and returned to his parents and three sisters in Manchester, and to meet and later marry Ellen Higginbotham. Ellen was one of four children born to Frederick and Ada (nee Scott), both of whom were 6 foot tall and always immaculately dressed even though there wasn't that much money around. But that was an age of traditional values, of pride in appearance, of good manners, where children were seen and not heard, where family was at the heart of everything. Ellen's younger brother Percy did not return from France, sister Annie committed the cardinal sin of marrying a Yorkshireman and "emigrated" to Pudsey, whilst the eldest, Walter, saw the world as a cook in the Merchant Navy before setting up a shoe repair shop and frightening Mancunians with his hair-brained exploits on every sort of motorbike known to man. In his black leather helmet, with goggles made out of ginger beer bottles, Walter was a fearsome sight. In the days before motorways and good roads, he would often shoehorn his wife Madge to his sidecar and drive to John O'Groats or Land's End. Real "Last of the Summer Wine" stuff!

Ellen spent the war on a Manchester airfield with the RFC (which became the RAF on 1st April 1918) and was involved with the record-breaking exploits of Alcock and Brown. Young Jack and Ellen met when Jack delivered his father's bespoke suits to the famous aviators. They married in 1925, and after the failure of the nursery, Jack did what he did best and liked most, became a professional gardener specialising in roses and dahlias. During the '30's they relocated five times in south Manchester before Mam found the place she wanted at 15 Orton Avenue. They moved in on the day war broke out, 3rd September 1939, and they both lived there till the days they died—Jack on 4th January 1969 and Ellen on 15th August 1986.

"The day war broke out." The Family Palmer—1939

As I've grown older I've come to appreciate the impact that Mum and Dad had on my life, on the sort of person I am, and how I've conducted my life. They were, I believe, the perfect parents. In spite of never having much money, they gave my brother and I everything they could and everything we needed. I was fairly bright at junior school and when I won a scholarship to the grammar school my folks had to fork out the very considerable sum for my uniform and accessories. I did not know that then of course and not once did they even hint at the sacrifices they had undoubtedly made. Mum was the sort that started saving for *next* year's holidays on the way back from Blackpool *this* year. She knew where every penny was, and Dad gave her virtually every penny he earned except the little he kept aside for an occasional Woodbine and a pipe of 'baccy. Mum went out to work herself most of her life; nothing was too much for her when it came to looking after her family.

Both are long gone, but I think of them both so often as if they were still here. I have nothing but happy memories of the childhood they gave me, or the way they sent me out into the world once they had done their jobs. I believe they were happy together; indeed, I cannot recall them having a serious row, but perhaps they did and perhaps they had problems that their sons were never aware of. That is how they were, how the world was then, and I wish in this modern age that we might retain those essential old family virtues.

I last saw my Dad alive at midnight on 3rd January 1969, but he was in hospital in a coma and although I would like to think that he heard the last words I spoke to him, I saw no recognition in his eyes. Only the previous day I'd taken my parents to Reading to catch their Manchester train. Even now, 35 years on, I can still see his smiling face and the tears on his cheeks as he waved goodbye for what was going to be the last time. He'd surprised me that New Year's Day as we stood in the first snow of winter by saying, "I've had enough Kel, it's been a good life and you've all made me very happy." To a 38-year-old man in the prime of life, and doubtless a million important things on my mind, I hadn't taken his words seriously. It occurred to me as we laid him to rest later that week, that he'd known his days were numbered even though he'd had no serious health problems for years.

I also missed the same message from my Mum before she died suddenly 17 years later. Mam was a very strong and independent lady who resisted all attempts to persuade her to move into accommodation where she'd have some help and supervision. She insisted on staying in the house she'd lived in for nearly 50 years where she could still welcome family and be in familiar surroundings. "I don't want to stare all day at a brick wall and live with a bunch of old people," she'd say.

So she looked after herself, visited us for holidays, and looked forward to our regular visits to Manchester to watch United or Belle Vue speedway. On one such visit, in a hurry as usual, I was going through the front door on the way to the car when she took my arm. I remember she suddenly looked incredibly small and frail as she said, "Thanks for everything Kel." I kissed her and rushed off, and have spent the last 18 years wondering how I missed her message and how I'd love the chance to play it again. Brother Derek called me three days later to say she'd died. It's odd how everyone of any age lives with the certain prospect of death, yet none of us believe it. Nevertheless, I'm sure that both Mum and Dad knew and accepted that we were parting for the last time in this life, perhaps to be beyond reach forever. I cannot help but wonder if I will know for whom the bell tolls, and how my sons and daughters will feel at the time.

Brother Derek

I'm aware that thus far I've said little about my brother. This I suppose is one of those dust bound boxes in the attic that one is reluctant to open for fear of what might jump out. I've always wanted my four offspring to stay good pals, or at least in close touch, just as close as they were when growing up. But it hasn't been that way with me and Derek—or "Spud" as I was wont to call him. Much of the problem is that we were six years apart, so I was always moving in different circles and with a different crowd of friends. Besides, I left home at 16 when he was 10 to join the RAF, so we didn't have much playtime together. I suppose, too, that there was cause for jealousy in that I was the big brother, I was the RAF officer, and when I came home, I was fed the fatted calf and my folks paid that much more attention because I was a rare visitor whilst Derek lived on the doorstep. At the time I didn't see it that way, and so I wasn't too bothered if he and his first wife were offhand to me and mine. More to the point, and to my shame and regret, I didn't care what Derek thought. We'd grown increasingly further apart and our lives were very different.

The animosity came to a head when Dad died and I put on his wreath the words "Up the Reds" in recognition of the exceptionally close relationship Dad and I had shared over our football. Derek's first wife saw that as irreverent, a hurt that opened a chasm between us that, try as she did, Mum never really managed to bridge. My problem, I'm sorry to admit, has been that I didn't care enough how Derek felt and in the ensuing years Rosemarie and I have spent barely any time with him and his super second wife, Brenda. But although I've never meant any slight or offence, to this day there is an uneasy feeling of confrontation, of one-upmanship by him whenever we meet. It's never really bothered me, but there remains a shadow between us that has never quite dispelled and I wish it wasn't so. The fault is mine; I must find both time and the will to correct that.

Early days in Manchester

Brother Spud and I grew up in the Garden Estate of Wythenshawe in Manchester where, in spite of WW II, we lived an idyllic childhood. Surrounded by beautiful open wooded countryside, those were days when the young could play anywhere without fear and without the lure of TV or PCs to detract from living a healthy outdoor life. I have vivid memories of running for miles through the fields and woods; the sheer exhilaration of being alive, of feeling the sun on my face and the wind in my hair. All I needed as I ran and jumped and communed with nature, was a stout pair of "pumps" or galoshes—before track shoes or expensive "trainers" were invented. There was little money, but great fun.

Today's middle aged and young can only think of their country being at war in terms of the two recent conflicts in The Gulf and Iraq, in Afghanistan and the Falklands. Long before that there was Suez and Korea, but none of those far-off wars had any real effect on the daily lives of people, or even where they travelled on business or holiday. Of course I was a mere boy in WW II, so neither did I truly appreciate the horrors and heartache of war. For instance, I cannot begin to imagine the pain of husband and wife, or of sweethearts, being torn apart with no idea as to when, if ever, they might meet again. Neither did my young mind ever have to consider how my parents must have worried for my safety from air raids and possible invasion, let alone try to carry on as normal and feed and clothe us all on the meagre rations of meat, dairy produce and confectionary, obtainable only via ration books. Fortunately my Dad was a professional gardener with access to greenhouses and allotments, so we weren't ever short of tomatoes and salads or green vegetables in winter. Most home produce went to feed the troops, and imported items such as bananas and oranges, coffee and tea, sugar and many varieties of meats and fish did not return in quantity until 1947 and beyond. Our staple diet was chips with everything that no one else wanted—or Spam, corned beef and a bacon substitute called Ulster Fry. At home we often lunched on bread and dripping using the particularly tasty brown crust of the latter liberally sprinkled with salt and pepper. Unless you lived on or near a farm, or kept chickens as many did, real eggs were like gold dust and only available via a flourishing "black market". There were dried eggs from a tin that made a passable omelette, dried milk and a sugar substitute. If you knew any American servicemen (of which there were millions it seemed after 1941) you might be able to scrounge a bar of chocolate or a packet of gum, plus cigarettes if you were old enough, or nylon stockings if you had the legs and a friendly disposition!

But as I was nine when the war started, I wasn't aware of being deprived. Thanks no doubt to our parent's sacrifices, Derek and I were well fed and clothed and certainly protected from the horrors of war except perhaps in 1940/41 when the Luftwaffe were overhead on many nights. There was no TV and only two radio channels that were heavily laced with propaganda, and so the only time you were really aware of what was going on was on seeing Pathe News at the local flicks—which again was always slanted towards good news to keep spirits high on the home front.

Another advantage, taken for granted then, was that parents could allow children to play out at any time with no fear of any harm coming their way. I never

recall any of my pals having any trouble with adults, the roads were not dangerous, and even though there was a total blackout from twilight to dawn, we all
moved around fearlessly and freely. In summer, there was "double British Sum-
mertime" which meant you could play cricket till 11 p.m. Looking back, it is easy
to endow one's youth with a false quality, but we certainly made our own fun and
entertainment in the parks, fields, woods and lanes of rural Cheshire—and if
weather or darkness did force us indoors, we'd play cards, ludo, draughts or
snakes and ladders, or I'd keep my wartime scrapbook up to date. We had no
electrical equipment other than a radio, but time never hung heavy—we were
content and happy.

There were times when it was best to be young and ignorant of the real danger. Often at night we'd camp out in our Anderson shelter listening to the AA
guns and the shriek of approaching bombs. Occasionally the explosions would be
so loud as to make us fear for our own house and Dad would pull back the blanket curtain to be reassured that the flicker of flames was not No15 going up in
smoke. On the way to school it was a great game to pick up jagged pieces of
shrapnel, and at school prayers every now and then we'd be asked to bow our
heads for one or more of our number that would not be coming back. One night
my insatiable curiosity to watch the celestial fireworks from our front door cost
me dear as a red-hot jagged piece of shrapnel some 4 inches long and half an inch
thick long buried itself into my thigh. I seem to recall being told at Manchester
Royal Infirmary that my successful treatment was crucially dependant on a new
drug called penicillin. Whatever, I was a real hero at school with a genuine war
wound and scar to show for it that has earned me many a beer and sympathetic
kiss since!

But as children, being at war meant little to us compared to what our parents
must have felt. I do recall one night feeling fear rather than curiosity. Dad took
me to "the pictures" in Withington to see his favourite actor Gary Cooper in a
film still shown called "The Plainsman". The air raid sirens sounded and patrons
usually had the option of staying in the cinema. But this night we were ushered
out to be told that a landmine was hanging on a tree by its parachute in the
churchyard opposite and we should evacuate the area quickly. Even as we hurried
down the outside steps, a voice yelled "It's going!" and I saw first the blinding
flash, and then fell flat as debris rained around us. I looked up to see a headless
body impaled on the railings only feet away as my Dad said, "Come on Kel, your
mother will be worried about us."

I now see that living through the war influenced my thoughts, feelings, ambitions and habits throughout my life. We were not aware of the value of money

per se, but we became resourceful and thrifty, believing it to be wrong and un-Christian to waste anything when so many had lost everything. Perhaps it's a case of *voir la vie en rose*, but I don't recall our deprivation leading any of us to beg or steal even though every door was open or unlocked and we lived in total darkness at night with no CCTV, security lights or police patrols to deter any wrongdoing. Scrumping apples was about as evil as I got, although I once nicked a pair of gloves at school and died a thousand deaths waiting for the heavy tread of the law and the sound of the front door knocker.

Darkness be my friend

> *The curfew tolls the knell of parting day,*
> *The lowing herd wind slowly oe'r the lea,*
> *The plowman homeward plods his weary way,*
> *And leaves the world to darkness and to me.*

Talk of darkness infers something furtive and secretive, of achieving surprise and avoiding detection before modern technology effectively turned night into day. Well, perhaps I did do a bit of that one way or another. But even though the Bible tells us "Men love darkness instead of light because their deeds are evil", it wasn't crime or sexual skulduggery that I had in mind. I came to like the dark through being a young lad growing up in that war of 1939–45. The world was a darker place then anyway, even though we were not aware of it being so. I imagine that applies however far back one goes. The Victorians who negotiated the streets of London by gaslight and flaming torch in the 19th century doubtless thought they were very fortunate to have their way so well illuminated compared to earlier generations, whilst those who had to travel by night in the pitch black of the country areas must have been grateful for any means of lighting their immediate path.

In 1939/40, my home city of Manchester at night probably looked like some of the remote towns I've seen in India and China; lines of identical dim yellow lights devoid of brilliant advertisements or flashing neons. There was relatively little traffic, house lighting itself was subdued, and so you seldom saw any reflection of light from the perpetual clouds or from the frequent fog and industrial smog that smothered southern Lancashire. When people talked of visibility in terms of "a pea souper" it really was like that; you literally walked into someone before you saw them. On top of this already dismal scene came the "Blackout", and very effective it was, too. It was necessary of course because German bombers then were navigating by dead reckoning; they had no electronic aids to guide them accurately to the target. To bomb a target they had to see it and were often thwarted by cloud as well as darkness, unless there was a moon—or the presence of life below was revealed by lights. As darkness fell, all over the UK the lights went out or the curtains were drawn. The few vehicles that there were had head-lights dipped permanently and were blinkered like a horse, not to shine outside a very narrow beam pointing dead ahead.

To enforce the regulations, a special force of Air Raid Precaution (ARP) war-dens patrolled the streets and shouts of "Put that light out!" reverberated through the night air. I didn't realise then just how easy it is to see a light from the air. A flash of car lights below or someone opening a curtain might be enough to cause the itchy finger of a bomb aimer, nervously scanning the blackness below, to release his bombs thereby causing a fire into which other bombers would drop their loads and turn thankfully back towards the Fatherland.

In such an environment, a young Palmer grew up loving the darkness in which he played and lived. We knew or thought nothing then of crime or vandal-ism. That was not our way, and the most mischief one ever got into was playing a game of running through the gardens in the dark, the odd broken window, or pinching one of Dad's Woodbines or Senior Service for a crafty drag. Our night vision was superb as we spent most evenings outdoors, there being no TV, no record players or computers, and very little on the radio to attract a teenager indoors.

The Man in Black

There was one radio programme that stood out, however, and thereby hangs a tale that convulses me in laughter to this day. It was a half hour weekly horror story narrated by a BBC chap by the name of Valentine Dyall. In the most sinis-ter of voices he would start his reading with "This is your story teller, the Man in Black, bringing you another tale of terror. We dare you to listen as we recount the tale of…" At the appointed time for this programme, the Orton Avenue gang of around eight 11/12-year-olds would gather stealthily under Mrs Conway's blacked-out window to listen to the broadcast and be frightened rotten.

Orton Avenue consisted of 34 houses set in a racetrack pattern, so that if you entered the back garden of No1 you could go through all the gardens and emerge at No34. Our chosen house for eavesdropping on the broadcast was No25 and I lived at No15. Remember, now, that it would be pitch dark and deathly quiet as our gang sat huddled against the wall like peas in a pod. The storyteller had begun to recount a ghastly tale of a man who took a bet to stay all night in a locked room with a dead body in a coffin. He had reached the point where "He heard the clock in the churchyard begin to chime the hour of midnight, when suddenly—from the coffin—there came a sound that chilled his blood…" As we waited with bated breath for the creaking of the opening lid, I looked up at the night sky and leaped out of my little skin! Silhouetted against the black velvet sky flecked with stars was the figure of a man in a dark flowing cloak and high brimmed hat.

I screeched and set off lickety-split in the dark through garden after garden, taking hawthorn and privet hedge in my stride, ploughing through cucumber frames, wiping out whatever flowers or vegetables came my way, sending cats and dogs scurrying for cover, and putting paid to at least one rabbit hutch and its furry occupant. I didn't stop until I arrived at No15 and sank down to get my breath on the grassy bank of our Anderson air raid shelter. I took a minute or so to divest myself of twigs, glass and other debris and opened the latch on our back door.

To retain the blackout when the door was open, my Dad had hung a thick blanket that I now pushed aside to enter our kitchen. Seated around the kitchen table were my Mum and Dad, younger brother Derek, and our next-door neighbour, old Mr.Dilley. "Sit down, Kelvie, and drink your cocoa. Poor Mr Dilley's just been scared out of his wits by burglars trying to get into Mrs Conway's." Hung on our airing cupboard door were a long black cape and an ARP warden's helmet! I felt a smug sort of satisfaction in knowing that it was "poor Mr Dilley's" prize cucumbers that I'd just wiped out!

My friend the Moon

Being a night owl it follows that I was, and am, a great lover of the moon. My lunar intoxication began when, as a young and callow fellow, I would walk along the river bank or through the oak and sycamore in our local park, and watch the silver crescent of a new spring moon, or marvel at the "full bright sail of a summer moon, tilting on the ocean-deep calm of heaven." My favourite moon in those days was what I called my "Harvest moon", a huge champagne moon that rose from the earth and slowly turned orange and opaque as it passed beyond whatever in the earths' atmosphere gave it its richer colour. I was a romantic soul, very much in love with love and believing that, somewhere in the big wide world, there was a girl who one day would share my thoughts and dreams and love me as I would love her. It was my time for imagining my perfect mate, even though I hadn't got the faintest idea what being in love really meant. I still see that harvest moon of my youth, rising over a field of golden English corn, becoming silver the higher she rose. I recall a moon over the Taj Mahal that looked as big, one that arose like a ghost from the dunes of the Sahara, a huge pale lemon moon rising over purple hills and distant water in Austria, and a second quarter moon lying on her back in the African bush. But most moons in most places seemed a lot smaller. As a lifelong aviator I realise that that is a very unscientific statement to make, but whatever her size or colour I am enchanted by her.

Some of life's magic moments for this amiable lunatic occurred during periods of moonbeam madness; unforgettable little memories to hide in a matchbox until a cold and rainy night when the world has turned colder. If I take a peek now I'll see my harvest moon over the fields of Cheshire, a silver pathway across the Mississippi, a deep red orb over the Oman Jebel, and a gleaming white, brilliantly cold lantern flooding the snow blanket of the Austrian Tyrol. And just one more, a memory and vision so evocative when you stand on a hillside and see her as the Highwayman saw her: "The moon was a ghostly galleon tossed upon cloudy seas." When you are lucky enough to experience such a night, I challenge you to refrain from uttering the line from the poem

Close relations

In the 1930's/40's, with or without a war, the world was a small place and most people did not travel or leave home early in life to find work elsewhere. Manchester was a great industrial city offering lifelong careers for men in various trades and occupations, whilst the war provided the opportunity or necessity for more women to work in the absence of the menfolk. Most of our relatives therefore lived within cycling distance or a penny bus ride, so we'd visit them fairly often.

Dad's three sisters had married well, one to a rare creature—a film director; one to a senior booking clerk at Victoria Station; and the third to the man from the Prudential Insurance. My mother's sister had emigrated to Pudsey "t'other side o' Pennines", and her brother, having served 20 years as a cook in the Merchant Navy, bought a cobblers shop and spent most days with a mouthful of nails and most nights with a mouthful of bitter. I remember them all with affection, especially the relatively affluent auntie Hilda and uncle Bill who took me in their caravan to Cheshire, the Peak District and even The Lakes. Uncle Walter the cobbler and his wife Madge lost their only son in a Halifax over Berlin and their daughter Marjorie ran off to India with a Sikh who ran a dubious bar off Piccadilly. Auntie Annie and Uncle Cyril in Pudsey were the posh side of the family. He owned a chocolate factory and she ran Bridge parties and Whist drives in their huge grey house in a grey town under grey skies. Their son Leslie failed in his attempt to become aircrew in the RAF and got thrown out for dealing in the black market. Daughter Elsie, a tall willowy blonde, ran a hairdressing salon and saw the rest of her relations as not good enough to sweep her floor. When she became pregnant, outside marriage, Uncle Cyril spent months looking for the star to rise again in the East!

In my young days children were to be seen and not heard. I spent countless hours in my Sunday best just sitting in a room surrounded by adults who supped tea and ate fruitcake, without ever bringing me into the conversation at all. Such formal gatherings were invariably held in "the front room", a room that was only used on Sundays or for major events. It had the best furniture, deepest carpet, luxury curtains and most attractive ornaments. If there were a piano in the house, it would be in that room along with a sideboard guaranteed to hold the special tea sets and other crockery, plus a drawer lined with green beige in which there would be packs of playing cards and various aids to keeping the score.

In winter, those front rooms were invariably freezing as, without central heating or a regular fire in the grate, you waited until the master of the house miraculously turned newspapers, firewood and soggy coal into a cheery blaze. This was usually achieved after almost smoking out the room by "drawing" the flames with a newspaper over the fireplace. Uncle Cyril's bright idea one Christmas of bringing in glowing coals from the kitchen fire, led to long term consignment to the dog house when he tripped and set fire to the Persian carpet. In reminiscing this way about people and incidents that I've not recalled in half a century, I realise I knew very little about my relations and whether they were happy with their lot or put on a show when in company. The best I can do is to remember them kindly, how they treated me with affection and left no pain or stain on my young life.

For me, junior school was a blur, but I somehow won a scholarship to Manchester Grammar at the age of 11 and proceeded to cover myself with glory as a centre forward, fast bowler (relatively speaking) and a speedy wing three quarter. Academically, the story did not read so well. My schooldays were a bit like a roller coaster, mostly unspectacular but punctuated with enough peaks of achievement to persuade my teachers to report "Has it in him to be a strong candidate for University", or, "If he applied himself he could do really well." In the senior forms, the comments changed tack a wee bit to "If Kelvie tackled Maths as well as he tackles opponents on the rugby field, we might yet have a scholar of note." And finally, the kiss of death: "We think Kelvie might be a late developer; worth watching." They might almost have added: "Out of sheer curiosity!"

I must say that at that age, I held no aspirations of achieving academic success. I loved the scholastic environment, the old buildings and their cloistral hush, the leather and the dark wood of the libraries, the masters in their flowing gowns, the majesty of the Main Hall when full, the singing of the School song. But I cannot remember looking forward to any special subject or lesson. It was as if I was on a different frequency, because things that I then found so difficult to come to terms with have often in later years seemed so obvious and easy to absorb. Oddly enough, since my late 60's I've been attending Old Boys Reunions and been astonished to find that many of those who were brilliant students, topping all the grades all the time, have led very ordinary lives, seem to have achieved little and are old before their time. I seem to be remembered most for my sporting prowess, setting the chemistry lab on fire, painting the statue of our founder Hugh Old-ham in United's colours, and for two spectacular girlfriends I had in the pleasing shapes of Norah Dalton and Joan Rowlands.

All sorts of things influence the way a person develops over 50–60 years, and I wouldn't presume to list the do's and don'ts—except to say, as I have to many young people in recent years, that whatever you think in your teens, and however obscure your future may seem from where you now stand, the day will come when you'll look back and wonder how you could have felt so low and been so blind. The world holds for each of us a million surprises, unlimited opportunities, countless paths we may follow to find our pot of gold, our own Shangri La.

It was that way when I left school in 1946 to join the RAF and, 59 years on, the opportunities for today's young hopefuls have multiplied many fold. When I left MGS, I'd never been out of England, hardly out of the North West. My knowledge of the World was confined to Geography at school and on keeping large maps during the war on my bedroom wall as I traced the great battles, linking everything through the BBC radio broadcasts. There was no TV, only the very rich travelled abroad, and overseas travel involved long and arduous journeys encumbered by strict passport and visa regulations, plus the need for inoculation and vaccination anywhere south of Dover. Many countries were accessible only by long sea voyages and most were totally unknown to residents of these shores.

Today you only have to watch a travel programme on TV or view the Departure board at an International Airport to see how the world has shrunk. In many ways that is a good thing; but I actually feel cheated in that the world has lost much of its attraction by being so accessible, by losing the once unique aspects of a city or country. What to me in 1949 when I first set foot in Malaya was the mysterious and magical "Far East" is now more like Dallas East. So many places, so much the same; that's not progress in my book.

Decision time for careers

But back to 1946, and to the surprisingly quick and ordinary end to my formal schooling. It was over in a flash and I can't help feeling there should have been a celebration or a tearful farewell from those who'd tried so hard to pump something into me. But no! One day I disappeared and 50 years later classmates couldn't remember whether I'd gone early or stayed to the end. That might explain why I've stopped going to the Annual Old Boys Dinner since they changed the venue from the School to a hall in central Manchester. It was the School itself, the bricks and mortar, its traditions and customs, which I felt in my bones. *"Laudator temporis acti."*

I was 16 with one of the most important decisions in my life to make, but in no way qualified or competent to make it. Where did I go from here? With shaky HSCs behind me, University was not an option with places at the very few Universities like gold dust. I'd had a few experiences that had given me the yen to fly—so I ended up in the RAF. Being so young, I wasn't allowed to enter flying training. So to be indoctrinated into the RAF way of doing things, I first had to learn a trade. I chose radar (back to the dreaded maths) and 3 years later amazed myself and half of Lincolnshire by graduating and being selected for flying training and commissioning. But I'm leaping ahead because the period between leaving grammar school as a boy, and to becoming a man with a trade and a future a few days short of my 19th birthday, constituted important formative days indeed.

It all started in February 1946 when an advertisement in the *Manchester Evening News* said that the RAF wanted bright young things to learn a trade at their expense before going on to greater things with a lifetime career. I filled out the form that was in effect an application to sit a qualifying written examination. That in fact was all I wanted to do—to sit a challenging examination to get practice for my forthcoming HSCs. I'd no visions of being a fighter pilot or travelling the world; my sights then were set very low indeed. When you don't know what the world has to offer, it's difficult to make plans and take sensible decisions. Perhaps subconsciously there were bells inside me urging me to fly, but if so they were muffled and I only had the faintest interest in flying. I didn't really have a clue as to what I wanted to do with my life, whereas my Mum would have told you, as she often told me, that there were only three honourable professions at which I should aim. In no special order, they were Doctor, Teacher and Bank Manager, but somehow none of those brought a gleam to my eyes in 1946. Financial rewards were certainly not uppermost in my mind; I thought more of a fulfilled life. With the benefit of 55 years of hindsight, I'd still duck the doctor and banker options, although teaching and instructing have often been part of my job in the RAF and industry, and by and large I've enjoyed doing that.

A Yen to fly

If there was something in my *psyche* in 1946 that aroused an interest to fly, it might have stemmed from a few incidents in my childhood. The first occurred in December 1941 when my Dad worked for Manchester Parks at their facility on Carrington Moss, five miles out in the Cheshire countryside. The site (now Manchester United's multi-million pound training complex) consisted of acres of greenhouses and beautifully kept bedding plots. In cold weather, the heat in the greenhouses had to be kept constantly high and the coke boilers, technology being what it was then, required de-clinkering and re-stoking around midnight every day. We cycled the 5 miles from Lawton Moor, at dead of night in the blackout, and through all sorts of weather, with our way lit by small battery pow-ered lamps on our bikes which threw a beam of yellow light all of 6 feet ahead of us. We couldn't afford dynamo lights (they cost real money), and I've just remembered that we had to stick yellow paper over the lamps to reduce the white glare from our powerful 1.5-volt batteries! Even so, I doubt if we ever made the journey without a voice from the darkness yelling: "Put out that light!" Dad made that journey every day for 15 years, and I can only marvel as to how he managed to do so. I can see him now hunched over the handlebars in his heavy brown overcoat and his favourite battered trilby, hurtling along at maybe 4 mph, or 5 with a following wind.

On this particular night we had reached the spot where the road became a cin-der track and we had to cut off to cross a couple of fields to the boiler house—about ½ mile in all. It was snowing so we left the bikes in a hedge to walk the rest aided by our cycle lamps. It's nice to recall that had we left our bikes there for days, no one would have touched them. The world was a much more honest place then. As we trudged through some four inches of fresh snow, the air raid sirens sounded and suddenly the black December sky was criss-crossed by the beams of dozens of searchlights and spotted with the explosions of anti aircraft shells. From our privileged vantage point we observed a wonderful firework dis-play, and a lad of tender years watched in awe, little appreciating that German men were dying in the air and English men, women and children on the ground.

A number of searchlights swung to focus on the same spot and at the intersec-tion could be seen a twisting silver object that looked like one of those little dart-ing fish one sees intermittently in a fast flowing stream. The AA fire homed in on it, but as we stood watching the drama unfold above us, the field through which we'd just passed literally burst into flames lighting up the night sky. "Come on Kel, leg it!" shouted my Dad as we ran to the air raid shelter, landing in about six inches of water but safe from the inferno raging outside. There was one enormous bang that caused Dad to demonstrate to me, a rare occurrence, the more lurid parts of his vocabulary. Then, miraculously, the glow from the fires faded, the all-clear sounded, and we clambered out to stoke the boilers as planned and walk, again now in pitch darkness, towards the road and our bikes. It turned out that many fields in the open countryside were full of fire decoys that were lit when an air raid was imminent, to fool the main force of bombers that these were the fires laid by their Pathfinder aircraft. That way, it was hoped, the enemy would dump most of its bombs in the Manchester mud instead of on the dense collection of factories in nearby Trafford Park, so important to the War effort.

But for Dad and I the night had only just begun. As we approached our bikes in the hedge, our lamps illuminated a huge black and silver mass displaying the German Swastika. It was the tailplane of a German bomber shot down by AA fire no doubt, and of course our bikes were somewhere under the mass of twisted metal. I recall that I bemoaned the loss of my wheels; I simply gave no thought to the probability that the wreck contained human remains. I never saw my bike again but Dad recovered his, changed one wheel and trundled around on that same bike for the rest of the war. I bought him a new one with my first wage packet in the RAF.

My second link with aviation came the following summer. I remember that summer as being hot and sunny for weeks on end which, with double British summer time in force, meant it didn't get dark until after 11 p.m. (Why is it that childhood summers always seemed so much better than now, I wonder?) Anyway, I was staying in my hols with my grandfather who lived just off the end of the runway at Ringway (now Manchester International) airport. One August afternoon with the sky half-covered by fair weather cumulus cottonwool clouds, I heard the staccato sound of canon fire and, looking up, glimpsed the distinctive silhouette of a Heinkel 111 pursued by a Hurricane. At that age, my aircraft recognition was better than when I later sat in my own cockpit!

Both aircraft disappeared from view and then the Heinkel spiralled out of the clouds to disappear behind a line of trees. Seeing the telltale pall of smoke and being a lad (what better excuse can there be?) I hurdled Grandpa's bottom hedge and set off at full pelt across a stubbled cornfield towards the smoke. As I ran I heard another noise above my head and, looking up, saw the Hurricane, or at least *a* Hurricane, pitching and yawing above me as its engine coughed spasmodically before, right in front of me and almost in total silence, it pancaked onto my favourite hedge and perched there rocking gently.

My first thought was for the dozens of birds that nested in that thick and deep hedgerow, typical of the hedgerows that then bordered the smaller beautiful fields so much a feature of the English countryside. But as I reached the port wing tip swaying above me, the pilot who had pulled back his canopy, shouted: "Sod off, lad, and find me some transport!" I didn't have to as a fire engine came bouncing across the fields from the airfield and I scuttled back to tell my Grandpa what I'd seen. At first he looked at me quizzically and I think he thought it was just another boy's yarn, and then he said, "If you like aeroplanes, Kelvie, we must show you the inside of one." True to his word he took me along within days to Ringway and for five bob I had 15 minutes flying in a De Havilland biplane. It wasn't the thrill of being airborne *per se* that impressed me that first time, it was how marvellous the patchwork quilt of the Cheshire countryside looked from 2000ft.

The third and probably the defining experience to whet my appetite for flying, happened when I joined the ATC and went on a summer camp in 1944 to the RNAS station at Stretton, near Warrington. I actually told Mum and Dad the camp was in Suffolk—just to make it sound more exciting. They never said anything but I suspect they knew the truth since we travelled in a converted bread van and the journey lasted all of one hour! I didn't know it then, but Stretton was a reception base for aircraft shipped in from the USA before going into operational service.

We ATC cadets were given an extra duty every evening from 6 p.m. until 10 p.m. of manning one of the perimeter gates. At 10 p.m. a bugle would sound to recall all personnel to quarters and—still only a wee lad—I was astonished to see the cornfield outside the camp literally come alive as dozens of sailors and WRNS dusted themselves down and came rushing through my gate. I had no idea what they were doing in that field! At 14 I didn't know girls were different from boys!

But back to the flying. The airfield consisted of a runway and numerous dispersals, all with parked aircraft. On this morning, having been on guard the previous night, I wandered down to a dispersal near my tent to be greeted by a pilot sitting in the cockpit of his a Grumman Hellcat (I think) waving at me urgently. I approached the powerful looking beast warily and climbed as instructed on the footrest below his cockpit. The pilot shouted: "I want you to give me a start, son. There's no other bugger here. Turn the prop till it sticks and when I shout 'Contact' pull down hard and stand well back—got it?" I nodded, only half understanding, and could only think he mistook my blue ATC uniform for that of an airman. But I followed instructions and needed no encouragement to stay back as the prop turned over slowly, and then to leap back as the engine fired, coughed and then roared into life. I moved to the wingtip to escape the blast, and watched as he donned his leather helmet. He gesticulated again, making it clear he wanted to talk, and pointed to the wheels. I realised he wanted me to remove the wooden chocks, which I did, but he was still beckoning me to the aircraft. I climbed the footrests with the slipstream battering my senses and bent my head.

"Are you bloody coming?" he screamed, pointing to the cramped space behind his seat. I squeezed in, being a thin rake of a lad, and he told me to duck as he closed the hood. "Put your arms around the back of the seat and don't touch anything else!" he shouted as he slipped the brakes and the monster lurched forward as a little bemused innocent fella prepared to be taxied around Stretton. We stopped to let another aircraft land ahead of us and sat there trembling, vibrant and alive, and tensing with energy. You can imagine my surprise when the enormous radial piston engine screamed up to top revs and we hurtled across the grass and up into the Lancashire sky. As we levelled off at about 2000ft, he throttled back and shouted, "Let's go see Blackpool Tower!" We flew for about 45 minutes along the coast and out to The Isle of Man, then back for a couple of "touch and goes" before landing. I'd spent most of the time on my knees or half squatting, but once the shock of getting airborne was over I found the whole experience exhilarating.

So exhilarating, in fact, that I played hooky from parade 3 days running, found my friendly "driver-airframe" and flew for the hell of it. One significant spin-off from those flights, which the reader may not fully comprehend, was sighting the Manx ferry that plied its trade between Fleetwood and Douglas. When our family had gone on holidays on that kipper boat we'd all been dreadfully seasick. But even being thrown around in the greasy smelly piston engine aircraft had given me no feelings of queasiness; I was over the moon even though no one else at the time believed my outrageous story. Strange, I agree, but 100% true.

Decisions-decisions

So come April 1946, when a very official OHMS letter plopped on our doormat, a young JKP was perhaps already primed to become a "Brylcreme boy". The letter said I'd passed the exams and should plan to catch the 10 a.m. train on 31st May from Manchester Central to London. Onward travel to RAF Halton in Buckinghamshire would then be arranged. Once there I'd be tested and attested, and allocated a trade after 3 days. Or, if I didn't like what I saw, I could return home. I was too young to recognise it as such, but this was one of those forks in the road that confront us all during our lives. Did I put the railway warrant back in the stamped addressed envelope and say "forget it, mission accomplished—examination practice gained"? Or did I rush about bragging to everyone (especially the girls) that I was joining the RAF and leaving school? I chose the latter—but to all intents and purposes obliterated the RAF from my mind. I went back to MGS and achieved acceptable HSCs. I digress to claim that to be a laudable feat in itself, as in those days one sat seven subjects in School Certificate and three or four at the Higher level the following year. The trick was that you had to pass every one, or you failed the lot! Astonishingly, I'd confounded my Maths and French masters and was still basking in the glory of success as my Mum began to gather advice as to what career her clever boy should pursue.

It therefore came as a great surprise in late May when another OHMS letter arrived saying, in effect, "See you at Euston at 1.15 p.m. on the 31st, here's another railway warrant in case you lost the last one." I'm writing this now at 74, but over the years I've replayed it all in my mind for various reasons and can honestly say that I left home on 31st May '46 with little more than the excitement of a journey to London and a step into the unknown beckoning me. Somewhere there was the moderate relief of not going back to school, but fundamentally I went through with something because I didn't know how to stop the bandwagon from rolling on. I did that again later in life when I first married; I went through with something half-heartedly and no one spoke up, advised me or questioned me as to what I was doing. With my folks, that wasn't carelessness or thoughtlessness. They wanted me to do what I wanted to do and did not interfere. But I can honestly say that had they argued, "Don't go to Halton, Don't get married", it's odds on that this autobiography would have been vastly different. But then life is full of "Ifs and buts" is it not, and who's to say until the last trump has sounded whether the turnings we take are right or wrong?

A Trip down a branch line

At this point, I'd planned to recount the beginning of my RAF life. However, I've fallen into the trap of all storytellers by opening up my matchbox of memories, tuning in to the frequencies of a youth so quickly and irrecoverably lost, and discovering things that have lain dormant and unconsidered for over half a century. They are mostly of no importance, but form part of a rich pattern that causes me to say, "Ah yes, I remember it well!" For instance, the mention of Central Station on the last page drew my attention to the fact that although my journey to London in 1946 was the only time I ever caught a train from Central, I knew that particular line quite well.

Going back to my earliest recollections, as a child I used to visit my mother's folks in West Didsbury. My grandfather, a very dim memory indeed, would take me to his allotments where he would perch me on a rustic wooden fence over-looking the railway line, set deep in a gully. We would watch for the arm of the black and white signal to drop before the London express silently appeared around a bend. Now some five miles out from Central, the powerful steam engine would have reached its top speed of around 90 mph and it was indeed a stirring sight for a boy as it suddenly appeared, wheel links racing, belching clouds of steam and smoke as it entered the tunnel with a massive roar and a piercing whistle, immediately below my vigil on the fence.

That childhood impression was so strong that in my MGS days, I would often get off my homebound bus at that bridge and wait for an express to recapture the thrill. The other reason for remembering that line with such affection, because I'd no real interest in train spotting as a hobby, was the route it took through Manchester. It first passed the holy of holies of Old Trafford football ground, before cutting east past the sports pitches along Princess Parkway. After negotiating my tunnel, it by-passed Stockport and reached the then open countryside near my other grandpa's house at Styal. I played there on its embankment often, looking for the nests of the abundant Skylarks, Peewits and Sand Martins.

I would cross an old rickety wooden bridge that led to a large well-concealed pond in Farmer Hankinson's fields, home to that beautiful and fascinating crea-ture, the newt. I can still remember the technique I developed for catching the lit-tle chaps when they popped up for a breather. That pond also gave me my first cobalt blue flash of a Kingfisher, and I'm embarrassed to say, of a girl's knickers when young Margaret Hankinson insisted on trying to educate me about the birds and bees when, like all sensible boys of my age, I was far more interested in the Greater Crested Newt! Her favourite place to lure young innocents like me was her father's barn and the fragrant comfortable haystacks in which we played and slept (as in sleep), and made a few nervous forays into the adult world hidden amongst the dry oblong bales of hay. Those snug little hideaways have long gone to be replaced by ugly round bales covered in black plastic. No wonder the kids of today say there's nothing to do!

They say one should never return to where small memories are. I regretted doing so some 50 years later when I took Rosemarie on a nostalgic trip to see the haunts of my youth. The railway embankment was now a rubbish tip, no one had seen a Skylark or Peewit for 20 years, my Grandad's back field was a factory, and a main road and housing estate had replaced beauty and tranquillity with noise and concrete. Farmer Hankinson's pond was still there, but old bikes, supermarket trolleys and beer cans had driven out my little crested friends. Margaret Hankinson, I discovered, found someone to take an interest in her nature studies and departed for Canada with him at the end of the war. Should you happen to meet a 75-year-old lady flashing her knickers in Toronto, please give her my love.

What is this thing called Love?

Unlike today's promiscuous norm, the great majority of young men in the 1940's were sexual pussycats. Of course we looked at girls, sniggered about their superstructure and legs, and even made outrageous claims about what we'd accomplished on a date the previous night. But it was all a mix of machismo and wishful thinking. The mysteries of love, passion and sex were safe with us; we knew nothing about erogenous zones and thighs had not yet been invented! I first noticed girls in a way that disturbed me when I was 17. Before then, a few of the fair sex had noticed me to the point of inviting me to partake of the forbidden fruit. At 13, it was the farmer's daughter of equally tender years who bared her all in a barn and left me wondering what all the fuss was about. At 15 a very smart and elegant Jewess who worked for my Mum insisted on showing me, on every conceivable occasion, the tops of her nylons. But there was no conceiving for me, only embarrassment. Even at 17, when another of my Mum's girls trapped me in the studio dark room, she was to find that I was as negative as the hundreds of rolls of film she handled each day.

The first time I recall having a feeling engendered in my loins by a female—as opposed to those funny physical urges that all boys experience when growing up—was under the Central Pier at Blackpool one warm dark night in August 1947. It was my first time on holidays without my parents. I'd taken a fancy to a girl from Huddersfield and, having fought off opposition from other young men in Mrs Duckworth's B&B, she and I walked out together for 2 glorious weeks. Strange though it may seem to young folk now, "walking-out" is exactly what we did. There was the odd preliminary nervous touching of hands and, after a decent introductory period, a hurried snatched kiss before the landlady locked us out for the night. Then one night, in a scene reminiscent of Deborah Kerr and Burt Lancaster lying in the seething surf of a Hawaiian beach, Maureen and I lay side by side in the darkness. My hand accidentally came to rest on her blouse and I felt the swell of her breast, a feeling that sent an unknown tingling sensation around my virginal frame. Covered in confusion I spent days apologising, but she didn't seem too worried and we continued to enjoy each other's company.

Just to show how fickle "love" can be, however, my growing ardour for her was wiped out in one fell swoop when I first saw her dance on the wonderfully sprung, gleaming floor of the Tower Ballroom. When dancing the quickstep, she dipped her shoulders to the rhythm—unforgivable! To a ballroom purist like me that was an immediate turn off, and in one fell swoop the fair Maureen lost all her feminine charm and not even the prospect of a heaving Yorkshire bosom under the North Pier could lure me back. Do not conclude from this, that I was totally blind and immune to the charms of the opposite sex. I'd go dreamy eyed at the likes of Jeanne Crain, Rita Hayworth, Joan Leslie and Teresa Wright—the sort of "girl next door" type rather than the brassy Lana Turner, Betty Grable, Dorothy Lamour image. But I didn't honestly look at any of them lustfully; I was more in love with the idea of love, and already beginning to believe that one day I'd meet my little miss perfect (except on the days when I thought my head was too small, my eyes too far apart, or my spots too off-putting for any girl to look at me twice).

So from early days I began to build up a sort of "identikit" in my mind of the features and characteristics of *her* that I wanted. The eyes of one, the hair of another; a smile here, a laugh there; long legs and a graceful walk, slim hands and waist, elegant movements, a proud look and a touch of defiance. I was to learn that even the slightest blemish or imperfection could negate all other qualities and virtues. Many times then, and since, I've stood admiring some gorgeous creature only to cringe when she opened her mouth to speak or pick at her salad with a fork. I've waited for some vision of loveliness to stand up and walk, only to become immediately disinterested when she did so on seeing that she was too short for me, walked with her toes turned out, or moved in short stabby steps.

This fixation with finding my Miss Perfect must have cost me many a good night out, many a laugh, and many a pleasant surprise. Often it has caused me to be pleased to find that someone who looked perfect in a photograph, or when standing still, loses that perfection once animated. Can anyone explain why that should be? Why should I have set myself a particular standard for which to aim, and then feel positively relieved rather than disappointed, when the object of my desire fails to score 100%? In recent years I've met a fair number of females off screen that looked gorgeous and desirable on it. The disappointments far outweigh the "Whows", and you truly appreciate that what puts a man into orbit about a member of the fair sex is far more than you see on a photograph or on a screen.

So I spent my teenage years as a celibate, first at MGS, then in the almost monastic life of an apprentice at Cranwell. I continued to lead a somewhat sheltered life in the pastoral ecclesiastical surroundings of Ireland until, at 21, I was let out on an unsuspecting world to start my flying training. There were occasions in those early years when I perhaps caught a fleeting glimpse of my ideal partner. In Alderly Edge there was a Dorothy, in Stockport a Joan, and in Ireland a Frances, but I never had either time, opportunity, or nerve to close in for a closer look, so they are but footfalls in the memory to doors I never opened.

I must be careful here not to give the impression that I was romantically or sexually abstemious, although I was far from being a rake or a Don Juan. In truth I was a novice, and the change after leaving Ireland was essentially that I was now moving in different social circles, in a very different working environment, and meeting with streetwise men and women. The nerve was rapidly improving whilst the opportunity count had gone off the scale. So now, you would have thought, all I had to do was to be patient and one enchanted evening, across a crowded room, wild fires would be lit in me by the eyes of a tall dark beautiful stranger and bells would ring. But no; not in fact for another 20 years about which you shall hear later. But back to May 1946, when I put away childish things and left behind the smoke and rain of dear old Manchester for the lure of the RAF.

4

FOR KING and COUNTRY

In committing memories to paper and opening doors that haven't been knocked on for many years, I've not found it easy to scour the past for key events that crucially affected the way my life developed. This Chapter proved particularly difficult to compile. It covers my leaving school to joining the RAF, and my service until I was commissioned in 1951.

Inexplicably, my three years at Cranwell had got lost in the mists. But the chance came in 1999 to pick up the faint signals from half a century back when someone who hadn't forgotten his RAF roots arranged a 50th reunion of our Apprentice Entry, having spent ages tracking us down. So it was that in Grantham in May '99, some 30 old codgers came together for the first time since 28th May 1949, the day when 96 of us had slow marched off the square at Cranwell to the strains of Auld Lang Syne played by our beloved pipe band. Although we were all trained as radar/radio fitters, few of us actually served together in our future careers; some left the RAF early, some served their 12 years before leaving, some stayed on until later retirement, others were commissioned either as aircrew or in non-flying roles, and some, sorry to say, had passed away.

If the survivors who made the reunion needed any reminding of the fragility of life beyond 70, we were given a sharp nudge when the chap whose idea it was died only weeks before the event. That sadness apart, it was a wonderful reunion, full of surprises and revelations bearing in mind that we'd spent 3 years living in each other's pockets and were the same age within six months. Some guys one recognised at once, others made you ask covertly, "Who's the bloke in the blue shirt?" There were some who, at Cranwell, had been the brightest, smartest and sharpest, but had not done much with their lives. Then there were others who had been technically "dim" and always in trouble, but who had been immensely successful in their service or civilian careers.

Most of us were accompanied by wives who had not been around in 1949 but had fascinating stories to relate how they coped with husbands who, for 3 years at least, had been expert at making their own beds, ironing, polishing, cleaning and scrubbing sinks, baths and toilet basins, darning socks, and cooking sausage, egg and chips at 2 a.m. in a "mess tin" over a meths camping stove. I thought it odd, perhaps I shouldn't have, that I still had most affinity with those who had been closest to me at Cranwell. But it was also a pleasant surprise to find that chaps I'd had little time for, remembered me with affection and had stories involving me that I couldn't remember. Oddest of all maybe was the marked divergence in how each of us remembered our 1000 days together between 1946 and 1949. There were some chaps in the Entry that I'd totally forgotten, incidents that caused great mirth when recounted that I had no memory of, and stories about our directing staff and instructors that went way over my head. But again I race ahead, so back to May 1945.

It was fun in 1999 to resurrect those youthful RAF days, to be surprised at how much of our past can remain dormant, yet spring into life as one rolls back the covers and takes a peep. But I soon realised I was falling into a trap. As I became more immersed in the past, I had to edit my writings increasingly more critically to avoid slipping into story-telling mode instead of being factual.

To see how others coped with that pitfall I read a number of autobiographies. Some were well nigh unreadable, most were ego trips, and many were clearly written, or at least structured and polished, by a professional writer. There seems little point in an autobiography if one perpetuates the errors, omissions, and fantasies of which you've been guilty throughout that life, or have someone else to write it for you, eh? I became suspicious of anyone writing much under the age of 60. Their offerings tended to read more like a CV, with a history of their achievements and experience directed to further their future careers or enhance their status. Of course there were exceptions, but by and large I've found the older writer more inclined to tell it "warts and all", often with startling candour and quite unafraid of painting themselves and their actions unfavourably. Joan Bakewell's beautifully crafted *Centre of the Bed* written at 70 is a classic example, as is Claire Bloom's autobiography, written at 65, that left me shaking my head and remarking, "Well, I never, and I always thought she was such a nice girl!" She was and is, of course, but it was a lesson I should have learned earlier. Life—especially someone else's life—is seldom what you imagine it to be.

And finally, one conspicuous conclusion from reading other autobiographies. Each writer believes his or her life, chosen profession, experiences, and time and place in the greater scheme of things, to have been the best, the most desirable, the most satisfying. How can any of us judge how our lives compare with those of others since we spend all our time living our own and always complain of not having enough time for that? Perhaps the answer to the puzzle lies in the fact that the autobiographer would not put pen to paper unless he thought himself or herself to be rather special if not unique?

Life as an Aircraft Apprentice

I left Manchester on my great adventure in May 1946, to be greeted at St Pancras by some very cheerful chaps in uniform who shepherded the dozen or so of us from my train to the then adjacent Marylebone Station. Thence, with our numbers in the hundreds by now, to Wendover in Buckinghamshire. It was a lovely summer's day, I was seeing places I'd only previously seen on a Monopoly board, and there were all these boys of my own age from all over the UK with different accents, different ways, different backgrounds. On arrival at Wendover, we assembled in three ranks and marched up the long hill to RAF Halton led by the massed ranks of the Halton Apprentices Pipe Band. I've loved the pipes and drums ever since, have always felt immensely proud when marching to them, and can never understand how Scotland can ever lose at any sport with the skirl o' the pipes to send the blood pounding through a man's veins. It's a bit like the passion raised in Wales by the singing of "Hen Wlad fy Nhadau" before great national events. Trouble is, then they all go home and forget what it is that makes a Land and its Fathers truly great!

Around 500 young lads arrived that day to start their new lives, few, I suspect, having any real idea of what they were letting themselves in for. As we hadn't actually taken any oath or signed our souls away, we were still in civilian clothes and being spoken to nicely by the NCOs. We took various aptitude tests and medicals before, on the third day, being given the ultimatum: "Sign here son, or sod off." I heard later that about 5% chose to do just that. The rest were placed into training categories such as Airframes, Engines, Armourers, and Instruments and—my allotted trade—Radar/Radio fitter. We were then "attested", issued with uniforms and other "small kit" equipment, and allocated a Service Number that depended entirely on where one had been standing in the queue to collect one's kit. Little did I realise then how that number would stick with me for the rest of my life. 583010 was abbreviated to '010 (Palmer), and I even now identify old buddies by their "last three". Smith '018 automatically identifies a scruffy ill-disciplined lad from Hayes, as opposed to Smith '973, a Brummie who was the smartest, best-behaved chap in the entry who rose to the dizzy heights of Sergeant Apprentice. Fifty years on at our reunion, no one called the Smiths Barry or Geoff; they were still '018 and '973 and responded immediately when so addressed.

Other Service Numbers issued that day, that would now be thought collectable, included '007, which ended up with a Halton-bound guy, Ted Guy by name, who left the RAF within weeks. (583)'111 went to a Geordie football-playing close friend who 5 years later went all the way to Kenya to be killed in a flying accident. 583010 was on the first piece of paper I saw in the RAF; it was on my commissioning scroll in 1951, on my retirement papers in 1983, is still on my Income Tax forms, and I quote it often to get reduced fares on British Airways!

RAF Cranwell

The first shock for those of superior intellect and intelligence chosen for a career in electronics was that our 3 years training would not be spent in lovely leafy Buckinghamshire, but in the windswept bleakness of Lincolnshire. Instead of being a member of the 53rd AA Entry at Halton, we were to become Cranwell's entry 9M5, which interpreted meant we were due to graduate in May 1949. So, having barely had time to think about our new life, the next morning we marched back down the hill to Wendover station, this time in uniform carrying a kit bag, and being verbally abused until we closed our tired young eyes that evening in Cranwell, East Camp. Talk about crossroads in life! I did not realise then that another was looming for me 3 months ahead.

Before I spin the yarn about the next three years, let's set the scene. In 50-odd years there have been so many changes that affect the way we all live and do things. One cannot now be critical of what people did then; it's a very different world and the past must be examined in the context of the time. Thirty-two of us started RAF life living in a dormitory with each being responsible for perhaps 7 square yards of floor space that held our iron bed, a metal wall locker and a small bedside cabinet. We were not allowed civilian clothes except on leave. We had 2 uniforms, one a "working dress" which felt like horsehair, and a "best blue" with brass buttons that felt like good horsehair. With the former we wore a forage cap, the latter a peak cap. To identify our Squadron, we wore black and green flashes or bands on the headgear.

We were confined to camp except for weekends when we were allowed off-base between 1 p.m. and 10 p.m. We paraded every day with rifle and bayonet, marched to and from work, worked on Saturday mornings and went to Church Parade every Sunday. Our contact with the outside world was minimal. We received mail each weekday, which was a little like the Prisoner-of-War routine with a food parcel from home being a major event. There were no phones, no TV, and a few of us had radios on which, hiding under our blankets, we tried to pick up the only good music channels such as Radio Luxembourg or the American Forces Network's "top ten".

We were paid half our wages every Friday, the other half being saved for when we went on leave; two weeks in August, one at Xmas and 5 days at Easter. My early pay was around £2 per week, but there wasn't much to spend it on anyway. There was a camp cinema where we minions had to sit in the front rows. The fee was 2p. The biggest drain on my meagre resources was the NAAFI where, for 6p, one could get a steaming mug of cocoa or tea (without the cookhouse bromide) and the most delicious cheese pasty that has ever been baked. The cookhouse food of course was awful: porridge made out of cement, scrambled eggs out of toilet rolls and rock cakes made out of real rocks. The only safe and plentiful fare was baked beans, and one morning 50 years later in a hotel in Brunei I enjoyed a breakfast with beans that I swear came out of the very same Cranwell tin. They tasted marvellous!

The NAAFI was also the place to see that rarest of creatures, a woman, and to get a nice smile. Believe it or not, it wasn't until our reunion in '99 that I found that some of my colleagues got more than cheese pasties from the NAAFI girls! It never occurred to me that there was anything else on offer and although I'd had the odd inkling in my younger days that girls were different, they didn't excite or interest me. After all, they couldn't play football or cricket, could they?

So against that background, the 9M5's settled down to learn to become highly qualified engineers and men. I suspect for most, the biggest challenge was the latter. We'd all come straight from school and probably a good home life. Now, in those early months (by design I'm sure) our little feet never touched the ground. We were awake at 6 a.m., each with a chore to do before preparing our own bed spaces to classic "bullshit" standards. Our blankets and sheets had to be folded in perfect lines to sit on top of our 3 biscuit mattresses. Our "small kit" of spare shirt, vest and pants also had to be presented immaculately for daily inspection. All rooms were inspected in our absence; any dust found meant the culprit was for the high jump. Our morning chores would vary according to a roster. One week it might be cleaning the ablutions, next polishing the brassware, sweeping the floors, or cleaning the windows. If there was a big inspection, there was a massive floor-polishing job to be done to the linoleum floor that gleamed like a mirror. That was a combination of pain and pleasure as it involved many of us wearing "floor pads" and doing a skating action across the floor holding hands. If done in the evening, that often turned into a game of hockey using broom sticks, the result often being mayhem and a few days on "jankers"(punishment) for those caught in the act.

Breakfast followed morning chores, then a parade, and then marching to the Technical school. March back to lunch, march back to work, march back to tea. If it was daylight—as it was in our first few months—we'd be on the square drilling before supper at 8 p.m., then back to more cleaning, polishing, and ironing. In such circumstances, certain of the Staff and some of the NCO apprentices from senior entries became hated, some were liked, a few respected. But above all, the Entry was established as a unit, as a team, with spirit, a common aim and a common enemy. The lessons learned from that character—forming process stay with you for the rest of your life.

But of course, under such a strict regime, there were casualties. For diverse reasons, some 12 of our number decided that RAF life was not for them and departed under a scheme by which lads could buy themselves out of training after one month. I cannot remember now exactly how I felt; I know I was unhappy in many ways but could not have faced the ignominy of quitting. I resolved to stay mainly through close friendships with a handful of like-minded boys who found solace and encouragement in similar adversity. That saw me through June and July, but as the summer leave loomed in early August, my new found confidence and independence led to me requesting a "personal interview" with our CO, a Flight Lieutenant.

I was to see a different side of two people I'd grown to dislike. The real authority of the Apprentice Wing was a hardened old (45-ish) Warrant Officer through whom my request had to be processed. He listened carefully to what I said and then told me I could see the CO, but in a kindly way explained that the first few months were designed to toughen us up and that after the holidays, the discipline would become easier as the technical side became more demanding. Our chat only lasted 10 minutes, but his kindness and words of encouragement had a positive effect on my attitude.

I saw the CO three days before the summer leave and explained that I did not feel I was doing well at the technical studies, and that I did not see the point of much of the discipline and "bullshit". Also in a kindly fatherly way, he explained the reason behind the service training and said I was doing fine in class. He asked if I had any other irons in the fire and I said, truthfully, that I'd had an invitation to join Manchester United as a professional footballer. I was however economical with the truth in that it wasn't the lure of United that was making me unhappy; I was simply homesick and feeling sorry for myself. The story of the United episode is covered elsewhere; suffice it to say that he made the promise that if I came back to him on 1st October with a repeated request to leave, he'd let me go. He simply asked me to look at the big picture, to remember that in the RAF I'd first have a trade, then a chance to fly, and have the opportunity to play as much football and other sport as I wanted. I went on leave with a great weight lifted from my mind. I later found that he'd written to my Mum and Dad.

The Summer of '46

Little could I know that my summer leave in 1946 was to be a defining period in young Palmer's life. A young man that has found his niche is seldom bothered with the rightness of what he is doing; he asks few questions, entertains no doubts and suffers no qualms or pangs of guilt. Exactly how the transition came about I can't say, but I started my leave as a boy and went back 21 days later something approaching a man.

The first lesson I learned was things seldom stay as they are; they change as people change, and in time what once seemed endless and changeless leaves you wondering where the magic has gone. I arrived back in the hometown and made straight for the old haunts and the boys I'd grown up with. They hadn't changed at all, I suspect, but to me they were now years younger than me, infinitely more scruffy and intent on childish things—not the grown up stuff I'd become accustomed to at Cranwell! Our traditional Sunday night entertainment was a trip to the Forum cinema where we consumed large quantities of ice cream and crisps (the ones with the little blue salt packet), and laughed exuberantly whether it was Laurel and Hardy or Frankenstein. On the way home, we'd play a silly game of jumping on and off moving buses that had no automatic doors in those days. We'd leap into people's gardens, either over or through the privet hedge, and derive enormous fun from racing each other to the top of a lamppost. On many homesick nights at Cranwell, I'd longed to be back with the boys; now I was looking forward to being back in Lincolnshire.

Then there was a girl who I'd always fancied from afar. She was a year older than me—a massive gap then—and she'd always treated me as though I were something on the bottom of her shoes. I'd just happen to be there when she came out of a shop or was walking down our avenue. "Surprise, surprise!" I'd say, and the haughty one would put her lovely little nose higher in the air and snub the hell out of me. In that first leave in the RAF I saw her walking towards me in a dance hall and as she saw me I saw her eyes say, "Oh God, not him again." But now instead of feeling crushed and turning red, I felt the anger rise within me, spun on my heels and vowed never to speak to that girl again. It was an insignificant incident, but it made me feel good. Many lessons we learn are salutary and the earlier we have them in life the better. But ignominious failure is seldom constructive; rather it cripples and destroys, resulting in so acute a lack of confidence that the effect is often terminal. Nevertheless, that experience made me say to myself, "You can do a damned sight better than that, Kel Palmer"—and with it I grew up a little.

Curiously, some 17 years later whilst serving with the USAF in Texas, I had to make an emergency landing at Stead AFB and was stuck in Nevada for 3 days for repairs. One night in a downtown bar in Reno, I sat quietly drinking my Martini when a familiar voice, albeit with an acquired accent, said, "Kelvie, it *is* you, isn't it?" I hadn't seen her since making that vow in 1946. She was unaccompanied and keen to chat to someone from the old country. She started in high spirits and, as I've often found with others when they first meet you, proceeded to convince me that her life was wonderfully happy and fulfilling, and she was only alone in the bar 'cos someone hadn't yet shown up. After a couple of drinks, she conceded she had a few problems, but after an hour it was all hands to the pumps as she poured out her sorrows. Her story was that she'd married a USAF guy from Burtonwood and returned to the US with him only to find that life there and with him, was not what she'd expected it to be. Now she was drifting and dreaming of going home to Mum—and she wished she'd married me instead. (Only she never let on, so nobody ever knowed it!)

That summer of '46 was also when I learned to dance and thereby lost a lot of the shyness I'd previously had. You could say I became more aware of the opposite sex, but you'd be wrong to think it was about sex. I was not to discover that for some years to come. But I had transcended as it were from being "a child, thinking like a child and acting like a child" to becoming a man and thinking as a man. I was now looking forward to returning to Cranwell, more focussed on my technical studies, and appreciating the fun to be had from working, living and playing with a bunch of fit bright young men with a common aim and a common enemy. Nothing better for concentrating the mind.

That summer leave was special in that it epitomised so much that was wonderful about one's youth, a mind sequestered and self-orientated, a body impervious to strain yet lazy and languid, a surfeit of zest but chasms of despair. It was a phase I was about to leave. The sun shone for every day of the 22 that I was home, learning to dance meant I felt so much more comfortable with girls, and I met a lass from Huddersfield that I was mad about (and thought I'd made pregnant because I once inadvertently touched her breast!). See—I told you I was naïve! Then there was one of those incredibly rare days of sport when on a Saturday in August I went at 10.45 a.m. to watch Lancashire play Yorkshire at Old

Trafford in "The Roses" match. At 2.15 I left to watch United play Arsenal at Maine Road with the Lancashire scoreboard reading:

1. Washbrook C..... not out 106
2. Place W............not out 101
Extras 28   Total 235 for no wicket

United beat Arsenal with a goal from my hero Jack Rowley, after which I went to Belle Vue Speedway to watch Jack Parker, Dent Oliver and The Aces beat our greatest rivals Wembley Lions. Yorkshire, Arsenal and Wembley, all duffed–up on the same day. If you sneer at those memories, you make a big mistake. You'd be looking at those events with old eyes and you can't possibly see what I saw and felt as I did when my world was much smaller than it now is, and I was little more than a boy.

A New Start

I didn't wait until October to give my CO the decision that I wanted to continue training. I saw him immediately and wrote to Matt Busby to say Thanks—but No Thanks. The effect on my enjoyment of life was staggering; I know I became a much more likeable person and could see more clearly what I had to do to succeed in the RAF. Perhaps that was the point when my mind was able to span the next 3 years and visualise a full career in the RAF. I already knew it would be a challenge, first to become an officer, and secondly to learn to fly. But now mentally, physically and emotionally, I was ready for that challenge. Moreover, I had a running mate in the shape of my bosom pal Norm who had joined specifically to become a navigator. Per ardua ad astra—here we come.

Learning to learn

I expected my time at Cranwell to be a difficult phase to write about. Not because I've forgotten it all—but because there's not much of interest to be said about the technical training to prepare us for the big bad world of the real RAF. Others in my Entry would wax lyrical about all things radar and radio and how becoming an extremely well trained and highly qualified engineer was the bedrock for what they did in their future lives. But not me, or my inseparable buddy Norm. Tehnically speaking, he and I were as dim as two Toch H lamps, and we struggled through our written and practical examinations.

But someone somewhere must have thought we were worth persevering with and so, on the 25th May 1949, we both proudly marched off the square at Cranwell to the strains of Auld Lang Syne played by the pipes and drums of the Apprentice Wing band. We were now fully-fledged Radio/Radar fitters, about to be released on an unsuspecting air force. We left Cranwell sadly yet joyously to await our postings whilst on leave. When I received mine 10 days later it was to RAF Ballykelly in Northern Ireland; Norm was off to RAF Lindholme near Doncaster. After 3 years of living within feet of each other, we were never to serve together again and only met twice before he stood as my best man at my wedding to Rosemarie in 1997. The other important outcome of that posting notice was that my lack of technical sharpness seemed to be more a question of aptitude rather than intelligence and an ability to learn. My Ballykelly posting was therefore described as a "holding post"; a prelude to being called forward to start flying training, and back to Cranwell, but this time as an Officer Cadet. Whilst I was doing a little jig in Manchester when I opened my OHMS letter, Norm must have received his posting notice in Portsmouth with acute disappointment. Bearing in mind he'd set his heart on becoming a navigator, his sad news was that he had failed at the final hurdle for aircrew selection, his aircrew medical. Norm served out his 12 years and left the RAF in 1960 to become a Civil servant.

A Royal Occasion

It would be wrong to dismiss those 3 Cranwell years completely because they were a very important part of my life. We worked hard under a fairly rigorous disciplinary regime, but we also played hard and enjoyed wonderful sporting facilities with opportunities to develop in other ways that few of us realised at the time. But I suppose it was the events away from the hard grind that one remembers best and with most affection.

Sometimes whilst writing, something will trigger my memory. This morning for instance, I was describing the severe winter of 1947 at Cranwell, when my TV screen displayed the simple stark unwelcome message "Princess Margaret has died". My mind went back to 1947, and to a gorgeous summer day when King George V1, Queen Elizabeth, and their two daughters made a formal visit to the RAF College. Some 50 Apprentices were selected from a cast of hundreds, to line a walkway across the beautiful lawn known as The Orange in front of the College. We young Apprentices were minions, of course, amongst the Royal Family, Clement Attlee, and the dozens of political, civil and military dignitaries that had flocked to such an occasion.

Nevertheless, small fry that we were, that day we enjoyed a grandstand view. Being 6ft 3 inches and a fraction, I was particularly lucky being first in line to the right of the Royal Party as they passed through our ranks. We were specially briefed not to move a muscle, turn our heads, or allow our eyes to wander a fraction from looking dead ahead. We had been on parade for hours, inspected by everyone but the King, and were standing "at ease" on The Orange for at least half an hour in the heat of the midday sun.

Suddenly there was a flurry of movement on the steps of The College and the Parade Commander's order rang out: "Royal Salute, Pre-sent Arms!" As we came to the Present in perfect unison, the Band of The Royal Air Force struck up "God Save the King", and as the music changed to a pastoral rendering of "Greensleeves", the Royal party began its leisurely stroll across the grass. I saw the King sharing a joke with Batchy Atcherley, the Commandant, and admired the Queen, all smiles and gracious hand movements. I kept rigidly to our briefing—still, ever so still, eyes unwavering—until, into my direct line of sight only some four feet in front of me and looking my way, came Princess Margaret with her sister looking the opposite way. I was so transfixed by her sheer loveliness that my eyes locked onto and followed her. As she drew level her eyes caught mine; she smiled, a gorgeous natural smile with a twinkle in her eye, and my young heart melted.

As if he could see through the back of my head, standing right behind me, was our drill Flight Sergeant. "Now then, you lads," he whispered (with a shout if you know what I mean), "keep your eyes front!" He might as well have told me to jump over the moon! On her 18th birthday, one of the few colour magazines of the time, probably *The Picture Post*, printed a full-page photograph of Princess Margaret on their cover. I kept that photograph as my pin-up and found it "amongst my souvenirs" fifty years later when cleaning out the attic of my house in Sussex. It is one of the oddities of life that special people become framed in our minds as they were when we first saw them; forever young, forever attainable and within reach of our dreams. I was to meet Princess Margaret on a handful of occasions later; two of them being especially memorable. I record them as they occurred, digressing from my main story but I consider that they belong together in the telling.

"This is not your day"

By 1953, a lot of water had passed under Palmer's bridge. I was now 23 and serving as a Flying Officer on my first Fighter Squadron at RAF Ahlhorn in Germany to where Princess Margaret came to present a Standard. With one of those quirks of fate that have dogged me, or blessed me, all my life, I was to meet her in two capacities. Firstly as Officer i/c the Station Guard of Honour, secondly as the Station Orderly Officer of the day, a secondary duty that came round about every two months for every young officer. Typically, the parade was held on the massive tarmac in front of the main hangers with the Princess and other dignitaries standing on a raised dais to watch the parade and take the salute at the march past. There came the time when the Princess was to inspect the parade starting with my Guard of Honour and she walked from the dais accompanied by the Station Commander and the C in C RAF Germany to where I stood rigidly and proudly at the front of my Guard. The order was given for the Parade to "Present Arms" which required the Guard to do just that with their rifles, and for me to first "kiss" the handle of my sword before whipping it down smartly to my right side with the blade flat and pointing forward. As I snapped my sword down there was an ear-piercing yelp and something rammed into my right leg. I stood rigidly, and doubtless red-faced, as the Princess exchanged words and laughter with the Station Commander, then came forward for me to be introduced and for me to tell her that the Guard was ready for inspection.

I turned to walk at her side as we inspected the Guard, and as we traversed the front rank she smiled and said, "You did awfully well—I'd hoped he wouldn't get in your way." At the very time that I'd wanted to say something clever, I was virtually inarticulate. As she left the Guard and carried on to inspect the parade, I saluted with my sword and returned to the front of the Guard. I was joined by the Station Warrant Officer who whispered out of the corner of his mouth that the owner of the Yelp was the Station Commander's black Labrador—but I was not to worry, as the dog was perfectly okay. I don't think that the SWO was one bit impressed with what I advised him to do with the dog!

Later that same day, the VIP's were in the Ladies Room of the Officers' Mess taking lunch and liquid refreshments. As Orderly Officer, it was my task to pass on any important messages or telephone calls for any of the assembled Brass. It's odd now to recall that in 1953 virtually all communication was by telephone or teleprinter; no E-mails, faxes or mobiles. So I either awaited a direct phone call, or one from our Operations Centre telling me what sort of message they'd received, for whom, whether it needed decoding for security purposes, and whether an answer was needed. I'd been briefed that any message for the C in C was to be passed to him immediately, which was routine in those days of a very hot Cold War. Flying Officer Palmer of course was praying that he did have a message to convey, as it would give him access to the inner sanctum and to the Princess. So when a call came from Whitehall for "himself", I took the gist of it and entered the Ladies Room with, I sincerely hoped, an air of importance and utmost urgency.

I manoeuvred around the small coffee tables that held silver buffet trays and glasses, and caught the C in C's eye. He beckoned me over. I whispered my message, to which he replied "All right, I'd better come out", excused himself from the Princess and half pushed me aside in the crowded room. In my anxiety to get out of his way, I stepped back quickly—Wrong! Just behind me was a short stubby coffee table that caught me behind the knees and I did a graceful but noisy back flip to land on my backside looking up at HRH.

The room fell silent—as it would. To my eternal gratitude the Princess, seeing I was unhurt, laughed merrily and said sweetly, "This *really* isn't your day, is it?" I muttered something like "I've had better", as my Station Commander with his wonderful charm and humour offered me a glass of Champagne and said, "There you are Johnny—I think you deserve that." "Hear, hear," said the Princess, raising her glass and touching me on the wrist. At that moment I wouldn't have cared if a nuclear war had started as for about six minutes we stood separated from the other guests and talked—as two twenty-one year olds—about life on a fighter squadron in Germany. What could have been a disaster became a wonderful and happy memory thanks to her sense of humour and human approach.

Lightning can strike twice

I admit my third tit bit sounds almost too far fetched after the Germany incidents in 1953. I'm not accident prone by nature; neither am I nervous or overawed by the great and the good. But, I said I'd tell it as it was, so I'll risk the odd comment of "A likely bloody story!" Besides, there were many witnesses as once again it was an air force parade, only this time I was a Squadron Leader at the age of 34 and was escorting the Princess back to the dais having inspected the Squadron. As we were walking and talking across the 50 yards of concrete, she stopped abruptly and, looking down, whispered anxiously, "My heel's caught in a crack." I remind the reader that we were in the middle of a huge parade being watched closely by a large and critical audience, some of whom were in a constant state of prayer that nothing would go wrong on a Royal occasion.

HRH tried a gentle wiggle of her foot—no good. I recall tight-lipped remarks about not wishing to lose the heel and having to hop back to the rostrum, and so forth. So, Sir Galahad, endeavouring to keep his trusty sword under control and conscious that this was a Royal ankle with which he was dealing, knelt and tried to encourage the wayward heel to dislodge. Only by holding the shoe in one white-gloved hand and the royal ankle in the other, was disengagement without damage eventually possible.

"I do hope that you're not enjoying that too much, Squadron Leader," I heard her say as she took her hand off my shoulder. I looked up startled, only to see the mischievous twinkle in her eyes and a smile that lingered at the corners of her mouth. Regaining my composure, we continued towards the rostrum where people keen to ensure that she was indeed okay, and that their heads were not for the chopping block, whisked the Princess away from me. I was fairly chipper about the incident. It hadn't spoiled the day at all and she took it in her stride, treating the potentially embarrassing incident as a laugh. Not only was Princess Margaret very beautiful, but also she had immense charm, genuine sex appeal, and a lovely soft girlish laugh. You were made to feel entirely at ease in her presence.

The reaction I faced from some of the senior officers present was not so enjoyable; indeed, some was distinctly poisonous: "What the hell do you think you were playing at out there, Palmer?" "What took you so bloody long anyway?" "Why didn't you signify there was a problem?" "What were you saying to the Princess, we didn't think it was so damned funny up here!" My Station Commander, a down to earth and very astute Ulsterman, hit the nail on the head when he said, "Pay 'em no heed John, they're all bloody jealous. Did yer get her autograph as well?"

Rumour has it that, particularly later in life, Princess Margaret was very protocol conscious and could be hard on anyone who overstepped the mark. When she was alive, so many people had so many unkind things to say about her. Now she's gone, they're singing her praises. I was fortunate enough to see her on only half a dozen occasions and to exchange but a few words with her in perhaps a total of 15 minutes. That hardly makes me an expert, but what I saw and heard, I liked enormously. "All of my memories are happy to-night." The romantic in me wishes she had married her Group Captain. They would have been happy, made a wonderful couple, and together been a great force for good in this country. That's how I see it on this sad morning in February 2002.

All for one and one for all.

Having digressed outrageously, I'm aware that you're agog waiting to hear of the courageous exploits of the 9M5's in the dark winter of 1947, the worst winter in the UK that I recall. My first wife would tell you that 1963 was far worse. But I don't know that because the wheels of my Javelin Mk9 were "in the well" at RAF Coltishall just as the blizzard was starting, and when the squadron landed back there from Singapore six weeks later in early March, the snow had all but gone!

Anyway, in 1947 the huge training station of Cranwell relied almost entirely for its supplies on the road and rail links to Sleaford and Lincoln. Anyone who has lived in Lincolnshire will automatically shiver as they recall the way that the wind comes straight from Siberia across the flat and featureless plain, with rain and snow driven horizontally, the latter to form deep drifts within a few hours.

We awoke one morning to find snow blacking out the windows of the barrack block. Our task was to clear the 3 miles of single line railway and narrow road to Slush (apprentice slang for Sleaford). It was backbreaking, cold, wet, miserable work, but it taught us how to work together, to keep a sense of humour and to respect the "management"—those who, whilst keeping us at the job, must also have felt considerable responsibility for our welfare.

It welded our Entry together. So much so that one night we returned to the barracks and carried out an unprecedented midnight raid on a senior entry dormitory, the occupants of which had been particularly brutal to us in our settling in days. We left not a single person in bed, not a bed left unwrecked, not a nose left unbloodied. I ask the reader to believe that in those days a fight, any fight, was "Marquis of Queensbury" stuff. If you thumped someone it was with a fist; not with a piece of wood, your boot or any other implement. You hit him above the belt, face on, standing up. The kick in the groin, a stab in the back, and the chains and screwdrivers are products of the modern generation. It was also one on one, not three or four on one.

If there was an unresolved conflict, a bare fist "Grudge fight" would be arranged. Usually in an empty dormitory late at night, lit by torches and candles, with a qualified referee, and as many spectators as could squeeze in. No staff or instructors ever came, but I was told years later that many a bet was placed on the outcome of those scraps and even the odd Officers' wife had been smuggled in to watch. We paid for our uprising by being given extra duties, more drill, loss of privileges and so on. But as we marched to breakfast the following morning after having had "the riot act" read to us, we went singing, not like whipped curs. We marched everywhere singing until the drill NCO's called it a day and stopped marching us. Above all, the senior entry we'd duffed up never darkened our doorstep again and the 9M5 massacre went down in Cranwell folklore.

Once Bitten…

In March 1948 there occurred an incident that provides the cue for me to state that, with the notable exception of the sport of Speedway, I hold a particular dislike of motorcycles. That dislike has peaked since coming to live in Wales where the peace of our locality and the state of our environment is wrecked by the mindless bikers that ride recklessly and fast on the footpaths and the grass areas. Between 1983 and 2000, I averaged over 125,000 car miles per year and watched with growing concern the motorcycle lunatics whose sheer stupidity raised the accident rate by the way they taunted and enraged other road users. In 1952, when converting from the Mosquito to the new Meteor jets, our Course started with 20 pilots and navigators and finished with 10 aircrew only. We killed four in flying accidents, and lost six through motorbikes—a terrible waste of life and careers. Later in the mid '70's when my two teenage sons got the bug, I spent many an evening dreading every phone call if they were out on their bikes. Fortunately both survived that dangerous phase.

Having got that pet hate off my chest, let me tell you about the weekend in March 1948 when United were playing Derby County in an FA Cup semi-final in Sheffield—a journey of 50 miles from Cranwell. I had an Uncle Walter living in Manchester who was a motorcycle buff. I believe he was probably born in a sidecar, and he was certainly capable of totally dismantling any machine, repairing, modifying and "mantling-it-up" again. He was notorious for returning home from his favourite watering hole, both drunk and asleep—miraculously without ever damaging himself or his bike. He and Auntie Madge had a soft spot for me, so soft in fact that one Monday evening in mid-March I was surprisingly summoned away from my dormitory to the guardroom by our flight sergeant ("Chiefy"). I arrived greatly agitated and fearful as to which of my nefarious activities had been discovered, to find the Chiefy accompanied by the driver of a van who said, "Sign here son, it's round the back" and drove off. Wondering what on earth was going on, I followed Chiefy around the back to find that my "parcel" was an enormous black gleaming beast of a motorbike, a Vincent Black Shadow, in fact. The Black Shadow was a name I'd only heard spoken by the real experts, reverently and in hushed tones—much as I would have described a goal scored by Jack Rowley or a sight of Cyd Charisse's legs!

With the bike came a premature Birthday card from my uncle saying he preferred his 250cc Norton, and I was to take good care of my VBS. Above all, I was not—repeat, *not*—to tell my mother (his sister) about the gift. I of course was staggered by the present and listened nervously as Chiefy reminded me that "Brats" were not allowed to keep motorcycles at Cranwell, that I had no time to go gallivanting around the Lincolnshire countryside, and I couldn't afford the petrol. He was right on all counts. He might have added that, besides, I didn't have a license, and wasn't there something about Insurance? However, now moving into "cunning mode", Chiefy pointed out that, as the van driver had left and my uncle had been so kind, he might consider letting me keep the bike in his shed—just until I could return it from whence it came, of course. Working on my well-known love of Manchester United, he hinted that an extremely rare 12-hour pass might be made available on the forthcoming Saturday and—if I liked—he'd be a real trooper and prepare the bike for my trip to Sheffield. I did like, and anyway what could I say? The deal was sealed.

There was the odd snag. Firstly, I had only ever ridden—and then rarely and recklessly—an old 250 cc clunker. Secondly, I didn't have tickets for the semi-final. I therefore offered the back seat to a professed Derby County supporter who also claimed to be an experienced biker. Abusing my advantage, I black-mailed Chiefy into giving him a 12-hour pass also and decided to play the ticket problem by ear. On the fateful morning, we set off from Chiefy's house disguised in flying Jackets and Biggles goggles and were soon streaking north westerly along a then deserted Ermine Street towards Newark. At Newark we turned north up the A1 where, in relatively heavy traffic, much of my bravado disappeared and the remainder of the trip to Sheffield was decidedly sedate. I ignored the ribald comments from the pillion about changing gear and being allowed to overtake a funeral. He shut up when he realised he might not get a chance to drive it himself.

As we drove through the centre of Sheffield, it was raining heavily. My inexperience showed as I tried to corner at traffic lights too fast and the bike slid away across the gleaming wet cobbles, dumping Bob and I in a very wet gutter. As we lay there, quite unhurt but fearful of the consequences and worrying about the bike, the dark shape of an enormous Yorkshire copper loomed above us. "Get up, pick up thee bloody bike, and get out of here!" We did so; only, Bob drove to Hillsborough as by now my nerve was shaky to say the least. At the ground, we paid a nice lady 2/- to leave the bike in her front garden, and went to find someone who could sell us two tickets. We accosted a seedy looking character who offered us two five bob standing tickets for £15. I was explaining that we might be able to raise a fiver between us when Bob grabbed the tickets and ran off into the crowd yelling, "Leg it, Kel!" Before I was able to take his advice I collected a black eye, left our ticket tout scouse with his hooter looking distinctly broken, and returned to find Bob swigging tea with the lady looking after the bike. United won 3-1, I was elated, Bob distraught, until I told him he could pilot our mighty steed back to Cranwell.

We rode back in the dark, another new experience for me, stopping at the odd hostelry en route and a Fish and Chip shop in Newark. As we mounted our machine for the last 12-mile leg of our journey, Bob was looking decidedly wonky so I said I'd drive back as the roads were now well nigh empty. We reached Leadenham with 4 miles to go and climbed the hill to see the rotating beacon of the College flashing across the flat and featureless terrain ahead. With not another light in sight, or any buildings of any sort, I opened up the throttle, put my head down and went faster than I'd done all day, exhilarated, and already looking forward to telling the rest of the chaps what a day we'd had.

Suddenly, right in the middle of the road, my headlights illuminated wall-to-wall cow. We struck amidships, and I recall vividly leaving the seat of the Black Shadow as we hit the bloody thing. I landed in a thick hawthorn hedge that broke my fall. I moved slowly to check I hadn't broken anything and then gingerly extricated myself from the thorns. I listened carefully, but could hear nothing except the murmur of the breeze that always blew in Lincolnshire. I stumbled along the hedgerow until some 20 yards on I heard a noise that I took to be groaning. I crashed through the hedge, saw a dark shape and knelt down to see how badly my friend was injured. He wasn't; the noise I'd heard was him laughing and he simply said, "You do have brakes on that bike, you daft sod!"

We were lucky; not so the poor cow or the bike. At around 3 a.m., the milkman who delivered milk to the camp came along and took the bike and us back to Chiefy's house. I never saw that bike again, and to tell the truth I didn't care. Uncle Walter popped his clogs very soon after so I was excused the acute embarrassment of taking the bike back. Just to show that human nature is often better than we think, when I went home for summer leave that July, I was handed a little stack of white £5 notes by Chiefy who'd placated all the offended parties, repaired the bike, and rewarded me handsomely to get his hands on his dream machine. Blackpool, here I come, with money to burn for once!

Did we do that?

In June 1948, the Entry went en masse to a Summer Camp. Before you say "lucky buggers"and your mind switches to tropical palms and blue seas, let me tell you that the tented camp was located in the sand dunes at Anderby Creek near Mablethorpe, famous for its bracing breezes. I have always thought of that as the world's biggest "con job" because to me that coastline is always cold and cheerless; the sea is either grey or brown and approaching freezing, and the local countryside is flat and dismal—as are the girls, incidentally. But beggars can't be choosers, and it was after all a welcome break from the Cranwell scene. We slept four to a tent and we named ours, romantically, "The Sweaty Sock" in honour of '018 Smith who could have stunk for England! We were there to develop field skills, improve our marksmanship and carry out various weird tasks that fell loosely under the heading of Initiative Training.

One lunchtime there occurred one of those incidents that you look back on and say, "Did we actually do that?" Our foursome had walked back from the mess tent to prepare our rifles for target practice, which involved chucking bottles and cans into the sea and blasting away from the sand dunes. Typically, one of our chums-lets call him Fred—managed to jam a live round in the breech. He was sitting on his camp bed opposite Norm and I with his rifle at an angle of about 10 degrees above the horizontal. To unblock the round, he began striking the bolt fiercely with the palm of his hand—oblivious to the torrent of condemnation he was getting from his colleagues.

Inevitably, the round fired and passed literally within inches of my face, followed instantly by cries of alarm and consternation further down the line of some 12 tents. We rushed outside to see people standing around looking for the culprit. The .303 bullet had left the Sweaty Sock some 3 feet from the ground and had gone through every tent in the line between 3 and 5 feet from the ground before knocking over a tea urn in the mess tent. We reckoned that Fred's bullet had passed within 4 feet of about 30 young men. Had you lined 'em up and asked him to miss them all deliberately he couldn't have done it. This was before the days of a million safety rules and regulations and before everyone faced a Court of Enquiry for any offence. An instant Investigation was carried out—like 20 seconds worth of deliberation by the drill sergeant. The usual procedure of search for the guilty, persecution of the innocent, was carried out, with the end result being that the Sweaty Sock four were put on latrine duties for the remainder of the detachment.

Nevertheless, there is a happy ending. Those readers familiar with tented camps situated in the *bundhu*, will know that on Day One an enormous hole is dug, perhaps 5 yards square and 10 foot deep, into which all the latrine and kitchen waste is dumped before being filled in with the sand and soil piled high on the sides. On the last Sunday afternoon, the other three sweaty sockers watched as Fred made his way to the top of the surrounding bank and began to empty his obnoxious latrine into the now brimming pit with his nose held high in the air to minimise the stench.

Suddenly, as if we were all praying for it to happen, the sides of the pit crumbled and Fred slipped before sliding slowly towards the mire. At first he said nothing, but as the awful realisation dawned on him, he clawed frantically at the loose sand, uttering desperate strangled cries of "Help!" We of course all rushed to save him, but somehow not one of us reached him in time and we heard the sickening squelch as our friend made his splash down. If the truth were known, we did consider just filling in the pit there and then. But instead we found a rope, tied it to a nearby truck and threw Fred the other end (from a safe distance, you understand). When he eventually pulled himself out, he tottered the 30 yards to the North Sea and stayed there until dusk. He did not sleep in the tent that night, and a much-chastened lad was never allowed to forget the lesson that abuse of firearms could land you in the deepest khaki.

Mens sana in corpore sano

As my wise Squadron Commander had observed, at Cranwell you could play as much sport as you wanted and the choice was virtually unlimited. In the post-war RAF, Wednesday afternoons and Saturday afternoons were dedicated to sport, Saturday mornings being part of the working week. I chose Soccer above Rugby because one could play for the Wing team on the recognised sports days, but also play for the entry in a Sunday league and play 5-a-side in the spacious gymnasium. In the winter season, I also played Basketball in the evenings and in the summer it was Cricket and Athletics. I was tall, thin and fast, so ran the 100 and 200 yards sprints and specialised in the Hop, Step and Jump (Triple Jump) and High Jump.

The benefits of so much sport are obvious; not so obvious now is the fact that there was little else available in the way of entertainment. There was no TV, no tapes or tape recorders; a radio was a noisy little box that supplied very little "pop" music, and the camp cinema did one show per evening at 6 p.m. and showed the same programme for three or four nights. I've mentioned that we were not allowed off camp, there were no girls available, and the NAAFI did not serve beer to Apprentices. A few of the "boffins" ran an amateur radio club, we had a dubious art class, and rumour had it that the camp laundry was a front for all sorts of skulduggery. But 95% of us played sport. By "sport" I don't mean what passes for sport today—things like darts, billiards, snooker, etc., which properly fall under the headings of Games or Pastimes and certainly not sport. If not the popular team games, one could choose boxing, wrestling, archery, gymnastics, swimming, small bore shooting, horse riding, fencing, or cross country running. So we were incredibly fit young men with our minds and bodies well occupied; so much so that we were all asleep at 10.30 p.m. before our young heads touched the pillow.

As in any military service, sport also played its part in team building, in engendering an *esprit de corps*, establishing a corporate identity for an Entry, a Wing or a whole Station. I suspect many of the young men who saw the value of teamwork at Cranwell, found it to be the fabric of effective business organisation later in their careers. Soloists are inspiring in opera and perhaps in small entrepreneurial ventures, but there is no place for them in large companies. That is not to say there is no place for the individualist, only that it is necessary for members of a team to suppress individual desires for the overall good of the team. At Cranwell, over a 3-year course, one could simply not be a loner.

Self-image too is important in sport, as it is in business. A corporate team like a rugby team must think of itself as a winner. Customers, like patients selecting their doctor, will seldom entrust themselves to those who do not exude legitimate, quiet pride and confidence in their own accomplishment and ability to produce. And then there's motivation. In sport this is often equated with mental toughness. How else does one explain the many occasions in sport when one team soundly beats another only to find itself thrashed by the loser the next time they meet? Motivation will almost always beat mere talent. We had motivation in abundance at Cranwell.

I learnt a lot about life from my sporting days at Cranwell. I also learned some hard lessons as some of the cockiness and arrogance in me was channelled in ways that greatly assisted me in later life. I particularly remember the satisfaction of expelling from our soccer team a number of prima donnas who, for all their skill and experience, were seldom able or willing to give of their best in the inter-Entry matches on which so much Entry pride depended. I replaced them with players with little natural talent, but immense enthusiasm and determination to succeed. We were hammered in the first few matches, but as the spirit and understanding grew, we became the team to beat. The Palmer who arrived at Cranwell would never have done that. It was a lesson that I benefited from a hundred times in my flying career, during my time in Industry, and am still using in Residents' Association and Youth Club management.

Who do you support?

In my day, if you played sport, it was odds on that you also supported your local professional team. Passion for sport defies logic: it is a disease that strikes early in life and becomes a magnificent obsession that stays with you throughout your life unmoved and undiminished by the inevitable peaks and troughs of success, failure and blinding mediocrity. Supporting a team isn't a question of convenience or expediency; it's tantamount to religion, a contract written in blood that is guaranteed to give sleepless nights and hours of nail-biting anguish as the in-vision scores flash up or you pick up a newspaper in the outreaches of the empire. What else could drive a successful and mature man to sit up a tree on Cup Final day until 4.55 in case he heard the cries or cheers that would signify a winning goal for the opposition? What else would cause that man to follow a cricket scorecard on Ceefax through his fingertips to see how many wickets had fallen? Strange indeed how those we think of as our greatest heroes can also seem the most vulnerable!

And of course it's not all about results. Sport has a way of affecting family relationships and friendships. There are days on which even the most loving of marriages come under severe strain as the clock ticks around to the magic hour and what seemed like an easy victory on paper suddenly becomes a life or death encounter. Long after I've gone, there will be friends, enemies and family whose memories of JKP will be aroused by a score flash or headline and fancy they hear me shouting

"Way-to-go-lads!" or "bloody Arsenal!" Some may curse me for those memories; others will find them an emotional trigger when they have all but forgotten what I looked like or how I figured in their lives.

My overriding passion, to which I refer many times in this journey through my life, has been Manchester United. It was handed down to me like some tribal ritual from my Dad and his Dad. But it was forged in Manchester and the RAF, in the 40's in the face of adversity when City were the more successful team and only the Jewish lads at MGS wore the red, white and black. At the tender age of 13, I learned how seriously even the old and illustrious took their allegiances when a red mist came down and I painted the statue of our founder, Hugh Oldham, in United colours. As I gritted my teeth against the stinging lash of the cane on my posterior, my addiction hardened with every gasp knowing that Him that inflicted my punishment was an avowed City fan.

My second love was cricket. Lancashire C.C.C. played at the other Old Trafford and before the days when TV allowed you to see the swing, spin and flight of every ball, I would sit in the cheap seats some 80 yards from the wicket and watch my heroes in white in what I can only describe as an idyllic setting with the game almost suspended out of time and space. Time and distance must lend enchantment because in those balmy days of my youth, the sun always shone, the meat and potato pies were always hot and crowds were friendly and appreciative of the finer points of our magnificent game. For all the excitement of a Test match or county final, cricket for me is a game for playing rather than spectating. I've played on many an English village green and on beautifully located cricket grounds the world over, and the abiding impressions are of tranquillity, gentility, and sportsmanship, and of romance with a cutting edge of competitiveness—all in a land of eternal sunshine. A warm breeze rustles the autumn leaves of my mind and the tears come easily as I recall a verse that was on the first scoresheet that I ever bought at Old Trafford:

> "For the field is full of shades as I near the shadowy coast
> And a ghostly batsman plays to the bowling of a ghost,
> And I look through my tears on a soundless-clapping host
> As the run stealers flicker to and fro
> To and fro
> Oh my Hornby and my Barlow long ago!"

With football for the winter and cricket for the summer, I found a third spectator passion so different that was enthusiastically shared by all my family—Speedway. Whereas soccer is about hours and cricket about days, Speedway is about 60 seconds of skill, noise, courage and danger as four men complete four anti-clockwise laps of a cinder track. Once again, it's about a commitment, being identified with one team, which in my case was the famous Belle Vue Aces who rode on England's largest track in the middle of the old Belle Vue Zoological Gardens in Manchester. Their home race night was Saturday, which meant no confliction of loyalties with what was happening at either Old Trafford. My love of speedway started in 1945 and my night out on my 75th birthday will be to the world championship at the Millennium Stadium in Cardiff accompanied by my two sons.

Rugby has played a great part in my sporting life, but much more as a player rather than spectator; except for a special interest in England and Sale, one of my old clubs and my local team as a boy. These four sports have given me so much pleasure as well as anguish, and I've been blessed to share the passion with my family and with so many good friends around the world. I was already firmly wedded to all four back in those teenage years at Cranwell and were you to ask any of the other survivors what they remember most about Kel Palmer, I'll guarantee their answer will have nothing to do with my intelligence, charm, good looks, cracking girl friends or all-round-good-egg qualities. It will be either "Bloody Man U", or some reference to one of my other sporting passions.

Time to fly the nest

I had arrived at Cranwell in 1946 with few ideas but lots of hopes and dreams. I left in 1949, with lots of ideas, reinforced hopes, and dreams that now seemed attainable. I was no longer a boy, but a young man, confident, passionate and dedicated to securing my future career. While some of the limitations I feared I might have had were confirmed, some fears proved to be quite unfounded. More significantly, I had found so many more interests, openings, outlets, challenges and goals for which to aim in my young life. I would wish for today's young to have the hope and ambition I had.

The euphoria of our passing out was tempered by the knowledge that few of us would meet again, that each of us would have to make his way alone in the adult world, and that those of us who were lined up for further technical training or as officers or aircrew, might yet fall at one of those hurdles. But as we travelled by coach for the last time together to Grantham railway station, we sang the songs we'd sung together, laughed at the same jokes, and ribbed the same unfortunates that we'd been ribbing for 3 years. The significance of that day did not really hit me until I was the only 9M5 left on the train as it later pulled out of Huddersfield on its way to Manchester. I suddenly felt alone and experienced a few moments of apprehension about the future. I knew I'd been selected for flying training, but would have to wait about six months for a course during which time I'd ply my new trade on an RAF station as yet unknown.

In a way, though, even that uncertainty was exciting. Besides, I was going home to swank off to my old chums; there were lots of stories to catch up on, and tomorrow night I'd be at Belle Vue Speedway to see my beloved Aces. I had money in my pocket, even some in the bank, and I scrubbed up well enough to guarantee that I'd persuade a pretty girl to come with me to the "Pictures" on Sunday night. To top it all off, there was Mum's cooking to look forward to. You could indeed say that Kelvie Palmer went home that June day in 1949, a happy and contented bunny.

"Lock up your daughters." RAF Apprentice Graduation—1949

5

THE IN-BETWEEN YEARS

Learning the hard way

It is said that Life is what happens to you whilst you're busy making other plans. Certainly that is what happened to me between June 1949, when I left Cranwell, and March 1951 when I started my Officer Cadet training on the Isle of Man. My final Board at Cranwell had said I would be recalled there to start my flying course "in about 6 months". Meanwhile, for me to gain experience and pay back some of my radar training costs, I would be posted temporarily to RAF Ballykelly on the shores of Lough Foyle, Co.Londonderry.

I knew little about Ireland. I'd been told that it was a country in which it was easy to believe in ghosts and goblins, in fairy tales, and the wee folk that lived at the bottom of every garden. Before the IRA became a disease on that beautiful island, it was still possible to walk through quaint villages with gay and lively street markets, expecting to be confronted around every corner by Barry Fitzgerald or Bing Crosby driving a jaunting car. The rivers were alive with salmon and the picturesque ever—changing landscape drew artists and photographers to capture the rugged grandeur of the wild Atlantic coast of Donegal and the softer beauty of Fermanagh and Killarney. So for me in 1949, leaving the academic and sheltered life of Cranwell, this was a thrilling adventure; an "overseas" posting that I anticipated with great relish.

The fun started when I caught the overnight boat from Heysham to Belfast. Those old clunkers were hardly the height of luxury as you spent some eight hours crammed down in the bowels with dozens of noisy drunken travellers, all praying for a smooth crossing—which was a rare occurrence. As I sat munching the obligatory cheese and tomato sandwiches provided by my mum, I was joined by a stranger and his lady friend. She proceeded to scoff my supper and he to entertain the lower deck with his marvellous tenor voice. He was the singer Josef Locke and he introduced me to the country of his birth with classics such as "The Rose of Tralee" and "Galway Bay" In the chill of a Belfast dawn, the cheerful pair accompanied me on the train journey west to my new home at Ballykelly. When they alighted at the little coastal village of Castlerock, I pulled down the window strap to wave them farewell. As my train chuffed its way along the ocean side, I could hear his voice fading as he sang, "Good bye, goodbye, I wish you all a last Goo-ood bye." It was a fitting and lovely welcome to Ireland.

On arrival at Ballykelly, no one knew anything about me only being temporary or bound for a pilot's course. As far as the Radar Servicing Flight went, Palmer was just another pair of hands. In fact, I was much more than that to them since, with the exception of a lazy skiving Sergeant, all the airmen were National Servicemen, a whining bunch of glum-faced malingerers with countless grievances who ticked off every day to their release after completing their 2 year service. As a Regular, and a highly trained one at that, I was virtually put in charge of them after a week or so and left to get on with it, whilst the sergeant nipped over the fence into the next field where lived a farmer's daughter. I was soon doing 90% of all repairs, driving the Section *garry* (truck) out to the hangers and dispersals, and installing, running up and servicing all the electronic equipment on the aircraft. Ballykelly was a Coastal Command station with 2 Maritime Patrol (MP) squadrons of Lancasters, 2 Halifax Meteorological Flight aircraft, 3 US built Privateer MP aircraft and a few Ansons and 1 Wellington—some 25 aircraft in all which operated round the clock and which needed their anti-submarine and navigation systems in top class order for their arduous all weather operations hundreds of miles out into the Atlantic.

I was therefore working like a one-armed paperhanger, but it was a wonderful introduction to RAF operational life and a comprehensive technical education. I became so immersed in the operation of the equipment in the air that, whenever I could, I would fly to see how well it worked and to make in-flight adjustments to optimise the systems to suit the needs of the navigators and signallers. I read the print off the Technical Servicing manuals, having found that they'd never been taken out of their covers before. I was able to improve the radar performance and reliability so much that I was driven down one day a week to the beautiful lakes of Fermanagh from which the RAF operated three Sunderland flying boats, to service their radar. Rare birds indeed, those Irish Sunderlands.

By the end of that first summer I understood why they say that if you want a job doing well and quickly, give it to a busy man. Above all perhaps, I had developed an understanding of my trade that I'd never felt at Cranwell. Strange, isn't it, how often in life that what once seemed beyond grasp and comprehension, later becomes so obvious and simple?

The Ireland of dreams

I fell in love with Ireland. From the airfield looking west are the Hills of Donegal with their ever-changing pattern of clouds and shadows. Lincolnshire had been flat, grey and windy. Here the coastline was rugged and spectacular with miles of golden sand and hidden coves where one could watch the Atlantic rollers crashing against the rocks, sending spray high up into the cliffs where thousands of seabirds wheeled and screeched.

When I had a complete day free, I would make the tortuous bus journey across to Donegal and to a lovely bay south of Malin Head where the Atlantic unwraps itself restlessly onto the curve of a deserted beach against a background of white cloud and blue distances. I would look along the long line of spray when the tide was full, listening to the grated roar of the pebbles which the waves first drew back and then flung higher up the strand on their return. The noise would begin, then cease, and then again begin with a sort of quivering cadence that had a hidden note of sadness, lulling my young mind into a melancholy daze. I've sat, alone or accompanied, on many beaches all over the world in the 57 years since, listening to the noise of the shifting shingle. Sometimes in the ebb and flow of the ocean or on the murmur of the wind, I've heard a whisper of human misery; sometimes a song of joy and often it has meant a reluctant exploration of my memory and of my faults. This man has made many more resolutions listening to the sounds of nature than he has ever made on New Year's Eve.

Inland from the airfield were rolling hills. Sparkling, dancing, busy rivers—alive with salmon and trout—eagerly winding their way over boulders and through small gorges that seduced you into taking a hundred photographs where one might do. My chief haunts in those hours of golden leisure were the banks of the Faughan that ran through a vale of green bracken. There came a point where one had to climb through leafy glades and oak and birch before joining a sheep track that emerged on the edge of a flat rock, projecting some hundred feet over one side of a chasm, where the river made a rapid roaring sound as it was swallowed up by a dark yawning gulf. Legend has it that a brave young man once jumped from the ledge to escape from the irate father of his forbidden lover. An Irish Lorelei if you like; but to all disbelievers and armchair scoffers I can vouch that when you sit in solitude in such a place, the line that separates reality from fantasy is faintly drawn.

From the ledge, the eye could catch the glint of the winding stream as it emerged a quarter of a mile away into an open course. In this place of inexpressible charm, the memories of the song I'd sung at Grammar School, the Londonderry Air, came back to haunt me. It was written, I later found, on those very banks where "so oft I strayed, ah many years ago". I was never a fisherman, but the words of the poet strike a chord in my heart and bring a tear to my eye.

> *"When I am alone, all existence seems to fade in a oneness with my soul and my memories. Eventually, all things merge into one—and a river runs through it. I am haunted by the sound and the sight of waters."*

Then there was sport. I now had the freedom to play both soccer and rugby; the former on Wednesdays with the RAF, the latter on Saturdays with the big boys in Ballymena. I was to understand for the first time what "being hard" meant, and after counting my bruises after every match I got the message and made sure I gave as good as I frequently got! I even found time for girls and through the local church contacts about which I've written elsewhere, I met a girl and started to see her regularly at the end of '49. So I was a very busy young man and a happy one. That was the time of course that I'd expected to be called forward for flying training. On hearing nothing, I asked Flight Lieutenant Carter, the Radar Section C.O, if anything had come through. He said not, but that he'd let me know as soon as it did. I was too gullible, too naïve to press him further. But also, I must admit, too contented with the life I was leading for it to seem a problem at the time. When I now look back across the decades at the half dozen or so choices in my life that have been decisive, I find that at the time I made them, I had very little sense of the seriousness of what I was doing. Only later did I discover that what had seemed an unimportant stream to cross was, in fact, a Rubicon.

Faith and Hope, but little Charity

Ireland was effectively my first brush with religion; it set the scene for the part that Belief, Faith, and Worship has played in my life. I'm quite unqualified to say anything sensible about the subject, except that in 75 years something must have registered. I'll start by declaring that I do believe in God and that no one could *want* to believe in Him more than I; to be able to say with 100% sincerity that "I'll cling to that old rugged cross, 'til my trophies at last I lay down".

My belief these days doesn't have a Church of England, Roman Catholic, Baptist, Buddhist—or any other label. Neither am I unduly concerned about this or that version of the Bible, Prayer Book or any other similar religious document. But, I've seen far too much of this miraculous, fascinating, beautiful and awesome world to believe that "it just happened". I've also met too many earnest, contented and happy people of all colours, beliefs and persuasions to suspect that they were living in a fool's paradise and did not feel, experience, know and love something or someone to whom they bowed in worship. I've been privileged to hear many wonderfully eloquent orators all over the British Isles; I've sat spellbound in a huge Church in Seoul seating thousands, joined a vibrant mixed race congregation in Cape Town, and met with the drug-ridden people in a dark and eerie Mission flat in the Walled City of old Hong Kong. I've been charmed and persuaded, frightened and encouraged, shaken and stirred. I've wept tears both of joy and of pity as people have prayed, sung and communed with their God.

Luke's Gospel in the Holy Bible recounts the Parable of the Sower. Some seed fell on the path to be trampled on and eaten by the birds. Some fell on stony ground, but withered as it grew for lack of moisture; whilst some fell amongst thorns that choked the plants as they grew. And some fell on good soil, and grew to yield a bounteous crop. It seems to me that in my life I've wavered back and forth between all four of those states, from the Agony to the Ecstasy. But for most of my life, sad to relate, I've dwelt in the desert of Apathy, or perhaps more correctly under a banner that might properly have read "I'm all right Jack". Worse still, I've been aware of it and regretted it.

In his wonderful 19th century verse "The Hound of Heaven", Francis Thompson wrote the words that often puzzled me, and always haunted me:

"I fled Him down the nights and down the days; I fled Him down the arches of the years.
I fled Him down the labyrinthine ways of my own mind; and in the midst of tears I hid from Him.
Up vistaed hopes I sped; and precipitated adown titanic glooms of chasmed fears, from those strong feet that followed, followed after..."

Thank God—it's Monday

Going to Church did not top my list of pleasurable experiences. Between eight and eighteen, Church meant dressing up in a Cub's or Boy Scout's uniform and being marched there on special occasions in a self-conscious gaggle. In my 'teens it was first an ATC uniform and then an RAF uniform with the added pain of hours on parade and intensely critical inspections of haircuts, uniform creases, polished brass, and white blanco-ed webbing. Everyone, irrespective of religious denomination or atheist, went on parade at RAF Cranwell. Everyone suffered the inspections, but before the parade marched to the Church, the "Jews and Roman Catholics" fell out, and anyone calling himself a non-believer was spirited off to work in the cookhouse. A Wing of Apprentices on the march was indeed a fine sight and the Officers and their elegantly dressed ladies would gaze on our arrival at the Station Church as if we were a Battalion of Guards. To tell the truth, we were a bloody sight smarter!

Apprentices were not however noted for their hymn singing, and in the back pews of the church during an hour long service, one might manage to read the *News of the World*, write a letter home, or even sneak a few hands of pontoon. Then it was on parade again to march past The Commandant and his entourage on the steps of the RAF College. On a good day, prayers might have been answered, and the march back to quarters would take the exhilarating form of an Apprentice "mutiny", led by the pipes and drums of the forty-strong Aircraft Apprentice Band. I never remember the "mutiny" being pre-planned, but if something had upset the senior entries, word got around and the entire Wing of some 700 apprentices (14 Flights) would march the half mile back to the square in "open order", stretched across the main road, to that most stirring and rebellious of marches "The Black Bear". Rabble-rousing and bawdy songs were sung, hats thrown in the air, and for maybe 20 minutes the Apprentice Wing ruled. Sometimes the drill NCOs made us pay with rifle and pack drill, but now and again some enlightened officer would see our belligerent behaviour for what it was, a real expression of spirit, and our corporate indiscretions were overlooked. Years later when I went back to the College as an officer, I looked forward to a mutinous parade. Indeed, had there not been one, I would incite one! The pride and passion in the march was something that stirred me then as the memory stirs me now. Even when I became a watcher rather than a participant, the triumphal Black Bear march was a spectacle that literally brought a lump to my throat, added inches to my chest size, and made me weep unashamedly. Oh that something in the Church during my boyhood days might equally have aroused my passion, or left a spark that might have turned to flame in due course.

Into the Fire

There could not have been a greater contrast to the religious voids of Wythenshawe and Cranwell, than that which confronted me on arrival at Ballykelly. The station personnel were probably no different than those in Lincolnshire when it came to religion. The difference was that I was no longer forced to go to church and I was free to go anywhere I wished when not on duty. Initially I was not aware of the unique problems that dominated religion in Ulster. I was far too busy exploring the beautiful countryside and coastlines of Londonderry and Donegal. My weekends were spent travelling to Buncrana on the Atlantic Circle where one could buy nylons for the girls, and butter, sugar and chocolate (still rationed in the UK). But best of all, one could sit down in an ordinary yet cosy little café to a huge plateful of steak, eggs, ham, mushrooms and tomatoes, washed down with unlimited mugs of strong tea, for around £1.00. After RAF food and the normal café fare in 'Derry, Buncrana was an island of privilege in a sea of tastelessness. It is strange that the Irish who can produce the most perfect porridge and soup, and the most wonderful "Fries", seem incapable of cooking meat. The Scots also cannot cook meat, especially venison—most of which finds its way onto boots for walking. But I digress. As the Buncrana novelty wore off and the nights began to close in, I found myself at a loose end and was "press-ganged" one Sunday by a trio of National Servicemen who worked with me and shared my billet. They had impressed me by their ever-friendly and cheerful attitude and, despite taking much verbal abuse, they openly declared themselves as Christians.

Mounted on four service bikes, we rode into Limavady in time for the 11 a.m. service. We rode back, uphill all the way, at 10 p.m. To put it mildly, I was overwhelmed by almost everything that happened that day. The Baptist Church was a quaint little place that was bursting at the seams for both the morning and evening services. The people made us extremely welcome, the hymn singing was vibrant and truly devotional, and the sermon of some 40 minutes could have gone on all day—it was that compelling. Surprise number two on leaving was to find that we were all farmed out to different families for lunch. Lunch was ready when we got to the house, prepared by the wife who left before Communion to feed her tribe.

Lunch finished around 2.30 which gave us just enough time to be at Sunday School at 3 p.m., finish at 4 p.m., High Tea at 5.30, Evening service at 6.30, end around 8 p.m., then up into a farmer's barn three miles out of town for a "country service" for the locals who couldn't get into town. Leave the barn at 9.30, in town 9.45, on bikes back to camp at 10 p.m. That was the regular Sunday routine with the occasional "away fixture" at another Baptist church on the coast or out to 'Derry, by a group of the young people who provided soloist singers or a choir, and perhaps a speaker, or the giving of "testimonies". During the week, there were various prayer meetings, bible classes, and fellowship groups that met in a different house each week. Religion was a fulltime occupation.

Seeing through the glass darkly

For an immature youth of 19, a long way from home and the friends I'd made at Cranwell, the situation that developed was inevitable. I was working exceptionally hard during the week under living conditions on the camp that were far from ideal. In 15 minutes I could be in the little market town of Limavady where I'd find a warm welcome, lots to do in a Christian fellowship, and the chance to see a bit of home life and taste home cooking in unusual surroundings. There were also many pretty Irish girls, and this was the first time in my life that I'd had the freedom, the inclination, and my own money to pursue that particular pastime.

And then there was religion. For the first time I was hearing about God and Jesus without any of the rituals to which I'd been accustomed in the Church of England. I was being led through the Bible to understand God's messages, and was hearing God being praised and worshipped with joy and thanksgiving. Love and forgiveness were replacing the messages of fear and damnation I'd so often heard proclaimed. Above all, perhaps, I was hearing a promise of Salvation, that sins could be confessed and forgiven. A question often asked upon meeting people for the first time was "Are you saved?" and if the answer was No, the retort was usually, "Then I shall pray for you to be saved." When one becomes locked into any programme of learning, the tendency surely is to be so engrossed with the good and attractive "pros" that one doesn't delve deeply into the "cons". I was hearing about a religion, a belief, that both made sense to me and pleased me. I was able to understand most of what I read, what I heard preached, and what was expressed in song and in open prayer.

For many months, that was enough and it was a while before I began to think more deeply about just what I believed and where the Baptist Church in Ireland stood in relation to other Protestant denominations and the Roman Catholic Church. That may have coincided with the demobbing of my National Service workmates and fellow travellers. All three left Ireland together and I was a lone "Godbotherer"in the Radar Section and in my billet, left to face the derision of some and the perfectly reasonable and genuine queries of others. I soon discovered that I was by no means an authority on anything much to do with religion and could do little more than defend my own newfound beliefs. I have to say that even if I managed to state those quite forcibly and persuasively, I did not always have the same degree of certainty deep down.

The Other Side of the Coin

But whilst I stayed in Ireland I was safe. I had the considerable might of the Baptist Church and its followers behind me and the distractions were few and not as "worldly" as if I'd been living in an English city. In 1950, Sundays in Co.Derry meant one activity, and one activity only—Church. There were no dances, no cinemas, no pubs, no sport, and only one café open at teatime that confined itself to tea and Irish currant bread. When I left Ireland in '51 I was briefly stationed in the Isle of Man. On the rare occasions that I could travel into Ramsey, I found the Methodist church (there being no Baptist church) a pretty cold and uninviting place. I was then posted to Portsmouth where again the "other denominational" churches were more like the Church of England with none of the friendliness and Christian commitment that I'd known in Ireland. I eventually found a niche in an Elim Church where I found the evangelistic spirit I sought with a large congregation of lovely people who worshiped in the way to which I'd been accustomed. But I knew before I left Portsmouth that I was now on the slippery slope—I was backsliding fast. I was by now a Pilot Officer, living in the splendour of the Officers' Mess, and thoroughly enjoying my flying and my usual sporting activities. Without the daily contact and fellowship of other Christians, my faith was not enough to sustain my commitment. I was still praying for God to make me good—but adding "but not yet!"

By the time I'd finished my flying training in 1952 and joined my first Squadron in Germany, I had drifted so far that when I returned on to Ireland on leave to see my fiancée, I felt distinctly out of place. Never again in the RAF was I to find any church that beckoned me; neither did I feel the urge or need to immerse myself in religion and matters of faith as I had in Ireland. I believe the same could be said of my then wife. She had grown up in a deeply religious family, in an equally religious country that put the church first above all. When, like me, she found herself cut off from virtually all Christian contact, she also fell away—though undoubtedly not as far as me.

Overseas at Last

In January 1950 an unexpected opportunity occurred for me to travel overseas for the first time. One of the units at Ballykelly was the Air Sea War Development Unit (ASWDU) which had aircraft and crews established to work up the tactics and procedures for maritime warfare and carry out development and operational testing of new tactics and prototype equipment. Two Lancasters were to fly to Australia to do joint service trials with the RAF on a new submarine-detection device called a sonobouy.

My hard work had paid off; ASWDU had specifically asked that I fly out with the detachment to look after all the aircraft and trials kit. I was thrilled, but also concerned that my aircrew course might come through, so I asked my C.O. again who said it was unlikely, but anyway we'd only be away for a month so I'd have lots of warning. In the event, we landed back in Ireland on June 10th! It was now a year since leaving Cranwell and I immediately asked about my aircrew course. Carter muttered something about delays, don't worry, we'll let you know. Once again I was both too trusting and too content with the life I had. But before I rush ahead, the Australian trip is worth a few paragraphs.

Older readers will remember how big the world was in 1950; younger folk would tend to ask, "What's the big deal?" In those days even France and Holland were "overseas", a visit to the eastern Med was a major undertaking, and the Far East was fantasyland to almost everyone but the troops who had served there until 1946. Australia was literally the other side of the world, a very long sea journey and a tortuous one by air in the slow, short range, altitude limited airliners of the day. With no TV, Australasia was never in your front room as it is now and very seldom even in the Pathe News at the cinema, unless there was a Test match down under. If anyone went to Oz, it wasn't a holiday or seldom for business; it was to emigrate.

So flying down to Darwin was a major adventure, a dream come true for a young man who'd never been further than London. We flew out via Gibraltar, Malta, and Tobruk in Libya. Then due south, clipping the corner of Egypt (Nasser's Corner) en route to Aden, on to Muscat in the Oman, Karachi, Calcutta, Rangoon and down to Penang in Malaya. I was virtually a passenger, having no aircrew role as such, so I spent most of my time lying in the see-through nose of the Lancaster, marvelling at the extraordinary scenery that passed below and often drifting off into a daydream of faraway places with strange sounding names. In later years I was often to fly those routes, either in the cockpit of a military aircraft or in the back of a 747, but that was always at very high altitude (30,000ft plus) and at high speed. In 1950 we flew much slower and much lower, often below 3000ft, seldom above 10,000ft. Presumably because the pilots had never flown the route before, and as most airfields then had no night operational capability, all our routes entailed a daylight take-off and landing. What a way to see the world for the first time!

The Lancaster was a noisy beast with four mighty Merlin engines throbbing away, and the ever-present pungent smelly mixture of aviation fuel, hot oil and a strange odour from the electronics that made one look suspiciously for smouldering wires. Air conditioning was not the top priority of those who'd designed it for destroying German industry in the war. Parts of the aircraft were boiling hot, real shirtsleeve stuff, but in other parts you were likely to freeze to death. Nevertheless, with the experience of the local flying I'd done, I was well prepared for my long hours in the nose. I'd been made a present of an American flying suit by an exchange officer on the Privateers, which was not only a sexy bright orange but had zips and panels everywhere that enabled me to keep warm or let out the heat when the sun was on the nose.

I'd also taken a sleeping bag, so if I wasn't looking down at the world I'd lie on my back and dream the dreams of a young man. I vividly remember looking up and back into the narrow fuselage and imagining what it must have been like on a pitch-dark night over Germany, perhaps on the run-in to the target. The sky potted with exploding shells, the gunners screaming about the approaching night fighters, and the pilots and navigator sweating to ensure they got their bombs on target. The forked piece of metal into which I jammed my coffee cup once held the bombsight; indeed there were many ghosts and memories to stir one's imagination. What luck; I was embarking on a wonderful adventure to see a world I'd never seen, from a bird's eye view in the heavens. By the time we'd reached our first overnight stop at Gibraltar, I'd settled in to a groove of activity—or non-activity. As we approached The Rock, I could see the coast of north Africa and, silly though it may now sound, I mentally ticked off Africa as "Been there, done that". I even had a dim and distant snap from my Kodak Brownie to prove it.

There were only four ground tradesmen between the two aircraft; an engine fitter, airframe fitter, electrician and me. The aircrew, far more worldly and experienced, were off like woolly bunnies into the local Spanish town of La Linea and, being good chaps, took us sprogs along. That was an education in itself. I did not know there were girls who did things like that. I'd never seen a donkey make an ass of himself, and I certainly was not familiar with the saying, "Nooky for love, money for souvenirs." We live and learn and I escaped from Spain with barely a blemish. Our electrician was not so lucky—he had too much of the local sherry, was beaten up for his watch, and would have heard the roar of eight Merlins in unison from his hospital bed as we took off for Malta the next morning. So now we airmen were three, and suddenly I was the expert Electrician as well as the radar man. If any reader thinks there's not much difference, try finding an electrical fault amongst 25 miles of intertwined cable with nothing more sophisticated than a clapped out voltmeter!

The leg to Malta was a bit of a blur; the previous night had taken its toll on a chap more used to Sarsaparilla than Sherry. Also, this was the time of year when the western Med. experienced its worst flying weather, with the aircraft unable to climb above the clag and so flying "down in the weeds" to remain Visual. This was no problem to the crew who operated most of the time around the UK in bad weather. But to me it was a very turbulent trip; moreover, I couldn't see anything of interest and, to make matters worse, the bloody radar started playing up. If someone stands at a blackboard and explains how to fix and tune the Transmitter/Receiver, or realign the scanner, it sounds so simple. To do it with the aircraft pitching, rolling, and hitting air pockets, it's difficult enough to hold your screwdriver or read the manual, let alone make sensitive adjustments whilst striving not to throw up into the scanner cupola. To hear the engine note change and the clump of the wheels lowering as we approached Luqa was therefore music to my ears.

We didn't hit the town that night, as the next day was to be one of the few days on which we flew two stages—the short trip to Benghazi in Libya and the longer desert route to Khartoum. But I got my tourist shots when we took off with the sun just coming up, and turned low and slow over Valetta. The sun lit up the bleached sandstone buildings around the spectacular harbour in which I could easily make out a number of capital ships, numerous smaller naval craft and half a dozen submarines. The flight was uneventful and dull before I was to set foot in Africa for the first time and to see how miserable the desert can look at first sight.

My appetite for the Aden leg was truly whetted when, during refuelling, the captain explained as we sat on huge oil drums that we'd see nothing but sand for hours. On approaching Khartoum, however, he would descend to 500 ft so that we could see the river life on the Nile. I picked out the silver ribbon of the mighty river in a shimmering haze. It spread from horizon to horizon and we seemed to fly for hours before we reached it and turned south. I sensed the heat and watched spellbound as we flew over the distinctive river craft, long lines of camels and small-tented encampments. My imagination told me I could hear the drums, the cries of the camel masters, and the sounds of the river. I was watching a scene from *The Four Feathers*, and was enthralled

Proceeding further east, the world unfolded before my eager eyes. By now I'd begun to feel as if I'd been born in the Lancaster. I sat up front on the flight deck, chatted to the navigator about our route and helped him take some sun shots with his sextant, and talked to the engineer about the way he "managed" the engines and was able to smell a fault long before it became a headache. I sat down the back amongst the new sonobouys and read all the literature with the Trials Officer, our navigator, who explained the technical features and tactics involved. My desire to fly as a career grew by the day, and I vowed to give officer Carter a hard time when we got back.

Leaving Khartoum, we skirted the Ethiopian highlands, over Asmara, and turned south down The Red Sea before heading east to the Yemen and the staging base of Khormaksar in the then Aden Protectorate. By now I was blasé about desert scenery, but Aden re-ignited my interest—first the view from the air as we watched the panorama unfold as in a Gary Cooper film, and later on the ground in the throng of weird and often fierce looking characters that contributed to the noise, smells, chatter and colour of the *souk* and feverish activity of the Arab traders on their dhows along the harbour.

By now I'd become accustomed to the way the aircrew operated on such trips. On landing, everyone—me included—would know exactly what had to be done to get the aircraft ready for the next stage. The captain would be busy checking that all the Customs and technical formalities were observed, the navigator would be checking the Met for the next leg and trying to find local maps, and the co-pilot or signaller would ensure that Khormaksar knew what pre-flight and in-flight catering was needed, and would allocate our overnight accommodation. Then it was back to the mess or barracks to get spruced up and head off downtown for shopping and the odd beer.

I suppose that was when I started doing my own thing. I was more than happy to have a cold beer or six, but I also wanted to see what made the rest of the world tick. I wanted to prowl around the harbour with my trusty little box camera, I wanted to look into those dark alleyways, go in shops that sold silk and gold and a million things one never saw in the UK. I decided that the most typical object I could buy in Aden would be a genuine camel stool—the thing the driver sits on atop the beast. One can buy cheap replicas, of course, but I wanted the real thing—sturdy, ornamental, and whipped and covered in leather. I persuaded a camel driver to sell me his and took it back to the airfield, well pleased with my purchase and related experience.

Later, when flying fighters, I was to realise how fortunate the Coastal and Transport guys were to have their own means of carrying large items, and I well recall on our return to Ireland how astonished the Customs man was to see what we'd stuffed into the Lancaster during a 5-month absence. My green leather stool was very special to me and it adorned our house for years until my first wife admitted she hated it and threw it out. Indignant, I recovered it, kept it in the attic and brought it proudly in 1995 to my second wife's house. Rosemarie humoured me for a few weeks, and then it was back to the attic! Sometimes women can be soulless; neither knew what I'd gone through. First, to buy that camel stool, then to protect it from thieving knaves for almost five months. Every now and then I nip up to the attic and promise it that it will be back in its rightful place soon. And so on to The Oman, Karachi, Calcutta, Rangoon, and finally into Penang in Malaya. As I write I ask myself how I can dismiss all those miles and all those countries in one line? I often felt like that too when, from the first class comfort of my 747, I could look down on the twinkling lights of a city, not knowing anything about the place and what sort of people lived there. Such a shame that we gloss over and miss so much in a new world of sound-bites and snapshots.

My strongest memories of those five stages include the long stretches over the Indian jungles and the Karachi-Calcutta leg on which the entire crew was ill with "Delhi-belly". We splashed down at Calcutta in a temperature of 105 degrees and a humidity of 95%. Guess who, as the only airman on board "C" for Charlie, had the honour of cleaning and fumigating it before we took off for Rangoon! But, as the saying goes, "It all jots up to experience" which stood me in good stead in the 60's and 70's when staging through the Indian sub-continent en route to and from the Far East in a modern fighter aircraft, strapped to an ejection seat. When shoehorned into a tight cockpit for over 12 hours when refuelled in-flight, you can't get up and walk back to the loo. If you have problems you either suffer for hours, or do as many of our formation did many times—make humble embarrassed apologies—and "divert" rapidly to the closest airfield. Palmer's experiences in 1950 led him to never drinking anything other than out of a sealed bottle, never eating salad or fruit, and being always armed with a box of rapid setting cement (until Imodium was invented!).

Our Lancaster made its approach to Butterworth over the beautiful island of Penang just before sundown on a Saturday evening. From my eyrie in the nose, I watched Penang loom out of the haze and marvelled at the brilliant turquoise of the shallows and the darker patches of deeper water or coral. I spotted the different shape of boats and sails from those off Arabia, enraptured as the sun sank in the western sky, first white, then yellow, orange and flaming red. As we roared in low over the palm fringed beach, I gasped at the richness of the lush tropical vegetation, the crimson carpets of Bougainvillea and the Wedgwood Blue blossoms of a tree whose name I can never remember.

By the time we'd reached dispersal and shut down the engines, that beautiful serene evening silence of the tropics was upon us, accentuated no doubt by having had our ear drums assailed in flight for hours. On the Equator, twilight is brief and the light fails quickly, so there was a great bustle around our Lancaster to get it tucked away for the night and then to whisk us all away to our respective messes. But the work had only just started for me. Our skipper said he wanted to leave at dawn on the Sunday and as we had a long over-water leg to Darwin, he wanted the radar and navaids to be checked over. He suggested I stayed to run up the electrics and he'd send a garry back for me at 7 p.m. Our engineer, who would normally have stayed to help, noted that there was a trolley acc. and a power trolley available, and besides, he was desperate for a cold beer. So I stood alone on the pan as a noisy bunch pulled away in the *garry*, leaving me looking at a Lancaster parked on the edge of an unfamiliar jungle with the only sign of civilisation being a wooden hut by the trees where, I'd been told, I could have a pee and a shower if I so wished.

It was a hot and steamy night, my first ever in the tropics, and I was fascinated by the cacophony of noise now coming from the jungle from unknown birds and animals. The breeze that usually comes shortly after sundown was hardly stirring the tops of the trees and the inside of the aircraft was like an oven. To get at the scanner I had to undo about 20 tight fasteners, lift off the heavy lid, and fiddle around in dim light with the old type power cables that had to be fully tightened and were difficult to unscrew. Without giving a lesson on the ASV radar, suffice it to say that I checked for faults, ran up all the electronics, put everything back ready to fly, removed the step, closed the aircraft door, and walked drenched with sweat towards the wooden hut, now barely discernable in the gathering gloom. My garry was due in 15 minutes. No phones, no idea where to go, no lights showing through the thick jungle. How about that shower someone had mentioned?

The shower I was about to use on Penang airfield in 1950 was not a chromium plated super spray enclosed in a white tiled closet with opaque doors. As I walked towards it in the gloom, I was expecting at best a line of Japanese style wooden buckets suspended from a beam with ropes attached that I would pull to tip the contents over my head. I was wearing my sexy orange flying suit that I'd worn for about 30 flying hours; I was extremely hot, dirty and no doubt smelly. I therefore chose to walk into the shower just as I was and then disrobe. I reached up and grabbed the nearest rope—and the bloody thing bit me!

For a moment I didn't understand what had happened. I backed out of the hut. Then, realising that my left hand was hurting and contained something that was still biting me and thrashing around like a long dark whip, I tried to shake it loose. But that only made it bite harder, so instinctively—there certainly was no cool decision—I tightened my grip and began to wield the thing around like a whip, beating it on the ground and against the side of the shed. I'd become aware that I was actually holding a snake, and a big, angry and heavy one at that. I didn't panic, but I was sure that I shouldn't let it continue to eat me and kept swinging it around until I felt no movement from it in my hand. I dropped it on the ground and immediately felt warm blood—*my* warm blood—dripping from my hand. That triggered the thought process. If bitten by a snake, the pamphlet said, stay calm, sit down, identify the type of snake and summon help. Well, I was staying calm, but I had no idea what sort of snake it was, whether it was poisonous or a constrictor, and there wasn't a living soul in sight or within earshot.

In the conflict my H.Samuel (Ever-right) watch had fallen off, but I reckoned the *garry* should be along to pick me up in about five minutes, at most ten.

But then as I sat trying to minimise the flow of whatever it was around my body, my head began to swim and my hand to throb agonisingly. Throwing caution to the winds, I got up and legged it in the direction in which I'd seen the *garry* disappear. I remember dimly being on my knees instead of walking and seeing the blinding lights of something before I blacked out. I was in luck, the driver of the *garry* was the station doctor, he being the only sober guy in the bar, I was told. He found me on my knees, saw the wound, and although it was torn rather than a single strike, recognised it as a snake bite and was experienced enough to try to identify the culprit so as to administer the correct serum.

He apparently threw me in the garry, drove to the dispersal, quickly found the snake where I'd left it, identified it as an ex-King Cobra, and gave me the appropriate jab. I awoke at 3 p.m. the following afternoon and was pronounced fit enough to carry on to Darwin two days later. The skipper admitted he'd have left me in Penang, but they needed my skills for the extended trials that followed. It was nice to feel wanted! I have the scar on my palm to this day of that encounter and a well-worn belt made out of the scaly chap that bit me. Forty years later I was to lay the ghost of that encounter when I sat in the dust of an Indian village near Bangalore surrounded by dozens of Cobras and marvelled at their beautiful arrogance and sensational colouring through my camera lens. I even saved one from death by Mongoose and somehow felt that an old score had been settled, the hatchet buried with another of God's frighteningly magnificent creatures.

An Anti-Climax

When the Far East trip came up, my greatest expectations revolved around seeing Australia and enjoying the hot weather. In the event, that part of the epic journey was an anticlimax. It started okay with crossing the Equator and then running into—and bravely straight through—an incredibly powerful tropical storm. I thought it great fun to start with. Seated in my glass house watching St Elmo's fire dancing on the nose and along the wings was a spectacular and thrilling experience, until the buffeting increased and the precipitation started rattling the Lancaster. Discretion then became the better part of valour and I moved up to the astrodome where I could hang on more securely and still see the fireworks.

Our sister aircraft, which had been delayed earlier in Arabia for 24 hours, had over flown Penang to overnight at Changi in Singapore. He'd hit the storm an hour ahead of us and we only discovered on landing at Darwin that he'd had to divert to Bandung on Java after losing an engine. In the event he never made it to

Australia, so until the RAF picked up the two ground crew on board and their sonobouy cargo, Palmer was Radar, Radio, Electrical, Airframe and Engines. Where do we get such men?

Having only one aircraft prolonged the trials, and we had early problems in recovering the buoys and keeping them serviceable. But that was all part of the experimental work and I rapidly became the world expert on sonobuoys. However, Darwin and Oz were disappointing. We only travelled elsewhere once, to Cairns in fact, and after the stunning scenery of Africa, Arabia and Asia on the outbound journey, Oz was a massive let down. I've been back dozens of times since to Sydney, Adelaide, Perth, Canberra and Melbourne, and I love the country and it's people. But I still like to irritate my Aussie friends by pointing out that Australian women are like Australian scenery. Hundreds of miles of utter boredom, then Wham—followed by hundreds of miles of utter boredom!

The uncomfortable Darwin climate and my even more uncomfortable billet (remembering I was then just a "boggy airman"), made it a detachment to forget. Our return journey took us to Singapore rather than Penang, Nagpur for Calcutta, Idris for Benghazi, and Marseilles for Gibraltar. That pleased me, as I was able to boast about seeing more countries. I was still in my teens and in five months I'd flown over 25,000 miles, accumulated almost 600 hours in the Lancaster, and been to 13 countries on 4 continents. I'd been bitten by the King of Snakes and survived, been well and truly bitten by the flying bug ("...and in a back room down in Flanagan's, done a lot of things that a gentleman never mentions").

Back to Ireland

We returned to Ballykelly, three months later than planned, on 10th June 1950, my 20th birthday. Within days, Flight Lieutenant Carter was telling me that my call forward to start flying training had not materialised. I didn't discover until months later that he'd actually received three posting notices for me but had replied with "Cannot be released for operational reasons, re-submit in 6 months". He'd told no one else. I was to stay in Ireland for another 9 months during which I was promoted (a little more cash), got heavily involved in religion, became engaged, and found myself sinking into a bit of a rut. The promotion excepted, the others were undoubtedly interlinked. I've written elsewhere about religion and about my first marriage. For now let's leave it that I married too young, under the wrong circumstances and for the wrong reasons. No one's fault; it's the way of the world and millions of young people have fallen into the same trap—some to prosper, some to fail disastrously, and some to make the best of it. I imagine I fall most aptly into the latter category.

When I eventually discovered Carter's deception, I was annoyed. But then one can never judge whether something is good or bad until you can look back and see it from a distance. Had I left Ireland in 1949/50 to learn to fly, I might have killed myself doing so. I may never have met my first wife and had four wonderful children. Neither would my career have led me to be posted to Cyprus in 1971 to meet Rosemarie—and so the last 34 years of joy we have known would never have been. Philosophically speaking, I believe the good and the bad have a way of evening out over the years, and after the bad I certainly enjoyed a taste of the good early in 1951. I was then playing rugby for the Combined Services and after a match in Belfast my Station Commander offered me a lift back to Ballykelly. He asked me why as a young, fit, regular airman with a few brains, I hadn't though of commissioning and flying. I told him, innocently, not bitterly, the Carter story. I didn't realise that Wing Commanders in the RAF used such language!

When I returned to my billet on the Sunday evening there was a note from the CO telling me to be at Air Traffic Control at 8 a.m. Monday in my "Best Blue" and overnight kit. I did so and was surprised when he drove out to one of the Ansons, told me to sit in the right-hand seat and said we were going to the aircrew selection centre at Hornchurch in Essex. My previous selection had been nullified by Carter's 20-month delay, so I really had to start all over again. At Hornchurch, I did the medicals, written tests and two interviews after which my CO took me into London for a slap-up meal, then back to Hornchurch for the Final Board at 10 a.m. on Tuesday. "You've passed," came at 11 a.m., back on the Anson by 12, landing Ballykelly at 3 p.m. "Right," he said, "get your kit packed, get the Station Warrant Officer to do your Clearance chit for you, say goodbye to the girlfriend tonight, and meet me here ready to go at 9 a.m. tomorrow." At noon on the Wednesday, less than four days after climbing into his car in Belfast, I was Officer Cadet Palmer about to start my OCTU course at Jurby in the Isle of Man. I owed that rapid and remarkable change of fortune to one man who was prepared to put himself out for someone he hardly knew, but in whom he had great faith for whatever reason. I was to enjoy similar good fortune on at least two other occasions in my life that I'll recount when I get to that stage in my writings. On a happy note, *Flying Officer* Carter was also posted that day!

"Straight out of Moss Bros." Cranwell 1951

6

AN OFFICER AND
A GENTLEMAN

Why, in the twilight of one's years, should one remember any period so much more vividly than another? I suspect that the most enduring memories relate to people one met at the time; also, that we see certain periods as mere staging posts to better things and, once past, they cease to arouse our interest much as the results of an examination are taken for granted once accomplished.

Whatever the explanation, 1951 had become a vacuum in my memory, a slice of my life that had started with my philanthropic Station Commander flying me from Ireland to the Isle of Man to begin my OCTU course. By 5 p.m. that April day, I'd been interviewed as an Officer Cadet, captained the rugby team against the Manx Police and made Flight Commander for the new entry. The latter honour fell my way because the Drill WO thought I'd got "A bloody good voice of Command"—doubtless a legacy from the College of Knowledge at Cranwell, whose teachings and comprehensive technical, leadership and administrative training were now about to become especially valuable in my officer and flying training and throughout my service life.

Time raced by. We were so busy picking up the basics of becoming officers and of rudimentary airmanship and aerodynamics, that before we knew it the Mess was being visited by the three military tailors, Moss Bros, Alkit and Gieves, for us to be measured for our first officer's uniforms. We each received an initial allowance, around £350, which matched exactly the purchase price of a Best Blue (No 1 uniform) in barathea, No 2 Working Dress (rough as old boots), one peaked cap, one forage cap, and a magnificent full length greatcoat with kid-leather gloves. I'd always been proud of my uniform, but this was special—even if I was made to suffer the most acute embarrassment on my first leave after commissioning as a proud Mum stopped everyone in Manchester to tell them that her Kelvie was now an officer.

Training in earnest

But of course the really hard stuff of flying training was yet to come, and the next 10 months were exciting, if often nail-biting. In practical work I had no real problems, but the RAF way was to teach you everything about the aircraft you were to fly and the equipment you were to use. The academics (bloody maths again!) stretched me to the limits, although I was later to thank those who drew up our rigorous and demanding curriculum. Realisation of the value of that training hit me when I served on my first operational Squadron. It boiled down to the fact that, if anything went wrong with aircraft or equipment, you knew enough to judge if it was dangerous, what you might do to fix it, and how you could minimise the effect of any malfunction by doing something in a different way to complete the mission. The training ensured that when you taxied in with a "u/s" (unserviceable) aircraft, you were able to explain the fault and symptoms, and point the servicing teams in the right direction. Such knowledge came to my aid many times; sometimes to save my skin, and sometimes to get something out of a sortie when the alternative was to take your sick steed back to base and hand it over to the engineers.

I was to appreciate the merits of the RAF system when I served with the USAF in Texas in the 60's. Their basic flying training was effectively by rote, almost all out of books with little "hands on" work. Their problem was compounded by that quaint old US belief that, by definition, no American is below average and none can fail. Thus, if a student failed to reach the required standard in a written examination or practical test, he was repeatedly re-coursed until he passed the test—or killed himself! The ultimate drawback to their system was that if an aircraft went u/s for any reason, it was usually a case for returning to base at once to get it fixed. If the mission was an operational mission, the penalties were obvious. At the very least, it meant that a high number of sorties were aborted with no practical training value accruing from the high cost of flying hours. Cynically, it meant there was always an excuse on hand for turning back.

One extreme example I cite occurred when I scrounged a ride on a B-58 sortie planned to fly south from Fort Worth to the Mexican border, west to El Paso, then up to Nellis outside Las Vegas. The B-58 in 1962 was the hottest ship in the US inventory, full of the latest technology. No one noticed for 10 minutes that we were flying north into Oklahoma instead of south. The navigator had set the Navigation System 180 degrees out, but neither he nor his crew had the basic instincts or training to sense or see that something was wrong. I tentatively asked the pilot why the sun was over our shoulders instead of high above, and why we were flying over Perrin AFB instead of Austin. The response was the classic American exclamation: "Oh my Gawd!" That said, some of the best and most professional aviators that I have ever flown with have been from the USAF, US Navy and Marine Corps, but the average capability was way below their opposite numbers in the RAF and RN. Unfortunately, that leads to the US military seldom operating as effectively and efficiently as their usually superior equipment should enable them to operate. Things may well have changed, of course, but in those days there is no doubt that the Americans were by no means deserving of the title "Top Guns".

So back to my early flying days and my relief on completion of the basic training at which stage we pinned on our wings, bought a Mess kit, and went to our advanced flying courses at an Operational Conversion Unit (OCU). Pilots and navigators were "streamed" according to their ability, aptitude, temperament, and other skills, to the role that the RAF—not them—felt they were best suited, or where they were needed most on the front line. Role selection was hardly a manhood issue, although there were some guys—especially in my fighter fraternity—who saw it that way. Many who wanted to fly the newest highest performance pursuit ships ended up in the right-hand seat of a bomber, in a piston-engined maritime patrol or transport aircraft, or even on choppers. The man who made an excellent Shackleton driver might not have done so well in a Lightning, but conversely being a Lightning ace did not guarantee you'd be equally proficient in a Vulcan or VC10. The navigator who worked as a pure navigator in a maritime patrol aircraft before the days of sophisticated systems, might not be anything like so expert in the back of a Canberra creaming around Europe at 500 ft and 450 knots.

In 1952, however, I cared not what anyone else was doing. I was selected to fly night fighters and started my conversion programme on the piston–engined Mosquito at Leeming in Yorkshire, knowing that I'd be finishing it on the new Meteor NF11 jets. It was an exciting time, with the slight disappointment that we didn't get many hours on the wonderful old Mossy before the thrill of the new aircraft. Looking back, that course can rightly be described as mayhem. Out of a starting line up of 11 crews, we lost over half to flying and motorbike accidents that either killed them or caused injuries that ended their flying days or retarded their training. We actually lost one pilot to an irate wife who literally walked into the crew room one night and dragged him out by the ear, never to be seen again!

It may have been a coincidence, but the crew numbers we lost were replaced on the course by three French crews, who always flew as a French duo as their English was decidedly dicey. With three of our instructors being Polish, two hailing from deepest Ireland and one a Highlander, there were nights when the circuit at Leeming was like a madhouse with the excited babble of the French clashing with frequent Polish cries of "Do bloody something!" Order and calm reigned only when we were under air traffic control or fighter intercept control by the soft voiced unflappable young WAAF officers. Not only was their pronunciation so good and their words so clear, but they took the trouble—not being aircrew themselves—to find out what it was like on a GCA approach at 300ft on a dark and dirty Yorkshire night, or trying to find another Meteor at 20,000 ft with a duff radar and the navigator throwing up his night flying supper in the back!

I recall one such night on our final check ride joining the Leeming circuit, in the fashion of the time, and being told by ATC that we were No 3 to land with one on Finals and one downwind ahead. It was a pitch-dark night with rain lashing against the hood and the brightness of the runway lights on the port side, making sighting of another aircraft's navigation lights almost impossible. Neither of us could see the aircraft ahead and as we turned onto the final approach (finals), a shrill French voice shouted hesitatingly: "Bellboy 20, downwind—at Leeming, Dishforth or Linton!" Apart from being somewhere in Yorkshire, he was lost and was actually in the Dishforth circuit some 12 miles south!

Almost simultaneously I heard the tower say, "Bellboy 22, you are lined up on the Great North Road, overshoot and rejoin downwind." Even as the exclamation "Bloody French" reached my lips, I sensed rather than saw a black shape loom out of the glare from the runway lights and pass so close over our canopy that I distinctly saw a spinning wheel extremely close to my right earhole. For a split second I waited for the noise or feel that would herald the departure of our tailplane. This of course was the third of our French farces that had tried to land in the wrong direction and had mistaken the overshoot command to 22 as being for him. Had he landed the wrong way and without the Tower knowing where he was, I suspect he'd have been very surprised at our arrival straight down his throat. That could have spoiled the whole day for at least four more of us.

It was a Friday night in early October. We had all landed from our second sorties that night at around midnight and after a quick debrief, shower and change of clothing, we dashed back to the mess for a traditional night flying supper of bacon, eggs, beans, tomatoes and fried bread. In the dining room sat the Senior ATC controller whose only comment about the mayhem that had been his circuit 45 minutes ago was: "If that daft sod Hervellyn (Bellboy 22 at Dishforth) doesn't get here soon, the kitchen will have packed up." Looking back I wonder why we weren't all nervous wrecks. Had that happened in the Honington circuit in the seventies when I was the boss, I'd have hung up a few guys by their buster-browns. If that happened today, the entire Air Force Board would sit on the Courts Martial.

The Folly of youth

As if that wasn't excitement enough for one night, for four of us intrepid aviators the night was far from over. Weather permitting; we flew every weeknight on the OCU. After our last trip on Friday, whatever the time, the four of us who lived t'other side of the Pennines, would pile in the only car owned by any of the students, a '47 Hillman belonging to Norman Spence, a navigator from Liverpool. Norm couldn't drive, so the driving was shared between the other three and divided up according to geography. That is to say that I, being the first to reach home in south Manchester, would always drive the Leeming to Manchester leg. Geoff Roberts alighted at Stockport, and when I got out Dusty Miller from Wrexham would drive Norman to Liverpool and then carry on to Wrexham. The reverse happened on Sunday night with Dusty starting out around six, via Liverpool, and picking up Geoff and I in Manchester at 8.30. Geoff then drove to Leeming. In retrospect, I cannot believe we had the energy. On a Friday we'd have flown 3 sorties starting around 2 p.m., with the last two at night, landing at midnight and arriving home around 5 a.m. for me, 7 a.m. for Dusty. There were no motorways, the roads were narrow and unlit, the weather over the moors often dreadful, and the Hillman prone to punctures. If you could average 30 mph in those days on any journey you were flying.

I don't claim that we appreciated then how fortunate we were to live the lives we led. But there's no doubt that we had it made. We were bright fit young men, flying the latest jets and living the social Life of Reilly. We were doing the world's greatest job, being well if not generously paid, owned one wheel each of a car that carried us home every weekend, and were living our lives to the full. Miraculously we all four survived and graduated in November '52 to be posted to Germany to start our operational lives; Dusty on 256 Squadron, the others on 96 Squadron.

Life on a front line RAF Squadron

The 12 young pilot officers that sailed on the Harwich to Hook of Holland ferry on November 13th, 1952, were lucky chaps indeed. At the age of 21/22 they were bound for a foreign country to fly the latest fighters in service. Germany then really was a foreign country with a totally different way of life and was still immersed in the aura of the defeated enemy. Few Brits spoke their language and, except for the occupation forces, even fewer had visited the country.

Our outbound sea crossing was memorable. The nightly military ferry carried hundreds of servicemen and women between the UK and bases in Germany, Holland and Belgium. The 12 bound for RAF Ahlhorn near Bremen, were to sleep in a large "cabin" filled with bunks. On the train from Liverpool Street, we'd met seven girls travelling together and around midnight they too ended up in the same cabin. In the ensuing party, the Captain was called down to reprimand us for our noisy behaviour, but when he saw the standard of our female company he stayed to join the party until the ship entered harbour at The Hook. One of the young ladies was the daughter of a Royal Navy Admiral who later became a famous model and married a titled German industrialist whose empire today is synonymous with enormous wealth. I know that Fiona will remember that night with great affection.

At The Hook we boarded a military train, again a novel experience, travelling through the flat Dutch countryside before entering Germany. I recall how neat and colourful the Dutch houses looked and how the styles changed once across the German border. Still neat and tidy, but not so colourful with most windows veiled by large green stemmed plants that I knew as "Stepmother's Tongue". We arrived for our induction programme in the fascinating old town of Buckeburg, where we were billeted in a large forbidding looking hotel by a castle. There in the old stone courtyards and dim wynds and closes, lit by pale lamps hanging above flights of grey steps, you could almost feel the history of the old town—grey, sinister and mediaeval. We walked out along cobbled streets; it was snowing heavily, the town was hushed, and the lights in the old shop windows left a great impression on me. I fell in love with Germany that night and I think it's true to say that it has been the European country I have enjoyed visiting most in the succeeding 50 years.

Life in Germany

RAF Ahlhorn turned out to be a very different station and Officers' Mess to that to which we'd been accustomed. Ahlhorn was an ex-Luftwaffe base, modernised in very comfortable style with sleeping quarters separate from the Mess itself, well-appointed and well heated in typical German fashion. Brits ran the Mess, but almost all the staff and those in the quarters were German and 90% female. Many a young British heart was broken by a pretty *fraulein,* I can tell you. Which is my cue to recount a story I've been telling for over 50 years; Rosemarie has heard it many times so she'll not mind a bit. The reader should understand that fraternising with German ladies was *verboten,* both on and off the station. But we were young and only human, easily swayed by a pretty face, good figure and appealing German accent. Faced with such temptation many fell; but I held out for six months until, one morning around 11.30, as was her custom, my bat-woman came in to wake me with a cup of tea and a slice of toast. I'd probably only got to bed around 4 a.m. after night flying, and every morning I would say *"viel und danke"* to Ursula and make some cheeky quip. She'd blush profusely and retire. Then one morning I awoke to find her leaning across me; our eyes met, our fingers touched, and sex reared its ugly head.

We were just reaching the point of no return when my door burst open and there stood the imposing figure of my Squadron Commander, a really old man of 28. He took in the scene and didn't need to ask the daft Hollywood question, "What's going on here?" Fixing me with a steely stare, he growled, "Best Blue Palmer, my office 20 minutes." Ursula, rapidly adjusting her clothing, said something like, "Mr Crowshaw think I'm a bad lady"—to which I, ever the gentle-man, replied, "Sod you, he'll probably throw me out of the air force!"

I cycled to the squadron hanger and reported to the Adjutant. "God, Johnny, what have you done this time! I've never seen the boss so angry. He's got the Sta-tion Commander and OC Flying in there with him." My heart sank; this was bloody serious; they're going to throw the book at me, I thought, as I wondered about the formality of resigning my commission. After what seemed an age, but was probably only a few minutes, I heard the boss shout: "March in Pilot Officer Palmer please, Adjutant." In I went, stood rigidly to attention and saluted. There, in front of me, sat the Squadron Commander peering at various papers on his desk. Ominously, he was wearing his hat, as were the Station Commander on his right flicking through Queens Regulations, and OC Flying on his left with The Manual of Air Force Law open in front of him. My first thoughts on seeing this intimidating array of brass and power, were that I was already in front of a Courts Martial. I was literally quaking in my boots as I surveyed the serious expressions on the faces before me. Then, agonisingly slowly, my Squadron Commander raised his head, jabbed his finger in my direction, and growled, "Ursula's mine—find your own bloody woman!"

My three judges, the three men most influential during my time on 96 Squad-ron, and thus on my future career, then fell about laughing like maniacs whilst I dissolved into a grease spot on the carpet, quite unable to share in their outra-geous sense of humour. That incident taught me two valuable lessons, however. The first was that a sense of humour should be one of the first things an officer should carry in his knapsack. The second was to make sure we locked the bloody door whenever Ursula brought my tea!

When we'd arrived at Ahlhorn in November, we didn't have a single operational aircraft on base. RAF Germany was expanding rapidly to counter the rapidly growing Warsaw Pact Threat, and new squadrons were forming every month with Meteors, Sabres, and Venoms distributed around the 12 northern airfields. The Meteors destined for Ahlhorn had been delivered to Wahn outside Cologne and the man destined later to tell me to find my own woman, gathered us all together to tell us that he would be delivering our first aircraft the next day. We sprogs were to gather at the "caravan", a mobile control point of those days close to the end of the active runway, to observe how to land a Meteor NF11 on an icy snow-covered runway. This of course was a splendid idea coming from an experienced pilot with many rare jet hours; a sort of mother hen teaching chicks that had been flying jets for only 4 months and picking up some 80 hours, but none of them in runway conditions such as these.

Early the next morning, Ahlhorn's entire aircrew population stood huddled by the caravan in driving snow as Joe Crowshaw's Meteor came screaming in out of the murk above the pine forest, touched down in a flurry of snow—and proceeded to go off the far end of the runway still doing around 60 knots. As the RAF bus passed the end of the runway on our way back to the squadron, we saw what was left of our first aircraft strewn between the poles of the approach lights with the cockpit embedded in a thick hedge and surrounded by curious German cows. Fifteen minutes later we all sprang to our feet in the crew room as Joe stomped in, glowered at us as if defying anyone to say a word, and growled, "I've just demonstrated how not to land a Meteor on snow; this afternoon I'll show you how it's really done"—and he did. I was never to meet a more capable and professional pilot than Joe in my career.

Those early days were golden days, days to look back on fondly during more difficult times. More importantly, I think we all knew they were special at the time. So often people say that such and such a time was the best, like ones' schooldays or "the Swinging Sixties", but you cannot remember thinking at the time that you were especially lucky or privileged. One lives life as it comes and it's only later, much later, that you can look back and say with any degree of conviction that "That was the best, the happiest, the most satisfying etc." We had so much going for us. 96 Squadron had 16 crews for 12 aircraft, and with the exception of the CO and his two Flight Commanders (ages 27/28), the rest of us were first tourists ages 21–23. Few were married and those that were, were too young to qualify for married quarters and it was not permitted to live off base.

"Where do we get such men!" 96 Sqn. Germany 1953

So the Mess was full of young men having the time of their lives, accentuated by having two identically equipped squadrons with intense but friendly rivalry. Being specialist night fighters, our daily routine was to fly a night-flying test (of radar) in the afternoon followed by two night sorties each of around 1 hour 30 minutes, which usually saw us finished by 11 p.m. in the winter or 4 a.m. in the summer. We carried out Armament Practice Camps for air-to-air firing (guns then, no missiles), and flew dozens of exercises to keep us in shape in case the Russian sabre rattling turned to all-out war. In the days before nuclear deterrence, the threat of a Conventional war was extremely high—much higher in fact than we believed as historical WP documents now reveal. We flew hard, but we played hard too.

The Mess bar was always hopping, and the okay drinks of the day, apart from the excellent German beer, were Pimms No1, Horse's Neck, and Scotch and Soda for the men, with the ladies favouring Port and Lemon and Gin and Tonic—and the gin had to be Gordon's. But of course we were also able to enjoy the wonderful German food and beer at the local hostelries. In England then, pub meals were virtually limited to sandwiches or at best a pie. In Germany one could buy the most delicious steaks, accompanied by *champignons* (small mushrooms), and *kartoffel salat*, preceded by the best tasting soup I have ever had anywhere. It was *Ochsenschwanz* (Oxtail) soup, so meaty and rich that one could stand up a spoon in it. If one's finances didn't run to a steak, and often they didn't, there was always *bratwurst* or *bockwurst* in a torpedo roll with *zempf* (mustard) that put most British bangers to shame.

I was never a drinker of UK beer; I'm still not, but Ahlhorn introduced me to lager, always served chilled in attractive stemmed glasses that bore the Brewery crest. It seemed that every town had its own brewery and distinctive *stadtwappen*. I collected them from all over Germany and came back with around 200 different ones. I still have around three dozen—each with its own history—because part of the fun was "borrowing" the ones you'd actually drunk from. They are mostly embossed, made from beautifully thin glass, and every one attractive enough to take its place besides the crystal in our display cabinet.

Before leaving the Bar talk, I'll tell you of one of those coincidences in life that seem far fetched, but simply prove that fact is more fanciful than fiction. I wrote earlier about an experience as a lad when I accompanied my Dad to stoke up the greenhouse boilers during an air raid on Manchester. It all came back one night after the Mess Bar closed and I was sitting in the cellar checking the bar stocks in my capacity as Junior Bar Officer, one of the many Secondary duties that a young officer was required to do. The Bar Manager was a German civilian by the name of Walter, and I'd been briefed to be fairly formal with him. But this night we sat down to have a beer and a chat and Walter revealed that in the war he'd been a Luftwaffe pilot. I began to take notice when he said he'd flown many raids in 1940/41 over England. This was surprising because many Germans said they'd served in the war, but it was always on the Russian Front. Walter was the first to admit to bombing England and even brought out his logbook to prove it.

I had the creepiest feeling as I flicked through the pages of the dates and missions and, sure enough, *there* it was. Whilst Dad and me were sheltering from the German bombs, Walter was in a Heinkel 111 dropping them! His own records showed that they lost three 111's that night over Manchester to AA fire, and then were hammered on their long way home by fighters that came up at dawn from the south-eastern airfields. We were to have many a beer and many a chat and I broke all the rules by getting him up in a Meteor two-seater trainer—as Flying Officer Smith, of course. In 1971, when he had returned to the post-war Luftwaffe, Walter returned the favour by giving me a ride in one of their F104's when the US dumped that high performance flop on half of NATO.

The guys who fly today's front line RAF fighters (or interceptors) would consider our trusty steeds of the early 50's much as my generation thought of a Sopwith Camel or Albatross. Theirs is an age when an aeroplane has become a System. A highly capable flying machine in itself, but one filled with all the latest technology in terms of aircraft handling, weapons systems, navigation, and all weather operation. The words often used to describe today's crews are highly professional, technocrats, automatic pilots, etc. And so they are and I certainly applaud their expertise, talents and operational efficiency. They must possess the ability to cope with a vast amount of information coming at them both visually and orally, and to absorb, assimilate and act upon it in a dynamic situation. That calls for outstanding mental capacity allied to great physical toughness. On the credit side, their aircraft are exceptionally robust, not east to break or bend, with every part of the system monitored and automatically protected. Enormous technological advances have produced astonishing levels of reliability and maintainability; and if things do go wrong, the crew enjoy zero/zero and high speed /high altitude safe ejection. You could say it's swings and roundabouts in comparing them with their predecessors. Pilots that flew flimsy wood and canvas contraptions in 1916, those that pointed their Spitfires at hordes of ME109's in 1941, and those of my generation, had different challenges and needed different skills and aptitude. Perhaps the physical/mental, experience/training, attitude/courage balance has changed; but who's to say who was or is the best and most accomplished when you're not able to compare like with like?

Ask a Swordfish pilot how he felt about his aircraft in the 30's and WW2, or ask a US Sabre pilot how he felt about flying in the Korean War. The answer you'll get is the one I'll give you about almost every aircraft I flew between 1949 and 1995. At the time it was the best, you were the best; flying the very latest to which there was always attached an element of risk, an awful lot of glamour, and enormous professional and personal satisfaction. In 1953 we didn't know that there would be aircraft and systems like the F15, Eurofighter, or F22; we were simply happy to be where we were, doing what the RAF required us to do. Happy flying is fulfilment-shaped.

Escape and Evasion

> "The pale grey phantoms of the slain,
> Glide nightly o'er the silent plain"

A criticism often levelled at the military is that they are still fighting the last war in preparing for the next. In the winter of 1953 in RAF Germany, we were certainly still doing that with frequent exercises to give experience should we have had to abandon our aircraft behind enemy lines and have to walk home. This story about one such exercise would probably have been relegated to the status of dream or hallucination had it not been shared by a sensible, level headed, intelligent pilot colleague who spent many years after leaving the RAF as a captain on Concorde.

On a bitterly cold February evening, he and I were dumped out of an army truck at dusk some 4 klicks (kilometres) east of the Rhine with a brief to make a rendezvous with a fishing boat on the Dutch coast 72 hours later. We were dressed in our standard flying suits plus an anorak, had no food, no money, could not use public transport, and our only map was an aviation chart that gave little surface detail. Germany and Holland were then awash with troops of all national-ities and there were thousands of soldiers and policemen looking for some 100 evading aircrew. If captured, interrogation usually involved being stripped and hosed down for hours in an outside compound with cold water. Pride apart, therefore, no one ever liked being caught.

John and I decided we should cross the Rhine quickly whilst there were still lots of people on the streets and the "defenders" were still getting organised. We found a railway line, jumped on the back of a westbound goods train, and rum-bled across the mighty river towards the Dutch border. We abandoned all hope of going further into Holland when the train stopped and began to reverse towards Germany. Nevertheless, we'd made a good start and so chose to rest up as we had to move, under cover of darkness, across totally unknown territory before hiding out during the day. Our planned rest came earlier than expected as we walked in the gathering gloom along the single-track railway line. We had a choice whether to match our stride to walk on the sleepers or between them. I went for the former, John the latter. He was a few yards in front of me, barely vis-ible, when he suddenly disappeared with a cry and a splash. What we hadn't rea-lised was that when these small branch lines crossed a stream or gully, they didn't build a full bridge—only the rail supports. John was unhurt, but soaking in a temperature of minus 5, so we found an open barn where he undressed and dried himself.

Somewhat nervously, I went to the adjacent farmhouse and explained our pre-dicament in pidgin Deutsche to the woman who opened the door. She welcomed us with open arms, dried John's clothes, and fed us thick hot pea and ham soup. I had the distinct feeling that we'd have been welcome there much longer but, hav-ing grabbed 4 hours sleep, we made our way up the hill behind the farm. It was now snowing, a soft gentle snow that sifted down in a slow dreamlike way to cover the fields with silence. It was exactly midnight when we stopped on the fringe of a wood to get our bearings and adjust clothing

I remind the reader that we were two very fit, well-rested young men; highly motivated to our task and to not getting caught. Our senses were razor sharp; this was not a game but a deadly serious challenge. The snow shower had passed and there was a pale half moon above high cloud that illuminated a silver grey mist hanging on the white surface; we could probably make out moving shapes at around 30 yards from our chosen vantage point. I'd just finished zipping up my flying suit in preparation to move out as I turned on one knee and said, "Let's go." John wasn't looking at me, but was on both knees staring down the hill and waving for me to keep down. I distinctly saw three shadowy figures on which his attention was riveted, heading silently straight towards our hideout. "That bloody woman's shopped us!" I hissed. "Let's leg it through the wood." He didn't reply or move an inch and when I looked again the figures had disappeared.

I grabbed his arm and pulled him back into the shelter of the trees, listening intently for the sound of footsteps crunching in the undergrowth. I stopped abruptly when I realised what I'd just seen. "They weren't Army or Police, John, they were nurses with red crosses on their uniforms!" I said incredulously. "I know," he replied, "and the guy between them was wearing a torn German uniform, carried a rifle, and had a bandaged head." In due course we talked about it and it seemed to affect John more than me. We even mentioned it to the "trick cyclist" who was present at our debriefing on the fishing boat days later, and to our de-briefer who muttered something like "hallucinations, fell asleep, bloody aircrew" etc. However, neither sceptic was able to explain how we both suffered from identical hallucinations and had precisely the same dreams. He was right about the "bloody aircrew", but was not giving us credit for our exceptional eyesight, acute powers of observation, and our pragmatic feet-on-the-ground makeup that accrued from our professional training and experience.

Being young men with busy and interesting lives, we jotted it down to experience and virtually forgot the incident until, one day that summer, our curiosity led to us bribing the only car owner on the squadron to drive us the odd hundred and fifty miles to the scene of our encounter. We found the farm and the lady who befriended us and recounted what had happened after leaving her that cold winter's night. First she took us to the approximate spot on the hill where we'd seem the apparitions and pointed out the features of the village below. Then she led us down the hill to a memorial in the small square that recorded the deaths in 1917 of over 100 troops, patients and nurses, from the explosion of an arms dump close to a military hospital. In the local museum was an oil painting of a nurse tending a wounded soldier in WW1; she wore a white uniform with a Wedgewood blue front on which was emblazoned a large crimson cross. That was the uniform I had seen for the first time in a snowy field by moonlight.

On that bitter February night, two young officers barely knew where they were, let alone the tragic history of the village through which they passed so briefly. In the same way that I still see my grandmother's ghostly face hours after her death in1936, I still can see those two nurses flanking a shadowy figure on that hill. In 1957 John joined British Airways and we lost touch until I bumped into him at JFK airport in 1993. His memory of the incident, especially his image of the wounded soldier, was equally vivid. Explain that if you can, but beware—you will have to re-programme two pretty sharp brains to do so.

Salad days

My memories of those early days in Germany are strangely clear. I remember where I lived and what I did, and can recall even little things that seemed important at the time. After a year of hectic and hilarious Mess life, my wife was able to join me, thanks to our being offered a flat in a Squadron Leader's off base hiring. This was a large German house in the lovely town of Cloppenburg, which meant we ate out most evenings locally. The Germans were very friendly; I cannot recall a single unpleasant word in two years. But it was the shops that fascinated me most with all sorts of unusual collectables such as the delightfully attractive Hummel figures, small coloured glass-blown ornaments and badges and emblems of all sorts. The Palmers couldn't afford a car in those days so were reliant on the odd lift from our host. Apart from a few days in Copenhagen, we didn't travel far by today's standards, but going anywhere then was an adventure and Germany was a wonderful place to explore. The car we travelled in was a brand new Austin A40—a pretty big car for its day. I saw one recently that hadn't rusted away and it looked like a kiddie car against a modern saloon.

It's not what you know…

It was a great time for my sport. I was still running, although now I'd found my distance at 400 yards rather than the sprints, and I concentrated on the triple jump, having decided I was a little too muscular and heavy for the high jump. As usual, I was busy with football, but my Rugby was really taking off as I moved to wing forward and I was beginning to feel the advantage of some excellent coaching and playing in the RAF pack with a couple of English internationals. My prowess on the rugby pitch came to my aid in a way that I least expected, another one of those twists in life that are welcome when they go your way. Let me explain.

95% of young officers then served on a short service commission of eight years from completion of training. The aim of the vast majority was to win a Permanent Commission (PC) that would secure a career for life. For this one had to be recommended and then undergo a series of interviews. This was a once-a-year ritual, and I believe there was an age bracket during which one might be considered with success linked in some way to the various promotion exams that one took at different ranks. If I seem a little vague about the procedures it is because we all seemed to be entirely satisfied with our lot in those days. We were in our early 20's, and no one ever had a thought for pensions, buying houses, saving for a rainy day and so on.

We knew—perhaps we'd been brainwashed—that our careers would be well looked after. We knew about promotion qualifying periods, about exams, advanced courses, and how we were expected to behave to be reported on favourably for promotion. More importantly, we trusted the system and I certainly never had cause to doubt that the system would treat me fairly and on merit. Back in the 50's I naively believed that if I didn't have certain knowledge or information, there was someone above me or above him that did and was thus able to make the right decisions. Much later in life I was to realise that you can seldom count on someone knowing more than you, still less on him or her doing anything about it.

But no such cynicism blurred my vision when, in the spring of '54, I went with two other hopefuls from Ahlhorn, to be interviewed by the Commander-in-Chief 2nd Allied Tactical Air Force at his Headquarters at Rheindahlen. This was the end of a filtering process that had begun in April with 9 young hopefuls at Ahlhorn and some 120 from the 13 or more RAF stations in Germany. There were 12 "finalists" reporting to the PSO's office and I was to be No 12, to be seen at 11 a.m. on the Friday. No 1 was a 96 Sqn colleague, a guy that everyone saw as a certainty for a PC; and No 2 was a titled gentleman flying Sabres at Oldenburg who was also rated a racing certainty. Indeed, the published order of interviews made it look as if the certainties were being seen first, with a dogfight following for the last of 6 expected awards. Imagine the consternation then at 12.30 on Thursday in the Officers Mess bar when candidates 1 to 4 inclusive all came to drown their sorrows instead of celebrating their forecast good news. When the bar reopened at 6 p.m., another 4 young men had tasted the bitter pill of rejection, leaving just 4 lambs for the slaughter on Friday.

That morning I waited in the comfort of the Mess until walking to the HQ at 11 a.m. On the way I met candidates 9 and 10, who had gone the way of all flesh and, as I climbed the stairs, was greeted by the second of my Ahlhorn buddies who simply said, "Miserable old bastard." With all the favourites gone it seemed clear that our C in C had no intention of giving anyone a PC that year, a fear instantly confirmed by one look at the straight face of his PSO who nonchalantly said, "Don't expect you'll be long Palmer, the old man is flying back to the UK after lunch."

I entered a sumptuous office where, behind an enormous highly polished desk, sat Air Chief Marshal Sir Harry Broadhurst. Sir Harry was a name spoken in awe, with a splendid war record and a reputation for being very hard but fair. He later became C in C Bomber Command at the time of the Deterrent and forged the V-force into an immensely powerful and capable strike unit. He made one bit of history that he'd wish to forget when, as co-pilot, he tried to land a Vulcan at Heathrow on its way back from a highly publicised trip to Australia. Tragically, he landed short and whilst he and the aircraft captain ejected to safety, the rear crew with no ejection seats perished in the crash.

I had met him in person only once before, and I was hoping he'd forget an incident that occurred during Princess Margaret's visit to Ahlhorn the previous year. He hardly bothered to look up as he waved for me to sit down. Head down in his files, or maybe mine, he did no more than grunt for a while and then looked up to say, "Why would you want a Permanent Commission, Palmer?" I was ready for that and prepared to launch into a stirring speech about high and windy career aims, when he suddenly said, "I remember you." Here it comes, I thought. "You're the clumsy young bugger who fell over the coffee table." But no—instead he said, "You're the open side wing forward who got that try against the Army this year, aren't you?" Taken aback, I admitted I was. He stood up and said, "Let's get a drink. I'm off to the UK after lunch; we can chat on the way."

On sweeping past his PSO, he told him to have his car at the Mess for half-one, and to bring all the other paperwork with him for him to do on the aircraft. He was only a little guy, but he walked at a cracking pace and never stopped talking about rugby. When we reached the bar he didn't ask what I wanted, but ordered two Brandy Gingers and kept on talking. Being the C in C, other officers coming in gave him a respectful smile but kept their distance, until an Air Commodore I knew well from cricket circles came in, smiled, and came across to shake hands. "This is the young scallywag who played the jape on Jack Ewing, you'll remember, Sir." "God, yes," replied Sir Harry. "I remember that, but I didn't know you were the perpetrator." Then, looking at his watch, he said, "Sorry, must dash"—and headed for the door nodding at the now crowded bar. I stood nonplussed. As far as I was concerned I was in the middle of a very important PC interview and he'd asked me virtually nothing about my career intentions or hopes. I therefore rushed out behind him and caught him as he was getting into his staff car. I mumbled something like, "Will I be called about the interview, Sir?" "Oh, don't worry about that, Palmer, you've got your PC. Tell Tim (his PSO) to call Peers Kelly (my CO) to formalise it. Good luck." I like to think my record and the personal impression I made at the unusual interview got me the PC deservedly. Nevertheless, I've often wondered what would have happened had I not scored that winning try against the Army.

The cricketing incident referred to is worth recounting. I was a childhood friend and schoolmate of a lad who became a much loved and famous England cricketer, J.B Statham—Dicky to his pals. When he did his National Service we met up again and played together for the RAF team. When I was posted to Germany we kept in touch. In late July he'd called me to say that Lancashire's planned pre-season tour had been cancelled and he wondered if the RAF might provide some opposition. I had no power or authority of course, but I knew a man who had—the Air Commodore who ran RAF cricket in Germany. To cut a long story short, the RAF arranged to fly the Lancashire team to and from Germany to play the RAF on Saturday and the Army on Sunday (with the rest of the long weekend being set aside for partying). The matches were to be 40 overs each side, with fast scoring being the name of the game.

We had a lovely man as Captain who loved his cricket passionately and had been an accomplished player in his younger days. He was now in his 50's, Pickwickian in stature, and unfortunately would bat nowhere but at No1. Even for limited over matches, Jack would take a good 5 minutes on his guard and prodding the wicket (I even saw him prod a matted wicket). Then he'd survey the field and proceed to take a good look at the bowling, perhaps for the first ten overs after which he might open his shoulders and sneak the odd single to avoid being arrested for loitering. A group of rebels decided that, on this occasion, we didn't want to see the familiar scorecard "J.R Ewing not out 5—in the 25th over."

The great day dawned, Jack won the toss and opted to bat, and the large crowd clapped enthusiastically as he and his partner made their way to the wicket. Jack took guard and eventually turned to face the first ball from Dicky who had doubled the length of his normal run in to the wicket. Dicky raced in with that smooth flowing run of his, wheeled his arm over and the entire Lancashire team, leapt in the air with "Howzat?"as the wicketkeeper clasped his hands high above his head. Without hesitation, the umpire held his finger up and a crestfallen Jack Ewing turned away from the crease and made his painful way back to the pavilion shaking his head ruefully. I was in the dressing room putting on my pads when Jack stomped in and said, "I knew he was going to try and york me and played straight down the line, but it swung at the last minute."

The match continued, the weekend was a roaring success, and big Jack bored people for years with his tale of how he caught Jack Ikin and stumped Roy Tattersall; with the odd mention of being dismissed by a real brute of a ball. It wasn't until eight years later at High Wycombe, on the night of Jack's official "Dining out" on retirement, that the guy introducing him let the cat out of the bag about his first ball dismissal. When Dicky steamed in and "bowled", he didn't even have a ball in his hand! Of course the Lancashire team and both umpires were in on the ruse. The scorecard that night in High Wycombe should have read, "J.R.Ewing (Captain) retired hurt—58."

A Friend in the snow

Of the few paranormal experiences I can lay claim to, the only one to make the hairs stand up on the back of my neck and to generate fear, as opposed to bewilderment or bafflement, took place in the Austrian Tyrol in 1954. Part of the Survival training given to all RAF aircrew in Germany in the '50's was the experience of living, moving and surviving in the harsh winter conditions of Europe. Training included downhill and cross-country skiing and rock climbing using, as a base, a large log cabin situated about 2 klicks above the inviting village of Ehrwald nestling in a beautiful Bavarian/Austrian valley. What wasn't on the course curriculum, but which was an essential element for young men who worked hard and played hard, was the *après ski* activities then concentrated on three hotels in the town. The nightlife was a far cry from today's frenetic chaotic club life, but the combination of a genuine Tyrolean atmosphere, good German beer and the attractive fun-loving frauleins and rich tourists made Ehrwald a heaven on earth.

A major snag, though one which probably added to the general flavour of the place, was that there was no transport between the Chalet and the town. There was a steep winding track, but that was usually covered with snow and ice and was a four-klick journey instead of the two if you went on skis via the deep snow in the woods and across the ski slopes. Having learnt or improved your skiing, one would leave the chalet after supper around 7 p.m. armed with a lantern and dive at speed into the woods to make your own trail or follow some other brave soul who had gone before.

Those who have skied in deep snow at night through a forest will appreciate the exhilaration and the dangers; heightened by the fear that with the promise of a hectic social night ahead, one didn't want to arrive in town wet and bedraggled! The consolation if you did fall was that it was because some other poor sod had come to grief and you'd fallen off laughing, or had been hit by someone totally out of control who'd wandered outside the ruts left by others. I recall that some wag had put a notice at the entry to the forest trail which read, "Choose your rut carefully, you'll be in it for 2 klicks."

The evening entertainment was invariably wonderful, but then came the bad news. After all the exertions, you were faced with a 4klick walk up an icy track to the chalet, feeling decidedly tired, with skis to carry and possibly blowing snow to contend with. Reveille was 0600, and you were out on the slopes or up in the forest by 0700. My tale concerns those late night/early morning journeys back to the chalet. On the first night that a bunch of twenty lean and hungry aviators were allowed to invade the village, there was a fancy dress party at the Gasthof Zum Baumweg. I latched on to a girl from Heidelberg who came dressed in the costume of a wolf, complete with long curly tail and flashing eyes. Her name was Adeletroud, but her odd name belied her stunning looks and ability to dance like a dream. Over the remaining 10 days, with the exceptions when the Course was out overnight "surviving", my return journeys got later and later so that I was almost always a lone traveller on the wintry route back to the chalet. On the third night I stayed very late. Adeletroud and I sat in her landlady's front room, watching the fire flickering over the ceiling and filled with that delicious drowsiness that is the half way house to sleep. I had to tear myself away as the church clock was booming the hour of 2 a.m. I opened the front door to be hit with a blast of icy snow borne on a half gale. Head down with skis on my shoulders, I began the long trudge up the mountain, thanking the foresight of those who placed depth sticks along the track. On leaving the edge of the village I was almost totally blind; visibility was nil, there were no lights and no horizon. My only means of illumination was the lantern shaped like a miner's lamp that threw a fitful beam for a few metres, no further.

I'd learned enough about survival to know that slow and steady was the tactic in physically demanding situations, so I didn't rush and I certainly was not concerned—until, about half way up, I stumbled. As I twisted to avoid falling, the beam from my lantern reflected from two glowing orbs to the right and behind me at a distance of perhaps 5 metres. From the height of the eyes, and the gap between them, I concluded that the animal was a large dog. I think I said "Good boy" and moved the lantern to see him better, but all I could make out was a shadowy shape. I started back up the hill with occasional glances over my shoulder, but all I saw that night were the two yellow eyes of an animal that made no sound, kept the same distance, and followed me until I climbed the chalet steps. The next two nights were carbon copies of the first except that on the third night I decided my companion during my lonely trek should be rewarded so I persuaded the chef in the hotel to give me a meaty bone. On reaching the chalet I turned and threw the bone towards the animal. The eyes disappeared, and the following morning when I went into the winter barn for my ski equipment, the untouched bone was still there. Every night on my lonely trek home my shadow dogged my footsteps, but never came any closer and never made any sound that I could hear.

In the middle of the course, after the classroom instruction and some field-work, we were all thrown into a personal survival exercise, pitting our wits against the elements and ourselves with no evasion involved. The scenario was that we'd bailed out over unknown territory and had to fend for ourselves with what we stood up in or had brought down in our parachute pack. In effect that was our normal flying garb plus a cold weather jacket, a dinghy pack, a bar of chocolate, a few strips of jerky, a weak torch and a whistle.

At 5 a.m. on the Saturday we were shown on a relief-free map where we were each to be dropped off, and where we had to get to without making any use of roads or of transport; we had no local money and couldn't speak the lingo. The rudimentary map showed two cardinal points. The first was an RV (rendezvous) at which I was scheduled to arrive at between 8 p.m. and 8.30 p.m. that night. There, I'd receive my instructions for the next leg and be given a warm meal. The second point was the spot I had to reach by midnight on the following night. The total distance as the crow flies was less than 10 klicks, but we were in the depths of the Austrian Tyrol in midwinter with some 3 feet of snow lying, heavy snow falling, and no knowledge of the actual terrain over those 10 klicks. Today, to send men out in such dangerous conditions would be unthinkable; it would break every regulation that has been designed to ensure that no one does any-thing difficult or dangerous and therefore that no one can be held to blame!

Our only safety briefing was that if we felt ill or overtired, we should make our way to the bottom of whatever valley we were in where we'd probably find a road along which, in due course, would come the Course wagon. I have a sneaking feeling that we learned a hell of a sight more in those days about facing up to adversity and recognising our own strengths and weaknesses than we'd be allowed to now. But then, I *would* say that, eh?

I left the relative warmth of the Course wagon around 6 a.m. and set off alone and in fine fettle into the forest. Our flying boots then were strong and comfort-able, but walking uphill in deep snow was tiring and by the time I reached the first RV at 7.45 p.m., I'd gone up and down two mountains, crossed three rivers without using a bridge, and roundly cursed those who had designed the exercise. I was desperate for the warm meal we'd been promised, to take off my boots, dry my socks, and sit down in comfort for a while.

I was beginning to think I'd missed the RV when I glimpsed a dim light in the blowing snow and reached a log cabin with a huge solid door on which was printed "Knock here—Loudly!" I did just that and a small shutter opened and a voice asked "Name—number?" "Palmer 96," said I. An envelope appeared with instructions to read the contents and keep them safely. As I fumbled with my zips to stuff the envelope away, a disembodied voice said, "Here, grab this"—and something was thrust into my grasping gloves as the shutter slammed shut.

I stood in a blizzard and almost wept. My "warm meal" was a live wriggling rabbit which I held disbelievingly in one hand as I tore open my instructions telling me to enjoy my dinner, and to be at my final RV by 10 p.m. Sunday—or I'd have to walk back as well! Now I'd never killed a rabbit before with my bare hands, let alone skinned one, cooked and eaten one. But by midnight I'd done all of that and warmed myself with the fire I'd managed to light. I was feeling quite proud of myself, but now came the task of surviving in the sub-zero temperature, in total darkness, in the middle of a forest. My thoughts drifted back to Ehrwald and to the hotel where Adeletroud—I hoped—would be missing me. I was certainly missing her and the other comforts of life.

Having concluded that to build some form of shelter in the dark—with branches I'd have to cut—was much too complicated, I opted to inflate my dinghy and sleep in that. Within 15 minutes I was as snug as a bug in a rug. I pulled up the hood, shuffled my backside around to get the right shape in the cushion of deep snow and, thus protected from the elements, soon dropped off to sleep. I must have been asleep for about three hours when I was rudely awakened with the dinghy rocking madly, a strange noise that I couldn't make out in my confused state, and a feeling that quickly crept up on me of cold—intense, painful cold. I came to my senses quickly and discovered I was virtually unable to move my hands or shoulders and my feet seemed dead. I couldn't tell at first why I couldn't move, but then suddenly the noise around and above me stopped and I felt the rush of cold air and wetness on my face.

With a rushing sound the dinghy deflated and I rolled to break myself free from whatever was holding me to it. I realised that I was half encased in ice; everywhere my body touched the rubber of the dinghy I was attached by ice to it. Warnings of frostbite flooded my brain: what if my feet were already too far-gone and I couldn't walk? A touch of fear spurred me to greater activity and I began to feel the painful tingling in my arms and legs and was able to first kneel, and then slump forward thankfully into the fresh winds of the mountain.

Very painfully I disengaged myself from the now tattered dinghy and stood up to feel my circulation returning. I didn't care that I couldn't see a thing. I was alive and everything seemed to be working, and I lumbered off into the blackness, looking and walking, I suspect, like Frankenstein's monster in the old films. There were many hours before dawn came, but I didn't care. I was just so damned pleased to be able to move, to feel some bodily warmth returning, and I was determined to keep moving slowly. As the sky lightened over the mountain my spirits soared and I made my way safely to arrive at the RV by the appointed time, munching my chocolate and jerky as if they would be my last meal on earth.

My lorry load of survivors arrived back at the chalet at 1 a.m. and within seconds I was fast asleep. Debriefing took place at breakfast at 8 a.m. My de-briefer was our Squadron Leader Medical Officer, and as I recounted my ordeal in the dinghy he reminded me that in our Course notes was a special warning about sleeping in ones dinghy. The problem was that if you completely shut out the outside air, your breath turned to condensation on the rubber and fell as water. As I'd erected the dinghy in the dark, it already had water or snow inside, and I'd just added to the water content. At 13 degrees below freezing, my body warmth when asleep hadn't been high enough to stop the whole shooting match from freezing up—me included. The Doc told me I was a lucky lad and said they'd better strengthen the warning about the dinghy. Then he asked me why or how I'd come to wake up since I must have been approaching the stage when people don't wake up whatever happens. I repeated how I awoke to a noise and a feeling that the dinghy was being tossed about. He then asked how I'd deflated it if I couldn't use my hands, and I told him that I couldn't and didn't—I couldn't have found my dinghy knife in the dark; but the truth was I never even thought about it at the time.

We worked out that I couldn't have travelled more than a few hundred yards from the first RV to where I'd spent the night. Sure enough, in spite of new snow, my track from the RV was visible and we entered the forest to find, first, my fire where I'd cooked the poor rabbit. 50 yards on, lay the remains of my dinghy spread out like a carpet of yellow flowers. Leading away were my ongoing tracks, and around the tattered remnants of the dinghy, the snow bore the marks of disturbance as I'd prepared to retire for the night and later departed. There were no tracks other than mine leading in any direction. But when Tom Dobie turned over the dinghy there were dozens of marks that had scraped the surface like a steel rake—and the unmistakable indentations of teeth, sharp tearing teeth that had pierced the dinghy shell, torn the rubber to shreds and given me an escape route. Marks made when I was fast asleep or totally motionless inside. Makes you think, don't it? Even after 50 years, I have no rational explanation.

After the physical exertions of surviving a Bavarian winter, it was good to get back into the daily routine of skiing followed by the evening entertainment. But it was all coming to an end, and on the penultimate night of our Course Adeletroud and I were both subdued, as we knew our time together was nearly through. The weather had changed and under a full moon the valley was a shimmering lake of silver-white as I walked her back the 100 metres to her rooms. I commented on the beauty of the moonlight and added that I wouldn't need a guide to find my way to the chalet that night. She laughed and said something like "the spirits look after those they love all the time". As I left her, she whispered, "Don't be late tomorrow, remember—I'll be watching you." I set off in high spirits and by now I knew every inch of the track. There was no need for the lantern and to walk on such a beautiful night with no wind and in almost total silence other than the crunch of my boots in the crispy snow, was a sheer delight. I was aware of my companion joining me without hearing a thing, but I sensed I was not alone and swung round abruptly. There at the customary distance stood a magnificent wolf, head raised and bushy tail swinging. I slowly knelt to one knee and said, "Come on then, let's be friends."

We faced each other motionless for maybe 5 minutes before I began to feel the chill and turned to walk more briskly up the track. When I looked again the wolf had disappeared. Mystified, I retraced my steps some 100 meters to where I could clearly see the impression left by my kneeling in the snow. I looked across the expanse of white clear snow and, for the only time in my life, the hairs on the back of my neck stood up. There were no footprints or the tracks of any animal off the track at all!

Friday was the only late lie-in we were allowed, but at 7 a.m. as the sun rose over the Alps, I skied across the crispy virgin snow over 2 klicks of open field alongside the track to the ski slopes. There was no fresh snow and the surface was unbroken other than for some wispy marks, such as a rabbit might make when moving in a hurry.

That night was our End of Course party and the last meeting for Adeletroud and me. She was leaving by bus at 11 p.m. for Garmische to catch the Munich-Heidelberg train. I told her of my wolf and of my uncanny response to seeing him there and yet finding no sign of his presence. She bent down from the steps of the coach to kiss me and said, "Why should you think it was a He? *Auf Weidersehn*, and always look behind you *Liebchen*." I was never to see her again and she is hardly likely to read this; but a man knows when he has experienced something extra special in the mountains of Bavaria. When I returned to the bar of the hotel, the barman we had come to know well said, "Your strange lady has gone

Sir. I don't think we shall see her again in Ehrwald." He waved me away with a smile when I asked him what he meant. Later that night, and for the first time in two weeks, I had no companion on the way home.

Confrontation

Any military man serving in Europe in the 50's was acutely aware that Winston Churchill's warning about the Soviet Threat to world peace was not "Crying Wolf". From the Baltic to the Black Sea, enormously powerful conventionally armed forces were arraigned against the NATO powers with the heaviest concentration being along the East/West German border. There were a number of obvious corridors of attack that would enable an armoured assault to make rapid inroads into Western Germany, and the NATO armies were deployed accordingly.

British and American aircraft were deployed according to their combat roles. Those tasked to provide close air support to the defending armies on the ground were based near to the border to minimise the flying time to engagement and for quick turnaround. The fighters were based some 100 miles from the border so that they could react to low/medium level raids against their airfields and take out any higher flying reconnaissance aircraft or WP bombers programmed for deep penetration to cities, Headquarters, Transport bases and vital Supply routes to the rear. As the quality and quantity of radar coverage increased, offensive aircraft were forced to fly ever lower to creep in under the radar beams. This gave rise to more sophisticated aircraft with advanced navigation, weapons and self-protection systems. This led to massively expensive Research and Development programmes and as aircraft cost rose, the R&D expenditure rose on developing weapons that created more damage and could be delivered more accurately.

This upward spiral affected both the NATO and WP countries and all their Services. The crunch problem for NATO was that, although they had the more advanced and more reliable equipment, they were greatly outnumbered on the ground and in the air. A conventional war would have resulted in much of Western Europe being overrun in a short time. Eventually this mismatch led to the policy of Deterrence which virtually said, "You attack us with overwhelming conventional force and we shall be obliged to respond with nuclear weapons." At first this was a threat to attack major cities and military establishments, but then as nuclear weapons were themselves improved, the bargaining—for that's what it was—came down to selected military targets. The basic message was: "We know you might have the advantage of surprise, and you are superior in numbers, but if you attack we'll give you such a nuclear pasting within minutes that there won't be many of you around to enjoy the taste of victory."

At the time, few of the young aviators at Ahlhorn had much idea about the grand strategy. It wasn't the big picture that occupied our thoughts, but rather what our part would be if war came. We knew our capabilities and our weaknesses, and how we would operate commensurate with the effectiveness of our equipment and the ceaseless training we underwent. We were also clued up as to what our immediate enemy was capable of—and that made us a proud and confident lot; many of us actually relished the idea of going to war.

Doubtless that was sheer bravado, like the bully who relishes a fight until he gets a punch on the nose and loses interest. And of course we were naïve, we really had little idea at our level how an all-out WP assault across the North German Plain might fare. Years later, when I attended senior colleges, I became convinced that had push come to shove before we took the nuclear stance, we could not have defended Germany or the Low Countries—and probably not France or the UK either. Everyone assumed then that NATO would never launch the first attack. Many historians believe that the Russians thought otherwise, and I have to say that after my final tour in the RAF as Chief of Nuclear Plans at SHAPE, it would not surprise me to find that the Americans had a different agenda from the rest of NATO. (Certainly President Bush in 2004, chose to dispense with the rule books and did it, as always, the American way.)

So we had a genuine confrontation that kept us on our guard with a dangerous enemy who was wont to toe the line often and stick his nose against the fence, if only to check our response through the resulting escalation of alert states. In such a stimulating climate, I was thrilled in 1953 to travel with the Command rugby team to Berlin, a city then deep into the Russian WP part of Germany and split into four zones—Russian, French, US and British. We travelled via the nightly military train from Hanover with blinds drawn throughout, and through the Russian Immigration/Customs post where the train was boarded and searched. We arrived at Charlottenburg Station around dawn and drove through a bewildering mass of rubble to the Guards' barracks where we were to play that afternoon. The next day we went on an escorted tour of East Berlin where we followed the precise route that the Russians stipulated and were only allowed to alight at an imposing War Memorial and the Brandenburg Gate.

My abiding memories of that tour were the incredibly tense atmosphere with a feeling that at any moment someone might ignite a spark, and the contrast between the Russian zone and the Allied zones. Berlin was still a massive bombed site, but there was a dull lifelessness and hostility on the Russian side that contrasted sharply with the bustle of life elsewhere. To hammer home that message, our hosts took us for the next three nights to get a taste of Berlin nightlife which was centred on a number of extremely lively clubs that for atmosphere, entertainment and excitement I've never since seen equalled anywhere. Perhaps it was a combination of my youth, the company I kept, and of being in such a famous city still bearing all the marks of war and surrounded by half the Russian army. But Berlin was a fun city; an exciting, friendly yet elegant place with none of the seediness or false glitter of today's so-called hot spots. (Her name was Heidi—and no, I didn't, but I know a Regiment that did!) I took Rosemarie there for a conference in 1997. The city had changed in many ways, but we found it to be a fascinating and friendly place and wandered down some of the old areas to find typically German pubs serving classic Berlin food and German beer and wine. Apologies to you wine aficionados, but a good German Riesling served chilled in a thin German glass is hard to beat.

> "*Lieb Vaterland, magst ruhig sein;*
> *Fest steht und true die Wacht am Rhein.*"

After the Lord Mayor's Show

After three wonderful years in Germany, I became an instructor on the night fighter OCU at North Luffenham in England's smallest county, Rutland. That tour was marked by the birth of my eldest son Kel, promotion to Flight Lieutenant, and my best seasons of rugby at Leicester. It was the first time that my Mum and Dad had been able to visit us in our own home and the first time I had the chance to show Dad what I did and what I flew. To give him an exciting first taste, I took him as darkness fell to sit amongst the approach lights at the opposite end to the take-offs that night. (You couldn't do that with today's regulations, of course.) The Luffenham runway had a dip in it about 600 yards from the threshold and so you hardly saw or heard an aircraft coming until it was on top of you. When the first Meteor hurtled over us at some 150 feet, Dad didn't say a word. I turned to see him lighting his pipe. "Is that what you fly?" he asked. "Yes!" I laughed. "Daft young bugger, no wonder your mother wanted you to be a doctor," he replied, stabbing the stem of his pipe in my direction.

That Luffenham tour somehow escaped my notice as I sped through the earlier chapters, but having opened the door all sorts of surprising memories came tumbling out to bring a sparkle to my eyes or a blush to my cheeks. In flying terms it was my least interesting tour in that we were simply a sausage machine for turning out night/all-weather fighter crews for the then dozens of squadrons in the UK and overseas. But there were other highlights that cause me to reflect on how the world has changed in 50 years. Let's start with drinking and driving which RAF officers, like everyone else then, did with barely a touch of conscience. One night nearing Christmas our squadron held an all-ranks party in a local hostelry some three miles from base. I won a bottle of brandy, but the bad news was that I had to drink it on the spot, which I did before staggering to my pride and joy, a green 2.5 litre Riley, to drive home via four miles of country roads. In the middle of nowhere I stopped to have a pee, fell into a ditch and lay looking up at the night sky. Suddenly a flashlight shone into my face and a gruff voice enquired as to my health. I told the good constable that I was perfectly okay and had tripped in the dark.

"All right Sir," said the Law, "Let me get you behind the wheel and please take it easy." I left him standing by his bike without any feeling of fear or shame. On another occasion the Officers Mess held a Sunday rally which was a sort of paper chase on wheels. Clues were left at a number of pubs and the idea was to collect as many as possible and end up in the mess bar, assuming you lasted that long. I didn't, and my three companions and I, including a strikingly attractive unaccompanied wife, landed in a ditch—which was quite a feat since it already held three other cars. I had one irate wife, but no one else cared overmuch—it was a jolly!

That tour also gave me my first real taste of flying with the Senior Service. The RAF trained Navy night fighter crews bound for carrier service on Vampires, Venoms and later Sea Vixens. So to teach us landlubbers more about the unique aspects of carrier operations, a few of us were assigned for two months to *HMS Albion* and *HMS Ark Royal*. Those were the days before the angled deck, automatic landing systems and ski jumps. Some aircraft were still taking off under their own power and those with propellers on the nose did a long curved approach before crashing onto the deck and grabbing a wire. Landings were guided by a batman, the deck-landing officer, who, with coloured batons, indicated whether you should go wing up/down, ascend/descend, cut/go-around again. Recoveries then were quite exciting and from a position on the Island called "goofers" one had a grandstand view of the skills and the disasters facing the naval jocks. I was immensely impressed at how the ship was operated when dispatching or recovering aircraft and was therefore delighted later in my career when I had the chance to fly with the US Navy and then again with the RN in my Buccaneer days.

One other flying incident will demonstrate how things have changed. My wife's family lived in Londonderry near the naval station at Eglinton. It was Xmas and there were presents to be delivered, so why not fly them there? A Meteor V11 was made available, the weather and landing forecast were checked and a flight plan submitted. The weather forecast at 10 a.m. was of good conditions en route and a landing forecast of 5/8ths cloud at 1000ft, wind 15 knots, gusting 25, at 30 degrees off a dry runway. Before beginning the descent over Belfast, a sweet female voice gave an "actual" of rain, but no change in wind speed or direction. Twenty minutes later at 700ft downwind over the Eglington hills, in severe turbulence, and with insufficient fuel to divert elsewhere, the wind was 90 degrees to the runway, at 30 knots gusting 50. By now the runway had taken so much water that it was splash down, not touch down, and Palmer's Meteor aquaplaned beautifully before going off the far end at around 45kts even though the undercarriage was retracted before leaving concrete. The Navy crash crews arrived, rescued the Xmas parcels, loaned me dry clothes and a car to drive to Limavady. The next day I was picked up by a colleague, flown back to Rutland where I got a slap on the wrist for ignoring a poor weather forecast (which I hadn't) and sent as punishment for another four weeks on the good ship *Albion*. Those were the days, my friends.

A Change of Tack

In 1958 came one of those posting notices that made you read it again and again, and ask, "How dare they post *me* there?" But they did dare, and it was to be instructing again, this time at the prestigious RAF Flying College at Manby in Lincolnshire. After all the years of grey gloom, grey walls and Siberian winds I'd known at Cranwell, I hated the thought of returning to England's most boring county. But as happened to me on other occasions, a posting I dreaded turned out to be a memorable one. My specialist instructional role was that of Air Defence to the RAF's most senior course, the Flying College Course. There were only 20 students on a 12-month course, of Wing Commander/Group Captain rank, who had either just completed tours as Station or Squadron Commanders or were bound for such posts on graduation. The students were selected as a mix of fighter, bomber, coastal, transport, recce and helicopter experience, with added variety coming from students from the Royal Navy, USAF, US Navy and Commonwealth airforces. The icing on the cake, before aircraft became too expensive to bend and break, was the provision of flying in the Hunter, Canberra and Lincoln with the twin seat Meteor V11 as the jet trainer.

The staff were handpicked for their instructional capabilities, officer qualities and role experience, whilst the status and seniority of the students attracted every top-ranking officer in the three services as visiting speakers, plus many prominent politicians, industrialists and foreign dignitaries. The course visited most opera-tional UK stations and many Allied units on the Continent, and a cross section of the most important and interesting Defence industries. As a young career minded Flight Lieutenant, I found my two years at Manby fascinating and later in my career I was to serve under very senior men who I'd instructed in the air and on the ground. It was the perfect "old boys' club", so much so that when, in 1978, I was posted back there as Director, I was overjoyed.

An interesting side benefit was that I acted also as Air Defence specialist instructor for the RAF's most intellectually demanding course, the Specialist Navigation course. This intensely academic course fitted navigators and pilots for key posts in the Research and Development establishments such as Boscombe Down and Farnborough. This link enabled me to be on a select team that crewed the RAF's two most prestigious aircraft at the time, Aries 1V and V, two specially converted Canberra's that carried out a number of new equipment trials and also were established for the purpose of competing for world records for time/distance flights. It was especially exciting to a fighter-jock as it meant flying to faraway places I would never normally visit on a Fighter Squadron tour.

Feeling the pressure

For one of the most interesting "record" attempts, we worked up with shorter-range shakedown flights using Aden and Nairobi via Tripoli or El Adem near Tobruk. I'm conscious that today's aviators would take for granted what we thought of as breaking the frontiers of science and aviation, but the aviation world then was very different, aircraft were far less sophisticated, communica-tions were rudimentary, airborne and ground based Navigation aids non-existent once away from Europe, and many airfields were almost "bare bases".

Nevertheless, we thought ourselves to be the latest and best; we knew not what the future held and were too busy living to care overmuch. Take for instance an episode that occurred on a shakedown trip to Aden, which I'd forgotten until my memories were aroused by a BBC TV programme last night. It concerned an incident in the Crater district of Aden city, a locality to become famous in 1967 when Colonel "Mad" Mitchell openly defied Army top brass and Whitehall to take his regiment, The Argyll and Sutherland Highlanders, into Crater to rescue British and Regimental pride.

We flew out on Friday and back Monday. The other two crew members in Aries V were a very experienced Wing Commander Canberra pilot and an equally seasoned navigator, both in their forties, with me a 28-year-old sprog unfamiliar with the Canberra and the routes down to Africa and beyond to the Far East. The flying was interesting, and the weekends were simply a "jolly". No work, just keeping in good shape to make a dawn departure on Monday. I was to find, as in many times later in life, that I had a lot to learn about life and about people, compared to which mastering the Canberra PR7 was a doddle. My crewmates knew Aden well and suffered from a common disease—they were inveterate gamblers. It had never occurred to my young brain that that was why they often flew together and had I been switched on, I would have detected the telltale signs when they both sported black eyes after a night out in Tripoli en route to Nairobi!

But here I was, an innocent abroad as we launched into the Arabian night to drink our way around the Protectorate, ending up around midnight in a smoke-filled cellar in Crater, full of a remarkable mix of well-dressed men and women, a fair number of unsavoury looking characters, exotic dusky ladies, and assorted uniforms that reminded me of Slim's bar in Casablanca. I was content to drink and watch the colourful and exciting floorshow, knowing that my colleagues were in a back room losing or making money. Around 1a.m., Tom the navigator whispered in my ear that they were "moving on to another game" and it might be fun if I joined them. Ever trusting and incurably romantic, I leapt at the chance and followed into the waiting jeeps outside. We tore madly through the town kicking up clouds of yellow dust and arrived at the harbour to be shepherded onto a sinister looking dhow that immediately slipped its moorings and headed out into the bay. We were soon out of the harbour, past the breakwater and line of shark nets, and out under a magnificent canopy of stars and a crescent moon tilting on the horizon to the south. I'd been given a beer, invited to sit on a mess of old ropes and blankets, and had seen my gambling friends escorted to the high stern of the dhow.

I was pleasantly happy in the warmth of a velvety Arabian night, talking cricket with an Australian schoolteacher and with two attentive Arabian girls providing cold beer and local snacks. Suddenly there was a violent commotion at the stern, loud shouts of protestation and two distinct splashes. I caught a glimpse of what caused the second splash and had no doubt that it was my redoubtable leader entering the Indian Ocean. Even as I jumped up to investigate, I was lifted bodily from behind by many hands and sent head-over-heels into the inky waters below. When I surfaced, I watched the red lamp on the dhow stern slowly disappear from view, heard the faint sound of voices carried on the water, and looked to see where I was in relation to dry land.

The water was warm with only a slight swell, but it bothered me that I couldn't hear any surf or indication of a beach. I was dressed in typical tropical kit; a thin shirt, light trousers and desert boots, and I was a good swimmer and very fit. But I was at least a mile from any shore, in waters that certainly held sharks and barracudas, and I'd no idea about tides or currents. Dawn was too far away to wait for, so I swam slowly towards the ring of yellow lights that twinkled on my northern horizon. It was a long swim and I staggered up a beach just as dawn was breaking. For three hours I'd seen or heard nothing and had no idea about the fate of those whom I'd joined in the drink. As I stumbled up the beach, I was picked up by an army redcap in a jeep who asked me where I'd like to go—as if he picked up fully clothed people walking out of the ocean every day! He ran me to the Mess where I quickly changed into decent clothing and went back to the main reception to phone someone—I wasn't sure who. Coming out of the dining room as I arrived, whom should I see but my Wing Commander who simply said, "Oh, good, I see you made it all right, John. Try the breakfast—the kedgeree is marvellous. We'll see you in the bar for lunch, eh?"

The events of that night were never discussed and five years were to pass before I found how deeply my two wet friends had been into gambling, and that they didn't know I'd been thrown overboard after them. Ironically, it all came out when an RAF visitor to our home in Texas told me that the navigator had since been killed in a boating accident—in Aden! Perhaps two and two made five in my mind, but I still believe that was stretching the arm of coincidence much too far.

Darkest Africa

My good fortune to be on the Canberra team took me next to Kenya, the weird story about which should carry a "Government Health Warning". When it comes to stories of the supernatural, I feel able to write only about things that have actually involved me and for which, then or now, I can offer no rational explanation. If I were to rely on someone else's word, then I might have to accept that they had been misled, deceived, or been vulnerable to an odd experience. In writing this in my seventy-fourth year, I see no value in recording what others have thought, felt, said or done unless I can endorse their experiences. The events described have been the subject of many a fireside tale and many a critical examination by intelligent and understandably sceptical people all over the world. No one, anywhere, has caused me to rethink these offerings, simply because I've told it as it was and described images fixed indelibly in my mind.

One particularly interesting "interrogation" of my tale took place in Waco, Texas, in 1962 when I was on an exchange tour with the USAF. With an Englishman being a real rarity then in the Lone Star State, I was invited to join in a variety of social activities, one of which was Toastmasters, a club dedicated to improving one's public speaking skills. With the aid of my "cute accent", I spoke often in the Dallas/Waco/Austin area, including the odd TV appearance. A spin-off from that was the "English Society" that pivoted on a series of 20-minute talks or addresses on virtually any subject. I spoke about my paranormal experiences, mainly because their English/European settings were foreign to the Texan environment, and were therefore of unique interest to them.

Their reaction astonished me. Allowing for the few John Wayne characters that never liked to be upstaged, the overriding outcome of my tales was to encourage those too nervous to tell their own supernatural experiences, to come clean, as it were. I had no problems defending my personal experiences, but after hearing some hair-raising Southern tales about voodoo and black magic, I was persuaded to recount the only experience I'd had in the tropics or in a hot and oppressive climate similar to Texas. After that session in Texas, I never recounted it to anyone. Even my wife Rosemarie heard it only last week for the first time, simply because sitting in an easy chair on New Year's Day in Wales, in front of a warm fire and watching the robins and chaffinches play in the garden, the whole episode still seems like a nightmare.

There are some parts of my life that I have only to begin to look back on to be at once enveloped in the very atmosphere of the occasion. This one in Africa in the late 50's is typical, but first I must set the scene with an "adventure" preamble to explain how one day in 1959 I found myself in a native hut in a Mau Mau village in Africa. When I first recounted this story in that College auditorium in Waco, it was a memory only three years old. Today, 42 years on, I cannot only see what I saw then, but can recall the stifling heat and the unforgettable stench.

The Canberra B2 (Aries 1V) touched down at RAF Eastleigh, Nairobi, one Friday evening in October. It had been a long flight in a cramped cockpit, strapped to an ejection seat or a canvas "rumble seat", and after a quick shower and change into the local Red Sea kit, it was direct to the Officers' Mess bar. One of our hosts, Tim Howard, a civilian member of the Mess, enquired what I wanted to do on our day off, the Saturday. Our boss was going fishing, the navigator was playing golf, but I opted for seeing the wild life, it being my first visit to Equatorial Africa. "Fancy shooting the odd croc?" asked my newfound friend; and the brandy and ginger answered, "Sure, love to!"

Resolutions not to drink brandy ever again were made at 5 a.m. when I was picked up in a Land Rover, and again many times during a 2-hour rough ride that ended on the banks of a wide, fastish flowing river. Let me ask you this. How many times in your life have you literally stepped into the unknown, into physical danger, into circumstances that could result in acute embarrassment and humiliation if you failed, out along a path that had no boltholes and on which you can't retrace your steps? Well, this was one of a handful of such occasions in my life as the two of us climbed into a long flat-bottomed wooden boat. Tim's briefing was fairly succinct. "Keep your hands inside the boat, don't stand up, and fire when I tell you when they're belly up." "What will you be doing?" I asked; quite reasonably, I thought. "I'll be in the bloody water, of course"—with a hint of "daft bugger!" in his tone. We pushed off and two things immediately struck me. One, the river was flowing a lot faster than I'd expected. Two, the crocodiles didn't behave as in Tarzan films where one saw them slide slowly into the water followed by a pair of eyes sticking up, before Tarzan leapt on their backs and duffed 'em up to show Jane how macho he was. These crocs literally galloped into the river, and then disappeared until a bloody great tail splashed the water near the boat and all hell broke loose. At this point I believe I may have been receiving further instructions, but I was far too interested in just staying in the boat and out of the seething water. Then, to my astonishment, my fellow boatman leaped into the water shouting, "Grab the sodding tail!" There were moments of unease you might say as I saw a white belly and fired, almost going in backwards as a result, followed by kneeling down and holding a scaly tail as the boat swung towards the bank. When we grounded, I was requested kindly to "pull the bugger ashore" as my friend emerged from the river and shouted, "Look out!" I turned to see a couple of crocs running down from the high grass and took steps to evade them—long ones at about 25 knots, in fact! Later, after what remained of the carcase had been cleaned (by him, not me), we launched the dreaded boat and floated serenely this time to where our native driver waited with the Land Rover. I have to say that the journey back via the game parks was absolutely fascinating and by the time we reached Eastleigh I'd almost forgiven him.

At 6 p.m. sharp I was at the bar again. Brandy and ginger never tasted so good, and as I sat spilling my tipple I was joined by some friendly soul who asked me what I'd been doing with my Saturday. "Oh God, someone should have warned you that Tim is not only a mad bugger, he's totally nerveless!" He then went on to tell me that Tim, a Kenya Police inspector, had been heavily involved in bringing the Mau Mau troubles to an end. He had masqueraded with the Kikuyu as a native for months and joined in their obscene rituals and practices, even taking their Blood Oath, before turning them in and being a key witness at their trials.

I've introduced Tim that way to better explain the events that took place two weeks later when we did a second proving flight to Nairobi. This time he'd been briefed to take it easy on us and offered to take all three of the crew out to Mt

Kenya. Once again my crewmates, different chaps this time, chose fishing and golf. So it was Tim and me who hopped in a little Beech something or other and flew to the foothills of that majestic mountain. The first surprise I had that day was seeing him climb into the left-hand pilot's seat. First, I didn't know he could fly, and secondly, I had a few reservations when I thought about his attitude to other things. A pilot's style of flying, in that sort of aircraft, tends to reflect his personality—in as much as the way a man walks, sits in a chair, or gestures with hands and arms. I half expected Tim to start up, impatiently wave away the chap monitoring his departure, and then streak out onto the strip and away without a glance around him.

But I was wrong. He started up and after doing his checks waved cheerily at the marshals, gave a smart US Navy "permission to leave the ship" salute, and taxied out slowly. When we got to the take-off point, he used just enough propeller blast to turn him into wind. There followed the little ceremony of engine run up, oil pressure and r.p.m. checks and a tap on the altimeter and compass. He adjusted his straps, waggled his controls through their arcs of motion observing the movement, then took off straight into wind and climbed slowly ahead to 1000ft before making a gentle slow turn towards our destination. On route I'd fully expected being hanging on my straps as he pointed out the interesting sights below, but we transited serenely and were soon making a smooth approach and touchdown in the foothills of the great mountain.

Once there, we didn't do much or see much, but there was an atmosphere about the place that I linked with stories I'd read by Ernest Hemingway. We saw a village that had been adapted as a set for an Ava Gardner film, and met an interesting couple called Armand and Michaela Dennis who were studying the behaviour of lions in the wild. I remember that she loved the local terrain but he couldn't wait to get back to life on the sea. We took off from Mt Kenya around 2 p.m. and Tim suggested I might like to visit a native village on our route in which he'd spent some time recently (He didn't know I knew something of his Mau Mau connections). I agreed, of course. Some pretty fierce looking characters greeted us as we came to a halt in a cloud of red dust. But all went well. Tim was clearly well liked and an enthusiastic crowd escorted us to the village. In the middle of the hutted village we met up with three men who were clearly the senior guys around and after an animated discussion, Tim asked if I'd like to watch a native ceremony, warning me that I might find it both disturbing and nauseating.

There was no brandy this time to help my bravado, but in the safety of my ignorance I welcomed the opportunity to see local life in the raw, so to speak. Tim briefed me simply to watch, not to talk, and not to move unless I felt the need to leave the bamboo/straw hut. We entered the dark interior that was lit by a number of burning torches. In the middle of the room, lain upon a rickety looking wooden table, was the figure of a man dressed only in a sort of towel around his waist. There were no women in the hut, only the three headmen plus Tim and me. As my eyes became accustomed to the gloom, my senses began to take it all in. First there was a foul putrid smell and a continuous hum from hundreds of large black flies. There seemed to be no life in the figure on the table; in fact, from where I stood some 10 feet behind his head, he looked distinctly green and very dead. Being under oath to say nowt, I had reached the conclusion that we'd been invited to some sort of pre-burial service when two more men entered dressed—for want of a better description—as I would expect witch-doctors to be dressed. At a sign from one of them, the table was lifted bodily and turned around through 90 degrees so that the body was now at right angles to Tim and me and much closer, perhaps 5ft. The new arrivals then began to chant and to wave various wands and sticks above the body—as if to demonstrate, I irreverently thought—that there were no strings attached.

The smell was now overpowering and the hut felt like the inside of an oven, but I was totally absorbed in what was happening before me. It was now clear to me that the man, not an old man by any means, was not breathing. I could also see that he had a gaping wound to his right cheek and jaw, his right arm was half-severed below the elbow and there was no foot attached to his left leg. One eye was closed and swollen; the other had the glassy stare of a dead man. I was looking at a ghastly, evil smelling corpse that was about to be buried or cremated—I knew not which—when, accompanied by a cry from everyone in the place, except me, the thing sat bolt upright from the waist and raised its uninjured arm. I half expected a rattle of unearthly drums and ghostly flute music, but silently, two headmen each took a shoulder and lowered the obscene figure to a standing position in which, with one leg trailing, one arm swinging and a disfigured head twisting and nodding, the three figures left the hut followed by the priests.

Tim and I followed and as we drank in the blessed fresh air, Tim waved to the headman walking behind the appalling looking figure and turned towards the airstrip. As we climbed in, he said, "It's best you don't ask, John; just come to terms with what you have witnessed. It wasn't a trick—no conjuring, no smoke and mirrors, no black magic—okay?" As we flew back to Nairobi, Tim pointed out anything of interest on the ground and I marvelled at how intimately he knew and understood the fascinating country in which he'd chosen to live. He left the aircraft quickly on landing, threw me the keys of the Land Rover, saying he had a dinner engagement and must rush.

We flew back to England the following morning. I was never to see or hear from Tim again. When we did our final shakedown flight to Nairobi three weeks later, I was told that Tim had taken his own life a few days before for reasons and in circumstances unknown. His request was to be buried in the African bush that he knew so well. I cannot add to the facts as I saw them, the ghastly things I had witnessed. I can only add that there were folk in Texas who saw nothing particularly strange in my revelations and were able to recount similar stories of—to me anyway—genuine horror.

A Career Limiting Experience

The long distance trial itself to the Far East was not without incident. We were using Aries V, a specially converted Canberra PR7 with 21 fuel tanks to give maximum endurance, thus reducing the number of landings necessary over a long haul. Shortly before the outbound journey, our most senior officer decided he would be captain. Understandably, the rest of the team were not overly enthusiastic because, although the old man was a vastly experienced and capable pilot, he was getting on a bit and not familiar with the Canberra.

But he was a nice guy enjoying the privilege of rank, so it was a happy crew that headed east. All went well until the last leg when we had effectively reached our ceiling, having cruise-climbed as the fuel was burnt off—a technique that meant you didn't expend more fuel to attain altitude. Our leader, as was his wont on long trips, had inserted his ejection pin, unstrapped himself, and put his feet up on the sill and gone to sleep. This left the aircraft to be flown from the rumble seat, a canvas seat that was rigged after take-off, for which the co' sat in one of two rear ejection seats next to the navigator.

At around 48,000 ft and approaching Timor, the snoring from the left-hand seat was suddenly drowned by a large bang. Sitting on the rumble seat, I was enveloped in a mass of yellow rubber that forced me over the back strap to lie horizontally with my head on the empty ejection seat. Our ace had inadvertently inflated his dinghy and was lifted out of his seat, away from the controls, and flattened half moon shape against the canopy with his back towards me. The Canberra began to turn, gently at first but then began to tighten up and descend. The navigator, comfortably strapped in his ejection seat, could do nothing to help without unstrapping himself, and I had the clear impression that he didn't intend to hang around much longer.

I had no such option where I was—and the captain was out of his seat and off oxygen. By now the "g" had built up and the only movement I found possible was to slide my right hand down my flying suit to where a serrated edge dinghy knife was strapped to my outer calf. I took it out as quickly as I dared—albeit ever so carefully—and brought it to where I could get a straight stab at the yellow mass. The lack of space and the aircraft movement made it difficult to aim properly with a knife shaped more like a potato peeler than a dagger. Asking the navigator to kindly belt up, I eventually pierced the dinghy that rapidly deflated and allowed our intrepid leader to get back on oxygen, regain control and put Aries V back on course and climbing again.

The only problem was that my aim had not been too good under the trying circumstances and, before I struck the telling blow, I jabbed a disgruntled senior officer twice in his ample posterior! Before reaching our destination he radioed to cancel the reception committee and asked to be parked on the far side of the airport. On shutting down the engines, I moved back to the ejection seat as he climbed out painfully through the door into the evening shadows. He left Manby shortly after and never spoke to me again until we met 25 years later when he was a defence correspondent and we met at Farnborough to talk about the threatened cancellation of Nimrod AEW. I had the impression that he didn't understand a word of what I was telling him and didn't really care much. When I tentatively referred to our experience at Manby, he acted as though he was totally deaf and I was talking gibberish. *Forsan et haec olim meminisse iuvabit.*

See what I mean about fearing the worst about postings or other happenings in life? Often what we dread turns out to be the best that ever happened to us. But if I was pleasantly surprised by my Manby experiences, my next posting surpassed my wildest dreams.

7

WAY OUT WEST

RAF officers in the 50's/60's would learn of their postings through the receipt of a small brown envelope telling them of their appointment and what they must do to wind up their present post. For senior officers, a gentleman called the Air Secretary would discuss preferences—or at least someone in his staff would do so—giving you the feeling of being well looked after. By and large, the Airsec's team did a good job. I was beginning my third year at Manby and as it was a training post, not an operational tour, was expecting to stay put for another year. So certain was I of that, that I went into Grimsby and bought my first ever new car. More significantly, I abandoned my obsession with the old 2.5 litre Riley (the one with the leather roof), and purchased a sensible family car. I actually owned the last 2.5 RMS series Riley ever built, the only black one I ever had, built in May 1953. Spares were difficult, the car was expensive to run, and I'd had a series of five Rileys that always kept me at odds with my bank manager. Also, I was now a dad three times over with the arrival at No 4 Hunter Avenue of son Chris. It made all sorts of sense to be more conventional and drive a reliable family saloon.

At 11 a.m. on Thursday March 14th 1960, I parked my new gleaming Morris Oxford outside the College. It had set me back £475, and the mileometer showed 18 miles total, the distance from Grimsby to Manby. As I entered the office, my Canadian colleague passed me a little brown envelope from which I pulled out a small memo that said quite simply:

> Posting notice: Flt.Lt.J.K.Palmer to James Connally AFB, Waco, Texas as flying instructor, All-weather interceptor OCU. Report to British Embassy, Washington DC, 25th March. Travel instructions to follow.

My first reaction was astonishment, which gave way to excitement, and the thought that in one year we'd be off to Texas. Unbelievable! It may seem odd to the reader that I couldn't phone home with the good news; but we didn't have a phone—very few did. So I held my impatience in check until I could deliver the new car and the posting news together when I went home for lunch. Just to be sure I wasn't dreaming, I called the author of the memo to glean any further information. A sweet young thing answered and said, "Oh, that's funny, I was just going to call you. The RTO at Southampton says they haven't got your hold luggage yet." "What do you mean, my hold luggage?" I asked. She explained that when you crossed the Atlantic by sea, they liked the hold luggage to be on board the day before sailing. I said that I saw no problem as we weren't going for a year. "Oh no, Flight Lieutenant Palmer, you and your family are booked to sail on the *Queen Mary* for New York *next* Monday. Didn't you know?"

I explained I'd just received the notice, and was about to say that it was impossible, could we delay going etc., when I suddenly found my brain working again and realised that a refusal or lack of interest might jeopardise the whole posting thing. To cut a long story short, sweet young thing and I agreed I'd have the five Palmers, complete with luggage, at Southampton docks at 1100 on the Monday; she promised to get the necessary rail warrants sorted out with my Personnel office. In this almost frantic state of mind, I rushed out to find my new car had been virtually wiped out by a refuse lorry—so left it there and told the garage to collect it. Next I told a surprised wife to clean the quarter ready for handing over on Friday afternoon, gave my corporal clerk my clearance chit to take around, went to see my bank manager in Louth, and hired a car to drive to Manchester on the Friday to see my folks before catching the overnight sleeper to arrive at Southampton at 7 a.m. on Monday.

At 9 a.m. we boarded the magnificent *Queen Mary*, joined in the farewell ceremonies as she slipped out of the dock on her way for a quick pick up in France (at Cherbourg I think), before heading out into the vast stretch of the Atlantic. I went alone to the front of the mighty ship, suddenly feeling a sense of utter peace. I was leaving behind a few problems that would now work out happily and was looking ahead to a tremendous adventure. In a sumptuous Reading Room cum library, I wrote a whole stack of "Thank you" and "Sorry we couldn't say goodbye" letters that I was to post in New York. There are so few times in life when one can see no clouds at all on the horizon and harbour no fears about health, wealth and wisdom. That moment was one of mine without doubt.

A New world

To a generation that can now cross the Atlantic in three hours or reach the US Pacific coast in eight, it is probably hard to understand why going to the USA was so special in 1960. "America"—the very name exerts the most powerful fascination over us. Is there any country more capable of producing such mixed reactions? People love it or hate it without ever having been there, they presume a level of intimacy with every state of that immense country and pronounce widely on American tastes, customs and opinions.

What is it that provokes so many of us to be hostile? It may be that we resent the sheer size and wealth of America and so try to decry it. It may be, even more now than when I first went there, that Hollywood and TV have distorted our views and made America and Americans so much larger than life, thereby relegating our ways, our standards, and our customs to something inferior. Whatever it is that makes the US special, I certainly felt it in abundance on that April morning. Before we were to see the Statue of Liberty loom out of the mist, there was a wonderful voyage to enjoy. My own experience of boats had previously been limited to the Manx kipper boats and the ferries across the Irish Sea and Channel. Most of those trips had been awful, but this was something else—sheer unadulterated luxury. The children had lots to do, there was free baby-sitting available and the food was never-ending and invariably delicious.

Had it not been for the thrill of seeing America, I could happily have stayed on board for months and so was over the moon three years later when we returned via the equally splendid *Queen Elizabeth*. As we entered New York harbour to see a skyline seen so often on a screen, my enjoyment of the view was overriden a little by the anticipation of all that lay ahead of us. We were to stay one night in the Big Apple, then journey by train to Washington DC for "acclimatisation", and fly on to Dallas and Waco the following week.

First impressions proved disappointing. We disembarked and waited on the quayside for our luggage to be assembled on a large trolley. Then we were pointed towards Customs and Immigration, but as I started to push the trolley, a porter, who told me in no uncertain terms that that is why he was there, snatched it from me. That didn't seem to bother him when, some hundred yards down the jetty he said he must now hand me over to someone else, and asked for $20. That to me was iniquitous and so I rowed with my first real American on American soil before rowing even more with my second who pushed the trolley to Customs and demanded another $20. We negotiated Customs with the help of an Embassy man who then deposited us in a cab via another porter—you've guessed it—another $20! We drove from the dock for about two miles, taking 10 minutes, and what could have been an exciting journey turned sour when I had to fork out yet *another* $20, and then start World War 3 over the size of the cabby's tip. That experience taught me two early lessons. The first was that tipping was a quite different way of life in the USA; you tipped to a set scale irrespective of the quality of the service you received. Secondly, that New York is a uniquely rude and brash city and one that, after seeing all the sights, I was careful not to make a habit of visiting on my frequent trips to the US over the next 40 years.

Hello Texas

After seeing and enjoying Washington, we eagerly boarded our American Airlines flight for Dallas and then a small commuter airline for the 70 miles to Waco to be met by the guy I was replacing. I didn't know him and was quite unprepared when this sunburnt chap with a Hawaiian shirt came over to shake my hand. "Knew it was you," he explained. "No other daft sod would wear a suit in Texas." I had this odd feeling that perhaps we had left civilisation behind in Washington, a fear later accentuated by the fact that no one seemed to think that a family of five might want somewhere to live in Texas. My countryman explained that we would normally have taken over his married quarter, but that he and his wife had opted to live in downtown Waco rather than on base. I later found that he lived in the coloured section of the city where rents were low so that he could pocket over half of his rent allowance. He also announced with great pride that whilst he and his wife had been there, they had driven only 1500 miles in a new Morris Minor van they'd bought in England, so it would be almost new when they shipped it back! He added that they'd saved around $4000, so were going home in great shape. I couldn't help but think that he and his wife had wasted the opportunity of a lifetime.

Anyway, the Palmers needed a roof over their heads and we took advantage of a USAF scheme whereby a few three bedroomed houses were made available for families on a short stay basis, maximum 5 days. This good idea contrasted with the thoughtless one of not allocating an *ex officio* quarter to Exchange officers, as all RAF stations did as a matter of course. This helped the foreign family to settle in quickly and not waste time in a strange environment trying to find somewhere to live. But glad to be there, we moved into the temporary house and I went to the base housing office the next morning.

"No"—the little coloured girl didn't know we were coming, and "No", the sergeant in charge could do no better than put us on a long waiting list. There were some 1500 officers on James Connally AFB so turn over was fairly good, but at No 66 on the list we had a fair wait ahead. I filled in a card and gave it to the girl who put it in the cardex, said she'd give me a week's warning when my turn came up and kindly asked if I'd like a "caw fee." I thanked her profusely and when she disappeared around the back, used all my devilish cunning and audacity to nip round the counter and change my card from 66 to position 3. At 11 a.m.

the next morning a sweet voice tracked me down at the Squadron to say "Loo-tenant Palmer, your turn on the housing list has come up, can you be at 306 Langley at 9 a.m. Friday please?" I could and I was and we were in. Lesson learned: Americans make millions of regulations, very few think of what they mean or understand why they were written.

"What do you mean, you lost the aeroplane?" Texas 1961

Life on a US air base

Settling in to my job and to the social life of the squadron and base was enormous fun. Almost everything was new; different aircraft, different equipment, different procedures and a different operating environment. I wanted to become operationally qualified quickly, so I'd get up at 4 a.m. and do the weather check ride, land around 6 a.m., have breakfast, fly an 8 a.m. slot followed by an 11 a.m. slot, and do my academics/technical work after lunch. This was made easy for me by a team of Squadron executives, to whom I was immensely grateful, who almost gave me *carte blanche* to do as I pleased. Within the month I was ready to go to missile camp down in the Florida swamps.

The social life was hectic too. As the only British family on base, we were invited to everyone's party. We'd be asked to accompany people going to watch the school, college or Pro-football games and the softball or baseball matches. Brits in Texas were very rare then, so we'd also find ourselves in the social pattern off base that included some of the state's richest and most influential people. Our "cute accents" earned us many a weekend in a palatial "Southfork-type" mansion or on a cabin cruiser on the lakes or rivers. In the dry heat of Texas, I was missing my sport, so I taught the entire base to play soccer. I qualified for a place on the College (American) football team by doing an evening course in Basket-weaving and did myself justice as a linebacker in which position I was able to spend more time on the field than off. I really took to softball and found my cricketing eye stood me in good stead for belting a lump of cowhide out of sight. I held the coveted field position of first base against fierce competition and revelled in weather conditions that guaranteed you played every match as planned.

I had my failures too. The first was golf, a game that I'd never been attracted to until Texas and then only because the local course was the only really green patch around. It was watered constantly and kept beautifully and provided a wonderful early morning stroll once you'd kicked the rattlers off the tees. The problem I fear was the spirit in which the Americans played the game. Sport for me has always been about physical fitness and prowess, applied through an intelligent mind. I have never bracketed sport and drinking together, even in my serious rugby days, and certainly I've never gambled in any of my sporting activities. The Americans at JC would bet on the match, on the half and on every hole. There were bars on the 5th, 9th, 14th, and 18th and many a club was smashed against a tree or ended in the water in anger or frustration; that wasn't what I wanted from my sport and recreation. Since then I have looked upon Golf as a disease and, in my days with Industry, as an opportunity for bribery and corruption by those who weren't too keen to work overmuch.

My other sporting failure hurt more because it was unexpected. From early Cranwell days I loved to play Basketball. At well over 6ft and very athletic it was the perfect game for me and I represented the RAF at every level up to Combined Services. Basketball is one of three national games in the USA, so I looked forward eagerly to showing them how well I could perform. I was sent on in a relatively unimportant match to gain match practice and for them to gauge my capability. They needn't have bothered; I knew myself within minutes that I was an utter novice by their standards. The game is all about teamwork, movement, speed and accuracy of pass, and the knack of working an opening to shoot. I was like a stranded whale and was so humiliated that I never set foot again on a court in the US.

Once I was on top of the flying, and the family and I had acclimatised and adjusted to the new and very attractive lifestyle, I began to widen my horizons. I was determined not to waste our time as my predecessor had, and started to plan on seeing more of the States. Being in the heart of Texas, we were almost equidistant from the Pacific and Atlantic coasts and from Canada. All were journeys in the order of 1500 miles, necessitating a lot of driving through uninteresting and sometimes hostile areas to get to the places you wanted to see. We decided we'd plan two main long trips to places that were uniquely interesting and would link a number of interests. We ruled out New York and DC as we'd be going back there on our way home, and we didn't favour the journey north to Canada. We planned for Florida on the Gulf Coast taking in New Orleans, the Everglades and southern Georgia, and the inevitable lure of the Wild West taking in El Paso (and Mexico), the Badlands around Tombstone, Grand Canyon, and Zion. We didn't fancy Las Vegas, whilst LA and San Francisco were a bridge too far.

A Means to an End

That itinerary meant missing huge parts of the States, so I sought ways of filling the gaps. Flying relatively short-range interceptors, I knew I might be able to visit a handful of other airfields, but would certainly not be able to achieve my ambition to visit all 50 states. A solution fell into my lap because of the way USAF aircrew then got their flying pay. In order to collect their substantial monthly increment of flying pay, aircrew had to reach a monthly target by the 15th of the following month, or lose that month's pay completely. This could not be achieved for all qualified aircrew on the base by flying the front line fighters, so the USAF provided "Training Support" aircraft in the shape of 4 twin engined T-29's and 2 four engined C54's, both able to fly legs of 1500–2000 miles.

The other peculiarity of the flying hour requirement was that the aviators didn't actually have to fly or navigate the aircraft; all they had to do was fly in it. So, every Friday lunchtime, up to four aircraft would set off loaded with aircrew for a longish flight to acquire some 6 hours time airborne. They'd stay overnight and then perhaps fly a shorter leg on Saturday or Sunday, flying back to Waco to be on the ground by noon on Monday. Accrued flying time would be between 12–15 hours, they'd play cards, shoot craps, read or sleep in the back, and have a whale of a time in Las Vegas, LA, New York or some other spicy city in the continental USA.

For a guy who wanted to see 50 States, and do the odd Embassy cheap liquor run to Washington or San Francisco, this was the bees' knees. The only snag was finding volunteer flight crew, which wasn't easy, there being only some 12 pilots qualified on type with the vast majority on base being jet jocks. Also, there was a great reluctance to "authorise" the flights, as the work involved in setting up the crews and backseaters, plus planning, weather and other clearances, was considerable. The scheme was about to be aborted when some bright spark suggested the British Exchange officer (having a form of diplomatic immunity) took over the running as a secondary task. I did just that, and used my competent secretary Wirda as the booking clerk-cum-schedule planner. To persuade flight crews to fly at weekends I gave each pilot his choice of route, whether it was to LA to hunt girls or to some hick town in north Montana or Wyoming to hunt the fearsome and dangerous Grizzlies that roam the mountains there. Sometimes the attraction was cheap booze, either mine from the Embassy or the Mormon's homemade whisky called "Leopard Sweat". The carrot worked like a dream, earned thousands of flying hours for the aircrew, and gave me access to every state in the union except Hawaii. It was of course unfair to my family for me to go every weekend and after the first couple of months I only took one trip per month. The day I left Texas for Hamilton AFB, Ca. "Johnny Palmer's airline" closed down.

One of the perks of an exchange tour was the availability of virtually unlimited amounts of very cheap booze. This came from the Embassy in DC or from a Bond Warehouse in San Francisco. Exchange officers either flew or drove to DC, or had their orders shipped by road or rail. For my first order, I followed the rules and had six cases sent by rail to Austin where they went to the Texas Liquor Control Board who doubled the price per bottle by putting on a 37 cent tax

I drove the 50 miles to Austin to collect my booty and found myself carrying the boxes from the 10th floor to my Rambler Station Wagon. They were all open for each bottle to be stamped and when I went up for the fourth box I found Hiram C.Potts, the liquor control man, with a bottle of Hankey Bannister in his hand saying what good whisky it was. He said it again on my next trip to the 10th floor and I said, "Well, if there's a bottle less when I come back, I shan't notice." There were actually two bottles less as I headed north to Waco. The following week I received a phone call from officer Potts which said, "Eh, big John, rather than send all that liquor through Austin, why don't you fly it in to Waco and I'll come up to stick a stamp or two on it?" I did just that and Hiram came down, put stamps on 12 bottles, left 60 unstamped and returned to Austin with three bottles of Scotch. I should point out here that I wasn't drinking all that liquor, but as the cost on base was about five times what I paid, I was letting my buddies have it at the price I had to pay, plus enough to cover Hiram's stamps. I made nothing but lost nothing, Hiram got his share, and my friends saved a fair bit of cash. Slightly illegal, but smiles all round, really.

Getting wise

Then came an incident that showed the other side of the American character that has always puzzled me. I took the C-54 to DC for a large order of 15 boxes just before Xmas. On the way back over Tennessee we lost the port outer engine; no sweat, of course. But then as we crossed into north Texas we had fluctuating power on two other engines and it seemed unlikely we'd make JC. Although there were diversions available, I was not too keen to land in another State on a strange airfield with what I had in the hold. So we decided, professionally and safely, to press on. As we approached Waco at around 8 p.m. on the Sunday evening, the tower asked to speak to me personally. "Sir," said the controller, "we have two Texas liquor control trucks awaiting your arrival. They wish to see you before you leave the aircraft. Oh, and Sir, the Base commander, Wing Commander, and your CO have all left the base."

We landed and taxied to the end pan where sat the two trucks. There was silence on the aircraft and the captain asked if I wanted him to accompany me. I said no, this was my problem and told him to sit tight. As I climbed down and walked across the pan, that enormous busy airbase was like Aberdeen on Flag Day—deserted except for Hiram C Potts and one other who strode purposefully towards me. "Hey, Big John," said Hiram, "am I glad to see you. I called your wife who told me when you'd be back. I'm in a real bind; tonight is our annual Hunter's Supper and all our liquor suppliers (they were in a "dry" County) have let us down. Any chance of a couple of dozen bottles?" So, in front of a worried crew and a base not wanting to be involved, Hiram loaded all the liquor in his vans, drove me home and took his 24 bottles plus back to Austin. I was relieved, of course, but my overriding feeling that night was that of watching people I was helping at my risk, walk away from involvement. It was to happen in other ways and I never fully understood the mentality involved.

I was fortunate to be able to explore America as I did, even though I couldn't see it all in the detail that, say a backpacker, would see it—the good, the bad and the ugly, and through meeting people in their everyday existence. But then a backpacker or a motorist would not be able to cover so large a territory or obtain a general impression quickly enough to filter out the unwanted and home in on the places and people of most interest. Such impressions are intensely personal;

and what I found fascinating others might relegate to a "been there, done that" category. I simply did it my way.

We visit places for the first time with preconceived ideas. Sixty years ago those ideas would have come from books or newspapers; now they come from films and TV which, for all their marvellous detail and coverage, can still distort the picture for a country as vast and diverse as the US. Watch a travelogue on Gibraltar or Malta, and in one hour's viewing you can get a real feel for the place and its people. Not so for the US, where history, colonisation, development, geography, climate and immigration have all stamped their mark in some way or another on states, cities, villages or the wide-open spaces whatever they might be. For over a century, writers, reporters and artists have misrepresented it, romanticised and sensationalised it.

My preconceived ideas of the US and its people included such gems as all Americans being generous and warm hearted, with the vast majority living in luxury in beautiful houses with swimming pools and a car for every resident. All College girls would look like Doris Day; long legs, short skirts and white knickers. All College men would be Ryan O'Neil look-alikes; except when they were wearing football kit when they all looked like Michelin man and played quarterback, of course!

If you were in New York, Texas, Los Angeles, or Salt Lake City, you'd be up to your backside in gangsters, cowboys, filmstars or Mormons respectively. Boston meant rain; San Francisco guaranteed fog, Phoenix wall-to-wall sunshine, and New Orleans sticky and clammy with a jazz band in every street. Las Vegas and Reno were towns to which men went to get away from their wives, and Florida and Palm Springs were where women went whose husbands had gone to Nevada. There is no such animal as an honest American lawyer or politician. The former cares only for his own pocket and the latter is without ideals, without greatness and is frequently held to ridicule.

Some of my preconceptions proved to be correct, but many were way off the mark. And that of course is what fired my ambition to utilise the three years I expected to be there in finding out more about their huge, violent, spectacular, heroic, inspiring and immensely rich land and the idealism, zeal and character of its people. I think I already knew that the standardised American was largely a myth, created not least by Americans themselves, so I began my exploration with an open mind. The mental blueprint I already had was amended on almost a daily basis. I was flying a lot in the Texas, Arkansas, Oklahoma, Louisiana, and New Mexico area and although I saw little in detail, it helped to draw a perspective. I also flew "land-away" sorties into Arizona, Kansas, Florida and Georgia, which broadened my horizons.

Then I was serving with people from all over the USA with their own backgrounds, lifestyles and accents, who contributed enormously to putting flesh on the skeleton. The guy who converted me to the F-89 was from Utah, his wife from Michigan; our next-door neighbours hailed from Mississippi, New York, Montana and Wisconsin. My crews on the weather ships came from Alaska and Maine. All in all, a tremendous fund of knowledge into which I could dip to make my plans to see more of the US, and home in on the places that interested me most.

Despite being able to draw on this fund of experience, it came as a surprise to find that, contrary to what I'd almost taken for granted, Americans themselves were not all that well travelled. I found many a comfortably-off Texan who had barely been outside his own State, and even more that felt that it was a waste of time to venture beyond the boundaries of the USA—simply because nowhere else could be as good! One of my pilot students, at the advanced age of 21, had never set his eyes on either the Atlantic or Pacific. Indeed, on his first ever visit to the seaside off Panama City in the Gulf of Mexico, he made the classic understatement of my life when he yelled at me from the shore: "John, there's a big fish in the water behind you!" Jerry Siderius's "big fish" was an 18ft Tiger Shark and I was careful to brief him that the next time he saw me swimming in the proximity of such a fish, he should shows some sign of genuine hysteria.

Years later when I was a regular visitor to the huge IBM plant in Owego NY, I was amazed to find that over 50% of the families I met had never set foot outside North America. By then, I knew the States pretty well and as I waxed lyrical about this or that scenic view, the food or climate, I'd frequently find the listener hadn't a clue as to what I was talking about. Then there was the oddity that some US military families when based overseas would never leave the base. Instead, they would confine themselves to "little America", the comprehensive on-base facilities provided by the US Government, and refuse to shop or travel in the local area. I knew an Air Attaches' wife from Dallas in Athens who would never visit a Greek home, and a US Marine's wife in Scotland who always boiled the water from the tap before drinking it or cooking in it. The fair Louise even made all her own bread and cakes because she claimed that Scottish bakers didn't fumigate their ovens daily!

Charity does not begin at home

Another myth quickly dispelled was that of American hospitality and generosity. Without exception every American exchange officer I met in the UK was a generous and capable host, but when playing at home that was not always the case. As an Exchange family and the only Brits amongst over 6000 people on base, we entertained often and fairly lavishly, thanks mainly to our entitlement to cheap booze. We realised however that over 50% of guests we had entertained frequently, never returned our hospitality. When I was in industry and working with a foreign company, it was customary to entertain visitors at home or in London. Hospitality when returned by Americans was superb, but it rarely happened. I was particularly disappointed in Texas when, even though I was saving my officer colleagues around $4 per bottle on liquor (over 60%), and went to the trouble to order it, pay for it and carry it, some 25% of recipients never paid me for their orders.

Setting the standard

But perhaps the most unexpected letdown lay in the proficiency and professionalism generally of the USAF and USN aviators. Exchange officers with the RAF were always exceptionally good aviators and the US military do have many outstanding officers and flyers. The disappointment came in finding that below the top 10%, the average was very low. Some of the fault lay in the training methods that assumed that if an aviator had good academic grades, he would automatically become a good pilot or crewmember. That assumption was carried to the point where an officer who failed a stage exam or flight check during a Course, was allowed to remain in training until he achieved acceptable grades, quit of his own accord, or killed himself.

Linked to that was the American method of Officer Effectiveness Reporting—OER's, which determined an officer's fitness for promotion, and thus the highest rank that he might attain in his career. The RAF equivalent, the Form 1369, had some 10 headings under which an officer was assessed with 9 grades against each heading. Every officer was assessed in the rank in which he was serving and against his peers. With written evaluations by the First Reporting officer and those above him in the chain, plus recommendations for instant, early or eventual promotion, the RAF system was fair and reliable. The USAF system however had only 5 evaluation headings with only 6 grades against each. Grade 6 was reserved for Generals and 5 for senior officers or exceptional officers of lower rank, of which there were not allowed to be more than a couple on a base with hundreds of junior aircrew. Next there was the problem that no American, by definition, can be below average, so no one can be graded 1 or 2. Thus if a reporting officer is assessing 30 Lieutenants or Captains, he only has 2 grades in 5 columns in which to sort out the wheat from the chaff. The USAF system was grossly unfair to the good guys. A belated promotion inevitably put an officer further behind on a promotion ladder that became steeper the higher one rose, with fewer posts available in the higher ranks. Late promotion also hit the pocket, as rank was the only route to an increase in salary except for small increments for time served. The other serious drawback of the system was that many very ordinary officers were promoted above their capability level, the consequences of which were only realised when it was too late.

As a Reporting Officer in Waco, I had gone along with their system on the basis that it was not my air force and therefore—"When in Rome". But when I was re-assigned and had to do my final reports on all 64 of my guys. I singled out 3 captains and 2 Lieutenants as "Exceptional", which meant awarding mostly 6s. This, I was told, was simply not permissible—it exceeded the entire base allocation for "exceptional" for the year, so please correct. As with the RAF system, if the second Reporting Officer disagreed with the findings of the first, he could explain, in red ink, why he disagreed. I never found an American prepared to do that, and on this occasion my own "end of assignment" report was placed in front of me as a form of blackmail to persuade me to sign. I held out, refused to lower the grades, and weeks later was called by my boss in Washington to explain why my 1369 from Texas contained eight 9s—top grading—and one 2. The 2 was for Tact!

My reward for my lack of tact came, when in 1980 at a NATO conference in Brussels, the list of speakers included two three-star Generals and one Brigadier out of my five USAF aces. The fourth made full Colonel and died in Viet Nam and the fifth retired as a two star to head up the strategic marketing arm of Westinghouse.

Guys and Gals

I found, and still find, American men to be little different to men anywhere. Nevertheless there were some surprises, or even shocks. It always shocked me for instance to find men with beautiful wives and lovely children eager to find sex with prostitutes and back street scrubbers whenever they went on TDY (temporary duty). That isn't to say that I didn't know RAF officers and Englishmen with an eye for a pretty woman, and I can hardly claim to be a saint. It was simply that many Americans seemed to discard all their standards of propriety, behaviour and dignity once they were out of sight of home, often drinking with the sole objective of getting drunk. Before you accuse me of being a prude, I have lived a lifestyle that has brought me into intimate contact with drinking and boozing of all types from the most elegant of cocktail parties to rugby clubs and sawdust bars in shacks the world over. But I drank in the love of the moment, the pleasure of the company and through an excess of high spirits. The American has a way of his own; he either takes a bottle in solitude or sits at a bar and proceeds deliberately and inexorably to get rat-arsed all on his lonesome. Either that, or he takes a real delight in a knockdown, drag-out, honking through your nose on your knees, type of party. I'm not talking about an alcoholic, just an ordinary Joe who will also take great delight the following morning in telling the world that he doesn't remember a thing after saying "fill it up again". There you are at liberty to call me a prude because I've never forgotten what I did whilst under the influence, and I cannot see any point in becoming oblivious *"non mi ricordo"*. If you don't feel anything, how do you know it feels or tastes good? I prefer to know when I'm having a good time. Sad to say, last night (2004) I saw a TV programme that made me realise how much the UK has changed in its drinking habits. The practice I had deplored in Texas in 1960, drinking to get drunk—"binge drinking"—is now commonplace here.

Other Americans I knew became irresponsible gamblers, a practice foolishly permitted on base when cunning and ruthless older officers often preyed on the young and innocent. As I say, I've known many RAF officers who have a flutter, just as they might chase the girls and hit the bottle. However, I never saw them sink as low as their US counterparts, or perhaps they were simply so much better at covering up their indiscretions and more aware of the need for circumspection.

Fools rush in...

As for the American female of the species, I shall have to pick my words carefully to the point where perhaps this should be written posthumously. But here we go—"once more into the breach dear friend." Before fat and obese became fashionable, most American females had that supreme confidence and assurance that seemed to be instilled in them through High School and College days. I noticed the difference from the moment I stepped off the *Queen Mary*. They usually had the money and training to dress well, were beautifully groomed, and carried themselves with poise, elegance, and even arrogance. They could usually talk the hind leg off a donkey, speak without restraint, interrupt their elders and betters, and invariably know everything about finances and real estate. It was as if they'd been mass-produced and programmed (Stepford wives fashion) to please a man at arms length, to adorn his house, and impress his friends, and in doing so to submerge their true feelings, concealed in *perdu* as it were.

I started to write that they flattered to deceive. But I was using the wrong term because what lay beneath their glossy exterior and often aloof attitude was something far more appealing. The overriding impression that I gained then and have experienced on so many occasions since, is that they are desperate to be female, to be women, with strong personal passions, capable of deep emotion, wanting things beyond the figments of reality, beyond the hardness of the world in which they live. They hunger for the power of affection, they long to be beautiful, graceful, fascinating and have sex appeal without calling it by any such name—but buy underwear with a view to it being seen! They weary quickly of men whose emotional content is that of a boy; they want to be loved and to have that great experience that eludes most of them.

To me in the 60's, they were a constant delight and a challenge. I would go into a gathering to see gaggles of, at first, serious looking and bored women. But as you engaged them in conversation, you were soon stimulated by the quickness of their minds, the sharpness of their wit, and impressed by the richness of their intuition. It was like watching an exotic garden spring to life after a shower of rain. In the social life of the US military then, the circumstances were perfect for a young-ish Englishman to be pleasantly surprised again and again by the female of the species. One would enter a house to be welcomed by the host and hostess, whereupon invariably the man would be guided into the kitchen to join all the other men whilst the lady went to the drawing room to mix with the girls. All the men would be drinking cold beer or neat Gin that they froze and called a Martini, and talking about the things that men talk about.

Women chat and gossip and talk rubbish too, but there was an underlying difference. The marvellous thing about good conversation is that it encourages us to express even our half-thoughts and thus sows the seeds for others to follow suit. Speech kindles the spirits, and soon a room is full of words and thoughts and ideas flying back and forth and you have a party instead of a wake. I found then in Texas, what I've found so many times since all over the world, that a man can get far more fun and become engrossed and involved in intelligent stimulating dialogue, when in the company of the women rather than a group of men.

That is how it hit me in the 60's and I'm not sure when the American pattern began to change. But I noticed when I started going back regularly to the US in the early 70's, that women were beginning to play a more dominant role in most things. As in Europe, they were getting more involved in work and in many more occupations, the myth of the dominant male and the submissive female had been lain to rest, and women were becoming persons first and wives second.

In the 60's I felt that most American women did not want freedom, but by the 90's they had taken it by the scruff of the neck and become more liberated through thought, work and dress. I have the sad feeling unfortunately that their independence has been bought by surrendering some of their beauty and grace, much of their integrity, and too many of their feminine qualities of spirit and mystery. Where once I might look across a dining table at a ravishing creature who smouldered with eyes full of expression and who made me dream of heaven in waiting, I now look across the same table to see an exquisitely groomed, intellectually sharp, business-orientated china doll—and feel nothing! Of course you could put that down to my advancing years, or to the wonderful mix of beauty and character that I have seen in Rosemarie every day for the past 31 years. So I'm now going to quit on this particular subject while I'm ahead, but let me recount one small episode that could only happen in Texas.

I earlier mentioned my secretary Wirda who I'd personally selected out of eight applicants, three of which were "honeys". I gave Wirda the job because she needed it and because she was amazingly truthful in telling me—a total stranger and a foreigner to boot—why she was as she was. She was a quiet unassuming lady of 34 who had seen better days and bore the marks of emotional suffering. I asked her if she was married or had been married, to which she replied No, not now, but twice in the past. Innocently, and not at all nosily, I enquired why her marriages had come to grief. "Oh, I shot them both," she said. That got my immediate attention, so I invited her to say more. She explained that she and her first husband lived on the outskirts of Dallas with their back "yard" overlooking open fields. There was a "coloured "problem in the area and so wives were invariably armed with a firearm of some sort for protection. One night around 2 a.m., she was disturbed by a noise in the yard and went to the door with a shotgun and issued a challenge. There was no reply, but as she turned there was another noise that made her ask again who was there.

No reply, so she hurried back into the kitchen and closed the door only for it to be smashed open. In the half-light she made out a figure and shouted that she'd shoot if he came any closer. The figure kept coming so she fired. Putting on the light she found it was one very dead husband. Her trial was a low-key affair on a charge of unavoidable self-defence for which she received a commendation for her bravery and paid a fine of $30 because her gun license was out of date. I hardly dared ask about the second, but it wasn't that different. Her second husband was a drunk who often beat her up. One night he smashed his way into her bedroom without saying who he was and received both barrels for his pains. This time the judge was harder on her, fining her $100 and suggesting she bought a burglar alarm or married a peace loving bullet-proof man of God. She turned out to be a wonderful secretary and a lovely lady, and I learned a lot about Texas girls from her and much more about the psychology of the American love affair with the gun.

Unidentified flying Objects (UFO's)

Talking about UFO's is like talking about ghosts; the moment you open your mouth a high percentage of your audience marks you down as a lunatic or a liar. Indeed, I'm equally sceptical and have frequently listened in disbelief to such stories, marvelling how anyone can possibly believe the outrageous claims that one hears. So why am I opening myself to similar ridicule?

Well, firstly, because my stories are true and, like Ghostly tales recounted elsewhere, have stood the test of time and scrutiny. Secondly, perhaps because I am a romantic at heart. At least that is what I have been accused of being, or complimented on being; one can never be sure which! For instance, I long for the day when some smart ass BBC TV film crew get publicly served up as smorgasbord for the Loch Ness monster, and to see Anne Robinson carried off kicking and screaming into the Himalayas by the Abominable Snowman. When Neil Armstrong first stepped down onto the surface of the moon, I was praying that a huge dark shadow would loom over him and for him to shield his eyes and utter that most famous of all American sayings: "Oh my Gawd!" Oddly enough, I once shared a dinner table with him in Paris during Air Show week. As the wine flowed, I felt this indiscretion coming on and told him (no offence intended) of my secret wish. "Don't think it hadn't occurred to me—the mike didn't pick up every word I said that day," he replied.

So—"lest men suspect my tale untrue..." I'm only going to offer one "ufoism" that occurred whilst flying operationally. I feel better qualified than most to give an opinion on UFO's, having spent 37 years of my life in the RAF, 25 of them in flying posts and all but the first three intimately involved with flying. All of my subsequent 17 years in the Defence Industry were directly associated with aircraft and I continued to fly frequently in military aircraft as well keeping up my p.p.l. Most of the major projects in which I was involved were about surveillance and reconnaissance—the airborne means of detecting and tracking unknown "targets" in the air on the surface. So I knew as well as most what could be detected, and the means of doing so.

A Pacific Puzzlement

The flying incident happened in 1962 on a night sortie in the F101B Voodoo out of Hamilton AFB, across the bay from San Francisco. The West Coast of the USA was then heavily defended by fighters and SAM against the long range manned bomber threat from the Soviet Union. As in Europe throughout the Cold War, every fighter base had its aircraft on various states of readiness depending on how Intelligence assessed the danger of attack. Being on a 10-minute alert state meant that you had to be capable of getting airborne within 10 minutes of being "scrambled". That meant the crews had to be seated in the cockpit with themselves and their chariots ready to go within seconds. If the alert state was 30 minutes, the crew could be resting in the comfort of the Squadron or alert facility, partially dressed to fly and with the aircraft already prepared. The USAF inevitably had only the best, and at Hamilton a custom built Alert Shed (mini hanger) was located some 60 yards off the end of the runway.

On the ground floor sat 3 fully armed aircraft, with power on and technical support to hand, and the ability to start engines automatically in the shed on "Scramble" and effectively start the take-off roll from the shed itself. (One didn't select reheat of course until clear of the shed.) Upstairs the flight crews waited in relative luxury. Not for them the long vigil in an often frozen and always cramped cockpit in the middle of the night somewhere along the East coast of England or Scotland. For them it was the perfect temperature, excellent food, TV, radio, all mod cons—and the *piece de résistance* when an alert sounded—straight down into the already prepared cockpit via a "fireman's pole".

My recollection of "pulling alert" in the RAF is that you were always delighted to be scrambled. With the USAF, it was a trifle inconvenient if you'd just started on the T-Bone or the '49ers were approaching the end zone! Being an Exchange Officer, I did more than my fair share of sitting in the alert shed, by choice. I couldn't get enough flying. At 1 a.m.on the Sunday morning in question, my pair of Voodoos was scrambled and within minutes was climbing away over the Golden Gate Bridge heading West with instructions to climb to 42,000 ft.

We were under "close control" which meant that we had one dedicated intercept controller on the ground (GCI) doing nothing else but feed us with information on our targets, guidance to get us to the point where we could take over the intercept ourselves, give us appropriate engagement orders, and aid our recovery. Because the targets were at high altitude, the ground-based radar was able to give us good heading/range/altitude information on them out to over 200 miles. 12 minutes after take-off we had a contact on our own radars showing a strong return at 70 miles, same altitude, and a closing rate of around 1000 knots. We were now out of range of primary radar on the ground, but in radio contact, with instructions to "Identify". To do that meant we had to get a "visual" on the target before deciding if it was friend or foe.

Our IFF transponder gave us no clue and by now the large return had broken to clearly show there to be two targets about one mile apart. We selected a target apiece and began to manoeuvre to close range at reduced speed to where we might see our unknown target silhouetted against the lighter backdrop of the western sky. By now our GCI centre would have eliminated the possibility that these were other friendly military aircraft or civil airliners, so the probability was that this was a pair of Soviet long range recce aircraft testing out the US air defences, without intention to overfly. But the blips on our radars were not behaving in the conventional fashion, bearing in mind aircrew then were extremely well-briefed on the capabilities of their potential enemy. As we manoeuvred, now close to our operational ceiling, the blips dodged around rapidly in azimuth and elevation, and suddenly our rate of closure decreased. Our F101's were now perhaps a mile apart and simultaneously we both saw above us a pattern of lights and shapes totally unfamiliar to us. We also lost radio contact at that point and the targets were out of our radar-scanning coverage. Levelling out at 47,000, I watched in awe, mixed with intense curiosity, as two strange shadowy disc-shaped craft flew a parallel track, well above us, synchronised in speed, for about two minutes. Then with incredible acceleration they headed west and climbed like rockets, disappearing from our radar in seconds.

With their departure we regained RT contact with GCI and each other. Our stilted conversation went something like this: "Did you see what I saw?" "Yep, and I'm on the wagon." GCI gave us immediate recovery instructions to Hamilton where, inside the hour, we were being debriefed by some very secretive guys whom I never saw again. Being an Exchange officer I was forbidden to see the classified report after I'd signed it and was advised to treat the incident as never happening. I only flew once more at Hamilton.

In 1992 at the Farnborough Air Show I met the pilot of the second Voodoo for the first time since our joint experience. Like me, he'd retired and was working in the Defence Industry. We chewed the fat for a couple of hours, flew old flights long since flown, recounted tales of loss and survival of mutual friends, and discussed his exploits in Viet Nam. When the climate seemed conducive, I asked him about that night and if he'd been involved in any follow-up action. I waited for the right moment because I knew only too well how paranoid the American military could be about security matters. I'm sure Phil was being truthful when he said, "You left at the right time Big John. We went through the hoop for weeks and then it was history, and always has been since." But when I asked him how he'd felt before he'd consigned it to history, his answer sounded like something a "trick cyclist" would persuade you to believe if he thought that you needed to bury a worry or a fear. He said that he'd put it down to tension brought on by the odd worry at home and flying a challenging mission at 1a.m.

Any airman knows that tension leads to fatigue, and fatigue to anxiety. Anxiety in an aeroplane can lead to some peculiar thinking, thinking that could get you into trouble and make you do the wrong thing at the wrong time. Sometimes when one looks back in cool analysis on the ground with the mind and body rested, the cause of anxiety and resulting actions can appear needless and silly. It's happened to us all. That night over the Pacific, Phil was one of only four men to witness the phenomenon. Others had seen strange things on their radar, but we were the only eyewitnesses. I certainly wasn't tired or worried, I knew the Voodoo well, I knew the procedures intimately and what we would have had to do had it been a hostile aircraft. Far from being jaded in any way, I was in my element and right on top of my job as an experienced aviator of 32 and in my physical and mental prime. I wondered how and perhaps even why, Phil had arrived at his odd conclusion.

When strange things happen to me, I try to find a logical explanation. If I can't do that, I almost always come round to accepting that it's beyond my ken, but that's nothing new so I won't let it bother me. This one didn't bother me, but it perplexed me. More to the point, I was puzzled by the way in which the US military and other interested parties handled it. And as of tonight, 10th January 2004, I can add another "curiouser" to that feeling, having watched a TV programme about UFO's only just released under the "50 year rule" which relates to the publication of classified data. The programme featured two incidents involving people I knew well in the RAF, well enough, that is, to have often sat down over a jug of ale and spun yarns about conquests, sporting achievements, flying and so on.

The first took place in 1952/3 in England involving a pilot who joined my squadron in Germany in 1953 as a flight commander. He clearly was under orders to say nothing about his experience, as in over two years in a very tightly knit community, not a word was ever spoken about a very strange occurrence that occurred to him and a pilot colleague whilst on a trials sortie from Gloucester. They both saw "Something not of this world" and were forced to "keep Mum".

The second concerned my head of department in 1958. Then a Wing Commander, he had come to Manby having just been an Equerry to the Duke of Edinburgh. I often flew with him on our overseas trips in the Canberra (he was one of the gambling pair in Aden), and spent many a night in far-off places in the sort of social atmosphere where confidences of that nature might well have leaked out. But they never did, and it was only long after we had both retired that I heard stories of him actually having met with someone described as "a visitor from outer space". When I heard it in the early 90's, I assumed he might have been wandering in his mind in his old age. But tonight's programme revealed that these incidents took place when he was in Royal service *before* I served with him between 1958 and 1960. Okay—there are certain things one does not discuss with anyone but closest friends; but is it not strange that in the social and working environments described, and over a combined period of 5 years, not a hint or even a rumour was ever in circulation? Funny—bloody funny, eh! Told you I'd digress.

America the Beautiful

Americans place enormous emphasis on youth, action and material success. Their land of plenty persuades them to believe in miracles with boundless optimism and quenchless hope; the American dream, if you like, whereby anyone can be what he or she wants to be. Their preoccupation with youth and action certainly means that they enjoy one hell of a good morning, although I now believe that means often they miss the lushness of the afternoon or the peace of the evening. But in 1960 I was happy to be in their morning mood, and caught their bug for "instant everything" in the one country in the world that probably does have everything that nature has to offer. I made my plans to see it all with enormous relish and mounting excitement.

I'll start with Texas which to be truthful is not the most attractive of states. There is some beautiful country down in the Sierra Madre/Rio Grande area along the Mexican border, but most of it is flat, featureless and dull, and there's not much to write home about. That said, it's worth recording an experience we had with one of the most violent displays that Mother Nature has to offer; namely the Tornado, a threat that occurs regularly in northeast Texas in the Twister season. It is so common that no one thought to tell the new British family about it, so one day shortly after our arrival we drove north to Dallas just as the storm sirens were sounding. The guard on the gate told us what the sirens meant and said, "Keep a look out for twisters." The warning itself was exciting to us and when I stopped for gas on the highway, I exchanged a few jovial words with a doctor and his wife that we'd met at a party and who were also driving to Dallas. We were in a beat-up old Buick and were in no hurry as we left the base behind us.

About 15 miles north, on a very flat straight piece of road, we saw a sight that I admit made my blood run cold as an enormous black funnel emerged from the low cloud to the west and snaked to earth, winding and twisting like a monstrous serpent. The tornado looked as if it would cross the highway a couple of miles ahead so we joined half a dozen other cars under a bridge and watched in awe and a touch of fear as the evil looking brute thrashed its tail around before crossing the road and lifting back almost to cloud base level. We were cautioned to wait as tornados were totally unpredictable and this one might well turn back towards us. Ten minutes later the skies were much brighter with the dark clouds now well to the east and we drove to where the funnel had crossed the road. The area was littered with all sorts of debris including a large truck and a tractor and the Highway Patrol told us that a private car had been sucked off the road. When we returned to Waco, it emerged that the doctor's entire family had literally disappeared. We always took notice of the sirens after that.

Have bug, will travel

One enthralling experience to whet my appetite for travel was a show I saw at Disneyland on my first visit to LA, using a huge continuous 360-degree screen on which was projected a travelogue around the USA. You stood in the middle and looked in one direction to see where you were going, and over your shoulder was where you'd been. I watched spellbound as all 50 States were shown to their best advantage. I think it was the last piece in my jigsaw plan for aiming to set foot in every state. I'm pleased to record that I visited every State but Alaska and Hawaii in the first two years and finally made both of those when I was with the Navy doing my F4 Phantom conversion and training.

There were many states and cities that, once I'd seen, I had no urge to return to. It wasn't necessarily that there was nothing attractive about them; rather that other places drew me back like a magnet. I can quickly dispense with the cities by saying that to this day I feel the anticipation if my airline ticket reads "San Francisco, New Orleans, Washington, Dallas, LA, San Diego, Pheonix, New York or Honolulu." I've recounted tales of San Francisco, Dallas and Washington elsewhere so I'll take a closer look at the others, either because of what the city has to offer or its significance as a gateway to other places. Like saving the most succulent piece of steak until the end, I shall work up to my favourites.

New Orleans

Cradled in a bow of the mighty Mississippi, the attraction of The Big Easy lay to me in the exotic blend of French/Spanish influence with Negro and Creole Indian cultures. Its lush tropical courtyards, hot and steamy climate, jazz and blues music to thrill the soul, and atmospheric restaurants in the softly lit streets of the old French Quarter, give it a character of its own. Someone once told me that Saigon and Tahiti came close. The former I was to find totally dissimilar; the latter far too French and expensive to bear comparison. The other attractions of New Orleans I found, albeit as a casual and infrequent visitor, were the proximity of "Ol' Man River" and the coastal swamp and Bayou country to the east approaching the Everglades. The Mississippi river has held a special fascination for me from the day at primary school when I put up my hand to boast that I could spell it and for which my teacher gave me a gold star.

Then I read books like *Huckleberry Finn*, heard dreamy melodies by Stephen Foster, and saw the stage show "Showboat". So much of American life, in books and song and theatre, was centred on the mighty river that "just keeps rolling along" In 1960 when I first saw it's silver thread below from our aircraft on route to Dallas, I marvelled at its length and most of all at its breadth when still some 500 miles from the Gulf. Perhaps the romantic in me saw a lot more than was there, and maybe if I'd looked more closely at the crime figures and at the fringes of New Orleans, especially the areas below water level protected by the levees, some of the magic may have evaporated.

But we can only tell of what we have seen and one night I saw a sight that has lived with me for 40 years, crystal clear, complete with background music and moonlit shadows. I had gone to a party on one of the large three-decked paddle steamers that took you out for about six hours for dinner, gambling, dancing and dreaming if you were so inclined. We were paddling back south when I decided I preferred the night air to the crowded noisy bar. I went on the top deck alone and looked out across the wide expanse of water as a full moon came up out of the river to cast, first, her golden path on the water, and then a silvery shimmering path as she rose higher. The band below was playing "Moon river—wider than a mile; I'm crossing you in style someday…" Sheer wonderful dreamy magic!

My other special relationship with that Louisiana/Florida coast arose from the captivating combination of sea, beach, outer islands and the strip of water between them and the coast known as the Bayous. Things that scare you often fascinate you and I found much to do that in the Sharks, Alligators and Snakes that abounded in the bayous and offshore. Neither was it a case of being lucky to come across one or more of the inhabitants. If you went to the inner shore, swam to an island across the bayou and then in the sea, you were guaranteed to get frightened. My curiosity ended after a water skiing incident when we were barbecuing at a friend's house that backed onto a bayou. I'd done my turn at skiing and was monitoring the engine when a colleague fell off in the rushes close to the edge. Of course there were the usual insulting remarks shouted in jest until we realised that he was in difficulties and in pain. We rushed to pick him up and I distinctly heard him say, "Goddamned barbed wire!" When we recovered him and rushed him to the house, then the hospital, we found he'd died from over 30 bites from Water Moccasins.

New York

I've made it clear elsewhere that New York is not a town I particularly like. But I'm prepared to accept that much of that goes back to first impressions and stubbornness in me not to change my mind. Rosemarie in fact was the one that made me reconsider my opinions in the 90's; she loves the place and we had some great times there together. Maybe by then the Big Apple had changed from my early experiences. I had one memorable weekend in 1961 when I attended an annual Night Fighter Conference, another word for a drunken brawl. The memorable bit was that I met a NY Yankee baseball player by the name of Mickey Mantle who, unknown to me, was a famous hitter of home runs. He gave me tickets for a game on the Sunday and promised to donate his bat to me should he hit a home run. He hit two so I got two bats, one of which was nicked from my hotel room, the other with which I hit the guy that was nicking it! I've only just realised that I haven't seen it for a while.

My next batch of memories came in the late 70's when I was visiting US companies on Long Island and Newark NJ. As part of the culture trip, we were driven around the dicey areas of NY in long black limos with tinted glass windows, escorted by men who felt more like bodyguards than salesmen or engineers. Around 11 p.m. we ended up in an Italian restaurant with our predominately Jewish hosts and were settling down to the starters when curtains all around the room opened to reveal big men in dark suits with odd bulges showing everywhere. Our hosts whispered or signalled for us all to get up slowly and leave quickly. No one ever bothered to explain!

Dusty bookshelves

Whatever my reservations about NY, NY, it was in one respect a Mecca for me. Elsewhere I've written about my 30-year obsession with collecting every book I could find by a particular crime writer, one Paul Winterton writing under a number of pseudonyms. NY was a wonderful hunting ground because it had a number of specialist crime bookshops and, above all, boasted the biggest and best collection of old and rare bookshops anywhere. I believe that is so because its closest rival would have to be London where I worked for many years and knew every bookshop backwards. But NY was special and I would wallow for hours in some of the enormous shops that had books stored twelve or more shelves high and so long that one drove a trolley along them. Another impressive feature was that they always kept a record of every book in the place—a facility that I often ignored because I enjoyed the thrill of finding a wanted book—hardback, paperback, first edition, dust cover, whatever, for myself. I also met so many people with similar interests but from totally different backgrounds and walks of life. So NY gets top marks from me in that respect at least.

Los Angeles

LA figures in my current list because of two ladies, Rosemarie and Cyd Charisse! But in the 60's I had no particular liking for a non-city that sprawled across half of southern California. My first visit didn't help when I went on one of those long weekends from Texas and landed our T-29 at the old Hughes aircraft airfield in Culver City. Hughes lent me a car for the weekend, which I drove to the beach at Malibu and the hotel they had booked for us. The rooms were actually in small chalets spread along the waterfront and so I parked in front of mine and started to unpack. After a few minutes I was aware of one helluva hullabaloo outside the chalet, which, as it couldn't possibly have anything to do with me, I ignored. But as the noise of car horns reached a crescendo I looked through the door to see, to my horror, that the car I'd parked outside was now smack in the middle of a major intersection surrounded by half of LA's Friday traffic.

I ran down the road to find the Chevrolet unmarked and slipped sheepishly into the seat and began, ever so cautiously, to drive away. Just when I thought I'd escaped, this police car with all sorts of flashing lights leapt out of a side road and hit me head on. As I sat in shock I realised I was going the wrong way in a one-way street, but it was my lucky day as the Police had also broken some law or other and the driver was so apologetic that they called Hughes and brought me out a replacement Chevy. Who said anything about a charmed life?

I was enormously impressed by Disneyland, especially as the same Hughes Company would always provide free tickets. Indeed, every time I've been to LA since, if I call Hughes (now Raytheon) I get free Disneyland tickets for all. Ironically, Rosemarie is not a Disneyland fan; her greatest fun in LA is to tour Hollywood and Beverley Hills looking at the wonderful homes and keeping an eye open for the stars. I was not nearly so keen, but was forced to admit that it was a truly attractive area to visit and—to make Roo's point—one evening in '98 between 6 p.m. and 8 p.m. we literally rubbed shoulders and shook hands with the likes of Warren Beatty, Faye Dunaway, Annette Benning, Dustin Hoffman, James Coburn, Goldie Hawn, Sandra Bullock, Arnold Schwartzeneger, and Patrick Swayze. Corny maybe—but fun, definitely. And then LA is home to my dancing idol, Cyd Charisse. Cyd gets a very special mention elsewhere, but the fact that she and husband Tony live in a penthouse/condominium in Wilshire up by the University, makes that city a very attractive venue on my travel itineraries.

San Diego

San Diego is a Navy town, the Portsmouth of West coast USA. Actually, that is not a fair comparison because the US Navy in the 1960's dominated San Diego with the massive presence of the Pacific Fleet and the number of huge and busy Naval Air stations in the area. As a Navy town, it is also a social town par excellence and I've yet to see anywhere that could boast the same number of high quality bars and clubs as there were on North Island and along the shoreline. The combination of the US Navy, the Californian climate and beautiful locality, seemed to attract a young female population of amazing talent and scintillating loveliness. Portsmouth, eat your heart out!

I arrived at NAS Miramar to start my conversion to the hottest aircraft then in service, the F4b Phantom, a truly magnificent and supreme operational aeroplane. Miramar was later featured in the film "Top Gun" and referred to as "Fightertown USA". The real star of the film was the F-14 that superseded the F4, but the Hollywood star who played the lead role, Tom Cruise, was guaranteed to have me screaming abuse at the screen. He portrayed the fighter pilot as brash, cocky and arrogant, totally prepared to risk himself, his aeroplane and backseater, to boost his own ego. I met and flew with many prima donnas and golden boys in the RAF, RN, USN and USAF, but I only ever met one who behaved remotely like Cruise's pathetic little creep. The words Pilot and Professional are synonymous.

Fightertown USA, USN F4 conversion, San Diego 1962

Converting to the Phantom on VF114 was excitement enough for me, but to then also become immersed in the stupendous social life of Southern California was the icing on the cake. I recall one amazing party held in the home of a famous female Hollywood star which you entered by lift from little more than a garage on the surface, and finished up in spacious luxurious rooms built into the rock face with the outside "walls" being huge windows looking out across the Pacific. I recall sitting sipping my Martini and watching our hostess dancing on a highly polished table to the rhythm of "The age of Aquarius". I could have got used to living like that.

On my first Sunday there I was invited to join my Squadron Commander and his family for a beach breakfast. We settled down around 10 a.m. in brilliant sunshine on a golden beach by the famous Coronado Hotel, equipped with the latest in BBQ equipment and stocked with fruit, frozen juices, ham, eggs, tomatoes, sausage and fried potatoes. The grill was soon sizzling and the plates coming out when suddenly mine host decided the conditions were not good enough to eat on the beach. It was around 75 to 80 degrees, but a slight wind had got up of around 5–7 knots and we scampered for cover as if on Blackpool beach when hit by another rainstorm sweeping in from the grey Irish Sea. "Sorry about that," said Jim. "We must try it again on a better day!"

San Diego always drew me back to its wonderful climate, its marvellous seafood restaurants, and the fascinating drives up into the high country to the east or Mexico to the south. Rosemarie loved it too and I well remember her cries of supreme exultation when I took her into Sea World and into the Killer Whale show just as Shamu was rising from the depths for the first time to do his tail flip and drench the audience with gallons of water. She loved too the displays of the Dolphins and Porpoise, and the whole setting of Sea World on the bay with the blue Pacific beyond makes it the ideal nature show.

Phoenix

My penultimate city is Phoenix; not the city itself, but as a gateway to so many magical and haunting places. Southeast of Phoenix are The Badlands, the most southerly part of Arizona that runs down to the Mexican border and is home to such Wild West cowboy towns like Tombstone and Bisbee. In the 60's, one could imagine, especially after sunset, exactly how the place would have been in the 1870's. There were no roads, footpaths were still sidewalks, and the dim lighting and all-wooden buildings took one's mind back to when the gun was the law and life must have been a pretty fragile thing. Outside Tombstone was Boot Hill cemetery with old gravestones with inscriptions like "Hung by mistake", "Shot by Indians" and "Caught where he oughtn't to be." In the main street was the fabled site of the OK Corral, and a small saloon in which John Wayne, Gary Cooper and Randolph Scott got the girl, wiped out the Bisbee mob, shot Billy the Kid or gambled away the takings from the noon stage robbery. How much was sheer fantasy or Hollywood's bending of the truth is hard to say; *quien sabe*. But of one thing I can be sure, that in 1960 before it all became too commercialised, there was a breathless, eerie, menacing atmosphere on the darkening streets of Tombstone that caused the Palmer family to cancel their hotel reservations and drive on up to Tucson instead.

The Grand Canyon

But it was the road to the north out of Phoenix that has drawn me back time and again to Arizona. Sometimes when time has not been critical, I would stop at the beautiful town of Sonora and nearby Oak Creek Canyon. Now there's a place to use up all your films in a hurry—on the spectacular red cliffs and the view across the river of the most perfectly proportioned rock peak formation that nature can offer. Further north as the road begins to climb towards Flagstaff, the scenery becomes boring, but the excitement grows as the Grand Canyon signs appear and you notice the fall in temperature from the baking heat on the plains below.

When I first drove along a narrow partly tarmac road that wound up the foothills onto the high plateau, I was impressed by the Arizona State Highways custom of putting a simple white cross at the edge of the road signifying a fatality. I was so smitten by Arizona, that I have been known to land at Phoenix at 9 a.m., hire a car to drive to the Canyon, and drive back to catch my LA or Dallas plane around 11 p.m. The white crosses, illuminated in the headlights, were a sharp reminder to me that I should drive with care.

There's no way I can adequately describe the Grand Canyon which everyone must have seen countless times on the screen and in books. It is a genuine wonder of the world, and I would recommend everyone to beg, borrow or steal an airline ticket to make the pilgrimage once; to stand astounded and speechless at the ever-changing pattern of colours, shadows, and shapes, to feel that breeze that comes up out of the enormous chasm as you watch the sun sink low in the west, and to experience the indescribable peace. However colourful and dramatic a film might be, you have to be there to allow all of your senses to take in and record what is happening in and around you. It is special, haunting and terminally unforgettable.

I saw it first without being able to use all of my senses, from the cockpit of an F89. It was before the days that flying in, or even over, the Canyon was prohibited. I was on a "chase sortie" from Nellis AFB near Vegas that meant that for about 60 minutes you chased someone else around the sky in a form of combat training. We followed our lead through wispy cloud down into the canyon and I was so astounded at the panorama below that I forgot all about the exercise and simply goofed at the amazing sights below me—and then above me and surrounding me. As we climbed away for the 200 odd miles back to Nellis, I was still in shock looking back over my shoulder to catch a last glimpse in case I never made it back.

But however impressed I was with the Canyon, I was even more entranced and enchanted the following morning when our "play zone" was between zero and 5000ft over Monument Valley—a place then quite unknown to me. As I glimpsed the enormous weird and wonderful shapes of the Valley sentinels below me I cheekily called our playmate, saying, "Sod off Carl, we're staying here for the next 20 minutes!" It was the beginning of a love affair with the State of Arizona, an affair so strong that it undoubtedly prevented me from seeing many parts of the USA worthy of further exploration. When I flew back to Waco days later, I sat down to plan our first long vacation—back of course to Canyonland.

That vacation was memorable because we were seeing scenery and places different to anything that any of us had seen before in person. Perhaps there was an element of so much of it being familiar from films, that we identified with it and accorded it more significance than it merited. The fact remains that we enjoyed a truly wonderful holiday driving our new Rambler Station Wagon across Texas for 600 miles to El Paso, then up to Albuquerque and on to the Badlands before turning north to the Grand Canyon and Monument Valley, although we never made it to the latter on that trip.

Monument Valley

To be honest, I doubt if the rest of the family fully shared my enthusiasm anyway as Monument Valley was a 3-hour drive beyond the Canyon in blazing heat across a featureless desert. But I had an overwhelming urge to be in that Valley so that months later, travelling by myself from New Mexico, I arrived in the deepening twilight when it was just possible to see the shape of the huge outcrops against the oranges and red of the western sky. It may have been my mood or the colours and shadows of the evening light, but I felt as if I were approaching Camelot, my appetite whetted for a dawn sortie into the heart of the Valley.

I had only a few hours to see my wonderland on the ground, but at the time that was enough. I was beginning to realise the true size and vast openness of this great country. I'd got the scent, been smitten with the Valley's own disease, and its spell has never left me. Over the years I went back a number of times, always alone because I was either on RAF business or on company business. My expenses were being paid for spending time in LA or Phoenix, and Monument Valley meant a considerable diversion, reachable only via a long car drive from Phoenix. So time was always at a premium and I only once stayed in the only hotel in the Valley overnight—until on our honeymoon in 1997 when Rosemarie made me very happy for yet another reason.

Thanks to the kindness of the two best bosses I had in 17 years in industry, I was able to take Roo on a joint business-cum-honeymoon trip to the States. Business was in Dallas, LA and San Diego and I was allowed tickets that included Denver, Las Vegas, San Francisco and New York on a 16-day itinerary with only three real days of work. We'd booked into our hotel in Vegas and paid in advance for 5 nights. Neither of us are gamblers but we thoroughly enjoyed the luxury of life amongst the casinos and ate and drank ourselves silly. On the third night we'd settled in to bed about 3 a.m. (early for us) when my bride said, "Didn't you want to go to Monument Valley on this trip?"

"Of course," I replied, "but it's 400 miles the other way and we can't get there by air."

"Well, if we left now, how long would it take us to get there?" I said it would take about 6–7 hours, but added that we were booked in until Sunday and they weren't likely to give us our money back.

"Why not ask them and if they will? I'll be packed in an hour."

Without any real hope I called the front desk of the MGM and related a sob story.

"No sweat, Sir. Let me calculate the finances and see what we owe you. Sir, we can offer you $485 if you leave by 6 a.m. today."

"Yes," I replied, "but what is our final bill? I paid you $475 on arrival."

"Sir, that is your final bill. We'll pay you $485 when you check out."

He then went on to explain that in Vegas they sell beds on a nightly forecast rate and that when we'd signed in, the Saturday and Sunday forecast had been $100 per night. It had since risen to $230 with Fridays' going rate up too. So we had stayed for 4 nights and paid $10 total for rooms and food! On that basis you cannot afford not to go to Las Vegas.

After wolfing an enormous breakfast of smoked salmon, scrambled eggs and kidneys, we pulled out of Vegas heading east at 5.45 a.m. We drove through the stupendous Zion Canyon and into Canyonland from the north, arriving at the Valley Lodge around 2 p.m.

We met the owners who showed us pictures of films shot there, met an old cowboy who had featured in Stagecoach and The Searchers, and quaffed the odd glass of Bourbon and branch, as we watched the sun go down over my magical mountains. We fell into our much needed beds around 8 p.m. and Rosemarie awoke me at 4.30 a.m. to tell me it was time to arise and watch the sun come up again and flood the spectacular landscape with its blood-red rays and warmth. I was about to experience a huge surprise. There is now a narrow tarmac road running north where once there was only a desert track and we drove to beyond the first of the towering monuments of rock to watch the sun's rays as they raced across the desert and began slowly to climb the mighty citadels. Awe inspiring though that was, I felt a slight anti-climax; I still wasn't seeing the Valley as it appeared in films and on canvas, or even from my bird's eye view from a cockpit. We drove south again to where a rustic old sign read "Monument Valley tour" and followed a dirt track up to a big log cabin that had various signs indicating that guided tours went from there. But it was still only 0530 and there wasn't a soul in sight.

We walked to the hilltop and looked down behind the lodge where a trail wound its way into sand dunes of sagebrush and cactus—and beyond I saw the peak formation that I sought, invisible from the road. We drove for perhaps a mile and I left the car to climb a sandy bank and stood transfixed at the sight before me. I gasped aloud. We seldom gasp or lose our breath for real—it's simply a figure of speech. But when your eyes alight suddenly for the first time on such a place, your mouth opens and you really *do* gasp. Rosemarie heard me cry out ecstatically. I was in raptures, treading on enchanted ground. Here was the Monument Valley of Indian folklore, their "Land of time enough and room enough". As we drove slowly on the view was kaleidoscopic, ever changing in colour and shadow, as we perceived from different angles and increasing levels of sunlight as the sun climbed into the clear morning sky. The dominant colours were red, sky blue and turquoise, and being April, some of the peaks still had snowcaps. I was too full for words and I literally danced on the spot with tears flooding down my face and thanked God for the beauty and majesty of His creation. I was enthralled by its beauty, and that morning I stood and drank in deep nourishing draughts of the magical panorama before me to sustain me in darker colder days ahead.

Monument Valley is unique in my experience; nowhere else on earth have I felt the same incredible sense of peace or been more aware of my insignificance on this earth and in God's universe. My heart literally leaps at the beauty before my eyes, and my ears become attuned to catch the music of the plains and the anthems sung in deep canyons by the desert zephyr. To my mind, people do not belong there; they detract from its primeval solitude and isolation and offend its timeless sanctity and mystic communion of sun and stars, mountain, sand and sighing winds. Scenically stunning though it is, and therapeutic its effect, I cannot imagine anyone wishing to live there to grow crops or raise any livestock. Hollywood placed settlers there, built ranches, and ran stagecoaches through it, but only, I suspect, to take advantage of the staggeringly impressive backdrops. Even the indigenous Indians located themselves lower down the plateau in the greener and warmer regions.

But that's okay by me; I prefer Monument Valley to remain almost inaccessible and certainly undeveloped. Those who run the tourism business in Arizona seem to have the same idea. They know what an attraction they have but they make it a well-kept secret. They used to produce, perhaps they still do, a classy monthly magazine called *Arizona Highways*. In its colourful pages they covered the scenery, the wildlife, the history, the geography and geology, and the flowers and fauna of the Canyon State. Both the Grand Canyon and Monument Valley figured prominently; I recommend that magazine and Arizona to the world and his wife. And oh yes, afore I forget, I must add that it pleased me greatly that Rosemarie was also enchanted by Monument Valley. Generally speaking, women do not like solitary places. Whilst an old soldier can settle down and make himself at home almost anywhere, a woman grows restless and begins to sigh for shops and hairdressers and crowds. It's only natural after all, I suppose, but Roo shared my love of the place and found it suited that part of her that is all about the soul and the spirit and of man's affinity with nature.

Hawaii

When it comes to naming a favourite State, I cannot separate Arizona (No 48) and Hawaii (No50). They are quite different; one is a single large area in the middle of a great landmass with no coastline, the other a string of islands over 2500 miles out in the Pacific. Hawaii to me meant tropical palms, sun-kissed beaches, girls in hula skirts, surfing, distinctive dreamy steel guitar music, and of course Pearl Harbour. When I thought of Hawaii I automatically thought of Honolulu and Diamond Head, I recalled a film called "From here to Eternity", and I had a vague notion that it was famous for pineapples and pig roasts, or *luaus*. My first acquaintance didn't tell me much more as it was a "one night stand" when my carrier moored off shore en route to SE Asia and I won a raffle to get a seat on a "Liberty Boat" helicopter ride to Hickam field. I liked the climate, the colour, the music, the girls, the dancing—but I could almost have been anywhere for what I saw of the island. I remember that a number of naval officers who had been based there complained that it had changed so much for the worse that they'd never go back—and certainly would not take their families. I was to have further short runs ashore in Honolulu during my time in the US. Later in the 90's, when travelling on business, I had the odd night's stopover changing aircraft on route to or from Australia and New Zealand before the extended range 747 was introduced.

Such visits were to Oahu or the big island. I admit that at that stage I could be quoted as saying that Hawaii was overrated and would not be on my visiting list—until my interest was aroused when Roo and I went to the island of Tioman in the South China Sea. I went, having read that the film "South Pacific" was filmed there, and I was keen to see the location and particularly the fabled island of Bali Hi. I was disappointed as it transpired that James Mitchener in his writings had, in effect, transplanted the beautifully spectacular island of Bora Bora in French Polynesia as the misty mountain across the sea from the US Navy base. The scenery did not exist on Tioman. On further researching the history, I found that the Director had anyway decided that Tioman was just too primitive at the time and too far away from the US of A. So he moved the set, lock stock and barrel, to Hawaii; more correctly to the most westerly island in the Hawaiian group—Kauai.

Before going into raptures over Kauai, let me admit why I enjoy holidays in the US so much. Irrespective of the usual and particular holiday attractions, Rosemarie and I are very fond of our food, of the places in which we eat it, and the comfort of the place where we sleep. Anywhere in the US, there is always good quick or slow food to be had, at reasonable prices, and in hygienic conditions. Similarly, accommodation is plentiful, cheap compared to the UK, and comfortable with most modcons as standard. I've been to many great spots in the world only to return to a hotel and find miserable sleeping conditions and lousy food. It's okay to rough it for the odd night, but not for an extended stay. Add the ease of hiring cars, getting quick and effective medical attention and understanding the lingo—and to me it really *is* America the beautiful.

Anything I write about Kauai will be an understatement. Like Arizona, some crafty characters have kept it a secret from the visitors that pour into Honolulu and the big island. Kauai is only 30 miles in diameter and yet the variety of its landscape is astonishing. It takes about two hours to drive around the three quarters of it that is served by roads. To the east are rolling hills and valleys, to the west a line of majestic mountains topped by Mt.Waialealein where in the shrouding mists of the volcanic crater waterfalls are born from the ever-falling showers. To the north is the staggeringly beautiful and awe-inspiring coastline of Na Pali, which is virtually inaccessible other than from the sea and by helicopter.

The eastern and southern shores are dotted with half moon bays of soft golden sand, perfect for swimming and snorkelling all the year round under sunny skies and gentle breezes. The west coast is a mix of exotic looking cliffs fringed by golden beaches, where on many days you will be the only inhabitants. The beaches change their moods with the seasons, as does the splendour of the sunsets with the lower angle of the sun. True paradise, however, is the northern shore which boasts arguably the finest collection of bays and beaches in the world, varying from open wide sweeps of golden sand ideal for surfing, to small cliff-bound beaches separated by *pahoehoe*. Spectacular rock formations abound with thick tropical vegetation running down from the hills, and a blue sea that sweeps in from the north to dance and swell and crash ceaselessly against the rocks sending dazzling spray hissing high in the air. Swimming can be dangerous due to the unpredictable currents and rip tides and even a walk along the cliffs can be hazardous due to the occasional enormous breaker that sweeps in from thousands of miles of open ocean. I can think of nowhere more exhilarating to be, a place that makes you feel alive and tingling whilst surrounded by sheer infinite beauty, colour and atmosphere.

Little wonder that Hanalei Bay was where Mitzi Gaynor "washed that man right out of her hair", or that Lumahai Beach was the setting for the Bali Hi scenes and a WW2 romp in the waves by Burt Lancaster and Deborah Kerr. Along the coast the magnificent Na Pali cliffs rise like dark green towers behind the golden sand of Ke'e beach, and here the explorers landed in the famous old movie to capture King Kong. Up in the hills, Jurassic Park was created and out in the bay Puff the Magic Dragon found his home in Hanalei.

Forgive me if I paint just a little more gold on this wonderful island. To truly appreciate its beauty you have to get a bird's eye view of the inaccessible parts from a helicopter and view the full majesty of Na Pali from the sea. The chopper will take you through a miniature Grand Canyon, up and up to the volcanic crater that gave birth to the island and is now officially the wettest place on earth; past dozens of glistening waterfalls hanging like slender silver ribbons through trees and rocks.

Out at sea your boat will be chased and escorted by shoals of leaping playful Dolphins; every now and then you'll see the dark triangular fin of a shark, an enormous sea turtle paddling its ungainly way, and the spin and splash of a Marlin or Swordfish. And if you're there in December through March, you'll experience the *piece de résistance*, the noisy flamboyant frolicking of the Humpback Whales down from the frozen north for their summer vacation. And again a promise, all of these sights and experiences on Kauai are guaranteed as normal everyday things, not just if you're lucky to be in the right place at the right time. Ask the guy who skippers your boat or the pilot of your helicopter if you'll see a Dolphin or Eagle on your respective trips and they'll look at you and ask, "Can a duck swim?" It really is that sort of place, a heaven on earth that everyone should see and experience. I guarantee there will be no feeling of anti-climax, no disappointment of finding that the camera lied or deceived—because no cameraman could ever do full justice to Kauai. What is more, for most of the time and in most of the places you visit, you have every chance of being the sole visitor, the only pebble on the beach. Now ain't that just perfection?

Verdict

I cannot call this a conclusion; furthermore, had I written a library of books about the USA, I could not have penned a meaningful conclusion. My schizophrenia about America and Americans will have been obvious, and even now, having just written in such fulsome praise of its scenic beauty and wildlife and my liking for so many things about the nation and its people, I'm seething over a

Tony Blair speech made this evening about the US leading a war on Iraq, in which our Prime Minister has decided to join off his own bat.

Iraq typifies the American stance of claiming that if you're not with them, you must be against them. It's their typically contemptuous way of saying that if their oil or other commercial interests are threatened, they will take military action or impose some drastic sanction, as they have done many times. They don't actually need British troops either in numbers or with specialist skills; in fact, they usually resent having them and seldom allow them any autonomy of action. They claim that Saddam is a threat to world peace and I agree in part. But I do not agree that the next line is that he must be emasculated and his regime changed to suit Washington. There have been many other cruel rulers; many other nations have had weapons of mass destruction for decades and have not been threatened with annihilation. Why do we have the "deterrent"? Is it not that if someone attacks us in some way, our retaliation will ensure that he can only enjoy his success for a very short time? Would even a dictator like Saddam risk total destruction of his country, let alone himself?

A great American once said, "There never was a time when some way could not be found to prevent the drawing of the sword." But General Ulysses S. Grant is no longer with us; there is instead an oil-rich trigger-happy Texan in the White House. USA versus Iraq is no contest; but I fear that the ripples from this short sharp war will lap on many shores for decades to come. I observed the American politico/military machine in action in NATO. If the rest of NATO did not agree with the American way, they would intimidate, prevaricate, lie, cheat and accuse until they achieved their own particular political, military or economic aims. They are the original Department of Dirty Tricks; they invented the custom of taking the ball home if they weren't winning, and had we ever gone to all-out nuclear war with the Warsaw Pact, it would have been fought from Washington and not from Brussels with all the years of joint planning overridden. The Americans always have a different and hidden agenda. They are the biggest Empire builders in history. There, you see, I told you I was "skitso" about them! But I must be careful not to tar with the same brush, because the soldiers who fought in Viet Nam did so with pride and immense courage; even though many of their countrymen who stayed at home hated the war they fought, and hated the men who fought it. The US public forgot the battles, discounted their sacrifices and even challenged their right to settle again into American society once the war had been lost. Perhaps that was the trouble—America had lost to an enemy that no one knew about or cared much about. It was not their war; it didn't suit the Hollywood version of glorious battle and triumphant flag waving. When it was over the dead didn't get up, dust themselves down and walk away; the wounded didn't wash off the crimson stains and go on with life. Viet

Nam left an awful mark on those that endured it, even those without a scratch returned home terminally wounded.

Writing in 2004, I have a sense of foreboding that Iraq will go the same way. The euphoria of the first military successes and the capture and shaming of Saddam will evaporate in the distrust and hostility of a country whose history dates back well before ours and long before the world knew of George Bush, the black gold of oil, and the United States of America. Our troops will be kept there to police and quell the terrorist uprisings that will foil the politico/economic aims, and the British and American public will know they were deliberately misled about the reasons for going to war by two men bent more on securing their place in history than pursuing the lost cause of converting the Middle East to Western ways. Yes—the world has shrunk, but Iraq is still the East and more in tune with the Indian Ocean than the Mediterranean. Once the home of great civilisations, she bears the scars of three centuries of a dying Ottoman Empire and a period of British mandated rule. Baghdad, the mud-coloured city on a mud-coloured river with its curious mix of Persians, Arabs, Afghans, Indians and Negroes, suffers the volatile cocktail of the divided faith of Islam with its two great sects, the Sunnis and the Shias. How can B&B talk so lightly of "regime" and "culture" change from their own ivory towers? History will record, I fear, that both are guilty of having made a sow's ear out of a silk purse.

> *"In thy faint slumbers I by thee have watched,*
> *and heard thee murmur tales of iron wars."*

But let me not finish on such a critical note. When, after three marvellous years Stateside, I received a signal informing me that my next post would be in the rank of Squadron Leader on No 23 Squadron, I was split between leaping with exultation and mourning our imminent departure. Overwhelmingly, it had been a wonderful experience and I felt proud and privileged to have represented the RAF and flown the Union Jack in a foreign country.

Experience of course teaches only the teachable and much of it cannot be expressed in words. We cannot afford to forget any experience, whether good, bad, indifferent or painful. So I came back from America to use both my professional experience and my added wisdom in a new job in a new place with new friends. Experiences lose their validity and influence unless we have the courage to recite and record them, and I did not want mine to remain secret. However, this is the first time that I've really given serious thought to so many of my experiences in the States, and certainly the first time I've tried to make sense of them on paper. But in one way or the other, I've been benefiting ever since from living in and travelling regularly to that great country, and from working and playing amongst its bewildering and crazy mix of people. God bless America.

8

THE SWINGING SIXTIES

Folklore has it that the 1960's in the UK were "The Swinging Sixties". I'm not sure that at the time any of us saw it that way, and I would not have been a good judge anyway as I had just returned from spending three years in the USA. I was still revelling in that experience as I re-acclimatised to life on an RAF Fighter Station in Norfolk.

Homecoming

To add to the anticipation of seeing family and friends again, England was a beautiful place in which to arrive on a clear morning in April. Unless you have lived abroad, you will have missed the comparisons that a returned wanderer might make. Texas and California have much beauty of their own, but England then and now has a unique beauty that brings tears to my eyes and a lump to my throat. The good ship *Queen Elizabeth* slipped into the mouth of the Solent and was painstakingly manoeuvred for docking at Southampton. We watched enthusiastically as our splendid new American car was unloaded and within the hour the Palmers were driving north to my parents in Manchester. I recall how beautifully green the countryside looked as we headed up through Hampshire and Berkshire into Oxford. It was almost as if we were seeing England for the first time, enraptured at the beauty of the small fields, the hedgerows and the colourful quaint little villages. There were no motorways then, of course, so we stopped at various places, ate food that tasted typically English, and held spontaneous conversations with total strangers.

Naturally we were suspected of being American visitors. The children and I talked with an American accent; we dressed like them, and drove a station wagon whose size and style were then strange to English eyes. We had a reunion with my folks to look forward to, then a trip to my wife's home in Ireland, and then to my new post on 23 Squadron at RAF Coltishall near Norwich. United were at home on the Saturday and that same evening Belle Vue would be riding on their magnificent old Speedway track in the middle of the now sadly extinct Belle Vue Zoo and Gardens pleasure park.

By the time I reached Coltishall two weeks later, I was again speaking passable English, driving on the left side of the road, and bursting to start my conversion to the Javelin Mk 9. I consider myself fortunate in that during my RAF career, whatever the posting, I invariably looked forward eagerly to what I'd be doing. Even when the new post was a ground tour rather than flying, I welcomed the challenge. I like to think that much of that was due to confidence in my own ability and my eagerness and determination to make things happen. My aim was to make the best of any situation, not merely to continue to do the new job in the way that whoever had held it before me had done. Conceited this may sound, but I always felt that when I left a station, squadron, unit, department, or office, it was in better shape than it had been on my arrival. How lucky I was to enjoy my working life from June 1946 to January 2000.

Being Unique

Before launching into my version of the Swinging Sixties, I'm going to mount my soapbox and state some self-evident truths about life that we frequently ignore. As I've dusted down half-forgotten memories, I have become increasingly conscious that my own life is both unique and worlds apart from the vast majority of other men and women. I can obviously relate to fellow RAF officers, to those I worked with in the Defence industry, and to those with whom I share a particular interest, be it social, sporting or vocational. I can understand the views and beliefs of most people, I am remarkably tolerant and I've grown to realise that "one should not criticise one's brother until one has walked a mile in his brothers moccasins".

But even my own countrymen, my own business acquaintances, friends, and occasional companions, lead lives so different to mine that I am in no way qualified to judge how good, bad, indifferent, or successful mine is compared to each of theirs. So there is little point in me dwelling on those differences; indeed, in much the same way that our Maker has fitted us all with a switch that blanks out constant morbid thoughts of death, I find he has also inhibited me from habitually comparing my lot with that of others. Perhaps that is what is meant by "ignorance is bliss?"

Only once in my life have I known real jealousy, and that was in sexual terms, and I am grateful to have been free of envy all my life. But life's greatest consolation perhaps is that there is a finite limit to human joy and physical pleasure, just as there is to physical pain and mental anguish. The ecstasy I experienced in the arms of my true love on a hillside in Cyprus could not have been any greater had she been the wealthiest woman on earth and I the Olympic champion in my favourite sport.

Neither could our feelings have been any more intense had we slept in the bridal suite of the Taj Mahal, and she been Cleopatra and me Le Beau Sabreur. And what event could possibly have made me more exultant and triumphant than seeing my beloved United score twice in the last minutes of the European Cup? Last month I saw a famous athlete win the world championship for her event after years of coming so close, and yesterday I watched Sam Torrance accept the Ryder Cup amidst scenes of great celebration. Their cup of joy was overflowing, and when the joy reaches the brim, the cup simply cannot hold any more.

Doubtless Winston Churchill reached the zenith of his emotions the moment that Germany surrendered, Neil Armstrong likewise as he stepped onto the surface of the moon, and Wellington as he rescued victory from the jaws of defeat at Waterloo. But I'll guarantee that the intensity, depth and persistence of their pleasure could not have exceeded that which I felt in Cyprus or in Barcelona's Nou Camp stadium. As for pain, well, I'm told that God in his mercy has made us so that when a certain level of pain is reached, a merciful mist descends to save us from agony we could not bear. In other words, when you reach a certain level of pleasure or pain, you stop counting. That is how I see it. Anyway, please read on.

The Red Eagles

My working life slots neatly into discrete packages of time. In the RAF, packages were of postings of one to four years in length, and in Industry to working for four different companies, each of four years in duration. If it's possible to select one out of some 20 packages in all, my tour on 23 Squadron stands out. My US tour was unforgettable and my tour in Cyprus when Rosemarie and I met must be counted as *"primus inter pares"*. But as a combination of job satisfaction, location, and the capacity to enjoy the life we had, the 23 Squadron tour first at Coltishall and then at Leuchars across the river from St.Andrews, is the one that provided most professional satisfaction. I was 32 years old, a newly promoted Squadron Leader, flying a new and exciting aircraft on a famous Squadron, and based in a lovely part of the UK. I had a young family, ages nine, six and three, and my career was progressing smoothly. I was very fit, a successful and accomplished sportsman, and full of ideas for adding to The Red Eagle's illustrious history and contributing to making life on the station even more attractive and enjoyable

What made that tour special was the indefinable ingredient that, if not already present, cannot be concocted. It's the difference between being merely a good team and the one that wins all the trophies. It is the mix of personalities, the chemistry, the interchanges and the characters of those that make up the team. On 23 it wasn't just the skills, style and experience of the aircrew, it was encapsulated too in the engineering and administrative support to the Squadron. The icing on the cake was provided by the Squadron wives who looked after each other when the men were away and organised and adorned the most elegant of dinners and the most riotous of parties when they were home. That feature was accentuated for me when, after one year at Coltishall, the Squadron moved to a new home at Leuchars. Being in Scotland with everyone living in base and there at weekends, gave an extra zip to Mess life. Wonderfully happy days indeed.

A big plus on 23 was the Squadron's role with 38 Group, a so-called Tactical group that was equipped and trained for deployment at short notice to the Middle and Far East in times of tension. That meant regular detachments; so instead of performing just the classic air defence role, the Squadron was in-flight refuelled over long distances to bases in Malta, Cyprus, Libya, the Persian Gulf, Aden and Singapore. Instead of flying Practice Interception (PI) or gunnery/missile sorties of some eighty minutes duration, we were flying non-stop legs of 12–14 hours with the help of tankers that sometimes accompanied us, or rendezvoused with us to top up our fuel. Falling on my feet again, I joined 23 as this new role was being introduced and had the job of leading the planning, training and eventual execution for a role that no one in the RAF had done before at squadron level.

"23 Sqn. Red Eagles—non-stop to Aden." RAF Leuchars 1964

In-flight refuelling (and de-fuelling)

My Phantom experience with the US Navy proved invaluable since, although the F4 was a roomier and much more capable aircraft and weapons system than the Javelin, it took time to get accustomed to sitting strapped to an ejection seat, shoe-horned into a small cockpit, for such long periods. In-flight refuelling is now commonplace and crews sit in aircraft for over 15 hours. But we were the trailblazers; we did it first and found out the hard way.

Not all the challenges were of major operational significance or technical complexity, but most were important. For instance, the tankers transferred fuel, but nothing else. What about engine oil and oxygen in an aircraft designed to fly for two hours maximum? There was no room to fit anything else, except externally under the wings, and those pylons carried fuel or missiles. There were no toilets in a Javelin, nowhere to cook food or store water, nowhere to stretch your legs, and no bunk or comfortable chair in which to grab some sleep or take off your bone dome for a rest.

In flight refuelling was relatively easy during the daytime in calm conditions, but could we do it at night, or amongst the tops of towering Cu-nims over the Indian Ocean with the nearest diversion being a dinghy if you couldn't get the probe into the tanker's basket? A solution had to be found to all the problems and we had perhaps the most fun (in retrospect) in solving that of having a pee at thirty odd thousand feet over the Empty Quarter or wherever we were at a given moment of need. One of our trial kits consisted of a tube joined to a condom, the lower end of the tube running into a plastic bottle strapped to the inside or outside of ones' calf. The first problem with this "penikit" was that it was a fairly fragile affair that often leaked or was knocked as you climbed in or out of the cockpit. The second, and decidedly the most annoying, was that having been strapped tightly to a seat for hours, one lost all sense of feeling in the family-jewel area and ended up cheerfully peeing oneself, until a warm sensation crept around ones' ankles. The expression "Fill your boots" suddenly took on a different meaning.

In the end, we abandoned any "stopcock" type solution and some bright spark designed an absorbent nappy. You simply had a hot flush followed by a long cold soak. When, in 102 degrees, you opened the hood after 12–14 hours, the groundcrew quickly dispersed and watched as you poured yourself out of the cockpit and waddled away awkwardly to the nearest shower. I'd rather not answer the next and obvious question, but suffice to say that a combination of pills and diet prevented most disasters except when one's last meal was taken in a part of the world renowned for Delhi-belly or Montezuma's revenge. On one memorable occasion in the early days, 12 Javelins over-nighted at Karachi and set off at dawn with the Valiant tankers for the staging island of Gan in the Maldives. One by one, starting soon after take-off, the crews of the fighting 23rd called in apologetically: "Red Leader, from Red whatever, making emergency diversion to such and such an airfield." They were spread out along the western coasts of Pakistan, India and Ceylon so that when I arrived at Gan I had only one other "chick" left out of 12. We learned, like thousands of Brits before and since, that when visiting certain outposts of the Empire, it was wise to take your own water and sealed sandwiches.

Thieves in the Night

One other 38 Group detachment deserves special mention, if only because of the contrast between the pain and the pleasure. The pain was the first 10 days of a detachment to El Adem, a staging post-cum-gunnery practice camp some 15 miles south of Tobruk in Libya. The climate and the terrain are awful, and just to make matters worse we were under canvas suffering all the deprivation that came with flying at night, and trying to sleep in the day when the day fighter squadrons of Hunters were doing their exercise flying.

When we flew by day on air to ground gunnery sorties, it was hell to climb into an aircraft that had baked in the Sahara sun for hours. By the time you were strapped in, you were soaking with sweat, eagerly waiting until you could switch on the cold air to clear the mist and cool down. Then when you landed and opened the canopy, first you got hot again and simultaneously collected a mouthful and a hair-full of blowing sand. When not flying, it was our nightly custom to leap aboard the Squadron Land Rover and drive into Tobruk. Tobruk is, or was then, a dump. A bunch of old dilapidated buildings, but nevertheless Heaven compared to an oil-lit tent out in the bundhu. On the night in question we did as all aircrew did—drank a few beers, laughed at anything and everything, and just enjoyed each other's company. I recall seeing an Arab girl do things with a coke bottle that put me off coke for years, followed by tricks with a donkey that made me vow never again to pat the little blighters on Blackpool beach.

But it was on the way back that a truly bizarre thing happened. The Tobruk–El Adem road was like most desert roads, narrow, dead straight, and flanked by open scrub. The Land Rover carried six that evening, the boss and me in the front and four others in the back. The boss decided half way home that he needed a kip, so he pulled over, put up his feet and fell asleep. He had developed the knack of instant oblivion, or so he told me, whilst awaiting scramble orders during the war. I recall reading that Winston Churchill was equally expert at it. I was rudely awakened by him shouting, "Come on Palmer, let's go for a beer in Tobruk!" There were groans of dismay from the back when they realised his intentions—and I wholly agreed. But the groans turned to ribald mirth as he revved up the engine, but all that happened was that the gharry rocked back and forth. We moved not one inch. We leapt from the vehicle, imagining, perhaps, a flat tyre, or that we were stuck in sand. We certainly didn't have a flat; in fact, we had no wheels at all. The gharry was jacked up on four piles of stones! Even allowing that we were all smashed out of our brains, it was still a remarkable feat, in pitch dark, to jack up a Land Rover with six men aboard, nick the wheels and leave it propped up on stones.

The following morning, like three hours later, we were out on the air to ground range. As we lined up on the cone targets in loose formation, the Arabs were actually scurrying around below us to pick up our discarded shell cases. Had they known what time we'd slumped into our camp beds, and what state we'd been in, I doubt if they'd have been so confident that we'd hit the targets rather than them.

Ridiculous to sublime

Ten days were more than enough in Libya, and I'll swear that 23 Squadron were so keen to get away that most of us got airborne before starting our engines. We were bound for the lovely island of Malta for a ten-day air defence exercise. Mid-June in the Med, no sand, living in the splendour of a superb Officers' Mess, and the fleshpots and restaurants of Valetta to look forward to. El Adem was soon but a dim memory.

As aircrew go, I was a good boy in Malta. Until, that is, the night we gave the traditional Cocktail Party that all visiting Squadrons gave for the host Mess. Other Messes or establishments were also invited on the basis of "Three officers and their ladies" or, in the case of hospitals, teaching colleges etc., "three ladies". We would have liked to add "gorgeous, young and funloving" but the Customs of the Service meant that we had to be formal and follow traditional etiquette. Many will now argue that etiquette and good manners are outdated, seeing the subtle nuances and time-honoured forms as snobbish and ridiculous. I prefer to think that courtesy and civility are not a matter of class or snobbery, but simply a way of showing consideration and sensitivity towards others. Suffice to say that in Malta in 1963 the social life on the island was as it was then on all British out-posts overseas—extraordinarily interesting and exciting.

Being a Squadron Executive, and he who organised most of 23 Squadron's functions home and overseas, I was in the reception line at 7 p.m. for our guests as they entered the large ante-room adjacent to the dining room where a sumptuous buffet was laid on. Dress for the men was "black tie", namely dinner jackets, and I daringly wore a white jacket that I'd bought when with the US Navy. The ladies predominately wore glamorous and colourful cocktail dresses with the older ones perhaps tending to wear full length rather than medium length or "Corr, look at that" mini skirt outfits.

The guests started arriving in that strange calm of a typical Mediterranean evening. The heat and shadows of the day fade at the going down of the sun, but the very stonework seems still to reflect its golden rays in a colour not of this world. It is a paint they use only in heaven and the world is hushed as if in prayer. It was a truly splendid occasion and I was feeling on top of the world, especially when the High Commissioner introduced himself, his wife and their guest. She was a smoulderingly attractive lady in a tangerine Ava Gardner-type dress that glowed and flowed as she walked to join the laughing, chattering, effervescent crowd on whom the Twenty Thirds' famous Red Eagle Cocktail was beginning to have the desired effect. I watched her go and waited to see if she turned. She did, and she smiled, and I had that rare feeling that makes everyone else at once invisible and seems to guarantee that irrespective of the crowds, your eyes never lose contact. But of course I had obligations and I did my tour around the room, ensuring that my boss and the visiting Fighter Command brass were being well looked after by my officers.

Then one of those moments you pray will happen, but which more often than not is a Walter Mitty fantasy. The High Commissioner and my Station Commander came over and said, "Johnny, we have a favour to ask. Admiral Rawlins's wife is anxious to be there when his ship comes into Valetta tonight. Would you mind awfully escorting her to Grand Harbour? You can use a staff car and doubtless you'll be back to join the party here. It looks as though it'll go on all night anyway." Being a good officer and a gentleman I said that of course I'd escort the lady. Inwardly I was cursing my luck and bemoaning the fact that I'd not even had the chance to exchange a single word with the mysterious lady in tangerine. My CO took my arm and said quietly, "We've asked you, John, because Al and Dave (the other two execs) are already half-smashed and you're much younger than them."

I was about to claim that I'd been drinking too, and that I was only four years younger when a voice with a distinct Texan sultry drawl said, "Gee, I'm so sorry to run out on your lovely party; it's really nice of you to drive me down to the harbour." It was of course she of the backward glance. Why had I imagined "The Admiral's wife" to be middle aged, regal and unctuous? Sue Rawlins stood with a mischievous twinkle in her thirty-five-year-old eyes and I was suddenly aware that if it became known that this gorgeous creature needed an escort, I'd be killed in the rush. I grabbed the offered car keys and almost carried her into the staff car before some other Sir Galahad could volunteer to let me off the hook. As we pulled away from the Mess it was 9 p.m. When safely down the driveway, I asked what time was she expecting her Admiral to arrive. "Oh, about 2 a.m I imagine, but he's a big boy and can find his own way home. I'd like to go and change anyway; our house is up in Rabat if you don't mind running me there?"

Rabat is an old town on a hill in the middle of the island, and it would normally take about 20 minutes to negotiate the narrow twisting roads. It took us I fear until 1 a.m., via a swim in the dark in St Paul's Bay, and I didn't park the staff car back at the Luqa Mess until 2 a.m. Well, we had a lot in common to talk about with me having spent time in Texas and the US Navy! The party was still going strong and, predictably, I got a barrage of "nudge, nudge, wink, wink" from the younger members of the Squadron, plus a distinctly icy reception from the other Squadron Leaders. At breakfast on Sunday morning I got a few questioning stares from the hierarchy with the odd pointed question such as, "That *was* Valetta Harbour you drove to, John?" and, "Did the Admiral pipe you aboard then?"

But it wasn't until we were all gathered in the bar at lunchtime that the murmuring breeze strengthened and threatened to blow up a real storm. "Squadron Leader Palmer 23 Squadron, there is a call for you on Line 2 from Admiral Rawlins." The Receptionist's voice rang loud and clear across the hubbub in the bar. Silence fell upon the room. I noticed a smirk on Al Black's face and a gleam of triumph in Bill Rosser's eyes. I picked up Line 2. "Hi there," said a familiar Texan voice. "If you're free, Lee would like you to join us on board for dinner tonight. I'll pick you up around six at the Mess if that's okay?" It was okay, and she did, and the dinner was excellent. Lee was a nice guy who sailed away the next morning, leaving his wife in the tender care for another week of a grateful RAF officer. Al and Bill hated my guts ever after. Sue could play Poker better than any man I have known. *Fecit!*

Farewell to Caledonia

My tour on 23 and living in Scotland ended as we converted from Javelins to the RAF's "hot pursuit ship", the Lightning. My finale was to head a small team of crews to ferry Javelins between the UK, Germany, Cyprus and Singapore so that the right "mark" of Javelin (those with a flight refuelling capability) would be based where needed. I chose the codename "Operation Heavenly" because it promised to provide some interesting flying to staging posts in countries that the RAF did not normally visit. In the event Heavenly never happened because the only IFR tanker then in RAF service, the Valiant, was grounded overnight and forever due to main spar fatigue, and the exchange of aircraft was delayed for months.

One story to come out of the planning phase of Heavenly may amuse you. The planning of this major deployment required me, as the boss, to divide my time between RAF Leuchars and HQ Fighter Command at Bentley Priory in Middlesex. That meant me spending every night on the overnight sleeper, 8 p.m. from Leuchars Junction heading south and 10 p.m. from Kings Cross going north. Northbound, the train did not stop between Edinburgh and Dundee; it went through Leuchars Junction at 5 a.m. at high speed that meant me getting back from Dundee hours later. If I could alight at Leuchars, I could be in bed in 15 minutes and grab some useful sleep before another working day.

It was therefore a very persuasive charming JKP who walked to the front of the train that first night to explain his predicament to the dour Scot who stood puffing his pipe on the footplate of the engine that sat simmering and steaming, before winding its screeching way slowly across the points to head north out of London. After acknowledging the seriousness of the situation and having his palm duly crossed with silver, the driver agreed that on approaching Leuchars, he'd reduce speed temporarily to "walking pace" thus allowing the safe exit of the chap who would be standing in the guard's van with its double doors wide open.

So far so good, and at around 5 a.m. on a dark cold Tuesday morning, the long train emerged from the tunnel some 300 yards from the platform at Leuchars Junction. Our intrepid traveller, awaiting his moment to jump, became increasingly anxious as he watched the platform slipping by at a much higher speed than he'd anticipated. Realising with some panic that there wasn't that much platform left, he launched into the Scottish night to land on the platform running at a high rate of knots and totally out of control, to plough into an enormous pile of BR parcels which broke his fall and certainly saved him from a broken something. Still slightly dazed as he sprawled amongst the wreckage, he looked up to see a wizened old face peering down at him incredulously, and to hear a voice say, "Did ye not know that train doesn't stop here?" His reply did nothing to enhance Anglo-Scottish relations. So it was that on Wednesday night he strode purposefully along the same platform at Kings Cross to see the same driver on the same footplate. "Do you remember, old bean?" he said in as civilised a manner as he could muster, "that we had an agreement on Monday night that you would slow down to let me get off at Leuchars?" "Ay," agreed the driver, taking a reflective puff at his pipe, "but did I no tell ye that we change drivers at Edinburgh?"

The Rough with the Smooth

When Heavenly bit the dust, my allotted 3 years in a "command post" was up and I received a posting that made me cringe—Administrative Plans at HQ Fighter Command. After 14 years on flying tours they were going to put *me* behind a desk. How could they? But one never knows what fate has in store, and little did I appreciate that my new post would afford me enormous satisfaction. Neither did I think then that I should miss Scotland so much, forever in my life to look back wistfully at my time in that romantic country. I fancy now I still hear the warm laughter of friends saying good night, a few bars of Auld Lang Syne carried on the breeze to seal the sweetness of my mellow mood. Another softer burst of laughter, a whoop or two and a volley of good nights fading into silence. "Better luv'd ye canna be."

A New Broom

High flyers in any capacity will recognise the truth when I say that you can have a far greater impact on any job if your predecessor wasn't too switched on, motivated, or committed to success. If life itself is what you make it, then any job is certainly that. For my first week in the famous old Battle of Britain HQ, I scanned the office files noting the telltale marks of an officer who had sought a quiet life, believed in passing files slowly and incomplete, hoping that someone else would run with the ball or pass it back when he'd left or he could delay progress indefinitely. *Manana* was good enough for him.

There was one glaring action outstanding, the essential planning for which had not been within the energy levels or innovative compass of my predecessor. The increasing importance of Cyprus as an operational base, staging post and exercise facility in the Eastern Med. had led to the need for an organic Air Defence system. My office was tasked to produce a Working Paper for implementation within 12 months. I wanted very much to go to Cyprus as most of the 23 Squadron Javelin crews had gone there to form 29 Squadron, so it was a Heaven-sent opportunity of which I intended to take full advantage. In spite of opposition from some quarters, I was soon in Cyprus, wrote my plan for the mix and location of air defence elements and tabled it a month later. There were to be surveillance radars on Mt. Troodos and at RAF Akrotiri, a SAM Bloodhound site on the south coast, a Lightning squadron to complement the Javelin squadron, and improved communications and fighter control facilities. My Air Commodore was so pleased with my efforts that he agreed to release me to attend Staff College after only nine thoroughly rewarding months in a post that I'd dreaded. Life teaches us so many lessons.

Back to school

Staff College was a "must" for any career officer, the penalty being that if you performed badly in direct competition with some ninety of your peers, you could kiss promotion goodbye. I enjoyed the year at Bracknell enormously. Not only did you receive a wonderful education to fit you for higher rank and high-pressure posts, but also you saw and learned a lot about the Defence Industry, gained a valuable insight as to how the other Services thought and operated, and were introduced to the then crucially important political and military aspects of NATO. Above all, you had the immeasurable benefit and fun of working and socialising with RAF officers from all roles and backgrounds, and with Navy and Army officers, the Commonwealth and USA, all of who were of roughly the same age and equivalent in rank.

I imagine we are all guilty of thinking at some time that we are the most important cog in any machine. It does us a power of good to find that we are just one cog, and that we must understand how the rest of the machine works if we are to do our bit most effectively. Bracknell benefited everyone, but I think it was especially useful for the 75% of students who were RAF aircrew. By and large, aircrew see themselves as a cut above the rest with pride and self-esteem to the fore rather than arrogance. But some tend to look down on other officers, and some aircrew even look down on other aircrew as inferior beings.

Sad to say, my own fraternity of fighter jocks were the worst offenders. They might acknowledge a Bomber pilot, but would consider a "Truckie" (Transport) or "Kipper Fleet" (Maritime Patrol) pilot as lowering the tone. It was therefore especially gratifying to watch the arrogant ones often being cut down to size by those who demonstrated that they were just as professional in their own spheres and equally gifted intellectually and socially. I felt it my duty to assist the fainthearted and took under my wing a very rare bird indeed in the RAF, an Education Officer. Students would gather in the bar at six to play "liar dice" for who would buy the rounds of drinks. For the uninitiated, five dice bearing Ten, Jack, Queen, King, Ace would be rolled and kept hidden for the roller to hand on to the next player. Using Poker hands, he could call high and pass on "birdseed" (a bad hand) or call the hand as it was, or under call it. The taker could refuse to accept the offered hand, or take it as called and secretly roll as many dice as he wanted to try and improve the hand. If you lost a hand, you were forking out for perhaps 10 drinks costing £12–£15, so in an hour you could either be broke or high as a kite.

As the name implies, the idea is to fool the guy next to you so that he or someone close to him pays and not you. You are therefore expected to lie. Graham the educator was a devout churchgoer and didn't lie, so he lost round after round that he could not afford. I played beside him and would deliberately finger the dice so as to pass him a "looloo" or at least a far better hand than I declared. This gave him the chance to offer a higher hand without rolling anything. Time and again, he'd refuse my under-called hand, and lost! So I was forced to withdraw from helping him, and one evening he was forced to withdraw when his wife—a terrifying woman—led him out of the bar by the scruff of his neck!

My other Graham story concerns football.1966 was the World Cup in England and I'd bought tickets for all the Wembley matches in advance. I invited Graham to join me for the Argentina game that featured an animal called Rattin, the Argentine captain, and Nobby Stiles, England's left half from Manchester United. This was a grudge match and tempers were getting frayed when, right in front of us, Rattin spat in little Nobby's face. 89,999 others and I leapt screaming to their feet and I turned to express my opinions to Graham. He wasn't there, and as I looked around was conscious of an affray around Rattin on the touchline. Out of the mass of shirts came Graham, being led by the ear again, this time by the law! Fortunately, no one got to know about this at Bracknell, Rattin was later sent off and England won. I kept Graham's secret for years, but whatever punishment he might have got from officialdom, it couldn't have been any more devastating than what he surely received from Her that ruled their roost. Until I met her, I truly believed that the days of human sacrifice were over.

Play up and play the game

That stimulating year at Bracknell also revived my rugby career. Although our average age was 33–35, by which age many boots have been hung up for good, Bracknell had to field a rugby team because the Army and Navy did. Our Commandant on the first day of the course asked, "Anyone play Rugger?" The unsuspecting students, wanting to impress, stuck up their hands. "Right, you're skipper (pointing at me); we play Camberley on Wednesday. Pick your team."

Not only were the Army guys at Camberley six months into their course, but also they used the quaint old Pongo tactic of counting Directing Staff as students. Our motley bunch, most of whom hadn't played in anger for years, were literally canon-fodder and we were first trounced on the field, and then subjected in their palatial Mess to the haughty false courtesy of which only a certain breed of Army officer is capable. As we boarded our coach, I asked all those of the team who were serious about playing regularly to gather in the bar on our return. I was delighted to find a 100% attendance but, above all, a fierce determination to gain revenge over the Army in the return fixture in April. I selected the squad on the same basis that I'd selected a soccer team at Cranwell 20 years earlier; motivation and mental toughness above mere talent. We trained hard and lost the odd guy through injury or anno domini, and we introduced two US Air Force guys who knew nothing about rugby but were natural ball players and as tough as leather.

"Conquerors of Camberley." RAF Staff College 1966

Revenge is sweet

On a typical mid-April day, a fleet of coaches arrived from Camberley, including their current Sandhurst courses that came to watch the Army's senior course duff up the upstarts in light blue. Sure enough, there were three directing staff again in their line up, two of them—just by chance of course—being Scottish full internationals and the other an Irish trialist. The pre-match banter in the bar was terribly civilised, led mostly by rotund gentlemen who'd not kicked a ball since schooldays but who proclaimed "haven't seen a better Army team in all my years of watching rugger"! The general impression was that we were privileged to set foot on the same turf as them.

The Royal Navy referee called the two captains together and gave us the routine brief, except that he added in jest "and come out fighting". My opposite number guffawed and said "no need for that" and jogged to join his team who were chattering like a troop of monkeys and performing exaggerated limb and muscle looseners. Our scrumhalf kicked off deep into enemy territory where their Irish trialist knocked on giving us a scrum some ten yards out. Our hooker struck quickly and the ball was at my feet at No 8. I could see the corner flag with only their scrum half in sight, so I picked up, ran over the scrum half's tackle and scored in the corner. Our full back miraculously converted and we were ahead.

That was the signal for mayhem. Suddenly it was high tackles, late tackles, elbows and shirt tugging in the lineout, boots in the back and in the face, and blatant obstruction in the days before that law was tightened up. Whilst covertly telling my guys to keep their cool, I was having difficulty in keeping mine as their skipper, playing in the second row, was marking me at the line out. When I say "marking", I mean marking my face with his nails, my back with his studs and my nose with his fist. A stiff-arm tackle that nearly decapitated me on half time gifted us another three points and early in the second half our one prima donna dropped a goal whilst running at breakneck speed. 12-0 with 5 minutes left, and it was all too much for the colonel with a double-barrelled name from a society regiment.

We won a line out on the half way line and as I brought the ball down, our gentleman hero kicked my legs away, grabbed me around the throat and proceeded to choke me. As I struggled for air under a mass of bodies, he put his fingers in each corner of my mouth and seemed intent on pulling my face right over the back of my head. So I bit him! I played rugby from the age of 11 to 47 and never bit anyone else, but I had a damned good bite at his finger that day. He of course ranted and raved and implored the referee to deal with "that sadistic brute", but the referee instead awarded us a penalty.

As our fullback moved to place the ball, I tapped him on the shoulder, saying, "This one's mine, John." I was not a reliable kicker, but that day I knew the gods were with me and from the touchline, on the halfway line, I put a wet greasy ball straight through the posts. I have to say that no sporting achievement of mine or anyone else's ever gave me quite so much pleasure. We won 15-0, and they were bloody lucky to score nil!

After we'd showered and changed we joined the noisy throng in the bar to be greeted as heroes by our Commandant and the Staff. A lot of congratulatory things were said; Camberley's Commandant was magnanimous in defeat, and I contrived not to sound triumphal. When the Camberley captain made his speech he followed all the customs and compliments and then simply said, as though he still couldn't believe it, "The bastard *bit* me!" Before he could utter another word, the Navy referee called out, "If he hadn't, I was about to send you off—dirty sod." Cheers all round. Collapse of stout party.

Silver tongues

It will not have escaped the reader's attention that although I see myself as a man of action, I also hold a special affection for things academic and scholastic. Perhaps I regret not having been a dedicated student in my early days at Grammar School, but certainly later in life I found a special affinity with the lecture hall, or more correctly with those who had a way with words and the manner in which they were expressed. Oratory was once cultivated as an art, with time for eloquence and leisure for those who wished to listen. Today public speaking is more a matter of expediency; speeches are brief and to the point because we are all too busy to listen for very long and are quickly bored by elaborate perorations. This is the age of the soundbite, the text message, and most people have an attention span of a few minutes. (Rosemarie swoons away after five!)

Verba volent, scripta manet describes the fate of men whose fame has rested on the spoken rather than the written word. In a sense, the life goes out of a speech once it has been delivered. The presence of the speaker and his gestures, the tone and modulation of the voice, the dramatic emphasis and pause; all are lost and cannot be recovered in print. Only the bare bones remain; even the most powerful imagination cannot conceive the form in which the words were delivered, or capture the greatness and magic of the occasion.

In 1962 I was privileged to hear General Douglas McArthur speak at West Point and in 1963 to sit spellbound through a Winston Churchill delivery in London. In Ireland, I heard many stirring stories and messages delivered from the pulpit by speakers who kept you riveted to your seat for hours. But Staff College was the first time in my adult life that I was to hear people give live talks or make speeches, as opposed to instructing me on some aspect of aviation or officer training. Accomplished and interesting speakers would "sing for their supper" before a captive audience of around 150, the interest and value of those evening sessions being a combination of the speaker himself, the words spoken, the location and the occasion.

Surprise, surprise

Two speakers stood out—George Woodcock of Trade Union fame and Denis Healey, then Labour's Secretary of State for Defence. I don't know what we expected when George Woodcock reached the podium. I do recall that he faced a degree of hostility even though there was a strict College maxim that all speakers be treated with respect and courtesy. I didn't feel any hostility then, although my present view of Trade Unionism is now vastly different in the light of recent bad experiences. I was just eager to hear a very prominent and well-respected leader explain what he did and how and why he did it.

No one interrupted his talk held under Chatham House Rules (which guaranteed all speakers non-attributable freedom of speech), but one could sense a deep undertow of hostility that was to flood the Hall when the Commandant invited questions. The first two questions caused a buzz around the room due to their content and the manner in which they were put. The visitor answered them comprehensively and quietly. But when the third question was almost spat at him, he moved from the podium, put his hand up to the Commandant who was about to warn his officers of their attitude, and walked to the middle of the stage. "Right," he said, taking off his jacket and making a come-on sign with his hands, "if that's how you want to play it, let's hear from you." He sat on the edge of the stage and pointed to the officer who'd asked the loaded and provocative question. "You first then, young man."

There followed a most scintillating exchange for over an hour until the Commandant had to call Time for us to go into dinner. George Woodcock received a standing ovation, and he continued over dinner to enthral those fortunate enough to be within earshot with the honesty and clarity of his views. When I complemented him on his performance, he replied with a twinkle in his eyes, "It doesn't really matter what you say; if you say it with conviction, they'll believe you whether it's true or not!"

Denis Healey addressed all three Service Colleges in the bigger auditorium at Camberley where 500 officers gathered to hear a Cabinet Minister explain to a wholly military and suspicious audience why his Government had just overturned the previous Government's Defence programme. The Navy's capital ship programme was to be devastated; no new build of aircraft carriers—worse still—their role was to be undertaken by land-based aircraft flown by the RAF. The RAF were dismayed at the cancellation of their low level strike aircraft, TSR2, and the emasculation of their VSTOL Kestrel to a short range Harrier, in favour of purchasing the US F111 and F4 (Phantom).

I can't remember what the Army lost out on, but I was sitting next to a prominent member of the Royal family who changed colour when he heard that his Cavalry Regiment were not going to ride horses again! Denis Healey was acknowledged to have been one of the ablest post-war Defence Secretaries and he gave a masterly presentation that day, seemingly without reference to notes. As questions rained in, he batted them away, nonchalantly striking a nice blend of firmness and humour. I felt an indiscretion coming on and asked him whether his "Far reaching blueprint for the next 20 years" might not mean the RAF would lose most of its promised new aircraft at the next Review as money ran out. I added that we seemed content to pour down the drain huge sums of money that we'd spent on R&D to develop and buy British.

He didn't answer my question at all, calling it first "tendentious" and then me a "chancer" for asking it. Then, "Let me ask you what your next assignment is when you finish this course," he said. "I don't know yet Sir," I replied. "I do," said he and asked for the next question. Two weeks later I discovered my posting was to the Operational Requirements Branch of the MoD in Whitehall. One of my first visitors in my new job two months later was himself. Grinning as he entered, he said, "Not so easy now, eh?" I only met him once after that, in 1999, when I went to watch the Maureen Lipman update of *Oklahoma* on stage. At the interval I stood to find him and his wife sitting directly behind me. I smiled in recognition and he immediately said what an enjoyable show it was, adding that he'd just returned from a visit to Oklahoma and Texas. "Do you know that part of the world?" he asked. "Yes," said I. "I spent 6 weeks there learning all about the F111 that you bought instead of the TSR2, and then cancelled the day I got back to London." He laughed uproariously. One of my all time favourites, Denis Healey!

Life as a Whitehall Warrior

On 4th January 1967 I walked up the steps of the Ministry of Defence in Whitehall to take up my post in the Operational Requirements Branch of the Air Force Department. Little did I know that it was to be the first day of 7 years that I would spend in that job during two separate tours in that imposing building, and the first day of 23 years that I would spend in the business of Defence Procurement, mainly for the RAF. That amounts to a third of my entire life so there's every chance that I shall bore you to tears with my memoirs and observations.

That January morn I was excited with the anticipation of doing what was generally recognised as the most interesting desk job in the RAF. In the MoD one wore civilian clothes, not uniform as in desk jobs at the various Command and

Group Headquarters or the Training establishments. It was also located in the "heart of *Londonium Augusta*. What a phantasmagoria; Big Ben was my office clock and I looked out at the then ungated entrance to Downing Street. I cannot think of another military HQ in the world that is so centrally situated with immediate access to world-famous stores, theatres, restaurants, tourist attractions, and buildings of historical interest. Bounded on one side beyond Horse Guards by a magnificent park, and on the other by Old Father Thames, a river that must surely have seen more of history and with more tales to tell over the last 2000 years, than any waterway on earth.

Internally, as with the War Office and Admiralty, the building was disappointing. At best pretty basic, at worst resembling a Victorian lavatory—unless you dwelt on the 6th floor amongst the political and military hierarchy. Many officers hated commuting to London, they detested the MoD and wanted to be back on flying, or at least on an airfield. When hearing such complaints I recall feeling guilty that I was enjoying my job. If you didn't subscribe to the "I'd rather be flying" cry, you were made to feel that your manhood was suspect, that you'd earned your wings and were drawing your flying pay under false pretences. I learned that those who complained most about the MoD, often volunteered discreetly to serve second or third tours in the Ministry. My view in 1967 was that I too would rather be flying, but that if I had to fly a desk, then Whitehall was the place to do it. After all, it came as no surprise to any career officer that he would be expected to spend time on the ground. If you had aspirations to command a squadron or station, or reach Air Rank, it was reasonable that you should know a lot more about your service, about those parts of it in which you hadn't served, and what the future might hold for it. You could not learn that seated in a cockpit where you were fully occupied as a front line aviator doing the job that everyone else wanted to do most. So began an extended 4-year tour in Whitehall, during which I changed my Project three times, moved offices ten times and was promoted once.

Flying a desk

Operational Requirements was a hugely satisfying job. On a Squadron, you flew the aircraft that had been specified, developed and procured by RAF officers like yourself based on their experiences, knowledge and expertise. However well that aircraft operated, you were always thinking of ways to make it better—perhaps to increase its sheer performance, to extend its range, enhance its weapons capability, or improve its reliability. In OR you could directly influence the equipment you might one day use in anger and draw on your flying background, combining the views of others and the help of many aircrew, technicians, designers, developers and planners, to decide what was required from an aircraft likely to stay in service for over 20 years. You'd look closely at the capability of a potential enemy, assess what technological developments might impact on design, and gauge a contractor's ability to produce what was required, in the desired timescale and at an affordable cost.

The beauty of being a Project Officer was that everything to do with the development of a new aircraft or other equipment, came across your desk. It also meant unlimited travel, both home and overseas, in order to talk to those who could help you and those who might wish to sell you something or buy the eventual product of your joint labours. NATO, being the organisation it was, it almost certainly meant serving on committees on the Continent, and in the USA if you were lucky. A wise OR officer would ensure that he had an open door to visit the relevant operational units to remind himself of the day-to-day things that were important to them at their level. When you left the front line you didn't automatically forget about flying and operating aeroplanes, but after a while the detail became blurred and it was often that detail that crucially affected the efficiency and effectiveness of a Squadron. If you could combine those visits with scrounging a ride in one of their aeroplanes, so much the better.

My firm belief in the principle of staying in touch with "the front line" got me into hot water with a new Director early in my tour. I'd made a one-day visit to a Phantom squadron to talk and fly, and the next morning he met me with both barrels blazing. Where had I been when he needed to talk, what was I doing out of the building, out of London, and didn't I know that talking to Squadron aircrew could only taint my work and affect my judgement as a Staff officer? I was never, never, to visit an operational station again. This was red rag to a bull; I knew he was hopelessly wrong as he was in so many things. He was like a fish out of water in OR and would perhaps have made a first class CO of a training station or been a world-beater behind a desk in a deadbeat NATO post in Brussels or Mons.

Shortly after the rocket, I visited Farnborough and brought back a small bottle of liquid that I smilingly put on his desk. Unscrewing the top, he sniffed the contents and recoiled, exclaiming "God, what's that?" "I didn't think you'd know Sir, it's Avtur, the stuff we burn in aeroplane engines," said I. That was a cruel thing for me to have done, but it was the culmination of months of frustration watching an incompetent senior officer flounce his way around the corridors waving pieces of paper that were written beautifully—but said absolutely nothing!

You could say my gesture was career limiting, but that was an occasion in my life when I did what I thought I had to do, and beggar the consequences.

But back to my arrival at the MoD. We've established that I saw London as a great place to work; the job was fascinating, the perks exciting, and I was bursting with enthusiasm. I didn't realise it at the time, but I was also very naïve—a flaw soon brought home to me when I had my first interview with the Director. My posting notice said I was setting up a new post as OR17, the post being a product of Labour's Defence review changes. But the AFD hadn't yet come to grips with all the changes so I assumed part responsibility for the F111 project that had recently replaced TSR2. Within months the F111A too was cancelled and my desk assumed OR responsibility for the Buccaneer, another aircraft handed down from the Navy with the demise of their carrier force.

No one in light blue was happy with the Buccaneer as a land-based, strike-attack aircraft, especially as it was in lieu of the British custom designed TSR2 that had been optimised for the high-speed low-level role, both aerodynamically and in system terms. Instead of TSR2, or the F111, the RAF was left with a relatively old, slow, and poorly equipped aircraft that had been designed with significant limitations in size, power and weight to operate off carriers. It was tantamount to trading in your old beloved mini for a Jaguar or BMW, only to have to resurrect the mini when you found you couldn't afford either of the others. But I was the new kid on the block and that was the hand with which I'd been dealt. It was a challenge that I accepted as I launched into a study as to how we might make the Buccaneer more acceptable to their "Airships", but more importantly to the crews who might have to go to war in it.

Essentially, the Buccaneer was aerodynamically well suited for relatively high-speed flight, "down in the weeds". What it lacked for long overland low level penetration, was a modern sophisticated navigation/weapon system that would enable it to fly deep into WP territory in all weathers, and to navigate and bomb with great accuracy. We'd designed such a system for TSR2, and the F111 had a similar capability. So I wrote my draft Requirement drawing heavily on those familiar systems, got a green light from my mandatory Staff circulation list, booked a flight to Fort Worth with my opposite number in the Procurement Executive (PE), and went to brief my new Director. He listened, expressionless, as I delivered my now highly polished blurb, and said, "Now look, Palmer, the RAF did not want the Buccaneer; we hate the bloody aeroplane and have no confidence that British Aerospace can do anything worthwhile that would make its performance remotely acceptable to us. I don't care how much extra fuel you stuff into it, or how you improve the flight system and electronics to make it all-weather, we do not want it and I won't have you or anyone else rushing around PE and the States spreading bright ideas. Is that clearly understood, Squadron Leader?" I walked out duly chastened, cancelled my flight to the US and asked my Group Captain, "What the F-treble-one do I do now?" "How's your AEW?" he asked.

My AEW was good; in fact, it was impeccable. I'd flown four consecutive tours on fighters with the RAF, USAF and US Navy, been an OCU instructor, worked closely with the fighter control branch and trained as a radar engineer in my early days. If I had to choose someone to write the RAF's first Operational Requirement for a land-based AEW system, I'd have chosen me! "OK, go and find yourself a new office, don't cross the Director again, and bear in mind that my daughter is getting married in Baltimore on 25th March, so you need the draft complete and validated by then." Puzzled, I asked, "Is that the date you're going on leave?" "No John, that's the date I take the OR to Washington to discuss it with the Americans; you'll be far too busy here to take it yourself, eh?"

I was beginning to see that my idealistic views about the purity of the Defence Procurement organisation were not going to sit well with the political aims and personal agendas of others. That of course was part of the learning process. I soon reached the conclusion—one that merely hardened over the subsequent seven years I served in Whitehall—that at least half of the people you met in pursuing your project were dedicated to making sure you did not succeed. Some of that was inter-service rivalry; some was single service competition for limited funds, and some PE's reluctance to buy anything except from a small clique of suppliers. Add the appalling apathy and ignorance of many politicians about anything to do with the Armed Forces, and you had a recipe for getting little done and a profound commitment to pouring money down the drain or into the wrong pockets.

Time out

Time now to halt my flow, pull off the main line and sit contemplatively in the sidings for a few paragraphs. Firstly, an admission that I hadn't looked forward to writing this particular chapter. However, as I've stirred up the old grey matter, forgotten things cry out to be recorded. I had thought that I would be able, without writing pages of solemn prose, to amuse and divert you, to convey information, and to find answering chords in your own life that might interest you. But I've found myself repeating trivial details of little interest to anyone. Is that egotism, or simply the fun of being able to savour again the highs and lows of a phase in my life that I forgot as soon as it passed because I was so engrossed in enjoying what followed?

A lovely literary lady in her 80's constantly reminds me to be ruthless with my words so as not to bore a potential reader. I remind her back that I'm still writing this for me and mine. So I shall continue to put more flesh on a skeleton of 75 years—and let the reader decide whether to burn the midnight oil or flick over the pages until a promising passage appears; reading part of it, as it were, all the way through. I do find it difficult to cut down on words because, as I rummage around in my memory, I am frequently surprised by how many interesting and funny incidents pop up. It goes against the grain to express everything in "sound-bites"; life is a sight too complex and interesting to describe on the face of a mobile phone! I do of course have to be selective and self-critical as I unearth an increasing number of recollections that make me wince or squirm with remembered embarrassment. I ask myself, "How did I overcome or survive that?"

Being critical of others is something of which I'm often accused. When one records a criticism of an individual, organisation, establishment, policy or action, it is difficult to strike a fair balance without going into a much deeper and wordy explanation. Someone once observed that it is easier to perceive error than to find truth, because the former lies on the surface and is easily seen, while the latter lies in the depths where few are willing to search. Those who say I tend to be critical really mean I'm a miserable sod who always sees the dark side of life and every glass half empty rather than half full. I reject that accusation because I have great love and liking for my fellow man and an unquenchable sense of humour. Remembering that I may not be here when this is read (so why should I lie?), what I will happily admit to is to being critical in order to be creative. Being critical to me is neither to praise or denounce, but simply to get nearer to my subject; and surely no man can rise above the judgement of his fellows. What say you?

A very senior officer that I'd known when we both were junior officers, and whom I liked and respected enormously, once remarked when I posed a tricky question at a symposium, "I see that age and promotion haven't curbed your critical nature, John." Even though he spoke with a friendly glint, coming from him the words stung. I asked myself if others saw me that way, and committed myself to a pretty severe self-examination. I knew that occasionally I would open my mouth without first putting my brain into gear, and sometimes I would unfairly pillory some poor speaker who was only saying what he had to say, and not perhaps what he believed. I consoled myself with the thought that I only asked questions to find out what I felt the speaker had failed to convince me of, or clarify that which I had misunderstood. Nevertheless, I promised myself to soften my tone and be less arrogant in future.

Then I took a closer look at what my old friend had taken offence at and why he'd felt it necessary to return my fire. I'd been critical of an AFD proposal, before it had become policy, and offered a suggestion as to how we might achieve the operational aim more quickly and certainly at less cost. I realised I had doubted the worth of a cherished AFD practice; I had challenged an assumption that was never questioned, a scenario in which my alternative was "unthinkable". I suddenly found myself saying "Cheeky sod" because, of the many talents my friend possessed, one that went with the high position he held was that of being a lateral thinker; one able to see many ways of skinning the cat. In my questioning mode, I too was looking at all the options in order to make things better, simpler, cheaper, easier—whatever; so why was I seen as a critical bugger and him as the sharpest mind in the AFD hierarchy?

"Oozing charm from every pore, I oiled myself around the floor." To the sixth floor, in fact, of the Main Building, to his splendid office, and took him out for lunch at Soho's most welcoming restaurant, The Gay Hussar. In those convivial surroundings, well into the second bottle of Merlot, I asked him to give it to me straight. Laurie was a quiet, thoughtful man who, had he smoked, would have taken a reflective puff on his pipe, before saying, "We all like someone who comes right out and agrees with us, and we all resent anything that may obstruct the path we wish to follow. It's all about where and in what position we are when being criticised. We may let criticism go over our heads, think of a clever answer, or come back with a cheap shot as I did with you. I knew where I could hurt you, but it wasn't personal. You always criticise fairly and courteously. Don't stop questioning, John; what you achieve is well worth the odd rebuff and bloody nose."

Quite a few ghosts like that have emerged from my shadowy memories; I shall try hard not to ignore them but am conscious that the self-criticism of a tired mind is tantamount to suicide. After all, I can't turn the clock back to heal an old wound, and I can't even find some of the friends I want to find, let alone resurrect some old and probably mythical adversary. In that context, I cannot help wondering whether one day there will be a time and place when we shall all be able to cure old headaches, wipe away old tears, and correct real and imagined hurts. I do hope so; there are men whose hand I'd like to shake and girls whose cheek I'd like to kiss. But back to 1967.

Airborne Early Warning (AEW)

Not the most interesting heading you've ever seen for a chapter, but it covers half a lifetime of stories, a few of which might interest you. So first a very simplified subject brief. AEW is about placing your detection sensor at a height above the surface where the radar beam looks around the curvature of the earth and "sees" objects moving on or close to the surface. If you point a radar beam upwards it will easily detect an aircraft against the open sky. If you point it towards the surface it will see the surface, and any object between it and the radar. The trick is picking out such objects from the mass of returns from the surface, buildings, vehicles etc. (i.e. you must be able to tell the difference between squawk and clutter!)

Since WWII clever chaps have been developing ways of making radar work whatever the background and properties of the target, and of making the airborne system powerful yet sufficiently small, light and affordable to be carried in a reasonably sized aircraft. Advances in technology have provided more power, at less weight, less volume and lower cost, with software development leading to enormous processing and memory capability, all with previously undreamt of levels of reliability. This isn't a technical paper, but to put that in perspective, the processor that now does the difficult task of sorting out the data you need from masses that you don't, is the size of your video recorder and weighs 10 kilos. In 1970 it would have been too large to be carried in an aircraft the size of a 747. In the 70's the reliability of our key systems was in the order of 8–10 hours (i.e. the system would fail before the aircraft had flown 5 sorties). With one type of aircraft we would take bets which of our systems would go tits-up before take-off! In 1999, the specification for reliability on a very sexy electronics system due to enter service in 2004, was 10,000 hours. With 2 years still to go, they believe they can now offer 15,000 hours MTBF (mean time between failures). The bad news is that the costs are astronomical.

But in 1967 my task was to find a procurement path for an effective AEW system to counter the Warsaw Pact's low-level bomber threat to the UK. The key was a radar that used new techniques to distinguish the attackers from other aircraft and all other radar returns. The research then was led by an extremely able bunch of "boffins" who resided at Malvern in the Royal Radar Establishment (RRE). Working in conjunction with Industry, they went through a cycle of design, development, and flight test aiming to prove the feasibility of the system, before defining the project in detail, more development, and then into production.

The staff work for that process was fascinating if frustrating. If the radar didn't work the project was dead, but you also looked at the platform in which it would be carried, at its many complimentary sensors, the way in which the RAF might use this unique capability, how other elements of the UK air defence system might be reconfigured to accommodate AEW and, above all, try to keep tabs on the costs. There one often fell foul of inter-service rivalries and during 1967/68 I witnessed the most vicious inter–service fighting of my 50 years in defence; squabbling that sometimes made my children's fights seem grown up and which were all the more vitriolic and damaging because of the influence, intelligence, intellect, experience and cunning of the combatants. The procurement process has always been long and tortuous, so many studies, late alternatives, technical hiccups and financial panics; so much uninformed political interference, intrigue and prejudice to complicate the already overly bureaucratic system. AEW was no different; nevertheless, we made excellent progress by listening to countries with AEW in service, and educating ourselves and the air defence specialists of the RAF as to how it would interface and be integrated. Then, in 1968, the axe fell unexpectedly when the development programme was zero-funded. The RRE development needed more cash than forecast and the technical risk was deemed as too great to continue. To sweeten a bitter pill, the usual rider to all cancelled or deferred projects, was tossed in: "We shall await the results of current US studies before reviewing the case for pursuing ASR 387." Politic-speak for doing nothing!

A Change of Tack

Please forgive me if I puff and strut a little about my intrinsic ability to rise from the ashes. When my boss informed me of the hiatus, I was dismayed. I knew development was not progressing and, though having great regard for Malvern's boffins, had little confidence in the British electronics company that was assisting them. Otherwise, though, the concept was sound, and the Requirement remained undoubtedly urgent with no alternative means of meeting it. With relief I concluded my job was safe and pondered the next move that I knew was going to have to come from little old me.

Firstly I went out into the real world and treated myself to a gargantuan plateful of fish, chips and mushy peas at a café under the Charing Cross arches. Then—"thus armed and thus engined, well nourished and fed"—I nipped up to the 4th floor, smiled sweetly at the secretary for the Committee that had made the decision to cancel, and read the draft summary Annie had prepared for approval. Acknowledging that technical risk and escalating costs were primary reasons for cancelling the radar project (and not Air Staff Requirement No 387 *per se*), two sentences brought a gleam to my prying eyes. One referred to our intended scrutiny of US systems and, since I was the Project officer with still a year to do in post, whose job was that going to be?

The second, and one that hardly registered as I watched Annie criss-crossing her silky legs, was the intention that, as with the Buccaneer, the RAF were going to take over the Navy's discarded Gannet AEW aircraft as their carriers phased out. Now that thought was laughable because, capable little aeroplane that it was, the Gannet had been designed to operate off Carrier decks under its own power, no catapults or ski-jumps—and was for local fleet protection. As a land-based AEW, it would have had problems protecting the fleet in Portsmouth harbour! Also, its search radar was only effective over the sea and very limited in detection range—a far cry from the RAF's ASR 387. I bought the fair Annie a thank you G&T at a pub since razed to make way for politicians' offices and, as was my nightly custom, ran across Waterloo bridge to catch the 1840 to Wokingham. On passing close to Heathrow, my attention was caught by an aircraft that I identified as an Argosy. My fertile mind rushed ahead. What if we put the Gannet radar in a sizeable RAF aircraft, one that was already in service but surplus to requirements, and then operated it from coastal airfields to give the Navy their AEW cover within, say, 400 nms of the UK? Using an aircraft already in service, we'd have all the spares and our engineers would know it well, we'd save the cost of a new aircraft, and provide the RAF with invaluable experience of the AEW role prior to the long-term solution to ASR387.

Brilliant, methought! Which airframes might be available? The Argosy wasn't popular, the Britannia was being phased out, the VC10 could be up for grabs and the Shackleton Mks2 and 3 were soon to be replaced by Nimrod MR. As a twin-engined aircraft, and notoriously short-legged, the Argosy lost its appeal. The Britannia and VC10 would need holes cut in their underbelly for the scanner—which would incur extra cost. The Shackleton Mk3 might be the best option as it had underbelly radar and a tricycle undercarriage for improved ground clearance. Promising, but first I needed to check the availability of airframes, then discuss conversion costs, and check the radar fit and performance when mounted differently.

Full of rekindled enthusiasm, I asked a PE colleague what aircraft types might be available in our timescale. He came back with Brittania, Shackleton Mk2, VC10, and Belfast and—amazingly—Concorde. He discarded the Argosy for which they had other plans, also the Shackleton Mk 3 as they'd been flying overweight for years and were knackered, and said there were only four usable Belfasts. Equally enthused at the prospect, he proposed the Shackleton Mk 2 as they had recently been refurbished and re-engined and thus had many thousands of flying hours left. With four rear-mounted engines, the VC10 was a non-starter whilst Concorde I immediately rejected for just about every technical, operational and economic reason you could think of. (Actually I kept that to myself for a wee while as I sniffed the prospect of looking at that majestic beast and scrounged three rides with an old pal Brian Trubshaw—just to keep the books straight, you understand.)

I'd also asked the Navy how many Gannet radars they had and what repair facilities existed. I had an engineer in Portsmouth before lunch and his summary was to hand at 4 p.m. when I left to catch the 5 p.m. train to Manchester for a meeting with BAe's "Mr Shackleton" at Woodford on Thursday morning. Five of us sat down at 9 a.m. and by 11 a.m. had agreed that it should be the MK2; the present radome would need only minor changes, the fitting of the Gannet radar was cosmetic rather than surgery, and BAe saw no reason why they could not convert 8 aircraft in around 5 months for the princely sum of £65K per aeroplane. We agreed the way ahead over a typical Deanwater lunch, caught the 2.30 from Wilmslow to Euston and wrote the OR paper before arriving there. It was typed early Friday, approved by my OR two star by noon, by Air Force Plans by 2 p.m., and in Controller Airs' outer office by 3 p.m. His Board met the following Wednesday to approve the conversion programme at the BAe estimated cost.

The Shackleton AEW MK 2 was a fully approved programme 8 days after I had glimpsed the Argosy landing at Heathrow. The "interim"system entered service within months in 1972 for an expected service life of 4 years but remained in service until 1991. Not bad for a capital outlay of under £1M! I often wondered what my bonus would have been had I done such a deal when with industry. By the time AWACS was bought in 1986, the RAF had amassed 16 years of AEW experience. But that's another story.

The Birth of AWACS

The Board that cancelled the UK radar study said we'd be examining equivalent US programmes, a move that suited me down to the ground. I'd be going back to a country I loved visiting to see exactly how the US Navy and Air Force were operating their in-service systems, but chiefly to assess how their enormously expensive overland AEW research was progressing. I was guaranteed regular visits to Washington DC, to Baltimore the home of Westinghouse, to Long Island the home of Grumman, and to Navy and AF bases along the east and west coasts of the US. I'd fallen on my feet again.

This interest in America and things American causes me to struggle to explain my transatlantic love/hate relationship, so I'll leave that until I reach the 1980's. But in 1969, I was delighted to be a regular visitor even though in those days we travelled by RAF aircraft and not in the luxury of British Airways or United. The flights operated from Brize Norton near Oxford into Washington Dulles, and I always felt like a second-class citizen on the return that departed Dulles at 6 p.m. on Friday. You'd arrive at Dulles, scan the board for the departure gate for "RAF-England", and wince at the thought of wrinkled sandwiches and acid orange juice as the dulcet tones of the Pan Am announcer would say, "Pan Am wish to announce the departure of their Pacific Clipper Flight 01, to Las Vegas and Honolulu, Hawaii. Gate 4, all aboard now please." You joined the motley bunch of dismally dressed Brits waiting to show their tickets and passports to the RAF Movements staff as the excited Pan Am passengers in multi-coloured shirts and crazy hats babbled and gurgled their way down to the gate like an eager mountain stream.

One such evening therefore stands out in memory. As the 90 odd VC10 passengers squeezed through the narrow doors to find their narrow uncomfortable seats, the Sergeant loadmaster was obviously in a tremendous hurry to close the door and get away. Unheard of in a service aircraft, there were people still standing as the VC10 slipped away from the ramp and headed towards the runway; even the flight deck crew were in a hurry.

All became clear as we waited our turn for take-off. "Ladies and gentlemen," the loadmaster announced, "you may have noticed our hasty departure from the ramp. That is because 20 minutes ago the company that delivers Pan Ams' in-flight meals delivered to us 135 first class meals destined for their Clipper flight to Hawaii. For sandwiches on your menu read Lobster Thermidor followed by Surf and Turf; for powdered orange juice read Champagne and Martinis. If you have any complaints about the food, please inform the duty officer." As the VC10 erupted into joy and laughter, my heart went out to the Purser on Pan Am 01 who was presumably about to ask his passengers whether they wanted corned beef or cheese sandwiches, lousy orange juice or water!

Langham's or The Connaught today?

Pursuit of a US option meant that the Project Officer would receive special attention from US industry reps in London. Taking bribes or being influenced by hospitality was naturally frowned upon, but I never did see any problem, either as a serving officer or when I was a marketing director, in discussing business over a good meal and a drink. It was an opportunity to understand each other better, and when working in an extremely competitive environment, I saw it equally as important to know that our bid was inferior as I did to be told we were favourites. I met some charlatans and crooks in my time, mostly in industry, a few dodgy politicians and the odd bent Civil servant, but overwhelmingly it was good to talk.

With the Government expressing interest in AWACS, the US sales campaign swung into action. In the USA, their principle target was the Joint Services Mission of the British Embassy in Washington. By cultivating the military and technical staffs there, American firms could inject their messages of advanced technology and superior in-service equipment to high quality and high ranking staff, who then came back after three years to influential posts in London and the military establishments. Their prolonged insidious campaign was effective and I knew RAF officers who were so brainwashed that they had an outright and avowed preference for US equipment.

When the resurrected UK Nimrod AEW programme was cancelled in 1985 in favour of AWACS, I determined to write a book about it. *Inter alia*, I would have been very critical of aggressive American commercialism, and of their methods and tactics to impose upon NATO a complete monopoly in aerospace and electronics system production. But my anger was tempered by my certain knowledge of political skulduggery in Whitehall, the inadequacies of our own Procurement system, and by the equally certain knowledge of the incompetence and subterfuge of some British industries. So I never went to print, but you may not be spared the ordeal, as I shall probably wax lyrical on that in my 1980/90 chapters. But in 1969 after the satisfaction of introducing AEW to the RAF via the Shackleton, I had one eye on the future system that we so badly needed. The competing US firms were Boeing and Westinghouse with AWACS, and Grumman with their Navy E2B/C "Hawkeye" systems.

Let's put aside the technical and operational pros and cons for now and concentrate on purely selfish issues, eh? All the US reps wanted to take me out to lunch or dinner. Those were the days before a massive US clampdown on entertainment of prospective customers, and I was fortunate enough to have one rep who adored the London dining scene. Once a week at least, he'd be asking me where I'd like to lunch and, after a shy period when I said anywhere that suited him, I bought Raymond Postgate's splendid *Good Food Guide* and experimented. My favoured restaurants obviously serve the type of food I like, but ambience, quality service, and warmth of welcome are almost as important to me. The overriding advantage of course was that I wasn't paying, just as years later it was the company's money not mine that went on entertaining my guests. When you're not footing the bill, it's amazing how much you can enjoy your food! After almost two years of being spoiled rotten, I knew London's troughs and water holes intimately and, strange to relate, the half dozen or so favourites I had then also topped my list when I again served in Whitehall in 1979/81, and later when I was doing the entertaining from industry between 1983 and 2001.

If in 1968 you were being hosted by GEC or Ferranti, you'd be lucky to lunch at a Commercial Hotel. If it were BAe, you'd end up in Joe Lyons—unless they were on home territory in Manchester or Blackpool where you'd be royally treated. The American companies had no such inhibitions. My man from Westinghouse was keen to push the boat out, and I wasn't about to stop him.

In no special order, I went for Stone's Chop House for their superb roast beef and English trifle. They closed down in the 70's—I know not why because their splendid restaurant off Leicester Square was always full. For unusual food in a wonderfully friendly atmosphere I'd plump for the Gay Hussar in Greek St. That most English of restaurants, Rules off the Strand, was an early favourite for their jugged hare, Welsh rarebit and bread and butter pudding. They became too tourist orientated and quality went downhill, but it remains a great place for décor and to impress the colonials.

The best Greek restaurant for dozens of reasons, and a superb place in which to entertain, I found to be Beotys', in St Martins Lane, and just up the road is the best place in town to see the famous—The Ivy, with a wonderful menu and fine cellar. I must also mention Motcombs with great affection and a bar in an old tea warehouse south of the river called the Boot and Flogger. I don't know if it's still there, but it once was a Mecca for me when in a certain mood. I have other good memories including Maurer's German restaurant in Soho that closed in '76, a fish and chip shop under Charing Cross arches, now long gone, and a corner café near St Giles that served up an English breakfast *par excellence* before TV bored us silly with diets and dire warnings about fatty foods. What about the feel good factor, eh? Of course I've eaten extraordinarily well in other places. But I've also looked too often at antiseptic white tablecloths and wooden waiters, picked up a tab for £250 for two when £50 would have been too much, and left an acclaimed and celebrated dining room only to pick up a burger on the way home to stave off hunger!

Not Brussels again!

Anyone who served in Defence Procurement will immediately groan and think of Brussels. We nearly all served on one or more NATO Committees, with regular meetings from which you returned vowing never to step foot in Belgium again. Of course, one seldom had a choice and became reconciled to having an excellent meal in the complex of restaurants around the Grande Place, but dreading the boring and seldom constructive work of the committees. I disliked the NATO circus because I enjoyed my work, was keen to see a particular project succeed, and felt that it was good to have a concerted view for defending ourselves from the WP hordes.

The snag was that few NATO countries were as committed as the Brits. Meetings were usually over 3 days, Wednesday a.m. to Friday p.m. Delegates arrived at 1000 to break immediately for coffee; so you started work at maybe 1115 and got through the preliminaries in time for lunch at 1230. Back at 1400, coffee at 1530, wrap up by 1630 (because you had to be in town to dine out that evening, didn't you?). The same pattern on Thursday, and on Friday you were going home so that meant an early finish with the last hour of work spent checking travel plans. The whole world seemed anxious to get away from Brussels on Friday evenings, and the airport was chaotic. Another major failing was that many delegates didn't speak even passable English. So although it didn't affect their understanding of the work, instant translations being available, those people could not lead on committee work between meetings. The bulk of the administrative work therefore fell to the ever-gullible Brits or Germans.

Above all, NATO was a classic example of American manipulation. They perfected a system whereby, if a project was not going their way, they would change their representative for the next meeting or field a higher-ranking officer to disclaim what the previous rep had said or promised. On major projects this led to months or years of US prevarication, until the Americans got their way, for their industry, by fair means of foul. Brussels thus became a chore rather than a pleasure; nevertheless the Moules a l'Escargot in Vincent's and the Portuguese Gambas au Citron were worth the hassle and frustrations.

A Chance missed

Meanwhile, the MoD continued to study means of meeting the ASR for overland AEW. The need was increasingly urgent. Far from lowering our sights, we were insisting that from a patrol line over the North Sea, we could detect targets approaching from the continent or the north at all altitudes, and continue to track them as they flew into UK airspace. Otherwise we were blind to anything flying much below 500ft once it left the European coast. Malvern and GEC Marconi were still looking at an "FMICW" radar, whilst Grumman were keen to assure us that their E2-based series of radars already had an overland capability with developments in hand to ensure a capability that met our ASR. Our expert advice on their radar however was that "if you wanted to get here, you wouldn't start from there" and that was proved correct over the next 20 years or more. So AWACS offered the only real hope, but like all US programmes it was focussed on US needs and on the roles it would play in the much more complex American air defence system. AWACS was to be an airborne control centre, not simply for the detection of enemy targets and the control of fighters. It therefore had different priorities; for instance it didn't possess a surface picture of the sea—an important issue for us in giving air cover to our Navy. Also, the US Navy had organic AEW in the shape of the E2—so they had no interest in AWACS, or it in them in terms of optimising its' performance.

So often the UK has been persuaded or obliged to buy American, only for their procurement to be cancelled or changed so that it didn't suit our needs or pockets. I was therefore wary of their claims, but there was a time in the mid 70's when, with development costs escalating and technical success hard to come by, the US offered us a share of the programme—under what terms I never knew. It was rejected by a combination of Malvern's "not invented here" stance, and GEC's insistence that they could develop the radar without US help. I saw little evidence that Westinghouse were going to meet our Requirement in the foreseeable future, however well they progressed on other elements of the system. But in spite of my suspicions about US motives, I could not see how Malvern and GEC, working and researching as they did with little cash and a team of one man and his dog, could expect to succeed where the Americans were failing with the help of an enormous research budget and a very large and strong technical team. I wasn't being unpatriotic, just downright practical. In the event, six years were to pass before any advance was made.

How's that for Intelligence?

In 1971 my time in London was up, and I had a posting for a Phantom Squadron in Germany—magic! But then the last of four new squadrons became one of Mr Healey's savings and guess whose job was the one that was axed? At the time I was devastated, but the consolation prize that I negotiated with the Air Secretary was to change the rest of my life. First, however, I'll close my version of the "Swinging Sixties" with two little stories that may interest and amuse you.

The Malvern/GEC Feasibility Study report on the new AEW radar had concluded that the ideal platform would be a modified Comet. Based on previous work for a carrier-borne AEW, GEC had decided that the optimum antenna system, to give continuous 360-degree cover, would be two synchronised scanners, one in the nose and one in the tail, rather than have a massive rotordome structure on the top of the fuselage. Flight trials of the prototype radar could be flown using just one antenna, so all they needed was a second-hand Comet that could be modified by BAe. PE found a suitable Comet from Middle East airlines with a good modification history and with sufficient flying hours left for use as a trials aircraft. The Comet was parked at Beirut, so an MoD team of four flew to Cyprus and took the short flight in an RAF Argosy across to Beirut.

Unfortunately our visit coincided with an Israeli air attack on Beirut and when some 60 miles away we were told first, to hold off shore, then eventually to land at our own peril! When all was clear, we did just that and taxied around the east end of the airfield looking at burning aircraft on every pan. Beirut tower told us where our Comet was parked and we followed an air traffic vehicle to where it stood with front steps extended. As the only serving officer in the team, I was volunteered to check if the Comet had been damaged. I mounted the steps to see a small notice flapping by the open door. Quite simply it read, "To the RAF with the compliments of the Israeli Armed Forces. Happy flying!" How's that for Intelligence?

But you said…!

The second story concerns a hilarious incident you would expect to see in a Spike Milligan or "Fools and Horses" sketch. The scene—the British Aerospace facility at Woodford, Cheshire. The occasion—the testing of the radome on the Comet trials aircraft to withstand bird strikes. Any radome fitted to an aircraft not only has to be aerodynamically correct, but also has to be optimised in construction for the power/frequency characteristics of the radar. The AEW radome construction was critical with the designers striking a balance between it being electronically compatible, yet able to withstand the rigours of flight under all conditions. The final test of this very expensive piece of fuselage was to see how it would stand up to being hit by a bird in flight. The standard test assumed a seagull or crow striking the nose on take-off at around 150 knots. A bog-standard UK seagull or crow weighs in at around 3 lbs, and a bird of this weight was to be fired from a small canon directly at the nose, followed by firings off the dead ahead position.

The assembled spectators watched in the pouring rain as everything was prepared for the test. Someone shouted "Fire", the canon roared—and the nose of the Comet rig disintegrated with a loud bang, sending a shower of radome debris high above the airfield to be blown by the Cheshire wind towards the backdrop of the Derbyshire hills. The engineers by the Comet huddled together, the rest of us climbed quietly into the waiting BAe cars, and drove in silence back to the Boardroom for tea and crumpets. After some 15 minutes we were joined by Woodford's technical director who explained to an incredulous audience that the wag whose task it was to procure the 3lb bird had done just that, only he'd bought it from the local supermarket—and it was frozen! The combination of relief and outrageous hilarity caused the teapots to be replaced by scotch as we heartily toasted British inventive genius.

During that first 4-year tour in Whitehall I had learned so much about my profession, about the political way of doing things, about how my own service operated away from the front line, and about myself. I'd come to know my capital city like the back of my hand, become an expert on where to eat and drink and even have pretensions of being a gourmet. I'd been so busy working, and travelling that I only really saw my wonderful young family at weekends. A few weeks later I was in Cyprus, and it took me weeks to stop feeling guilty about walking to work every morning in brilliant sunshine along the cliffs, no more rushing for the 0810 to stand in a cold uncomfortable corridor for an hour before being trampled on the tube. At 6 p.m. I could stand on my patio as the sun went down, nursing a brandy and ginger as we gathered the sprogs to go downtown for a wonderful Cypriot kebab. Gone were the nights of burning the midnight oil in Whitehall, of arriving back in Wokingham just in time to go to bed. I felt grateful that I had chosen, or fallen into, a career that gave me the best of both worlds. Variety really is the spice of life; and freedom the fuel of life.

The Cyprus Rugby team with a star guest at no. 9—1974

9

CYPRUS 1971–4

I admit I was extremely disappointed to be going to an Air Staff job in Cyprus rather than commanding my own Squadron; every aviator worth his salt would consider being a Squadron boss as the zenith of his career. That said, from the family point of view, the "plum" job that I negotiated with the Air Secretary as a consolation prize, was much the better posting. Firstly it was to the guaranteed all year round sunshine of the Eastern Mediterranean and to a way of life that was fast disappearing. As a key executive I had an ex-officio married quarter that was high on the cliffs with a sea view and some 400 yards from a private beach. My wife had full time domestic help, the children were in an excellent Services School, there was a vibrant social life for all the family, and we enjoyed the benefits of tax-free booze and cars.

Gone was my dreary commuting to London, the late night working, and the way I missed out on the children growing up in their younger years. Had I got my dream posting there is no doubt that for another two years I would have been so committed to the Squadron that the family would have come second. Indeed, had we gone to Germany, the boys would have stayed as boarders in their Day School and our eldest daughter would have stayed in England also. Little did I know however as I settled in to a new job in strange surroundings, that fate was about to change my life and the lives of those around me so dramatically. All the family enjoyed that tour immensely. The impact on them came later, but it would have nothing to do with my job or career. It had everything to do with love.

What is this thing called Love?

Perhaps I should start by saying what love isn't, even though for the first 41 years, 5 months, 5 days and 12 hours of my life I thought I had a pretty good understanding of what people meant by being in love, or feeling love for another.

Meeting Rosemarie Yvonne Knight (nee Evans) on June 6th 1971 in Cyprus turned my world upside down

By then I was reconciled to believe that the vast majority of people met someone who they liked the look of, someone with whom they could have fun, share life's pleasures, enjoy making love to, or accompany to the ballet or theatre or support the same football team. In the days when commitment through marriage was important, a relationship that was based on these and other attractions usually resulted in offsprings that, in most cases, drew a couple closer to provide much valued security. That security often became an impregnable rock on which the marriage survived and even prospered, even though one or both of the partners would often have little compunction in having affairs and potentially disastrous sexual relationships outside the marriage.

I could never gauge exactly how good a marriage was. Some couples clearly settled for what they had, presumably after early passion had subsided and they were fortunate enough to be good pals. Others were always sniping at each other in public, but always went home together and behaved impeccably. Some lived together but lived separate lives—him in the bar or on the sports field, her in the Thrift Shop or tied up with the children. Then—and especially when I lived in the States—there was the perfect father and husband at home who, as soon as the wheels touched the ground in some other place, would be hell bent on having sex with anything that moved as often as possible before he returned home to be Dr Jekyll again. The female of the species was often equally able to be a Jezebel, a wanton "lush" one day and a prim and prudish "butter wouldn't melt in her mouth" lady the next.

Life was a succession of "Well, I never's!" "Who'd have thought it's?" and "Really—and I thought she was a nice girl". But just to keep the flame of hope alive that there was such a thing as true love, that one could fall in love at first sight, and that the high passion of one's early adulthood could last and become an even greater passion in later years, every now and then one saw a couple whose love for each other shone like a beacon, making them stand out from the rest. So hope sprang eternal.

When He Fancies he is Past Love…

I obviously became one of the settled and contented brigade that I've described. I had a lovely young and growing family. Significantly, too, I was enjoying every day of my life in the RAF. As I commit that to paper, I find myself questioning the truth of that claim. Was it like that, or do I just see it that way from the distance of time? The unqualified answer is that it is true; I honestly cannot recall a day in my post-Ireland RAF life when I did not get up and look forward to my working day.

Were there any Miss Perfects in those 18 years? Well, there was a possible sighting in Bavaria in 1953, another in Texas in 1962 and a Scottish experience in 1965. But all were unopened doors. That did not mean I never found anyone else attractive; a certain smile, the shape of a mouth, the lilt of a Scottish accent, a flowing head of titian hair, might all lead to a dance too many, a word too indiscrete, or a look too lingering. Lost opportunities, lost chances, lost love—who knows; at a different time, in a different place and under different circumstances, who's to say how any perfectly ordinary and proper relationship might flourish or founder? Then, of course, for every sighting of a possible target, there were unknown numbers of ships that had passed in the night. If Miss Perfect *had* passed my way, I'd missed her.

On April 14th 1971, the six Palmers arrived on the beautiful island of Aphrodite. I was thrilled to be free of the pressures of Whitehall and the noise and bustle of London, with the whole family delighted to exchange the rain and cold winters of England for the warmth and year-round sunshine of the Eastern Mediterranean. It was an exciting prospect for me professionally, whilst the guaranteed sunshine meant a new lease of life for my football, rugby and cricket pursuits in the twilight of my sporting life.

I had the enviable job of looking after the RAF Air Defences on Cyprus and also the Near East Transport Wing equipped with that most versatile of aircraft, the C-130 Hercules. This gave me a fascinating working mix of the Lightning fighter squadron at Akrotiri, the Bloodhound SAM site at Paramali and the high power long-range radars, 6000ft high up on Mount Troodos. The transport role offered extensive travel around the Mediterranean to the major NATO and CENTO HQs in Athens, Naples, Izmir and Ankara. The icing on the cake was the special responsibility I had for the UK's support of Omani and British seconded forces in the Dhofar War against the Yemen. I was able to experience the fascinating and totally different environment, the atmosphere and culture of Arabia and the Persian Gulf—a region that I'd only seen previously from my cockpit at 40,000 feet and 500 knots en route to and from places further east. So I was by no means at a loose end, and certainly not in need of any excitement.

Similarly Rosemarie, although in a bad marriage it transpired, was in her element in Cyprus. The living was easy, the RAF provided domestic help, and she lived the exciting and socially-orientated life of an RAF officer's wife abroad. My family, ages 7 to 19, loved the sun and sea and all the cultural and sporting attractions of Cyprus. I was a happy and contented bunny with no thoughts whatsoever about a new love life, or even about the vastly different often-hectic social life of an overseas posting. Nevertheless, I should perhaps have heeded the words of a wise old writer of songs:

At 17, he falls in love quite madly with eyes of tender blue.
At 24 he gets it rather badly with eyes of a different hue.
At 35, you'll find him flirting madly with two or three or four.
But when he fancies he is past love, it is then he meets his last love, and he loves
her as he's never loved before.

A Collision Course

So many people have written so many words about love, but few count for much unless the writer has experienced love for him or herself. True love is a lot rarer than the romantic novels and 1940's Hollywood would have us believe. Bertrand Russell said that three great passions governed his life: "The first was Love because it brought ecstasy—ecstasy so great that I would often have sacrificed all of the rest of my life for a few hours of that joy. Next it relieved my loneliness, and finally, in the union of love, I saw in a mystic miniature the prefiguring vision of the Heaven that saints and poets have imagined." He concluded that it was that true Love he had at last found and I know what he meant because that is what happened to me on Sunday June 6th at the Officers' Mess RAF Episkopi.

Without any warning or premonition, the earth moved, the sky fell in and time stood still. I was alone on the veranda when I first saw her. There *she* was; a gorgeous 29-year-old, impeccably dressed as she always is, with a long elegant stride and a proud look guaranteed to turn heads wherever she goes. She walked up the steps from the courtyard into the open corridor leading a young girl to the buffet table. She walked and moved and held herself, as I knew she would, her dark hair falling on one suntanned shoulder and down one side of her proud and beautiful face.

She smiled to the girl, a radiant smile that outshone the noonday sun and delicately, ever so delicately, chose her food and walked back to her table with the graceful walk of a ballet dancer or elite model. I fell in love at first sight and knew at once that I'd not waited in vain. Minutes later we met for the first time as her husband introduced us. We were later to admit that our initial reactions at that handshake were identical, although neither of us revealed that until almost 6 months later when we kissed for the first time in the entirely proper context of a New Year's Eve party. I was 41, she 29—and we stood that night in the middle of a mob of screaming revellers and heard or saw nothing but each other, conscious of a love that it was now far too late to deny. The six months that preceded that kiss were, in effect, our courting days. I'm not sure whether there is such a phase as "courting" today; people live together on a trial basis and walk away just as easily. Right or wrong, that wasn't our way in our circumstances in that enchanted summer of '71. The encounter that had taken place that June lunchtime had left us both bemused. Neither of us, we later agreed, had been looking for an affair, yet in a second our lives had been changed forever.

I introduced my wife to her and her husband, and now walking on air, moved on to our own table ensuring that I took up a position from where I could see more of my vision of delight. She was perfect; in fact, she was more than perfect as I watched her every movement and expression, heard the dulcet tones of her voice carried on the warm sea breeze and, whilst the orchestra was between pieces, caught the distinctive sound of her laughter bringing her own brand of music to my ears.

From that day on, we later agreed, we must both have begun to wear that abstracted, dreamlike look; lips half parted, eyes unable to focus as if in a trance. All my life I had yearned for something beyond the figments of reality, a steady passionate flame, and a single-hearted ecstasy. And here it was. "Through the gate into the garden, up that enchanted mountain, and out into the glory and splendour of Heaven itself". As she and her family left she glanced back discretely, and I knew that we had a destiny together; we had just set up the first milestone on the road towards each other.

Military life in Cyprus being what it was with all its customs and protocol, our meetings after that, and until New Year's Eve in fact, were few and invariably confined to exchanging brief nervous exploratory remarks. But we were innocently embarked on the journey of love, and it was no ordinary journey. In those early months, all of my dreams about the perfection I'd sought, or my obsession with my "identikit" lover, were turned into reality. Rosemarie was all of those things, but the more we met—albeit so publicly—the more I saw in her to love. When we kissed for the first time at that New Year party, I could not believe that a kiss could mean and say so much. I'd kissed hundreds of girls, but it was as if I'd never kissed or been kissed before. We still had said nothing about love, we were still being circumspect and proper; but we both wore the look of love, feeling more like sixteen than forty-one and twenty-nine.

Rosemarie and her husband and 6-year-old daughter Sarah, had been on the island for 2 years when I arrived. They lived in downtown Limassol with a social life more hectic and different to ours, centred on those families who by rank, lack of seniority, or few children, had not amassed enough "points" to qualify for a married quarter on the station. This meant she moved in a younger social set, mainly the junior aircrew from Akrotiri, who tended to combine the more formal Mess social life with the Turkish and Greek bars and restaurants that provided wonderful food and entertainment at ridiculously low prices. Rosemarie loved the sun and the beauty of Cyprus and had settled easily into the wives routine of Coffee and Bridge mornings, sunbathing and swimming, with the children home from school at 1 p.m. along with most husbands. The constant round of formal and informal parties gave her the opportunity to do what she loved doing, dressing up. The men folk on Cyprus were truly spoiled rotten by the glittering array of female beauty that adorned the dance halls and bars of Cyprus. The summer and Christmas Balls in the Officers' Mess were akin to watching a fashion show in Paris or Milan, except that the ladies in Cyprus were more attractive.

The lifestyle she led often made me unhappy. I didn't know initially that her marriage was not as it seemed, so although we were both fatally smitten from the moment we met, we had to endure six long months of uncertainty during which we each loved from afar without knowing—even imagining—that our love might be returned or acknowledged. We both would create opportunities to be where we thought the other might also be. Her husband worked in the same HQ as me, so we routinely met at social functions, but of course that wasn't enough and the 12 miles that separated our homes might have been 12 million. In the hope of catching merely a glimpse of her, I'd drag my family into town on any pretence. Rosemarie on her part would nag her husband to drive into the Sovereign Base sports complex in Happy Valley—in the hope that I might be playing rugby or cricket. "On the street where you live" might have been written for us. Functions in the Mess or house parties were truly pain and pleasure. One didn't always know who else was invited, and remember that we were both oblivious then to the others' feelings. So the first one to arrive would invariably face acute disappointment, and then watch the entrance with increasing anxiety to see if the other showed up. If not, the next step in this tortuous ritual would be to ask the host, or a known friend of the other, if the other was expected at the function. This question of course had to be put in the most casual offhand manner, as if it wasn't of the slightest interest—but merely a matter of polite conversation.

Passion and protocol

For those not familiar with the social life of the time out in the far reaches of "The Empire", it should be said that behind the façade of passivity, courtesy and impeccable manners, lay a seething mass of intrigue, suspicion, and gossip. Folk were always on the lookout for some tasty titbit to add to the annals of the outpost. It may seem odd today with lifestyles and customs so different to those I describe, that Rosemarie and I should want—or have been content—to love in secret and not to reveal our feelings. But there were practical difficulties in the codes of behaviour, formalities, and conventions of the day that we could not ignore.

We were both married with families on the island; affairs with other officers' wives were not simply frowned upon—they were *verboten*. If such outrageous conduct came to light, it usually meant the immediate posting of one family and a career "black" for the offending officer. In our case the danger was compounded because, not only was I two ranks above her husband, but also shortly after we met I became his head of department (a move incidentally in which I'd had a hand as it would bring Rosemarie more often into our social circle!).

There was the ever-present danger; initially of suspicion that mischief might be afoot, and later of actual discovery when we were meeting clandestinely. Life in Cyprus was like life in a ghetto. You lived in each other's pockets, used the same mess, clubs and cinemas, shopped in the same NAAFI and local markets, and were subject to the same strict rules and code of conduct. There were matriarchal women, full of benevolent majesty, who made it their duty to know everything about everybody. They helped fuel the gossip, inspire the envy and jealousy, all of which was accentuated by the hot humid climate that seemed to turn many a shrinking English violet into a man-eating tropical plant.

A significant threat to the secrecy of our affair was a powerful Police and Intelligence presence, primed to identify anyone in high office and with high security clearances, who might be vulnerable to blackmail by the foreign agents that infested the island. Being at Russia's back door, Cyprus was then of immense strategic defence importance. My position made me a prime target, but in those first 6 months Rosemarie and I were truly innocents abroad. I couldn't call her at home, there were no mobile phones then, and writing was out of the question even had I picked up the courage to make the first move. At parties, the limit of my indiscretion would be to help her light her cigarette and to venture the lightest touch on her fingers in so doing. Dancing, in the old fashioned way, provided the occasional moment to talk and make nervous reconnaissance into her feelings. But even in the intimacy of a tango—a dance designed to make men and women very aware of each other—there was a room full of eyes and ears alert to the merest hint of an illicit relationship.

Occasionally, someone would be caught in the act, so to speak. The rules and regulations would be dusted off, and some poor soul would be on the next VC10 back to the UK. Others would heave a sigh of relief, "Dear John" letters would be written, and many a budding romance would bite the dust. In the nature of things, all would soon return to normal and it would be monkey business as usual. Sad to say, most of the passions aroused in such surroundings between men and women in the prime of their lives, were soon burnt out. Even if they survived the days when both were on the island, they seldom lasted once one or the other or both were back in the UK. It was odd how some people, especially ladies who would never have a hair out of place in English society and who thought of themselves as veritable pillars of virtue, became sexually loose under the Mediterranean sun and stars. If only someone could have bottled it, they'd have made a fortune!

The point of no return

But whatever the rest of Cyprus got up to, Rosemarie and I were far too engrossed in each other to notice. The disease had struck and there was no turning back even though, before we each knew of the other's feelings, we also dreaded that when one of us left Cyprus that might be the end for us. Our fate was sealed in the Spring of '72. I was always seeking ways to exchange even a few words with her, and at a cocktail party I'd mentioned that I had influence as to who might get on RAF "indulgence" flights, a scheme whereby serving personnel and families could use otherwise empty seats on RAF passenger aircraft for a nominal fee. Rosemarie had expressed an interest in indulging to Istanbul, Teheran or Athens, some of our local runs. So I composed a short letter (on specially bought Wedgwood-blue paper) to advise her of forthcoming flights. Just to "spice it up" a little, I addressed her as "my favourite witch" in reference to a sensational Halloween costume she'd worn at a Christmas party.

I scented a unique opportunity to get either a "proceed with caution" Amber light, or a "dead stop, forget it mate" Red. So, to the list of flights I added," If you can make any of them, please call me on Episkopi 301". Her husband was away (as well I knew), so I sent the letter via her next-door neighbour's husband who gave me a curious look as if to query why I was sending a lady a letter in a sexy blue envelope. Being senior to him, I haughtily explained it was merely an Indulgence list. He didn't look too convinced, and ironically when I bumped into him and his wife in London some 25 years later, they both laughed and said that however well Rosemarie and I had imagined we'd hidden our feelings, our passion was so obvious from Day One that people took bets on which of us would be on the VC10 first!

The following day, a voice I'd never heard on the phone said sweetly, "How's my favourite warlock?" I was so taken aback that I had to ask her to repeat it. She did so, and went on to thank me for the offer, but said she wasn't able to get away at the time—but maybe later? All flustered and tongue tied, and not wishing to blow what was already a massive step forward, I said I understood and "see you soon, eh?" I put down the phone in a daze, stood up, walked around my desk concluding that I'd certainly got an Amber, possibly even a Green, and let out a huge "Yahoo". Turning around I saw the august figure of Sir John Aitken, our C in C standing at the open door. Smiling, he said, "Whatever you're on John, save me some of that."

I spent days and nights analysing every word she'd said, and how she'd said them. Was she just being nice to someone who'd made a friendly gesture? Perhaps she'd mentioned it to her husband who'd said, "Better keep the old man happy." Any reader who has known the tortuous pangs of loving, yet not knowing if love is returned, will understand the bittersweet agonies I suffered.

Mercifully soon after, the Operations Branch held a dinner in one of the luxury hotels in Limassol. I was already seated when Rosemarie and her husband came in. She didn't look where to sit or ask her husband; instead, she made a bee-line for the seat next to me, arriving as she always does, looking deliciously feminine, with a laugh and cheerful words of greeting. I sat unable to believe my good fortune, although I suddenly realised from looks I was getting from across the table that warning bells were ringing loud and clear.

Prior to that dinner, there was the Christmas season to be negotiated. I could hardly wait for it to come with its endless round of parties at which you were guaranteed to see everyone from the RAF and Army on the island. No one went home for Xmas; Cyprus *was* home to thousands of military folk and the lifestyle was exceptional. Looking back on 37 years in RAF uniform, I've no doubt that the 60's and 70's were the best time to serve. The flying was that happy mix still of fun and high technology. Station life was both comfortable and exciting. Virtually everyone lived in married quarters, especially overseas. It was before the days when the conversation in a Squadron crew room was more about mortgages than last night's trip to Hero Square or the Pat Pong. Wives stayed at home instead of working, you moved stations every three years, and the social life was centred on an extremely well run, comfortable and happy Officers' Mess. The closeness of the families was reflected in the spirit of the aircrew and of those who supported the operational task, the engineers and administrators. How lucky we were.

But with those Christmas festivities of 1971, came the inevitable pangs of frustration and—for me I'm afraid—of jealousy. Rosemarie has always been beautiful; vivacious, friendly, and popular and quite unperturbed at talking to anyone anywhere, however important and famous. She was invariably the centre of attraction for men of all ages with intentions both honourable and distinctly dishonourable. Watching the wolves prowling and the bachelors freelancing, without having any overt claim myself or being able to dissuade a too-persistent pursuer to sod off, was like being on the rack.

Rosemarie was never a flirt and in 34 years she's never given me cause to doubt her. But at that time, before she and I had any commitment, I admit to agonising for hours at parties and even more when I knew she was at parties elsewhere. We were to discover later that she had the same sort of anxieties, and if I weren't at her function would concoct some excuse to be taken home early. If it were me and my wife who were out socialising, Rosemarie wouldn't be able to sleep until she could be reasonably sure I was home. All lovers will know the special torment of knowing that the one you love is with someone else. Distrust is not the pre-dominant feeling. It's the fact that the loved one is in an environment where someone else has the opportunity—and perhaps the right and the desire—to be close to and intimate with the loved one, without him or her being able to object.

Ironically, I'm drafting these notes (in 2002) on one of our beautiful quiet beaches on the south coast of Cyprus. Rosemarie has wandered off to do a bit of beachcombing whilst up on the sand track a Cypriot truck driver (miles from the main road) has come down to do his daily girl-spotting act. He gets out of his truck, displays his hairy torso as God's gift to women, and then scuttles back to his cab as I appear on the beach. Thoughts like that once drove me mad. As Maurice Chevalier sang so perceptively and melodiously, "I'm glad I'm not young anymore."

A Touch of Israel

Staying in the present, I watch our Gay Lothario's truck dwindle in the distance along the hot and dusty track fringed with carob trees and the bundhu scrub. Beyond the cliff line are rolling hills which now, in July, are an incredibly colour-ful mixture of golden corn and luscious green vines. The women were out in the vines as we drove down picking the early grapes to reach the European markets before the Israelis and Egyptians. We learn something every day, do we not? I never knew the Egyptians grew grapes, let alone exported them.

That mention of Israelis leads me to digress to a remarkable incident yester-day. We'd driven up to the beautiful old village of Omodos, high on the road to Troodos. All cobbled streets, whitewashed walls, old ladies making lace, and old men sitting in the shade taking their mid-morning beverages. Into this peaceful haven and its many souvenir shops, came a coach load of Israeli tourists, mostly middle-aged women but with young and old alike in a group numbering perhaps 35–40. They proceeded to swamp the little shops, completely overwhelming the handful of assistants, and set about stealing whatever they could slip into their bags or handbags. Even when confronted by a shopkeeper for stealing, they still had the audacity to argue about the price they should pay for the goods they'd attempted to steal. In all my years of travelling, to over a hundred countries worldwide, I have never seen anyone steal so blatantly and *en masse*. I've been to Israel often and had many dealings with their air force, government and industry. I've always seen them as intensely proud and very professional people. Yesterday we saw them as the Cypriots must see them, and I must say that an illusion for me was shattered.

Mediterranean Disappointments

One more short digression and then I'll move on to the defining moment for Rosemarie and I. My gaze has switched from the sun-drenched cliffs to the turquoise sea now flecked with white foam as the midday breeze gets up. I look across this beautiful seascape, as I have many times in 45 years, and realise what is missing from such apparent perfection. It is the absence of any obvious maritime life. Now and again one sees a Seagull or a lone Cormorant, a Swallow skimming the waves, or a Griffon Vulture majestically patrolling the skies off the Episkopi cliffs. But never have I seen the surface broken by the fin of a shark, the leap of a dolphin, or the splashdown of game fish or whale. I remember someone telling me that it's all to do with a lack of food in this part of the sea. Few shells on the beaches, no barnacles on the rocks, no profusion of underwater vegetation, Pity, really, but then on this scintillatingly beautiful morning, I think I can put up with it!

Many will be pleased that these waters contain nothing more dangerous than a mean sardine, but to me its a serious deficiency when one looks at other sun-blessed corners of the world. I have always been fascinated when sailing or swimming in the Indian Ocean, off the Oman coast or further down in the Maldives. The ocean simply teams with sea creatures of all shapes, sizes and colours. With Rosemarie, I've enjoyed similar marine life extravaganza off the coasts of Australia, Malaysia and South Africa. Perhaps the most rewarding of all has been off the northern coast of Kauai, the garden isle of Hawaii. There in the shadow of the stupendously majestic and beautiful Na Pali cliffs (Bali Hi in the film South Pacific), a boat journey becomes the stuff of which dreams are made. Spinner and Bluenose Dolphins surround and play with the boat, flying fishes skim the waves, and massive sea turtles wallow their ungainly way to who knows where. A Tiger

Shark takes one for lunch and leaves the scraps for a flock of screaming gulls to squabble over. Should you make the journey around Christmas, you'll be royally entertained by the huge Humpback whales and the twisting turning leap of a Swordfish or Marlin. In the restaurants, local lobster, scallops and abalone bring the taste right out of the ocean and, I'm sad to say, leave even the tasty Cypriot fish mezzes well behind in their wake.

No holds barred

But let me return to the early minutes of 1972 when two lovers stood shell-shocked in a Limassol nightclub, intensely aware of the impact that one lingering kiss had made on their lives forever. Our rapture was broken by my wife grabbing my arm asking to be protected from a local who was pressing her to dance. There was no problem, but of course I could not argue and Rosemarie saw the danger more quickly than I and said I must go with her. I did go, but her intervention was nothing to do with any Cypriot; it was a ruse my wife had pulled a hundred times in our married life—and outside she called me every name under the sun and I was told never to dance with Rosemarie, ever again.

I recount this because it had a profound effect on how our love affair proceeded from there. Our next opportunity to meet seemed an age, but was only 3 weeks. It was at a supper party held in our married quarter at which, unknown to me, my wife brainwashed Rosemarie by giving her a wildly inaccurate view of our marriage, craftily warning her off by claiming we were wonderfully happy. Bearing in mind that Rosemarie and I were still in shock after the wondrous happening on New Year and hadn't had a moment to discuss it further, she despairingly concluded that we were doomed to be star-crossed lovers. In an attempt to save me and stabilise her own marriage, she was soon to dismay me by revealing that she was pregnant; we mustn't—couldn't—be any more than friends. I was devastated, so my Wedgwood blue letter penned a few weeks later in March, was a last desperate attempt. It made Rosemarie realise that I'd not given up hope and so when I called one day to ask if I might call by her house one morning, she said of course I could. The die was cast forever in that first rendezvous at her flat in Theseus Street in Limassol.

Our first illicit meeting was a very tame affair, but it's effect on us at the time and on the rest of our lives was tantamount to a nuclear explosion. For some 20 minutes, we kissed and blurted out breathless admissions and secretly held fears, now able to express our relief that the waiting, as we loved from afar, was over. We hadn't been in love in vain. I well remember feeling that this was something so rare, so precious, that we shouldn't grasp it too tightly in case it slipped from our hands. It wasn't an instant prize for instant gratification, but the beginning of a courtship, of learning to love for the sake of love.

Already I was experiencing emotions and responses which—at the age of 42—I'd never known. It was as if I'd never loved, never touched anyone else, never felt as though the world held no one but her and me. For the moment that was enough, and I didn't want to say or do anything that might break the magic spell and spoil it for her. I simply could not do enough to please her. I was actually flying to Germany that same day and as I walked away from her front door she stood looking stunningly beautiful and smilingly said, "Hurry back now." As I walked away, impossibly feet off the ground and head in the clouds, I was already anticipating the reunion.

The months that followed were idyllic, even though I now look back in disbelief and wonder how we escaped discovery. Some things were in our favour. Rosemarie lived in town so we had few British neighbours to worry about. I was her husband's boss so I had every reason to know exactly where he was since often I sent him there! I lived on the senior officers' "patch" some 12 miles away and my wife seldom drove into town alone. When we left the vicinity of Rosemarie's flat, within a mile we were in the beautiful open hillsides of Cyprus with only the occasional shepherd and the tinkling of goat bells to disturb the mesmeric tranquillity.

Alone together, we were overwhelmed with new sensations; a window had opened on a world of experiences and excitement that neither of us had ever known or imagined. When I held her in my arms it was as if she hadn't a bone in her body; her skin was softer and smoother, her hair like silk, her voice so soft and sweet that I felt I could kiss it. Long before Jeffrey Archer referred to his lovely wife Mary as "fragrance", I used that endearment about Rosemarie; feminine and fragrance describe her to a T. Today, after 34 years, I am still unable to turn away for love of her beauty.

But beyond the nature of the sensuous feelings that pervaded us, we were enmeshed in something far deeper whether we wished it or not; moments between a man and a woman which no pen can write or tongue tell; when nothing happens on the physical plane but the eyes spin an ethereal web. Everything was alive, from the stones under our feet on the sun-drenched hillside, to the mountain peak of Troodos that shimmered in the morning haze on the horizon. We were ultra conscious of the shape of a tree, the fall of a leaf, the cry of a bird, the tinkle of goat bells in an otherwise silent world. We believed in omens, portents, and talismans, and we invoked the supernatural spirits that roamed our seashore, our hills and our woods. We mourned the death of a carob rat, saved butterflies from drowning, and ushered flies out of the door instead of spraying them or knocking them for six. All of nature had sprung alive to become a meaningful part of us.

We were in harmony, both well and truly stricken by the disease that overtook all our thoughts and feelings, consuming us as with a fever. It was unique to us, a lovely and delicate counterpoise, neither love alone nor sex alone; everything alive, everything a shooting star. We had stopped worrying. Our prayer was to love each other better and more perfectly; to be content, not to grasp that which we'd been given too hard but neither to demand too much from the future. What we had was enough. For some reason, way beyond our ken, we had been brought together, to our moment of fusion, to be ourselves. We knew how the world would view us; nevertheless we both utterly believed that what we now shared could have come from nowhere or no one but God himself. We were grateful to God, to life, and we were not ashamed.

But obstacles there were too. I walked to work or caught an RAF bus, so I seldom had a car. That meant borrowing my boss's staff car for official journeys. I needed a reason to do so which was easy with my far ranging responsibilities, but I could easily be recalled if there was a panic. To get to Limassol, I had to drive through miles of Sovereign Base Area roads, then along a 5-mile narrow stretch of back road through the orange plantation along which all the RAF wives from Akrotiri would be driving. There was always the chance at every function of someone coming up and saying quite innocently, "Hello John, saw you over in the plantation on Monday morning; what on earth were you doing there?" In Limassol itself it would be Rosemarie's friends who might see us, or surprise us if we were at the flat. Which is why we much preferred to run the obstacle course up into the hills. I was invariably in uniform, so I wasn't out of place in town or between bases, but would have been out in the hills. I never took the car close to the flat for obvious reasons, so we'd meet somewhere easy for her to reach, as she didn't drive. Occasionally she'd catch a taxi, remembering that the temperature was usually 80+, but neither of us liked her doing that as the Cypriot drivers could get fresh with service wives. We had our own special reasons for keeping a low profile and in taking as few risks as possible.

Most of our trysts were in the morning as between April and October most of the men only worked until 1 p.m. and the children finished school at the same time. It was amazing how much we'd pack into a few precious hours. I'd be in work at 7 a.m. for morning "prayers", work like a one-armed paperhanger until around 9 a.m., borrow the boss's car and be at Rosemarie's by 9.30, leaving white-faced animals and motorists along my route. We'd arrive at our favourite spot in the hills by 9.45, leave at 1045 for me to be back in the office by 1115 with 2 working hours left. I would set my main meeting times at 0730 or 1130. That way I could wind up my early meetings by 9 sharp, or arrive wonderfully refreshed and as cool as a cucumber at 1100 for the later one. A couple of notable "flying visits" spring to mind. One morning at 8 a.m. I jumped out of a C-130 by parachute into the Med off Akrotiri, wrote to Rosemarie during the descent, was picked up by a launch and met her at 9 a.m. on the town bypass. Another was a rare nocturnal visit when at an Officers' Mess Dining-in Night—full Mess Kit and all the formalities—I rushed out after the speeches at 1030, was with Rose-marie by 11 p.m., left at midnight and was back in my Mess Kit playing Mess games by 0030. You had to be fit in those days! Time and place had nothing to do with the way we felt. You can't plan passion.

I've said that neither of us were looking for an affair; and had Rosemarie been looking there would have been no shortage of candidates for her affections. We were simply both taken unawares and when Cupid's arrow lodges in your heart, it doesn't come with a guilty conscience or concern for innocent injured parties. Both may come later as the realities bite, but when the madness strikes the over-riding thoughts are not for others. I have explained my own marriage elsewhere, but about Rosemarie's marriage I knew little. I saw them as a handsome and pop-ular young couple, but did not know her husband either professionally or socially. After we met, I obviously took a closer interest in him and began to hear things that concerned me. He was clearly a womaniser and not too particular about where he sowed his wild oats. When officially I was told of misconduct that endangered his security clearance, I was reluctant to mention it to Rosemarie as I wasn't sure whether she knew or whether it would be a shock. Selfishly, I feared it might at that stage cut across our flowering, albeit still innocent, rela-tionship.

When, after seven months of brief encounters and snatched cautious words on the dance floor, we were committed and had time to talk, I found how bad a marriage she had. His womanising had been well known to his colleagues and superiors. He'd been an uncaring, untrustworthy and cheating husband, not averse to raising his fist to her. After being humiliatingly forced to attend a formal Admonishment for his conduct with the Station Commander, she had decided that divorce would follow as soon as they left Cyprus. As far as her husband was concerned, therefore, neither of us had any reason to feel guilty of our affair or of the long term consequences that now appeared inevitable.

In the ensuing months, we did have one other slight encumbrance. In Octo-ber 1972 Rosemarie gave birth to Robert. We had actually had a morning meeting the day before he was born and I saw her next, slightly demented (*me* that is), 24 hours later as she recovered in Akrotiri hospital. So for the next 6 months we sometimes had a baby's cot with us on our nature travels and oddly enough it never seemed a terrible inconvenience. Now that we were so much closer, there was a price to pay. Each meeting was magic, but every social event became more painful and time spent apart or out of touch was torture. Weekends and holidays were especially bad and there were times we both took outrageous risks. But fortune smiled on us and although many must have harboured suspicions, no one was ever able to say "Gotcha".

Leaving Cyprus

The day we'd both dreaded came when Rosemarie's husband was posted back to the UK. We'd known each other for eighteen months and had been lovers for twelve. I knew that I'd remain in Cyprus for another year, so my overwhelming problem was trying to come to terms with being out of touch with her and the fear that once she was back in England, she might settle down again and commit Cyprus and me to the memory bank. That wasn't because I doubted the sincerity or depth of her love. It was simply an acceptance of the facts that she had a husband and a young family and I had a wife and 4 children. Cyprus and the UK are 2000 miles apart, but light years apart in other respects.

Life in England, on a new RAF station, would be very different, and she'd have to acclimatise and adjust to that whilst thinking of me still in the place where we'd met and fallen in love. Telephone links, only 35 years ago, were so different. Mobile phones did not exist, and even to set up an international call required an advance booking, hours of waiting, and then usually a garbled line that cost the earth for a couple of minutes. I well remember the first time I was able to do it from the office; it was like Mafeking all over again. We hardly spoke, so overjoyed to hear each other—live, if you like—and not having to look at a postmark to see how long ago the letter had been written and fret over what might have happened in-between.

How lovers managed to stay sane during wartime separations I cannot imagine. Rosemarie made contact more achievable by choosing to live in an RAF married quarter away from her husband, one close to the Wiltshire airfields into which I would fly whenever I could get a duty trip to the UK. With her husband home only at weekends, the mail was pretty safe at her end. But I had to be especially careful at mine to make sure that some well-meaning neighbour didn't take my mail home from the Mess, or my wife pick it up before me. God, the agonies we went through!

But before then we had the harrowing episode of Rosemarie leaving Cyprus. Overseas, the RAF postings system worked well. On posting, the husband would be given a specific date, time and flight number well in advance and do his "Clearance procedure" from office and home accordingly. Rosemarie and her family were booked on a VC10 flight leaving for Brize Norton at 11 a.m. on July 10th, 1973. She had to do all the things service wives did on posting—clean the house for handover, give and attend farewell parties, last minute shopping, and the drudge of packing; in the middle of which she had to make time for a guy slowly going around the bend. I simply could not face the idea of standing on our sandy beach watching her VC10 climb away into the blue morning sky. "Now the harbour light is fading, this must be our last goodbye. Though the carnival is over, I shall love you 'til I die." No way, I thought—that's asking the impossible. So, abusing my power, I concocted a meeting in London and booked myself on the same flight and in a seat immediately in front of her. During the flight, with her husband asleep, she stretched out a long brown leg to touch my elbow. I looked around surprised to see the open mouthed look of disapproval on the face of an Army colonel seated across the aisle. I glowered back "Mind your own bloody business" and he buried his head in his *Horse and Hounds* for the rest of the flight.

I knew how chaotic it would be for Rosemarie on arrival in the UK. There were Customs to be negotiated, her husband would be sorting out his hire car and trying to keep an eye on luggage accumulated in almost 5 years overseas. Rosemarie with a baby and a young daughter would be overwhelmed, and I'd be attempting to look normal when in fact I felt as if I was being torn in two. Even as her husband was beckoning to her to push through the crowd, a girl I knew well who was also leaving Cyprus for good, waylaid me keen to chat. As Rosemarie neared the exit with a look of desperation on her face, I rudely excused myself from the girl and made tracks towards Rosemarie and just had time to mouth "see you in Cardiff" before she disappeared.

Knowing there'd be no time for goodbyes, Rosemarie had promised me that 2 days later, come Hell or high water, she'd meet me at Cardiff station at 1 p.m. I arrived from London and she was there to the second, looking more lovely than ever in a pink two-piece suit as she started to run towards me, tight skirt and high heels, and literally flung herself into my arms. My cup runneth over. That meeting was so important to both of us. I never doubted how much she loved me, but now she was in a different world, back with her family with a new baby that none of them had seen, and having to acclimatise to a country so strange to which she'd been accustomed. I would have known within minutes if she'd had any second thoughts or doubts. I need not have worried. I only had about 5 hours to spend in Cardiff, but for us five hours was a lifetime. We'd often met—and were often to do so after that—for only an hour or so, with hours of travel for one or the other or both, to make our rendezvous. We had become experts in filling every second of our time together. I'd hired a car and we drove to a hilltop near to where we now live and spent a couple of hours consolidating where we were and what we wanted the future to hold in store for us. Looking back now I recall that we never argued or had differences about the things that mattered. We were then as we are now, almost like a pair of Siamese twins.

Rosemarie had arranged some sort of subterfuge with her sister to cover her day out, and I finished up dropping them both in their hometown before starting my lonely drive to Cardiff and a desolate train journey to London. But we'd negotiated that first massive hurdle of leaving Cyprus, and that night she phoned me at the RAF club in Piccadilly to joyfully tell me she'd broken the news about us to her Mum. As I flew back to a lonely empty Cyprus, I was already writing to her and eagerly anticipating the first letter that I'd receive from her in my pigeon-hole in the hallway of the Mess where I'd first seen her almost 2 years before.

Days without Rosemarie

My solution to easing the pain back on the desolate island was to throw myself into my work. When you're miserable, you cannot forget why you're miserable or ignore the pain in your guts. But work is the surest palliative, the only medicine that, taken in large and frequent doses, can bring some comfort. I should tell the reader that, even when my attention was focussed on seeing Roo as often as possible, I did not allow my work or duties to suffer. God has blessed me with boundless energy and I can truthfully say that the RAF more than recovered from me any time that, in their time, I had devoted to Rosemarie. Someone had to suffer and of course it was inevitably my wife.

I was aided in my need to be totally occupied by the escalating involvement of Cyprus-based forces in supporting the war in the Dhofar. I spent hundreds of hours in the air flying the Ankara, Teheran, Bahrain, Muscat route down to our Omani bases on Masirah Island and Salalah, which once served as the vegetable and fruit garden for The Queen of Sheba and her Sabaean people. When I reached the forward base at Salalah, I then took every opportunity to go up on the Jebel to monitor the fairly vicious fighting that was going on between the Yemenis infiltrating the border and the Sultan of Oman's forces that were strengthened by UK elements and mercenaries. It was a strange and extraordinary, often surreal, chapter in my life. I felt like a modern day Lawrence.

Whilst in Arabia I was virtually out of contact with Rosemarie, but then that wasn't much different from Cyprus because even there, strange now to relate, calls to the UK were very difficult to come by and expensive. We had the added problem that we needed "secure contact", so I didn't feel any more out of touch in the Oman than I did in Cyprus. I must have written a million words to her from desert and mountain hideouts as my affinity to that part of the world evolved. I am by no means a desert-lover as some men became, particularly those who were there with something to leave behind and forget; usually a woman or money troubles. But I understood the feeling that crept over one, especially around sundown. It was a feeling, maybe even a calling, that persuaded many to stay there for the rest of their lives, to turn their backs on whatever threatened, and often to turn their faces to Mecca at the appointed hour.

Occasionally, I'd have a legitimate or contrived meeting in the UK that meant me flying into Lyneham or Brize Norton near Swindon. Rosemarie lived at RAF Abingdon, only a short drive from either. Her husband was stationed at Doncaster and came home only at weekends, so we could arrange a few uninterrupted hours together and sometimes an unbelievably rapturous night together. We really lived on scraps of time, of which we had so little as I was always travelling on duty and thus had to fly according to the tight and infrequent RAF schedules. But such problems seemed no great hardship. If we could be together for a little while, we could recharge our batteries for lonely months apart.

It is a Puzzlement!

To derive so much pleasure from the body, mind, voice and mere presence of another is one of life's greatest gifts—if not the greatest. I could fill this book listing all the things that made me love Rosemarie then, and all the things that have led me to love her increasingly more deeply to this very day. But were I to scan in detail every year since we met, peruse every dictionary and thesaurus, and sit before a hundred glowing firesides with her at my side and a glass of cheer in our hands, I could still not explain the inexplicable. For every attribute, quality and virtue that I might identify in her and ascribe to our love for each other, there will be another ingredient that I cannot define and that I've yet to see any poet or writer able to put into words. The very qualities I try to define are those that defy definition.

Call it mysticism, black magic, witchcraft, enchantment—what you will. But it is the reason why true love is not something one can design, plan for or prepare for; neither can it be evaded, declined or ignored. It either happens or it doesn't, and when it does it is terminal. After the virus, the leaf is never the same.

A final word on my totally inadequate personal description of true love. In spite of its delights and its ecstasy, love does not consist in merely gazing at each other in wonder, love and praise. There are still disagreements, still differences, still raised voices, enragements, accusations, frustrations and discontent. Indeed perhaps arguments between lovers are more vicious than those between strangers as each knows where best to slip in the sword and probe for a weakness. To hear how Rosemarie and I tackled that problem, I invite them to read about a character called Bear in Chapter 17. But for now I state my conviction that to love deeply in one direction makes us more loving in all others; and to love truly is to be able always to then look outward together in the same direction.

Breakpoint

Looking back, some might point to 1974 as the perfect opportunity for me to have made the break and left my wife, but that conclusion would have been in ignorance of all the facts. There were too many obstacles, too many obligations that could simply not be overlooked. I had four growing children that I loved dearly and wanted to see make a good undisturbed start to their life at school and hopefully University. I had my RAF career to consider; not from a selfish ambitious point of view, but because promotion meant more money and a step towards better jobs and further promotion. I've often heard people who have been faced with and taken hard decisions say that money is unimportant compared to love, and that one can always build a new career or business. I'm sure that's often true, but I'm also aware that what is a financial disaster to one person would seem like a pretty normal situation to another.

When an Army colleague in Whitehall said he was broke and walked around half-demented, what he meant was that he might have to sell his ocean-going yacht and buy a speedboat to get him between islands on his third Caribbean holiday in 12 months. When I said I was broke, it meant I couldn't afford a chip-butty for lunch, and I'd be dreading the next letter from my bank manager in the days when that gent held the power of life and death over us all! I had no other income. No one then or since has ever given me a penny or left me anything in a Will. I've never had Great Expectations, or expectations of any sort. No one has ever sidled up to me and offered me a fortune to tell them my country's or company's secrets.

Had I divorced then, and adultery with another officer's wife was cited either by my wife or Rosemarie's husband, I would lose career, salary, and pension—the lot. Rosemarie accepted my rationale and much besides, and so even when I returned from Cyprus in 1974 and she was divorced soon after, we knew we faced a time of waiting. Many times since I have regretted not taking that major step then, or even later in 1982 when I left the RAF. But both for reasons still obvious and some lost in the mists of time, I did not and cannot now undo the past. I do know that without her in 1973 I was desolate, but of course life did go on.

Arabian nights

My frequent visits to Oman provide a number of stories made special by the location. Early in the war, we landed a Hercules on top of the Jebel on a sand strip and went to the tented camp for sustenance whilst the cargo was being unloaded. I walked out back towards the aircraft to be met by an Arab frantically waving his arms. I didn't speak a word of Arabic, but looking beyond him I saw the aircraft rocking from side to side accompanied by a horrendous noise. Puzzled and concerned for the safety of the aircraft I ran forward to find that the noise came from two camels that had been tied to the floor rings whilst their drivers had a kip. The mess was awful and the stench never left that particular aircraft.

On another occasion I was taken up to one of the Jebel outposts by Skyvan, a rugged little piston-engined machine that could operate from short unprepared strips. I'd signalled ahead that I was coming and whom I needed to talk to. Because the strip was on top of a cone shaped mountain and the surrounding peaks were occupied by the Yemenis, our approach technique was to arrive overhead at 8000ft, do a tight and rapid spiral descent to minimise exposure to small arms fire, stop, let the passengers out, dump any stores, and depart rapidly via a steep upward spiral. We stopped in a shower of sand and stones, engines screaming, as I yelled "see you at four" and ran from the Skyvan towards an arm beckoning me to a hole in the ground as the aircraft leapt back into the sky. Hearing that echoing "ping" as bullets ricochet off rock, I threw myself headlong into the black hole and arrived amongst the inhabitants, all arms and legs. My language suited my bruises and cuts, and I looked up to see the open mouthed astonishment of four combat clad men.

"Sorry guys" I panted, "I thought you'd have been used to that kind of language."

"Well, yes we are, Sir, but not from a Minister of God."

My message that Wing Commander *Palmer* was arriving had been corrupted to Wing Commander *Padre!* They thought I was a Sky Pilot.

And then one of those happenings that make you wonder if it's you that has lost the plot. Masirah Island was the UK's major staging base in The Persian Gulf through which was delivered most of the supplies for the Oman/Yemen war, either by air or by the occasional Fleet Supply Vessel. A hazard to air traffic came from dozens of donkeys that roamed the island and had a nasty habit of standing on the runway. So a donkey fence was built to keep the little blighters out. Came the day when the fence was destroyed in a storm and, in the absence of local trees, a replacement was ordered from the UK to be delivered by sea. The War Committee I ran in Cyprus kept tabs on delivery of the fence, which, due to a succession of cock-ups, was delayed for some 4 months. When it eventually arrived I wrote in the Minutes (tongue in cheek of course) that whilst the fence had been down, the donkeys had disappeared—so how did we justify the fence? Before I knew what was happening a very senior, rather elderly, officer arranged for 50 donkeys to be shipped to Masirah from Sharjah in the Gulf. I would have hated to be President of that Board of Inquiry!

If envy were fever, everyone would be ill

The last months of my Cyprus tour were soured by the attitude of my new boss who was a V-Force navigator newly promoted to Group Captain. He took exception to my reports from the Oman, a procedure I'd followed throughout the campaign, as, with the Dhofar being a war zone, visitors were not encouraged. I held fortnightly briefings on the supply situation, including my personal knowledge of what was happening and from photographs that I'd taken in profusion. He attempted to sabotage my popular briefings, and refused to accompany me to Salalah so that I could show him the ropes. Six years after I left Cyprus, and he had retired, he sent me photographs that he'd taken himself, adding, "You never went there, did that" etc. I thought he was joking and returned the photos with a note that said, "Is this all you know about the Jebel campaign? See me after school." The silly bugger actually threatened to sue me for that!

In the Arab/Israeli War of '73, Egypt's surprise air strikes had left Israel dangerously short of fighters. From our lofty vantage point on Troodos, and from radio and intelligence sources, we had a pretty accurate account of Israeli losses. Applying my Phantom background, and as the senior Air Defender, I wrote a "battle summary", the main conclusion being that Israel could survive no more than four days. If Israel were defeated, the impact on the UK's position in the Middle East could have been dramatic. My new boss strongly objected to my initiative, said he also knew all about the Phantom from his course studies, and who the hell did I think I was? I merely thought I was doing my job and was therefore quite chuffed two days later when the US 7th Fleet sailed into Cyprus waters and unloaded their entire complement of F4s to Israel! QED.

The last laugh was mine on the day the family Palmer left Cyprus. There existed a top secret Operation Order, the details of which were known to only four people on the island; the C in C, a helicopter Squadron Commander, the senior Policeman, and whoever sat in my chair as the writer and custodian of the Order. The plan was for the emergency evacuation of a very important politician. Four days before I left, I took in the updated Order to the C in C, replacing my name with that of my successor, and getting the two signatures required. My new boss, who was not privy to the content, said something about a last fling and smirked when he overheard the C in C say as he signed, "I don't expect we'll be needing that in a hurry." History records that days later a certain Archbishop was snatched from Nicosia by helicopter and transferred to the safety of the British Sovereign base area.

I've been critical of someone that I haven't given a moment's thought to in 30 years. Perhaps I rubbed him up the wrong way, maybe I wasn't his type or he supported Arsenal? But I found it sad to be criticised for attempting to do a job that I'd been doing well, by someone who didn't know me. Oddly enough, it has brought to mind something that I noted often in my working life; namely the attitude of many people once the word was out that you were on your way. Somehow you ceased to be of importance, to have any say or to make any further contribution. Or maybe it's me, eh?

So in 1974 it was back to Blighty, to cold wet and windy Lincolnshire, and to Rosemarie. I bade a fond farewell to our beautiful island. Since then, Rosemarie and I go back whenever we're able to scrape together the airfare. It's our second home, Cyprus the magical isle.

Postscript

Forgive me, folks, if, in 2003, I confuse your train of thought by adding this postscript to the Cyprus chapter. Roo and I have come back on a holiday that I never thought would happen. We're on our favourite beach that looks exactly as it did two years ago, 20 years ago and probably as it did 200 and 2000 years ago. We're sitting on a rocky shoreline looking east along a line of cliffs and headlands stretching some 10 miles into the morning haze. At 10 a.m., 88 degrees and 8% humidity, we haven't seen a single soul since we left the main road three miles away at 8 a.m. I remind myself that this is what relaxing is all about, putting behind you those things that cause the worry and stress, and being part of nature rather than part of the rat race.

The problem with the rat race is that it's hard to give up, like being on a tread-mill that encourages you to go faster and further until you burn out and lose interest in life. Last night we met a couple of old friends in Paphos who had taken the plunge; sold up in England and chosen the simple life. They've found their special island and I've no doubt they'll live out their days here. They told us that they went back to Sussex briefly and were astonished and frightened by the aggression that has become part of everyday life in England. In Cyprus the roads are dangerous because, technically, the Cypriots are lousy drivers. In the UK the roads are dangerous because so many people drive aggressively and without care for other road users. They noticed how often they heard the F-word and we noted that we'd not heard it once in the last 14 days. In Cyprus there is little crime or vandalism and the towns and villages are kept neat and tidy in sharp contrast to the UK, which is now Europe's biggest rubbish dump.

As always there's a downside. The "ex-pats" bemoan the rise in the cost of living, the deteriorating exchange rate, effects on UK pensions and property prices. Many, like our friends last night, still see the good far outweighing the bad, but many that have been here for a long time have become bitter. There always was an element in the military and civil service overseas that treated the locals as distinctly inferior and therefore kept strictly to their tight communities and national cliques. That age, which I suppose was linked with "The Raj" in India, the tea planters in Malaya, the farmers in Kenya and the white dwellers of colonial Hong Kong, was snobocracy at its worst. A social round of Bridge, cocktail parties, Band Concerts and White Mischief all behind a façade of excessive courtesy, gentleness and good manners. Now that the locals are doing their own thing and becoming affluent beyond their wildest dreams, the ex-pats are bemoaning their loss of influence and authority.

I once had an active dislike of such folk and such behaviour, but now my predominant feeling is one of pity for they are certainly the most boring people on earth with lives full of senseless chatter, forced laughter, daily doses of the bloody Archers, and the overseas service of the BBC. Terribly English, with their past lives stamped on their faces, they usually sit in a chill silence eating stonily at dinner. Army, RAF, civil servants; there aren't too many of them left and as they fade away I fear I shan't be all that far behind. But come what may, I do not intend to let those thoughts detract me for one second from enjoying this heavenly sun-kissed beach and the already copper coloured vision at my side.

Where were we? Oh yes, back to Lincolnshire. What a contrast!

10

BACK TO FLYING

The College of Knowledge

In 1974 I swapped the sun-baked cliffs of Cyprus for the flat featureless windy plains of Lincolnshire to attend the RAF Air Warfare College at Cranwell. After WW2, a career officer might be selected for a number of Staff courses designed to fit him for further promotion or to hold a particular post. Such courses were additional to the specialist courses related to one's category or trade. For instance, all aircrew would undergo an Operational Conversion Course (OCU) on the appropriate aircraft before joining a front line squadron, or a pilot might specialise and become a Test Pilot, and a navigator become an Aero Systems graduate to fill a more technical research and development post.

For staff training, the first course as a Flying Officer/Flight Lieutenant was the OATS (Officers Advanced Training School) course; as a Squadron Leader/Wing Commander you went to Staff College, and as a Wing Commander/Group Captain it was the Flying College Course that became the Air Warfare College in 1974. Later you might attend The Royal College for Defence Studies (RCDS) where your fellow students would be drawn from all services, as well as from the Government, industry and foreign sources.

Most of those courses have now disappeared or been combined and amalgamated with similar courses from the other services. But at the height of the Cold War the most sought after course for General Duties (aircrew) officers was the Air Warfare Course. The course with only 18 students was focussed on Operational matters rather than Staff work, and was socially superb. As with Staff College, the interchange between students was a key ingredient with every RAF operational role represented, plus one officer from each of the Royal Navy, Army, USAF or USN, RAAF or RNZAF, Canadian forces, and one RAF Ground Trade, either an Engineer, Fighter Controller, or Equipment officer. I was looking forward to it immensely, and to the posting at the end of it that was guaranteed to be a good one.

I've said I enjoy the academic environment. Cranwell had it all with splendid working accommodation, a fully equipped Lecture auditorium and the RAF College library. The main Mess was a beautifully located 1920's building, with elegant internal decoration, and a Mess staff of mainly old seasoned retainers who gave the place a special charm, not to mention a level of service seldom found elsewhere. The post-war grandeur and ambience of an RAF Officers' Mess had begun to decline in the 60's, and Cranwell was among the last bastion of the forces of civilisation, a bygone age that only lasted half a century. Even so, it wasn't everyone's cup of tea but it suited me perfectly, especially as I was also able to have the family resident on base. The children suffered a little in that they were only going to be in the local schools for 6 months, but eldest daughter Cherrie was off to Bristol University to study law so we had one less to worry about.

Occasionally I find myself acutely conscious of the atmosphere of a building or a particular room that I once knew. Cranwell is one such recollection—more specifically—the College library, the College dining hall on a great occasion, and the Lecture Hall of the AWC named after a famous and popular old boy, Air Chief Marshal Sir Augustus Walker; "Gus" to everyone. Mentioning him makes me wonder what was so charismatic about many of those old guys; why do we look back and believe that we shall never see their like again? Is it perhaps that they came back from WW2 loaded with medals to bask in the glory of what they did as young daredevils cum heroes, or are we fooling ourselves and seeing only what we want to see? The popular TV conception of the typical wartime RAF officer is a lean six-footer with a cultured accent and the obligatory moustache. They are usually pretty toffee-nosed, have an eye for the ladies, and turn out to be some sort of cad or bounder whose sole aim in life is to nick the family jewels or someone else's wife—whom he then ditches when he's got her dosh.

Well, I was in the RAF when all those types were around and I don't remember a single senior officer who acted like the TV archetype. Of course the war heroes nearly all faded away in the 50's and 60's, leaving us with a very different sort of leader at our helm. We moved into an era where the high ranks were full of the great thinkers and planners, rather than the operational doers and men who would be the natural leaders in times of war. Between 1965 and 1990 I can think of only three Chiefs of the Air Staff who would have attained that position had there been a ballot; most of us, I suspect, would only have followed the others out of sheer curiosity. A few were, to put it bluntly, miserable sods who seldom stood up to the politicians when it mattered, who would never have resigned out of principle, and who were still protecting their six o'clock when they retired to treble their pensions as non-executive figureheads of leading defence companies.

The good guys, real leaders combining operational nous with the human approach, often ended their careers at two or three star level just missing the top jobs they deserved. Of course they were rewarded handsomely; most received knighthoods, and they could regard themselves as enormously successful in their chosen career. All the same, I'll wager that many who fell one or two fences short will, if they write their autobiographies and are honest, record their disappointment and indignation at having been usurped by a less capable man. I didn't mean to bang on about that because it sounds as if I'm bitter about my own career and promotion limits, but nothing could be further from the truth. I was promoted to my level of competence judged on my performance. I believe I had the talent and overall capability to have risen a couple of ranks higher had I managed the rest of my life in a different way. But I didn't because other things took pride of place at crucial times in my career, and looking back I wouldn't exchange what I've had for the privilege of reaching two star level. If the reader doubts my sincerity, I ask him to remember that I promised to tell it as it was. The laddie's not for turning.

In 1946 I'd started my RAF life at the foot of the ladder at Cranwell. Thirty years on I was back, but at the top and delighted to find the course memorable for a number of reasons. Pride of place must go to receiving the OBE "gong" from Her Majesty the Queen at Buckingham Palace in the presence of a doting mum and proud family. Then a treat that came from a unique mix of coming home after three years in Cyprus, being free at weekends, and having a family that were Manchester United and Belle Vue speedway mad. We travelled to almost every home and away match that season and were rewarded by United winning the league and Belle Vue's captain becoming world champion.

In the lecture hall, I was particularly obnoxious to the RAF's Operational Requirements supremo when he informed the Course of the Air Force Department's decision to go ahead with development of the AEW Nimrod, but with a very limited overland capability. I mention that incident because Nimrod AEW was to play a huge role in my life later. The *piece de résistance* was my end of course posting to fly the Buccaneer, the aircraft you'll recall that gave me so much grief in my first OR post. Talk about chickens coming home to roost! Someone had a great sense of humour.

It seems odd to look back now and recall that, having got such a plum posting, I was almost a nervous wreck by the time I went to the Aviation Medical school to get my personalised flying kit for the Buccaneer. The problem, you see, was that not only am I six foot three and a quarter inches tall, but I have a thigh length of over twenty-seven inches. Before you accuse me of boasting, allow me to point out that the maximum thigh length permissible for the ejection seat of the Buccaneer was twenty-five inches, and I knew that the Aviation Medicine doctor would note the problem as soon as I sat in the bloody seat. He did and said, "Ah, we seem to have a problem Wing Commander." "I won't tell if you won't," said I. He stroked his chin as doctors often do and said, "Well, you'll look awfully silly walking around without any knee caps, but I see you've ejected before so perhaps the law of averages will come to your aid." I arrived at Honington determined to get in shape to play rugby and soccer that season—just in case.

The big drawback during my series of courses, due to the tight programme and the many nights we spent away, was finding time to see Rosemarie. For the sake of the children, she'd moved to join her husband who was stationed near Doncaster. After a few weeks, she realised she couldn't live under the same roof and went to live near Grimsby. We were in adjacent counties, but finding the free time and availability of transport was a major headache. Nevertheless, we made it and had some truly wonderful reunions that usually ended with me legging it to catch the last train at night. I can remember running like a maniac in the pouring rain and fog of a Lincolnshire night as the train approached, and slumping down in my seat with passengers wondering what crime I'd committed. Rosemarie was worth every discomfort and inconvenience—I'd have cheerfully walked back to Doncaster had there not been a train. See what I mean about looking at the big picture and not worrying overly about the incidentals? Anyway, I finished all my courses to retread me for flying and set off gleefully for the Buccaneer base at Honington in Suffolk.

The Honington Buccaneer Wing

There is no gainsaying the enormous pleasure and satisfaction to be derived from running a busy operational low-level strike/attack station in the 1970's. I must be careful not to go over the top in my enthusiasm, but I have the benefit of 56 years of working experience to back me up. To have some 1200 men and women all working together with a common aim and dedication to do a well-defined and important task in a particular way, without the backbiting subterfuge and politicking that typified work in industry and the Ministry—that was some achievement. First then, it might help to say a wee bit about the aircraft and its role before taking a closer look at my experiences.

In spite of the RAF's initial rejection of the Buccaneer, the OR staff and the guys responsible for its eventual introduction to squadron service, had done what the RAF is well used to doing and is rightly renowned for; they had made a silk purse out of a sow's ear. Blackburn Aircraft, based at Brough near Hull, had built the Buccaneer to operate in the extremely demanding Carrier environment, off catapults, short decks, heavy landings and staying on deck in all weathers. For maintenance purposes it had to be "lifted" below decks, which incurred the extra design penalty of folding the wings.

The Buccaneer, like all British built aircraft, was too long in the pipeline from think tank to squadron pilot, and by the time it reached Navy service it was already outdated, both aerodynamically and as a weapons system. In fact, it didn't really have a system, more a number of separate aids that an experienced crew would optimise for the specific purpose and circumstances. Nevertheless, the Mk2 version, much improved over the Navy's original underpowered Mk1, fortuitously met a special need at the time, referred to in my AEW writings. Namely, it could be flown very safely and comfortably, very low, and quite fast at a time when surface or airborne radar could not detect aircraft down in the weeds.

The RAF used the Buccaneer in two distinct roles. One was its intended role in the Navy of offensive action against maritime threats to the Carrier and accompanying ships; the other the standard RAF role against land-based targets requiring deep overland penetration. The tactics were significantly different, the maritime role usually involving co-ordinated attacks by a formation of up to nine aircraft, the overland role being mainly nuclear using pairs or fours of aircraft. Both roles, operated by separate squadrons, were exciting and demanding, and it would have been hard to find a more professional and dedicated bunch of aircrew anywhere. All the RAF Buccaneers were based at Honington including the OCU. It was a wonderfully exciting and challenging job for me and I settled down to my conversion with relish.

The Palmer sprogs at Old Trafford—1975

A Personal Dilemma

Have you ever noticed how something you anticipate from afar, which seems attractive and in which you feel that success and satisfaction are assured, suddenly looks quite a different prospect when you meet it face to face? Things always turn out differently than anticipated; sometimes for the worse, sometimes for the better, but almost always differently. The Honington posting was to give me unforeseen headaches and for some quite unexpected reasons. Read on.

I'd enjoyed my Staff tours, however, like any aviator I was always keen to fly. That was my reason for being in the RAF; that's what I enjoyed doing most and was paid extra to do. In my annual assessments, I always put down flying as my first preference, ideally in a Command role and on an Operational outfit. When my Honington posting had come through I was therefore exultant and went through my "retreading" flying course and other related courses with enthusiasm.

I arrived at Honington to take over from an old acquaintance, impatient for him to hand over the keys and depart. Meanwhile I started my abbreviated conversion to the Buccaneer with a mix of ground school, simulator and flying, along with moving into our ex-officio married quarter. I was literally champing at the bit to start in earnest.

The first snag was all to do with me. I had last flown operationally ten years earlier at the age of 34, since when I'd been in constant contact with aeroplanes and the way they were operated; but those posts had been a mix of all sorts with flying not my primary function. As any professional aviator will tell you, that isn't the same as being on a front line squadron, or being a flying instructor, and flying the same aircraft on a regular basis and often to its limits. Furthermore, neither the Buccaneer nor the low-level strike/attack role were familiar to me. I'd been on fighters from Day One; a wholly different culture as you might imagine. My Canberra experience had not been in an operational role.

So here was I, a very rusty airman indeed, flying a new aircraft in a new role, and trying to do that in competition with a bunch of extremely professional, bright and cocky guys 20 years younger than me. Professional pride was very important. I wanted to prove myself again after years of being on the ground, and by proving I mean that I wanted to have the respect of all the crews so that when I flew with them I was flying as part of a competent team and not as a hanger on. I remembered with remorse how I'd behaved as a flight lieutenant when senior officers spent a short time of familiarisation on my flying unit before taking up their Air Staff post. How I'd been so bloody sure that I was the greatest ever to strap myself into a cockpit, and been a cruel sod who laughed at how long it took an old chap to strap in, prepare to taxi, and then taxi to the runway as if he was hoping a snag might occur to excuse him from taking off. I would be critical of his RT procedures because they sounded more like "Tally Ho, nail the bastard" rather than the clipped professional communication style we used.

Keeping older aviators up to speed in the RAF was a phase that didn't last long. It became clear by the mid-1950's that aircraft technology and performance were advancing far too quickly for those who had been out of the cockpit for years to keep up. It wasn't simply a case of embarrassing them, but of killing them. Even an uncomplicated aircraft can be a killer when things go wrong, when weather turns from blue skies to low cloud and poor visibility, and lack of practice has dulled a pilot's natural sharp instincts. I recall a Friday evening in 1953 in Germany when Station Commanders from the many RAF bases were converging on Wahn near Cologne for a Command Guest Night. What better way for the boss of an operational station to arrive than in one of his squadron's latest fighters? On that fateful wet and gloomy German evening, no fewer than three highly regarded experienced pilots were destined never to see another Guest Night.

My post at Honington was a flying post, but with the complication that, as I was going to be the Operational Executive on that station, I'd be scrounging rides in the Squadron or OCU aircraft whenever I could. Everyone was extremely helpful and friendly, no one took the Mickey, and the course went well even if it did mean burning the midnight oil more than I'd ever done in my life. I managed that first hurdle with a mixture of relief and intense satisfaction, but now I was confronted with another that involved a conflict of interest, with repercussions that raised a number of important principles for me and led me to sticking my head above the parapet.

It was the dilemma faced by many senior officers in my position to which I've alluded, a conflict between manhood and safety. In a nutshell, did I concentrate on being seen as a capable member of the aircrew fraternity, or, concentrate on fulfilling my primary role as the guy responsible for ensuring that if war came, the entire station would be able to do the job for which it had been established, trained and equipped. In the case of Honington, that was the planned and timely delivery of weapons of mass destruction, to planned primary or alternative targets.

To be sure of doing that, the entire station had to be geared to a war footing including ground defence to protect the aircraft and facilities. The capability to perform the war mission was tested by no-notice exercises when a large team would descend at any time, any day of the year, to carry out a Tactical Evaluation. Every aspect of the station's preparedness for war and its ability to perform its operational task was tested, including the launch and turnaround of all aircraft with assessments of navigation, timing and bombing accuracy made via various bombing ranges. To fail Taceval was the kiss of death for those deemed responsible; the chief fall guy was invariably the man who sat in my chair.

I may well have been better able to manage my own flying as well as the operational supremo task, and to satisfy both Strike Command and myself, had I been the boss on a Fighter station. First I would have been in a familiar role, and secondly I could have flown more in that role without nearly so much time devoted to pre and post flight planning/debriefing and to the mission itself. In the fighter world the standard sortie time was around 1hour 15 minutes. Allowing an hour to brief and kit-up, and an hour after to debrief and dress, you could start at 0800 and be back in the office by 1130. In the Buccaneer world an 0800 start would get you walking to the aircraft at 1030, airborne by 1050, back by 1315 and in the office by 1530; assuming you had no delays or problems. In other words, one relatively short Buccaneer sortie meant a whole day out of the office. For guys on the V-Force or Nimrods, the airborne times would be between 6 and 10 hours, so for one day out of the office they'd pick up a lot more flying hours.

I had no doubt as to how I'd be judged. If I failed in my primary task of having the station at a constant readiness for war, no one would thank me for it. So I ran a bloody good station; ensuring that if the balloon went up when I or any of the key executives were off base it would still operate like clockwork, and I flew as often as I could in whatever role the flying units could offer me.

However, having achieved my own professional compromise, I was to put my head above the parapet when, some months into the job, I was asked to write a letter of support for the chap I'd succeeded. Unknown to me he'd received a very poor and damning final report from his Station Commander, since promoted to be a very senior officer at the HQ under which he served. The adverse report was based on a combination of a poor Taceval result and having flown too little. Even though he'd been a Vulcan guy with similar role experience, he'd fallen between the two stools, embarrassed his station commander, and was now being bullied with his career prospects in tatters.

My letter outlining my own experience of settling into the post went down like a lead balloon with said senior officer. But after some early trepidation, I was prepared to back it up as he had left so much bitterness behind him when he'd left some months before I arrived. He was of a type, fairly rare but still too many, that expected everyone else to be as sharp as they thought they themselves to be. They tended to gather a small bunch of adoring cronies around them and treated everyone else with contempt. I had no doubt as to the competence in the air of these prima donnas—they were very capable aviators. But they were only good at managing people who were like them; they could not instil confidence in lesser mortals and the effect they had on so many others not so gifted was often disastrous. They had many a career, and even the occasional life, to answer for. I was always wary when our paths crossed in later years.

I was fortunate that during my tenure, my boss was a charming laid-back David Niven type of guy obviously hand-picked to restore morale and repair the badly dented relationships with the local landowners. He got on with looking after the wider interests of a busy station and left me to run the operational aspects. When he flew, he flew one of our twin seat Hunters and kept away from the Buccaneer. Between us, and with the wisdom and help of a trusty old kipper fleet navigator as OC Administrative Wing, we made Honington a happy place again as well as gaining top credits in the Tacevals.

Hearts and minds

An example of the importance of our relations with the local Suffolk populace occurred one beautiful balmy Friday evening in that incredibly warm and dry summer of 1976. In addition to our own squadrons, we hosted the one surviving RN Buccaneer squadron when they were not embarked on Ark Royal or Illustrious. Whilst on shore, they practiced deck landings on a small section of our runway marked out like a carrier deck complete with arrester wires. This system, called MADLS (Mirror Assisted Deck Landing System), gave us some operating problems. The system required the aircraft to fly a fairly precise circuit pattern around the deck that was a much tighter and lower pattern than would be used for normal airfield operations. This meant an aircraft landing, overshooting, going round again, and returning to land and overshoot for perhaps thirty minutes. With maybe three Buccaneers in the pattern at any time, all constantly changing their engine power and configurations, the locals were driven scatty by the noise. The problem was exacerbated because we couldn't mix Navy practice with the normal daytime flying, so MADLS was usually done at the end of day flying.

On this occasion, I received a call in my house at around 6 p.m. from a very irate but terribly superior lady who was "Trying to have a Cocktail Party before dinner in our garden, Wing Commander, and can't hear each other talk because of your bloody aeroplanes!" Scenting a chance to improve local relations, I invited myself to the cocktail party and took a two-way radio set to the "Local" channel. Arriving at a most imposing mansion, and recognising a few famous public faces, I encouraged the hostess to talk to the pilots herself and tell them how to adjust their overshoots, circuits and engine power to minimise the noise. Of course it worked like a treat. The Navy crews were invited to come as they were and join the party, the local politician got his name in the press by calling the Buccaneers "the sound of freedom", and I joined a social set that really knew how to rough it in the Suffolk countryside!

Apart from the daily buzz that one got from being at the sharp end of operations, being the boss of an airfield with *carte blanche* to travel anywhere on it at anytime had other distinct advantages. Elsewhere I've recounted tales of my Afghan Hound and his exploits chasing hare and pheasant on the airfield. I also had unique access to the largest and most prolific mushroom patch in the area; early mornings full of magic, first sightings in the low grass and the touch and the smell of a perfect cold white dewy mushroom. However, I was soon put in my place by the Station Warrant Officer who tactfully but firmly told me, "Mush-

room picking on the airfield was allocated long before you arrived—Sir." I didn't
of course want to change the natural order of things, so I made do with a bag of
fresh mushrooms being left on my doorstep every morning. Well, it saved me
getting my feet wet, eh?

After Dark

Honington in those days never closed and so I spent a lot of time on the airfield
or in the vicinity at night. I explained how I loved the dark as a boy and that continued in my flying career when I spent some eight years on night fighters, until
they were equipped with the various electronic aids and instruments to be called
"all-weather fighters". We called them "night fighters" because they were fitted
with airborne interception radar that helped you find aircraft in the dark that carried no lights and didn't wish to be seen. The radar took you close enough to get
a "visual", to see the shape and silhouette of the other aircraft to decide if it were
friend or foe, and what to do if it were the latter. In those days there were specialist "Day fighters" that were ill equipped to operate in the dark, leaving the night
fighting to those who were equipped and trained to do that role. Depending on
the time of year, you flew most nights starting about one hour after sunset and
often landing around dawn. The hours were somewhat anti-social, the children
always woke you up on their noisy departure for school, and sleep was hard to
come by as everyone lived adjoining the airfield on which flying continued during the day. Nevertheless, those were enjoyable tours of duty and I always had a
preference for night flying or, later on, for flying in adverse weather on instruments. To me it was more challenging, there was more professional satisfaction to
be gained, and more often than not you went back to the mess for a drink or
breakfast feeling you'd earned your flying pay.

Apart from the flying itself, I found the atmosphere in the crew room or on
the airfield so much more exciting at night. A fighter airfield in the 50's and 60's
was a very busy place, just as was Honington when I would spend hours out by
the runway and around the dispersals watching aircraft being turned round, taxiing, taking off and landing. Anyone who has done that job will know how for
two to three years one is so obsessed and so intimately involved with the flying
heart of an operational base that there's little time for anything else. When it ends
it's a relief in a way, but for a long time you miss the thrill and excitement of
commitment and satisfaction that goes with the job. I found myself identifying
with the Battle of Britain pilots and heavy bomber crews of WW2 who went
through the same routine day after day and night after night. And when it came
to an end, you almost wished you were starting again, just to be able to do it bet-

ter than the first time, because now you knew so much more about the job—but chiefly about yourself.

Being on an RAF station usually meant being in the middle of nowhere, whether it was Suffolk or Scotland. That also meant that the surrounding area was virtually deserted and one could ramble cross-country at dead of night without ever meeting a soul. Many will recognise the way that one's senses of sight, sound, touch and smell are engendered by solitude, and even accentuated in the dark. You learn your bushcraft skills, about the art of concealment, of moving swiftly but silently; you are aware of changes in the direction of the wind, you discern and distinguish between the noises made by the wildlife and the natural movements at night in the woods and the fields. Knowledge of nature and the land is a respectful and a deep, almost possessive love.

I'm not a great walker, although I could be called a "loner" I suppose. But I was invariably accompanied on my night walking by one of my greatest friends, one with four legs and a positive hunger for being out in the dark with me. Sometimes it would simply be a stretch around the married quarters or across the airfield if it was closed to flying, but often it would be through the local fields and woods. In Manby days my companion was a Springer Spaniel, later in Berkshire a faithful mongrel, at Cranwell a Labrador, and later two Afghan Hounds over a 20-year period. As a boy in the war, I ran and leaped through the open fields of Cheshire with a crazy Saluki called Tattybogle who belonged to a loveable old lady; my folks being unable to afford a dog in those carefree young days of mine.

Oh, what times we had, what fun we shared! "Those little ghosts that trot behind us, venturing from the past…" I think of them all so often, I miss them all so much, and I recall with stabs of pain and conscience those times when I didn't treat them as they deserved to be treated. Perhaps the final lines of that poem will come to pass one day and make me very happy: "Will in some glittering corner find me, and know it's Heaven at last…" Of course, they were all different characters as are all the dogs that own us humans. Rusty the Springer was a bundle of energy, rooting in every hedgerow and ditch, chasing anything that moved, and a dab hand at nicking meat off the butcher's van that came around on a Saturday morning. Another Rusty, the mongrel, was a tearaway that waged a personal war against cats and newspaper boys. I was then commuting daily to London and on at least three occasions had settled down on the train to read my *Telegraph* only to be joined by an excitable mutt that spent the rest of the day in my office in Whitehall.

Dodger was a golden Labrador, the sort that pinches toilet rolls and is picked from a litter by one's youngest daughter—who never takes him for "walkies" once he's no longer a puppy. I know, with a pang deep in my heart, that I treated him roughly at times. He was a loveable little ball of flesh and muscle but was so naughty that he caught the brunt of my tongue and my flat hand on his ample posterior. We once put him in the servant's room because he was too destructive to be left to roam the house alone. When we returned that night, he had literally eaten his way out of the room through a very solid door. He was also a wanderer who, given a sniff of freedom, would be off like a woolly bunny and come home disgustingly filthy and smelly. Rosemarie told me that she had one like that when she lived in Lincoln. "Sandy" was well known by all the farmers within a five-mile radius of Scampton, and having lost him she would make the rounds hoping that he hadn't met the fate that many of the farmers said they would mete out if he ever showed his face again. I've no doubt that Sandy owed his longevity more to Rosemarie's looks than to his cuteness.

But back to Dodger and our walks together through the fields and woods of Suffolk. I say "together" but it wasn't like that. We'd set out together, whether on foot or in the car, but then he'd be off like a train and as I walked he would operate out of sight and hearing in a sine wave pattern around me. Every few minutes he'd appear briefly at breakneck speed across my path and disappear on the other side. Sometimes he'd actually brush my legs at speed and my cry of "bloody dog" would awaken half of Suffolk. But he was my pal and however badly I treated him he came back for more, to look at me with big brown adoring eyes and to lick me to death. One day his wanderlust took him under the wheels of one of our refuelling bowsers and I cried for a week at having lost as trusty a friend as a man could have.

It was through losing Dodger and trying to replace him that I became a devotee of that beautiful canine aristocrat, the Afghan Hound. The family were so upset at losing Dodger that we embarked on a tour of all the kennels in the eastern counties to find his double. Of course we couldn't, even though we saw Labradors of all ages, colours and sizes. At one kennel we visited I saw this long lean half-starved Afghan who looked as if he were waiting for the man with the box to arrive. I didn't say anything because I didn't want to be disloyal to Dodger. But one night after a week of fruitless searching I happened to say I'd liked the Afghan. "So did I!" the kids chorused, and we realised we'd all wanted the Afghan, but thought it would be letting the side down. I phoned the kennels and later that night we had an Afghan, one Khazir of Arouka that we promptly abbreviated to "Khaz". It took about a month of TLC by the entire family before Khaz was fit enough to join me on my nightime sorties. I was soon to learn that he was a totally different companion to Dodger. If I took him on the airfield,

Khaz would not only raise and chase hares, he'd catch them by surprising them with his lightning fast acceleration and then panicking them to evade by using fighter pilot tactics to tighten his curve of pursuit until he caught them in mid leap as their strength waned. About the only way Dodger would have caught a hare would be for the furry ones to die laughing at him trying to keep up!

At night, the Afghan was different again. When I let Khaz or his successor Saxon, off the lead, they would streak away out of my sight and hearing until, having established their independence, they would return like rockets to run around me in ever decreasing circles. Initially I was wary of letting Khaz free, as he was an expert in rounding up sheep. On one holiday in Wales, he stampeded an entire herd of cattle from halfway up a mountain to the river in the valley. At that moment, I could have cheerfully killed him, but it gave me such a thrill to watch him at speed with his jinking run as he evaded the flying hooves of horses and cattle, as well as me and a highly irate farmer. I lost Khaz abruptly when one day he literally seized up in our front room, unable to move. The vet came at once and said she could keep him alive for a few months, but his walking days were over and she recommended putting him to sleep. I lay at his side watching his life go out of my reach. The suddenness was awful; the fleetness of his run, the pride in his eyes and the elegance of my spectacular hound have stayed close to me ever since.

Saxon, who took me over in 1987, never enjoyed the benefit of an airfield or the miles of open countryside around one. He arrived when we moved to Sussex, but what looks there like open countryside all belongs to someone, usually a someone that builds fences and gates and discourages use of his land by man or beast. My best walks there were in the National Trust wood that ran for some 4 miles along the South Downs. Saxon's favourite stunt was to accompany me deep into the wood and then suddenly turn and hurtle back towards his house. If I didn't follow, he'd eventually come back. I was to be very grateful for that one night when we'd gone out after an unusually heavy fall of snow up on the ridge. He left me as if shot from a gun to follow the winding path down through the woods. I decided to be a clever sod and surprise him by cutting him off at the bottom of the hill. I set off across the snow but the combination of slope and ice caused me to fall and I slid out of control, falling over a 10-foot high ledge and coming to very solid earth about half way down the hill. I lay with all the breath knocked out of me, afraid I was going to die. Then, as feeling returned, I wished I had, as my 60-year-old bones began to tell me that they objected to being propelled through the air. As I lay literally seeing stars, I felt a hot breath and a silky tongue on my forehead as he lay down beside me and waited until I recovered.

He never moved more than an inch from my side. Not long before the poor lad died as Afghans do around 10 or 11, I noticed a difference to his normal routine of nocturnal strolls. Instead of crossing the old road into the woods, he'd nip around the side of the house where we had a half-acre field bordering a small thicket by a streambed. There were lots of trees and bushes down there, pitch dark and easy to fall; so not being a believer in the use of the electric torch by night I would let him roam and he'd return after half an hour or so. One moonlit night, however, my curiosity got the better of me and I crept furtively along the stream bank until I could view the thicket. There, frolicking in the grass, was Saxon with a family of foxes. He played with the cubs as if they were his pups and even when on his last legs he seldom missed his nightly playtime visit.

Those two beloved Afghans were my friends and companions for over 20 years. I cannot begin to say what they meant to me and my nights were never the same without their shadowy presence. I still ache for them and hope they loved me and enjoyed being with me in return. The pleasure I found in their company is engraved in gold on my heart.

So the darkness has always been my friend and I yearn for a night under the stars of heaven undimmed by the lights of earth, whether on a Cyprus beach, on the high plateau of Arizona, or beneath the stupendous soaring cliffs of Kauai. But even if the setting cannot be exotic, warm and spectacular, I should be content to be in Britain that boasts the most beautiful countryside that this world has to offer. I'd happily settle for the cold hills of Scotland, a night on a Welsh mountain where one can reach out and touch the darkness, or the misty wet fields of Suffolk where all of one's senses become razor sharp as you melt into the blackness and become one with all earthly things and the music of the night. The darkness, too, for obvious reasons, was a friend to Rosemarie and I as we often sought to be together away from prying eyes. I've covered that story elsewhere, but I'd be surprised if one or two reading these pages were not to find a tingle somewhere inside to remind him or her of the thrill and loving comfort of a secret rendezvous in the folds of the night.

> *"So we'll go no more a-roving, so late into the night*
> *Though the heart be still as loving, and the moon be still as bright.*
>
> *For the sword outwears its sheath, and the soul wears out the breast*
> *And the heart must pause for breath, and love itself have rest.*
>
> *Though the night was made for loving, and the day returns too soon.*
> *Yet no more shall we go a-roving by the light of the silvery moon."*

Human nature?

I've probably confused you by digressing to tales of the night and our canine friends, so let me return to my Honington days. Life teaches you that you're never too old to learn, even though you can still be surprised. I certainly had an enlightening but disturbing experience at Honington, which was accentuated during a "Disaster Management Course" that I attended some months later. We are all guilty perhaps of turning a blind eye or a deaf ear to a problem we don't wish to face, and built into us all I suspect there is a safety valve that prevents us taking a line of thought or fear that we could not withstand. Whatever, I was dismayed and shocked by my experience one morning in an English pine forest.

It started during my morning round of the airfield when I talked to my officers and airmen at their workplace to ensure they knew the value of their contribution to the operational well being of the station. There was an ethos on an RAF station, as on a Naval vessel, that I never found later in industry. This particular morning I'd stopped to chat to two airmen mending a hole in the perimeter fence. I had half an eye on a pair of Buccaneers that had joined downwind and were turning "finals" to land. As the lead aircraft flared out and smacked down hard into the concrete, I sensed that No 2 was in difficulties. He'd overcooked the turn, lost height and was now in an irrecoverable situation. Sure enough, as the nose dipped, the canopy flew off and the two occupants ejected seconds before the Buccaneer hit the pine forest in a sheet of flame.

I headed towards the fire and shot through the gap in the fence into the forest, telling the tower on my radio where I was. I raced down a firebreak and immediately saw one of the crew staggering away from the flames. I asked him if he was okay and about the other crewmember; he wasn't really listening so I told him to sit in the car and talk to the tower. I hadn't seen the crew actually land, but both chutes had deployed when they were very low, and they'd ejected sideways (rather than vertically) so I wasn't sure what I'd find past the conflagration. Some 30 yards from the aircraft I found the pilot hanging four feet from the ground with his 'chute caught in the trees. He told me where he was hurting. I undid his harness and lowered him slowly to the ground and then carefully yet quickly helped him away from the flames to sit by a tree. I knew he'd broken one arm and almost certainly a leg, but he could have had other injuries. Both crewmembers needed urgent attention and I rushed back to the radio. The Buccaneer of course and a few dozen trees were beyond help.

The navigator in my car had passed out. I needed help quickly and asked the tower where the ambulance and fire engines were. Neither could access the woods to the crash site from the airfield and were coming via the main road, a journey of some 3 miles. The fire crew called to ask which path they should take once in the forest and I gave them directions as best I could. I gave the tower more details, saw the fire engine approaching, and went back to the pilot who by this time had also passed out. There was nothing I could do to help him medically, so ran around the fire to see if the ambulance had arrived. The sight that met my eyes was unbelievable! The fire engine was pouring water on the trees, but there was no sight of the ambulance. However, the forest path was totally blocked with private cars and vans that took no notice as I tried to make them clear a path for the ambulance. I saw one man trying to put a piece of the Buccaneer's tail in his car, and I was told to Foxtrot Oscar by another who was carrying away the pilot's discarded helmet. I called the tower to ask about the ambulance and they confirmed he could not get into the wood because of parked up vehicles. I told them to call in a helicopter urgently to evacuate the crew, whose injuries were still undetermined.

Whilst I was calling the tower, there were men trying to talk to the semi-conscious navigator and pulling at his flying suit. They stole everything removable in the car including my hat and only withdrew when a formidable lady brandishing a spanner declared herself to be a nurse and sat in the car. I found the pilot being pulled at by another two idiots, who were apprehended by the fire crew I'm pleased to say. The chopper arrived to evacuate the crew, a guard was posted on the site, and the fire crew stayed until the fire was out. It took the combined efforts of Police and Forestry Commission to clear the crowd and allow the fire engine to leave. Let's put that into perspective with timings. From aircraft impact to the crew being separated and safe—5 minutes. Arrival of fire engine—9 minutes elapsed time. Forest path blocked totally—15 minutes. Arrival of Chopper—20 minutes. Clearance of forest paths—75 minutes. This was an August morning in rural Suffolk; where did all those people come from in so short a time and why did so many act like ghouls and grave robbers, and the majority do nothing but gawp and hinder the emergency crews?

Man's inhumanity

Because of that nasty experience, I amended our Emergency Orders at Honington and circulated all flying stations to alert them to the dangers if they had a similar accident close to the airfield. I found that my experience was anything but exceptional when I attended a course appropriately entitled "Disaster Management". The course was aimed at Officers of organisations that might become involved in attending "Disasters" during their normal course of duty—Police, Fire, Ambulance, Armed Forces, Coastguard, Oilrigs, railways etc.

The course was divided for syndicate sessions (now called workshops) where smaller groups shared experiences and ideas informally. My fellow syndicators included a Police Inspector from Cambridge, a London Underground safety officer, and a Pathologist from Belfast. The latter horrified us with his entirely factual and unemotional accounts of the atrocities and torture carried out by the IRA on their military and police prisoners. I expect we have all winced at reports of kneecapping, elbow spiking and fingernail burning, but what that pathologist described was indescribably horrible. Sadistic burning, barbarous mutilation and slow torture under extreme pain, were the norm at a time when part of Ireland and an evil few of its sons returned to the Dark Ages.

The policeman from Cambridge told a very different but fascinating story of the infamous Cambridge rapist, who was not actually caught until a couple of weeks after our course. It was the early days of DNA and of a number of new ways of collecting irrefutable evidence. Within the confidentiality bounds of the course, he gave a pen picture of what this man was like, both physically and in his mental make up. He even volunteered the way in which he might make his first mistake and be caught. When the TV programmes and reports came out following the capture of the evil little creep, about the only thing our friend hadn't shown us weeks before was his photograph!

But it was the Underground man's story to which I was best able to relate after the Buccaneer accident. He was a senior member of the first rescue team that had gone into the Underground after the Moorgate tube disaster. I don't recall the date, but the main feature was that a train was diverted at speed into a dead end tunnel with horrific consequences. There were many dead and horribly injured with a major problem being that this all took place deep underground in a narrow tunnel, with the front carriages virtually telescoped. In a scene of unimaginable carnage, the rescue teams were attempting to first administer aid and then recover bodies. Unbelievably, whilst doing so, there were men posing as rescuers, climbing into the front carriages to rob the dead and even take human remains as "souvenirs". How sick can you get? I thoroughly enjoyed the course; but nothing in life has ever really shocked me since.

The Red Arrows

The RAF Red Arrows formation display team are so well known that everyone must have seen them for real or on TV. I was immensely privileged during my time at Honington to have them on board for a complete season whilst their home runway was being re-laid. For those who have seen them from afar, let me assure you that in real life the team and the people in it are just as impressive on the ground as they are when making those beautiful patterns in the sky. Now I'm only too aware that there are at least two ex-colleagues of mine who will say, "What the hell does John Palmer know about the Red Arrows?" My answer to that snide remark would be, "Very little, compared to some, a great deal compared to the vast majority of readers." They flew from my airfield for six months when the Gnat was their aircraft and I flew with them a dozen times. I looked after them when they visited Cyprus in the early 70's, and during my industry days joined them for social occasions in the Mess at Farnborough after their conversion to the Hawk. My conclusions over 35 years are that they have always been professionally superb display pilots, they have always worked effectively as a team under a Team Leader, been models of smartness, punctuality and military correctness, and brought immense credit to the RAF and this country. Whilst the display teams of other nations have waxed and waned, come to grief, and fallen on hard times, the Red Arrows have been out there as *the* act to follow.

They were formed at a time when it had become too expensive in operational aircraft and pilots to put the display role in the hands of a front line squadron. In the 50's and 60's, many squadrons had display teams flying the Hunter and the Lightning mainly. Both were excellent display aircraft, they looked good in the air and the Lightning of course had the noise and power and reheat to give a display that little extra humph. Treble One had a superb Lightning team that at one stage was nine strong and I seem to recall a nine-ship Hunter team from either 19 or 92 squadrons painted in royal blue, or was it black?

The good teams make it look so simple and smooth, as if the wing tips are tied together and the pilots sitting on velvet cushions with no noise, no buffeting, and no turbulence. Anyone who has flown in such formations will know that it's not like that; the guys earn their money and the praise.

When formation displays really took off after the war, it was all about the actual flying. But as the game became more competitive—especially with the Americans—it began to matter how colourful or mean-looking were the aircraft; then it was some fancy taxiing routine, next the line up on the pan, the way the canopies opened, coloured smoke, flashing lights, and eventually how the pilots dressed and how the team was marketed. Great showmanship, yes—but it had to be great flying or it didn't make the grade. Many national teams bit the dust—some because of money, some because their aircraft were not suitable, some because they were not disciplined enough when the display rules tightened up after a few air show tragedies.

In the Arizona desert I once watched a US Navy team of four follow each other in sequence into the ground coming out of a loop, and I was in the stands at Ramstein when the Italians suffered a mid-air collision and hit the spectators. I was at Farnborough the day John Derry's DH110 disintegrated and landed amongst the crowd, in Paris when the SU29 crashed, and was taxiing for take off at Leuchars when our own solo aerobatic expert went in nose-first 30 yards away in his Lightning Mk3. Not all were formation accidents, but they, and others similar, had a dramatic effect on what a display team is allowed to do today over an airfield and in the proximity of spectators.

So I enjoyed that season with the Red Arrows. I was so sure of their professionalism and skill that I was prepared to allow them to do things on the airfield that I would not have authorised my own crews to do. I'll refrain from saying what at this point, as a few may still be around. Being on the spot and available for an hour or so, I scrounged rides with them often, as did my eldest son, and I was chuffed to do the same again at Farnborough 20 years later just months after my triple heart bypass. As an RAF officer and a raving patriotic Brit, I am immensely proud of the Institution we know as The Red Arrows.

My Honington tour was special and it came to an end all too quickly. If you got a flying tour as a Wing Commander, it was two years on the dot. There were too few flying jobs for people destined for further promotion to spend more than two years in any job. It had been a real challenge for me at a time in my career when I might have expected an easier ride, but there was the satisfaction of knowing I'd left the station in a much better shape than it was on my arrival and I was given a splendid send off that made me feel my contribution had been appreciated. The icing on the cake was when those from whom I'd been scrounging my Buccaneer flying, laid on a pair of aircraft to fly out to Cyprus for the week-end with the added perk of transiting via the good ship Ark Royal on the way out. It was great to again sample "a life on the ocean wave" and to return to Cyprus after four years away and see the changes resulting from the Turkish invasion.

I recharged my batteries in the Cyprus sun and my wine cellar with demijohns of Cyprus wine and brandy that I carefully stashed in every spare and safe bit of space on the Buccaneer. I was astonished to watch as the pilot of the other aircraft, a very experienced Buccaneer man indeed, loaded his loot into the bomb bay. My surprise escalated to incredulity as we swung into the dispersal at Luqa in Malta and he selected bomb doors open before shutting down the engines, and bombarded the welcoming groundcrew team with flying demijohns. A propelled gallon of brandy could spoil your whole day!

A lot happened to our family during those two years at Honington. Cherrie was at Bristol University reading Law; at first doing well, but then making one hell of a mess of the opportunity she had and sowing the seeds for problems later in her life. One Sunday morning big son Kel left for Warwick University, leaving an enormous hole behind, and Chris left school to start work without any real idea of what he wanted to do.

I'd like to have done the job ten or five years earlier and I'd have liked Rosemarie to share it, but regretfully we never had the chance to be together as husband and wife during my RAF career. We'd have made a marvellous team. When my posting came it was to the Department of Air Warfare, the old Flying College, at Cranwell. Cranwell seemed to draw me back into its clutches time and again, and however much I dreaded the thought of living in the bleak, grey, cheerless countryside, I knew that, armed with the marvellous tonic of enthusiasm, I'd settle in as always like a duck to water.

Family gathering at Kel's passing out—Sandhurst 1981

Inspecting officer at Chris' passing out—Swinderby 1982

11

ALMA MATER

My Alma Mater must properly be Manchester Grammar School, but I spent so much of my RAF career at Cranwell, undertaking or administering some form of instruction, that I have also to think of it as my "fostering mother". The tour that I started there in 1977 was to be the last I would serve on an RAF station. After Cranwell I went back to the Ministry of Defence and completed my service by retiring voluntarily and prematurely from my post at SHAPE in 1983.

I returned to Cranwell, first on the staff, then as the Director of the College of Air Warfare, and can unashamedly say that I was immensely proud to do so. I would look at the Rogues' Gallery of the many famous and popular airmen who had sat in my chair since WW2 and feel honoured to be in such company. I believed I could acquit myself well, and was even surer of that after "inspecting the books". In the three years since I'd been on the Course, a gentleman who was what I might call an "academic" had run the College, and he had surrounded himself with senior staff of similar background and inclination. I doubt if he'd sought the position and his approach was to do that which he did best. Unfortunately that was not what was best for the Air Warfare course, although the Aero Systems Course, a very technical course, was in good shape.

The AWC, to recap, was for officers of Wing Commander and Group Captain rank and equivalent, who had come from or were bound for senior posts directly associated with flying operations. Such posts would be Squadron or Station Commanders, Operational Requirements and R&D posts at research establishments like Farnborough and Boscombe Down. The aim was to broaden their experience beyond the roles in which they had specialised and thus fit them for higher promotion. For instance, to cover the role of Maritime Patrol, there would be in-house lectures, the C in C Coastal Command (18 Group) would address the course, and visits made to a front line station and to firms involved in producing aircraft or systems for maritime air needs. But instead of having a concentrated phase on each role, the sequence of lectures and visits had been based more on a geographical reference to cut down travel costs, whilst senior visitors all came in a gaggle at the end of the course. I changed the curriculum and the sequencing and watched with the utmost satisfaction as the life and value returned to the AWC.

Included in the shake up was a revamping of the Continental tour. NATO was then the cornerstone of all military activities, so it made sense to visit NATO HQ's in Brussels, SHAPE, a Regional HQ, and a mix of RAF, Army, US, German and Dutch bases. We extended the tour from 6 days to 12 and I plead guilty to ulterior motives; one being a Gasthouse deep in the Black Forest that served the world's best charcoal-grilled steak and veal cutlets, another being my favourite *Moules a l'Escargot* and *Gambas au Citron* in a noisy vibrant restaurant off the Grande Place in Brussels.

Eins, zwei, drei, vier...

You'll not mind if I digress to tell one story of our European tour that stirs fond memories? The city is Heidelberg, the place the old Red Ox Inn made famous in the film The Student Prince. Places like Der Roten Ochse can become tourist traps where you pay through the nose for inferior fare, but we were just a bunch of guys roaming a lovely old town who found a pub where one could drink cool German beer in a convivial atmosphere, made special by German drinking songs and frequent cries of "Prosit!" About twelve of us lasted the pace to find ourselves around 10 p.m. competing in "schooner races" with students from the nearby University.

Schooner racing involves a team of any number, each member of which drinks a measure of beer (without spilling a drop), in sequence. We had drunk maybe six races against the students when Herr Ober called "time", it being a weekday. Honours were even, and so the students invited us back to the University until honour was served. We were deposited in an eerie medieval cellar with some of their female guests whilst the students excused themselves. After a while the huge wooden doors at the end of the room burst open and we were confronted by ten or more extremely smart looking gentlemen in grey Prussian uniforms and hats, each wearing a duelling sword on his belt. This was the Heidelberg University beer-drinking team, and they were bloody serious!

The basic rules were the same, with some added formalities. First, you wore bibs that, if wet, meant disqualification. Secondly, you were only cleared to drink when the referee behind you shouted "Ya!" Third, alongside each drinker was a *Honkatorium*—a large bowl into which one could throw up at any time and continue drinking. By now we had the odd guy the worse for wear, so our team of 10 dwindled to six and I found myself drinking at No1 and No 10. I should say that I am not a beer drinker, but I can drink it very fast indeed—or could then. After a further six races honours were still even and, as midnight was the stipulated closure time, it was decided that the victors be decided by a final duel between the respective nominated champions. I drew the short straw to represent Great Britain.

We both retired momentarily for a leak, and in my case a quick fingers-down-the-throat, and returned to the duelling table. I was relieved to have taken the chance to unload a little as I saw the vessel from which we had to drink—an enormous hollowed bone horn which later I found held over two litres. For this competition, if you spilt anything, the referee topped up your horn. The bone was so smooth and thick at the lip that it was difficult to gauge the flow and my guzzling technique did not work. But we had a short practice—the Germans were scrupulously fair I have to say—and then we were off. I thought I'd never finish, but was only penalised with a small top up right at the start. As I began to feel the beer running free on tipping the horn, someone by my left ear was yelling, "You've got him boss, take it easy!"

I felt the last surge of liquid leave the horn and triumphantly turned it upside down on the table to a round of applause and much-appreciated kisses from the ladies. The *piece de résistance* however was yet to come. I was led to a long tube-shaped room with a low ceiling along which, set into the wall, were small plaques of some 4 inches square, each with the outline, caricature style, of a face. This was their roll of honour; the tiles represented the University's drinking champion for that year. Much to my mortification, the tile for that year was carefully prised from the wall and replaced by a temporary "J.K.Palmer—Champion" tile. Once again I fancy I hear hoots of derision from certain quarters, but that was a great night and a memory of Heidelberg that few will have experienced, or perhaps wished to talk about.

Beware of the little guys

Meanwhile, back at the ranch, I was revelling in my job. But of course there is always a snag and this time it came in the rotund pear shape of the new Deputy Commandant. His post was really a sinecure, almost always filled by a man on his last tour who could sit back in his large office and comfortable married quarter, join in the hectic social life of the many training departments on the station, and give the mainly young officer element the benefit of his considerable experience. Unfortunately the new incumbent was a spiteful miserable little man, both in stature and personality, who went out of his way to be obnoxious. It started within days of his arrival when he insisted on joining our Continental tour. We flew into Wildendrath for a cocktail party after which we hurtled off in a fleet of mini-buses to nearby Munchen Gladbach. We were settling in nicely at a splendid German bar when my arm was tugged and smallbore Sid took me aside to say, "Group Captain, I want *him* and *him* (pointing to two of my students) sent back to Cranwell tomorrow. Right!" I only knew of this senior officer by reputation, so tentatively asked him, "Did they nick your girl then Sir?"—said with a smile and in obvious jocular mood. "You know bloody well they did," said he. "They have no respect for rank." Still in jovial mood—after all it was supposed to be a night on the tiles—and showing all of the tact for which I am renowned, I said, "Perhaps the *fraulein* didn't realise you were our leader?"

I might have succeeded in calming him down had one of the errant students, a dashing handsome fighter jock, not come over with his slinky prize and said, "No sweat sir, Heidi's mother is longing to meet you." I had no wish to be in perpetual head on conflict with a man who could make life uncomfortable for me; but I was now 47, feeling secure in my rank, and sure of my views. I did not suffer fools gladly, and neither was I about to sacrifice two very capable officers to satisfy the envy and jealousy of a mean little man. I told him that if after sleeping on it, he still wanted me to send the guys home, I would first call The Commandant to express my objections—then take everyone home. I meant it, too. That set the tone for the next 12 days and created a situation unique in my RAF career. I respected rank, I recognised the need for and the value of a pecking order, and if I disagreed with someone senior would still treat him with the respect due to his rank. But this little man was different; I despised and disliked him intensely and we parted the bitterest of enemies one year later.

I went for my final interview on posting and stood in front of him waiting for him to look up at me. When he did, I simply said, "Air Commodore, I have no intention of listening to any more of your vitriolic comments. I actually don't give a damn what you have written about me. You could have made an enormous contribution to the value of what we do here and to the enjoyment of the Staff and Students; instead you've gone out of your way to be a miserable little sod and are quite the most unpopular officer that I've ever known. The sooner you retire the better for everyone." I recall leaving my beloved building walking on air.

This particular gentleman's nasty attitude was all the more pronounced because his predecessor was just the opposite. He was one of the influences in my life that I have referred to earlier; someone who one met quite by chance but who went out of his way to be considerate and fair. This will sound self-centred, but this is my autobiography so I have to record that my boss and my friend David saw me as few others had when he referred to my sometime apparent indifference and aloofness as shyness. He was absolutely correct; in certain circumstances I find myself being incredibly shy and I've always put it down to being a bit of a loner.

In spite of the excellent RAF system of annual reporting, many officers would not take the trouble to get to know the men on whom they were reporting well enough to be fair and just. The harm in that was that competition for higher rank was fierce and if you missed promotion and slipped behind your peers you probably could never expect to make up lost time. I don't have a personal axe to grind on this topic as I feel my life has really been swings and roundabouts, but I have felt for many good men whose promotion has gone by default, with the undeserving often benefiting. My colleague David made sure that all of his guys got the assessments they deserved and was not afraid to tell them if the news was not too palatable; again, a rare trait.

The Demon Drink

But I introduced David for an entirely different reason. He was an alcoholic and as a result he died tragically, well before his time, after personal humiliation and expulsion from the Service he loved. The odd thing was that I knew him well for some 14 years and had not the slightest suspicion of his affliction for the first 12 of those years. He was a very dapper and smart man both in and out of uniform, whose previous tour had been in command of a high profile Harrier station in Germany. So he was held in high regard by many and was quickly promoted to Air Vice Marshal rank after leaving Cranwell. At Cranwell he was the perfect leader of the Air Warfare department. He was a very easy man to talk to, impeccably behaved and I never saw him looking the slightest the worse for wear for drink. Had I been a caricaturist, I would have depicted him smiling with one foot on a bar rail, dressed in blue blazer and grey flannels, and sipping a half-pint mug of bitter. When he and his wife entertained at home, a frequent occurrence in his position, everything was as it should be. On our visits abroad and to industry and other stations, I never saw him even slightly under the weather.

I was sad to see him go and was not to see him again until 5 years later when I had left the RAF and he came back to London from another German tour. David was a pragmatist; he always said that when promoted he felt he would only be able to perform well in a handful of posts, two of which he got as a "one star". He dreaded going into a "high quality" staff post, such as Air Plans or the Central Staff, where he'd be found wanting and unable to give of his best. Perhaps it was his first post as a two star that brought his fears home to roost—I cannot be sure.

When I phoned to invite him for lunch it was on the pretext—though I really did not need one—of discussing the problems of a mutual friend. When he arrived at the restaurant, I couldn't believe the difference that five years had made. He was drawn looking, hesitant and unsure of his words, his vital spark and sense of humour had gone. We both ordered the culinary disaster that we'd often said would be our choice before going to the gallows—sweet anchovies on melted White Cheshire, Jugged Hare with roast potatoes and boiled onions, English trifle, and a sizzling Welsh rarebit with a glass of port. I'd chosen Rules, the atmosphere was wonderful, and I anticipated a memorable reunion. He picked at his food, barely spoke and left claiming an early afternoon meeting.

Puzzled, and wondering if I'd been to blame, I called an old mutual friend who agreed to meet me; same time, same place, same menu—two days later. Spike told an astonished JKP that David had a history of alcoholism, that he'd usually managed to conceal his disease, but that whenever he was stressed he'd slump back into the pits. He'd bought a house near Spike in Lincolnshire and when they met socially, David would have gin and vodka stashed in every conceivable place around the house to drink secretly whilst drinking tomato juice openly. Deceit is second nature to the drunkard. On hearing the story I could only marvel at the loyalty of friends who had protected him for years.

Two years later Spike told me that things had got worse and our friend had received a formal warning from the MoD. Shortly after, he called to say that David had been asked to leave the service after being picked out of a Whitehall gutter. It was not a total surprise, therefore, to open the *Telegraph* obituary page soon after to see the smiling face I'd once known. Spike told me how horribly he'd died in an accident at home and how it had affected his family. I tell this sad tale because as so often in life it's a case of "there but for the grace of God…"

I've never been a heavy drinker, but the RAF lifestyle often put you in a position of regular and serious drinking. In industry, the business lunch and dinner circuit led to many a knock down, on your knees, honking through your nose-type of affair, whilst overseas, potential customers and clients would be only too happy to ply you with every liquor known to man. But, in spite of the temptation and practice, I've never had to say, "God, I need a drink!" If I have, it's been water or strong Lancashire tea! Seeing the disasters wrought by alcohol makes me even more fearful these days when I see the damage being wrought by drugs—and that seems to start at age 10 or less now. I suspect that I shall have much to say about that subject much later.

Spring turning to autumn

What turned out to be my last tour on an RAF station proved memorable. I played my last game of rugby at the age of 48 on a pitch where I once scored four tries as a fleet footed winger against our bitterest enemies, Halton. I stood as the Reviewing Officer as an entry of young flight cadets marched past where my 9M5 entry and I had marched off to the strains of Auld Lang Syne. I scored my first and only "first class" century on the College Orange where I'd fallen in love with a 17-year-old Princess Margaret. I made my first visit at 200 feet a.m.s.l. to the North Pole on the annual Aerosystems flight that then landed in Northern Greenland. The highlights of that, apart from the utter grey desolation beneath the aircraft at the Pole, were watching the Arctic foxes fighting over my bars of chocolate and buying 100 cans of my favourite Coors beer for just $1 US—funny the things that stick in your memory, eh?

It was the last time I was to engage in team sports and have the opportunity to fly on a regular basis. Having done so much of both I was surprised by my own reaction to that. When people have asked me since if I miss flying or miss my sport, the answer I have been able to give with 100% honesty is that I haven't. Of course, there have been times when I've walked across a newly mown field, caught the scent of the grass, and imagined a young Palmer running for the sheer exhilaration of running. Times that I've watched a formation of Tornados or F-15's line up and thrilled at their ear shattering roar as they streaked away down the runway and climbed away on their reheat pokers.

But I have not missed those things, I've not ached to do those things again, simply because—I believe—that whilst I was able to do them I never missed a chance to do so. I never recall opting out of flying anything, anywhere, at any time, and I always looked forward with great relish and confidence to every football and rugby match I ever played. Even when the odds were we might get a hammering, I always believed we could win—or at least I could win my own local private battle. I looked at all the young starry-eyed Cranwell officers around me and thought, without envy, I've been there, I've done that. "Don't cry for me young lovers, I've had a love of my own like yours, I've had a love of my own."

Whitehall—the second time around

1980 was in many ways a watershed in my life. I'd had a taste of the Operational Requirements and R&D world, and the AWC had accentuated that with the many visits to industry and the broader spectrum of defence activities to which we'd been exposed. Little wonder then that my next posting was back to the OR world as a Deputy Director; back too to my first love, air defence, which I'd temporarily spurned during my Buccaneer days. That urge to be involved in things new was probably the growing pains of someone keen to start a new career, albeit one that stemmed directly from what I'd experienced and enjoyed doing so much. It was also a belated end to my naivety in that I was about to learn that other people did not share many of my dearly held principles and standards. Indeed, I would find a hostile reception when I tried to live up to them, and many who by fair means or foul would be intent on shaking my faith.

Ten years had passed since I'd left Whitehall. The RAF had changed, I'd grown older and as a Deputy Director I was now expected to be only one-third airman, the other two thirds being politician and accountant. The naivety of which I spoke came from my firm belief that it was the job of everyone in the OR corridors to give the front line the aircraft and equipment it needed to emerge top in any conflict. No, that didn't mean damn the cost and to hell with timescales. But it did mean setting certain standards of performance—of capability, reliability, and interoperability—below which you were not prepared to fall. It is likely I admit that I erred on the side of wanting the best rather than accepting merely the good, but I still believe my approach was to be preferred over those who lived by compromise and cared little for the quality of what equipment entered service, just as long as *something* entered service. I was now working for and in the company of people with a quite different agenda to mine, people whose sights were set on achieving stardom, the tap of the sword on their shoulders and a splendid office on the 6th floor.

Understandably, the 34 years I had spent in the RAF had sheltered me from the big bad world. A military life is very different to a civilian life, with its own customs and rules, working environment and social life. But then, whatever our lot, others live lives vastly different to ours depending on their family backgrounds, education, social status, financial circumstances, ambitions and so on. How often do we look at the homes and locations of others on TV and remark on how unattractive they would be to us? Come to think of it, I've lumped all military men under one heading, but I know that life in the RAF was vastly different in most respects to the way that the Navy and Army operated and lived. Throughout my life I have found that however accomplished and confident I may have been in my job and circumstances, I could be like a fish out of water when confronted with the strange and mysterious. Age of course plays a part; there is a great difference between the high passion and questioning of youth and the mere petulance and cynicism of old age. But whatever way I describe it, that Whitehall post in 1980 did a lot to destroy any residual naivety I had and taught me that I must tread far more warily if I was not to be frequently disappointed with the words and actions of my fellow man.

Whilst lashing out a bit, I should confess to one other type of individual that was always guaranteed to get my goat. I can't say whether they were peculiar to the military, but that was the environment in which I saw them operate. They were officers, mostly Army but with a smattering of Navy and RAF, who were independently wealthy. The Army seemed to attract the upper class twit, whereas the RAF and Navy selection and training processes weeded out such individuals at an early stage. But anyway, these were chaps that didn't need their military salaries and lived a life style that was way beyond most others. Their wealth and family connections gave them an exaggerated idea of their own capabilities and importance and they often intimidated more senior officers by their superior attitude. One, an RAF Squadron Commander took the most outrageous liberties with the way he flew and allowed his crews to fly, simply because he didn't really care whether or not he stayed in the RAF. As I say, the Army had the lion's share of such individuals to the point where I despaired of what might happen if such pompous idiots ever took men into battle.

You'd be wrong if you believe you detect a touch of envy or sour grapes in my attitude; I didn't suffer from either at the time and now 25 years on I have no regrets. I see little wrong in having money *per se*, or in being ambitious. It would be a great honour to be knighted, and a leather chair is more comfortable than a wicker one. But in 1981, my own experience and instincts were telling me that politics and financial cuteness were replacing operational knowledge and nous at far too low a level in the Air Staffs of Whitehall. I can't say now how long it took to put me in that frame of mind because I certainly returned to the Holy of Holies full of enthusiasm for the task and looking forward to renewing my acquaintance with attractive spots abroad, the wonderful selection of London's eating places, and the freedom of movement and travel I would enjoy thus enabling Rosemarie and I to see more of each other. The family were living in a splendid RAF house on the outskirts of Maidenhead so my commuting consisted of a one-mile walk home to station, Great Western to Paddington, Bakerloo Line to Embankment. One hour door to door, and three hours to Rosemarie's, making a day trip a piece of cake—not at all bad.

My Directorship included equipment with which I had vast experience. The Nimrod AEW that I had started 15 years earlier was well into final development. The front line fighter was the Phantom that I'd flown in the US and was about to be replaced by the F3 Tornado that carried a mix of air-to-air missiles that had an international procurement tag with the US, France and Germany. There was a multi–national IFF programme (back to Brussels again), fixed and mobile radars, and mobile surface to air missile systems. I inherited a splendid team of pilots, navigators, fighter controllers and engineers. If you couldn't be flying, this was as good as staff jobs went.

Even though I knew air defence as well as anyone, there was a lot to learn. Technology was advancing rapidly, the UK was co-operating within NATO on equipment procurement, but the competition between UK firms and with foreign firms for the lucrative contracts was never fiercer. There was still inter-service rivalry for the tightening budget; the procurement process gave the illusion of being efficient, but actually prolonged the time between initiation and entering service to the point where costs inevitably escalated, whilst the capability of the end product fell short and in-service dates were delayed. Whatever the contributory reasons for the unsatisfactory state of defence procurement, they do not belong in an autobiography; but some affected me directly, so I can hardly avoid giving my observations.

Before I slip into turgid prose mode, there was that first hurdle to overcome of finding out what your predecessor did, settling in to the mould he'd created, getting to know your team, and becoming familiar with the myriad military and civilian contacts in the UK and overseas. In that acclimatisation phase, one massive advantage of the RAF that one never had in industry was the existence of a comprehensive filing system. If I wanted, for instance, to read about Nimrod AEW progress, there'd be a file or files on which everything was recorded, in chronological order, and with minute sheets to link the staff actions so that a complete picture was readily to hand. Doubtless those records are now on disc, but I imagine they are no less comprehensive.

But before I could begin reading myself into the job, I needed an environment in which I could sit quietly and comfortably to meditate with few distractions and no noise. Don't ask me why, but I like a cosy office with a view and a door that I can leave open or close. I dislike the present day "open plan" where everyone oversees everyone else and conversations are held in little tight huddles. I'm showing my age there as I imagine E-mail has replaced most human conversations!

So I was not impressed to find that my splendidly isolated office overlooking the Thames and Old Scotland Yard was furnished with one desk, one hard chair and one plastic visitors chair. No other furniture, nothing on the walls, nothing on the floor and nothing on the desk other than current files that would be locked away at close of play. The incumbent wanted it that way; he was a cold fish, less like a fighter pilot than any Lightning jock I ever knew, and he epitomised the general view of a "staff officer" as one who knew nothing about the real world, but who gave the impression that he knew everything. I changed almost everything about the way he did things, not that I ever knew whether he'd been successful or not; I simply could not work as he had done. On my first day in charge, after he'd bought me half a pint and said he must rush, I sat in his miserable cell and planned the transformation. First, I went to a little man who occupied a dismal grimy office in the sub-sub-basement, surrounded by heating pipes, some ten feet above the Circle Line tube which made his teeth chatter every three minutes, and adjacent to Henry the Something's old wine cellar. I pleaded and cajoled for new—or better furniture. But in a building that houses hundreds of officers of higher rank than I, plus hundreds of civil servants who always came first in the pecking order, all he would promise was a wooden chair to replace plastic and a waste paper basket.

I left the grey little man to his dusty dungeon and commenced a tour of all eight floors of the building. That meant looking into 800 offices along three miles of corridor, just to see how the other half lived. Of course I couldn't see into the offices of the great men—they would be well furnished anyway. But it was obvious that the Army and Navy, and most of the civil servants over a certain Grade, were generally much better equipped than were we poor RAF junior-service officers. It was an RAF trait; we were the only ones following the rules. I noted that about 5% of offices were unoccupied, some of which were well if not sumptuously furnished, mainly in the Army environs. The Army imported their own desks, carpets and curtains and most Army officers had the obligatory spaniel or other gun dog that curled up in leather chairs which the little man in the dungeon swore did not exist on his inventory.

On that first night I waited until the third exodus of staff. The first exodus was of civil servants whose heels disappeared into the London night on the last chime of Big Ben striking five. The second exodus around 6 p.m. was mainly military staff in the middle and higher ranks that usually waited for their bosses to go and then shot out hoping to have created the right impression. The third exodus were those hard working guys who had deadlines to meet, and who wanted to catch the 9 p.m. news and see the kids before they went to bed. They would depart between 7 and 8 p.m. leaving only a handful of sad souls to pore over their papers.

At 8 p.m. I retraced my steps to rooms where I'd earlier noted items of furniture that were not being used—or were far too good for the guy whose title was on the door! I cunningly earmarked rooms that gave me easy access to the lifts, a bank of four of which were within yards of my office. By 9 p.m. I had a beautiful office, I had avoided detection by the eagle eyed security men with their white sticks and wheelchairs, those being the days before CCTV invaded every corner of our lives. I sat in my resplendent surrounds the next morning and awaited the onrush of enraged pongos or the man from the dungeons. I never did see him again, or anyone in fact for weeks, until a noisy Colonel barged in and said that my yellow leather armchair looked "awfully like the one the Regiment had provided for General David". I invited him to look at the sticker on the base that read "John Lewis—Oxford Street" and he left mumbling "Sorry old chap" all the way down the corridor. On my final visit to that building in November 1999 to hand in my security pass and say farewell on my retirement from industry, that yellow chair (which *was* General David's) and 90% of my ill-gotten gains in 1980, were still in the same office.

My next priority was to get to know my chaps and their particular projects sufficiently well to give them my support, as well as ensuring that I could brief upwards when required. The upwards bit gave me most trouble because I did not work like my predecessor. For reasons best known to him, he had concentrated on only two main projects, leaving his Project officers to handle the others. That was not my way; I believed passionately in delegation and in allowing officers to use their initiative and to run with their ideas. But the MoD was, in many ways, a jungle, a building in which you seldom knew your true supporters and opponents, and where one had to protect the inexperienced from the devious, cunning and lazy. In trying to do so, and not for the first time, I felt a touch of cold steel 'twixt my shoulder blades. In Whitehall, when you made enemies for whatever reason, you were up against some clever people. Not for them a quick punch on the nose or a simple Foxtrot Oscar; the most dangerous were often the most charming, the deepest cuts usually coming with a smile and even a handshake. Well-dressed ignorance went a long way in SW1.

Don't you find that the world and the people in it are rarely what they seem? I am frequently revisiting these pages to check I haven't recorded anything that might be seen as a sham and which would misrepresent me to you. You may not think that important, but if you volunteer to pen an account of your life for you and yours, what is the point of telling a fairy story? Undeterred, therefore, I'll keep trying to tell it as I saw it, fully expecting others to have seen it very differently. If they have, I'd like to read about it.

Cynicism or newfound Wisdom?

I was soon to witness an example of how the AFD appeared to have lost its way over procurement. A Moratorium on defence-spending had been imposed and an urgent meeting was held at DD level to decide which funded projects were to continue, be cancelled, or be subjected to delay or reduced funding. As usual, the target of savings was not given, so every DD turned up to fight his own corner. With air defence I had to think in System terms; that is as a combination of Interceptors, AEW, surface radars, ground based and airborne weapons, IFF and Specialist communications. If the capability of one part of the jigsaw was to change or disappear, it followed that the gap left had to be compensated for by adjusting other pieces of the jigsaw.

The *ad hoc* committee took no heed of such basic truths. Projects were selected for the chop simply because they were not high profile, possibly because there was no specialist there to defend them properly on the day, or that the sum able to be saved was conveniently acceptable. These were not new and high-risk projects, but projects that had been fought through to an advanced stage of procurement over many years as integral elements of a complete system. As usually happened—and I'm particularly sorry to say this—the top priority fighter projects were never allowed to suffer. Even when a strong case could be made for buying something off the shelf that had a proven acceptable performance at lower capital and running cost, we always stuck to an inferior more expensive British buy. I am of the fighter fraternity and as patriotic and as keen to buy British as anyone, but when serious cuts have to be made, even the unpalatable must be considered. Thus a suggestion that we might buy the proven F-15 instead of a lesser performing, more expensive, late in service suspect Tornado, was not even allowed to be discussed or argued on paper.

In any event, the carefully selected brainwashed Chairman was not inclined to enter into deep discussion and quickly arrived at a list of sacrifices that naturally pleased those whose pet projects had been spared. I was dismayed that two of my key projects were to be axed and I pointed out that this was major surgery; his indecently fast decisions were cutting arteries—not making cosmetic changes. I was first politely ignored and then accused of being disloyal when I persisted. To which I answered that I did not count loyalty as meaning that I was required to conceal my impatience or annoyance when the demands on my enthusiasm became farcical. I saw loyalty being used as a conception to blackmail me into silence when faced with the incompetence and sheer folly of the Chairman, or of those who briefed him. Not for the first time was I said to be tactless, and this by my immediate boss who should have been supporting his projects, or at least giving his guidance prior to a major policy meeting. A compromise was eventually negotiated, which I suspect cost me dearly—although no one would ever admit to that.

NATO frustrations

I also lived up to my tactless tag on one of the NATO committees that my staff and I sat on. The project was the NATO Identification System (NIS), that was intended to be fitted to all operational aircraft and control units to identify friend from foe and give the control authorities a complete "air picture". By definition, everyone in NATO had to use the same system and, by procurement rules, the industries of all 14 nations were eligible to compete for the very attractive contract It had taken many years to agree a Specification to meet the Requirement so everyone knew exactly what was required and by when. The US tended to bid as individual companies for such contracts, whereas the Europeans usually bid as a consortium, both to share development costs and combine the best in national technologies. The NIS winning consortium was European, but even though the capability had been of the utmost urgency for over a decade and they been its' greatest advocates, the US declined to sign a contract on the grounds that they had to confer with US industry and confirm with their military that the chosen system was acceptable. They agreed to return to Brussels in six months to table any desired amendments, but predictably came back with alternative US proposals for equipment made in the USA.

Admittedly, the US had by far the largest number of platforms to fit and refit would therefore cost them heavily. But that was known going into every industrial competition and, to put it bluntly, US policy was that all NATO contracts should be competitive, just as long as they won! They were past masters at confusing NATO meetings that were not going their way, they would change their delegate, or up the rank of delegates so that the more senior guy or newcomer could claim that his predecessor did not have the authority to have said what he did or commit the US to a particular line. They would undermine the activities of European firms by withholding items of hardware or software only available in the US, and would try by fair means or foul to create disharmony in a non-US consortium. When they met opposition to their dirty tricks, they would insidiously intimidate through some form of diplomatic, commercial or military skulduggery. One had to admire their professionalism and determination in a ruthless campaign directed to impose a complete monopoly for western defence equipment.

There was a lethargy about British industry, a lethargy even more marked on the Continent, that contrasted sharply with the US's natural urge to compete. We and the rest of NATO let them get away with it and they were, and still are, the world's biggest bullies. I received much support from British industry over my complaints on the NIS fiasco. In Whitehall few really cared because most pre-ferred to buy American anyway, and as it wasn't a new high profile aircraft, ship or tank, no one was prepared to die in a ditch to take on the Americans. Reading that may cause some to suppose that I am anti-American. Nothing of the sort. I have enormous affection and respect for many aspects of the American achieve-ment. I simply bemoan the fact that so many roll over and allow US commercial aggressiveness to prosper without challenge. I shall enlarge on that when I talk about my 17 years in the defence industry, but before that let me add that we would gain enormous respect by competing aggressively ourselves. The greatest respect if we did would come from the Americans themselves.

All sides of the Pentagon

Whilst knocking the Americans, I must recount an amusing story suitable for all ears, told many times, usually in the convivial aura of a good restaurant. To set the scene, I explained earlier that Air-to-Air missiles came under my wing. In 1980 it seemed a good idea to form a four-nation committee to conduct a com-bined study of existing designs and current developments for two new missiles; one a short range (dog fight) missile, the other a long range (stand-off) intercept missile. Commonality was the buzzword; we should all use the same weaponry and save billions in development and spares. The four nations most concerned with development, operational use, and production, were the UK, US, Germany and France. The Committee were to meet first in the US to draw up the Memo-randum of Understanding (MoU), and then meet every two months alternating between Washington, London, Paris and Bonn. I was delighted to be the RAF representative, with an engineer from the Ministry of Technology and a high-ranking civil servant who was a self acknowledged expert on the drawing up of international formal MoUs and contracts.

For all the fun it gave us and all the hard work accomplished, the high hopes of that first meeting in Washington were to end up on the rocks, as did so many NATO projects. The French pulled out after the second meeting in Paris to do their own thing (but wanted free copies of all that the other three did!). The Ger-man and UK industries were only interested in using their own outdated technol-ogy, and then only on the short-range weapon. American development was already well advanced; they wanted to do the long range weapon themselves agreeing to buy from whoever was the short range winner, knowing full well that we and the Germans would never agree and they'd be able to buy their own prod-uct on the grounds that they couldn't wait any longer. That is more or less how it turned out. The US produced both weapons, sold both to most other countries, and one German firm and two British firms picked up a few crumbs from the US table. The French stole all the ideas they could, claimed to be world-beaters and eventually produced an all-French inferior missile. But at least it was French.

Now the story, which came from the inaugural meeting held in the Pentagon in an impressive room on the 4th floor, prestigiously furnished in mahogany and green leather. The Chairman was a USAF three star general who had taken over the Operational Requirements job after a high profile command job in Tactical Air Command. Bob was a very capable and likeable guy who had one disarming habit; he always held an enormous cigar in his hands that he ate-he never smoked it—he bit off a chunk at a time and chewed it. He talked quietly but firmly and you were always aware when he was getting upset as the tobacco was chewed more and more vigorously. At 10 am on Tuesday, the full committee of around 20 members sat to put together the MoU, and by Wednesday at 4 p.m. had only reached the middle of page 3. The culprit in chief for the snails' pace progress was our civil servant mandarin who objected to almost every sentence on the basis of grammatical purity. To make matters worse, when he objected he had a nasty habit of quoting Gower's Plain Words or Somebody's 19th century manual of English speaking.

Shortly after coffee on the Wednesday he produced a real purler—something along the lines of "Mr Chairman, the British delegation cannot possibly accept that sentence. It is imperative that a colon be used, not a semi-colon. You see…". Chairman Bob had been working up to a fair old chewing rate and he held up his cigar to halt the flow of words and said in his Texan drawl, "Okay, okay. Tell me Doctor North, exactly what sort of school were you at?"

Our good Doctor wasn't taken aback in the slightest and immediately retorted, "Well, Mr Chairman, the sort of school to which I went taught us never to finish a sentence with a preposition." Silence fell upon the room. The US staffs held their collective breath; one simply did not talk like that to an American three-star general. The Germans grunted, the French muttered and shrugged their shoulders, and the rest of the British contingent had visions of Reg North being rushed to Sing Sing. The Chairman's expression changed not one bit. Reflectively, he rolled his cee-gar in his hand, took a slow bite and pointing it at Reg, said, "Okay, let me rephrase that, Dr North. Exactly what sort of school were you at—arsehole?" As much in relief as mirth, the Pentagon boardroom erupted with screams of laughter and Bob said he'd see us all at 9 a.m. the next day.

An amusing sequel occurred in the Sheraton as I was dressing for dinner. A knock came to the door (funny how they do that, eh?), and I was surprised to see a sheepish Reg North standing there. Civil Service mandarins did not normally stay at the same hotel as *hoi polloi*, never mind knock on their doors. "May I come in for moment?" he asked and, again surprisingly, took the cold beer I proffered him. I let him get out what he was obviously trying to ask, which was, "John, do you remember that little altercation I had with Bob Russ this afternoon over the MoU? Would you say that I lost?" We took him that night to a well-known Speakeasy in Georgetown to help him relax. Around 3 a.m., and very much the worse for wear, he asked me the same question. "Reg," said I, taking advantage of the relaxed atmosphere, "he beat the crap out of you." "No, no, John," he said. "You can't say *beat*; it would have to be flushed; you see…"

The following lunchtime I was privileged to shake the hand of President Ronald Reagan. Our 4-power committee was informed that The President was making a surprise visit to the Pentagon to present deferred Viet Nam war medals. The ceremony was to take place in the inner courtyard and Pentagon staff were invited to watch from windows or from the external stairways that led down to the garden. I watched from a 4th floor platform and was surprised when The President then chose to climb the staircase I was on and came up beaming past the spectators with that boyish charm he never lost. As he reached my level, he held out his hand and asked me which service I was from. I said I was actually an interloper from the RAF, in town for a conference. He asked how I liked America, how long I was there for and I joked that my friends would call me "a bad actor" (a common US expression in those days for a rogue). "Don't let that bother you," he laughed. "They've accused me of that all my life."

Early Warning indeed

If you've stayed awake, you'll know by now how big a part AEW played in my career. I was delighted to see how successful had been my bargain-basement buy of the Interim AEW Shackleton, and some of my staff had served on 8 Squadron based at Lossiemouth in Scotland. But initially I didn't get too involved with the new Nimrod AEW project, partly because I knew it so well—but mainly because I didn't want to tread on the toes of my very capable AEW desk officer. I only became involved at major Project Review Boards. It was clear however that problems were just waiting to happen. Some related to development of the radar, some to the lack of co-operation between the two joint prime contractors, many due to MoD PE's management of the project, and not a few due to RAF cynicism that they would get what they had specified on time at the right cost. The Project was in Development, the penultimate phase of procurement before moving into full Production. This was the time when contractors were perfecting their designs, producing prototypes, and putting together hundreds of different items of equipment and software to make it all sing as a System. Inevitably there were problems, for which contingencies were built in to the programme to allow for extra costs, slippages in timescale, or even adjustments to delivered performance. But the realisation was dawning that Nimrod had more than its fair share of snags.

At BAe Woodford, the home of the famous old AVRO Company, two trials aircraft were being assembled. Aerodynamically the Nimrod airframe was sound and the bulbous extensions to nose and tail for the radar scanners caused no real concern. There was the usual problem in all new aircraft of finding available space to fit everything, of ensuring that you had enough electrical power and cooling, and that you could carry as much fuel as you needed without exceeding the take-off weight parameters. Adjustments and compromises to the aircraft fit and configuration would carry on through production and beyond.

The crucially important item both in terms of the AEW role and the optimum external and internal configuration of the aeroplane, was the new GEC radar system. The system included the integration, interface and interoperability of many different pieces of equipment, and involved computers and software packages more advanced than any then in RAF service. It was no secret that the transmitter programme was in trouble, as was the main computer that most engineers believed was not going to have anything like the capacity needed. It followed that if you couldn't transmit, you couldn't collect and analyse the enormous amount of sensor data, and therefore you had no sure means of knowing whether you could achieve the essential detection and tracking performance.

The technical problems highlighted other major drawbacks. There was no single Prime Contractor; BAe and GEC were joint leaders between whom great distrust existed. GEC were faced with the major problem that their much-vaunted radar was a long way from being proved and during the time that GEC were being seen as responsible for delays to the programme, BAe were only too happy to hide their own shortfalls against the more critical AEW system failures.

The MoD Programme Review Board, which effectively managed the programme, was reluctant to accept that Nimrod was in deep technical trouble. Their Chairman, Controller Aircraft, fired warning shots across the bows of both main contractors but failed to force either, particularly the chief culprits GEC, to put more effort and money into meeting their obligations. MoD PEs' weakness, some said conspiracy, was transparent to the Air Staff who began covertly to explore other ways of satisfying their AEW Requirement.

This AFD stance, seen by MoD PE as tantamount to treachery, was exacerbated through a parallel failure by the same division of GEC on the high profile Tornado F3 intercept radar. The AFD at the time was more frustrated than angry—that was to come later in full measure. Both lucrative radar projects had been awarded to GEC in 1977 after intense lobbying by Lord Weinstock and his opposite number at BAe. After the earlier failure of the Nimrod Radar development programme, the RAF had set its' sights firmly on buying into the US AWACS programme. But the Buy British campaign had secured the work for British industry and, it has to be said, saved thousands of jobs. I was to get a far better view of the mess a year later, but at the time I admit I was as bamboozled as everyone else as to the seriousness of the problems and whether they were temporary or terminal.

Have you ever tried looking into a can of worms? If so you'll know what it was like trying to make sense out of the radar project which, as I keep repeating, was the critical feature of the programme. Could the radar detect aircraft flying between it and the surface and be sufficiently uncluttered and accurate to guide fighters into a position to identify an enemy and destroy him? If it couldn't, you were pouring good money down the drain. The specialist MoD Radar Establishment at Malvern led the research into the new techniques in the UK. Malvern had a famous history and undoubtedly housed the best technical brains, in research and development terms, in the UK if not in Europe. They came up with ideas of their own and worked closely with the contractors to turn those brainchilds into operational equipment. The work that the R&D teams did was so technical that most ordinary mortals couldn't hope to do anything but understand a few basics. Everyone else therefore had to take them at their word and trust what they said. Naturally, they were both proud and secretive, and usually confident that the object of their ingenuity would work properly. They were unfortunately seldom able to guarantee that they could produce what was needed at an acceptable cost and timescale.

Next, to understand the nature of the problems, you had to look at those in industry responsible for turning the R&D output into hardware or software, again with cost and timescale in mind, plus now the need to produce a reliable and easily maintainable system with emphasis on the "system". It is one thing to have a piece of kit working by itself, quite another to have it working properly as one small cog in an enormous wheel. Probably the most difficult of all, was getting a true picture from those with a vested interest in the outcome of a project. There were people protecting their rears, preserving their jobs, guarding reputations, defending previous decisions, building audit proof trails, and ensuring that their doorsteps were clean. Taken together at that stage of development-and however suspicious one might be as to the outcome-there were too many uncertainties to make a viable case for cancellation. So both Nimrod and the Tornado F3 lived to fight another day, but the seeds of doubt had been sown in the AFD that were to bear bitter fruit two years later.

Let's hear it for the Lady

In 1982 there was the slight distraction of a war in the Falklands. All else rightly took second place and the aftermath of job reshuffling led to me leaving the MOD a few months early to take up a post in SHAPE (Supreme Headquarters Allied Powers Europe), at Mons in Belgium. I don't want to add to the many stories about the Falklands War except to say a few words about a lady that I've often criticised for what she did when in office, the damage she wrought in the lives of so many ordinary folk, and the legacy that she left through some of her policies.

But I was privileged to see her as "The Winston Churchill of The Falklands" and a mighty fine sight it was. She held twice daily briefings to which she almost always came in person and ran those meetings as I suspect Churchill would have run his; brilliantly informed, straight to the point, and aware of exactly who in the audience could answer her piercing questions. If someone else tried to answer and "pull rank" she was devastatingly severe, and she always asked the questions that mattered; questions that you wished—if you were trying to avoid an issue—that she'd ask the First Sea Lord or her Secretary of State. She really was a "hands-on" leader, and she got the full ten out of ten when she threw a cocktail party in No10 after the return of the Fleet for those involved in the briefings and meetings. And she helped serve the drinks! Cometh the hour, cometh the woman.

Last Things

Many pages ago I recorded that my time at Manchester Grammar ended with anti-climax. I hadn't exactly expected to go in a blaze of glory, but I felt let down that someone—anyone—hadn't lied and said, "Gee, Kel Palmer, we're really sorry to see you go." The same thing was to happen in December 1982 when I decided to take premature retirement from the RAF and left my post in Belgium to go straight into civvy street. Had I left from a Station or RAF HQ, there'd have been a big dinner (Dining Out) for me and a lot of folk would have said nice things even if they didn't mean them. But that didn't happen in a NATO slot and one day I packed the car and a removals van, drove to Calais and awaited my retirement papers after 37 years in the RAF.

But before I move onto that wholly different life, you'll not be surprised that I have the odd comment about my final RAF tour, as Chief of Nuclear Plans in SHAPE. I admit that when I arrived in Belgium I already had thoughts of retiring which stemmed, not from a wish to leave the RAF or being unhappy, but from the number of offers of jobs I'd received on leaving the MoD. I had received only a few days' notice of my posting, so hadn't had the time to invite my work friends and colleagues to a farewell party. I therefore wrote an apology and said that after I'd settled into the new job, I'd be back to throw a party. From those letters I received a number of offers. The one that attracted me most was with BAe in Washington as their man on the air-to-air missile programme that I'd had a hand in. I wrote back saying thanks—but no thanks—which made them think I was after more money, which I wasn't.

It was left like that until I flew over to Farnborough in early September for the Air Show when, by lunchtime, many of the previous offers had been repeated. This time I listened because by now I knew what my job was all about. Frankly I hated the job itself and could not reconcile the general atmosphere at SHAPE with the succession of high pressure but enjoyable posts I'd enjoyed with the RAF. I was in a very onerous post, one that carried a lot of responsibility and meant being very precise in what I wrote and said, and very diplomatic in dealing with the Nuclear set up that was dominated by the Americans. They treated SHAPE as an overseas club, as a pleasant way of being able to travel the Continent without doing too much work. They had all the typical US cut price shopping facilities on the base and were able to take advantage of the many holiday resorts run for the American military throughout Europe.

I had 24 officers on my immediate staff, twelve of which were American, few in whom I had the slightest confidence. One, a USAF full colonel, would spend two hours every morning in the SHAPE bank queues changing money between the many European and North American currencies to gain maximum exchange rate profits. Another was an immensely wealthy US Marine colonel who would drive from Mons every Friday morning in his Porsche to be in Berchestgarden with his Italian model girlfriend by 6 p.m. He arrived back at 2 p.m. each Monday, having averaged over 110mph for the return journey. We'd all like a go at that, eh? But it wasn't his car, his bird, or his lifestyle that hacked me off; it was that as an officer on my staff he was as useless as tits on a bull.

Clearly it wasn't what I was used to, but I was even less used to being told by our American four-star general that I shouldn't chastise Colonel Lee for wanting to let his hair down after an exacting week's work! I realised that I was beating my head against a brick wall when I approached the Deputy Commander, a three-star RAF guy, with my concerns, to be advised, "Let it go, you'll not change their attitudes." He was a nice chap and a very capable one who had been put in a high profile post, but he held no real power in the US-led nuclear regime. Britain was the only other NATO nuclear power, but we were a mere token force at SHAPE; all the real decisions were made back in Washington. I'm sure that the Supreme NATO Commander at the time knew exactly why I held such a jaundiced view. When asked by the Press, "General, can you tell us please how many people work in your HQ?" he answered laconically, "On a good day, about 25% of them."

It's all water under the bridge now and all those folk, the organisation that existed and the enemy for which it existed, have long gone too. I'll content myself with recording my totally unshakeable belief that had we ever gone to nuclear war with the Soviet Pact, all the NATO plans would have been overridden by the US as we could never have effectively used the complex and lengthy procedures necessary for the release of nuclear weapons in trying to fight a controlled and escalating nuclear campaign. So I was professionally very disillusioned and dissatisfied, knowing full well that if I chose I could see out the rest of my career in Mons until normal retirement at age fifty-five. I could join the US party set, the Golf circus, the long weekend/short working week brigade, buy a cheap new Mercedes or BMW every year, and put the rest of my overseas allowance in the bank.

Actually, that doesn't sound bad, does it? But the clincher for me was that had I stayed there for three years, my current OR experience and knowledge that industry was interested in would have dissipated. The decision was relatively simple in the end. I received a firm written offer from BAe to be their air missiles man in Washington. I was enthused until I looked more closely to find too many ifs and buts that always seemed to be attached to jobs with that Company. Then there was the almost impossible dilemma concerning Rosemarie, even though I probably saw too many phantom problems at the time. Also, I would have to leave at least two of the children behind, if not three, and I changed my mind before my last day in uniform and accepted an offer from GEC for what else-the Nimrod AEW programme.

We returned from Belgium on 1ˢᵗ December, took retirement leave and end of tour leave and retired formally on 23ʳᵈ March 1983, having served almost 37 wonderful years in the mob (36 if you discount SHAPE). Anxious as ever to get my feet under the table, I opted to join GEC at Borehamwood three days before

Xmas, bought our first ever house 12 miles away in Luton and settled down to make a new life.

Ironically, I recall the first words spoken to me at GEC by the Managing Director who'd been trying to lure me out of the RAF for years. I cut short my leave and thought it would be a good idea to meet all the folks with whom I'd be working in the social run up to Christmas, and then be ready to start in earnest in the New Year. Thinking he might welcome that too, I broke the news enthusiastically; he turned with a sallow smile and said, "Oh, I see, you're joining us for Christmas." A funny feeling told me that I was now just another worker, not a blue-eyed boy whom they wanted and needed on their side.

12

GEC-MARCONI

This is the first of four chapters covering my second career in the British Defence Industry. I've avoided technical detail unless necessary to explain an issue. Should you suspect I have picked on some individuals or organisations too pointedly, I submit that my views have stood the test of time and of scrutiny from the safe and calm haven of retirement. This is how I saw it without prejudice, without grudge and certainly without vengeful intent. Others have been free to have their say over the years, but then I suspect you wouldn't want to be overwhelmed and confused with everyone's point of view. I offer you mine.

I once thought of writing specifically on the Nimrod AEW project; not because I was involved with it for 20 years, but because the programme epitomises so many of the problems that have beset UK Defence procurement since WW2. However, I decided it would best be subsumed in an autobiography which I shall enjoy writing and a reader find less boring. I want to be fair and factual about my time in industry, although experience teaches there is precious little fact that when closely examined is indisputably fact. Not so?

Acclimatising

My first surprise on joining GEC was to find that obtaining the information I needed in order to do my job was not readily available. The usually garrulous Managing Director had lost his tongue. The Marketing Manager, an ex-RAF officer who I thought of as a friend, was clearly playing hard to get, and my Divisional Manager was unable to give me any idea as to the talent and backgrounds of the team I was taking over. The Mission System team itself seemed nervous as to how I was going to approach my work with them and, instead of the Company compiling a briefing folder to introduce me to their ways of working and what they wanted me to do to help their programme, they were being positively negative.

My suspicions were aroused, or perhaps I should say I had misgivings. But my enthusiasm was unbounded to get stuck into my new career. After all, I was still tuned in to trusting people and concluded, quite reasonably I thought, that a Company that had been head-hunting me for years might just want to make best use of the truly vast current knowledge and specialist experience I had to offer.

Hang on Palmer, I say to myself, this running away with harsh bitter reflections will not do; why are you dwelling on the red entries rather than those in the black? I admit that I find it hard to view objectively something that is wholly subjective, to intellectualise something that carries a lot of emotion. Also, I doubt if even my friends would have any interest in reading about the everyday things that happened at the various GEC sites; the storms being more newsworthy than the calm seas. But let me try, after all this time, to stand aside and assess the actions of the major players and give credit where it is due before I deliver a few quick kicks to some deserving backsides.

The AEW team in Hertfordshire in 1983 were a friendly bunch of excellent engineers, some at the top of their profession and motivated to getting Nimrod AEW into RAF service as an operational system of which they could be proud. When the programme came under serious threat of cancellation it would be hard to find a more loyal and dedicated team anywhere, and that spirit flowed down to the administrators, secretaries and even the normally invisible bean counters. If by some miracle anyone of that team ever reads these words, I'd like them to know how much I respected them; it was not their fault that GEC eventually lost the contract in humiliating circumstances.

The Tangled Web

Nimrod's problems were born in 1977 when the MoD was persuaded to award a development/production contract for their evolving ten-year old Operational Requirement. Much of the lobbying originated in the all-powerful BAe whose aircraft was an acceptable platform and had been used for trials since "DB1", the first trials aircraft had been bought from Middle East Airlines in the late 60s. The Aircraft Office in PE (The Procurement Executive) naturally supported an aircraft that had a proven maintenance record in RAF service. Intense parallel pressure was clearly exerted by Lord Weinstock whose GEC empire was in the process of amassing a money mountain. He convinced the Ministry to go ahead with both the radar for AEW and the Intercept radar for the Tornado F3, the fighter version of the strike/attack Tornado that replaced the V-force and Canberras. To get his way he would have had to impress the technical side of PE, plus the specialists at the Royal Signals and Radar Establishment (RSRE) who would be providing much of the brain power, many of the trials facilities, and underwriting the viability of the technical solutions.

Contributing to the decision would be a laudable wish to retain leading edge technology in the UK, to fund RSRE's facility at Malvern, and to find suitable export markets to challenge the US and France. Not being in Whitehall in 1977, I don't know what the AFD reaction was then to the Tornado radar, but few believed that a hastily home-developed AEW could succeed against the progress made by the USAF with AWACS and the US Navy with the E2B/C Hawkeye. Cynically, even had their "airships" voiced reservations, the politico/industrial lobby with the ultimate threat of "It's either this or nothing" would have overridden them.

However good their original intentions, GEC were doomed to fail. They had neither the numbers nor quality of people to run two such programmes, perhaps a legacy of waiting for years and diverting scarce resources to other projects. Suddenly, one Division owned two major developments. Inexperienced engineers with little specialist knowledge and even less management experience were promoted overnight beyond their levels of competence. Executives were faced with running two technically-demanding developments, of working closely with the MoD establishments, managing their own large teams of relatively inexperienced people, and working with BAe as joint Prime contractors. It was a recipe for disaster. The men and women who were handed the poisoned chalice doubtless did not see it that way. They would have realised their good fortune and believed themselves capable of rising to the challenge for which, it probably seemed then, they had time on their side.

What couldn't have been foreseen below Managing Director level was that their GEC masters under Lord Weinstock did not properly understand the MoD's Requirement or, if they did, had no intention of spending a penny more than they could help to meet it. The workforce, delighted that their future was guaranteed with five years of development, six in production, and twenty in service, could not have imagined that their executives would not be able to work in a joint Prime Contractor capacity with BAe. Neither would they have suspected that those in Stanhope Gate and Rochester would be prepared—indeed committed—to hiding problems and failing to reveal the true state of difficulties arising during development. In following that duplicitous path, many an unholy alliance was formed with people in high places in MoD PE and even the odd senior RAF officer was not above suspicion.

So where did I stand in this chaos and what could I do about it? My allegiance was to those who paid me in GEC, but I'd spent 37 years in the RAF and been involved with this particular programme, on and off, since 1966. As GEC had been so keen to get me aboard, I naively thought that it wasn't a case for me of taking sides, I believed that we were all working together to give the RAF what they wanted and what they had paid for. I saw my real value to GEC as being best able to translate the RAF's needs and priorities and take any GEC problems back to the RAF, thus smoothing out the development process in a mutually satisfactory way. If you think that naïve of me then I must tell you that no one in GEC, either when I was being wooed or after I'd joined, ever briefed me on my precise role. No one, not even the MD who must have been feeling the pressure, ever said formally or informally, "Now look John, this is how it is and this is how we'd like you to play it."

As I became familiar with GEC's pecking order, I talked to key people in Marketing, Engineering and System integration. I met the Trials team at Woodford, and with BAe and Malvern. I knew the programme structure intimately, counting most of the key people as friends. To a man, they were still friendly, but it was as if a steel curtain had come down on information transfer. I didn't like the picture that was emerging, but I was unsure as to whether I was facing sheer incompetence or something more sinister arising from dubious Company policies. In the RAF I'd had a lot to do with industry, but visiting a company for briefings and a business lunch is not the same as working for one. The first shock came when I asked my Divisional Manager to tell me about more about the team I'd been allocated. I'd be finding out for myself in due course, but it was nice to know which particular individuals were being groomed for stardom, how long I had them for, and whether there were personal matters I should be aware of and keep an eye on.

He was an exceptionally nice guy, so his response amazed me. He was surprised that I should have asked the question at all, saying no such assessments or records were kept—but that the Personnel Director might have something. The sign on that gentleman's door should have read "Anti-personnel". He haughtily advised me that the only staff records were disciplinary records, and besides, who the hell did I think I was for daring to approach him? Here was a man with whom I was obviously going to cross swords, a man who turned out to be part of an internal GEC Gestapo. The pieces of the jigsaw of doom were beginning to fall into place.

I then went to open the box on Company policy. Where better to start than the Marketing Director who was ex-RAF, had wined and dined me dozens of times and who, with the MD and Chief Engineer, attended all the meetings that mattered. I simply wanted to get an early feel for the big picture and, again naively, thought that if I read through the Company Policy files it would provide the essential framework. I went to his secretary as he was away for two weeks. She was very reluctant to show me anything until I spoke to the Chief Engineer in the next office who gave her the green light. She need not have bothered—I gleaned nothing. A GEC "Policy File" was a bunch of assorted papers kept between the same cover in no particular order, and with no interconnecting minutes or actions. I was later to find with all the companies for which I worked, that there was no such thing as a genuine Company Policy file. Individuals kept on "personal" files, only the records that it suited their purposes to keep. No omnibus Company policy file existed because a comprehensive record might mean someone accepting responsibility and to whom blame could be attributed. The practice of building an audit proof trail was a GEC trademark.

Drawing that blank led me back to the Chief Engineer. He was effectively the programme manager, so if anyone could give me a sensible summary on the project it should have been him. You'll have noted that I didn't go to him first because I was still following my air force teachings of following the chain of command; you didn't go to the top if the answer was available lower down. However he was unable to tell me anything that I didn't already know and was clearly under pressure not to reveal the true state of the development, either to the MoD or even to someone on his own team hired and tasked to help pull his chestnuts from the fire.

The real eye opener came when the Marketing man returned to launch into a scathing attack on me for "stealing his files" the contents of which he said had nothing to do with anyone else. Okay, so that was the administrative practice in GEC and I apologised for my innocent error, but that incident created a wedge between us that was never removed. We live and learn, but I was left pondering: "Methinks thou doth protest too much." Having failed to get any sense from the leaders, I was forced to do it the hard way. I first got the latest state of play from the MoD, and then carried out a thorough trawl amongst the many System specialists to see if they were happy with their part of the ship. Most were, and were actually delighted to talk to someone who was thinking in System terms rather than of separate specialist elements. But what concerned me most was the abject lack of understanding as to what performance the RAF wanted, especially those performance parameters that were essential and non-negotiable.

This ignorance started with the Manager of the Systems Group who, a mathematician by trade, had been placed in a uniquely important post and was well out of his depth. The Transmitter team by now had overcome early snags but now had a serious reliability problem. It seemed to come as a surprise to many that the system had at last proved capable of detecting targets at long range, and they were so chuffed with that success that it inhibited significant progress on the tracking and intercept functions—the *raison d'etre* for the system.

At another site under the same MD, the Tornado F3 radar was in even more trouble and the MoD were beginning to lose patience. I could confidently claim then to be an expert on using interception radar (AI) systems, and put my head on the block by offering to look at a video of the performance obtained in recent trials. I found it hard to believe that I was being asked to make any favourable comment on the evidence before me. Again, it seemed to come as a surprise to the GEC hierarchy that their radar could actually see a target. They pointed to the screen to show where it was detected and how it was tracked, little caring that as soon as the target or the fighter changed heading, the tracks disappeared. They had edited the tape to eliminate the worst features but even so, here I was in 1984, watching a new technology radar destined for a new generation fighter, that was substantially inferior to a radar I'd operated 20 years before! Admittedly, there was much development still to be done, and the new technology had the potential to perform a lot better. But the damning feature with both the AEW and AI radars was that GEC did not seem to know or really care what the RAF wanted, and were not embarrassed by their failure to meet the Requirement and to be running way over time and budget. Somehow in late 1984 the message eventually got home. In typical GEC fashion, the MD left overnight, followed by a handful of key figures that were probably partially responsible, or were simply fall guys following a well-established pattern of search for the guilty-persecution of the innocent.

A Reprieve

The new MD was a breath of fresh air and he made immediate staff changes that put AEW back on the rails and kept the Tornado radar programme alive. The team were given a new sense of purpose, whilst the MoD accepted a delayed In-service date and proving of the main performance features that had now been slightly emasculated and called "Cardinal Points". We even began to see a way that we might produce an export version of the radar for fitting on the C-130 with potential markets in The Far East and Australia and a short-range version with European aircraft companies in Italy and France. We were forced to look at foreign platforms because however sensible the choice of Nimrod as the RAF's platform, it was unexportable. These "scaled down" systems, less capable than the Nimrod fit, were based on our belief that the performance requirements in less populated parts of the world and over the sea could be met by the present radar when fully developed and configured. But the RAF system remained in trouble because, between them, the combined talents of the GEC and Malvern engineers had not managed to enable the radar to distinguish between targets moving above a certain relative speed on the ground and airborne targets.

In other words, the sensor detected too much and a radar map of the UK looked like an AA motorway map. Changes were needed to the computers, the software, correlators, filters and processors-all of which involved time and cost with high technical risk. These deficiencies had been pointed out frequently to GEC; they had chosen not to implement them. The RAF reluctantly accepted that for their limited money and in the timescale, they would not have an over-land/overland capability. However, they did need, expect, and had contracted to being able to detect, track and intercept targets flying overland when the AEW was itself over the sea (The North Sea patrol being crucial).

It was humiliating to watch the GEC hierarchy try to wriggle out of their con-tractual undertakings. Once, during a demonstration to top executives, I had to acknowledge its limited overland performance. I was told very forcibly that I couldn't say that to the bosses of GEC—even though it was the 100% truth and directly due to their failure to invest sufficient cash into development of the main computer and the other vital elements. They refused to face facts even when pre-sented in house by those who worked for them and had total commitment to get-ting it right.

In February 1986, in a final attempt to achieve the minimum acceptable oper-ational capability, the MoD funded the programme for a further six months to the tune of £50M. Meanwhile, they also invited other companies to tender for the programme in the event that GEC were unable to satisfy the MoD that they could develop the System to the cost and timescales now set. In their customary arrogant way, GEC's scoffed at the idea that the MoD would cancel at so late a stage, and pointed to there being no alternative system available. The six-month Competition went ahead under protest, with GEC relying on the influence of the formidable Lord Weinstock—supported by BAe—to win the day with the Prime Minister and her Cabinet.

Home to Roost

March to December 1986 became one of the most intense periods in this man's life. From 26th February when the Secretary of State for Defence announced the extension in the House, I went on a veritable roller-coaster of a ride that plumbed the depths and reached the heights, one that portrayed the best and worst of Companies, Civil Servants, MPs, service officers, organisations, and individuals.

By calling it "intense" I'm not pleading pressure. Pressure is something that can destroy a man, tear at his reason and undermine his confidence and persistence. I'm talking about the intensity of facing a challenge, of leading a team in a worthy cause with real hope of success, of countering opponents who'd been waiting in the wings for a chance to bring you down, and of restoring a sense of pride and achievement in a team badly let down by top management. Those nine months in 1986 were intensely satisfying for me, irrespective of the score at the end.

This isn't a story, so it matters not if I put the cart before the horse. But let me spell out the task facing GEC in this competitive stage. Our aim was to convince the MoD that we (now as Prime contractor) and BAe, could meet our contractual commitment within the budget and revised timescale. By now the entire GEC team were fully aware of where we fell short of the RAF's Cardinal Point specification and what we had to do in order to satisfy it. In effect we had to turn the on-going development work into hardware and software in time for flight trials and demonstrations to be given within 6 months. To achieve that aim meant little more than spending money that GEC could and should have spent years before. But some of the enhancements meant parallel improvements in a number of areas that complicated the proving of the complete system-a little like the annual chore of getting the Xmas tree lights to work by trial and error! But now we had a clear plan with tight but manageable timescales that, now acting as Prime Contractor, we could carry out without hindrance. Above all, we at last had the right managers in the right jobs.

Mass briefings were given to everyone on the affected sites, specifying what had to be done and what the penalties were for failure. The response was unbelievable and as the life, drive, and enthusiasm returned to the division, I couldn't help but rue the wasted years of mismanagement. The new found confidence and technical advances coincidentally led to the birth of a C130—based export system with Lockheed of Georgia, and even as the development was proceeding at pace, combined GEC/Lockheed teams were visiting Pakistan, Singapore, Australia, Taiwan and Malaysia; heady stuff indeed. At the mid point in June we were well on track.

At the outset of the competition, we had briefed a specially formed MoD evaluation team on our programme, the sequence of work, and milestones for being able to prove how well we were doing. Being centrally involved, I had insisted we be totally open about our programme as many of their team held misconceptions and misgivings that had been allowed to gain currency in the previous year. I argued that GEC were seen as having hidden the truth and ignored the RAF's warnings, and we should start with a clean sheet. I still believe that that was the right policy, though I was later to be dismayed by the underhanded actions of senior RAF officers who I had trusted implicitly, but who had simply had enough of GEC's subterfuge and fairy tales and were out for blood.

In parallel with observing our progress, the MoD were now being courted by a number of aircraft and radar companies who saw their chance of scuppering GEC's dominance and BAe's sales of Nimrod. This feeding frenzy was led by the producers of the only two in-service systems, Boeing/Westinghouse with AWACS and Grumman with the Hawkeye. Another Lockheed group teamed with Thorn in the UK to offer a system based on the P3, and others offered variants of the E2c radar on larger airframes to achieve the RAFs' specified time on patrol. On 25th September, the Minister of State for Defence Procurement announced that in the light of GEC's successful interim demonstrations, and after a concurrent evaluation of other contenders, the evaluation was to be narrowed to Nimrod and AWACS. Both systems, he stated, had the potential to meet the CPS and accordingly GEC and Boeing were to submit their specifications, terms and "best and final price offer" for meeting the Requirement, by 10th November.

A False Dawn

Within GEC it was Mafeking all over again at this announcement. Congratulations rained in and the GEC hierarchy adopted the haughty disdainful air of "What else did you expect?" In their eyes it was all over bar the shouting, their policies had been vindicated, their strength as Europe's biggest and richest Electronics Company had been bound to prevail. I was under no such illusion. I expected the elimination of all the other contenders; they had never been a threat. I watched the body language of men I knew well, I saw as eyes were lowered and people were keen to change the subject. I noted how the MoD evaluation team, allegedly anxious to be fair and open, did not return for further updates as our trials progressed, and how their leader became impossible to contact. With the open access I still enjoyed to the MoD, I found it odd that so many of the team so often were out of their offices and out of the country in Washington or Baltimore, or the AWACS bases at Tinker in Oklahoma or Geilenkirchen in Germany.

My suspicious mind drifted further. BAe were getting unusually cosy with Boeing, and although that might seem innocent I have never known any company so accomplished in offsetting its bets. But the clinchers for my suspicions that it was a done deal for AWACS from 26th February were twofold. First, the deeply held preference in Whitehall at 2 star level and above for AWACS based on a history of dislike and distrust of GEC. Secondly, the odd coincidence that every time we flew a Nimrod trial, we were tracked from a distance by at least one of the NATO E3A's. We had undertaken to give MoD our flight plans for the trial flights so they knew exactly where we planned to fly and what our radar picture should be. They could have no other purpose to shadow us than to compare radar performances in similar scenarios. Entirely legitimate-except that we were in trials mode being compared with a proven operational system supposed to be in competition. We didn't get their flight plans and once, when we set a trap and turned unexpectedly towards them over the North Sea, they turned and high tailed it back to Geilenkirchen. Okay, nothing too sinister, but it all added up to the outcome being a foregone conclusion. The MoD had decided; I briefed my GEC masters accordingly.

The GEC hierarchy, with rare exception, were a cold and unapproachable lot. Bad news was unacceptable, facts confused them, warnings given by underlings—even by very knowledgeable experienced underlings like me—were scorned and renounced. They had it on the very highest authority that all Lord Weinstock had to do was to turn up at No. 10 and Maggie would roll over and award GEC the contract. A particularly insufferable BBC man ran a Panorama programme in the final weeks of the evaluation. His prime witness was the Group Captain who had taken over from me, who of course I knew very well and who I respected as an extremely knowledgeable officer with a very impressive television presence. I knew he would come across as an honest airman simply asking for what the RAF had agreed to procure and pay for. He would speak very clearly and precisely and, without actually saying so, would leave the impression of "Are we being unreasonable?" I could have written his speech for him.

I persuaded my own MD that GEC must be very careful whom they selected to appear against the MoD's champion. It must be someone who did not offend, who knew the programme and the issues well enough not to lose their cool, and who would be able to speak convincingly and persuasively on all the good things that GEC were now doing. He must be able to play down past errors in a slightly humble way whilst majoring on new development, emerging technology and keeping the cutting edge stuff in Britain. His trump card would be to ask if the UK really wanted to pour over £900M down the drain. I was dumbfounded when they chose the executive most despised and distrusted by the MoD. He was the head of GEC's electronics empire outside HQ, and the man on whose shoulders lay most of the blame for years of sheer incompetence. If that wasn't enough, he was a scruffy, furtive looking individual who had no personality and was guaranteed to give the crafty Panorama producer the very image of GEC that the latter wished to create. Knowing my reputation for tact, you'll know that I made my feelings clear. But having tried to persuade many others to help, the best I got was an agreement that I would have the job of briefing and coaching our man to put up a good show.

It was like trying to try to teach a one-legged man how to win an arse-kicking contest. Our 60-year-old top executive in a pinstriped suit with egg-stained tie knew it all. He didn't want to know what the RAF wanted or why; he believed that all they deserved was what his Company chose to give them. I knew what the RAF would say; how it would be said by a clean-cut smart officer in uniform young enough to know about modern technology and modern aeroplanes. I also knew that they'd film each of them for around 20 minutes, but cut the film to five minutes and show statements out of sequence. That was one reason for the guy being interviewed to be able to think on his feet and be wary of making statements that could be distorted with clever editing. I offered to question him, as I knew he'd be questioned, so as to get him thinking on the right frequency and in a cool calculating frame of mind. He threw me out twice for being "disrespectful" and hardly heeded a word I said. The result was as complete a disaster as could be imagined. The Group Captain came across as an honest intelligent man who deserved the best equipment the country could afford; our man made everyone squirm with embarrassment and say they'd never buy a used car from such a rascal, never mind £900M of AEW!

My next unwelcome message up the chain in November was that the battle was lost and a policy of damage limitation should be followed to seek offsets for the blow that was about to fall. If we gave in gracefully, we could be spared the humiliation of our faults and incompetence being announced formally in the House. After all, this was a decision that was bound to draw heavy criticism because of its impact on British industry and the loss of hundreds of jobs. GEC was a huge company with many successful divisions; a defeat of this magnitude with maximum exposure on the international stage should be avoided. Once again the answer from on high was a lemon; Lord Weinstock still had to play his trump card. Well he did, and he lost, and the whole sorry tale came out in a long speech in the House and the following day almost the entire workforce in Hertfordshire received their brown envelopes. I said earlier that Nimrod brought out the best and worst; no one emerged as real victors, there was skulduggery on all sides and the Ministry of Dirty Tricks worked overtime. That said, there can be no doubt that the guilty men in the Nimrod disaster were the top executives of GEC. After over half a century in the aircraft/electronics business, I can think of no Company that deserved its comeuppance more on that fateful afternoon in

Westminster in December 1986. I went back to Radlett and sent out hundreds of Xmas cards with the message, "Let nothing you dismay."

The Aftermath and consolations

Personally, I was not about to sit back and mope. I was being kept on to run the C130 export programme with Lockheed that would benefit from the many improvements made during the trials. We retained one of the Woodford Nimrods and satisfied Lockheed's electronic experts that we had an export winner on their aeroplane. Some 40 air forces all over the world operated C-130's and the radar fit in the extra wide fuselage with a roll-on, roll-off capability, was well nigh perfect. When about to start conversion of a C130 to the role, the edict came from Stanhope Gate that we could not proceed. Lockheed offered to meet half of the development costs, but "himself" had finally killed a programme that went back 20 years. To the rest of GEC and British industry that was a decision based more on Lord Weinstock's pique rather than his renowned business acumen.

I saw the writing on the wall and began to look elsewhere. Taking my time, I considered six offers from industry, one to run a Tramways museum, another to be manager of a Scottish estate, and one to run a County Football Association. Remarkably, a GEC financial mogul covertly sidled up to me and suggested I might run some sort of illegal arms deal for him. He even brought along my first months wages in the form of a 1987 Jaguar. I declined of course, but can't help wondering every now and then! On the grounds of salary, location and doing something I knew best, I boringly and predictably opted for another defence company, moved house to Sussex and started work at Crawley. I was to stay there in the same building until I retired in 2000, although I worked for four different companies. More of that later, but first a trio of cameos in GEC days that I hope you find amusing.

Prior Knowledge

When the evaluation competition started in 1986, GEC decided that none of their Directors or technical heavyweights was suited to portraying GEC in a suitable image. It would be necessary to face the media from time to time, give rousing speeches in the City, and whip up enthusiasm for buying British and so on. The then Chairman of GEC drew the short straw and I became his minder, accompanying him whenever he was likely to face difficult questions about the programme. He briefed me on my duties along the following lines: "I know bugger all about aeroplanes and radar, I'm just a dumb farmer. It's likely that some of those who interview me will take advantage of that and trick me into saying something that you and the rest of the company wouldn't want to be on record. If that happens, just come out with something really rude and crude—and they'll not print it or screen it—okay?"

I understood very well. Our first interviewer was a lovely lady who turned on her considerable feminine charms before we went on air; they clearly knew each other well and had jousted before. She smilingly chatted him up, reminding him of the questions she was to put when the red light came on. He retorted by saying he'd seen it all before, and "For God's sake Angela, why must you always wear white knickers?" The red light came on; she said how nice it was to have such a distinguished representative. He with charm oozing from every pore replied that it was always a sheer delight to be interviewed by her. At that our fair lady launched into a question that was loaded with danger and venom, quoting a sum of taxpayers money that would be "squandered by GEC's negligence and incompetence" if Nimrod was not chosen. He was stung by the sharpness of the question and began to answer by challenging the amount of money and simultaneously criticising BAe. From over his shoulder I saw her eyes gleam as he took the bait so I stood up and uttered words that would have made Billy Connolly blush. "Good lad," he said, and had cause to repeat it four times in a ten-minute session. When the interview stopped and Herself had summarised it for the TV audience, I was handed a whisky and was feeling quite pleased with my performance. The sweet smiling lady walked sinuously towards me and I smiled a welcome—as even bitter opponents often do once the swords are sheathed. She slunk up very close, smiled demurely and said very quietly with eyes flashing, "If you ever screw up one of my interviews again like that John Palmer, I'll have your balls in my next curry." I do believe she meant it too.

No expense spared

When we marketed the C130 AEW overseas, we had to put a brave face on the competition going on in the UK, explaining to potential customers that this was merely a blip that had nothing to do with the system bound for the C130. We needed a touch of credibility that, to be effective, could only really come from our RAF customer. By fair means or foul, someone persuaded the RAF to let us have an RAF two-star who was in a Defence Sales post. His task was to join us on our trips overseas and support our radar claims and promises without perjuring himself or the MoD. He was tailor made for the task; tall, smart, affable, well spoken and socially perfect.

Our first stop was Kuala Lumpur and the best hotel in town. I had the job of looking after our VIP who strangely, for an RAF officer, had never been further east than Bahrain. On the first evening, a Thursday, he rang me in my room to ask if the hotel service entitled "massage" in the directory was administered by men or women. Did they come to your room or did you go down to the sports centre? Would GEC pay for it and would I go with him as he'd never had a massage before and as he was playing golf with the Sultan on Saturday he needed to be in good shape—and so on. I answered, "Both, either, yes," and if he wanted me to.

So down we went. I introduced him to Anna, the girl who ran the parlour, and said he was an important guest—so please treat him well. I'd had a shower and was sitting talking to Anna when the door burst open and two very agitated Malay-Chinese girls stood shrieking something that I couldn't understand. When they'd been hustled out, Anna explained the cause of their panic. It seemed that my colleague had gone in with one of the girls and she'd asked him to undress except for his towel and lie down. Then she'd asked, "Oil or powder", "front or back first", "softly or rough". Oil-back-soft were his choices, apparently. She had then asked him to turn over on his back and noticed he was "looking naughty" in her words. Thinking he had more in mind than a massage, she asked him if he wanted her "to finish him off". He'd replied, "Yes please."

The poor girl assumed this meant he wanted the *a la carte* menu, called in two other girls and they finished him off in no time! At this stage it appears my charge was so overcome with what had happened to him, that he left in a great hurry. Anna's concern was that the girls had embarrassed him and he might lodge a complaint. I told her not to worry, I'd check it out. He must have heard my door bang because within seconds he was hammering to come in. "John, I can't tell you how embarrassed I feel," he said. "By the time I realised what was happening it was too late. Whatever will those poor girls think?" I told him not to worry, these things happened and I'd ensure that all was well. He thanked me profusely and said something about behaving himself. We stayed in KL for six days before flying on to Tokyo, and when I paid his hotel bill it included charges for no fewer that 12 massages!

I told him discreetly of course that I was delighted to see he'd got over his embarrassment and that GEC were only too happy to see him keeping himself fit for his arduous duties. So taken was he by the charm and utter femininity of the Oriental ladies that the night we arrived in Tokyo he eagerly scanned the Imperial Hotel directory of services and dialled the number for room service massage. If only he'd asked! Massage in Tokyo was delivered by ladies weighing around twenty stones, built like sumo wrestlers and committed to anything but a western gentleman's pleasure. I was so pleased for him that we returned to the UK via Bangkok or else he'd have been scarred for life.

Into the Lion's Den

Nimrod AEW bit the dust, overwhelmingly due to GEC's appalling negligence, parsimony, and incompetent management at the highest level. When the C130 AEW was also cancelled and the GEC workforce disbanded with only a handful retained, I was not about to hang on to the bitter end. Someone liked me and I was well treated on my departure; however, before leaving I had a few things to tidy up. As I'd decided to stay in Defence I was keen to find out if I'd blotted my copybook in the MoD and might be *persona non grata* in the odd place. So I wrote and telephoned a lot and ended up perfectly satisfied that people had seen my efforts as in the company interest, but also as loyal to my RAF roots and to getting the right equipment to the front line at the right price.

I was keen also to tell GEC top management what I thought of their performance, even though I did not expect them to be interested in anything constructive I had to say. I just felt that someone should speak on behalf of the Hertfordshire hundreds who had lost their jobs because of Company policies and mismanagement, and were then subjected to a scandalously mean and callous redundancy scheme. The middle managers had lost their heads too, and only those who had managed to protect their backsides and run for cover to another division were still around. But they were not the culprits anyway. There was little point in going to him of the Panorama debacle, the buck stopped firmly at Stanhope Gate on Lord Weinstock's desk. So I wrote a four page letter, suitably crafted I thought, to get my points across without bitterness and rancour but being overtly critical of GEC's failure to meet its commitments to the RAF and its employees. I also tossed in GEC's failure to have any sort of career structuring that would help safeguard the company's future in the increasingly competitive world of electronics and aviation.

Again remembering my upbringing of following the chain of command, I went to see a non-executive GEC Director who was the highest-ranking ex-officer in industry. I knew what I wanted to say to Lord Weinstock and hoped that with his experience at the very highest level he might be able to give me some helpful advice. Instead he pleaded that he had no real authority, could not be seen to be rocking the boat, and felt I should retire hurt rather than carry my bat for a last knock. I left his office cursing myself for having approached him and disappointed that a man of such stature, private wealth and position, was too frightened to stand up and be counted or too aloof and comfortable to give a damn.

The letter dispatched, I was pleasantly surprised to receive a call from the great man's secretary summoning me to attend on the following Monday. I was met by the Technical Director, a charming man who warned me what to expect and how I might best make my points. He took me into the lion's den and withdrew, leaving me stood opposite the desk waiting for Himself to look at me. Looking down at what I could see was my letter; he said, "Well, Group Captain, you are absolutely right." For a split second I was taken aback by such honesty and endorsement of my opinions, until he added—looking at me, "It *is* above your pay grade." In my letter I had acknowledged that neither I, nor anyone else beyond Stanhope Gate, could be privy to all the intricacies of running such a huge empire, and had written, "I appreciate that much of this is way above my pay grade." He had gone straight for the jugular to put me in my place whilst knocking me off balance.

Fortunately—and I well recall the atmosphere in that room—I was a man that day totally on top of my subject, sure of my facts and certain that I was repeating the views of hundreds who would not have the same chance to state their case. Quietly and respectfully, yet firmly and confidently, I gave him both barrels and waited. "Have you seen our latest balance sheets?" he asked. Then, "Would you not say that I was running a successful business?" I talked eloquently about teamwork, self-image, motivation, integrity, treating people like the decent important people they almost always are. I added that if his Company had done more in that way, his profit margins might have been even higher. I suppose we agreed to differ and after some 20 minutes he was clearly getting restless. He said something to the effect that there were lots of jobs in GEC that I might consider, without any suggestions, and raised an eyebrow as if to say, "What do you think of that?"

I heard myself say with a smile, "Thank you Sir, but I believe the days of human sacrifice are over." We shook hands and I left to get a cheery pat on the back from my newfound ally outside. I wondered in retrospect if my closing words might have been different. Perhaps so, but I had a spring in my step when I emerged into the Park Lane sunshine and experience has taught me that when I have that instant feeling of achievement of a job well done, I should stick with it. 18 years on and GEC's empire has crumbled; food for thought, eh?

13

MEL PHILLIPS

How often does one explain a decision with "It seemed a good idea at the time"? Looking back, it's difficult to say just what swayed my choice of my next employer, but I think I chose MEL over three other contenders because the money was better, the company in size, culture and attitude was refreshingly different to GEC, and because its location at Crawley was much more attractive in terms of local housing and environment than that of my second choice of Thorn EMI based at Hayes. I'd been "head-hunted" for the post, which was a nice feeling anyway, and found myself welcomed with open arms, albeit confusingly as three different directors thought I should fill three quite different slots. The director who wanted me most spoke eloquently and persuasively at my initial interview, but I was to discover—as so many ex-military men have done—that those first interviews should all begin "Once upon a time…"

Military men find industry to be a culture shock because during their service lives they are left in no doubt as to exactly what is required of them. When however they arrive to take up a new job in industry at middle or senior management level, they find that they are expected to build their own empire, possess psychic powers to understand all previous company activities (without any records of course), and to know the professional skills, capabilities and experience of a bunch of men and women they've never even met. Of course there are advantages in that a new man can plough his own furrow and not be stuck in a rut created by his predecessor. It also means that one need not be too sensitive about the feelings of one's staff and fellow managers since you have no idea what pay and perks that even someone of your own "pay grade" is getting. In the military you would know to within 5% what a fellow officer had in his wage packet; in industry the differential in salary might be 70% and one might drive a BMW with running expenses paid, whilst another of identical grade makes do with a middle range "dry" Ford.

Being a new kid on the block also provides the opportunity to shine at everyone else's expense, to make oneself indispensable, and jump the queue for promotion over people probably more committed, loyal and capable, but without your ruthless streak. Again, I see the sneer on certain faces from my past when I write that and hear them saying, "Bloody Palmer, where does he get these odd ideas?" Well, we all have our own *bete noires* do we not? And the two or three men I'm thinking of, thought the sun shone out of their buster browns and they could do no wrong. I saw them, as Machiavellian characters, unscrupulous thick-skinned men that bullied and schemed their way through life leaving more pain than pleasure in their wake. Come to think of it, I never saw them on the rugby field where a scrum in the mud can sort out the men from the boys, neither did I ever see them put their head above the parapet or stand up to be counted. Okay, it's a personal thing; but those three colourful characters (Black, Brown, and White-I kid you not!) did get up my nose and as this is my autobiography, that's how I saw it-and them. There, I've got that off my chest.

My start with MEL was not an auspicious one, although until they sold out to Thorn EMI in 1990, I thoroughly enjoyed working for them. I'd been hired to run an AEW programme that MEL had dreamt up in the wake of GEC's Nimrod disaster. A lot of foreign countries had been persuaded that AEW was an essential element of any air defence network and were looking for something less complex and a lot less expensive than Nimrod or the available US systems. MEL had leapt on the bandwagon with a cut-price system for India which, to be attractive to the customer, had to be mounted on the HS 748, an Indian-built version of the twin turbo-prop Andover in RAF service. The deal was that MEL would build the radar, help re-design the Indian 748, and the Indians would install, flight test and introduce the system into service with MEL help. There was nothing wrong with the idea of a moderate performance AEW for the Indian scenario, or with the HS 748 since long range and mission endurance were not of paramount importance. The problem was that MEL did not have a radar; now that *was* a problem!

MEL (Philips) specialised in small lightweight radars for maritime patrol—a very different technical challenge to that of AEW. None of their radars could be used for AEW, so the director who hired me had gone to the mother company in Holland to obtain radar for modification to the role. It gets better since the radar he intended to use was designed and built by the Dutch for fitting on their naval destroyers. For what it was designed to do, it was a decent piece of kit, but it wasn't designed to detect and track airborne targets moving at high speed against a clutter background, nor to be mounted on a moving platform on which power, cooling, space and weight limitations were critical. Somehow this director had persuaded a well-respected senior radar engineer to go along with his crazy idea, and he in turn had persuaded the Indians—anxious to get involved in high tech radar development—that it was a feasible programme. Within days of joining I was sent as part of a large team to make the final R&D arrangements with Phillips, and was equally amazed to find on arrival in Eindhoven that I was to be the programme manager.

Without any briefing as to previous agreements, I was expected to negotiate a deal that gave MEL the right to modify the Dutch radar and then incorporate it into the Indian AEW system which had to include a reasonable element of Indian R&D input. My reaction to this ludicrous situation was one of disbelief. I'd been in the front line of AEW development for 20 years, I'd watched a number of heavily funded projects by capable engineers come to grief and only recently had a grandstand view as a £945M, nine year programme of the UKs' biggest and richest company, was cancelled at the death by the Prime Minister because it failed to meet the Requirement. I clarified a few issues in principle before bringing the meeting to a dignified early end on the pretence of clearing some pseudo legal aspects with BAe and HAL in India, arranging to reconvene three weeks later in Eindhoven. Back at Crawley I discussed the feasibility of developing the radar with the few engineers that appeared to be in the know. I detected little enthusiasm for the venture and even less confidence in the outcome. My director was keen that I shouldn't ask too many questions, but I pointed out that as he'd hired me for the job it was my head on the block, and before I could move the project forward I needed to understand what the Indians wanted and were expecting from MEL. I was to discover how many knaves there were in the MEL hand that I'd been dealt.

A Real Indian rope trick

India—the very name spells fascination and yet repulsion. Fascination takes the edge as I think of the magical plains in the north stretching up to the majestic Himalayas, of looking across the Jumna in the twilight to the splendour of the Taj Mahal that Shahjehan built for the love of a woman. I marvel at the immensity of the country, its teeming millions, their poverty and humility, and the mysteries and secrecies of a land once the jewel in the crown of the British Empire.

It is no good pretending that the repulsion does not exist; India is a clash between what you see, hear and smell, and what you feel in your heart, your soul and in your unconscious. Sitting in this grey cold February in Wales, it's easy to think that one exaggerates the Indian environment. But there is no doubt that our brains and bodies work differently at different temperatures. Unless you live in the luxury of a modern hotel and travel everywhere by air conditioned car, you will usually feel like a hot wet sponge, be too hot to bear a sheet or a collar next to your skin, be subject to fiery surges of temperature, and find your brain addled and temper volcanic.

I once berated our sub-continent marketing manager in Crawley when I heard him abusing our agent in Delhi over the telephone. I asked him when he'd last seen Gupta, to be told that he'd never met him, neither had he ever been to India after two years in post! Where India was concerned, he'd been living in a smug mental sanctuary, hiding from unpleasant reality and content to communicate via fax or E-mail. Whilst he sat in office luxury, surrounded by secretaries and all the modcons, Gupta was in a ground floor office, with chicken wire for windows, a telephone that worked maybe 25% of the time, the swish of a single battered fan for air conditioning, a room full of flies and dust, and a constant brown tide of people passing by his miserable office. I told our office-bound shirker, that when I was last there drinking Gupta's hot sweet tea, I counted half a dozen bodies being carried high on skinny shoulders en route to burial, burning, or the river.

Hysteria hangs in the very air of India. I visited often over a period of 30 years and when the choice was mine, I was usually happy to send someone else. However I would not have missed the experience and cite India as a place to which everyone should go at least once. I tried to persuade Rosemarie to come with me but, given the alternatives, she refused and still has no wish to go. I digress but will return to some thoughts of India later. I knew India and the Indian Air Force from RAF days and from various talks (on AEW) that we'd had at GEC. So when I was offered someone to escort me around India on my first visit in MEL colours, I declined on the basis of saving the company a few thousand pounds. I knew exactly whom I wanted to see and where I wanted to go; I also knew that both of the very senior officials I would meet would want to talk in private.

Every country requires a different approach to marketing, and each operates a different procurement system with multifarious procedures. India was pretty straightforward; you persuaded a high-ranking Officer or politician that he should buy or co-develop your equipment, and he did the rest—probably via many channels and many handshakes, but it was a top-down process, never bottom-up in my experience. This meant that in setting up the foundations for doing business, you had to enjoy a close personal understanding and mutual trust with usually one, seldom more than three, key individuals. I'd held meetings in Delhi and Bangalore, and with the aircraft manufacturers, and was about to fly home when I had a call from The Man in Delhi. Over a weak and noisy tele-phone line, he sounded angry and suspicious and suggested I caught the first plane back to Delhi. I did and we met at 4 p.m. in an out of town bungalow that he always used (i.e. not the MoD).

Exceedingly politely he welcomed me in and bade me to sit, offered tea and waved his man away when I declined. As he leant forward and fixed me with his piercing eyes, I was reminded of the Indian Rajah in a favourite old film of my Dad's, "The Charge of the Light Brigade." I half-expected him to say, "Well, Major Vickers, we meet again." Instead, he said, "Well, Group Captain Palmer, I thought when you came to see me last week, we had reached a good understand-ing. But after receiving unexpected visits from two of your colleagues this week I am wondering who I am supposed to be trusting." He could not have surprised me more had he called me Major Vickers because I hadn't the faintest idea what he was talking about! Ingenuously I asked him what he meant, to which he said, "Oh, come now, you must know that Mr Jekyll and Mr Hyde have both been to see me separately and both asked that their visits should not be made known to anyone else"—"Jekyll" being MEL's senior marketeer, and "Hyde" the South East Asia area manager. Neither had spoken to me about Indian AEW, nor had they revealed their plans to travel to India at a Board meeting only a day prior to my departure.

My host saw this was news to me, and because he and I had met on a number of occasions before, asked if I could be frank with him. I said that I always had been, and enquired whether the others had talked about AEW. When he assured me that they talked about nothing else, I asked if I might telephone my office (no mobile phones then). I was still trying to find a legitimate reason for their being there and for avoiding each other and me deliberately. If they were in country on different programmes to their own agendas it would not be necessary for us to confer. So why all the secrecy? It was 6 p.m. in Delhi, 10 a.m. in Sussex, and I made contact with the director's secretary with whom in three weeks I had man-aged to strike a rapport. She told me that both had left the UK within 48 hours of my departure, they had been seen separately by the director, and each had phoned every day to update the director on whatever he'd asked them to do. She had been tasked to book different hotels for us all and to ensure that our flight paths did not cross at any airport. She obligingly told me where they were stay-ing, gave me the rest of their itinerary and asked if she was to tell her boss that I'd called when he returned from Holland the next day.

"Oh yes please," I replied sweetly, "and tell him that we are all taking the Air Marshal out to dinner tonight; and blame me—don't you be seen to have been involved." I had previously given the Air Marshal an overview of the reasons for my visit without being too forthcoming about my reservations as to the way MEL were planning to meet his Requirement. I had wanted to talk to his R&D people about their ambitions for shared development and work and to the aircraft firm about the technical modifications and forecast performance post-conversion. Now I felt I could trust him with a little more about MEL's intentions and summarised my concerns so that we could all feel comfortable. In return, I sniffed out some idea of his budget and how he wanted the eventual contract to be drawn up.

We hit it off beautifully. His electronic experts were no mugs and already had sussed out the potential problems, and he made it quite clear that he did not expect a world-beating system, but one that would give cover against the obvious potential enemy and in which Indian industry would play a major development role and pick up the lion's share of production. I couldn't fault his aim—how he achieved it was up to him. My job was to ensure that we could complete our initial development satisfactorily and then transfer our technology to India in a way that gave us both credit and profit. I had major concerns, but now I knew what the customer wanted, I knew what Phillips wanted; all I had to do was sort out our own guys.

The first step in doing that was imminent; the MEL guys to be sorted were in Delhi that very minute and were to get the surprise of their little lives in the exotic dining room of the Maurya Sheraton. A few phone calls and faxes and Jekyll and Hyde were separately made aware from Crawley, not from me, that they were expected to dine with The Man, one on one, at 8 p.m. in one of India's most authentic national restaurants.

Slowlee slowlee catchee Monkee

I briefed—as in bribed—the splendidly attired Sikh Head Waiter to show my two friends to the selected table and to show my guest to a different table if he arrived before I was free. If this all sounds too cloak and dagger-ish, let me remind you that I had only just been hired to do a particular job for which I'd been poorly and misleadingly briefed. With the agreement of my director and the Board, I was now using my unique experience to familiarise myself with the customers aspirations so that Phillips and MEL could put together a credible package. Unknown to me, two senior company officials were also in country, armed with my itinerary and visiting my contacts ahead or after me. I smelled a rat. However, at that stage I had no idea whether it was just one or a swarm, or whether I was merely seeing another industry example of the rat race whereby knowledge was power, so people kept important facts to themselves. Whoever was doing what to whom, I was in a strong position because—whatever else my critics might accuse me of—I was invariably open and honest in all my dealings. If for good reasons something had to be kept under wraps for a while, I would never offer a false alternative. That was how my RAF working life had taught me to be, and during my years in industry I was frequently grateful because I never had to bother about tangled webs or about breaking promises that I'd made and forgotten about. I simply told it as it was.

Hyde arrived in the dining room and sat down. He selected his customary cigar, which was always the most expensive in the box when he was on expenses, and his usual tipple of malt whisky. An unsuspecting Jekyll arrived minutes later and, as I'd picked an alcove table, the two were on each other without warning. I gave them enough time to try to find out what the other was up to, and to make excuses at which both were past masters, and then joined them. I watched their faces—Hyde brash and arrogant, Jekyll sly and furtive, and asked sweetly on whose authority were they interfering in my programme. Both were flummoxed because each thought that they were the one specially selected to track and upset the new boy, whereas our director with more faces than a town hall clock had set up both of them to provide him with intelligence.

As they dug their respective holes deeper, they of course were not aware that I was about to be joined on a nearby table for two by The Man, and when he walked across and I went over to him I'd have given anything for CCTV in the room. I left them with, "I've faxed Crawley a report of our meeting tonight and copied it to the Board. I'll see you back there next Monday if you can tear yourselves away." Jekyll never spoke to me again, and Hyde left to join Thorn who then bought MEL and he and I crossed swords for years. The scheming director swore that he'd not briefed anyone to do anything, whilst I informed him that everything about the project was fatally flawed and there was no recovery path. The Board agreed even as the director fled to Holland to try to repair the damage to his corrupt plans. Whilst there, he got drunk, smashed up a few cars, three motorists and himself, spent weeks in jail and hospital and left ignominiously. I wasn't triumphant in the least; I was simply shocked that the fortunes of such a well-respected company were in the hands of a few charlatans.

A Ban on Hunting

However, I must not close this piece on India by prattling on about the dubious practices of big business. India, where time means little and *Karma* rules all, is too immense and fascinating to be overshadowed in such a way. So let me pick out a few special memories that I treasure—amongst my souvenirs as it were—that show how our enjoyment of this world is immeasurably enhanced by meeting people that think, look, talk and dress differently and live in places and climates that dictate a different life style. No one reading this could doubt my love of nature and of wild animals. India for me meant snakes and above all, the tiger. I had hinted outrageously about wanting to see a tiger in the wild and one day I received the exciting news that a place had been obtained for me on a wild boar hunt in an area where there was a good chance of seeing the King of the Jungle. We flew by courtesy of the Indian Air Force to an airfield near Bareilly, thence south by Land Rover, camel, and finally elephant to the Ganges basin with its dense river grass and bamboo thicket. The briefings were very professional, by men who knew the boar and the tiger, the need for preservation, and all the attendant rules about who could hunt and when and with what. I knew that my safety would be seen as paramount and my hosts, however keen they were to show me how a pig-sticking and tiger-shoot were conducted, would keep me off the ground and out of harms way. I was handed a splendid rifle that I found perfect in weight and feel for me, and I had little doubt that I could hit my target should the opportunity—or the need—arise.

Technically and physically I was primed for the hunt. Mentally I was not. To explain that I must take you back first to Kenya in 1959 when I found myself shooting crocodiles—or at least frightening the hell out of them and me! I had asked myself then what right I had to fly 5000 miles to butcher such dramatically fearsome but magnificent creatures in their own environment. They posed no threat to me unless I invaded their domain. Next I'll take you back to Rutland in 1955 when I was hauled before my Station Commander because I was nicking the foxes from the local Hunt. The Hunt would sweep from Uppingham down the valley, which is now Rutland Water, and the quarry would have to cross the narrow road outside my house before running into more open ground specifically landscaped for the passage of dozens of horses and the pack. One day returning home for lunch I'd come across a fox that was close to total collapse. As the Hunt came into view with the horns and the cries of the riders echoing in the distance, I picked him up and shoved him into my MG and whisked him home. When he'd recovered, I put him back in the woods and tried to be home whenever the Hunt met. Over some eight months I rescued five foxes, but was caught with number six. My CO told me I was offending the local landowners and numerous bigwigs and that, for the sake of community relations, I should cease. For the sake of my career, I did cease—well, at least I didn't take the car and found another way of helping the furry little chaps.

But it was in Texas in 1961 that a switch in my brain moved decisively from the apparent pleasure of shooting something to "Never kill one of God's creatures". In Texas there is, or at least there was then, just one day in the entire year set aside for Dove Shooting. The Texas brush that day was alive with red-hatted hunters who'd fire at anything that moved not wearing a red hat. Men keen to show how it was done introduced me to the quaint custom and I was soon caught up in the thrill of blasting away at innocent Jack Rabbits and fast low flying doves. Then, as so often happens when gripped with excitement and intent on filling the sky with lead, one gets careless. I caught a glimpse of movement to my right, wheeled and fired. At my feet fell the largest Hawk I have ever seen. He sprawled there, critically wounded, screeching at me and defiant. Seeing him to be past help, I pointed my gun at him, closed my eyes and fired. I cried with anguish at what I'd done and vowed I would never again shoot a living thing.

So it was in the lush green high grass at the edge of an Indian jungle in 1989 that a beautiful male tiger in full lustre merely heard the whistle of shot that passed over him, rather then taking the lead in his proud magnificent head. I thanked my host for giving me the chance to see my tiger; he replied that a man was more of a man for choosing not to kill rather than killing for the sake of it.

Land of the Ghurkhas

My second tale concerns visits I made to Kathmandu in Nepal, an adequate description of which is beyond my ability to pen. There is a small central city, full of bustle, noise, colour and people—a city of astonishing buildings, most of which seem perilously close to collapse, where limbless and blind beggars swarm in the streets, dogs snarl, fight and mate, and where children seemingly lie dead in the excrement of goats and cattle, and yet in which one feels perfectly safe and amongst friends.

To the north tower the gigantic peaks of the Himalayas, white and holy, a place of infinite serenity with a constantly changing pattern of cloud, sunlight and shadow. Climbing out of Kathmandu, you pass the tiered gardens where women and children in the brightest of colours tend the crops and rickety looking houses totter on the edge of deep drops. But it is the scenery that meets your eye as you leave the foothills that leaves you gasping at its sheer magnificence. You reach that level where the silence becomes almost unreal and it's easy to believe in places like Shangri La and the Kingdom of the Gods. With mountains, there is no argument. You've either been there and felt their wild implacable spirit—or you haven't. I do not have the words to describe what is a human contact with this rapture of reality. I've felt it twice, once in the Himalayas and once in Monument Valley. You can't see it on any photograph because it's deep in a confusion of senses, it's about light and space and looking out into a blissful eternity. I know nothing of Yoga—indeed I admit to being nervous to peel back the layers to view it more closely. But I do know that it deals with the three brains of man; the cerebral, the abdominal and the pelvic, and is realised only by the senses and can never be explained by words. Something tells me that there are forces astir in this world of which I know very little.

> *"Thine eyes shall seek the solar orb, thine earthly part shall earth absorb.*
> *To guide thee through the trackless night, to yonder sphere of love and light."*

Twenty-five miles to the east is the literal top of the world, the mountains that peak with Everest at over 29,000ft above sea level. Twice I went up Everest by helicopter to the service and hover ceiling limits of the machines and weather. Once I made it on foot with a small team to what I think they called Snow Camp, and then beyond to 21,500 ft and a breathtaking view of the peak. It looked so close, but that final 7600 feet held a million challenges and dangers that had sent many to an icy death. Most at Snow Camp saw it as the first rung on the ladder; their climb had hardly begun. But as my team headed down, I did not envy them. I've sometimes watched men embarking on some exciting and brave venture and wished that I could join them. I didn't feel that way about climbing, as much as I exulted in the panoramic views and the sheer physical achievement. Nowhere did this man feel so alone as he did on the side of a great mountain.

On my last day on Everest, a special treat lay in store. Seeking refuge from the icy wind and grateful for my *pashm*, I was gingerly negotiating a narrow path when I disturbed an eagle that had just finished a meal on a ledge. He was heavy with food and I was astonished to see him run some distance like a Harrier doing a short take-off, before he could launch himself. Then with a beat of enormous wings, curved at the tips, he lifted and circled so close above me that I could hear the wind in his feathers, before slowly and majestically he flapped his way below me into a gorge to become lost in the fastness of the jagged rocks. Perhaps in great things it is enough to have tried, to have breathed the same air as heroes. I greatly admired the bravery and skills of those who climbed that majestic mountain of rock and ice to fulfil their personal ambition or dream. I was not envious—to each his own; but as a non-mountaineer, the feeling of achievement I felt is one of the highlights of my life. Experts say that Everest is now too highly populated, but on my three trips I hardly saw a living soul. That suits me, as such places to me are special for their remoteness, mystery and inaccessibility. I resent them becoming commonplace.

Indian Night Life

My experience of Indian nightlife had been restricted to an Officers' Mess or a luxury hotel. I found no attraction in the nightlife that lay beyond the atmospheric restaurants and culinary delights. I was not naturally attracted to Indian girls and women, most of whom were light of frame and usually dressed so that only the eyes were visible. I thought of them as very feminine, facially often very beautiful with eyes so deep that you felt you could dive into them—but for me there was something missing. I was never tempted. Until one night I was taken to a small town that sat under the moon shadow of the great mountain of Annapurna. An Indian town at night is a far different place than the noisy streets and colourful bazaars of the daytime. When we entered the dimly lit rooms the atmosphere took my breath away. There were some people, well dressed, occupying lush comfortable chairs around a circular low stage, but elsewhere many sat cross-legged on the floor chewing what I was told was betel nut, or taking a pull at a hookah. I was reminded of the smell of "Arab's trousers" and of my grandfather's greenhouse obsession with geraniums.

The nautch-girls moved silkily and silently amongst the customers, and I declined the offer to partake of whatever so many were chewing or smoking, and left untouched the drinks that were poured for me. I needed no stimulant to appreciate what was happening before my eyes in the shape of a tall beautiful dancer who was barefooted, with red and orange voluminous skirts, bare at the waist and with a decent tight top garment that accentuated her exquisite figure. Her body was adorned with rings and bracelets, reflecting the light like mirrors to make it seem as if she were dancing inches off the floor at times. She danced to the music of flute and drum. Entering to a murmur of appreciation and expectation, she stood perfectly still momentarily, deliciously feminine, and then with leisurely sinuous movements began a sequence that started at her curved fingertips, before moving into her hands and wrists and arms.

As the tempo of the music quickened and heightened, her shoulders took up the rhythm that seemed then to transform her whole body like a writhing serpent. She seemed not to have a single bone in her flexible body as her feet began to move, rising on her toes like a ballet dancer and then moving her hips in the way of a Polynesian dancer to show glimpses of bare leg and trim ankles with her skin gleaming like burnished gold. My attitude changed from casual interest, to curiosity, to fascination and then to an intense feeling of being on the stage with her as the drumming reached a pitch of noise and excitement. I found myself looking into her eyes from perhaps six feet away and had the strangest sensation that they never moved or blinked, whilst her body melted into the rhythm of the drums. I could feel as well as hear the drums, and watched in rapture and ecstasy as her infinitely subtle movements slid into my soul as they went back down the rhythmic scale, through her body, into her shoulders, down her arms and wrists and back to her fingertips from whence they had started. I was enchanted and intoxicated—not with wine or hashish as many in that room, but simply with the dance that was so much more than a dance. "He who is intoxicated with wine will be sober by dawn, but he who has lost his senses to the bearer of the cup will not recover until the Day of Judgement." That night taught me the extent of my ignorance over the philosophies and ways of India, so mystical and so material that they baffle this Western mind of mine. I should have liked to explore further but now I fear the time has gone.

Working to strengths

Meanwhile, back in Crawley, the aborted Indian project had sucked the life out of everything else and there was tremendous relief that the company could get back to a product line that it was good at; small lightweight maritime search radars for the smaller aircraft and predominately for overseas customers. It was a good time to launch a new drive as technology advances now made it possible to enhance the effectiveness of a small system by integrating other sensors and displays. Protecting ones' own maritime, land and air approaches had become more popular than offensive systems and weapons. So at last I turned my back on AEW and concentrated on overseas markets and the development of custom-built maritime patrol (MP) systems. My suitcases began to wear out quickly as I literally toured the world outside Europe, but also had much to do in Europe as most of the suitable airframes came from the UK, Italy, France, Spain and Sweden.

Most of what I found fascinating on MP systems will be boring unless you've been in the marketing or aviation business. But, as with everything one does in life, you learn as you go. I learned for instance that it didn't really matter whether the product we were selling was as good as we intended or made it out to be. With equipment for fitting to an aeroplane, it mattered more to a customer that he was buying a good reliable aircraft at the right price. If you convinced an airframe manufacturer to fit your equipment, it didn't matter how many more capable or better value systems came along, the manufacturer would always sell yours. I also learned that in many countries, it mattered more how much you paid in backhanders rather than how well your kit performed. In Indonesia the going rate for inducements was 25%, in Brazil it was 15%, and in a notorious country in Africa it was a luxury flat in central London and a season ticket for Highbury. Many countries had no such overt practices, but few did not have some way of ensuring that certain people did very well out of a big commercial deal.

Even in countries calling themselves "squeaky-clean", there would be inducements, carrots, trade-offs, sweeteners, consolation prizes or whatever. I was never able to avoid the feeling that however hard I worked and however honest I was, someone who had done very little was reaping enormous personal benefits. I accept it is the way of the world, but I was not brought up or schooled into being part of that particular gravy train. More fool me some might say. But whatever I felt of the "funny" deals at the time, or how I saw them with the benefit of hindsight, there was no gainsaying the enormous pleasure I derived from travelling to so many countries. One bonus from entering the maritime patrol market was that it took me to the smaller countries whereas AEW had been a capability more for major powers. Even the small nations wanted to protect offshore oil and mineral rights and fishing grounds, and prevent smuggling and piracy. Some only wanted one or two aircraft, few wanted more than six, so I searched for the most attractive aircraft platform and designed a basic radar and system to which any customer could add his own extras of sensors, communications or armament.

With enormous enthusiasm, I drew up my marketing campaign, conscientiously arranging the itineraries so as to get maximum coverage from the visits without incurring unnecessary travel cost. Looking back I admit that I followed many false leads simply because none of my industry masters ever said I shouldn't go to such and such a place because my chances of success were nil. I had unbounded confidence in what I could offer a customer, otherwise I'd never have packed a suitcase. But at the start I was not aware of the political pressures, for instance, that made it inevitable that a particular country would only buy from France and never the UK, or that a foreign airframe company could not use foreign radar if a home produced one existed. I had to find out for myself that when Palmer went alone to spread his MP gospel to Algeria or Argentina, he would be confronted by "Mr France", a French combined team of industry, military, civil servants and politicians whose government would subsidise their bid and make it impossible for me and others to compete.

When trying to get a Spanish aircraft manufacturer into bed with the UK, rather than buy American, I discovered he wouldn't do so because Boeing might then decide to move their European 747 repair facility from Madrid to somewhere else in Europe. I enjoyed accumulating the experience, but I wondered then why the intelligence department in the companies for which I worked did not give me better guidance at the time. I don't like some of the conclusions I've reached with the benefit of hindsight.

South America

High on my list to visit was South America, a continent to which my RAF duties had never taken me. Before we set foot in a place, we all have notions and impressions formed over many years from a variety of sources, increasingly from TV travelogues that in shrinking the world often leave misleading images. Briefly, my preconceptions of South America were the Amazon, Copacabana beach, Carnaval, the Samba, the anaconda and the jaguar, the Andes, Peruvian mountain ruins, incredible waterfalls, tall beautiful *mulatas*, Argentinean beef, Eva Peron, a sea battle in 1941, constant political unrest and much poverty. South America is all of those and so much more; a few disappointments but so many more wonderful surprises with a touch of the unique that always has appealed to me.

In the late 80's and early 90's I was almost commuting to Rio de Janeiro and Sao Paulo on a weekly basis. When you travel to any place so often it's hard to avoid the "been there, done that" attitude, especially when, however much you enjoy it, you're not with the one with whom you want to be. It would be hard for anyone not to enjoy the scenic splendour of Rio. The spectacular rock formations of Pao de Acticar (Sugar Loaf) and the enormous statue of Christ who scans the whole of the sprawling city from high on Corcovada Mountain. The beautiful beaches of Copacabana and Ipanema with wide esplanades along which walk, run, skate and glide some of the world's most gorgeous creatures ogled by suntanned men who pose and preen, but seldom enter the water or join in the continuous games of football and volleyball taking place on the firm golden sand.

The drive from the airport to the luxury hotels along the southern beaches reveals a magnificent open city with parklands and tree-lined avenues. The shops that you see from the main thoroughfares are bright and modern, people appear happy and prosperous, the traffic heavy but not congested like New York, London or Rome. Bars and restaurants abound; the former serving the local poison *caipirinha*, and the latter specialising in the most succulent beef on earth cooked Argentina-style. For those fortunate enough to live and work in shop-window Rio, life is indeed sweet. I got to like the Brazilians very much. It is when you go behind the façade into the *favelas* of Rio and out into the provincial cities that the country loses much of its appeal. In few cities anywhere is there such close proximity of wealth and squalor, ostentation and misery as in Rio. Rich and poor often live harmoniously as intimate neighbours, which I found remarkable when one sees the violence and confrontation in other South American cities such as Caracas and La Paz.

Our man in Rio

I promise not to write another technical word about MP systems, but forgive me if I tell a wee story that occurred in my pursuit of a contract in which we were in head on conflict with the French. They had an inferior system but a very powerful marketing strategy including 100% loans from the French government. To demonstrate Government support for British industry (not always a given), we obtained the assistance of a then prominent MP to assure the Brazilians that we could be trusted to fulfil our contract and also offer some trade incentives to swing the deal our way. It fell to me to be his keeper for four days in country; I must withhold his name as he is still inclined to hit the headlines now and then, albeit for the wrong reasons.

We landed in Rio on the Thursday morning and drove to his five star hotel on Ipanema beach. Our Brazilian commercial partners provided his transport and made most of the social arrangements. I was to provide him with spending money, accompany him to all the meetings and social engagements, and keep him out of trouble. My hotel was about 2 miles away and I took time in the limo to give him the do's and don'ts of life in Rio. One of the main warnings was the very real danger of being mugged; in fact. over a period of four years and visits by over 20 different people from MEL, I was the only one to escape being mugged. Neither was it a case of simply avoiding dark and lonely places, or even darker and less lonely girls. In Rio, daylight muggings were a national pastime. If you walked alone on the beach or esplanade you would find yourself surrounded by a happy bustling mob, under the cover of which you were divested of everything including any decent clothing you might be wearing.

So as I handed our esteemed colleague £500 in local currency, I advised him not to venture out of the hotel grounds by himself, but if he did go onto the adjacent beach he should wear nothing but shorts and a shirt, and carry no wallet, no jewellery, no watch, and no cash. I suggested he rested after the long flight and I'd collect him for cocktails and dinner at 6 p.m. About 4.30 I received a panic call from my secretary to say that our MP wanted to see me urgently. I'd been working downtown since 9 a.m. and now had to drive the six miles through early evening traffic to go via my hotel to change into my DJ before picking him up as planned.

It was a very hot day and by the time I reached his hotel I was just a little frayed at the edges. He met me in the lobby, dressed immaculately, to tell me that he'd been mugged on the beach. "Lucky that I briefed you not to take any valuables," said I. Crestfallen, he told me that they'd nicked his best watch, designer sunglasses, wallet and the £500 I'd given him! I heard the old old story: "Nice boys and girls, playing volleyball, surrounded, knife on throat, don't shout or leave the beach till we have." I summoned my not inconsiderable charm and asked him to get a drink at the bar whilst I made a few calls. I drew out another £500 in local notes, briefed the duty manager to look after him and give him anything he wanted (except companionship in the room), and asked him to call me if there were any problems. I returned to the bar, handed over his spending money and said we'd be leaving in five minutes. "Just pay a quick call," he said and disappeared towards the gents.

I went to the checkout desk to make sure they had understood my instructions as he returned, saying, "What do you think of those for a pair of beautiful sunglasses?"—laying them on the counter. Even as he put them down, he was elbowed out of the way by one of those overbearingly pompous grey haired American Airline captains who slammed his flight bag on the counter and demanded his bill—now! Showers of brown glass flew high as the proud owner of the spectacles cried, "They just cost me £300!" I almost reminded him they'd just cost me and MEL £300, but instead I had the distinct pleasure of calling the Captain a clumsy arrogant sod and telling him that AA was undoubtedly the worst major outfit then in operation—which it was.

That night our VIP fell asleep in his Lobster Bisque, spilled port over Madame Ambassador's white dress, had his face slapped by a *passistar* who didn't welcome his roving hand, and finally got laid out by a transvestite who objected to having its' equipment tampered with on the dance floor. Similar disasters over the next three days culminated in him missing his BA flight on the Monday and suggesting he'd have to stay until the next BA flight on Thursday. I suspect he was slightly peeved when I changed his ticket for Iberian to fly him to London via Lisbon that same night. He'd waffled on about an important meeting he had with the PM on the Tuesday; I merely made sure that Mrs Thatcher was not disappointed! He was inebriated most of the weekend and looked like death every morning, but I admit that his performances at the meetings that mattered were the best of British. I could not help but admire him for that, but when the world fell around his ears a decade or so later, I could only say, "I told you so."

The Stuff of dreams

I've admitted elsewhere that I have always been on the lookout for doing something different, taking advantage of the situation to do something that I might otherwise never get a second chance of doing. Those with lots of money can look at a map of the world and decide where they want to go next. They can travel in style, live in style, change their mind if it isn't what they want and do something else that is. I've never had that financial freedom, so going to one of my Meccas has always given me exceptional satisfaction and I was to seize that chance in Brazil to go to the depths of the Amazon. I had six free days and opted for the adventure rather than accepting an all-expenses-paid week of Carnaval.

I'd never seen anywhere quite like it; I still haven't. The unimaginable beauty, the immensity of the jungle, the sheer size and power of the river over a 1000 miles from the ocean, and the way of life of those who lived there. Sometimes a much sought after or longed for experience is an anti-climax, but this one was magic from the time I set foot on the twin jet that took me via Brasilia, the political capital of Brazil, then on to Manaus. On the Brasilia leg I sat next to a senior politician who gave me an invaluable insight into Brazil's financial jungle, and to Manaus my companion was a Canadian helicopter pilot/cum dendrologist based some 100 miles up the Negro river who promised me an interesting ride if I could get up to his base camp. I'd no idea if I could as I was going strictly "on spec", but it was another option that was to prove rewarding.

We landed in Manaus in the middle of a ferocious thunderstorm that, due to its intensity, I expected to last only briefly. It actually rained at the same intensity for 9 hours. But of course that was the norm, and people there lived almost underwater just as those in the frozen north work, play, and live normal lives in the snow and sub-zero temperatures. In the friendly clamour of the bar that night I met the skipper of a riverboat going up the Amazon the next morning who said he'd drop me off at a small village and pick me up on the way back. I met a woman who lived in the same village who had a canoe for going deep into the *igarapes* (jungle creeks) and I made friends with a cultured Indian who knew everything about the wild life of the Amazon basin. By midnight I was an expert on a place I'd yet to see through the stair rods of continuous rain. The atmosphere of the bar was unbelievable; every time the door opened I expected Humphrey Bogart to walk in, shake his hat free of rain, fix me with a baleful glare and grunt "Whisky".

Love interests and Cup Finals aside, I don't think I have ever gone to bed looking forward to the next day with such eagerness and interest. My early call was at 6 a.m., and by 7 a.m. the tub that my skipper friend pretentiously called his riverboat was chugging out into midstream with visibility less than 10 yards in the driving rain. Standing next to him on his "bridge" (made from an aero-engine crate with a Perspex sheet) I remarked that I wouldn't like to taxi an aircraft in that visibility. We couldn't see either bank and the water was more like open sea than a river. He explained he could tell where he was by the feel and flow of the river and the pattern of the vegetation debris floating on the surface. I wasn't convinced, but as the sun came up and the rain eased, we were exactly where he said we were on his dog-eared chart.

We turned off the main stream into a backwater and eased gently alongside a rickety jetty from which a narrow track led off into seemingly impenetrable jungle. I'd decided to take up the offer of the woman with the canoe and followed her on a mainly wooden walkway with handrails, which soon deteriorated to criss-crossed logs with no handrails. Two things immediately struck me. The first was the incredible dawn chorus coming out of the jungle all around and above us. The second was that although now hundreds of yards from the river, the crystal clear water was flowing above the jungle floor at about 3 knots and 3 feet deep. Yet on that fast moving base, enormous lilies and other plants were growing as if in the tranquillity of Kew Gardens.

As the light improved and the rain ceased, I was enthralled by the vivid colouring of the birds and butterflies, at dragonflies the size of swallows, and by the myriad of slimy slippery creatures that flashed through the shallows at great speed. My self-appointed guide led me proudly to a ramshackle wooden/bamboo structure in which sat two small children, one of whom offered me a steaming cup of brew that looked like oxo, but almost blew off the top of my head. "We grow," said my hostess, pointing to the forest that enveloped the hut. "You like?"

A moment's digression here to bemoan the fact that I have been so busy rushing through my life that often I've not taken the time to savour what I've seen or said or done with other people. I have fulfilled so many of my ambitions, but having done so have committed my memories to the archives or Recycle Bin and not revisited an experience that I once cherished. Now, time and again, I'm finding new delight and satisfaction as my memory, except for some tedious examples, improves all the time. I'm able to recall places so easily, and even emotions and my state of mind at the time. I count that as an enormous privilege and wonder if, as one grows seriously old, whether those embers of memory will still glow brightly inside a body that has grown cold, both to its owner and those who live with it. I do so hope that grey eyes, grey hair, and wrinkles are belied by a fire burning deep below. Where shall we old folk be if it that is not to be so?

But back to 1990 when I was still sprightly and in the depths of the Amazon. The woman gestured for me to climb into her canoe as her young son pushed us off and then leaped aboard making me fear for a moment that I was bound for the dark fast flowing waters. I was reminded of my crocodile-hunting episode in

Kenya 30 years before as this river simply oozed menace as I imagined what lurked beneath the smooth surface. It wasn't long before my worst fears (or should that be eager wishes?), were realised. We were on a stretch of sluggishly flowing black water some 25 yards wide with the banks covered in dense high grasses and I had a distinct feeling that my companions were expecting a visitor. I saw it first some ten yards away and thought it was an animal swimming with head held up out of the water. But it disappeared only to surface alongside the canoe and be immediately lassoed by the boy who began to wage a tug-o-war. This was one of my "must-see" creatures of the wild, a large—perhaps 12ft long—Anaconda. It wasn't so much the length that impressed me, or the soaking we all received as it thrashed and twisted, but its sheer body size or girth. The bit that almost joined me in the boat and which I pushed back into the water must have been nearly a foot thick. That's a lot of snake, and I was more than happy to see the boy loosen his noose and watch the monster sink below the water to re-emerge heading away.

The little brown family were greatly amused at my reaction to their playmate and the woman explained that as they lived with the snakes, they also respected them and treated them as fellow-jungle dwellers, and not as enemies. I could have listened to her talk such commonsense for days, but after one day on the rivers and backwaters that left me breathless yet elated, the woman took me back to where the riverboat had dropped me and I spent a none too comfortable night in a sort of houseboat that seemed likely to destruct any second under the weight of water that poured incessantly from the Heavens.

I was glad that I refused the "oxo" because, as all the other occupants of my floating greenhouse slept oblivious to the raging night, I was able to witness the most spectacularly frightening thunderstorm activity I've ever seen from the surface. On the silver/black stage of brilliant lightning flashes and forks I could see a world of twisted waving trees and of shadowy shapes and white water flung high. I could imagine other terrors out there in the tumultuous violence of the storm and its endless peals of thunder. As the storm moved away the wind dropped, the houseboat stopped shaking, and I sat fascinated as the clouds broke to reveal a huge full moon that illuminated a beautiful scene of magical tranquillity. Suddenly I was Peter Pan, watching the swooping circling flight of hundreds of birds or bats against the silvery backcloth of the moon. I tiptoed past the dreamers to the front of the houseboat and gasped audibly as I looked up at the dark sky away from the moon and at the sensational celestial show above me. Where the tree-tops met the horizon, distant silent lightning flared like bubbling hot lava and for a while I fancied I saw the silver/grey/white arc of a "moonbow". Satiated with that wondrous spectacle, I fell asleep huddled in the bows of the damp and dirty old boat and awoke to the warmth of the sun on my face and the Viet Nam style clatter of a chopper landing in the clearing behind.

It was my friend from the flight from Brasilia who'd been told by the riverboat skipper where I was and had come to keep his promise. I remarked that, in this vast wilderness, it was surprising that the jungle drums were so effective. But he explained that in the dangerous and violent climate of the Amazon basin it paid everyone who lived and worked there to be in regular touch with a recognisable pattern to their activities so that others would be alerted if the pattern changed. As much as I was enjoying life on the water and in the weeds, I leaped to the chance of seeing more of the country from the air. We flew to remote villages, to lumber camps, to a diamond mine, to a place that I swear grew "oxo", and to three of the most spectacularly beautiful waterfalls that you could imagine. Only the Victoria Falls and Foz do Igauaco can compare in my experience.

But my real treat was yet to come, and I heard about it at daybreak on the Monday morning. I'd told Charlie the Chopper that I'd seen my Anaconda and wished I could see a Jaguar or a Black Panther. He admitted he'd seen neither, but knew a man who had and we'd be staying with him on the Sunday night. "Hicky" turned out to be a bit of an odd ball for me. He had been FBI or CIA and had left the fast lane for a lifestyle that only involved meeting an occasional human being. He was not short of cash and his tree house, appropriately named "Canopy Cabin", was a splendid structure with a river jetty and a helo pad. After a sumptuous dinner served by two native girls wearing little more than a smile, we began some serious drinking and telling of "war stories". I watched as our host's early joviality turned to being morose, then to bitter and self-destructive. Charlie knew him well and turned the conversation to my liking for big cats. "Jaguar's easy, they fish at my landing stage. Panther—you'll be lucky to see one if you spend a year here," said Hicky. Ever hopeful we kept drinking until one of the girls crooked a finger at me, and gave a sign for me to hurry—but be quiet. I followed her to the side veranda to see a young Jaguar bound away from the river's edge with a fish in its mouth. I was thrilled; I had no camera ready, but for that image I don't need it. It's locked there in my precious memory bank.

We were leaving for Manaus at daybreak for my noon flight to Rio, so we retired early and I slipped out onto my section of the veranda to get a last feel of the jungle at night. I sat in darkness and silence except for the noises of the forest around me and a single dim light that half lit the jetty and helo pad. Remember, we were some forty feet from the ground, and I must have sat silently for an hour almost dozing off when I had the sensation of not being alone. The clearing was empty, there were no lights behind me, and only the moon just rising over the far bank of the river was giving any light, but not yet brightly. Something, I know not what, drew my attention to my right and I stared at the lower bough of the next tree. Using the night-fighter pilot's trick of never looking directly at something in the dark, I slightly offset my gaze and my heart missed a beat as I saw two bright yellow orbs looking at me. I assumed it was our little friend the Jaguar, but as the moon shone more brightly, the eyes disappeared and the black gleaming shape of a big Panther crept along the bending bough before slipping silently to the ground and into the forest.

I realise how extremely fortunate I was to see my "big three" in such a short time and a warning voice keeps niggling at me: "Lest friends believe thy tale untrue, keep probability in view." But I'm finding again and again as I recount my experiences, not fantasies, that I'm occasionally being inhibited from telling all because the world has so many doubters and so many ready to decry and keen to pour scorn on the achievements or experiences of others. Take it or leave it folks—this is an autobiography and this is how it was. I vowed that night to return to the Amazon and spend a lot more time becoming immersed in its magic and mysteries. But as happens in life, even the best of intentions go by the board. I was often to fly over that incredible part of the world and to look down at the green carpet, the increasing areas of brown destruction of the forest, and the mighty rivers that flow through it. How much we miss in our comfortable airline seats at 35,000 feet, and how grateful I am for having had the privilege of being there for a little time at least.

Been there, done that

After Rio and the Amazon and the odd trip to Recife, there wasn't much in Brazil or the rest of South America to attract me back. Venezuela and Colombia I found intimidating and violent, Ecuador and Bolivia uninteresting, Uraguay passable, Argentina good for a fun night out with excellent food, and Chile well worth a few visits to the craft markets of Santiago and the icy wilderness of northern Antarctica with the whales and walruses being the scene stealers. My memory of Peru I suspect will be the same as many travellers; the sharp contrast between Lima and the mountainous and the jungle beauty of the Andes and Amazon. Lima was a city that I disliked intensely, so often shrouded in the gloomy mist of the *Garia*, and one where I never felt easy about eating and drinking—not even from bottled water! True, I had few business prospects there so never stayed long enough to really see the country or meet the people. I did go up the un-missable Inca trail, through the Sun Gate and on to *Huayna* and the magnificent citadel of ruins at 8000ft above sea level on the Ancient Peak, *Machu Picchu*. But I did the boring bit in a Peruvian Navy helicopter, and felt guilty and a bit of a fraud when talking to tourists that had tramped for days to get where I stood. I didn't feel envious of their journey; there were many sore feet, aching muscles, and nasty insect bites that I was quite prepared to forego.

Isn't it just a crime to write off so many countries and so many places in one page? But then that's how I saw them against the lure of so many other wonderful parts of this globe. My penalty for having seen so much was, I suppose, that I tended to find real interest and fulfilment only at the top of the mountain, or in the extremes of nature and excitement. I often found myself asking "Is that all there is?" when others were using miles of film and going into raptures about a 600-year-old temple or a view that one might see in a hundred mountain ranges across the world. I can only say that I never wasted a minute, so if I was missing something in South America, I was seeing something different on another continent, a different ocean, or in another town.

Small is Good

A final tale from MEL days connects my marketing ventures with Brazil, Chile, Ecuador and Venezuela, and concerns the choice of aircraft platform for our radar system. All four countries had previously bought a second hand American aircraft, the Grumman Tracker, under a US scheme so generous that no one else could compete. Like all aircraft built for carrier operations the Tracker was a rugged dependable aircraft, big enough to carry our system and achieve a reasonable time on patrol. They were nevertheless old aircraft and needed a major overhaul plus replacement engines as well as modern electronics. Such work could only be done in North America by two firms specialising in Tracker conversions. Having been to the Canadian outfit in Nova Scotia, I knew what could be done at what cost and in what timescale. I next headed south westerly to Phoenix to the other, which was no hardship for me because I love Arizona. I was to be delighted by what I found, not so much because Arizona was wall-to-wall sunshine compared to the grey/green of Halifax, but because of the laid back casual professionalism of the guy who ran the outfit.

In the boardrooms of the huge aircraft manufactures one often felt that you were in Saville Row or in one of those Berkeley Square showrooms that purveyed only new Rolls Royce or Bentley cars. Everyone wore an expensive Bespoke tailored suit, usually blue pinstriped, with a white shirt or a striped shirt with a white collar. British Aerospace led the way in the UK whilst across the Atlantic the leading aircraft-cum-fashion houses were McDonnell Douglas and Lockheed, albeit with shiny suits. Smaller aircraft firms like Marshal's and Gulfstream were much more relaxed, but this man in Phoenix was something else. I drove out of town under clear blue skies and found the small airport at the end of a paved track. I drove into what appeared to be a car park, but which also accommodated half a dozen beaten up Trackers.

I parked and walked under the folded wings to what I took to be the front door of the main offices and entered a splendid air-conditioned office area to be welcomed with a huge welcoming smile and greeting from a Doris Day look-alike who warbled, "You must be the English gentleman that Jim is expecting? Please come through—caw-fee or a coke maybe?" She led me through a large square room, grandly furnished with green leather and dark wood furniture, a deep pile carpet, one wall tastefully dressed with western paintings of Indians, cowboys and stagecoaches, and the back wall with various aircraft pictures and paintings.

"He's in his Aspen office today," she said, and led me out onto a patio of the same size of the room, with the same furniture and an enormous desk, the twin of the one inside. Bordering the patio was a line of trees, variety unfamiliar to me, with straight white trunks and broad light coloured leaves that twisted and twin-kled in the desert breeze. I took his firm handshake, said I liked his pad and his dancing trees, and told him I'd just flown in from Halifax.

"Tell you what we'll do if you have the time," he said. "Drink your coffee; then I'll show you the aircraft I have here, and then we'll go fly in whichever one you want. How does that sound?"

I took a sip of my coffee and looked down startled at the mug because the con-tent was more like treacle than liquid.

"You like my coffee I see. The trick with this brew is that it don't take as much water as you think it do!" said Jim.

Still working that one out in my mind, I sipped his blackjack and watched a pair of skylarks climb singing into the morning sky, felt the warm kiss of the sun on my face and felt downright contented. I don't know how to describe a silence so beautiful—it was as if the world were waiting for something wonderful to hap-pen but was in no hurry. It wasn't total silence, but what sounds there were, were hushed and unobtrusive.

I then detected one sound that I didn't recognise and listened intently as it recurred every few minutes—a sort of swishing sound. As we toured the Trackers I identified the source of the swishing. It came from a steady stream of ladies driv-ing their golf buggies from the car park to a golf club on the edge of the airfield.

The swishing of their tyres on the grass and the colour and sparkle of the drivers seemed tailor-made for the place and the occasion.

I showed Jim our ideas for fitting the system and he calculated how many aircraft he could do on base or down in South America. Then we flew, using as an excuse to fly low the other configuration he had in mind, that of the Tracker as a water bomber for brush and forest fires. We landed hot and happy two hours later, chatted up a bunch of golf widows who came to watch us taxi in, and then proceeded to drink Coors beer until we fell over. I knew I could do business with this man and agreed a conversion contract with two of the customers down south. In the end neither went ahead as the French scuppered the finances and then pulled out of the corrupt deal they had made. I was really chuffed a few years later to read that Jim had sold all his Trackers in the water bomber configuration and had bought in all the now discarded South American ones to convert and sell on. There was a man who deserved every cent of his success.

14

THORN EMI

Same Office, different Company

It was fortuitous that I had opened up the South American market for MEL, as in 1990 they were bought out by THORN EMI, the company I'd turned down in favour of MEL. Thorn had lost their way in the radar business after producing an excellent MP system for the RAF Nimrod. Having failed to sell it overseas, they ill advisedly tried to persuade customers that it was easily convertible to an AEW system. (Where had I heard that before?) They moved their HQ to Crawley and brought in their radar teams. Their first mistake was to treat the MEL engineers and staff as unimportant to Thorn's vision of marketing their products; keeping their Nimrod cards so close to their corporate chests that no one could see the spots. They had a distinctly different style of management to the friendly laid-back approach of MEL. Their directors nested only on the top two floors of the HQ; to walk around the engineering areas and talk to the workers wasn't in their game plan. It was a throw back almost to GEC, and for 6 months the MEL and Thorn guys worked as if competitors rather than colleagues. Eventually, the top man lost his head and commonsense prevailed with the new director being a very hard-nosed businessman, but also a very shrewd one who I regretted having crossed when I'd turned him down four years earlier. But it all began to slot into place and business was good.

On my home front, however, the storm clouds were gathering. I went innocently into a meeting at work with my MD to be confronted by two CID men who'd had a report from a private detective hired by my wife, that I was selling Company secrets to South Africa. It was all total rubbish, but it led directly to a period of immense turbulence that almost cost me my job, virtually bankrupted me, separated me from my children (at least one for ever), and nearly cost me my life on the operating table. But that's another story.

Back to Church—a Second Chance

As one falls in love again, so one goes back to the Church. But it was not until we moved to West Sussex, that I went back at the ripe old age of 58. My inner resurgence started in 1986 when I left GEC when the Nimrod AEW programme was cancelled. I was faced with finding a new job to support the lifestyle I'd developed that included purchase of an expensive house. I probably worried more about the job than I needed to, but there were financial problems brewing and I desperately wanted to start a new life with Rosemarie. I returned to contemplation and prayer and miraculously I ceased to worry. Job offers flowed in and I found a house in Sussex that seemed to provide the long-term solution to my compendium of hurdles.

My wife's relations in Ireland still had a great influence on her. She was always looking for a new spiritual home, as it were, and found it in a non-denominational Tabernacle in Worthing that seemed to combine all that was good from the Irish experience with a Minister who was both a great orator and a charismatic leader. I could listen to him speak for hours and he was so full of Christian energy and drive that it was an honour to be invited to speak from his pulpit. Many fascinating and compelling visiting speakers did so. With him at the helm, I began to recover much of my dormant faith. I joined in the weekly activities of the church and acted as Linesman on Sundays. I was then travelling frequently worldwide on business, and so helped provide the Pastor with a link to his many overseas contacts. I'd carry messages, videos, tapes, and literature in both directions and met with some wonderful people.

I have the fondest memories of an enormous church in Korea, filled every Sunday with thousands of people—you actually could book your seat in advance! Then there was a rare mixed race church in Cape Town and a thriving church in Kuala Lumpur that suffered greatly from acute religious bias. Perhaps the jewel in the crown was a mission held in the Walled City of Hong Kong run by a lovely English rose, Jackie Pullinger. Her book *Chasing the Dragon* was a wonderful testimony to her incredibly dangerous work amongst the criminals, Triads, and drug barons that ran that amazing city in the 70's.

It was my experiences with so many different Christian people throughout the world that confirmed my beliefs, my faith in God, and in the foundations of the Christian faith. I had never felt happy with the labels of the different faiths and was always wary of the way that many Protestant Christians were critical of other faiths, practices and ceremonies. Going beyond that, I had also had the privilege to witness how other people worshipped their God in their way, probably never having heard about the God that I knew. I concluded a long time ago that in the end we are really talking about the same God—we simply have our own different ways of getting to him because of where we happen to live and practice our faith.

Bell, Book and Candle

> *"A Bell is rung, the Book is closed, a Candle is extinguished."*

During the period when I returned to the church, 1988 to 1996, my commitment and contribution were overshadowed, diminished and—according to some folk—totally destroyed and negated by the inescapable fact that I was an adulterer. Adultery has affected all levels of society since the Garden of Eden. The very word itself condemns; people can light-heartedly discuss affairs and "a bit on the side", but Adultery comes dressed in a black shroud and evokes crippling images of broken trust, loss of faith, deception and failure. I've explained how I met Rosemarie in 1971 and that we fell in love at first sight. We were kept from marrying, first by my conscience to want to see my four children through to adulthood, and later by my wife's refusal to grant a divorce. Rosemarie and I are now sailing in much calmer Christian waters and I'll cover that in due course. But first I must record some of my thoughts and disappointments—admittedly as a sinner and unworthy believer—about some of the people I've met under the banner of religion and Christianity.

I accept that I am hardly qualified to criticise anyone else, but—like it or not—this is what happened to me. Apart from a few certainties and many hopes, I cannot be sure I'm right, being fair, or justified in what I say. People will accuse me and dispute what I say I have no doubt, but there are thoughts and feelings inside me that I do not like and cannot understand. Perhaps the reader may be better placed than I to do so.

I find it hard to be critical of those I once counted as friends and fellow Christians. Yet my overriding feeling is not one of bitterness, but of disappointment. One is frequently disappointed in what people do and say, but there is an added dimension to the hurt when a professing Christian lets you down. In a word, it's hypocrisy, and has something to do with a "holier than thou" attitude. In the early days in Ireland I suppose I was simply naive. I would go to church and hear the wonderful messages of salvation, of "Loving Thine Enemy" and about forgiveness. And yet those very same people virtually ignored and often hated the Roman Catholic community—a feeling that was of course returned in good measure. Occasionally, two or more Protestant churches might interlink for some purpose, but it was overwhelmingly a case of "never the twain shall meet". Baptists had little time for Methodists, who mistrusted the Presbyterians, who poured scorn on the Church of Ireland, who didn't recognise The Brethren—and so on.

In Ireland, the Baptist church was well funded, especially by the local rich farmers. It didn't seem to matter to those who sometimes preached fire and brimstone from the pulpit, that the man who gave most was the biggest philanderer in Co. Derry with half a dozen look-alike offsprings in Sunday school from different mothers. Nor that their respected and much loved minister was "having it off" with a female RAF officer from Ballykelly, and that members who ran the most profitable shops and garages in town were in all the rackets. Okay—so that's the way of the world, in any town or village you can name. However, it always seemed the height of hypocrisy and unfairness to me that when some poor lowly parishioner put a foot out of line they got both barrels of condemnation from the hierarchy. I can't say that I suffered under that injustice then; at least not that I knew of. It was later in life that I faced the full force of the Church's censure and it saddens me to this day.

In Worthing, I became a very active member of the church and made a great many friends of all ages, including the Pastor and his deputy. The cause of my literal fall from grace was my love for Rosemarie and hers for me. She and I had discussed our faith often. She was a regular churchgoer in Wales and had, as now, very strong beliefs and commitment. Acknowledging that we were sinners in the eyes of the world and of God, we found it possible (some might say convenient) to justify our misdeeds on the strength and truth of our love for each other. We argued with great conviction that nothing so beautiful and fulfilling could be so wrong. We took our love to God, confessed our sin and accepted that we might never be fully accepted, but hoped that we'd be understood as would any sinner whatever his or her crime.

My wife had known about Rosemarie since 1979, but as already mentioned, in 1990 she covertly hired a private detective who bugged my house and my car, followed me around the country on my many business trips and even tried to obtain money from the company I worked for with the claim that I was selling their secrets to foreign governments. Now alerted to what had been going on, I began some sleuthing of my own, remembering that this is a chapter on Religion, not about divorce and things legal.

I discovered that my wife had told the Pastor about Rosemarie. Fair enough, you will say, but it was the Church (of which I was also a member) that lined up the crooked detective and recommended the solicitors who were to represent my wife. It became clear why, over a period of about six months, I was first refused baptism, why I was then made unwelcome as a Linesman, and told I should not take Communion. I arranged to see the Pastor to talk privately about the situation, knowing full well that it would be a difficult interview, but had to be faced. When he ushered me into his office I was confronted by my wife, which of course totally sabotaged my reasons for talking to my minister. He had turned it into a marriage guidance meeting.

The next surprise from this man that I admired enormously was to find that he had had me followed during one of my visits to Cape Town. This he did through one of his church contacts there that reported back that I'd had Rosemarie with me. When I explained that Rosemarie was at her daughter's wedding in Wales that weekend, and that the only woman I spoke to in South Africa was the wife of an old colleague now living in Cape Town, I was told that even that was very indiscreet of me. In my job I met and worked with dozens of women of all ages and colours, fat and thin, ugly and beautiful, dull and sexy. I had to ask what it was I was being accused of.

I next contacted a very senior member of the church Committee—an extremely successful and rich businessman with whom I had got on well and with whose wife my wife was very friendly. I wanted to talk to him, "warts and all", about my genuine concerns, to tell him as a trusted friend and seek advice. His response was that he wouldn't talk unless I gave up Rosemarie. I was then informed in writing that my church membership was terminated, to which I'm afraid I replied that I understood how uneasy people must feel, but that perhaps the sign outside the Church should now read "Sinners not welcome here".

So despite my facing up to the obvious problems that the church—any church—would have with my ongoing affair, I had been ostracized, condemned by that Man of God into a spiritual darkness. Even though there was never any overt scandal, Rosemarie was 200 miles away, and the rest of the world knew nothing about the situation, not a single person of the hundreds I knew at that Church over a 7-year period ever called me, wrote to me or attempted to communicate with me in any way.

The final straw, if you like, came in 1996 when my prolonged divorce proceedings were approaching a climax. The stress of the past years had taken their toll and I needed an emergency triple heart bypass operation that I underwent in Midhurst, some 20 miles from Worthing. My children all came down to see me, as did my brother, a number of close friends from the RAF and business colleagues. However, neither before the operation, immediately after it in hospital, or when I returned home to convalesce, did a single member of my church contact me or even send a get-well note. Their utter silence was mirrored by my wife's Christian family and friends in Ireland, many that I'd known for almost 50 years. To this day, that silence remains unbroken.

In the eyes of all those good folk, I might have been the devil himself and they may well have thought of me as 100% in the wrong and my wife 100% in the right. But not one of them ever bothered to ask for my version of events, and I faced a barrage of lies and unproven accusations every time I went to Court for the divorce. I have never been able to reconcile their attitude with the very foundation of Christian belief "Forgive us as we forgive them that trespass against us". Were they all so perfect, so full of goodness, benevolence and knowledge, so indoctrinated with the superiority of their own brand of belief that I was not worthy of the odd prayer and the occasional kind thought? *"Si j'ai faille, les peines sont presentes."*

Sad and disappointing though my experiences were, I am bound to say that they had no adverse effect on my belief in God or on my trust and understanding of the Word of God. If anything, my faith was enhanced. I was simply perplexed but able to see things in a different light. Most Christians I have met are just ordinary folk—well meaning, earnest, hard working; not endowed with more wisdom, knowledge or virtue than anyone else; not gifted with more vision and not always more tolerant. They are concerned, as are all healthy self-centred people, with family, children, home, security, salaries, pensions, etc.—all the mechanics of existing. They are eminently likeable folk, converted and mellowed to humanity and tolerance, who have quietly jettisoned belief in the infallibility of their own idea of salvation and with the wrathful aspects of the Deity they profess to love.

Because I liked and respected the pastor in Worthing so much, and because I'd been content and happy in the community he'd led so well, I wrote to him constructively and at length, either side of my operation. No answer ever came. Rosemarie and I had been open to everyone and to God about our love. We were anxious to have His blessing on our marriage shortly after my divorce. We attend her church together in Wales, even though it does not wholly fulfil for me the vibrant evangelistic mood I once enjoyed. But then, to us, loving and believing in God does not rely on formal Services, splendid Churches or all the trimmings of worship. We are at peace with our thoughts and with our consciences. Perhaps that is as much as we can hope for and as much as we need.

THORN in the doldrums

In the midst of all my domestic turbulence, I was starting my eighth year in industry with new masters THORN. But I still had an awful lot to learn about the ways of business or—put another way—to unlearn from my 37 years in the RAF. As at GEC, my background was such that I had unique operational experience together with intimate knowledge of MoD procurement procedures as well as knowing most of the officers and civil servants in key posts. My new boss chose to ignore my credentials which had led to me receiving over a dozen offers on leaving the RAF and then a further six when leaving GEC, including being headhunted on four other occasions. In any efficiently run organisation, you would have expected me to-at the very least-have been briefed to walk the corridors of Whitehall on behalf of the Nimrod team. Even more odd, Thorn was pursuing the sale of an AEW variant with China and despite my unrivalled knowledge of AEW and having been to China promoting GEC's radar, I was excluded. Their attitude was one of possessive conspirital secrecy; there has to be one word in our vocabulary to describe that but I'm hanged if I can bring it to mind.

Thorn's possessiveness was inexcusable, and only served to make the ex-MEL engineers suspicious of the performance claims being made and of the dishonesty of much of their salesmanship. In an industry and a specialisation where good engineers were keenly sought after, most of the best left for pastures new. Had I been a young man, I too would have gone. But I was then 60, had already worked for two companies in 7 years, and anyway I knew exactly what programmes we should be pursuing, with or without Thorn's co-operation. I concentrated on two winnable RAF programmes; one a smallish but high-profile navigation training aircraft using an MEL radar, the other the Nimrod MPA replacement that was sure to be a massive international competition with US aircraft well to the fore. The first had to be won by 1994, the second by 1996. To stick to my principle of always having something in every stage of the procurement pipeline from development through feasibility to in-service, we also joined a US led consortium for a ground—breaking new system for airborne battlefield surveillance. If we could win the contract for the Feasibility Study, we'd be paid to do leading edge research and be well placed to win the following lucrative Production contract. I'll talk about that programme, ASTOR, in due course.

First out of the traps was the Dominie Navigation radar for which our MEL radar was perfectly suited with minor modifications. Our team of six did the development work, liased with Marshals the airframe contractors, and demonstrated to the RAF in the air how we could exceed their Requirement. Even so, winning the contract was not all smooth sailing and it was here that my knowledge and my contacts in the MoD were decisive. I was in my element with so many contacts in London and was back on the lunch and dinner scene with a vengeance. I make no apologies for that even though wining and dining are seen by some as tantamount to bribery and corruption. What better way to exchange ideas and make progress than sitting across a table whilst eating well and drinking sensibly? I often found that those who were critical of the Lunch Club played a surprising amount of golf or just happened to meet the key people whilst on a shooting trip in the wilds of Scotland or on a day out during Cowes week!

The hiccup on Dominie was revealed at just such a lunch two days before Christmas. Skulduggery was afoot. The Company about to be awarded the contract had tendered at a ridiculously low price, as well they might because they'd done nothing to adapt their already inferior radar for the far more demanding role in which it was now to be used. They'd guesstimated what the other five contenders would bid at, and knocked 20% off their price. The RAF was about to get a pile of cheap useless junk for the purpose for which they were procuring the Dominie.

The choice of winning contractor is based on overall cost-effectiveness and value for money. When I flew with the US Navy, there was one aircraft type that had a notice stuck below the instrument panel reading, "Beware, this aircraft was bought from the lowest bidder." That said, a more expensive piece of equipment is not necessarily the best; indeed the best is often the enemy of the good. In 1938/9 the best design for the RAF's new fighter was rejected because it could never be technically achieved. The "second best" was achievable, but would be too late into service for a war that was imminent. The third best was adequate, in time, and won the Battle of Britain. It was called the Spitfire.

My lunch companion that December day was equally concerned that the RAF was about to be handed a pup. He wanted to be armed on the first day back at work in the New Year with questions on basic radar design and technical operation of the antenna, the answers to which could not be fudged. The design offered was not capable of doing the job, neither could it be modified cosmetically, or it's inadequacies offset by the use of some other technique or kit. Those who understood prepared the questions, and we won the contract fairly with the best system at a price smack on average over the seven bidders.

The success pleased me greatly because I'd been able to combine my own professional aviation knowledge with a sound understanding of engineering, marketing nous, urint (a feeling in the water), knowledge of how the MoD procurement system worked, and how it could be influenced even at the eleventh hour. It was a matter of great personal import throughout my industry career that the Government should get value for money and, especially, that the guys who had to operate or fight with a piece of equipment, should get what they had specified. I was even more pleased when our system proved a resounding success in service, far exceeding our performance forecast. The £26.5M success gave Thorn a great boost, helped retain many key staff that now saw real prospects of winning other major radar contracts. The company re-organised, and for once it was not merely to give the illusion of progress, but to put together a much more effective engineering team.

Out of Sight

Having stressed the importance of meeting specifications, I reluctantly cite a major failing of every company but one that I worked for; namely, After Sales Service. The rules and procedures on this were tightened up in the 90's so that when the ASTOR contract was signed in 99, over 50% of the total contract value lay in the long term (15–20 year) support of the system in service. But before then, it was more often the case that once equipment had been delivered and passed its acceptance trials, the supplier took little interest in his product unless a lucrative update or maintenance contract beckoned.

There were notable exceptions, especially where the giant aircraft companies were concerned, and later when technology advanced so quickly with miniaturisation, low weight, low volume, and power savings resulting in quantum advances in reliability and maintainability. The customers that suffered most were those with small orders, especially foreign customers who had to buy high-tech equipment from overseas without a sophisticated procurement agency to handle the deal or an in-country Support capability. I had many bitter confrontations with managers who worked on the basis that once sold, they could forget that product because by the time problems emerged, they would be in a different post, or, due to changes in the Company, it would be impossible to track down the culprits. Indeed, many such charlatans put effort into building audit proof trails to ensure that it was always the customer that suffered. I had one humiliating experience that epitomised the management cancer affecting the defence industry.

When Thorn reorganised, I inherited Turkey as a marketing area and went with our man in Ankara to a huge naval base to discuss putting our Dominie radar on their updated helicopters. As was my custom, I contacted the relevant departments with interests in country to be briefed on any problems, or be tasked to make contacts. For Turkey I had no takers, and my predecessor had not left any files or data-which by now you'll know was par for the course. I was astonished to find that the standard fit on ten helicopters was a Thorn radar. None were working and some had the inners stripped out and were being used for coffee cups, map stowage etc. I visited a rudimentary workshop where a few young

Turks were pottering around on a workbench with assorted tools, trying to make sense of a Maintenance Manual (in English) that was not even for that model of the radar. I was told that the radars had been in service for some six years, but when faults occurred and the equipment was returned to the UK (at the customers expense) the sets took around six months to be returned, and usually came back with the faults uncorrected. I was incensed at this news and vowed to come back within the week with an explanation and a solution to their problems.

At the main gate en route to the airport, the guard told our agent in Turkish that the Base Commander wished to see us. I had visions of being welcomed warmly with typical Turkish courtesy, being offered a drink and a "thank you for coming". I should have smelled a rat when I was ushered into the dining room where, along the top table, sat the Admiral flanked by his six senior officers. I was guided to a single chair in the fashion of the Mastermind inquisition, and given both barrels in perfect English! I was asked why anyone would want to buy anything ever again from a company that had sold radars that had never performed to specification, that were technically unreliable, and for which servicing support was virtually negligible. He went on to say that the Americans always overcharged and the French were always a day late and a dollar short-but only the British failed on all counts.

The assembled officers clearly saw that I was surprised and not a little angry. I said I would not blame them if they never bought British again, but that I get a full report with appropriate apologies and return to grovel, talk and hopefully negotiate a face-saving deal. I felt fortunate to get out of there alive and returned to search for the guilty parties. I made myself even more unpopular, and as always as you tried to follow the trail to apportion blame, there were too few records and too few honest people around prepared to help. The buck should have stopped with the appropriate Director, but as I had already discovered people at that level in the Defence Industry seldom shouldered the blame for their appalling dishonesty and mismanagement.

I did manage to get a "field team" out to Turkey to do repairs and some training, but once a foreign government or service has lost trust, marketing becomes an impossible task in that country. The Turkish experience led me to look at other support contracts and I was to find serious fault in our dealings with Australia, Indonesia and Malaysia, in all of which we had otherwise excellent prospects of success. That aspect of the defence industry in my time was a national disgrace and was one of the few instances in my life when I was ashamed of being British. We pride ourselves on being a world leader in technology and there's no doubt that we have some of the best minds and the most efficient and capable engineers in the aviation and electronics fields. Our failure lies more in the integrity of top management. Integrity is the *sine qua non* of all human endeavours including business. Customers deserve the very best, they deserve a quality product, and to be treated fairly even when it costs. The British Defence industry since 1960 often fell well short of meeting integrity standards and it's failure in the export market is a damning indictment that has cost this country dear.

Another Nimrod battle

Of all Thorn's programmes, the one most vital to their long-term sustainability was the radar for the RAF Nimrod MPA replacement. The combination of Nimrod airframe and Searchwater radar had made the RAF the world's most capable force to meet the surface and submarine threat posed by the Warsaw Pact. It was crucially important that their updated radar be selected for whatever replacement airframe was chosen. As usual it came down to a head on conflict with the USA. When the Nimrod was getting long in the tooth, the RAF had intended to buy whatever System the US Navy bought to replace its P3 Orion fleet. But the US cancelled their programme thus leaving all other potential purchasers of their new system high and dry. With no new US system in the offing the UK had to go it alone for a capability of immense importance to them. The battle was to be fought between BAe with an updated Nimrod, the French Atlantique, and US updates of the P3c. But before the battle was joined in earnest, Thorn sold out to Racal.

15

RACAL ELECTRONICS

Racal were a company with an enviable record for straight dealing and responsible management. Out went the majority of the Thorn directors eagerly clasping their golden bowlers having milked the Company for years, and in came a veritable gale of fresh ideas, open and friendly management, and creative thinking matched with prudent conservatism. It was a joy to work for them. For the third time in 10 years, I'd changed companies but not moved an inch. Everyone wanted to work in Crawley it seemed.

Elsewhere, I've covered the turbulence in my private life that came to a head in the year of Racal's takeover. But concentrating on the work in hand, we were now able to proceed as one Company rather as we had done under divided loyalties in Thorn. Nimrod MPA was our prime immediate objective, an AEW system for China was an on-going side issue, and we were involved in a consortium to compete for the new and exciting ASTOR project for Battlefield Surveillance, more popularly known in US terms as J-Stars. Dominie had given our small-radar team the leg up to develop that system for other export markets, and a combination of experience and aggressive marketing led to success in the AEW/ASW mix of systems for the RN Sea King and the long term development for the new carrier borne helicopter circa 2010. Racal in 1996 was a good place to be indeed.

Nimrod MPA

So on to the Nimrod. Fear not because I shan't bore you with technical features, but rather concentrate on what became a typical major programme battle, full of dirty tricks, political intrigue, and dubious claims and promises by those competing and those making procurement decisions. The stakes were high in this high profile international MPA competition. A similar competition for the US forces would involve many more aircraft and therefore be of far higher value, but such competitions were virtually all-American and it was a waste of time and money to compete. But this one was wide open and whoever won the platform competition would reap the benefits of development funding, plus production and support profits making them very competitive in the world market.

If a new build P3 were chosen, Lockheed could offer that at an attractive price to the US Navy and to foreign customers operating older P3s that would then be bought back, reconditioned and resold to countries too poor to buy a new version. If Loral's second hand refurbished cheaper system were successful, all the foreign countries operating older P3s could benefit from the low price and update their fleet. If the French could sell the Atlantique overseas, that could open up the market for an aircraft that had consistently been overshadowed by the P3 due to a US foreign sales policy that almost gave away the aircraft. BAe had no real foreign sales hopes, they'd blown those many years before, but if they had to close down the Nimrod line that would effectively be the end of building large aircraft in the UK; all their other large aircraft ventures such as Airbus involved only part construction in the UK.

Similarly with the radar and ASW System. A highly capable system could compensate for shortcomings in the vehicle, and if successful would be attractive to other users in terms of performance and price, plus the benefits of guaranteed long-term support. US giants like Raytheon and Hughes already had monopolies in certain countries or on certain platforms and would be keen to stamp out any threat to their superiority. In the UK, GEC were making a despairing last-ditch effort to stay with the big boys whilst Thomson CSF in France saw this as their last chance to sell their system that had been very difficult to export previously. Racal had the undoubted advantage of being on the current Nimrod and being highly thought of. Plus there had been an enlightened development programme to dramatically reduce the size, weight, power and cooling requirements of Searchwater through the use of new technology, and at the same time enhancing its performance. Operationally we were in good shape, but faced the problem of competing on every one of the five platforms because the final decision would be made on many factors including total package price and perceived cost effectiveness over which Racal, as a sub-contractor to any of the aircraft giants, had little say.

Two of the options were US aircraft so they'd be under pressure from US companies to buy US radar, as would Dassault be drawn to a French product for the Atlantique. Also, we were under no illusions that if BAe were offered a better deal by a US manufacturer, they would not hesitate to buy American. Does that shock you? It would have shocked me once, but that's how it is I'm afraid. I had every reason to suppose that our intelligence assessment of the radar opposition and of the RAF's view of the platforms on offer was accurate. We decided therefore not to bid on the Atlantique, neither on the refurbished P3 from Loral, which we left to GEC. That left us with a hearts and minds job to do on BAe to offer our radar, a sales job on Lockheed to convince them that the RAF wanted Searchwater, and a political job with our own Government who always took a squeaky clean approach so that every competition was truly international, a quaint notion that few other countries even bothered to pay lip service to.

The uninitiated or trusting soul might consider that a contract for over £1B being fought for internationally would indeed be squeaky clean and a model of sound professional practice and judgement. If so, you'd be disappointed. The British military knows what they want and are experts at committing that to paper and getting agreement in the MoD. Their wishes start life as a Target and become a Requirement as flesh is put on the bare bones to say what is realistic in terms of affordability, timescale and technical risk. The Requirement, then refined to be a Specification, is then put out to tender, sometimes with financial provisos included. Bidders then tender their price to meet the Specification in the given timescale. Now the fun begins as the Prime Contractors seek to find out what the other contenders have bid and how well their bid has been received. If you are a sub–contractor, it is unlikely that your Prime will tell you anything at this stage because he's too busy playing his financial cards close to his chest to gauge what he might do to offer a better deal to the MoD. That might include dumping your contribution in favour of a cheaper solution or to please the customer if he thinks that is what the customer prefers.

As a sub-contractor, you won't know the Prime's bidding price; in fact you won't even know what price tag he has put on your system in his submission. It would not be unusual for him to have raised the price you gave him by as much as 50%, the danger being that if the customer starts looking for savings, he might see you as too dear and opt for another supplier. So, this is a time for the sub–contractor to keep all the balls in the air whilst protecting his own, where detailed knowledge of the programme, the customer, the procurement system, and the decision makers becomes invaluable. On Nimrod we had all that in place and eventually secured our guaranteed slot with BAe and the new P3, which were really the only games in town. We then waited patiently knowing that we were winners whoever won as Prime and with mixed feelings as to who we wanted to win.

Being a patriot through and through, my heart was in Lancashire with BAe, but there was potentially a bigger sales potential if the P3 won due to its greater export appeal and the fact that the US would probably insist on selling a US radar to everyone but the RAF. As decision day loomed, London was awash with US salesmen and bean counters, MPs and other dignitaries were being wined and dined lavishly. Hunting, shooting, fishing and golf weekends were all the rage, and trans Atlantic weekends had never been so popular. By now the RAF and most of the MoD had had all the say they were going to have, the senior Civil Servants still involved were very senior and the decisive battles were being waged at the west end of Whitehall. When you follow a programme that closely, you can almost smell the answer; you can certainly detect the body language that brings either a smile to your lips or a cold feeling in your guts. Uniquely on Nimrod, I was all smiles; with weeks to go the only uncertainty in my mind was whether I'd be a regular commuter to California or Manchester. I appreciate that in recording my part in this and my experiences, I'm barely scratching the surface. Tied up in a major contract were the fortunes of huge companies, and the personal reputations and futures of politicians, high ranking Civil servants, serving officers, barons of industry, and key men in the R&D world. For many there was much more at stake than a single contract, some were desperate to win, others fearful of losing because their reputation and credibility might suffer. There were men involved in making crucial decisions who knew nothing about which aircraft or which system was best for the RAF and for this country if it ever went to war. Their minds were on bank balances, the balance of trade, retention of a special relationship with the USA, and so on.

Doubtless the intentions and actions of the vast majority of the people involved in competing for a major contract were honourable, certainly up to the point where evaluation of all the bids had been completed by the MoD. Their resulting recommendation would have stated that the chosen bidders solution met the RAF Operational Requirement, that it would meet the designated in-service date, and that the total programme cost including long term support, was within budget or deemed acceptable. The evaluation and recommendation would have been expertly carried out and elegantly spelt out in an impressive and convincing format and style. Typically, the paper would rule out quickly and firmly those submissions that did not come up to scratch leaving two, perhaps three, solutions where the pros and cons needed to be compared and argued through for the final decision to be taken at the highest level.

This was the stage in the process for serious skulduggery to begin. For instance, you might have an offshore bidder that best met the performance, timescale and cost parameters, but a British bidder whose total cost was, say, 5% higher. Question-is it worth saving 5% if by doing so we put the British bidder out of business or have a detrimental effect on his capability to export? Put another way, what if this programme is the launch pad for a new area of development that needs success now to be able to expand. Do we want that technology to stay here or do we let it go overseas?

It is entirely proper that such questions are fully explored in the decision making process, but now the evaluation has moved from people who knew what they were talking about operationally, technically, and economically to involve people who are merely bean counters or have some vested interest. This Government body, or rather sequence of filters, may well look at the pros and cons and ask what if Bidder A was to change his engine supplier, or if Bidder B was to review his disproportionately expensive support package. These and many other questions would be put back to the expert evaluators for assessment, but the problem now is that a great many people, including the bidders, have a much better idea-if not the complete picture—as to who has bid what.

Bidders are then called on to supply supplementary information or clarification. They will know why they are being asked and may now take the opportunity to inject other improvements to their original bid about which they may have received covert intelligence, as well as sensibly interpreting the new questions. Bidder A might report that since completing their bid 9 months ago, further discussions with a British engine supplier have revealed that their new mark of engine now meets the specification and, due to weight and volume savings, the aircraft fuel capacity can be increased to give an overall 10% increase in endurance.

Hearing of this on the grapevine, usually accessible via a £90 bottle of Claret in The Ivy, Bidder B may suddenly discover that he can now move his Wisconsin production line to Northern Ireland, thus creating 400 new jobs and relieving poverty in one of the Government's difficult areas. This might even induce Bidder C, who by now knows he was almost dead in the water, to pool resources with Bidders D and E and reduce the total programme cost by £100M and put all Production in the Prime Minister's constituency ('cos the folk who live there are such nice people you understand). At this crucial stage of re-jockeying for position, the US President suddenly remembers he's always wanted to visit London in mid November, and the Select Committee for Defence are torn between accepting invitations to attend two conferences of "Immense strategic importance"—one run by the USA in Hawaii, the other by the French in Tahiti. They ultimately accept both, only to withdraw gracefully when the venues are changed to Scunthorpe! Okay, I'm exaggerating, but only a little because now there are no holds barred and every dirty trick you can think of is being played, every little piece of blackmail, bribery and corruption is used as and where it can be most effective. This is the time when companies make promises they know they can never keep, make claims about equipment performance improvements that cannot be realised, and take the trade-off battle away from military equipment into areas of Government concern perhaps of even greater import than defence.

When all bidders have responded to further questions, the decision—making becomes real cloak and dagger stuff. It is now at three star and above level and, for Nimrod's replacement, the decision was to come from the Cabinet itself. Even then, it's all about picking the right time to announce it. Before or after Christmas? Before or after our unpopular announcement about Pensions? Monday a.m. or Friday p.m.—so we can nip off for the week-end and avoid the critics? After a late Cabinet meeting, during which I was at The Ivy sipping that £90 bottle of Claret, the word zipped down Whitehall that the decision was in favour of a re-furbished, re-engined, heavier Nimrod with our radar on board. Having called my Directors and ordered the second and third bottles of grape juice, my first thought was for the abject misery that the losers would be feeling at that moment. So much honest endeavour—so little reward. Cheers!

The China adventure

Racal's bright management team had blown away the Thorn cobwebs. My main programme now was ASTOR, but first there was the interesting side issue of Chinese AEW from which I'd been frozen out by Thorn. I suspected that our engineers were still dubious that our excellent MP radar could be upgraded to provide an adequate AEW system. They were naturally anxious to reap the benefit of all the work that had been done, but also knew that the Chinese were a very difficult customer. GEC had found this to their cost and were still spending millions to persuade the Chinese Air Force to take the old Nimrod AEW kit, albeit suitably modernised and modified.

The Chinese Procurement system was vastly different to NATO's and ours. When I first went to Beijing in 1986 with GEC, it was to offer AEW fitted to a Canadair executive jet. The USA would not sell to China and we had the only operational AEW other than them. The facilities for our presentations varied from day to day. One day we'd have a quiet room with comfortable chairs, good projection equipment and window blinds. The next we'd have a bare room with no projector or no curtains or blinds. We got used to being self-sufficient, belt and braces stuff, but it was difficult to give professional presentations especially as every word had to be interpreted.

One never knew the status or speciality of the audience as no one wore uniform or rank badges. I recall giving a simplified explanation about the subtle differences of detecting high and low flying targets. I noticed that the most attentive man was one dressed in the standard dark garb, but wearing one green sock and one blue sock that were easily visible as he still had his cycle clips in place! I was thinking to myself "What the hell am I doing here?" when this guy who'd not opened his mouth for days said in perfect English, "Tell me then, Palmer, why is it that in Skolknik on page 67, the author explains that there is no correlation between...etc." Skolknik is, or was, the bible on radar techniques and I was to find he knew it backwards. GEC's engineers became very wary of the Chinese ways of compiling information, and the ex-Thorn chaps were equally careful because you could not waffle or "bullshit" a Chinese technical audience. They were academically astute, but also never forgot a word you uttered and each was anxious to do his or her best as there were literally hundreds queuing behind them to take their place if they screwed up.

I once asked an accomplished and pretty interpreter where she was trained, and she told me she was never allowed to leave China. I promised to send her a dictionary of technical terms, which at first she thanked me for, and then in panic said she could not accept. In the end, I sent it via our Air Attaché who handed it over covertly and months later I received her prolific thanks via the same circuitous route. Another snag in 1980's China, was that a foreigner could not travel anywhere by himself. There was one main hotel for foreigners and very few restaurants unless you went with Chinese hosts. You were taken to all the local tourist spots like the Great Wall, Tioman Square, the Forbidden City, the Pearl Market and the old tombs. Unfortunately you were obliged to do the same tour every time you went. Almost every meal was taken with the Chinese, either as hosts or as guests when you were throwing a so-called "Banquet". The Banquet was a particularly dicey affair because you invariably sat at a huge round table with all the food piled onto a circular revolving tray (lazy Susan style) from which the host on your left would serve you. Anyone who has not been to China proper should not confuse the "Chinese" he takes away in this country, with the Chinese food on offer in China. Some of it is unspeakably horrid and pungent; much of it is presented in a way that we foreigners will never understand, and it is usually washed down with an obnoxious rice wine and toasted with a Chinese rocket fuel from a Sichuan village called *Maotai jui*. However, the biggest danger of the Banquet is that everyone around the table is constantly toasting you. Whereas you (as honoured guest) are expected to stay for the entire meal, your hosts will eat in shifts so that they are relatively bright whilst you are hoping to die at any moment. This quaint custom might be because by changing shifts, perhaps three times, more of them get a chance to eat more food and to meet you. Nevertheless, after a few visits and exposure to their poisonous drinks I took to taking in large quantities of malt whisky and good Cognac. With these on the menu, their drinks were left off and if you had to drink so much, it was nice to get smashed on the best liquor available. It also slaughtered a few of them.

When I returned with Racal ten years later, Beijing was transformed. New western style quality hotels had been built, roads widened and repaired, the city modernised and painted, and the people looked happier and more prosperous. But there was a down side. Many of the distinctive and ethnic features of the old city had gone completely or were made to look unattractive and shabby in comparison. The military and Government people had also been spruced up. The true rank and importance of some was still withheld, but one could now discern a pecking order and detect the difference between the military and the civil servant regime. Sadly, the *maotai* had not improved with age!

I was now on a quite different marketing tack, only too aware of the shortfall in performance between what the Chinese (Navy in this case) wanted and what we could provide. There are few dummies left in the world now. Everyone goes to the Air Shows, reads the aviation publications, surfs the Internet, and receives briefings from ex-Warsaw Pact military who are anxious to sell their old and unwanted equipment. The Chinese knew as well as we did that they'd not be permitted to have AEW to AWACS or even E2C standard; neither was the Russian version being offered of much use as it relied on old technology that could not now be supported.

So, they'd bought some fairly new Russian aircraft, suitable in size and performance for the role, and wanted Racal to fit the radar with their help. I saw this as a mutually beneficial venture. The Navy would be operating long range land based aircraft for the first time, both in the MP role (for which Searchwater has no peer) and in an over-water AEW role which was not too demanding on the system. The Chinese aircrew would get invaluable operating experience, whilst their own very competent scientists and engineers could develop their own capability for a follow on system. I found myself lecturing on anything and everything to do with the RAF, and found the Chinese remarkably enthusiastic and wonderfully friendly people. I hope as I write that the French company that bought out Racal in 2000 kept our promises to China. It could be en export goldmine if we treat them fairly.

What's in it for me?

I've made no secret that where I could, within the bounds of honesty and fairness to my employers, I would take advantage of my foreign visits to visit places I otherwise would not have the time or the money to visit. I'll mention two in relation to China; the first of which was a visit I made to one of those special places that you have in your mind and set your sights on seeing. Chinese paintings and decorative ornaments often depict tall mountains clustered together with mist wreathed around the sharp peaks. This spectacular scenery is not a touch of artist's license; it exists in Guilin in the northeast of Guangxi Zhuang some 500 miles west of Hong Kong. The river Lijiang winds through hundreds of hills like a blue ribbon from Giulin to Yangshuo. As your boat moves downstream, the individual hills stand like jade hairpins, cliffs hang down to the river, and the green hills seem to be floating in the water. I suppose the magical journey is no more than a meandering 35 miles, but it is 35 miles of sheer unceasing poetic flow as the river twists and turns, bending back on its course as if reluctant to leave so fair a land and lose its identity in the ocean.

Guilin itself is famous for its green hills, beautiful waters, spectacular caverns, exotic rocks and the fragrant osmanthius that fills the town with its aroma in the autumn. It is indeed one of those rare places on earth that looks equally enchanting in the morning sunshine or in the sunset's glow, with flowing rosy clouds, misty waters and dreamy hills. I'd long had that "must-see" feeling about Guilin, but warning bells reminded me that whenever I've had such a feeling about anywhere, I also have a moment of fearful anticipation just before I see it. Will I gasp in astonishment or feel I've been cheated? I remember feeling the latter when I first approached an African game reserve, only to realise that I must see it from the inside, from eye level, and be where the animals are. Most of the world's great waterfalls are like that too—totally uninteresting until you reach the edge or hear the thunder of the waters from afar; but when you see them, the memory stays with you.

With Guilin I wasn't kept in suspense long. The scenery hit you as the aircraft broke cloud in the twilight. From 5000 feet one could see the winding river and from the runway, the airfield itself was surrounded by the beckoning pinnacles. I remember the surge of relief and expectation at the sight; this was not going to be another Ayres Rock anti-climax.

I booked into my hotel, reserved a boat for 6 a.m., dined alone and watched the moonlight play on the Lijiang River before retiring. As I boarded the boat the heavens opened and I sat frustrated and bemoaning my luck because it felt like one of those days they always choose for the Old Boys cricket match! Then suddenly, in the middle of cream cheese and bagels, the clouds cleared and the whole magical tapestry was laid out in front of me. I was busy taking photographs of everything with a particular flurry of activity as we anchored by a Cormorant fisherman who displayed the prowess of his six birds that sat on his bamboo raft and shoulders and fished to his command. Later when we arrived in the fascinating town of Yangshuo I also noticed his prowess as a businessman. He was waiting at the jetty to ask, nay demand, his fees from those who'd taken his photograph 10 klicks downstream.

Like a journey through the Highlands of Scotland, every turn in the river revealed new vistas of beauty; every hill different, drifting mist and cloud patterns, diffuse shading and shadow, a land of aquatint. Magic—sheer, enchanting magic. I left Guilin the next day vowing, as I have done many times in life, that I'd be back one day. I never have had the opportunity, but it's one of those places that I can recommend to anyone that they should see—it's unforgettable.

Life being what it is, there was a sting in the tail. Six weeks later my credit card bill showed that I'd spent £2600 for one night in the Guilin Sheraton. My bill was actually $130, but someone had copied my card and hammered the account. Had it been for a small amount I may have missed it, but not £2600! The credit card company of course investigated, but they took 2 years to wipe that fraud off my account! I was forced to say that that would not do nicely and dropped the account like a hot brick.

My second China story involves Rosemarie. As we neared a contract in 1998, the Chinese were keen to talk about anything that would help them in managing the programme. They therefore paid my fare and hers to Beijing, and also picked up the hotel tag for the 14 days we spent there. China was a great disappointment to Rosemarie. Our hotel was not the one we'd chosen but one the Chinese moved us to. There was nothing wrong with it in terms of comfort and facilities, but we had the interference that made Rosemarie genuinely cross; our rooms were searched every time we went out. I'd experienced that often in China; also in Malaysia, Taiwan and Venezuela. So I set a few traps and derived much fun from tracking down where the nosey blighters had been looking. Rosemarie also disliked the food, but she was marvellous in not showing it, especially when picking white whole chicken feet and still-moving snails out of her soup. We did enjoy some of our dinner dates for all that; dinner now having replaced the old term "banquet" it seemed. Due entirely to her presence, I'm sure, we dined one night in a 1200-year-old Lake Palace. We were treated to magnificent fare in a dramatic setting with an army of gaily-attired servants and authentic displays of Chinese dancing and pantomime. This was clearly the manner of dining to which the rich Chinaman was accustomed. And of course we had the obligatory tours to The Great Wall and the tomb of Mao Tse Tung. But I think her favourite visits were to the Pearl Market, the backstreet shopping bazaar and the Friendship Shop that sold everything that was uniquely Chinese. Rosemarie would not place China on her list to re-visit, but we made up for it later that year by visiting Australia and Bangkok, the latter being her idea of a shopping heaven.

Before enlarging on our travels, I must tell you that the period between mid-1996 and the Millennium was as hectic as any in my life. I developed diabetes, underwent a knee operation, had a triple heart bypass, was divorced acrimoniously, re-married at once joyfully, and worked like a one-armed paperhanger on a fascinating new military programme that was to demonstrate that however old you may be, you're always on a learning curve. The programme was ASTOR (Airborne stand off radar) that I'd helped initiate in Thorn days as our long-term ace-in-the-hole. ASTOR was my swan song in industry and in my paid working life, Racal exceptionally retaining my services beyond my 65th birthday until midnight 1999 when I was approaching 70. I'll cover ASTOR later and how Rosemarie and I took advantage of the travelling I did in support of that project to see more of this wonderful world. But first, a mention of other things in the 90's.

Tales of silk

Let's start with a couple of cameos about flying, or more correctly about what happens when you stop flying and commit to a parachute. The first involves my brother Derek who, in 1993, asked for a spot of help on an RAF Squadron history that he was writing. He'd served his two years national service in the RAF as an engine mechanic, but had retained an interest in his old Squadron, No 19(F), that had been equipped with Hunters in his day. Having not been an aviator, he was delving through masses of statistics and personal stories of ex-19 chaps and was a little unsure as to how best he might edit and present some of the "war stories". Having a fighter background myself I knew 19 pretty well, had met most of their CO's, and had easy access to those that had risen to high rank. But my main task was to chat to old boys who had sent him personal accounts of particular incidents and suss out if they would make good material for his book.

Two attracted me at once, with stories involving combat and parachuting that I found both interesting and perplexing. Both men lived nearby on the south coast and I rang to ask if they'd be prepared to talk to a fellow-aviator. Both invited me to visit them without hesitation. So it was that one Sunday morning I arrived at the front door of a bungalow near Shoreham to be met by a fairly wizened old fella well into his nineties who had been on 19 in the RFC days of WW1, before it became the RAF in 1918. I sensed we were going to get on when he met me with two glasses in one hand and a bottle of Remy Martin in the other. We sat on his veranda at 10 a.m. and I spent a while trying to tune my mind to his frequency and to how things were in France in the RFC almost eighty years before, days when combat flying was in its infancy. Putting my own past into perspective and into context has been one of the fascinating aspects in compiling this autobiography. Taking others back to theirs proved equally fascinating.

My particular interest with this old guy was that he had described flying "at 19,000ft over Ypres on our morning patrol". Remember that this was 1917 when an aircraft was a flimsy structure of canvas, wood and glue, braced by a maze of wires and struts. I'd said to Derek that I thought he'd put one nought too many on the altitude. Not so, my interviewee assured me, he *had* meant nineteen thousand. "What on earth were you doing at 19K in a Spad?" I asked, mindful that it was an open cockpit, there were no oxygen masks then and most of the action (in my experience via Hollywood and war books) took place in the first five thousand feet above the battlefield.

He looked at me incredulously and said, "Because—you daft bugger—by 1917 the Germans were patrolling at 18K. They had parachutes and some even had oxygen!" Duly chastened at this gap in my knowledge, my thoughts turned to the next obvious pilot-type question. "What did you do if you had a flamer up there?" He gave me an old-fashioned look that said, "Didn't they teach you anything at Cranwell?" The answer was that they taught me a lot and I'd asked knowing that the British did not have parachutes during WW1. (Astonishingly, our medics believed that the human body would not survive leaping into the luft at speeds of 100–130mph, whilst our politicians refused to fund provision of parachutes on the grounds that "If we give 'em parachutes, they'll be over the side every time an engine splutters, and we can't afford two hundred quid for new aeroplanes!") So the Americans had 'chutes when they eventually joined in at the end, the Germans had them in 1917, and even the French had ordered them. The RAF didn't introduce them to service until hundreds of pilots had been killed in peacetime.

But back to the answer to my query as this old guy poured another brandy. "In February '18 I was caught up in a thin air battle and was on fire. My choice was either to stay and be barbecued—not really a choice—or jump over the side and hope I'd black out before hitting the deck. I had one other option, namely to use the revolver we all carried for protection if we landed in enemy territory. I opted for a speedy end, pointed the revolver to my forehead and pulled the trigger. I bloody well missed! Well, not quite missed, but ploughed this furrow into my scalp (pulling back his patchy grey hair) which stung so much that I lost control of the aircraft, spun like a corkscrew and came out around 2000 ft still smoking but no fire. I limped back to the field and poured half a bottle of this stuff (pointing to the Remy) over me head and the rest down me throat."

The second cameo, from WW2, featured a Battle of Britain Hurricane pilot in the summer of 1940. Derek's reservations on this tale were that it would take up too much valuable space and should be drastically shortened. Having heard it, again on a brandy flavoured Sunday morning, I recommended that it went in verbatim and if any cuts had to be made he should make them in the boring statistics. The following is what the ex-Squadron Leader had written for Derek and he repeated it almost word for word to me:

"I was returning from an escort sortie and found myself just off the French coast at 5000ft with about five eighths cover of cottonwool cu (cloud). I'd fired all my ammo and was thinking of hot toast and tea back in the Mess when I was suddenly aware—being a sharp fighter pilot—that my shoulder and right leg were hurting and the cockpit was filling up with smoke. I could see nothing in my mirror, but saw that my starboard wing was beginning to curl up towards me. I remember thinking that was a poor show as it was a brand new aeroplane, when smoke turned to flame and I wanted out quickly. I opened the hood but it jammed above my head and wouldn't budge. I tried to stand up but something was holding me down, and I then saw as I struggled that my right leg was actually spinning around in front of my nose and my left leg was trapped in a bloody mess on the cockpit floor. Putting all my weight on my left leg I thrust myself up until my shoulders were pressing the hood and pushed like hell! Suddenly, I don't know how, I was out of the aircraft tumbling like a top. I looked down for the D-ring; there was the sudden jolt as the harness bit into my crutch and the crack of the canopy deploying—and the startling silence known to every parachutist once he clears the aircraft. I knew I must be within ten or fifteen miles of the English coast, but I was still surrounded by fleecy cloud and caught glimpses of the white tops of the waves below. I was not a good swimmer and now had the added problem that I only had one leg, and that was spewing out blood into the air at an unacceptable rate. I tore off my squadron silk scarf and tied it as tightly as I could to stem the bleeding, looked up and saw that I was below cloud and approaching a beach with white cliffs at an alarming rate. How was I going to land on one leg, as I'd never done it on two? The answer was painfully as I hit the beach moving sideways, breaking the good leg and turning over on my back to be pulled along by the billowing canopy. My ride across the beach was halted as I hit a waterlogged tree trunk and lay there with all the wind knocked out of me and my blowing 'chute trying to pull my shoulders out of their sockets. I banged the release box and heaved a sigh of relief as the canopy and harness were whisked away on the wind. I adjusted the tourniquet and looked up just as a farmer arrived with a pitchfork, stuck it into my backside telling me what he thought of bloody Jerries. I advised him in good old Anglo Saxon that I was English and that if he looked at my leg he'd see I was injured and needed a doctor urgently. He looked—and obligingly fainted!

Seeing no one else on the beach or on the cliff, I slapped his face until he came around and was able to stagger off to find help. I remember thinking at the time that I wasn't going to be much good at the tango and, with a sudden pang of dismay, that my big date on Saturday had gone for a Burton. After about 20 minutes, the farmer arrived accompanied by a policeman pushing his bike (I can still hear the crunch of the pebbles), and a little later an ambulance crew that whisked me off into Battle Hospital. I was in dock for six months, spent another six recuperating, but was back flying within 2 years of being shot down."

I then asked the ancient aviator a few questions out of genuine interest, such as why he'd allowed himself to be taken unawares in a very dangerous piece of sky and how he explained his wing folding up like a roll of carpet. "Day dreaming" and "beats the shit out of me" were his answers, said in a tone that brooked no further comment—and to which he might have added, "I've been telling that story for half a century; that's how I remember it old chap, take it or leave it."

His was a particularly vivid story, but I'd heard many like it from men who'd flown in the war. Perhaps some were "Irish stories", some had improved with the telling and some had called on poetic license. But I had no doubt that the vast majority were essentially true. There was a feeling of pride, mutual respect and comradeship that lasted for the rest of their lives between men who had lived, fought, known fear, felt sorrow and elation, and been a closely knit bunch both in the air and on the ground. They were happiest in their own clique. Personal experience has taught me that there is a downside to those days of fulfilment and achievement. I've seen it in men coming back from wars in Europe, Viet Nam, Korea, Suez, the Falklands and the Gulf when their adjustment to normal service and family life proves difficult. A few ease their way through it, many take time to acclimatise, but some never make the transition and make themselves and those they love unhappy and unsettled.

War leaves its mark on us all, but perhaps only those who fly can understand the peculiar sense of involvement with aeroplanes, the moments that have an intense effect on you. The way the ground trembles with the surge of power as a formation takes off, or as a mass of vibrating metal screams off the catapult from a carrier deck in a cloud of steam and flying chocks. The feeling you get inside a close formation of aircraft, or the knowledge that danger lurks above or below or over the next ridge. I've no doubt that men who served in Ulster in the IRA active days will too have a special bond, as will those that drove their ships across the wild Atlantic through the wolf packs, or took their tanks into Alamein, Caen and Kuwait. Memories forged in the heat, tension and anticipation of combat or danger, have a way of staying with you for life. For some tragically, the nightmares born in combat never fade.

Rather them than me

I suspect that might apply to a XV Squadron crew who in January 1991, flew the Tornado GR1 in the Gulf War (Operation Desert Storm) and wrote a vivid account in 1992 of their experiences, entitled "Tornado Down". I had met them weeks before the war when I visited their base at RAF Laarbruch in Germany to get myself up to date on how the aircrews were using the Tornado's radar. My company had just won the contract to build the radar on which future RAF navigators would be trained, and it was important to remind myself of the technical performance and operating procedures that my engineers should aim for in the equipment we produced. Little did I or they think that only months later their battered faces would be shown on TV worldwide as the Iraqis paraded them triumphantly as captured aircrew having been shot down by a SAM on their first mission.

On reading their story I found it easy to relate to their normal Squadron lives, the gradual build up to war and the disbelief when they found themselves in Bahrain about to put their operational training, multi-million pound combat system, and their own skill and courage to the ultimate test. I understood their desperation in wanting to be there, anxious and fearful of how they might react to tension and fear, but even more fearful of missing out on this chance of glory, mindful of the St Crispins Day message and their privileged position "whilst less fortunate men at home in England slept peaceful in their beds". Many men would envy the normal lifestyle of RAF aircrew, flying the latest and most potent weapon system in service; but now they were about to step up a gear, into the unknown, about to go to war.

I followed them easily through their pre-flight preparations, the hectic moments when forced to change aircraft, and then the exhilaration of taking off at dawn with a full warload to rendezvous with the tankers before descending into enemy territory. Now down almost to the deck in bright sunlight over the desert floor with the aircraft bouncing in the increasing turbulence, and then the adrenalin flooding, heart pumping final approach to the target knowing that, coincident with you needing to be very precise and sure for weapon release, the sky around you has suddenly become full of flashes, trails, smoke and coloured confetti. You hear nothing of the bedlam outside, but you know it's there as the aircraft is manoeuvred to that final critical point in space at which, with bombs gone, you depart that little corner of hell as quickly as possible.

But for this crew on this day it didn't happen, the bombs didn't release and now low and heavy over the angry hornets nest of an intensely defended airfield they had to escape or perish. Having jettisoned the bombs they had the misfortune to collect a SAM in one engine that virtually made their craft unflyable. Both ejected at around 400kts and under 500ft to float down in almost total silence into an empty desert. That sounds simple doesn't it? But in the course of just a few minutes this pair had had more excitement than most men experience in a lifetime. They'd picked up a few knocks and bruises, but were in good shape considering the nature of their arrival in Iraq. I could still relate having had the ejection experience, but from then on in their book I could only read page after page and wonder how I'd have stood up to the pain, torture, and humiliation they were to suffer for 7 weeks as prisoners. I found myself baulking at reading every page, at the painfully honest accounts of what each felt and feared, and I coiled up inside myself and thanked God that I'd never been tested that way. Prisoners see war without glamour; the courage and comradeship are missing as they meet cruel men determined to humiliate and coarsen their very fibre.

The half dozen veterans I talked to on my brother's behalf told tales of what happened to them, at a different time in a different world. Most didn't realise that they were making history, that they would be considered heroes, and that their deeds would be recorded in letters of gold. They did what they had to do, they did what their country expected them to do, and they did so within their own particular small piece of the world. For soldier, sailor or airman—hell is a small place and the world consists of only what they can see at the time, or as measured by the flight time of a bullet or missile. Often they surprised themselves with how they performed in exceptional circumstances, at how being afraid they had overcome fear; looking back in anguish hoping there might be a replay—a chance to do it again differently. Life doesn't allow that particular escape route unfortunately.

"You cannot choose your battlefield,
God does that for you
But you can plant a standard,
where a standard never flew."

Animus non integritatem sed facinus cupit

In 1996/7, heart operation, divorce and marriage all took place over a 5-month period. So many things coming together at once, with the attendant realisation that I'd had a fairly strong medical warning, that my working days would be at an end in two, at most three, years and then I'd be on a pension and into my 70's. On the credit side was the fact that Rosemarie and I could now be together, able to live our lives to the full as man and wife. I held an enviable position in the company. I'd been key to their recent success with Dominie and Nimrod and we were well down the road in winning the prestigious and potentially lucrative Feasibility Study on ASTOR. I was a sort of father figure, I suppose; certainly respected, hopefully trusted and not likely to break any rules. The events of autumn 1996 almost put an end to it all—and this book would never have been written. It was a difficult yet immensely fulfilling chapter, so before I recount what Roo and I did after the operation, here's how that all came about—out of the blue, as it were.

The Operation

"It may seem a strange principle to annunciate as the very first
requirement in a Hospital, that it should do the sick no harm."

It's an indisputable fact that hospitals are bloody dangerous places in which to hang around for long—which is why I've always avoided them like the plague. But that autumn, life came up and hit me right between the eyes, like the handle of a garden rake when you step on the teeth! I have had the extreme good fortune to be healthy all of my life. Until the mid 90's, I'd only spent the odd day in hospital; once as an apprentice with 'flu in 1946 and a knee operation in 1991. Since 1946 my days off work could be counted on the fingers of one hand and as RAF aircrew I enjoyed the benefit of annual rigorous medicals that continued until 1993. So there wasn't ever much cause for concern; until that day in 1996 when I took the Gatwick express to Victoria.

I arrived to discover that the Underground was on strike, but with only a mile to go to my meeting in Whitehall, spurned the idea of a taxi and set off on shank's pony at a brisk pace. After about half a mile, I suddenly felt very short of breath. No pain, just breathlessness, so I sat on a wall for few minutes until all appeared to return to normal and carried on to Whitehall without any further discomfort. I had my meeting, enjoyed my customary splendid lunch at The Ivy and forgot all about the incident. Until exactly one week later the same sequence of events was repeated, and I vowed to do more exercise as I obviously wasn't in very good shape.

However, I still was not concerned, as they seemed to be two isolated incidents; inexplicable, but nevertheless innocuous. That week I had a scheduled appointment with my doctor, David Whitehead, when I asked for "other sins to be taken into account."

"Can't detect anything wrong," said he in his usual cheerful but always professional manner. "Better safe than sorry though, I'll send you to have a treadmill test as soon as I can get a slot."

This was Thursday p.m., eight days after the first scare, and the treadmill test was set for 7 p.m. on the following Monday. I duly boarded the treadmill in the presence of a physio and was congratulating myself on this being a piece of cake when he said, "Hang on now, I'll turn it up to a brisk walk." Sure enough, after about three minutes everything started to go pear shaped and I was really struggling for breath.

The following morning David called to say that he'd arranged for me to go that afternoon to the King Edward VII hospital at Midhurst for an angiogram, which I gathered involved stuffing some sort of camera inside my chest to see what was causing the poor breathing. By the time her in the dark stockings had brought my tea, the specialist was at my bedside to advise me that I did indeed have a problem that could not be cured by medicines or by blowing up my arteries. I would need a quadruple heart bypass. He went on to explain—still to a disbelieving patient I must add—that the walls of my arteries had begun to collapse, fortunately in such a way that none had been completely blocked—which also explained the absence of pain. He went on to say that although he'd be there, the operation would be done by "himself", the great man in London, and I was to see him on the Thursday, D-Day plus 12, as it was.

This was now all moving a bit too fast for my liking, but I remained unconcerned. I arrived at the London hospital to be welcomed by a tall leggy blonde nurse who ushered me into a sumptuous waiting room, plied me with coffee and biscuits and eventually into an equally sumptuous office to meet "himself". He reiterated the cause of my discomfort, said nonchalantly he was probably only going to do a triple ("as one was a bit too close to do without great risk") and that he'd need a fair length of new artery—so could he please have my left leg? Did I have any questions?

At this point one has to bear in mind I was still very sceptical that there was a damned thing wrong with me. So I asked him in genuinely jocular mood, "After the operation, will I be able to play the piano?" He looked at me as if I were some sort of idiot and replied that of course I would. "That's some operation," said I, "I can't play a bloody note now." The blonde vision of loveliness hurried out laughing as if she'd wet herself. "Himself" was not amused and said dryly that he'd heard all the jokes, so could I pay attention (in a tone such as M might use to a frivolous Bond).

He went on to put me down in that very superior way some doctors have, and then said that a place on his table had been reserved for me on the following Tuesday at Midhurst (D plus 14 in effect). I would need to check in on Monday evening for pre-op prep. "All right with that?" he asked. To which—doing a rapid mental scan of my diary—I replied, "Oh no, can't make it that day." "Why on earth not?" said he. "Well," I replied, innocently and firmly, "I've got tickets for United against Liverpool on Saturday." This time the sense of humour failure was absolute. Glowering at me from behind his mammoth desk he said, "If you and I cannot meet at 9 a.m. next Tuesday in my theatre, I want nothing more to do with your case—do we have a date?" "Yes Sir!" I replied, realising that the game was up.

But my respect for him and my concern about the operation *per se* were as nothing compared to what I was faced with as I drove home to Wales on the Friday evening. Not wishing to worry her, I'd told Rosemarie nothing about the problem and the rapid escalation of events. It was Sunday morning, still in bed, when I finally blurted out that I had a wee problem and had to go into hospital the next day. Rosemarie was devastated, but as always after the initial explosion she settled down to organise everything. She was coming with me, she would stay as close as she could after the operation, she'd nurse me back to recovery—and she even persuaded cousin Judy—an exceptionally highly qualified nurse with vast cardiac op. experience—to accompany us to Midhurst.

So it was that on the Monday evening at 6 p.m., just 13 days after the first symptoms, I checked in at Midhurst with Rosemarie and Judy—both who were to stay in the hospital that night. They kept my spirits high and before I knew it I was being wheeled into the operating theatre being told by a nurse that I'd soon lose consciousness. I remember as they swivelled my bed through the swing doors I caught a glimpse of Rosemarie and waved. My last thoughts, very distinct memories, were that I really should be worrying at this very special time, but that I simply hadn't got the time to do so!

My next conscious memory is of opening my eyes in a dimly lit room and feeling Rosemarie's hair brush my cheek as she said, "You're going to be okay darling." I remember seeing other people in the ITU ward who all looked bloody dreadful, covered with pipes and tubes and oxygen masks, and surrounded by flickering TV-type screens.

"What about them poor buggers then?" I thought.

My overriding memories of the next few days were of pain and discomfort and especially that awful time in a hospital shortly before dawn, taking your pills and medication and feeling as if you were lying in a fish tank. The pain of course was all to do with the fact that a bunch of doctors had been prising open my ribs to get at the important bits and then stuffing it all back together and stitching me up with steel wire. The pain wasn't too bad when you were propped up with lots of pillows and could get to sleep. If you couldn't, the discomfort factor escalated, and if you coughed, worse still sneezed, the pain was acute.

I'm enormously impressed by our current hospital-based "soaps" that have heart op. patients drinking tea, arguing with spouses and walking two hours after surgery. Personally, I was delighted after 3 days to be able to take a few tentative steps and to be able to lie down rather than sit bolt upright. There was the joy too of going to the loo unaided, instead of the ignominy (or was it frustration?) of having a nurse hold your willy. After 6 days I was allowed home to be taken care of by the world's most attentive nurse. She and I had the odd confrontation over the following weeks, due entirely to my short fuse at being so bloody helpless. One hilarious incident was my first real bath. When it came to getting out, without having any power in my arms it was simply impossible as Roo couldn't take my dead weight. We were within minutes of calling the fire brigade as the water got colder, until we hit on the wheeze of stuffing pillows and blankets under me until I almost rolled out like a great landed whale.

On the 10th day after the op, I attended a "vital" Board Meeting at my company at which my short temper led to me calling the MD of the mighty Lockheed Corporation a "miserable sod" much to everyone else's immense delight and satisfaction. Within 18 days I was back to working full time. I owed my recovery—indeed perhaps my life—to a very sharp GP, a wonderful surgeon and a loving caring wife. Also, it must be said, to having private insurance (taken out only 2 months before), without which I'd have been on the long waiting list for the Pearly Gates like so many unfortunate people.

There's probably another chapter on things medical in me, but suffice it to say now that it cannot be right that seriously ill people have to wait so long for life-saving surgery in one of the world's most advanced and civilised countries. I find it odd that the one certain thing in life is death, yet so many of those who should be pumping money into our Health Service, appear to think that only the poor are destined to pop their clogs, and that they are expendable. Three years later I've revisited this chapter and decided that so much has been written about the NHS and the quality of our medical staffs and hospitals, that my opinion will be of no real interest. Nevertheless, my experiences in Wales have given me an itchy pen!

My knowledge of the medical profession was confined effectively to the Palmer family doctors when I was a boy in Manchester, and then RAF doctors from 1946 to 1990. That experience installed doctors in my mind as dedicated, capable, and caring human beings who allied their education and intelligence to a work ethic and genuine concern for the welfare of all. If any of us were sick and incapacitated by a physical injury, or running a temperature, the family doctor would be at the house almost any time, day or night. They were all professionals that we respected without question and who would be prepared to listen to what you told them and explain in a kindly understanding way what you must do and what they would do next. Should you be hospitalised, the hospital—any hospital—would be welcoming, clean to the point of being spotless, and staffed by men and women who looked and dressed and acted the part of people whose main aim in life was to help you. They prided themselves on their "bedside manner" but were no slouches when it came to reading the riot act to a reluctant or difficult patient.

Ill health, pain, and discomfort are not tied to a particular season, day or time of day. The dedicated vocational medical folk of yesteryear were literally open all hours because that was when the sick needed them, and they knew that and accepted their duty when they embarked on a long and demanding course of training. Because they were a well-educated and hard-working profession, they enjoyed a lifestyle and a quality of life well above the average, but of course no one ever begrudged them that; they were amongst the most respected and best-loved members of any community.

In the 90's in Sussex, I had the enormous good fortune to have an NHS doctor like that, working in a splendid surgery complex and supported by excellent local hospitals. I was so impressed that even when I moved to Wales, for two years I would drive the 450-mile round trip to Worthing for any medical treatment. But a combination of cost and age forced me on to the local NHS, from the sublime to the ridiculous indeed.

So what do I see now, alarmingly as I get older, as the medical panorama in Wales? Firstly, Doctors who don't want to work unsociable hours, who are reluctant to get up from their desk and computer to actually touch and examine a patient, and—sad to say—whose ethnic background means patients are treated as prescription scroungers and layabouts instead of the ordinary decent folk that most of them are. So many people are wrongly diagnosed, so many useless and inappropriate medicines prescribed, so many sick and needy people are left frustrated to grow old and falter long before they would elsewhere in Europe and England. In spite of all the political promises, waiting lists to see a handful of specialist consultants are disgracefully long and follow-up treatment schedules outlast the patients! Hospitals, never popular places of course, are all too often now forbidding, unwelcoming, shabby places with shabby staff and shabby treatment. The fact that very few display the dedicated professional qualities needed and expected, only serves to accentuate the generally appalling standards to which we've sunk. In 1961, when living in Texas, I delivered many talks and lectures on radio and TV about the wonderful medical services we enjoyed in the UK, proud of a service that was of the utmost importance to everyone living in our country. If asked now, I should have to bow my head in shame and frustration at what has happened to the jewel in our social crown, more appropriately now called the National Sickness Service!

A Second Chance

12 weeks after the operation, my surgeon told me cheerfully, "Your diabetes will kill you long before your heart will." Thus heartened, I demanded that my divorce now be completed (they'd refused it in case I died from the operation!) and hastened our marriage. Roo and I planned our immediate future. Now she could accompany me on business trips and attend Cocktail Parties, Air Show lunches and dinner parties when entertaining Racal's guests. Also to Squadron reunions and RAF social functions that we had always longed to share as partners. We had a lot going for us, except money after a ruinous divorce. But I'd been collecting Air Miles on my many travels so Rosemarie virtually travelled free. Another plus was that overseas if you rent a room for one, it's the same price as for two. So the only extra expense was her food and at my "expenses grade" we lived extraordinarily well. Shamelessly, after a wilderness existence, we sought adventure rather than purity. I knew this was the time, even if Rosemarie didn't, that we should see as much of the world as we could whilst still reasonably healthy and capable of arduous travel. We were strapped for cash, but I'd have a damned sight less when I retired, and then there'd be no more air miles or company-assisted hotels.

I knew where I wanted to take her; she'd spent so many lonely years waiting for me without complaint and now was the time to show her the places I'd been seeing for years. She's a funny lass; by that I mean she has very firm and definite views about most things and if she's made her mind up that she doesn't like a particular country or culture, she just won't go there. In 1993 I'd introduced her to the States and I remember the thrilled look on her face as she emerged from Customs at Dulles Airport. Just flying out alone was a great adventure and she was to do that later to meet me in Philadelphia, New York, Singapore and even Honolulu. She was flying westerly from London to San Francisco to Honolulu as I was coming from Perth easterly via Sydney and Fiji. I arrived just in time to slip my lau over her head as she stepped from the Wicky-Wickey car. Life doesn't get much sweeter than that moment. She loved the USA and I was determined that she'd see a lot more of it including Hollywood (her choice), Grand Canyon, Dallas, Niagara, Monument Valley, Las Vegas, San Francisco, San Diego, Atlanta, Tombstone Territory, the Badlands and New York City, and the border towns in Canada and Mexico.

I wanted her to see Singapore, KL, and Bangkok and drive through the jungle and walk on palm fringed beaches. I wanted to take her to Australia and feed her scallops and white wine at Doyle's across the bay from Sydney Harbour, to see her cuddle a Koala Bear, squeal with delight as a Kangaroo bounced across her path, and jump in the breakers at Manley and Bondi. Selfishly, I wanted to watch her body turn golden brown and her face light up with the warmth of the southern sun. I wanted the tropical flowers to see her and know the true meaning of beautiful and exotic. Then there were targets closer to home; the ancient glories of Rome and the wonderful treasures of the Vatican. The bustling life of Istanbul, historical Egypt, the Holy Land, and Athens where I knew she'd feel at home after years in Cyprus. I wanted her to know why I loved the little villages and great mountains of the Alpine region, why Berlin, Budapest and Heidelberg attracted me, and why I had a love/ hate relationship with Paris. I knew Madrid would surprise her, I wanted her to see Copenhagen as I saw it, and have at least a glimpse of countries like Poland, Sweden, Switzerland and the far south of Ireland.

That's a long shopping list to cover in three years, as well as having an eye on one or two other special trips if the opportunities arose. I passionately wanted her to visit Cape Town and a Game park; she loved nature and animals so much. I wanted her to see Rio where—apart from sunshine—she'd adore the scenery, the food, the music, and the joy and energy of the Brazilians. Above all, I wanted to take her back to Kauai, that most perfect of holiday retreats, for her to continue her love affair with the dolphins and whales.

We all have our own unique curiosity; things that we have as priorities to see or do because of some connection of thought or action or hearsay in our lives. When you're in the mood to see something you've not seen before, I've found that it's almost as satisfying to have had the experience, and not liked it, as having had it and enjoyed it. Mentally you cross it off, say, "been there, done that", and get on to thinking about something new. By experiencing things we do not wish to repeat, we actually enhance the things we really like; being able to compare fairly and more sensibly, I believe.

All lovers will know there is something magical about being in a foreign place with the object of your affections. You notice things that previously made no impression; you react to a place so that the sum of the whole is immeasurably greater than the sum of the two parts. We travelled, we saw, and we enjoyed it all, but there were places that I knew would not impress Roo and might even frighten her. I would never have taken her to Nigeria, Venezuela or Viet Nam; the violence, sinister undertones and poverty would have unnerved her. I'm pretty sure that she'd have seen Moscow, Manila, Bucharest, Karachi, and Teheran in the same light as she'd seen Beijing; once was enough. Then there were other places that I knew would not be at the top of her list, but which I felt she should see at least once, because they are uniquely different. India and Nepal were my favourites there, but deep down in Roo's nature was a dislike of the Indian sub-continent that I was never able to overcome. I didn't try too hard, mind you, because we had such a long wish list; but India, Japan, Korea, and Indonesia—all fascinating countries in their own right—held no attraction for her, whilst North Africa, Algeria, Morocco and Tunisia would not have been her cups of tea.

She was keen however to visit the Persian Gulf, especially Dubai, but a planned visit for me to chair an Air Show Conference there in 2001 was cancelled after the Twin Towers tragedy. The Gulf is not my favourite part of the world, and I suspect Roo's wish to go has much to do with inexpensive (unaffordable) jewellery and gold. But I would have liked to take her to Muscat, up into the Jebel and to spend a couple of nights in what she refers to as "The real desert; you know, Lawrence of Arabia stuff". If I ever find a few shekels, I'll take her. ASTOR gave us access to the States, and the other great provider of 747 seats turned out to be my Nimrod MPA work with the RAF. As the company's lead man with the RAF, I helped run the annual Fincastle Competition between the Commonwealth aircrews which is held every year in one of the Commonwealth countries, Australia, Canada, New Zealand and the UK. We therefore enjoyed two splendid visits to Kinloss near Inverness, one three-week trip to Adelaide, and a related Air Show visit by Nimrod to Pretoria. Just to show how spoiled rotten we were, we turned down the Canadian trip to Vancouver Island due to a prior engagement in Rome!

I was about to apologise for forcing more boring prose on you, but then I told myself I should write my story because it's what I want to do. I shall therefore recount a wee story from Scotland, one about a very special trip to South Africa, and tie up our global wanderings with something on Australia. Wanderings all the more special because we were lovers, and all lovers know the magic of sharing somewhere new and different.

A Cup o'kindness

The former concerns a pre-Fincastle gathering in a Forres hotel, where all the Nimrod contractors supporting the event gave freely of their marketing funds with expense accounts taking a fair old beating. Fifteen Company marketing men, many ex-RAF, sat down after dinner in a splendidly old-fashioned bar and followed their annual custom of sampling whatever the local brew might be. The previous year in Adelaide it had been particularly potent Australian Rum, and the following year Moosemilk was to leave a trail of bodies across Vancouver. But this was Scotland, and where better to be on an October night than in a bar tended by an expert on "The Malt" and with a vast array of single-malt whiskies behind him to prove it.

Already I feel my wee story extending into a tale, but it is New Year's Eve as I write—so apportion some of the blame to the odd dram of "*uisge beatha*", the Celtic water of life, beginning to bite. Scotland is a country of geographical contrasts; from bleak mountainsides to sun-dappled river valleys, from crystal clear icy lochs to shores and peat bogs fed by the Atlantic Ocean, brushed by gentle breezes and torn by mighty winds. From the wild grey Highland mountains to the softly rolling green hills and the subtle sweetness of the Lowlands. When you take a dram of malt, you're sampling the beauty of that Scottish landscape. You'll recapture the aroma of the heather flowers, the scent of peat, of seaweed and of woodsmoke, and you're tasting the finest barley, the purest water, the perfect yeast, to which some genius has applied simply heat and cooling, plus the magic wrought by the slow working of time.

> *Let other poets raise a fracas,*
> *'bout vines, and wines, and drucken Bacchus,*
> *And crabbit names and stories wrack us,*
> *an' grate our lug—*
> *I'll sing the juice Scotch beare can mak' us*
> *In cask or flask or welcome jug.*

There, I told you so! I've only to start thinking of Scotland and things Scottish, and I'm under a spell, with my heart and mind following my old golden roadways of years gone by. Scotland the brave, Scotland the ever present tingle of life at the flood with the spell of a wild and untameable country whose every nook and cranny is marked on the map of romance. Where else is a country's music and poetry carried on the breeze, where else will you find it curled up like a faithful friend in front of the fire? Where else have men embroidered a landscape more richly with daring deeds, where else has passion, love and pride soaked into the grass and heather and rock, making them so different from other grass and other rocks?

Whilst you're engaged in that fruitless search, let me take you back to the bar and note that another time-honoured, but very rare, custom of these contractor gatherings was that everyone bought a round in turn. We were all on expense accounts, the justification was audit proof, and we were all playing away. We started to imbibe the single malts in the order recommended by the expert—Jimmy the barman; a sequence based on a trawl through the five distinct Malt regions of Lowlands, Highlands, Western Highlands, Speyside, and Islay and the Islands. I'd be the first to admit that a Talisker, Balvenie or any classic malt, is at its best when drunk under a threatening sky in the shadow of a Scottish mountain, but it's still a lot better drunk anywhere in Scotland than in a London pub or New York nightclub.

Wee Jimmy, being a true Scot, worked on the belief that as our tongues became loose so would our wallets, and by the time we were all singing and reciting the songs and poetry of Robbie Burns we were almost into taking out a mortgage for each round. At this propitious moment, the bar door swung open to reveal the jovial face of the Almighty; in other words, the British Aerospace senior director who was not exactly renowned for pushing out the boat. He apologised for being late and then asked the fateful question, "Anyone like a drink?" Someone—trying to be helpful, of course—said that for the last three hours we'd been following the malt whisky trail through Scotland and wee Jimmy would know what we hadn't sampled. Silence fell upon the room as we waited for wee Jimmy to make his suggestion. "We-e-ell," he said thoughtfully in his thin piping voice, "you've had the 10-year-old McWhatsit, and the 20-year-old, so perhaps you'd like to try the 30? I do have a few bottles in the cellar." "Capital!" beamed our new benefactor. "Since I've missed a few rounds, why don't we make them doubles, and perhaps our friends would join us as we've taken over their pub?"—waving generously around the room that contained another fifteen or so people in addition to our group.

I expected Jimmy to be out of the bar like a shot, but he nonchalantly walked through to his cellar and emerged walking gingerly and blowing the cobwebs off his store of "30 year old". He began to pour doubles, ever so carefully, and it was noticeable that even a few that had stopped drinking (or might even have been tea-totallers) were now awaiting their glass of the golden nectar. Lifting his glass high, our ace wished everyone Happy Days and looked down approvingly at his glass saying, "My God, that's smooth!"

"Shall you be putting that on your hotel bill sir?" queried Jimmy.

"No no, I've got some cash on me—what's the damage Jimmy?"—taking out his wallet with a flourish.

I'll swear that Jimmy sent up a little prayer with thanks before he announced in his broad accent: "That'll be Wun thoosand and wun hundred poonds exactly."

The sound of a penny dropping was broken by a very brave—soon to be redundant, I fear—BAe marketeer, who inquired, "Shall we have another round, boss?"

Happy Wanderers

Cairo 1997

Cape Town 1998

Monument Valley 1999

Hawaii 1999

Cyprus 2000

South Africa

The South African venture was, from start to finish, one of those happenings that you have to rub your eyes and pinch yourself to be sure it wasn't a dream. South Africa was my marketing patch, but after a few visits it was clear there were no immediate prospects to pursue, and although it was high on my list of places to take Rosemarie, I didn't have the cash to go it alone. Then, out of the blue, an opportunity arose during a quiet spell on ASTOR starting with a phone call from a Nimrod Squadron Commander at Kinloss telling me about a trip to an Air Show in Pretoria and asking whether Racal might sponsor them, and would I like to go on the Nimrod. (I ask you—can a duck swim?)

I checked with our agent in Pretoria to find the Air Show had suddenly become a big political issue as the Government had invited virtually everyone that built small jet fighters to demonstrate their aircraft. He wanted my support at the Show anyway and Nimrods' presence clinched it. But the timing wasn't quite right as Nimrod would be arriving three days into the show, and I was needed earlier. So I now had to say No to the Nimrod ride and book BA instead, which of course had me counting up all available air miles and finding I had enough to get Rosemarie from London to Johannesburg, and back from Cape Town. We only needed £62 to get her from Jo'burg to Cape Town.

We were off! I was to be at the Show in Pretoria for six days and then down to Cape Town to join the Nimrod crew for another four days. I'd be busy, but we'd see a fair bit of SA with the very important exception of a Game Park. You can of course see animals in zoos and compounds all over SA, but the big thrill is going out into the bush and seeing them in totally natural surroundings. Those places were a long way from where we'd be, but we couldn't have everything; or could we? Two days before our planned departure a huge diplomatic row blew up about some aircraft being banned from the Show, and a 72-hour delay was imposed to sort it out. Suddenly, I had gained 4 spare days before work began—time to hire a car and drive the 200 odd miles to the Kruger for at least three days.

Frantic phoning followed, but no UK travel company could offer accommodation in or near the Park, and even our agent's secretary in Pretoria reported that there were no vacancies anywhere. Then—at the last minute—I got a call to say that we could have the luxury suite at Leopards Hills due to a late cancellation—but they needed instant confirmation. I persuaded our agent to book it on the company account, crossed my fingers, and rushed to pick up Roo to catch the night flight to Jo'burg. Even for me, a truly hardened traveller, this was an eagerly anticipated adventure. I wasn't sure whether I'd be seeing anything new, but I was taking Roo to see things she'd certainly never seen and that was the object of the exercise. We drove east from Pretoria across fairly featureless country but even that was interesting in a different country with people who acted differently. A two-hour stop in a busy market town was a real experience before we reached the hills and mountains and began a steep descent towards Leopard Hills, located at the northwest corner of Kruger. The entry to the Park was not very impressive—that said, I don't know what I expected, but apart from a 12 foot high fence there was nothing to show it was a game park. There were no turnstiles, we didn't pay. Everything would be explained at the Lodge some 15 miles ahead, said the gate guard, and he said nothing else except we should turn left at the sign after crossing the river.

At this stage I didn't tell Roo that I felt that this was a bit of an anti-climax. The terrain around us was bush and scrub, very few tall trees, nothing at all like a jungle and no feeling that we'd ever see anything of any interest in the place. Perhaps it'll improve down by the river valley, I kept telling myself, but I wasn't that hopeful as we only had about five miles to go. Suddenly I had to brake sharply when, on rounding a bend, we were faced with huge lumps of earth in the road. I started to drive slowly around them, remembering I was driving a BMW saloon, not a 4-wheel drive, when Roo said disbelievingly, "The lumps are steaming!"—and it hit home that these were elephant droppings. Suddenly the apparently empty bush was alive with strange noises, half-glimpsed movements and some obvious signs of recent animal presence.

We didn't see another soul until we reached the hotel, which quite simply took our breath away. It was comprised of a series of small buildings joined together across trees and rocks by wooden walkways. We were shown to magnificent quarters perched high on a rocky bluff with a panoramic view of the river and open game areas. We had a beautiful set of rooms, with a vast veranda, an antique but very modern bath out in the open air, and around us the sight and sound and colour of nature. Signs warned us not to walk out at night and to beware when we went onto the veranda—and just to demonstrate the need for the warning, a large green snake flashed across the room and into the rafters as we stood spellbound. In the middle of the complex was a splendid bar and dining room and we were introduced at lunch to the other twelve guests.

The viewing pattern of the park was based on two main forays per day out into the bush—one at dawn, the other at dusk and into the night. After returning from the morning drive around 9 a.m., there was a bush walk for the brave to look at the signs left by various creatures and to see some of the less obvious residents like spiders, lizards and snakes. Other strange pastimes included breaking open elephant dung to see what the blighters had eaten, and even smoking the dried variety in a clay pipe. But it was the two journeys in the open four wheel drives, each seating two guides, a rifleman and 6 tourists, that were the icing on the cake. They surpassed my wildest expectations. If the reader hasn't been on such a visit, I must explain that Leopard Hills is not like the Kruger where animals roam across open spaces and are viewed from the road, usually surrounded by many other vehicles. In Leopard Hills, you are the only vehicle around and you're driving along tracks, not roads, and across fields and open scrublands. You are right there with the animals and often passing them within a few feet before realising their proximity. The many thousands of acres includes a major river, so there is ample cover for the animals and they have the freedom to move throughout the Park with some access to adjoining special private reserves.

What I hadn't appreciated until we drove out was that, except for the giraffes whose heads were often above the trees, all the other animals were well protected and disguised by the fairly dense bush and the variety of vegetation. As we were to discover, you could be in the middle of a herd of elephant without even knowing it until you were surrounded by angry bulls and mums protecting their little ones. When that happened it was frightening in a way, but immensely impressive to see over a hundred elephants walk by your vehicle within feet with the bulls flaring their ears and telling you to clear off. Remarkably, when they'd gone the signs of their passage were virtually nil to the untrained eye. Leopard Hills prided itself on being able to guarantee to show you "the big five"—Lion, Leopard, Cheetah, Rhinoceros and Buffalo, in addition to elephant, giraffe, hippopotamus, crocodile, hyena and all varieties of deer, antelope and the smaller rarer cats. The wardens of course knew where to look and how to follow and even anticipate certain animals being in a certain place at a given time. The need for the rifleman, who sat on an extended front bumper, was tragically demonstrated when the big friendly African that we'd had on our vehicle was attacked and killed by a lion the week after we left.

After the dusk vigil at the watering holes, the drive through the bush in the dark was fascinating. The guides knew their environment intimately and would often stop to point a powerful search light to illuminate some creature hiding off the track that they had heard or sensed was there. Most animals accepted the presence of humans in a vehicle, somehow not seeing that as a threat. But there were occasions when we saw a potentially dangerous animal whilst on foot and the whole demeanour of the animal changed. You suddenly felt that you were on a menu, not on a sightseeing trip. Those who haven't shared our wonderful experience will have seen it all, and more, on screen. There is so little of the world that is a mystery these days, and that I think is a great pity. But the screen doesn't show you everything; it can't assail all your senses and give you the feeling of being there, so privileged to have been in the midst of God's marvellous creatures. I recommend to anyone who hasn't yet done so, and can afford to do so, to put a visit to a private Game reserve like Leopard Hills at the top of your travel list. I promise you an experience of such pleasure and interest that you'll be doing what I've been doing ever since—pinching myself to ask, "Was I really there?"

Australia

Between 1986 and 1999, I visited Oz on an average of four times a year for periods of a week or more. So I could say that I know Australia as well as most non-residents. I confess that, apart from a few late editorial tweaks, I had considered my autobiography complete before adding these paragraphs, from which you may conclude that I didn't have any experiences screaming out to get a mention. Even I am surprised at the omission because so many Brits see Oz as a prestigious holiday target on the other side of the world, where the sun shines constantly and everyone is either a sun-tanned beauty or an athlete par excellence. I didn't even think about Australia when narrowing down my choice of subjects to those most memorable to me, or those in which a reader might take most interest.

How do you explain that? Familiarity breeding contempt perhaps, or worse still indifference; neither love nor hate, closer in fact to apathy. Well, first I admit that I always looked forward to going there. My most frequented spots were Sydney, Canberra, Melbourne, Adelaide, Perth and Brisbane in that order. I usually flew between them, but I also drove through most of New South Wales, Victoria, South Australia east of Adelaide, and Queensland up to Brisbane. I visited Alice Springs occasionally, Ayres Rock (once was enough) and Tasmania, which I found stupendously beautiful in parts. And that is another puzzlement because so many Australians had given me the impression of Tasmania as a cold wet miserable place, rather like the far north of Scotland and with a population so sparse that sheep were invited to most parties to make up the numbers. I found the area south of Hobart around the original settlements, easily the prettiest spot on the continent. I suppose I always felt comfortable there because the climate was mostly good, the people were friendly and spoke reasonable English, and the food—especially the sea food—was very high quality and often well-cooked. Hotels were invariably comfortable, clean and well air conditioned, providing good food at reasonable prices. But perhaps the overriding attraction for me, bearing in mind that I was there on business and was always a conscientious sort of bloke, was that compared to the UK and US, everything was so laid back.

When travelling by air, the queue at the desk was long if you waited more than five minutes, the executive lounges were sumptuous, flights went to schedule, and there was no heavy drinking, rowdy passengers, or the usual hassle associated with airports. When I left the hotel at 8.30 for my appointment in the MoD in Canberra or a company office in Adelaide or Perth, it was a busy day if there were more than three cars waiting at the traffic lights. Canberra was the only capital I knew where you didn't have to make appointments weeks ahead. You just called that morning and 90% of the guys you wanted were not only in, but would be delighted to join you for lunch or dinner.

RAAF officers on exchange with the RAF were invariably very sharp individuals, good officers and very socially adept. In their own country they were equally impressive, but there were many frustrations when trying to sell defence equipment. Firstly, they always stipulated the best performance that was technically available; but never had enough money to achieve their aim. Secondly, they were far more likely to buy from the USA. That may have been due to British Aerospace's arrogant pushy way of marketing, or because they took the US carrot of Foreign Sales benefits enabling them to buy better products on the never-never. British companies cheerfully paid the enormous travel expenses in trying to get a part of the Australian market because they were a prestigious customer. But the fact is that they seldom purchase more than a few items of equipment and the long-term cost of supporting them from the UK is ruinous. No marketeer will admit that, since 14 days in Sleepy Hollow is a rest cure compared to flogging around the Middle East or most European capitals. Australia is not exactly in anyone's front line. They have no natural enemies and they couldn't defend themselves if Indonesia or China for instance decided to duff 'em up. One never felt the Australians believed they needed to defend anything, and I always looked upon their Strategy Plan as more of a Walter Mitty novel than a statement of their defence plans. I would often sit on an RAAF base hoping that someone-anyone—would actually fly that day just to show willing, whereas on most airfields in the UK and US, there'd be a constant flow of traffic.

But enough of dull defence, more about things that really matter. I found that many of my preconceived ideas were wrong. First take the Australian character who comes across as a very confident, often brash, superman. In fact, those of European ancestry always seem to have an enormous chip on their shoulder, believing that foreigners—especially Brits—see them as country bumpkins with corks in their hats and a surprising number of otherwise intelligent and capable characters see themselves scorned by outsiders. Then there's the myth about Australian scenery and the beauty of the Australian "Sheila". In many ways they are similar. You'll see something that makes your eyes pop out, then drive hundreds of miles through complete boredom, until it's eye-popping time again—followed by even longer periods of boredom! Finally on the debit side, a word about food. Australians have some of the finest natural ingredients in the world, but all too often the size of the portion seems to be more important than the taste, or than its place in the meal as a whole. I'd rather have a succulent well-flavoured 8oz fillet steak than a half-cooked steer with only its horns and tail cut off. I want shellfish prepared with herbs and sauces that enhance the natural flavour rather than a lobster so big that I need a DIY kit to prise out the usually bland flesh. Okay, that's me, but Oz is not my idea of a gourmet's delight.

Sydney

I like Sydney; it has all the features that attract me in a coastal city—a wide river flowing into a beautiful bay, with an attractive waterfront featuring the Harbour Bridge, the Opera House and dozens of different types of water craft that buzz around the place affording spectacular views from almost any angle. Add the friendly climate, a dozen or more sheltered bays and ocean beaches nearby, and a wide range of good restaurants, and Sydney is well worth a visit. As a city there's not much of it, the centre shops are nothing to write home about and you're soon out into suburbs that hold no real attractions for me except when searching for Australian editions for my crime book collection. Heading north beyond Manley there are some beautiful residential areas tucked into the many tight valleys and spread along the coast with its sandy beaches and wild waves that knock the breath out of you but challenge you to take them on. The warmth of the water I found makes one hell of a difference as to how you enjoy that experience; being beaten up *and* frozen to death would be very different.

I found nothing particularly attractive about the other major cities, but neither can I say I disliked any of them. They were more like big coastal towns than cities with no discernible city centre and no heart or character. Life just ticked along pleasantly, but you almost wished that there would be something just to bring a sense of life and purpose to the place. Oddly enough, Rosemarie felt the same about the shops, about fashion and about the food. "Is that all there is?" she would ask. And in 1999, just to show that Roo and I were not alone in our underwhelming views of Oz, the family that I lodged with in Crawley went for 3 weeks—and came home after two through utter boredom!

Of the State capitals, I liked Melbourne best. That might have been because many of the defence industries were located there and because their restaurants had a strong Greek and German influence which suited my taste. Adelaide's main attraction was the vineyards in the hills north of the town, again with a very rich German heritage. Perth was just beaches and sunshine, a combination that seems hard to beat except that you feel totally unchallenged and unexcited. Canberra was a one-off. Being the centre of government and the home of the Ministry of Defence, it was a must on almost every trip. I went regularly, stayed at the same hotel, ate at the same restaurants, and met the same people so often that it became like Brussels had been in my time in Whitehall. Essentially very boring, but nothing to really upset you one way or t'other except when the place was black with the sheep flies. You'll gather that I'm struggling to make this even the slightest bit interesting so I'll recount the odd cameo tale and leave Australia in peace.

First a mention of one of the few memorable parties that I went to out there, a remarkable statement because the general impression conveyed by all the films and soaps is of a really swinging place, especially with beach parties and "barbies". That could be because I moved in social circles not given to wild parties, excessive drinking and sexually nimble women. But this was the same social circle of the military, government and Defence industries in which I operated in the UK, US, and Europe—and that scene was far from dull. Nevertheless, there was stiffness about the social life that I experienced, so this story of an impromptu party in a top Melbourne hotel stands out.

It was Friday—and not a moment too soon! The occasion was "a few drinks" in my hotel room at 5 p.m. with "a few RAAF officers" with whom I'd been negotiating a contract. The deal was done and I invited our local team of two to join half a dozen air force guys for a mini-celebration. I made the mistake (some might say stroke of genius) of calling my ex-Cranwell secretary—then married to an RAAF officer at a nearby base—to tell the guys about the invitation. I suggested we kept the party simple by having only beer and champagne, supported by oysters, smoked salmon and abalone; nothing greasy or crumby, you understand. I told the hotel kitchen I wanted the oysters to be a mix of both raw and "A l'escargot", and asked the fair Maureen to set up the room for 5 p.m.

When, at 4.45, I exited the lift on the 22nd floor opposite my suite, you can imagine my surprise on being met by a wall of music and females gyrating in the corridor. Maureen explained that around twenty officers had arrived, plus the odd wife and girlfriend, and that the other girls had been hijacked from the debris of an earlier wedding party in the hotel! We therefore had around 50 people instead of 10 and she hoped I didn't mind, but she'd upped the order for the refreshments! At midnight I signed a bill for 100 dozen oysters, the hotels' entire stock of abalone and smoked salmon, 6 crates of champagne and 300 cans of Fosters. I was glad to have a signed contract to accompany my expenses for that small tasteful and refined carousal.

What else? A few evenings spent cooking one's own steak and sausages, grilling fresh fish on the beach, watching the 'roos at dawn, and viewing the marine life from the majestic cliffs west of Melbourne. The rest is all about a pleasant place to be if you want to be away from the rat race and not be too challenged intellectually. That I realise is damning with faint praise, but that's how I see Australia compared to much of the world. I'm forced to admit that the same applies to New Zealand, another place that always attracted me perhaps because it is effectively the furthest away one can be on earth from England. It is undoubtedly a beautiful country in many ways, a sort of southern hemisphere Scotland with particularly majestic scenery on South Island. But for a well-travelled (spoiled rotten) chap like me I must conclude that I'm pleased to have been there a few times, I liked what I saw, but it would not figure in my top list of places to visit, or hold any special memories.

The disappearing Far East

An Englishman defines the Far East as starting at Burma and taking in those countries south of China and north of Australia. When I first went there in 1950, places like Rangoon, Singapore, Kuala Lumpur and Jakarta were so different from anywhere else on earth and each had their own unique character and culture. Their equatorial climate, exotic vegetation, daily lifestyle, architecture, shopping, oriental influence and eating customs, were all so different from those in Europe; appealing often because they were so distinctive. You ate in circumstances that you'd never countenance back home, you travelled in the most dangerous and uncomfortable of vehicles, you dressed to stay cool rather than look elegant or smart, and you looked at the locals as if they were from another planet—which in a way they were. It was all part of, or had been part of, the British Empire. As a Brit you were a bit special and were treated as such.

In the second half of the last century, most of that changed. Singapore and KL became rich and modern, replacing their ramshackle buildings, tiny market stalls, muddy roads and rickshaws, with towering skyscrapers, huge and affluent shopping centres, broad multi-lane highways, and more luxury cars per mile than you'll see in London, Paris or New York. Sadly, for me, as the locals moved to an undreamt of standard of living and lifestyle, much of what I had found attractive and fascinating about the Far East was eroded. My interests became almost entirely business-related, although I gratefully embraced the new standards of fully air-conditioned luxury accommodation and the upgrading of the local cuisine with an international flavour. As the cities lost their character they also began to swallow up the surrounding countryside; one could no longer walk to the Singapore River and watch the salt-water crocodiles basking on the banks. Gone were the days of finding a cobra on your patio or having a gaily-coloured bird walk nonchalantly through the condiments as you ate your curry or noodles. Many would welcome those changes, but for a man that likes things to be different and exciting, much of the charm and mystery that was special in the Far East had gone by the 80's and 90's. Notwithstanding my age, would you believe that I now see sameness replacing distinctiveness and characteristic when it comes to the fair sex? With so many women now having perfect teeth and having body bits added, taken away or reshaped, they're beginning to all look the same. A woman's attraction is often in the curve of her mouth, the way she smiles, talks, pouts and moves the muscles in her face. Now that they seem to come out of the same pod, gone are so many of the unique almost indefinable physical features that fascinate us gullible impressionable males. By 2050 at this rate, all love-making will be done on the Internet, or whatever succeeds it, rather than in person I fear.

But in the 1990's I had my 100% woman, and when I started taking Rosemarie to the Far East it was to show her some of the natural beauty of the places I'd spoken of. Needless to say, there was something everywhere for her to enjoy in the shopping malls, whether she was getting low price watches, jewellery or clothes, or finding items peculiar to that particular country. But we also travelled out of the cities to where you are in the forests and jungle and able to see life much as it was when the Japanese army flooded down from the north in 1941. I shocked her the first time there by driving from Singapore to the small Malaysian seaport of Mersing and hiring a boat to cross to the islands of Rawa and Tioman. The splendid launch she expected was a beat up fishing boat driven by a scurvy looking knave who wore a turban and a kukri in his belt. Roo doesn't like boats smaller than the QE2, but she warmed to the journey as we watched the flying fish and occasional shark fin before landing on the rickety jetty of a genuine desert island complete with bowing palms and golden sand.

Her favourite city was Bangkok, which held a special attraction for me with so much that is still uniquely Siamese and Far East about the place. She thought the street market shopping out of this world and was intrigued by the exotic nightlife and the bars and nightclubs of Pat Pong. Knowing how often I'd been there I got the odd funny look, but she quickly realised that the Thai ladies are far from the scrubbers and tarts that frequent our city centres and that one can mix with them without coming to any harm or feeling intimidated or threatened. Bangkok is a city of splendid temples and related architecture, many of which are best seen from a river that is a quarter of a mile wide in the city, with banks festooned with some of the world's most luxurious hotels. Across the river are islands and floating constructions where live a high percentage of the population. A favourite early morning pastime of ours was to take breakfast on the Regent Hotel patio above the river and watch thousands of young girls arriving on the river taxis. They came from appalling living conditions, but stepped off the gangway looking incredibly smart in their light coloured frocks and business suits. Thai girls are a bit special. They are usually quite small but almost invariably slim and feminine with a higher percentage of pretty and gorgeous than any nationality I can think of.

Rosemarie poses with her favourite aircraft. SBAC Show 2000.

ASTOR—A procurement classic

Now where was I? Oh yes, back to ASTOR, into which programme I can say with total honesty that I gave 100% throughout. I knew precisely what the MoD wanted it to do, what their budget was, what the sequence of procurement would be, how the radar Establishments would figure, what Thorn had done in a 10 year Feasibility Study with their work underwritten by Malvern, and what other UK and American companies wanted from a hugely important operational tool, one full of innovative and leading edge technology. In a nutshell, ASTOR is designed to look down from a great height (50K feet) and to detect moving and static "targets" on the surface at long stand-off range (200miles plus) in order to detect a potential threat, and when one exists, to guide offensive forces to the right place at the right time and in appropriate strength and composition. The system is intended to differentiate between different types of parked aircraft, between wheeled and tracked vehicles, show movements of ground and air elements, identify them, and determine their speed and direction of movement. In order to do this you need a high performance long endurance fair-sized aircraft as platform. But the most important single piece of equipment is a dual mode (moving and static target) radar system that has unprecedented power, detection, resolution, tracking and correlation capabilities, plus a complex communication system to disseminate the processed data in near-real time.

In other words, the sort of programme with immediate and long term benefits to make any defence contractor die for. Many were prepared to do so, either as the all-powerful Prime Contractor (PC), or by getting a slice of the cake as one of many specialist sub-contractors. Because of the capability involved, it had to be led by Americans who will never surrender or delegate any intelligence gathering to anyone else. Also, only the big US companies had the resources to manage a big aircraft programme together with an even bigger and lucrative System programme that combined so many different technologies and had a 30 plus year in-service span with many potential export derivatives and updates.

Clearly, when involved in any fierce competition, you try to pick the team that will give you the best chance of success. When ASTOR advanced to the Project Definition phase in 1993 we, then as Thorn, touted our unique experience and credibility to a number of companies. We chose LORAL of Owego NY to be Prime and lead our consortium, and signed up that very capable company Texas Instruments and a number of small specialist firms before other consortia could do so. On performance, cost and availability, there were only two suitable platforms, both twin engined executive jets. We selected Gulfstream of Savannah because they already had similar aircraft in service and were developing the Mk V that would be exactly what we wanted by 2001. The other contender, Canadair's Global Express, was still in development and well short of meeting performance targets. To keep as much work as possible in the UK, we joined with Marshal of Cambridge to fit the system to the Gulfstream. Our consortium won the Project Definition Study contract with some ease against five other consortia. Second and third came consortia led by Raytheon and Northrop Grumman who also won a PD contract. Battle was now joined in earnest for the Production contract of well over £1B.

Know your friends

The three primes reviewed their teams. With two teams eliminated there were small specialist companies now looking for a team to join and the primes had a field day signing up desperate firms at the lowest cost. Don't ask about loyalty; that's a dirty word in industry. If a PC can find another firm that will offer a lower price, a better delivery date, promise of performance improvements, or with offsets or sweeteners in other areas, then they'll be snapped up and the original partner dumped. Indeed, the American giants will win a contract with a team deemed to have the best overall package, and then re-bid parts of the programme thus cutting out even their longest running mates. I know, I know "that's business"—but it's often dirty business and, not being a ruthless sod myself, I find much consolation in that I have yet to see success that has been achieved that way, make the successful bastard any happier! Although this was a UK programme, the PC's were American committed to gaining a lead in the US across a range of related projects and to keeping the bulk of their work in the US. That made economic and political sense for them, but this was a programme for the British services, and both the Government and industry had poured money into a decade of research and development. The Americans therefore had to strike a nice balance between offering the UK a large share of production and transfer of advanced technology, whilst ensuring that they maintained total control of the project with as much spin off benefit to the US as they could decently protect. I've said this before and it was equally true about ASTOR; whilst we proclaim that our international defence competitions are squeaky clean, our two major competitors, the USA and France, work solely on behalf of the USA—period, and France—*point final.*

I expected ASTOR to go like all international projects; everyone looking for an edge and prepared to promise performance that relied enormously on successful timely development and research in other programmes. I knew someone would promise to place work in Northern Ireland and Wales, that "research centres" would be funded out of the goodness of American hearts, and that our gullible Government would have the traditional carrot dangled in front of them by the Pentagon that they'd be given access to US programmes so secret that no one had ever heard of them. Such games and fantasies are par for the procurement course, and I enjoyed sussing them out and countering them through knowing what was technically feasible, homing in on the often unsubstantiated risk element, and forcing them to reveal their true long term costs. So on the premise that all is fair in love, war, and procurement, we dug in for a bitter and protracted fight.

The biggest cock-up since Arnhem!

The real disappointment on 15th June 1999 was not so much losing the contract to Raytheon, but why we lost it. No one can "win 'em all", but even in this cynical age one can get consolation from having done ones' best. We'd known we'd had a mountain to climb for 18 months and were fortunate to have stayed in the game for that long. There's no way of fudging this, we lost because our PC screwed up big time. Firstly he put in a proposal that was so poorly written and formatted that it obscured the technical superiority that our system undoubtedly enjoyed. Secondly, he bid at a price substantially higher than our competitors. Thirdly he ignored the advice of his British partners who knew exactly how to write a British proposal, and he hid the true pricing in his bid so that when all the British members of the team were trying to gauge how well we were doing, we had no idea that his price had virtually killed us from the outset. His deception also included certain provisos he had made concerning the number of aircraft included in his bid, and the cost of the vastly expensive through life support package. It would be hard to find a better example of defeat being snatched from the jaws of victory by sheer corporate incompetence. At the time, and in many inquests since, I have tried to seek justification for Lockheed's folly. It's too easy to put it down to typical American arrogance and I'm forced to conclude what I said at the time to their hierarchy. Namely, that it was bloody awful management riddled with the American tendency never to disclose the full picture, to always keep something up their sleeves. Time and again I've seen that in operation and it only serves to hoodwink and confuse themselves whilst giving them a false sense of security.

There are key stages in the evaluation of bids when a bidder has the opportunity to know, guess, estimate or feel how things are going. Even when warned after the opening bids that the signals were not in our favour, our PC still held back the vital information that could have dramatically changed the direction of our campaign. When he finally listened and believed us, with his top US masters involved, the instant reduction in price and the clarification of key features of his bid were far too late and too dramatic to be treated as credible by the MoD.

The old adage "When in Rome…" applies here. The US procurement system is very different to ours, their government gets involved in a different way and their rules, procedures and business laws differ. Naturally, we Brits know our own system. We know who the key people are at any given stage of the project, and—by fair means or foul—often by "urint"(a feeling in our water), we know how we are faring at any stage of the evaluation. The folk most closely involved understand the operational, technical and financial features, the reaction between them, and are best able to, first, write the bid as our evaluators expect it to be presented, then to sniff out problems requiring attention. Knowing the MoD's ways, there are occasions when reading between the lines will be preferable to someone telling you up front what your problem is. In a big competition MoD play the cards close to their chest anyway; security is good.

Even when, at the end of the first major round of evaluations, it was obvious that we were falling behind, our PC still did not listen and still kept the truth of his financial bid hidden. When you don't know something as fundamental as that, you waste valuable time and effort searching for the inexplicable and you begin to doubt the fairness of the evaluation. Your suspicions are aroused; you start asking whether the Government, or individuals in it, might be making some deal on the side with the Americans, and why does the UK spend so much money on R&D only to let the really high tech stuff go to America?

ASTOR was due to enter service as No 5 Squadron at RAF Waddington in 2004 under it's new name of SENTINEL. I shall be watching carefully, as I'm watching other major programmes, to see if the American contractors keep all the contract-winning promises. When AWACS replaced Nimrod AEW in 1985 it was supposed to be costing £1.2 B compared to Nimrods £975K. When I last counted in 1995 it was over £2.8B and still rising. It's proved a good system and I've said what I felt about that change of programme at the eleventh hour. But ASTOR interests me even more. I do not believe the RAF will get what it wanted in full. I believe the Americans will hold back on the capability provided, and I do not believe that British Industry or the British economy will reap the benefits promised by the competition winners and the US government. I hope I'm around to check it out. As a late postscript (December 2005), SENTINEL is running late to unknown specifications and BAe's Nimrod Mk4 MPA is 6 years late and countless millions adrift. What's the betting that no one will carry the can for fooling the RAF and clobbering the British taxpayer on Nimrod and Sentinel?

23 Squadron reunion, RAF Waddington 2001

Another reunion, with a Tornado F3—2002

The Old Forge

Meanwhile, back on the farm life went on—so stand by for a Palmer digression. If this were a script for theatre or film, I would have to follow the unities of time and place and tell the tale in a logical sequence. But an autobiography is different; many experiences need fleshing out separately from the chronological flow rather than being woven into the main text and are thus better dealt with thematically rather than historically. That way one can digress and later resume the thread of the narrative without putting the reader out of his or her stride; please forgive me if I'm wrong.

For a number of reasons, the 10 years in which I lived in the Old Forge deserve special attention, not least because it was by far the longest occupancy I've had in one dwelling. Four years was my longest RAF tour and six years the time I spent with my parents in Manchester as a boy. When Rosemarie and I left the beautiful old cottage in 1998, we were too excited at just being together to be over-concerned about swapping leafy Sussex for the Cynon Valley. But the cottage remains much in our thoughts, as many of its inhabitants over four centuries must have found during its early days as an Inn and as merely a home since around 1850, the year Dickens penned Bleak House.

> *Whoe'er has travelled life's dull round*
> *Where'er his stages may have been*
> *May sigh to think he still has found*
> *The warmest welcome at an Inn.*

The idyllic English countryside that sweeps up to the South Downs in Sussex, a landscape that attracts artists, poets, and composers, is also famous for its magnificent homes discretely hidden by hills and woods from the thousands who stream down the motorways to the South Coast. Of course it wasn't always like that in the beautiful valley of the Storr. Centuries past, the main highway from London to Arundel and Portsmouth was at best a well ridden track that wound its way through the rolling hills via a series of posting-houses where passengers and coachmen would take a short rest from the discomfort of their journey and take their repast. Horses would be fed and watered, teams changed, and post-chaises could be hired by the passengers for completion of their journey off the main coach routes.

Adjacent to the "London-60 miles" milestone stood a small Coaching Inn, open 24 hours every day, to which were attached a Forge and a Smithy. The kitchen would be hung round with gleaming copper and tin vessels; hams, tongues and flitches of bacon would be suspended from the low ceiling, and a clanging smoke jack would sit beside the fireplace. In it's heyday, the place must have been chaos; loud with shouts and sounds of sizzling fat, the yelp of hounds kicked away from the fire, and the gossip and banter of the passengers as they ate and drank from foaming tankards of ale. Trim housemaids would have hurried to and fro under the direction of a bustling landlady, but still seizing the moment to exchange a flippant word and a laugh with the group around the fire.

When the building was first constructed, Shakespeare was only two, Bacon still five, a young man called Francis Drake was about to go to sea with Hawkins, and the crews that would man the Great Armada had already been born in Spain. Had you stood then at the front door of the inn and looked north, you'd have seen in the distance the square grey top of a Norman church that had been there since 1214—the year of Magna Carta. Looking south towards the sea you'd have seen, just 100 yards away at the intersection of the Brighton-Petworth track, a gibbet from which would often hang the body of a highwayman or footpad. And in the middle distance to the west, your eyes would have focussed on the Chanctonbury Ring, a spectacular circular copse of trees that had dominated the skyline for centuries. The bones of the highwayman have long since blanched in the sun and been scattered by the wind. Chanctonbury Ring was uprooted *en masse* the night of the Great Storm in 1986 when a BBC weatherman scoffed at any suggestion of gales that night. But the Norman church is still there and still holding Sunday services 800 years on. The old Coaching Inn has not fared so well, it's main purpose having been overtaken in the mid 1860's by the invention of steam power. Now there remain perhaps three of the original rooms, joined in the 19th century to what was the Forge, to comprise a cottage now known as the Old Forge, proudly dated 1553, and owned since the mid-1930's by a family that grew old there before it was sold in 1986.

With the inevitable bypass having been built to protect the quaint village, the cottage was now located on a side road, a cul-de-sac, bounded by a gurgling trout-rich stream on one side and a National Trust oak, sycamore, bluebell and fern wood on the other. At night, the road and surrounding area are in total darkness with barely a hum from the traffic on the main road. Foxes run in the gardens, bats flit over the twisted chimneys, and on a black velvet night it is easy to imagine the creak of harness and to blame the groaning one hears on the timbers of the ancient house and on the sighing of the wind that funnels up the valley from the sea to move amongst the boughs of the old trees.

As the new owner in 1986, I was not a man disposed to bothering about things that went bump in the night. I'd travelled a lot, seen a lot, and heard a hundred tales about ghosts and goblins, poltergeists and evil spirits. I'd sat up all night in the Navajo desert with the Havasupai Indians, tracked the stars with Aborigines, and chanted to the Crocodile God with the Kikuyu in Mau Mau days. My feet were planted firmly on the ground. Nevertheless my interest was aroused in 1990 when an old chimney sweep asked if I'd ever spent Christmas Eve in the Old Forge. I said I had and received an old fashioned look from the sweep who asked, "Didn't you find it a bit chilly?"

The old man went on to confide that the main hallway, an original part of the inn, always became dreadfully cold on Christmas Eve. And in that icy graveyard wind, at least three ever-so-sensible people had seen a figure, the same figure of a lady in a pink and white old-fashioned garb, on the staircase. The sweep duly got his glass of whisky, and the incident was forgotten.

Strange to relate, the vault-like chill was again in evidence in the years that followed. Our mature Ginger Tom would never go or allow himself to be taken upstairs in the Old Forge; whereas he'd virtually lived there in our previous house. My beloved Afghan Hound would sit rooted for hours silently looking up at the same spot in the ceiling, even to the extent of allowing himself to be carried out into the lane at dead of night—still in the sitting position. But this phlegmatic, pragmatic philosopher refused to be impressed. There was bound to be a bloody good reason, even if I didn't understand what was going on.

Until, that is, I found myself living, firstly alone in the cottage, and later with Rosemarie. With the house now all mine, I moved into a smaller bedroom that necessitated a longer walk along the ancient corridor and gallery to the bathroom. The house, sparsely furnished, was noisier than before. My previous wife had gone with most of the furniture, and *anno dominie* had seen off Saxon the Afghan and Tigger the Tom. I effectively had no neighbours, the nearest being a house-bound old lady of 90 who lived halfway to where the gibbet once stood. There was little or no traffic at night and no house or street lighting was visible. Only the foxes and the occasional Barn Owl triggered the security lights. I might as well have been on a desert island.

A man living alone is not the tidiest of people, but there was so little furniture in the upper rooms of the cottage that anything out the normal was instantly detected. On this particular night, I awoke in the early hours to visit the bathroom. I walked across the empty gallery, by the dark wooden banister rail, and into the bathroom. Twenty—maybe thirty—seconds later, I emerged into the well-lit passage only to stop abruptly. My fresh towels and underwear were neatly folded and draped meticulously across the banisters. They had been in the airing cupboard, which I hadn't opened at all. I knew there was no one in the house or anywhere near it, but nevertheless wandered around puzzled finding all doors and windows firmly secure, as I knew they'd be.

From that night, the event recurred a number of times with the contents of the airing cupboard being transferred to the banisters in the twinkling of an eye. I never felt fear or disquiet, but there was more to come as Rosemarie became a regular visitor. She is a much more sensitive person, a great believer in "the other world", and she began to lay traps as it were for whoever or whatever was making its presence felt. Sure enough, if she put out one of her scarves or her underwear, it would very quickly be displaced or even hidden. Only *my* clothing was allowed to be on the banisters. She became aware of a presence that, although not sinister, made her feel that she was not welcome. Simple tasks like putting on her makeup to go out became a real trial of effort, for she was made to feel listless and slow.

The time came for the Old Forge to be sold and everything that week seemed to move up a gear. In broad daylight one early evening, the gallery was suddenly filled with a black impenetrable mass that moved slowly away over the banister rails. Black, black—in spite of the brilliant beams of the evening sunlight streaming through the great window. I admit my blood ran cold; the incident coming close to being hair-raising. On the last night I spent in the house, I was awakened about 3 a.m. by the sound of—well, yes, it must have been the wind. But as soon as I opened the bedroom door to investigate, the noise ceased—only to start again when the door was closed. Of course, in the morning sunlight there was nothing to be seen to explain the noises—except a change of underwear transferred from the airing cupboard to the banisters; clothes I'd put there to air before going to bed!

That is exactly how it happened to two sane and sensible people; one a true cynic and disbeliever of the occult, the other sensitive enough to detect goodness and mischief rather than evil or intent to harm. We did not tell the new occupants, a young couple with three small children, about the strange happenings. Firstly because they may have pulled out of the transaction—and it was a bad time for selling houses. Secondly, because with young children such a tale may have disturbed them. Based on our experiences and the multiple sightings over 50 years made by the previous owners and their guests, we were persuaded that the presence was benign; probably a serving wench or housemaid from the days of the old Coaching Inn. Disturbing, perhaps—dangerous, no.

But as happens, a chance meeting with the new owner in 2002 led to the tale being blurted out in jocular fashion. The young man turned white and left without saying a word—but it was abundantly clear that the news was not totally unexpected, and that two and two had suddenly made four. The Old Forge went on the market again, looked after by one careful owner for many hundreds of years you might say!

Vipers in our midst

Two other happenings in those last few months of my paid working life gave concern to someone with my delicate nature! The first was the power game played by a senior Company marketeer who walked the Whitehall corridors as I did, but who operated at a couple of rungs up the ladder from me. This meant that he seldom understood much about the detail of the project neither did he address the big picture. Instead he concentrated on the politics and therefore on a very few key individuals; he also made sure that No1 was covered! In my book he committed two unforgivable crimes. The first was that he had early vital information on pricing that confirmed both my belief that we were struggling, and the amount by which I'd assessed we must be behind. He kept this to himself. Secondly, when the rest of us were trying to analyse exactly where we were and feeding our thoughts openly to him, he would concoct bogus explanations rather than admit that he didn't have any reliable pertinent information. His deceitful way of working was to cause severe embarrassment in the MoD who were blaming serving officers and MoD PE managers for releasing information that had actually come from one very senior Civil Servant. Had that ex army officer of ours ever gone to war, I have no doubt that the first bullet fired would have lodged in his ample posterior.

I learned a sharp lesson from that episode. The careers of an RAF officer and a civil servant, both excellent officers and good friends, were jeopardized by suspicions that they had leaked vital contractual information to affect the choice of winning consortium. The injustice of that angered me and I made it known, ever so discretely, that they were not the culprits. Suddenly, I was being asked to meet with serious men in dark suits and zero sense of humour, who gave me the distinct impression that I was in the wrong for opening up a can of worms that others were happy to leave shut; their scapegoats already being in the bag! "Why have you waited until now to blow the whistle?" "Has money changed hands in getting you to speak?" My wish to see justice done was seen as far more of a crime than that of the guilty senior civil servant. I would not have wanted to pillories said civil servant, he was only doing what many others had done in the procurement business, but I was not about to let him and our poisonous Pongo put the blame on innocents. The experience nevertheless has since paid off in voluntary work in Wales where, when faced with bare-faced corruption and lies from two unprincipled rogues, I have had the courage of my convictions and the persistence to scupper the scoundrels!

Final thoughts

It would have been nice to have gone out in a blaze of glory, waving the ASTOR flag of victory. But I'd had a remarkably satisfying and successful 5 years beyond the normal retirement age and couldn't complain. The day I stopped, I was still learning. My friends at RACAL gave me a fine send off and I felt they were genuinely sorry to see me go. I knew on handing in my keys and passes that I'd done my level best for people who had stood by me during the most difficult times of my life. They had restored my faith in human nature and I will always think of them with fondness, gratitude and pleasure for the successes and happy times we shared.

During my final 14 months at Crawley, I lodged with a local family. My working life spanned 54 years from the age of 16 to 70, but that was the only time I ever spent in lodgings. Rosemarie was in Wales and The Old Forge had been sold. The Whalleys were a lovely family, living in a very comfortable and warm house, and who left me alone to do exactly what I wanted. I was out most evenings and every weekend so I wasn't cluttering up their front room every night—but that really was down to my shyness, not their inhospitability. I owed them an enormous debt.

My retirement was sadly preceded by the unexpected departure of my Marketing Director and friend for many years. John fell foul of the same ex-Army officer I spoke about earlier and was despatched without warning. Later I explain what I felt about him, how I tackled the unknowns of retirement after 17 years in the Defence industry; a quarter of my entire life that flashed by unbelievably quickly during which I saw and did what most men have only dreamed of. Now there is less time ahead than behind—so little time, precious time.

> *When as a child I laughed and wept, time crept.*
> *When as a youth I dreamed and talked, time walked.*
> *When I became a full-grown man, time ran.*
> *And later, as I older grew, time flew.*
> *Soon I shall find while travelling on, time gone.*
> *Will Christ have saved my soul by then?*

Live now my friend, wait not for the morrow. *Carpe diem.*

◆   ◆   ◆

Mountain Ash
23 December 1999

On Retirement

Dear Friends and Colleagues,

Having tottered on the brink of final retirement for a number of years, suffered the slings and arrows of outrageous fortune, and struggled manfully through self-induced disasters and the subsequent cross-examinations, I've decided to run for cover.

Well, not quite "decided"; more like prompted, cajoled, propelled or laid aside—as in shunt. But at soixante-neuf, with the Millennium almost upon us and life and people generally turning colder, it's probably time to ride off into the sunset.

The 17th century (fully modernised) cottage sought by my bride and I will have the beaches of Kauai at the front and the Bavarian Alps to the rear. Steps to the right will lead to Old Trafford (via the Ivy) and winding away to the left will be a sort of Rodeo Drive cum Knightsbridge along which Rosemarie can browse in a constant 82° F, 12 % humidity—and no bugs!

Inter alia, we shall ban mobile phones, computers, motorbikes, solicitors, The Sun, Bruce Forsythe, Ruby Wotsername and Arsenal supporters. We shall welcome beautiful music, the green of an English spring, the warmth of the Cyprus sun, the grace of an Afghan Hound and our milk being delivered—in bottles—every morning by Cyd Charisse driving a lady's silver Mercedes.

But meanwhile, we're going to live in Wales! No doubt from time to time, we shall venture out of our country retreat and cross the Severn Bridge to try and pick up the pace in the fast lane. If you're not careful, we might just look you up and bore you with tales and lies of our retirement.

One never knows who or what is likely to move in or out of one's life, and we may yet have some moments to share. But for now let me say how much I've enjoyed your friendship and our relationship, in good times and bad. Someone told me recently that one of the perks of growing older is that you remember so vividly things that never happened at all! Perhaps so, but whether it was back in the 40's at Manchester Grammar, during my 37 years in the RAF, or my subsequent 17 years in industry, I'm so glad that you and I met.

There is of course a great difference between the high passion of youth and the mere petulance and cynicism of maturity and old age. I hope that I've managed to bridge that gap reasonably well and succeeded in bringing tone to what otherwise might have been a vulgar brawl. I commend the text that follows to your attention and hope I can practice what I preach.

JKP

◆　　◆　　◆

A CREED—for youthful attitude

"Youth is not a time of life. It's a state of mind. It's a test of the will, a quality of imagination, vigour of emotions, a predominance of courage over timidity, of the appetite for adventure over love of ease.

Nobody grows old merely by living a number of years. People grow old only by deserting their ideals. Years wrinkle the skin—but to give up enthusiasm wrinkles the soul. Worry, doubt, self-distrust, fear and despair...these are the quick equivalents of the long long years that bow the head and turn the growing spirit back to dust.

Whether 70 or 17, there should be in every being's heart, the love of wonder, the sweet amazement of the stars, and the starlike things and thoughts, the undaunted challenge of events, the unfailing childlike appetite for 'What next?'

You are as young as your faith, as old as your doubt, as young as your self-confidence, as old as your fear; as young as your hope, as old as your despair. So long as your heart receives messages of beauty, cheer, courage, grandeur and power from the earth, from man and from the Infinite, so long are you young.

When all the wires are down, and all the central places of your heart are covered with the snows of pessimism and the ice of cynicism, then, and only then, are you grown old indeed—and may God have mercy on your soul."

(General Douglas MacArthur to the Cadets and Officers of West Point)

◆   ◆   ◆

My Friend John Wilson
(Written on hearing of JBW's death, December 2002)

Today I lost a good friend forever. An ex-colleague called to say, "Bad news, John is dead." My first reaction was one of disbelief; he was only 54 and it seemed like only yesterday that he was jesting with me on my 69th birthday. "*Soixante neuf, soixante neuf,*" he chanted. Adding, with his quiet smile. "How does it feel to be that old?"

My second reaction after a moment's reflection was to promise myself that, for the rest of my life, I will not leave unsaid any words of affection, of kindness, of regret, of apology, of forgiveness, to anyone who I love, like or respect. I hadn't seen John for two years and was about to write his Christmas card, thanking him for all that he had done for me a few years back. But suddenly and unexpectedly, the chance has gone. *"The moving finger writes, and having writ moves on. Not all thy piety, nor all thy wit, can move it back to cancel but half a line."*

John Wilson was born very close to my birthplace on the Manchester/ Cheshire border. I know that he went to Altrincham Grammar, but I don't know much more about his early days or even what he did before he joined Thorn EMI at Wells in the late 80's. I met him when Thorn bought out MEL in 1990 when he would have been 43 and I was 60. I recall him telling me that his early manhood was spent in the Navy, or was it the Merchant Navy? I know he had an uncle who scouted for Manchester United and who occasionally fixed me up with tickets, and that John lived and worked in the USA and Singapore for a number of years. I also knew him to be the fastest and most dangerous driver I'd ever been driven by—he ran through a new set of tyres and brake drums every 12,000 miles! But that just about sums up my knowledge of JBW's history.

John provided classic proof of a long held belief of mine, which I have seldom had the interest or courage to proclaim, that first impressions can be very misleading. When he arrived at Crawley as Marketing Director with the Thorn takeover I, and almost everyone else I think, saw him as a slightly pompous, aloof, and out of touch Director—much like the rest of the Thorn Board. Although Thorn had acquired in MEL a successful and progressive company with strengths in the civilian and overseas markets, they seemed to take little interest in building up the new Company; except for ensuring that all their directors would receive a golden handshake when Thorn in turn were bought out!

But John proved me wrong when he took over all Defence marketing and I became his chief man with the Ministry of Defence, as well as having special responsibilities for the USA, Australia, South Africa and Turkey (the last two because no one else wanted them). We worked together extremely well and became good friends, which was surprising in view of my initial impressions, but also because we were so different in many ways.

I'm over 6ft 3ins tall and reasonably well proportioned. John at around 5ft 8ins., was of Pickwickian stature due perhaps to his love of good food, and the good wine that he quaffed by the barrel without ever being drunk or adversely affected in any way. He was a man who shunned exercise of any sort. I don't believe he owned a raincoat, topcoat or even umbrella, since he never had any intention of walking anywhere! From the House of Commons to the MoD Main Building in Whitehall is about 300 yards; even on a dry day John would call a cab. He was also a dedicated and heavy smoker, never unhappier as when he was strapped to his business class seat on a 747 for 12 hours without the chance to have a quick drag.

I suppose we got on so well because we were so different in many other ways. Where I was comfortable, John would be uneasy; where he was often in his element, I was often bored. Where he would sit quietly at a high level meeting (getting even rather than angry), I'd be throwing rattlesnakes on the table to stir the dead and dismal into some sort of life. He had a small clique of buddies in the defence world with whom he spoke and lunched often, whereas I tended to spread my contacts net much wider, both in the UK and overseas. We both enjoyed entertaining, particularly at lunchtime and especially in London, a city that boasts more quality restaurants with a wider range of cuisines than any other in the world. John liked to take his "full English breakfast" at Simpson's in the Strand, and his favourite lunch haunts included Motcombs, L'Escargot and Langhams. My tastes in food and atmosphere led me mainly to The Ivy, Beotys, the Gay Hussar, or Rules especially if my guests were from the Colonies. Overseas our tastes were probably closer, but I don't think John shared my obsession with Texas barbecue, Creole cooking or the local *Caipirinhas* (country girl) rocket fuel of Rio. Once, as we sat watching the sun set behind the Sydney Harbour Bridge from his beloved Doyle's on the Beach, I committed sacrilege by deriding his favourite Australian fish dish. To me the Aussies, like some famous American eating-houses, tend to put size of meat or fish helping above quality of taste. John of course was not of that school; indeed in many ways I was peasant to his gourmet.

Likewise, I think it's true to say that we didn't share the same likes and dislikes about the countries we visited in our marketing ventures. We both liked Australia; it's climate, food, wine and generally relaxed way of life. We were in accord too that female beauty in Oz is a bit like their scenery; hundreds of miles of utter boredom—then suddenly—wham! (followed by hundreds of miles of utter boredom).Oz apart, we were poles apart in our tastes. John loved Singapore; I found it insipid and steamy and much preferred Cape Town. He liked Kuala Lumpur whereas I went for Bangkok; his Hong Kong was my Rio, for Paris read Berlin, for Madrid read Rome. In the States his favourite towns were Washington and New York; mine are San Francisco, San Diego and Honolulu. We neither of us liked China or India overmuch, but—as he was the boss—I went. (Returning via Kathmandu or Budapest just to get my own back!)

Perhaps because I was some 17 years older, and due to my strong military background and relevant experience, John placed a great deal of trust in what I said and recommended. He would often discuss the merits and faults of our younger marketeers, and I was frequently surprised at the strength and severity of his opinions of others when, with me, he was invariably the most affable and reasonable soul. He did have what I can only call a stubborn streak. He would make up his mind that a particular person was not really acting as part of his team, and would give said person a very rough ride indeed.

Or, as with me on one occasion, he would make up his mind about a potential project and simply refuse to budge. With me it was an Australian Coastguard system which I'd pursued for a couple of years and was actually in Canberra to complete the contract before flying to Perth to sign it with the aircraft suppliers. He phoned from the UK to say that I was not to travel to Perth or complete the contract. He would not say why then, nor when I returned to the UK. The rest of our department were equally bemused as to why he should spurn a lucrative turnkey project. Our only logical conclusion was that it somehow clashed with something he was doing elsewhere and with somebody else. As Curly sang about Jud Fry in Oklahoma, "But he never let on, so nobody ever knowed it." However for me that was a one-off, and I trusted the guy. The bottom line is that we worked together extremely well, perhaps because we were so different, yet complemented each other. Whatever the essential ingredients of a successful working relationship and friendship may be, John and I had them in spades.

But overriding all of the "chemistry" and professional bonding, John was much more than a good friend and boss to me. When Racal took over Thorn with John as sole surviving Director, I ran into the most difficult period of my life with divorce and financial problems that threatened to overwhelm me. Racal's incoming Board did not know me and a clear decision was taken that I should leave. I was already at the normal retirement age of 65 so finding another job would have been well nigh impossible. But unknown to me, John went in to bat on my behalf in the difficult climate of a company takeover with many people wondering if they'd survive the night of the long knives.

One day, within a couple of the date set for my departure, I took a call from John. He said, "Are you sitting down? Well, you've been re-instated." It was obvious at the time from the attitude of others that this was not a universally popular move. But John had stuck his neck out for me, working for weeks to do so and without ever giving me a hard time or chiding me for my transgressions. He had no need to have done anything, and undoubtedly made the odd enemy in so doing thereby jeopardising his own position. I believe I justified his faith in me by helping win three major defence programmes with the RAF over the next three years amounting to some £350M for Racal alone, and another £1.4B for British industry. But John had made that possible by believing in me and fighting my corner when the safe and easy thing for him to do would have been to buy me a dinner and wish me God speed. In July '99 I returned from holiday to find that he'd not been so lucky. He'd not had a champion, and without warning he'd been made redundant and was off the site within the hour. I discovered later who had masterminded John's downfall and I look forward to the day when that pompous and poisonous Pongo asks me to pack his parachute!

I saw John briefly five months later when he returned for the annual Christmas lunch, by which time he'd done what he'd always threatened to do—retired to become a relaxed, laid back, contented soul who easily exchanged his pin-stripes for a pair of jeans, shaggy sweater and hairy face, and swore never to work again. I remember that he told us with relish that he planned to apportion his time between six months in Australia (their summer of course) and "t'other six months living in a long boat on the cut", in which he'd cruise around at an average 2 knots from pub to glorious pub. He arranged for his boat to be custom-built up in God's own county of Lancashire, and waxed lyrical about the labyrinth of waterways that were being re-opened throughout England and Wales.

When last I spoke to him, he appeared to have moved seamlessly from the jet-set to the wet-set, from Barclays Bank to canal bank, from the constant hum of Marketing to the peace and tranquillity of the English countryside and to backwaters where no one does today what they can put off until tomorrow. Had I been able to write to him this Christmas, I was going to suggest we met for a chat and a chop before he migrated south in the New Year. I wanted to thank him again for what he'd done for me, and for his friendship. I wanted also to explain to him why I hadn't told him at the time about my triple heart bypass in '97. He only found out at my farewell party in '99 because I'd told a few folk for the first time earlier that day; only my secretary had known before. He had said to me with a hurt expression, I recall, "You could have told *me*."

My response was simply that I hadn't wanted to put him under pressure because I knew he would have insisted I took things easy, curtailed my trips to London, and probably grounded me from running around the world. Above all, I'd not wanted my good and trusted friend to have the burden of trying to protect me in Racal's political jungle, which like every Company I worked for had a fair smattering of would-be assassins. I also wanted to see him to learn whether he was as truly happy in his enforced retirement as he appeared to be. I had some disquiet there because, in spite of a new lifestyle that seemed to suit him well, with a social round that he certainly enjoyed, I knew he would inevitably be spending a lot of time alone. Some men can do that happily; I'm glad to say that I'm one of them, but I knew from him and other close friends that his divorce in the early 90's had left him emotionally and financially shattered.

The latter he recovered from; the former he never did as far as I could see. Indeed in my socialising with him all over the world I never saw him take the slightest interest in any female however interesting, attractive or intelligent. He'd make the odd joke of course, as we all do; the girls in the office thought of him as a true gentleman, and he could be an absolute charmer; but there was no real interest that I ever detected. I'm convinced that he saw his ex-wife as the only one for him, and I'm pretty sure that he carried a torch for her until the day he died. I have never met her or his children, but I know how he cared for them and how he helped them in every way he could as they grew up. I expect that I am now about to meet them all as we say goodbye to my good and true friend. I'm hoping that, in some way, I shall be able to find a convenient opportunity to convey to them the respect, comradeship and love I had for their young old man. "*Cinquante Quatre* John, *Cinquante Quatre*." You have left us far too early.

16

IF MUSIC BE THE FOOD OF LOVE...

Try as I might, I could not do justice to this subject by spreading it across 15 chapters and 70 odd years. So let me start by admitting that one of my greatest regrets is not being able to play a musical instrument, or for that matter, not be able to express my thoughts and feelings on canvas, or to be able to shape, form, figure, fashion, carve or mould some sort of material in a creative way. When it comes to art I haven't a clue. If you gave me a canvas, a box of paints and a palate and told me I'd be shot at dawn unless I produced a painting, I'd tell you to go ahead and shoot. I really would not know where to start. Yet I have a great appreciation of other people's artistry and am most contented looking at and studying paintings, watercolours and photographs of all sorts of subjects.

Sculpting, carving or chiselling are equally foreign to me. At Grammar School, my woodwork lessons taught me only how to get splinters. When everyone else had finished their pencil box, made a letter stand for their Mum, and were constructing tables and chairs, I was still trying to get the lid to fit my pencil box. To this day—as Rosemarie will be only too happy to tell you—if I put up any shelves or other fixtures in the house, the animals will go into hiding.

As to music, I would above all love to sit down at a piano and convey my mood and feelings via the keys in the way that Roger Williams or Ronnie Aldrich might do. If not a piano, then perhaps a guitar played semi-classically like John Williams or in the more popular style of John Denver. But again, I wouldn't know where to start. During the war, my Mum paid money she could ill afford for me to have piano lessons with a loveable old biddy by the name of "Miss Primrose". Her small cottage backed onto the sports field and her attempts to teach me the boring scales and notes were emphatically thwarted; partially by my attention being diverted outside, but more due to my then total lack of interest in music.

Whatever there is in my make-up that inhibits the development of any musical talent in me, I am happy to say it has not spoiled my enjoyment of music or of dancing. Both have had an enormous influence on my life since I was around 15. I think I can remember how it started.

First Awakenings

One day in 1944 when Mr Chips (the Woodwork master) decided I was too dangerous to be allowed to use any implement other than sticking plaster, he led me despairingly into Daddy O'Rourke's music class and offered me as surplus to requirements. Of course it was a put up job, but the kindly music teacher encouraged me by asking me to sing a solo whilst seated at my desk. Some of the others had already sung, and I flicked through the little blue book and chose "The Londonderry Air" for no better reason than I liked the title. Mr O'Rourke played it through first and then accompanied me on the piano. I began "In 'Derry Vale, beside the singing river, so oft I strayed ah many years ago..."

The first to be surprised was me. I didn't recognise my own high-pitched voice that owed much I expect to sheer nervousness. As I finished "...for your green Isle my exiled heart is yearning, so far away so far away, across the sea..." Mr O'Rourke applauded, as did the entire form. I was quickly whisked away to perform for a gentleman by the name of Pollard who had been heavily involved a few years back in a famous rendering of *Nymphs and Shepherds* by the Manchester Schoolchildren's Choir. For a couple of terms I was a really popular little creep as Mr Pollard coached me as a soloist and in a choir—until one sad day my voice broke. Thereafter all my singing was done in the bath or at the Stretford End at Old Trafford. But the corner had been turned, and inside me I knew the beauty and romance of music, I felt a rhythm and a belonging with many types of music played on many different instruments.

Invitation to the Dance

The next big step was to do something with my newfound interest, and that was forced on me in a way when I joined the RAF. I've mentioned elsewhere that when it came to girls, I was a late developer. But when I was home on leave, it eventually dawned on me that the best way to meet girls—the only way if you didn't live amongst them—was to go to a dance. There was a girl named June Hill that I fancied (correction—drooled over!). I used to see her regularly at the Youth Club before joining the RAF, but had never dared to ask her out. In fact, to tell the truth, it took all my nerve to try to attract her attention and, if I got a smile in return, I was walking on air. Her boyfriend was the School Captain at everything but tiddley-winks, and I was but a shy and callow youth. I would watch them dancing and hear people say what wonderful dancers they were and how well they danced together. Oh woe was me!

But now I was in the airforce, I was in uniform, and when I went eagerly to the Youth Club on the Monday of my first leave, Fred the boyfriend seemed a lot less formidable. So, mustering all the machismo I could and wearing a 'take it or leave it' smug smile, I strolled nonchalantly across and asked June if she'd go out with me. Demurely and sweetly, she tossed her mass of black silky hair and answered, "Yes please." Then, when bewitched and bewildered, I asked her what she'd like to do, she said sweetly, "Can we go to the Ritz on Saturday?" "Okay, I'll pick you up at your house at six o'clock," said I, and strolled off as though clinching a date with the most gorgeous girl in Wythenshawe was something I did every day.

Now for any male readers who were not 16 and living in Manchester in 1946, I need to fill in a few gaps. At that time there were literally dozens of dance halls in any big town; even now I can think of six within 3 miles of my Mum's house. The dance would start at 6 p.m. and finish around 11 p.m., certainly by midnight. There would be a live band (no discos then) and the pattern of music would be three quick steps, break, three waltzes, break, three slow fox trots, and the occasional Latin American session of rumba, tango and samba. On rare occasions; the bigger places would be really adventurous and toss in an old-fashioned waltz, Palais Glide or other novelty dance.

Boys and girls in roughly equal numbers stood around between dances, with the boys making a beeline for their favoured partner as the next session was announced. A girl could, and often did, refuse politely, especially if she was there with a partner. Many girls not blessed with good looks or impressive dancing skills, were left unapproached all evening and became known as "wallflowers". Many boys, similarly disadvantaged, were rejected so often that they went home or to the pub, disgruntled and disheartened, some never ever to set foot on a dance floor again. Never were the words "No thank you" so final and humiliating as you turned away head down and red of face.

The last dance was always a waltz—the last waltz. Protocol had it that the partner you danced with then was the one you took home and from whom, with a little bit of luck, you stole a goodnight kiss on her doorstep. Many a tear was shed, many a heart was broken, and many a dream shattered, after the last waltz. The music stopped, the lights went out, and the world fell cold and lonely. So when Kelvie Palmer asked June Hill to go out with him that Monday in July

1946 and she nominated The Ritz, it might have appeared like a dream come true for him. But was it? There was one big problem—he couldn't dance a step!

One Step at a Time

The enormity of this inadequacy hit me even as I turned away from June, having secured my date for Saturday. I'd already had a taste of feeling like an outcast when going to a couple of dances in the NAAFI at Cranwell. I went because everyone else went, hoping in spite of not being a dancer that I might meet a girl whom I could talk to and invite to the "pictures". But all the girls that I fancied wanted to dance, and when the statutory "Ladies invitation" had attracted a girl to ask me, I had to feign a serious ankle injury—from football of course. I wasn't even sufficiently streetwise to blame my incapacity on something that sounded more glamorous, like an aircraft or skiing accident. Like everything else in life, the longer one puts off doing something, the harder it becomes to break the ice. I was in serious danger of my timidity becoming terminal.

The situation was bloody serious. The girl of my dreams, in the palm of my hand so to speak, and me about to humiliate myself one way or the other. If I called to say I couldn't make it, she'd get the wrong message, and if I took her to the Ritz, she'd be asked to dance every dance by someone else and I'd lose her for good. The shame would be all the greater, as the Ritz was *the* dancing venue in Manchester, with a beautiful large polished well-sprung dance floor that attracted the best dancers and the best looking girls. I'd just about reached the conclusion that suicide was the only honourable course, when I realised I was walking behind a girl who lived in "our avenue". I hadn't seen her since joining up and she was interested in what I was doing and invited me in to see her Mum and have a coffee. We'd hardly started chatting when her mother said, "Mildred's going to stay with Eileen (her sister) in London for a week. They'll take her out dancing, so Mildred's taking lessons everyday this week to learn the basics. Can you dance Kelvie?" I blurted out my predicament and so it happened that Mildred and I went together for 5 hours, Tuesday through Friday, to the Chorlton School of Dancing.

We had a wonderful teacher, a tall willowy lady, who had me doing all the popular dances by Friday. I would still have to call on my football injury to decline the tango, but we were up and running. Mildred and I turned out to be a well-matched dancing pair—for training purposes, as it were. The upshot was that I arrived at June's house in confident mood at 6 p.m., spot on, that Saturday evening. My Mum, typically, had bought me a new suit from Burtons "on the coupons". Fred Astaire, eat your heart out!

The evening went like a dream. We danced every dance—I even limped through the pain for the tango—and danced the last waltz with June locked firmly in my arms. It was all so wonderful that I went mad and hired my first ever taxi for the 4 miles back to June's. I duly got my nervous goodnight kiss, and a breathless "See you on Monday" promise, as her mother's voice crackled down the stairs: "What time do you call this?" By gum, we knew how to live in those days!

Terpsichorean Temptations

But this is a statement about me and my music and dancing. So I'll leave June for a different chapter and record that, lovely girl though she was, the star of the show was she who taught me to dance. Pat Sheppard was no oil painting. I suppose she was 32 to my 16, and if you saw her walking down the street she'd not deserve a second glance. But on the dance floor, as we danced then with our bodies in perfect unison, she was a dream—like dancing with one's shadow. As I became increasingly adventurous with my steps, and even when I crossed feet and got the balance all wrong, she followed me effortlessly and gracefully. When it came to those steps that demanded the close, almost intimate contact of thighs and hips, she felt like a woman should—a feather one minute, a tigress the next.

Apart from the footwork and patterns, Pat taught me another lesson about the way I was to enjoy music and dancing throughout my life. She made me realise it was perfectly possible to appreciate and absorb the sound of music, and to experience the timing, balance and grace of dancing, without any emotional or sexual involvement *per se* with those who played, sang or accompanied you across the ballroom floor. Of course, if you do love or lust after your dancing partner, the pleasure is that much more intense. All this and Heaven too indeed.

"La grace, plus belle encore que la beaute."

The classic example of that is my friend Cyd Charisse who is the most graceful, elegant and utterly feminine dancer I have ever seen or known, as well as being a beautiful and sensual woman. At one and the same time she feels in your arms as though she hasn't a bone in her body, yet where hands and bodies touch, she feels like whipcord vibrant with extraordinary life and rhythm in every move. That said, I can write with absolute honesty that having watched her and met her many times over 60 years, I've never had the slightest evil thought about her that would deserve a smack in the mouth from husband Tony.

So in that enchanted summer of '47, there was no denying that my crash course of dancing lessons, aimed at getting me in June's good books, had actually given me a whole new outlook on life. So much so that I spent the rest of that leave having dancing lessons with Pat during the day at five bob a throw, and then hitting the high spots at night with June. Pat, swept along perhaps with my enthusiasm and keen that I should progress, took me to private sessions during the day at the Ritz where, alone most of the time, we chose our own records, and danced and danced and danced.

Most popular music then was written for strict tempo dancing and we must have wore out the old 78's of Mantovani playing "Jealousy", Glenn Miller and "Moonlight Serenade" (perfect for the tricky slow foxtrot), Artie Shaw's "Wood-choppers Ball", and The Andrews Sisters version of "Rum and Coca Cola", that enabled one to mix a quick step with the more exotic Latin American beat. My liking of the tango "Jealousy" was probably an omen because years later my first wife and I argued often and bitterly about me dancing "with every woman in the room", as she put it. I simply enjoyed dancing and when the opportunity was there, I much preferred to dance rather than drinking or propping up the wall.

Ballroom dancing of the 40's/50's was my idea of true enjoyment. I also enjoyed the "Swingin' Sixties" and the in-between era of the 70's. But I have to admit that I'm not overly impressed with today's frenetic frenzy on a packed floor where a female partner is so remote that she might as well have been left in the taxi. Uncivilised discos have replaced elegant formality, and if a mere man bemoans the change, think how the ladies feel who used to get such a thrill out of dressing up to go dancing. That's not to say I don't enjoy variations from Ball-room. I became fairly accomplished at Scottish dancing, I used to do a mean Twist, and Rosemarie and I are no sluggards when it comes to Line Dancing, Texas style. Early in 2005 she persuaded me to find a school that taught tradi-tional ballroom dancing. After much searching I found one that ran a 10-session course covering the "social foxtrot" (as opposed to the slow foxtrot), the cha-cha-cha, rock & roll and waltz. I quickly realised that although I'd been dancing my socks off for 60 years, it was difficult to go back to basics and to keep to the for-mat of steps they are now teaching. When it comes to plain enjoyment of the art, I don't suppose the steps matter that much. Nevertheless I just wish the young of today could enjoy dancing as we once did.

My music tastes are wide and varied, and I have hundreds of CD's and records. I will sit for hours listening to music; always appreciative, often wistful, sometimes sad, and occasionally so emotionally charged that I weep out of sheer pleasure and identification with the music. Rosemarie is 12 years younger, so the era she missed out on—effectively the war years—is one on which our tastes tend to differ. I love the Big Band sound with a specialist clarinet or trumpet feature. I enjoy the superb artistry and timing of vocalists like the younger Frank Sinatra, Dick Haymes, Peggy Lee and Dinah Shore. She hears much of that as "old fashioned", but of course appreciates the melodies and the music spawned during six years of war that kept the spirits high for the millions of lovers who were kept apart.

Nowadays, technology has made it easy to play what you like, for as long as you like, with wonderful tone and clarity and without having to move much more than one finger. That's good—of course it is. Yet I doubt if the wonders of modern technology could make me more content than I was in 1945 when I listened to Tommy Dorsey's "Sunny side of the Street" over a crackly old crystal set, or to the first 78 I ever bought, "It might as well be Spring", and my Dad's favourite "Hungarian Rhapsody No2", all played via a well worn rusty needle. In their day, at that time, they all sounded well nigh perfect. What you've never had you never miss, eh?

The cat's got the cream! With Cyd Charisse—London 2001

These we have loved

When I penned the previous pages, I ended with the paragraph that still brings this chapter to a close. But having listened to Desmond Carrington's programme this lovely Sunday morning in May, I realised that there was so much more I could and should say about my musical preferences. For anyone who is reading this, please remember that right now I'm doing this for me. I hope nevertheless that you won't find it boring.

All of our memories of a particular melody or song are clearly based on our enjoyment of the sound or the words or the picture that is created in our minds, especially if we listen to an instrumental or classical piece. But what we like is also intensely personal in that music can blow away the cobwebs to remind us of a particular person, place or occasion. It may even remind us of a dream rather than a reality, perhaps an echo of a feeling or emotion, or for that matter something feared and disliked.

If I now sit here and ponder, I'll guarantee that I'll not write a word today! I'll be thrashing over all the candidates in my mind, searching through hundreds of CD's, and will change my mind about my top 10, or prefer another rendition—and so on. So not in any order of merit, but as "musts" for my desert island sojourn, I'll certainly take along the following discs.

Oh What a Beautiful Mornin'

There are mornings now and then, rarer as a man grows older, which come steeped in the wonder of youth. Everything is sharper, lovelier, more desirable, so that, alive to one's very fingertips with the beauty of the world, one seems to tremble on the verge of a discovery. On such ecstatic occasions, my heart invariably begins to sing "Oh what a beautiful morning!"

My first recollection of hearing it sung was in April 1948. At the age of 17, still more cot-wise than street-wise, I had just watched my team Manchester United beat Blackpool in the FA Cup Final at Wembley. Head in the clouds, I'd travelled back by Tube into London intending to catch the 8 p.m. from Euston to Manchester, there to share my joy and outrageous tales of victory with my Mum and Dad.

London was a strange and awesome city to me then, and around 6.30 I got off the Tube at Covent Garden, simply because the name conjured up all sorts of images to a raw young Northerner. I joined the throngs of people along Long Acre and soon found myself walking past a queue outside a theatre (I think it was the Theatre Royal in Drury Lane). Suddenly a man in doorman's uniform shouted, "Eh young fella', if it's just one ticket you want come on, the rest are couples." I can only think that he picked me out because I was in uniform. Once inside, bemused and fearful of how much I might have to pay, I began to turn away, but he grabbed my arm, pointed to the stairs and said, "Up to the top, stand at the back", winked and said, "Here's a tanner for an ice cream."

For the second time in a day, I'd proved the streets of London really were paved with gold. I'd talked my way into Wembley free, and now I was about to watch my first ever show at the same price. I thanked the doorman and said I'd been to Wembley. "I know that, you daft young bugger, you've still got your rosette stuck in your hatband!"

I was enthralled by the atmosphere in the theatre and soon forgot that I was expected in Manchester at 11 p.m. I stood dreamy eyed as Curly and Lori sang "People will say we're in love" and "Surrey with the fringe on top". But "Oh what a beautiful morning" was the one that struck the most chords and since then hundreds of people all over the world must have been rudely awakened and winced as Palmer has walked out into a beautiful sunny morning and felt that overwhelming urge to burst into "There's a bright golden haze on the medder."

I can't really explain it. It's rather like that distinctive feeling I had as a young-ster about Saturday mornings, or about Friday evenings when I lived in the USA. For some reason that I can't explain, they were different, there was something in the air and, without looking at a diary, you just knew it was Saturday or Friday. In Ireland you always knew when it was the Sabbath. Just as in a city you can *feel* a fall of snow; the world is wrapped in a soft hush, normal early morning noises are muffled or absent and even time seems to stand still. At such times, God is in his Heaven; all is well with the world. So I sing!

For many years I lived in Texas, the "next State down" as an Oklahoman would say sneeringly. I've been back there often in my industry days, but I don't think I've ever seen "the corn as high as a elephant's eye", and besides it's not the corn we English think of as a cornfield. But the joyful exuberant feeling that brings on the song is the same in Sussex, as in New Zealand or Bavaria or Argen-tina. But if I had to choose, I would anyway choose a field of golden wheat, on a golden hillside, waving in an English summer breeze. I can feel its warmth and hear it rustling amongst the adjoining oaks, as I watch the Skylarks rise to meet the sun.

One Friday night in 1994 in Melbourne, I made one of my impetuous "must see" decisions. I'd always wanted to see Tasmania but, for some inexplicable rea-son, Aussie friends had made the island sound like Aberystwyth or Skeg-ness—grey beaches, grey skies, grey sea and grey people. A business acquaintance drunkenly offered me his Aztec for the weekend, so I flew off to Hobart the next morning before he changed his mind. I drove down to Georgetown on the southern coast and found Tasmania a wonderful mixture of green hills running down to sandy beaches and magnificent cliffs. On that Sunday morning when I awoke, the residents of my cliff top hotel were treated to a very heartfelt emotional rendering of the song written for a Plains cowboy. It has been lurking there in my heart and vocal chords for 57 years of my life.

Aces High

My next musical companion would be something to stir my patriotism, with a strong flavour of sport and a heavy whiff of flying. It being a desert island, no one would be there to watch me as I paraded along the sands throwing up salutes to an imaginary VIP on a dais. Neither would they see the tears in my eyes as the stirring martial music of "Aces High" took me back to the pomp and circumstance of a military parade, to the brass bands that used to play before every football match and at half time, and to the roar of powerful piston engines before the days of jet propulsion. (Shades of the film "Battle of Britain".) Folk to day don't recognise or think too highly of military or martial music. Perhaps it smacks too much of the glorification of war, of the days of Empire, or of a class-ridden society. But I'm not ashamed to say that it has long played a big part in my life, whether whilst wearing a uniform and the pride that goes with that, or through the sound and spectacle of a great sporting occasion.

A close contender to Aces High for my military band slot would be the marching version of "The Yellow Rose of Texas". It's one of those tunes that can be given the "dreamy south" treatment, or dressed up in banners and costumes, with high stepping, baton-twirling girls in short skirts, and delivered with a stirring mix of trumpets, drums and pipes reminiscent of the American Civil War (or at least the Hollywood version of same). That tune would also be my spur to thoughts of Texas, which always has a special place in my heart. Barbecued beef and potato salad (with a Bavarian twist), the annual State Fair, Coors Beer, Dallas Cowboys, Dallas Cowboys' cheerleaders, summer rodeos, rattlesnake roundups and exhilarating flying weather. Then there are the native Texans, so often derided by other Americans, but people who epitomise the American image of friendship and generosity and who are amongst the most civil and courteous people on earth.

In 1960 I attended a Pool Party (as in swimming) at the Browns—whose house was later used as "Southfork" in the Dallas TV series. It started with Happy Hour on Friday evening and I arrived back at my base in Waco just in time to fly the morning "weather ship" sortie at 5 a.m. on Monday! Finally, and you must have been waiting for this, I can't leave Texas without noting that on 8th March 1921, in Amarillo Tex. was born Miss Tulla Ellice Finklea—Cyd Charisse to you. Big State, Big Heart, Big memories for JKP.

Will ye no come back Again?

The answer to that of course is always and forever, at least in my heart. I have always felt that if I were to jump out of an aeroplane at dead of night and without knowing where I was in the world, when dawn broke I would say at once, "I am in Scotland." Especially if I'd landed somewhere to the north of Stirling and the west of Dundee. The roads go north to Pitlochry, Drumtochter, Blairgowrie and the Spittal of Glenshee. But best of all, turn your face West and head for the Highlands of Romance:

> *...As you tread my golden roadway of the days of long ago;*
> *Will you realise the magic of the names I used to know?*
> *Clachnaharry—Achnashellash—Achnasheen and Duirinish.*
> *Every moor alive with coveys, every pool aboil with fish.*
> *Every well-remembered vista, more exciting mile by mile.*
> *'Til the wheeling gulls are screaming round the engine at the Kyle.*
> *Think of cloud on Bheinn na Gailleach, jagged Cuillins soaring high.*
> *Scent of peat, and all the magic, of the misty Isle of Skye...*

Scotland has always held a special charm for me; perhaps because of the wee dram of Scottish blood in my veins, certainly because the Scots have maintained their uniqueness, protected their culture, and strengthened their pride in all things Scottish. In contrast, we English are an unpatriotic lot, the Welsh have totally lost the plot and have no identity other than the unenviable variety, and the appealing and distinctly Irish culture has been long obscured by those who in claiming to save Ireland have all but destroyed it in the eyes of the world.

Scotland is a land of incredible scenic beauty; even its frequently atrocious weather has advantages in that it provides an ever-changing pattern of sunlight, colour, cloud and shadow. You can be in a driving rainstorm one minute, turn the corner and be in Brigadoon. Their music is like that, too, with something for every mood and occasion; from the stirring invigorating skirl o' the pipes to the melancholy beauty of a lament with all the pride and all the grandeur. The pipes are not so much something in the air as something deep in the heart. Grief opens the Scottish heart. The Celt has a genius for the glorification of sorrow. All his sweetest songs are sad; all his finest music is sad; all his greatest poetry springs from tragedy. I think of the heart-wrenching "The Flowers o' the Forest" born from the disaster of Flodden, and in a melancholy way I'm reminded of Texas country music.

Then there are those particularly haunting tunes that reflect the country's natural beauty or tell about the ecstasy of love or the pain of unrequited love. There's softness too in the female tongue, like a highland breeze playing through the bracken and the grass. It was enough in the late 1700's to send Robbie Burns into raptures and leave him often burning the midnight oil. To me in the early 2000's, there's magic in the very names of places and features that make every Scottish journey an exciting prospect.

One day in 1995 I was acting as a "referee" in a Maritime Reconnaissance competition held annually between the air forces of all the Commonwealth countries. Flying out of Kinloss near Inverness, I was assigned to the Australian crew and invited to fly with them on their pre-competition "sector recce" trip to familiarise them with the area and the ATC procedures etc. It was a rare day indeed for Scotland, scintillatingly clear and blue across the country; only when we climbed aboard the P3 did the Navigator realise he'd brought no local topographical maps, only flying charts. I was therefore asked to act as a tourist guide around Scotland using the only map I had in my briefcase that showed golf courses, whisky distilleries and castles—and not much else. Fortunately I knew Scotland well both from the air and on the ground, so I was delighted to take on the job with the weather as it was.

It was actually a revelation to me because I was seeing the beauty of the country in late autumn from between 1000–1500ft at 160 knots, instead of my accustomed high-level view in my fighter days or at 500kts and 300ft in my low-level strike attack days. One had a rare bird's eye view of the terrain for some 5–10 miles around you, a perception of course that you never could get in a car or on foot, or at the speeds I'd been used to. I took them to all the famous golf courses; at St Andrews I got permission via the local tower at RAF Leuchars to circle the Old Course for about 15 minutes whilst the RAAF guys took photographs.

Similarly at the beautiful rugged castle of Eilean Donan, we were cleared to fly around it approaching from the loch and the sea to get the most photogenic views. Even I was surprised when the prints were displayed to find that we were actually looking up at Eilean Donan, and not down! We went down Loch Ness past the ruined shell of Urquhart Castle where the loch is deepest, willing the monster to appear, past Ben Nevis with her summit as always in cloud, and on to the misty Isle of Skye to gasp at those stupendous terrible towering spires of rock—the "Black" Cuillins, and the grey ghost of Dunvegan Castle. The distillery of Glenmorangie got a special visit as we were taking all the overseas crews there to a dinner as part of their culture enhancement. I even managed to persuade the gung-ho skipper of the P3 that it would not be appreciated if we flew *under* the Forth Bridge! The Australians could not believe that such a small country had such a rich and bloody history. To give them a momento of this very special place, I scoured the dusty bookshelves in Inverness for a 1930 copy of H. V. Morton's *In search of Scotland.* (Now that's a real piece of writing which makes me have serious doubts about ever putting mine in print!) Everyone should *see* Scotland as we saw it that day. Just as anyone who wants to *understan*d it must walk the great hills in the sunlight, or in the teeth of a westerly when vast clouds sail overhead sending their shadows racing over the moorlands. Mornings when the hawks are tossed and turned by the winds, when your footsteps are printed black behind you in the thick dewfall; the hills brown with dead bracken, grey with sleek silvery heather stems, and soggy with the little peaty streams that tumble excitably to cascade between boulders down the slopes.

So another of my discs would be to remind me of Scotland, its great natural beauty, its culture, its poetry, its mysteries, its people and its music. I'm torn between the Phil Coulter version of "My luve's like a red red rose" with its heartrending lines of "I will love thee still, my dear, while the sands o' life shall run" and that lovely melody from Brigadoon of "Heather on the Hill". Maybe I'll just take 'em both, eh, and sneak in the massed bands of the Highland Regiments with "Scotland the Brave" to remind me of a truly magical mysterious country. I never think of Scotland without warmth of feeling and a great depth of love for the friendly faces, the friendly voices, and the generous Scottish welcome. I think of its glens and deep dark gorges, the white torrents, and the way the mountains lie in purple against the wide and open sky. I can even forgive the millions of "midgies" that rise from the heather as I picture the little white cottages in the western hills, smell again the flavour of the peat reak, and recall the taste of good Malt after a hard day's walk. "Better loved ye canna be" indeed.

> *For auld lang syne, my dear*
> *For auld lang syne.*
> *We'll tak' a cup o'kindness yet'*
> *For auld lang syne.*

I Left my Heart in San Francisco

A song for "the wee small hours" would have to be the beautiful piano version by Roger Williams, or the silky vocal by Tony Bennett. It's difficult to describe the emotion that lives in this song, late at night with the piano covered in empty glasses and a gorgeous creature coiled sensuously in a chair. I never did leave my heart in 'Frisco in the sense that someone special was waiting there for me, but the City on the Bay is one of the few cities that cannot be exaggerated and has always held a great attraction for me; even the name evokes magical memories. The melody itself is what dreams are made of. I have listened to it so often, usually with the lights dimmed by the glow of a fire, and never been able to sing the words because I've been so choked with emotion. Most big cities are similar; busy, noisy, flashy, dirty, impersonal—but 'Frisco is different. I love cities on the coast or on a bay like Rio, Cape Town, and Sydney. San Francisco is right up there with them; a car-honking, boats-hooting, ferries—churning, trambells-ringing delight, with the spectacular Golden Gate bridge, the teeming restaurants around Fisherman's Wharf, and the steep hills up and down which the trolley cars jingle and rattle to make it a real fun city. Judy Garland did a great publicity job for the city when she opened its Golden Gate on the Broadway catwalk.

In 1960 I was attached to 84F Squadron flying the Voodoo out of Hamilton AFB, across the bridge in Marin County. I was introduced to San Francisco by a USAF pilot colleague called Neil Franklin who took me to Chinatown, to a downtown area famous for its jazz clubs and cellars, and to a bewildering range of bars and restaurants that combined superb food with great character and ambience. It was all the more enjoyable because there was no violence, very little obvious drunkenness or—to my knowledge—any drug problem. People were just there to enjoy and be happy. I was looking forward to just such a pleasant evening one Saturday in December. I'd been alone to Candlestick Park to watch my first US pro football game, the local 49ers against the country's then top team, Green Bay Packers. I'd arranged to meet Neil at 7 p.m. in a bar (on California I think) called The Yankee Doodle. The place gradually filled up with men and women mainly in their 20's and 30's, and as I sat contentedly sipping my Martini at the bar, the place was humming. Into this cauldron of excited noise walked a bunch of very confident smiling young men who were obviously recognised by the partygoers, thereby putting up the noise level by many decibels, mostly from girlish shrieks. I sat unconcerned until a group of three of them came and stood behind my bar stool and I began to be pushed and jostled. I turned to see who was doing the pushing to find a guy leering at me and saying,

"You're sitting on my barstool friend." "I think not," said I, and turned to continue sipping my drink, at which point my elbow was struck so violently that I spilled my drink. I rose slowly and carefully to my feet. As I turned I knew instinctively that the elbow nudger was about to hit me and just had the time to duck and turn so that his fist grazed my ear instead of flattening my nose. Stung with pain rather than anger, I lashed out at my assailant, catching him smack on the jaw. Now I had not set myself to punch him and the place was crowded, so my blow was not exactly one of shattering force. Unfortunately, as he fell back his legs were taken from under him by a long low cocktail table and he slid back along the highly polished floor to hit the wall with glasses and ashtrays crashing around him, and Miss America screaming as only American girls can scream.

As I looked at the devastation, my shoulder was grabbed by a barman who yelled, not as you might expect "Don't break up my joint", but "You can't hit *him!*" He kept repeating "You can't hit *him*" leaving me slightly bemused. Before I could work out what he meant, I saw the biggest of those still standing, with a face full of scars, pushing his way towards me. "My God," I thought, "here I am with a broken wrist in a foreign bar about to feel like General Custer at Little Big Horn." Scarface was now in my face as he quietly said, "If he gets up, please hit him twice as friggin hard! Have a drink, friend."

That party went on in the Yankee Doodle for hours, then me and Neil (who had arrived to find me being fêted as a hero) were taken around the town until being poured into a cab around 6 a.m. to drive back to base. The guys who had become our buddies were the Green Bay team and the gentleman up to his backside in cocktail glasses turned out to be their very unpopular (though brilliant) quarterback. Scarface was their captain, and he introduced me to Green Bay's commercial manager who promised to send me two season tickets for the next two seasons. He kept his word and I stayed in touch with Paul the captain for over 30 years and last saw him in Paris in Airshow week 1993.

But my story did not finish there. When Neil and I got back to Hamilton an urgent message awaited me to call my boss in Washington DC. I had no idea why an RAF Group Captain should want to call me at 7 a.m. on a Sunday morning, unless it was bad news about my family. I called him at once to be greeted by a northern Irish voice saying, "Palmer, what the Hell have you been up to this time? Have you read the morning papers?" I said I hadn't, still confused. "Well, just to give you some idea of the trouble you're in, how about this for starters"—and quoted from the Sunday Washington and New York papers:

"Packers slay the 49'ers, Palmer slays the Packers"
"Limey floors Packers QB in 'Frisco shoot out"

There were lurid accounts of a bloodbath, eyewitness reports of how I'd hit him with a barstool, and tearstained pages from a broad who'd cradled the smitten hero in her arms as he lay following his savage beating. All rubbish of course, but isn't that what newspapers usually write? "Don't say anything now," continued the Group Captain. "Just catch the noon flight to Washington; your ticket's paid for and my driver will pick you up at the airport. Bring your best blue (uniform), we have an appointment with the Ambassador at 9 a.m. tomorrow."

On arrival at the Embassy, the Group Captain met me with such a look on his face that I wondered why he didn't don his black cap there and then. "Just tell the Ambassador the truth; if it was the drink then just say so," he said. With those cheerful and encouraging words of Ireland ringing in my ears, I was ushered into the Ambassador's office. Smilingly he came towards me and held out his hand, which I took unthinkingly. I winced with the pain. "Sorry old son," he said. "What a splendid war wound you have there—you must tell me all about it."

So instead of the grilling and possible expulsion I'd feared, I sat on the Ambassador's patio and was fed bacon, eggs and kidneys whilst I recounted the story of Palmer's last stand at the Yankee Doodle. I was so popular that an impromptu cocktail party was laid on at lunchtime, by the end of which I'd slaughtered the entire Green Bay team, was being touted as the next contender for Sonny Liston's title, and had received a surprising number of Green Lights from ladies to whom I'd not been properly introduced. I was to fly back to San Francisco that night and on the way to the airport the Ambassador said, "Of course, John, I don't suppose with you being on the West Coast you'll be able to use your season tickets for Green Bay very often." He was right, I couldn't—but *he* could and did, bless him.

My love for San Francisco was such that I wanted Rosemarie to see it for herself as I'm sure she must have suspected when I banged on about it, that I'd had some secret love nest there in my past. So it was that in 1998 on returning from Hawaii, we stopped over for the weekend and sampled the seafood at the Wharf, drove over the bridge to Sausalito and danced till dawn at the Top of the Mark. Perhaps the city had changed a bit since those halcyon days of the 60's, and maybe one should never go back where small memories are. But to all my other cherished memories of that unique city, I can now add Roo's hair blowing in the Bay breeze and remember the look on her face as I drove our hired Cadillac at speed down the terraced street made famous by Steve McQueen. Cadillacs just don't bounce like 57 Chevrolets!

By the time I get to Phoenix

My next musical treasure takes me back to the States again to a moment of nostalgia that has stood the test of time since 1968. I was on a day flight from San Diego to Washington and had luckily been upgraded to first class. About an hour out we passed over Monument Valley, one of my favourite places on earth, and I was able to pick out many of the landmark features. On my in-flight radio channel there was a tape by Percy Faith with such tuneful pieces as Special Angel and Both Sides Now, followed by Andy Williams singing "By the time I get to Phoenix". Below me I could see the ribbon of highway along which one would drive from LA to Phoenix and eastwards, and as I sat eating my lobster salad and sipping champagne I felt the most privileged person on earth. The magic of that moment remains with me and I have to say that in millions of air miles flown since, it has never been repeated. I'd take the Andy Williams vocal, but I also love the Williams/Aldrich piano versions that transport me to a gleaming dance floor where I'd be accompanied by a long legged girl in a black dress with a slit in the side. Dark hair piled high on her head, we'd slow foxtrot our way to heaven. Can anyone explain how I loved her in San Francisco long before we even met?

John Denver

Every now and then one hears an artist with whom one immediately identifies. Johnny Denver was such an artist for me with his relaxed country style and beautiful melodies. He was a rarity in that you could hear every word he sang, and his words—words written by him—were worth listening to. On stage, John didn't need an enormous band, flashing lights, a bevy of half-dressed girls, or fancy gimmicks to support him. He just sat down quietly on a stool and tore your heart out.

Rosemarie and I were driving through Arizona when a local newsreader made the simple statement that "Reports are coming in that an aircraft piloted by the singer John Denver is overdue on a flight off the Pacific coast". Somehow I knew there was no mistake and that the world had lost a very special man and musician. I never have heard the full story of his "accident" and all news about him seemed to dry up as if he'd never been amongst the world's top entertainers. But his music lives on and my choice of a single track is almost impossible because he sang about life as we all live it, about the pleasure and the pain, the past and the future. I'd take his "Sunshine on my shoulder", "Some days are diamonds", "My sweet lady" and "Annie's Song"; whilst "Leaving on a jet plane" would remind me of the many times I had to leave Rosemarie on my travels around the globe. My son Chris was one of his greatest fans and I was so sorry that having got tickets for what proved to be John's last visit to England at the Albert Hall, Chris and his wife Trudy had to drop out at the last moment.

A Choice of Classic

To my first six selections, I would certainly add my Dad's favourite classic, Liszt's Hungarian Rhapsody No 2. I'm no connoisseur of music as you can tell, but that piece I find intensely satisfying and I only wish Dad could have heard it now played with the clarity, contrast and pure power that is possible with modern recording equipment. The Rhapsody also holds a special meaning for me; an enduring and fond memory of my childhood days when I would get up early on an autumn morning before going to school. I'd go into the nearby Park woods to collect the "conkers" (horse chestnuts) that had fallen from the trees during the night. There was something in the music that transported me back under those trees and the wildness of an autumn day. Of course it had to be a windy morning to unseat the hairy spiked nuts, and my abiding recollection is of the noise of the wind in the branches and amongst the leaves, and of looking up to see the huge tree whipped this way and that as I waited for the sight or sound of the large brown conker shell hitting the ground and spilling its shiny red treasure across the soft carpet beneath the tree. It seems to me that we were all closer then to nature than we are now, and that is to be regretted. What a wonderful childhood I enjoyed, to be sure.

The Best of the Rest

I'd be keen to have with me the beautiful melancholy music from "Somewhere in Time", and a dreamy instrumental version of "This guy's in love with you" which Roo and I adopted as our theme song in our early days. Two other orchestrals would be "Moon River", to remind me of my dreams as a young man watching the moon rise up across the Mississippi, and a haunting tune dripping with tropical nights and exotic sounds called "Quiet Village" that I once had on a *Readers Digest* LP.

   To remind me of the matchless green beauty of British hills and dales and our rivers and lakes, I'd pack "The Londonderry Air", the string orchestral version, to remind me of days spent alone with nature in that beautiful Isle across the Irish Sea. I specify that to exclude the vocal version of "Danny Boy", which to me and many others have become synonymous with that bunch of hooded terrorists, thugs and murderers called the IRA who have used religion and patriotism to cloak their evil warped activities—some who have the gall today to sit in our seat of democracy in Westminster!

I could not leave behind the equally romantic Hawaiian style "I'll remember you" by Andy Williams, nor a young Sinatra singing "South of the Border". Tommy Dorsey's "Sunny side of the Street" would sneak in my short list, as would Eve Cassidy's "Somewhere over the rainbow". To come right up to date, I've been enchanted lately by the loveliness and the voice of Katherine Jenkins who sings "Land of my Fathers" in a way that brings tears even to these old English eyes. Also—for some unknown reason—the hauntingly sad refrain of "What a wonderful world"; best listened to as the shadows lengthen, the sun shimmers out of sight, and the hills change colour through the whole blue spectrum. It is a sentiment that I now relate to more than ever before.

But I'm way over my allotted 10 and I could think of hundreds more, and change them as I listened to others. Perhaps after all I wouldn't need the actual music, because my heart and mind is so full of the melodies and the words. Indeed, I often find myself bursting into song and beginning to sing in the street or in a superstore. That's what music is all about really, isn't it?

Recently I sent Cyd Charisse a card on her 85th birthday in which I wrote "May you always be dancing in your heart". I would wish that everyone could enjoy a life enriched by its fair share of rhythm and romance, of the sound of music and the delicate, sensuous exhilarating passion or exquisite expression of the dance. I cannot imagine how much poorer my own life would have been without them. Partners forever without a doubt.

17

RETIREMENT (Jan 2000)

"Twixt the Gloaming and the Mirk"

The world has turned over many times since I walked out of the gates of MGS in May 1946 and whatever hopes and dreams I had have either been realised or become shrouded in the mists of time. But I can truthfully state that at no time in my working life between school and vacating my last office on 31st December 1999, did I ever spare a serious thought about retirement. I was far too busy enjoying what I was doing that day or planning what to do tomorrow. A Chinese poet wrote, "There's always a place kept for an old horse though it can take no more to the long road." It never occurred to me that anyone would put me out to pasture. I had not come face to face with my own mortality then—and indeed I still haven't.

I remember in my late 40's and early 50's listening, sometimes incredulously, sometimes cynically and often with amusement, to successful and hard working RAF colleagues who waxed lyrically about their plans for retirement. There were a few whose sights were set solely on earning money to first secure and then improve on the very attractive lifestyle they'd enjoyed in uniform. Others—and probably the majority—were happy to have the chance at the relatively young age of around 55, to start a second career that would earn them just enough to live a comfortable and worry-free life. But there were many who made no bones about retirement; meaning they would take on no commitments whatsoever, live a life of ease on the earnings of a high-born lady, and spend most of their time in the sun, the bar, on a yacht, or in a garden—providing it was maintained by somebody else, of course.

Increasingly, in writing this autobiography, I have come to realise that we each live lives so unique, so different because of our peculiar circumstances, that most comparisons are meaningless. We each of us start and finish our day with ideas, doubts, fears, pressures and hope, whilst our outlook, temperament, mood, and feelings will all have been influenced by what we've been doing over the previous

24 hours, and with whom we were doing it with. More significantly, none of us has the faintest idea what is going to happen in the next few minutes, let alone weeks or months. Experience tells us that it is probably as well that we never know what is around the corner.

Whether category our thoughts about the future fall into, there will be times in everyone's life when we look into the crystal ball. I recall one such occasion in 1972, sitting under the Bougainvillea in a garden bar in Cyprus, chewing the cud and putting the world to right with the four officers that made up my Air Defence staff. A non-stop supply of ice cold Brandy Sours had obscured all traces of rank, loosened all tongues, and seduced us into revealing our hopes and plans for the future.

As high as I ever get these days! Cyprus 2003

The oldest of the five was my SAM expert who'd been an air gunner during WW2 and was due to retire the following year. He was returning to his beloved

Scotland to a farm that grew berries for a famous jam manufacturer. He would use his terminal pay to modernise his granite cottage, create a special garden of water features and run the farm with his wife. He asked no more than to do just that, to smoke his pipe and to quaff the odd jug of bitter. He and his wife had been saving for years to realise their dream and had let pass the many opportunities for travel that came with the RAF life. Four months after retirement at the age of 58, soft amiable Dougie died from cancer.

The second oldest was my Transport Squadron Leader who was one of those guys I always admired, capable of turning his hand to anything practical. He wanted to buy a plot of land somewhere in the Cotswolds, build a house to his own design, and perhaps pick up a few bob here and there with the RAF Benevolent Fund or similar service-linked Charity. He did all of that, wasted thousands on a useless ungrateful son, looked after his ailing wife with incredible cheerful dedication—and died of a heart attack before he was 60. His wife is still alive.

I was the next oldest of the bunch of five, and the second youngest was my Ground Radar expert. That drinking session was the only time I ever got close to understanding him. He saw himself as God's gift to women, thought Fred Astaire was a clumsy oaf on the dance floor compared to himself, and yearned for the day when he could earn so much money that he could put two fingers up to those of his superiors who had consistently over the years failed to recognise what a genius he really was. He actually was good at his job and he and I got on well, although he was constantly at war with those who shared his office. He left Cyprus and the RAF and carelessly at the age of 55 I heard, finished up in jail for embezzlement and fraud.

The youngest of the five surprised me most. He was then in his early 30's, a Cranwell-trained pilot with the self-confidence of all fighter jocks and good prospects of promotion to high rank. He was adamant that he'd retire at 55 whatever rank he'd risen to, and retire to somewhere in Cornwall where he'd spend his time sailing and enjoying the social life of a gentleman in a small village where everyone knew everyone. He had no interest in any occupation outside the service and no intention of joining even a Christmas Club once he retired. I met him last in 1989 as a 49-year-old Group Captain; his plans had not changed one iota and I heard on the grapevine at a reunion that he's now a part-time painter of seascapes in St Ives.

You could say that our look into the crystal ball was a total failure for two of my friends and a partial for the third. Only one followed the path he'd planned and hoped for. Of the five Brandy Sour drinkers that day I suspect I gave away least of my plans for the future. That had something to do with me being the boss and letting the guys have their heads, so to speak, and much to do with the fact that I saw my future as being with the then wife of one of our junior officers, a situation that Rosemarie and I were than working very hard at keeping a secret.

But even so, I have to say that as a 42-year-old, retirement and what I might do with it seemed a lifetime away. I was enjoying life to the full; I enjoyed my work, the life in Cyprus, had four wonderful children and was head over heels in love. That love was the be-all-and-end-all when I finally retired on the last second of the 20th century after drawing a wage non-stop from the age of 16 to my 70th year. I'd enjoyed an enormously interesting and satisfying working life and closed the office door for the last time feeling I'd done my bit; most of it my way, and most of it for the benefit of those I'd worked with and for. I was going to live with the woman I'd loved for 30 years and circumstances meant that we'd be living in Wales. Just to be together was enough; I thus entered retirement with a completely open mind; no burning desires, no targets, no trepidation. I don't mean that to sound like the customary happy ending of an old Hollywood movie; life isn't like that. But Rosemarie and I never doubted that we could make it work, we knew our love would not recede like the tide leaving behind the debris of a love affair. Whatever obstacles emerged, we looked forward eagerly to retirement but recognised early on that we would need to make adjustments. Perhaps we couldn't change the wind, but we could adjust our sails.

BEAR and Forbear

My Dad oft quoted an old northern saying, "They're all queer but thee and me, and I'm not too sure of thee." My uncle, a pompous tyke from Pudsey, would say, "There's nowt as queer as folk." In effect they were acknowledging that each of us is unique. Do we not all follow the demands of our own nature? I am what I am and cannot now change my personality. Surely none of us can? We can change our aims and aspirations, curb our desires and lusts, quell our fears and rein in our anger, but we cannot change our temperament. So how do we adjust our relationships with others to create an atmosphere that enables others to express their feelings and attitudes and live harmoniously?

The acid test comes when we decide to spend every living moment with someone else; sharing our hopes, fears, ambitions, money and probably our bed. But however hard we work to secure the relationship, we may still need help to cater for our human unpredictability and impermanence. That is never more true than with a second marriage. Frank Sinatra sang melodiously of Love being "more wonderful the second time around". Millions would agree; nevertheless, a second marriage can be a minefield, even when a couple are very much in love and have the benefits of maturity and tolerance on their side. The challenges of raising a family may be behind them, as may be the stress of "keeping up with the Jones'" and wanting to do everything and to go everywhere. But whatever the circumstances, it's fair to say that if two people have been married before or have lived without a partner for many years, they are certain to have developed habits and ways that may well cause friction with a new partner's own *modus operandi*.

Previous relationships would have left their marks creating potential flash points that would be exposed as the couple each began to be their true selves and had stopped acting to please or impress. Friction thus created might express itself on one end of the scale like a nuclear explosion, or at the other as a silent hostile gloom. Every couple's experience of love is unique but where Rosemarie and I are concerned, you should know that our quarrels are closer to the nuclear explosion end of the scale. Why should that be so? Well, I was married for over 30 years to a woman with a very different temperament to Rosemarie. In that time, whatever the shape of our individual personalities and our intellects, some degree of harmonization and blending must have taken place. I would therefore behave in a certain way when sharing a house and doing things together. Similarly Rosemarie would have developed her way of behaving when she was married, and we both had many years of living alone or, in my case, out of suitcases in hotels and other people's houses. You could summarize all that by saying that we were both set in our ways and, as we began to spend more time together—instead of the all too brief but wonderful hours we'd been so used to—we began to find that some of our deep rooted ways could cause irritation.

Then there is a culture difference that cannot be ignored—not a gap, you understand—but a distinct difference. I'm English and Rosemarie is Welsh with many of the inherent peculiarities of that warlike race. But she, wise Psyche, was the first to recognize the dangers and the first to attempt a realistic sensible solution that didn't involve stag nights, girlie nights out in a stretched limo, or wanton and random infidelity. She decided we must have a go-between, a mediator, a domestic diplomat if you like to guide us through choppy seas. Our solution may not be perfect or even innovative, but we opted to enlist the help of a small furry inanimate intermediary; to wit-a Bear. Read on now keeping tongue well in cheek.

We're not talking mascots here or talismans; neither are we talking oracles or soothsayers. In effect, we're talking about someone (not some*thing* mind you) who intercedes whenever the seeds of a disagreement are sown. He is the ship's cat, the first in line for the proverbial boot up the backside; he's the one that takes the blame, has the stupid ideas, forgets the car keys, misses the last post, and spills brown sauce on the cushions. He is the bridge between critters and humans; you can read to him, he knows all your secrets but keeps *schtum*. Blame him for anything, and he won't deny it. When Rosemarie or I say "Bear sez", you know we're pouring oil on troubled waters, taking the edge off a cutting remark. Amid the trials and tribulations of life, he's the ever-present, ever-loving quiet little presence.

Rosemarie bought him for me for Christmas. Although handpicked for his fine features, obviously superior intelligence, and matchless temperament, he was not of the carnivorial aristocracy. He was not, for instance, a haughty expensive rockhard Steiff or an ugly Hermann. Neither had he appeared in Disney films, advertised porridge, or been apprehended for poaching salmon. He was simply a cuddly, common or garden little critter whose character Rosemarie began to fashion so that he gradually, ever so discretely, wormed his way into our affections. When he joined the Family, it was not yet the Family Palmer. Those were difficult days, with prolonged acrimonious divorce proceedings affecting his Dad whilst his Mummy lived alone in Wales, to where he and his Dad would commute from Sussex each weekend. To start with he resided mostly in his Dad's office in Crawley, but he didn't like that as the secretaries would cover him with perfume, pass unkind comments about his parentage and his regrettable tendency to fall base over apex whenever he was caught by a gust of wind. So he moved back to Wales where Rosemarie coached him in the art of diplomacy and the skills of mediation.

That is how Bear fits into our love story. He is not what he is and where he is because he's cute and well behaved, or because he sees no fault in us, makes no reproach and will stay with us forever. He possesses those attributes, but they are of secondary consideration against his constant and imaginative contribution to marital peace; he has an uncanny knack of nipping trouble in the bud, of calming and cooling the ripples of disagreement before they can become roaring waves or sinister currents.

From time to time, usually after the odd gin and tonic, Rosemarie and I have confided in our close friends about the little fella. We found to our surprise that some of them are also lunatic fringers; one couple write 'em down and put their bones of contention in a box, another pair of political persons agree to give a fiver to charity if cross words are uttered, and another play silly games in the bath—but we'll not go into that. Then there was the guy in an Atlanta hotel who caught us talking to Bear when the lift door opened. We explained ever so seriously that we were just telling him (Bear, that is) to be careful of the crush in the lobby, as we didn't want to lose him. "Gee that's okay," responded our American cousin "Everyone should have a Harvey."(Now, who in his right mind would want a bloody six-foot rabbit as a mediator?)

If you sneer at my revelations about Bear, you make a big mistake. You'd be looking at these golden words through jaundiced eyes and cannot possibly see what Rosemarie and I have experienced as we have been spirited away, our imaginations stirred and our world made a happier place. Perhaps we exaggerate his personality, but there's no harm in that providing he succeeds in his primary mission eh?

Bear is just Bear; not a Teddy bear, Ted, Edward, or Pooh, just plain unique Bear. He has degrees from Oxford, Cambridge and Harvard, all of which he obtained in under 24 hours. He has a seat in the House of Commons (the one with teeth marks on it), has played premiership football (for Man.Utd of course), and is rapidly overtaking Heath Robinson as an inventor of ingenious and technology defying gadgets. Bear is the fruit of Rosemarie's loins, a chip off my old block, and we his parents are both true Arctophilos (from the Greek *arkos*—meaning Bear, and *philos* meaning friends). Think of him engaged in some of his favourite pursuits, that strangely may reflect all that you will have imagined many times in your childhood dreams—which you'll find when it comes to Bears—last your whole life through. *Q.E.D.*

What is this thing called Wales?

This bit needs an introduction all to itself. I can't just treat it as I once believed-like an afterthought—because it's about the present and the place where I shall now probably see out my days. When I embarked on this tome, I hardly thought I'd get this far, and anyway I had the safety net of expecting it to be read when I was no longer around to face the flak. But now it's not the flak that I'm concerned with; it's the dilemma of highlighting some of my genuine concerns about Wales and the Welsh and of being seen as unkind and critical out of context if I lump everything Welsh under the same label.

Earlier I warned about attempting to generalise about a country and people as vast and diverse as the USA. Well, Wales would fit into the USA some 4300 times and its population of 3 million be dwarfed by the USA's 281 million. Yet even in this small appendage of the British Isles, there are enormous differences—if not in the topography, geography and climate, then certainly in the people and in their culture, customs and language. To a man from Cardiff, a resident of North Wales might as well be an Eskimo, who in turn would see himself as vastly different and much superior to a fisherman from the South West or a hill farmer of the Central Borders.

Homing in on where we chose to settle, the Valleys, intense tribalism exists. The Rhondda is very different to the Cynon Valley, an Aberdare "snake" barely recognises a Pontypriddian, and those on the other side of the same valley are often strangers—with grave misgivings about the residents in the next street! Having only lived here for five years, been a regular visitor for six and an occasional one for twenty, I do not qualify as an expert. However, I have a Welsh wife and in-laws, have immersed myself in local affairs, and made a great many friends. So I have an opinion, made all the more valid by being able to compare with the other 25 places I have lived in these islands and five countries overseas, not counting extensive travel to 110 countries worldwide. I can only speak as I find and without any intention or wish to offend. Does that sound ominous?

So what did I know about Wales before settling on a Welsh hillside in 2000? To be truthful, very little. I knew from my flying days, zipping around the low level routes at 500 feet and 500 knots, that much of the countryside north of the southern cities was incredibly beautiful. I knew from my rugby days that Wales produced the game's finest backs, albeit quite the dirtiest and most malicious forwards. I knew of their music, their male voice choirs, and appreciated the power and eloquence of politicians and of actors like Richard Burton and Anthony Hopkins. I knew of the importance of coal and steel to the Valley communities and the terrible legacies of that era. I knew that Welsh lamb was deliciously sweet and I saw a striking Spanish influence in some of their women that made them exotically attractive. I was vaguely aware of a bizarre national costume, of what to my ears was an ugly native tongue, and that there were days when daffodils and leeks were the traditional adornment. I'm scratching around a bit now, but as a change from Blackpool our family occasionally went to Rhyl for our hols in the 40's and my brother thought Betws-y-Coed another name for heaven in the 50's.

On the debit side, my Mum said she'd never trust "The Welsh", that "welshing" on someone meant that you'd broken a promise or left unpaid a debt. I was never quite sure which, or of the derivative. So I didn't know much—and much of that was wrong. I could not have believed how complex this country is, how it can take you from dizzy heights to utterly despondent depths, and how different are its people from any I've known. Here I sail in dangerous waters, because I only want to write about Wales and the Welsh, more specifically the Valleys, as I see them now. I don't want to go back as many do, researching history to find why a man from Mountain Ash should in 2005 blame some dastardly deed by an English monarch or minister in 1600 for the enormous chip on his shoulder and the dilapidated state of his town.

It may well be that some ancient ancestor of mine spent his life kicking Welsh backsides, but there's nowt I can do about that now if he did. Neither am I qualified to look at the reality of life in these valleys in the days of coal and steel. Those industries have virtually disappeared, never to return. More significantly perhaps, they slipped into extinction in so short a span that many of those involved were unable to match the rate of change in their lives. I never meet anyone that wants them to come back. Of course they want the jobs and prosperity to return, and there are still many who speak nostalgically of the appeal of community life then; of the sense of belonging, of solidarity, and of the workers banding together against the common enemies of poverty, owners and politicians. There were good things, but the participants know they were far outweighed by the bad.

Sticking out my neck in my old fangled way, let me endear myself to the scarlet masses by observing that in many ways, the Wales of yesterday on which people now look back fondly, never actually existed! It was and is largely a myth, an illusion, mainly created, sensationalised, and romanticized by writers and filmmakers who look back nostalgically from a safe distance at lives they themselves couldn't wait to leave behind. Films like "How Green is my Valley" are no more accurate representations of Valley life than the legends of Robin Hood and King Arthur depict life in England centuries ago, or how most Hollywood Westerns glamorise the era of the cowboy. The harsh realities of life have been air brushed out or removed via computer software, to be replaced by a sentimental fog to obscure the unpalatable.

So however good, bad or indifferent were the old days, I'm going to avoid them in my snapshot of Wales today. Otherwise I'll be submerged by the bitter resentment and irrational thinking that always occurs when dearly loved thoughts and objects have to be renounced. Bitter experience tells me that I'll face enough modern day abuse without digging up the graveyards of the past.

Writing this chapter earlier in a different mood, I began recounting the utterly normal and boring things that I did as I tried to come to terms with a new life; one without work pressures and outrageously fast long range commuting, and one with dramatic social and environmental differences. My energy and inquisitiveness naturally led me into the Voluntary Sector which means you get lumbered with countless requests to chair this, be a secretary for that, and lead a motley bunch of sincere folk, do-gooders, the lunatic fringe, and reluctant public sector people, to pursue lost causes or raise money for schemes that mostly go tits-up as interest wanes and people see they can't make any money for themselves. I shan't elaborate, but I'll pick out some of the highlights—which even so may send you to sleep before your partner brings your cocoa, or you cry out for whisky in sheer desperation.

Why put up with it?

That group of my RAF contemporaries in the 70's that looked ahead to retirement, had all sorts of ideas as to what they wanted to do. But their occupational desires were overshadowed by where they wanted to live and in what sort of circumstances. "Location, location, location". Most would have foreseen living in a small country village such as they saw near most RAF stations, or some quiet little spot on the coast or in the hills. Uppermost in their wishes would be peace and tranquillity, appealing countryside, good dog-walking country, proximity of a village pub and local shops, and good road and rail links to major cities and recreational pursuits.

Given that, the local village committee would see the Annual Fete as its biggest task, with a Christmas concert, the odd auction and society wedding as other items of interest. I led that sort of life for twelve years in Sussex, even though I hadn't then retired. Whether you were rich, moderately well off or living in rented or public accommodation, it was an easy and graceful sort of existence that contrasts sharply with life in the Welsh valleys. There is of course a well-heeled section in the Valleys, and also a thriving middle class that lives there, but is more likely to work in Cardiff or Swansea, or even further afield. But they are islands of privilege in a sea of poverty since Welsh history has created an "underclass" in the Valleys, seemingly unable to break out of the stranglehold of deprivation and apathy. Let me say again; the Valleys are not truly representative of Wales, especially of Cardiff which is little different in character and lifestyle to most British provincial cities and is not steeped in the brand of "welshness" that has left the Valleys still struggling in the last century.

As a weekend commuter here I saw little of the surrounding area. Now I travel all over the Valleys and am still asking why the people here put up with their lot? The simple answer of course is that two generations have known nothing different. They were shabbily treated when the work disappeared from the area, and they have become so used to inferior housing, inferior services, and mis-management of their towns and estates, that they know no better than to live in perpetual conflict with authority and suffer from an aggressive inferiority complex.

They accept a rail system that virtually blanks them off from Cardiff after 9 p.m., they accept bus services that seldom run on time and allows drivers to decide what routes they should follow missing out many roads and stops at their whim. They put up with too many doctors who wouldn't know a bedside manner if it jumped up and bit them, whose medical knowledge might be acceptable in the far flung reaches of the old Empire, but which is dangerously inadequate in the 21st century. They have become accustomed to hospitals that are the seediest and shabbiest in Britain and which would simply not survive elsewhere in the UK. They are served by a dedicated dynamic Police force, but one numerically inadequate for the tasks it faces and abysmally supported by a toothless and senile legal system that penalises the good and protects the wrongdoers. The Social Services, so admirable in concept, are woeful in practice because their staff cannot make headway in the quagmire of human misery and apathy in which they work.

True, there has been a breeze of change blowing from the Welsh Assembly leading to local authorities improving their infrastructure and strategic planning. But with some, the old culture still predominates. There's a "tick in the box" mentality that produces millions of words, all of which give the illusion of progress whilst ensuring that nothing gets done. It will take a wind of hurricane force to bring real change, and men and women of a calibre and a passion that usually takes them across the Severn Bridge or the Atlantic to where their talents are recognised and more suitably rewarded.

Amidst his constant tirade of criticism of all things English, one of Wales's most celebrated poets asks, "What is wrong with us in Wales that we have to look back continually as if to better days, even though some people who are old enough to remember, remind us how hard those days were?" In his poetry, some that I understand but most of which is beyond my ken, he seems to blame all the ills of Wales on anyone but his own countrymen—as if the world is in some conspiracy against this little country, when in fact the world hardly knows of its existence and even less of its culture. In his own words, R.S. Thomas tells us that

> *There is no present in Wales and no future.*
> *There is only the past; brittle with relics, wind bitten towers and castles with shy ghosts.*
> *Moulding quarries and mines, and an impotent people sick with in-breeding, worrying the carcase of an old song.*

Adjustments

You will have noted that I have not actually retired, but simply changed the way I spend my time. I don't fly for a living or fun anymore; write operational requirements, design weapon systems or market high technology products. I still talk, argue and disagree with the good, bad and indifferent, but now it's about the quality of life, housing conditions, youth clubs, the environment and ways in which this part of my adopted country can drag itself almost reluctantly towards a quality of life that most inhabitants of these islands take for granted. Whilst my life skills enable me to retain a sensible balance most of the time, my moods see-saw between delight and despair; the latter because those who enjoy the fewest privileges seem determined not to do anything for themselves and to be hell-bent on confusing and thwarting the efforts of anyone who tries to improve their lot.

One flaw that I see as particularly damaging consigns many to always being a day late and a dollar short. In a word it is "grudge", an inbuilt persistent resentment that often allows even minor disagreements to result in people being ostracised and ignored for years even within families. Those who practice it tend to so blinded with hate and perceived offence that they stubbornly refuse apologies, reject the offered handshake, and turn a deaf ear to even the kindest word. I don't say I've never experienced such behaviour before I came to the Valleys, but here it is a disease that seriously affects the quality of life. There's something more, albeit far less sinister. Historical injustice has left Valley folk with an obsession for illness and disability. People positively wallow in thoughts of doom with every sniff a harbinger of pneumonia, every headache a potential tumour and every pain in the gut the threat of the big C—instead of a surfeit of beer or a dicey prawn working its way through the system! Local TV and radio follow the same dooms-ville pattern, concentrating on the bad which they repeat bulletin after boring bulletin. Where else is the late news on Monday night still telling you what the local rugby or football team did last Saturday?

I hear howls of protest at my next statement, but there is a strong vein of racism in South Wales—when it concerns the English. They'll drink with Aussies and Kiwis, party with the Irish and Scots, and even back the French or Germans against their closest neighbours. But where the English are concerned, the Welsh have more chips on their shoulders than Harry Ramsden. Journalists everywhere have always had a megalomaniacal streak, spinning delusions for the masses under the pretext of giving news, but Welsh papers are in a class of their own in their bitterness to England and the English.

These customs have no cosmetic solution, only surgery will suffice; I admit to not even being able to understand them, let alone have a solution. But both Celt and Cambrian are fated perhaps to be misunderstood by the Saxon, so maybe we should leave it there, eh? Nevertheless, I'm still in the frame of mind of believing that I have much to offer my new compatriots and I still am, thank God, full of energy and ideas for making a telling contribution. More significantly, in spite of my cynicism about that part of the Welsh character that borders on the self-destructive, I can see in so many of my new friends an awareness as to what they and their country can achieve. Their efforts are all the more meritorious because they are succeeding whilst rowing against both current and tide; I do so hope that this patronising sod—as many call me—will be around long enough to see the fruits of their labours and vision.

There, I told you that I had to get a few things off my chest. But let me put that in perspective and summarise by saying that I see the Welsh Achilles Heel being that 5% of the population are a pimple on the backside of progress for the other 95% who are as bright, friendly, hardworking, caring and forward thinking as any nationality I know. Finally, I implore the Tourist Board to play down the old myths and their language crusade, and concentrate on promoting the real attractions of this fascinating country. Welsh scenery deserves to be talked about in the same breath as Scotland and Ireland and sceptics should start by taking a drive from Anglesey to Aberdare via Port Meirion, Harlech, Barmouth, Machynlleth, Rhayader and Llanwrtyd. There's lovely—and while we're at it, let's aim for Taffy to be spoken with the same affection and humour as we treat Jock and Paddy.

As I write that I find my mind filling up with a roadmap for the next few years. But I'd be surprised if you'd be interested in that, and anyway it belongs in a quite different sort of book to what this one might be—should I ever decide to go to print. Perhaps there is another book in me, perhaps there'll be time and God will provide the energy and the spirit so that the old mind and matter continues to be interested in what is happening in the outside world. We'll see.

A Silver Lining

Was I deceived, or did a sable cloud
Turn forth her silver lining on the night?

During 2004, Milton's silver lining came to the rescue twice in quick succession to more than offset my growing sense of frustration with the deceit and flagrant dishonesty I was encountering in Community affairs. On quite different tickets as it were, Rosemarie and I were invited to two Royal events in London about which I had no inkling, making the surprise even more satisfying. The narratives tell the tales, but I must record that the shock was greatly outweighed by the feeling I had of my efforts being recognised and the gratitude I felt for those who had sought fit to champion me. Above all, I was ecstatic for Rosemarie. She'd not been there when I'd previously attended such events and now she would have the thrill of dressing to kill, meeting The Queen and other members of the Royal

Family at two world–famous addresses, and experiencing something of how the Crown is ingrained in our culture and heritage in countless ways.

There'll be those reading this who will sneer at my recollections, just as some folk seething with envy and jealousy and a dislike of anything English or Royal, have shown their displeasure. I care not a jot for their opinions; I felt honoured, privileged, proud to be British, and immensely proud of and happy for my wife who purred her way through both occasions with beauty, style, grace and inexpressible charm.

Buckingham Palace

On a bright sunny morning in June, the postman hands you a Christmas Card-size buff envelope saying, "Don't see many of them in these parts." Taking care not to deface the red E11R Buckingham Palace postmark, you open the envelope to read, "The Lord Chamberlain is commanded by Her Majesty to invite (you) to a Garden Party at Buckingham Palace…"—giving date and time.

It won't have come as a total surprise because weeks before you'll have been asked whether you would accept such an invitation if extended. Nevertheless, until the formal invitation is to hand, you'll be wondering if it will actually happen and who might have plagiarised himself or herself in recommending you. You might well utter "Thank God for that" as you remember the amount you had to shell out weeks back on a new outfit for herself "before all the new summer stock is snapped up" (she'd implored). And then there were those from whom you couldn't keep the secret; how would you have explained that you weren't after all going to take tea at Buck House if you weren't now handling a card that said so? But it has come, so you savour the moment and start planning for real; assuming of course that you count it as an honour and a privilege to be invited by your sovereign.

Not everyone does. There are some with advanced political views that are genuinely and passionately opposed to the monarchy, believing it serves no practical purpose and to be a waste of public money. When sounded out about being invited, one would expect such folk to decline, but I have never met anyone who boasted of or admitted to doing so. Then there are those whose social, political, business or financial status guarantees occasional contact with members of the Royal Family and who would not welcome mixing with *hoi polloi* at a Garden Party.

At the other end of the scale, some might decline simply because they view themselves and their circumstances as not being compatible with the splendour of the occasion; people who would not feel comfortable with dressing, acting and behaving in a fitting manner. However, experience warns me against speculating how people from different walks of life might view a Royal invitation and the occasion itself. We are each of us unique, living and moving through the social strata, belonging at different times in different categories. However clever we are, how much energy we have, and how blessed we might be with the riches of life, there are finite limits to what we know and comprehend. So this account this can only be about a Buckingham Palace Garden Party as Rosemarie and I saw it; our personal sketchy impressions wearing the blinkers of our own knowledge in recounting a very special day and event in our lives.

We've covered the invitation bit, except to say that you may never know how you came to be recommended. On previous Royal occasions I was a serving RAF officer, but the civilian list is different and to tell the truth I'm content not to know. The next pre-event hurdle is the reaction when you tell folk of your good fortune, which can range from genuine delight to frozen horror and a one way ticket to Coventry. Few social events trigger off so much envy and jealousy and, as with any awards and honours, with the possible exception of those given for bravery, there is a fair smattering of "What the hell's he ever done to deserve that?" Or, "God, there'll be no living with him now." And, the inevitable, "Who did he pay, or she sleep with, to get that?"

One gets used to being told that "The first time we went, the Royal Family were queuing up to shake hands with us". Or the lightly veiled malignity of "My mother said she'd never go again", citing the appalling lack of dress sense, the wrinkled cucumber sandwiches, or the indignity of waiting outside for the gates to open. Then that well-meaning advice guaranteed to keep you awake for nights of "It rained incessantly and ruined my hat, shoes and new dress—in spite of my £100 umbrella from Harrods." The weather is unquestionably a major factor as there is no "wet weather" alternative and one cannot shelter in the Palace. Then there are decisions as what to wear; where to stay, dress and park; how to behave if "presented"; and what medication to take to avoid being caught short or becoming a nervous wreck. Customary decisions about which camera lens and mobile phone to take are made for you—neither accessory is permitted. If such qualms seem fatuous to one who hasn't had the experience, I submit that however philosophical and laid-back one might be, it is impossible to face such an occasion without some disquiet as to the potential pitfalls and disappointments, if only because there's little chance of a replay!

We who visit London often tend to take our capital city for granted, but having visited some 110 countries worldwide, I place London without bias at the very top as the tourist Mecca. Rome has its ancient history, Paris a certain charm,

New York a tingling vibrancy, and Rio, Sydney, Hong Kong, Cape Town and 'Frisco their beautiful harbours and spectacular scenery. But no other city combines the centre of Government and the Military, with a mix of history, architecture, the arts, theatres, hotels, sporting venues, restaurants, shops, parks and ethnic enclaves to attract the famous, the notorious and the interesting.

Thus it was that at 2 p.m. on a brilliantly sunny afternoon in July, with all the decisions and much of our apprehension behind us, Rosemarie and I tumbled out of a taxi and joined the small queue at the main gate. The immediate impression was similar to joining a joyful family occasion. Everyone in the queue seemed keen to talk, exchange credentials as it were, and to be looking eagerly forward to entering this magnificent famous building around which thousands of happy tourists and sightseers were gathered. The Palace guests were excited, the crowd colourful, good humoured and well behaved, and the Police and military unobtrusive, friendly and helpfully efficient. The official photographers were having a field day, recording a special event for people who felt privileged just to be there. Buckingham Palace that day was a great place to be.

At 2.30 the gates were swung open and an orderly crowd filed past the Police checks showing entrance cards and proof of identity. A wizened Margaret Rutherford look-alike had brought her invitation card instead of the mandatory entrance card and almost swooned away before the kindly policeman quietly reassured her that she would not be sent to the Tower this time and gave her a pretty policewoman escort into the Palace. One felt that had she sinned similarly in Beijing she'd have been abruptly and rudely ignored, in Paris she'd have been led dramatically to the exit, and in Washington DC she'd have been surrounded by tall men in dark suits and spent her summer in Guantanamo Bay. Behind her, a cheerful soul from Shropshire exuberantly pulled out his card from his morning suit—and then chased the confetti of banknotes that swirled away across the pebbled courtyard in the brisk summer breeze. A proud lady in tartan garb with a Rob Roy accent, turned to wave to envious companions at the railings busily snapping away at what had become something of a fashion parade.

Now one joined another smaller queue under the arches leading to the inner Courtyard. It was a relief to be out of the glare of the sun and for many ladies to relax a little and discreetly ease their pinched toes from shoes that suited the occasion, but were not too comfortable in which to stand around for perhaps 6 hours. There followed an orderly procession across the Courtyard to the steps leading into the Palace itself and its red and gold opulence, 20 seater settees, and large portraits of serious looking ladies and gentlemen on most walls. Then out onto the patio and down steps into the garden. A glorious Arcadian scene with the white marquees bordering the main lawn and the music of two military bands blending with the excited banter and laughter of the chattering crowd as the available chairs were occupied.

Surprisingly there was little colour in the main garden, the green of the well manicured lawn contrasting with the darker greens of the high trees and, somewhat intrusively, the seven or so top floors of the London Hilton overlooking the scene. At the rear of the garden there is a beautiful lake, again with an unexpected lack of colour, but on this day the skies were blue and the sun shone brightly on a crowd now beginning to find its feet and voice and spreading its own carpet of colour across the green sward. Now was the time to watch the ladies and to admire the fashions, the hats especially, and the way the supposed weaker sex steals the show and turns the heads. Here there was elegance, there a disaster; sitting cross-legged a beauty, standing munching a sandwich a vast betoxed lump of womanhood. Those in the know took up their seats or their station along the expected two routes of the Royal walkabout, or where they would have a good view when the Royal party entered their tented enclosure.

The Queen was scheduled to arrive at 4 p.m.; it was now 3 p.m. Suddenly, around 3.20, came a flurry of activity. Tea was being served and within seconds a dozen or more queues had formed to collect their soft drinks, tea in china cups, sandwiches and sticky cakes. Another myth dispelled; the buffet was excellent and there was no need to rush as tea was still being served along with ice cream at 5.30. The mood now among the guests had changed perceptibly to that of a party spirit, almost as if the tea had been Champagne and the lemonade Pimms No1.

Then at 3.40 came that feeling that spread like wildfire amongst the crowd. It was as if a wind had sprung up to rustle the branches of the great oaks and chestnuts and flutter the feathers in the ladies hats. Something was happening on the steps. The gentlemen of the Royal Household splendidly attired in morning suits with black hats and wearing different coloured buttonholes (to indicate their duties perhaps?), were beginning to prepare two separate channels through which The Queen and other members of the Royal Family would pass. Now the jockeying for position began in earnest and many a marriage was put to the test as he or she lead the way to where he or she wished to stand. Would it be in the line where Her Majesty would walk, or where the Duke of Edinburgh would be along with Princess Anne and Prince Edward? Could we get in the front row or be stuck at the back and not see much? So many decisions—but at least it was not going to rain on our parade!

My days of rugby line-out jostling with judicious use of elbows and knees have come in handy; Rosemarie and I are right at the front and about to witness a wonderful example of how we British plan, control and manage our royal and state occasions, observing the formalities and protocols, but making the procedures friendly in an atmosphere of sophisticated social behaviour. The resulting illusion is of everything being so simple and natural, but such success derives from careful planning, attention to detail, and practice, practice, practice. The key players at this stage are the elegant gents of the Royal Household, men in their 60's and beyond who quietly and without fuss move down the lane before The Queen, ensuring that a passageway of some 5 yards wide is kept clear and no one encroaches beyond the imaginary line set by them. Whilst doing this, they engage the crowd in polite conversation and those appointed to do so select individuals or groups, seemingly at random, for presentation to The Queen.

At 4 p.m. the Royal Party appear on the patio, the National Anthem is played, and the Queen descends to make formal presentations to recently appointed Lord Lieutenants and chaplains. Then she moves down the channel to meet those being presented, and as she advances the channel behind her is unobtrusively closed by the gentlemen of the Royal Household and, one suspects, by a fair number of totally inconspicuous security staff. Overwhelmingly, the crowd is good-natured and perfectly behaved. But, as always, there are a few who must push to the front and don't mind whose feet they stand on or whose hat they knock off in so doing. Again, there is no substitute for a sharp elbow, a strategically placed thigh and a warning smile that brooks no further infiltration.

The choice now is whether to dash over and line the second channel, go back for more tea and cake, or find a comfortable seat that gives one a grandstand view of the Royal Party crossing the only roped off piece of turf en route to their tents for tea and then back to the Palace just before 6 p.m. We chose the latter, drank more tea and had a splendidly close encounter with the Queen, Duke of Edinburgh, Princess Anne, Prince Edward and sundry members of the Royal Family. I get a dig in the ribs for describing Princess Michael as "a real red-blooded woman"; whatever "they" say about her, she oozes a rare mix of arrogance, femininity and sex appeal. With me suitably chastised, we followed them slowly back to the Palace steps to a rendering of "Greensleeves", then joined in the appreciative warm applause as the National Anthem signalled the end of activities. To the strains of pastoral music, we all made our leisurely way back through the Palace to spill out into The Mall in the late afternoon sunshine, to seek the comfort of a warm bath, before dinner at The Ivy and time to reflect on a memorable day.

When it's all over, you wonder why you worried about so many things and whether you might have done things differently. You hope the professional photographer was professional and that you might appear on the video you've ordered. But then a memory of such an occasion needs no printed proof; it is something that you experienced in a very personal way, a pride and a pleasure that you felt in just being there and a satisfaction that someone had thought you deserved to be there. I've written about our day, not to preserve the experience *per se*, but to savour it and make it even more real, more visible and palpable. As I wrote earlier, Royal occasions in general and Garden Parties in particular are not everyone's cup of tea. But my pride and enjoyment at being there is reflected in Rosemarie's unbounded delight and our store of precious memories, and I'm glad to be able to share our experience with others not so fortunate to be at Buckingham Palace SW1 on July 5th 2004.

Scrubbing up well for a Royal occasion. Buckingham Palace 2004.

The Queen's Award for Voluntary Service. St James' Palace 2004.

St. James's Palace

Were I a composer or an artist, I'd be putting this on canvas or to music, both to describe and do justice to a grand occasion and to store another cherished memory. But my talents I fear are limited so I must write before the fog of everyday routine and the ticking of the clock obscure the sharpness of the events in a Royal Palace on 19th July 2004. It all came about like this.

Every year around one hundred voluntary groups throughout the UK receive The Queen's Award for Voluntary Service. The process, of which the receiver may not be initially aware, begins in the autumn of the previous year with nominations by local people. After much staffing and assessment, the organisations chosen to receive the award are advised in May that the Award of a certificate signed by The Queen and a commemorative crystal will be presented on Her Majesty's behalf by the Lord Lieutenant for the County in which the group operates. An added bonus is that the group is then entitled to use the emblem of "Unsung heroes" on its stationery etc. The full list of those fortunate enough to have been recommended and approved is published in the *London Gazette* in early June.

Whilst still experiencing the heady mixture of surprise, elation, incredulity and gratitude that someone thought you were worthy of nomination, you read the *piece de résistance*—a paragraph informing you that Her Majesty wishes to invite three representatives to a reception in St.James's Palace in July, and you are to reply whether you would wish to receive an invitation. This really is the icing on the cake, but even as you post the note saying "not arf", the practicalities begin to bite. Are we here on 19th July? Do we go by car or train, stay the night, two nights, where and how much? What on earth to wear, do ladies wear hats, is my old suit up to it? Will we meet or just see The Queen and other Members of the Royal Family at close quarters? How do we address them if presented? Do I still have a copy of *Debrett's Etiquette*? Then the most daunting thought of all; only three of your group can go, who do you ask, how should they be chosen, how will folk respond who don't make the trip of a lifetime?

In a nutshell, in June our group held a splendid presentational lunch to receive the Award from the Lord Lieutenant of Mid Glamorgan, which provided the opportunity to say thanks to our proposers, and to all those local people and organisations with which we operate. We enjoyed good coverage in the local press and the three representatives fell like ripe plums off a tree; myself, Rosemarie my wife, and our trusty hard-working Treasurer, Emily. We travelled by car on the day, stayed that night—and my old suit cleaned up well! At 5.30 we arrived chirpy as a box of birds in The Mall and joined the growing throng at the Friary Gate entrance to St James's Palace. At this stage, all is still conjecture. Is the reception to be held in the Palace itself or in the marquees outside that we saw from the road, and why are those two ladies in blue wearing hats when we're not? Other questions spring to mind about the history of this splendid building that is still the official seat of monarchy. Wasn't this where the Queen Mother lived in the latter days of her life, didn't Princess Margaret live here for a while—or was that Clarence house, and what about Prince Charles? I knew we should have read up on it before coming

In the balmy July evening, there's a cheerful intoxicating expectancy about the mood of the waiting crowd, standing in small groups with other friends who have travelled to share this event, but who will stand outside ruefully when those invited have disappeared through the imposing doors. Tourists and other sightseers look on curiously, wondering no doubt what the occasion is and whether they'll see anyone famous.

An American gent with a Texan drawl asks audaciously where he must pay to go in, and on being told that it is "By invitation only" and that invitation comes from The Queen, retorts, "Hell, don't your Royals like making money anymore?" A charming lady passing by, mistaking my slightly bemused reaction to this typically North American remark, asks if she can help. "I work here," she reveals, and kindly tells us what the procedures will be, promising us a lovely time and says she'll see us inside as she is the Royal Nurse for the event. Taxis and private cars disgorge more excited little packets of humanity including the disabled and blind, all primed with nervous anticipation. The setting is beautiful, the mood exhilarating, but above all you realise how extraordinarily friendly and helpful everyone is. There's no shouting, no quarrelling about parking, no pushing in the queue, no one dropping litter, no boisterous yobs and even the taxi drivers talk nicely to their passengers and never hoot their horns. If only we could bottle this and take it home!

5.45 p.m.—and those closest to the entrance start fishing for their entrance cards and means of ID. An orderly flow follows past unobtrusive security into an imposing wide corridor; a distinct buzz stemming from interest in the Palace décor and plush red and gold interior, but above all a cheerful friendliness of folk just feeling privileged to be there. Next up the green staircase with the ladies pointing to the furniture and tapestries and the ceilings with curves and coves in gold leaf, and the magnificent chandeliers. On into the Gun Room, walls emblazoned with the weapons of mediaeval warfare; swords, pikestaffs, pistols and body protection of a bygone age when fighting meant man-to-man conflict and almost certain death from even minor wounds. From there into the three main rooms on the first floor overlooking the garden that we are told was so beloved by the Queen Mother. Sighs of relief that we're not en route to a marquee as feared when we see a set of tables groaning under the weight of glasses containing water, orange juice, white wine, scotch and gin and tonic—with ice and lemon, of course. Somewhat surprisingly we are to find that these beverages are served throughout the evening, borne skilfully on silver trays by a team of footmen who always seem to be on hand with a top up or a new glass, and later on with trays of delicious bite-size crudités.

The middle room again is a riot of crimson and gold with a number of huge portraits around the walls. One is of a Monarch dressed in his regalia, which painting one of the Household staff points out contains a fair amount of artists license in that a mere mortal could never have worn all those garments, medals, and regalia at the same time without sinking to his knees under the weight. The Throne, a truly beautiful piece of furniture that looks surprisingly comfortable for its size and shape, dominates the third room at one end and is crowned by a huge canopy of sumptuous gold braid and tassels complementing the red of the silken damask walls.

And then one of those cameos that made this occasion so special; a member of the Queen's Household takes a young blind man to the throne and lets him see it in the only way he can by running his hand over the frame and the material. Beside him, his trusted friend, a black Labrador, lies passively on the scarlet carpet with kindly head resting on golden feet. Oh for a camera.

At the far end of the throne room is a small door through which we are informed Queen Elizabeth II, the forty-second sovereign of England, will soon emerge. Purely by chance we have positioned ourselves advantageously and are soon joined by the first folk destined to be introduced—the disabled, the blind and a handful of other groups that have been selected apparently at random to be presented. Our threesome places bets on what colour the Queen will be wearing. Rosemarie plumps for pink, Emily says pale green, and I say blue.

Whilst waiting, I seek information from Vice-Admiral Tom Blackburn, Master of the Household, as to how the Royal Party will circulate amongst the guests. He gives me a simple answer: "They will all circulate amongst you in every room until 8 p.m. It is a party given for you; just enjoy yourself as will they." Another affable and erudite chap reminds us that this palace was built by Henry VIII and that it became known as a raucous place of ill manners and debauchery, particularly under Queen Anne. It seems out of place in this very grand building and in an air of such dignified gentility, to hear that Anne's claim to fame was her unseemly appetite for food and drink that resulted in frequent embarrassing bodily noises for which her courtiers reluctantly accepted responsibility! A sort of, "Have that one on me, your Majesty."

The gold-leafed clock in the throne room has moved on to 6.15. By now all the guests, some 252 we are told, are spread evenly through the three spacious rooms. There is ample space to circulate; none of the jockeying for position that typifies a larger gathering or one where constraints are imposed by rank and status. One is conscious of a unique atmosphere that our hosts generously attribute to their guests all being "Volunteers", intimating that label to signify a certain level of behaviour, which I found most complimentary. A professional photographer is doing his bit and everyone seems keen to talk to everyone else. Typical of the thoroughness, we have all been given a small booklet with the names of Groups and individuals, plus our personal nametags. I speak to a group from Stockport who support the restoration of a grade 2 listed cinema; Rosemarie chats to a man from Weardale who provides water-based activities, and Emily to another group from Wales that provide riding facilities for the disabled. I look around me and feel enormously privileged to be there in the presence of my Sovereign, and also with so many of my peers who give much of their lives for others.

The wine has now been flowing for 30 minutes and the excited chatter has become a laughter-filled cacophony as we await The Queen's arrival. I'm sure that the atmosphere would have been just as buoyant had we all been drinking milk, but there is no doubt that when Her Majesty, unheralded, entered the throne room, she created an immediate aura, a sense of occasion, a charisma *par excellence.* Although there was at first a respectful hush, the atmosphere was electric. I was wrong about the colour; Her Majesty is in a muted pink silk chiffon dress set off by diamonds and pearls. Rosemarie squeezes my arm in delight and Emily whispers in awe "Isn't she beautiful" as The Queen, accompanied by David Blunkett in his capacity of Secretary of State for the Home Department, stops immediately in front of us. The black Labrador that sat by the throne makes friends with David Blunkett's guide dog and tails begin to wag furiously. "I do hope that's all right," quips the Queen to a round of spontaneous laughter. As The Queen and Prince Philip move deeper into the room, we move into the middle room and immediately meet the Duke of Kent who shakes our hands firmly and asks where we're from and what we do. He takes a special interest in what we say about overcoming apathy and about current trends in vandalism, and looks you straight in the eye as he talks whether the matter is a serious one or said in party spirit. If that sounds unimportant, I can only tell you that I have met many famous and infamous people all over the world who are so busy looking over your shoulder at someone else they wish to meet, that they never make eye contact and barely listen to what you're saying.

As the Duke moves on with a cheery remark, we are joined by Prince Philip looking shorter than one expects but with those piercing eyes and ready grin that at once put you at ease and able to talk freely. He has a reputation for not being much interested in small talk and I am wary of slipping into boring mode, so easy to do when trying to make the most of a fleeting encounter. But he asks if we're enjoying ourselves and we comment on how wonderfully effortless and well organised it all is; yet so laid back and relaxed. He laughs and mutters something about "enough practice" and picks up on a reference to keeping our patch free of rubbish. "You've solved the rubbish problem in Wales," he jests. "Better come to London—we need you."

We then meet Her Majesty's Lady in Waiting who, as well as keeping an eagle eye in the direction of The Queen, takes time to tell us something about the Palace and its recent history. She comments on The Queen's amazing energy and resilience in having so many formal and social commitments and meeting so many people, all of whom wish to engage her in conversation. She admits that she doesn't know how the Queen does it, but she does do it so successfully that all who meet her know that they have been in the presence of greatness, yet have been with a friend. She tells us that this function is normally held in Buckingham Palace, points out a seat by the window where the Queen Mother would often sit, and is just telling us that she is travelling by train with The Queen the next day to the Royal Welsh Show at Builth Wells when The Queen moves to our group of three. It is testimony to the informality of the occasion that it seemed perfectly natural for her to join us in that casual way. I bowed from the neck and shook lightly the proffered royal hand. As The Queen looks beyond me to Rosemarie and Emily, my two lady companions curtsey in unison beautifully—as if they do that every day.

The Queen asks where we come from and what we do, taking greatest interest it seems in what we said about our local problems of vandalism and drugs threatening our young people. She says how valuable is the contribution of volunteers and encourages us to keep up the good work. She puts us all at ease so naturally that it didn't seem at all out of place for Emily (who's never been to London, let alone seen the Queen) to say, "Excuse me, your Majesty, may I say what beautiful eyes you have." The Queen thanks her for the compliment and laughs engagingly in a way that I recall when I first saw her and heard her laugh at the RAF College in Cranwell in July 1947 when she was 20 and I a mere lad of 17.

Rosemarie, with her wonderful eye for style and grace and fashion, is immensely impressed by The Queen's perfect complexion, immaculate hair, and eloquently gracious hand movements. (Things my mother taught me, eh?) Had the party ended there as The Queen moved away smilingly, we would all have been more than pleased and content with our lot—but there was more to come. As we stood by the window, feeling the cool evening breeze, surveying the tranquil garden and quaffing yet another cold gin and tonic, we were joined by the Duchess of Gloucester dressed in a pale beige skirt and a sequined top overblouse. There followed five fascinating minutes or so of relaxed dialogue with the Duchess expressing her very firm views and taking a keen interest in what we had to say about our work and how we tackled the problems. Some of our most important issues are not the stuff of which parties are made and I remind myself that this is a party and not a workshop. But the Duchess—dazzlingly attractive—is a great listener and conversationalist, and as her lady in waiting whisks her away we look at each other joyfully and marvel at how magical has been our evening.

We stand absorbing the relaxed informal atmosphere, collecting our thoughts and savouring our Royal palaver when we glimpse Princess Alexandra moving into the middle room. This time—I admit it—I make a beeline for her, as I know how much Rosemarie wishes to meet her. As a girl, her looks had often been compared to the Princess and I knew that to talk to her would be the crowning moment for Rosemarie. Remarkably we cross the room without being ambushed; the Princess turns to greet us; tall, slim, and elegant in a gorgeous ivory and gold cocktail suit matched perfectly by tasteful jewellery that made one's eyes glisten. That is Rosemarie's description; mine would be simpler—exquisitely beautiful and feminine. But even that impression was eclipsed by her personality; she positively radiated intense and unfazed enjoyment in where she was and what she was doing. We spoke, laughed, joked and put the world to right for around six minutes. It was like standing in a warm breeze on a hilltop, refreshed and bubbling over with life.

It was 8 p.m., the party was over, but truly for the Fernhill trio "our cup runneth over". We unashamedly savoured every last moment and were amongst the last to leave. The Palace staff with perfect manners and good humoured tolerance answered our departing queries, replenished our glasses, and made us feel they'd enjoyed hosting us at one of the best addresses in the country and in the most exclusive organisation in the world. We took a last and longing look at the red and gold grandeur that represented a huge slice of English history and took our vivid and precious recollections out into the warm summer evening and the exciting bustle of a great city. After the famous people with whom we'd been privileged to share a few hours, and the wonderful company of our volunteer friends, we opted against joining the rich and famous clique at The Ivy and dined at our favourite Greek restaurant to reflect at our leisure on our second truly incandescent experience in two weeks.

Epilogue

I can't say whether I'll have the time, energy or motivation to expand on these memoirs—we'll see. But for now I'm going to pull the curtain down on this part of the show and hope you've found something to arouse your interest, passion or amusement. I hope too that I might have thrown more light than heat on things outside your own experience; and I'll even take the odd touch of pity as a compliment! I am particularly conscious of the fact that I will have left my reader often dangling in the air where I have related a story to my satisfaction, but not to his or hers. I may not have been able either to record the opposite view or the view as seen from a different angle. I will certainly have puzzled some about my tales of when the world was simpler and values so different. I will have been too heated to be objective on occasions, too set in my mind to have acknowledged that the opinions and views of others were worthy of consideration.

But then, that's life, isn't it? So many of us live such busy lives that once something is passed, however cruel and painful, we tend to let it sink to the depths of our memory and get on with today's living. I also know that there are a few (could be many, I dunno) who would be highly critical of what I've written, just as they were critical of what I did, albeit seldom to my face. Criticism is easy; achievement is the difficult bit. I've tried to stay honest in the time that I've had and in my present frame of mind and circumstances. This might have been a different story had it been written in 1983 when I left the RAF, and it could be different again if I survived to pen it on my 80th birthday. Who knows and who cares, eh? This is my story; others can do as they wish.

Robbie Burns knew a thing or two when he remarked, "Oh the gift that God had gi'e us, to see ourselves as others see us." And I wonder how many times in our lives we have felt the niggling fear that John Denver expressed in one of his many poignant lyrics:

> *The face that I see in my mirror*
> *More and more is a stranger to me.*
> *More and more I can see there's a danger*
> *Of becoming what I'd never thought I'd be.*

I've often found it difficult to end a letter, a service paper or an article; this tome is no different. I've enjoyed writing it so much, it has given me a little pain but enormous pleasure, but now it is finished, up to date, I've arrived. There's nothing "final" about it. I'm not solemnly facing my own mortality or about to pop my clogs (that I know of) but I'm pretty sure that I should quit whilst I'm ahead. I'm persuaded to put it that way because of late I've begun to comprehend what my Dad meant the day before he died when, seemingly in perfect health and happy, he said, "I've had enough, Kel." Had I been tuned in to his frequency, I might have heard him telling me that he'd seen enough, heard enough and knew enough before "leaving for new affections and sounds".

It's not like me to be depressed over anything for very long. But lately I've become disenchanted with those with whom and for whom I've been working closely since my retirement. I'm fed up with the constant bickering, the underhandedness; with the jealousy and envy shown by those who seldom put their heads above the parapet yet criticise the actions of those who do. Astonishingly, that has recently included me being morally blackmailed by people in high places with whom I've clashed in trying to improve the lot of folk in these valleys. I'm dismayed at a culture that claims the young need no guidance or discipline, at the way our Government cleverly evades the drug menace, and the way it avoids noticing the creation of an underclass more distanced from the privileged and wealthy than ever before.

Looking further afield, I recently watched the News bulletins 10 days after the 2005 *Tsunami* in SE Asia. Instead of horror and dismay at the appalling human misery being my prime emotions, I'm appalled that the greatest natural disaster in modern times has already sunk to becoming a media shop window for reporters and broadcasters to display their vocabulary and acting abilities. I find myself cynically eyeing the sudden US interest in countries they've hitherto ignored and suspect that there isn't a spare hotel room in Singapore, Jakarta or Bangkok as the vultures and hyenas gather ready to gobble up every scrap of the commercial spoils of regeneration and rebuilding.

Could it be that the high passion of my youth, that certainly lasted until my early 70's, has now turned to irreversible cynicism? Has the rawness and brutality of the 21st century done that, or is it aided and abetted by my body refusing to do what I'd like it to continue to do? Is my mind failing to keep abreast of new technology, unable to accept new ideas without relinquishing the old and proven values of honour, integrity, manners and civilised behaviour? More to the point, now that I'm getting closer to finding out what this life has been all about I realise that I'm no clearer on that score than I've ever been—despite my periods of earnest faith, my quest for the truth, and a deep conviction that there is something wonderful and mystical to follow. I find myself asking as a man of Old Arabia did:

> *Strange is it not, that of the myriads who*
> *Before us passed the Door of Darkness through*
> *Not one returned to tell us of the Road*
> *Which to discover we must travel too?*

Si Jeunesse Savait, Si vieillesePouvait

I was reminded recently that it's not easy for an old guy like me to remember his age; I may look 75 from outside, but inside my thoughts and feelings have aged little. A young lady that I often meet on Council business asked jestingly, "Kel Palmer, are you chatting me up?" In a way I was because I have always felt the attraction of a pretty face, a trim figure and a feminine laugh. I still do not see myself as "past it", by which I mean past having the pleasure to look upon female beauty and be moved emotionally, not lustfully. Few young folk I suspect understand the occasional longing of an old man (or old woman?); the unkind labels of "silly old fool" or "dirty old man" come all too easily to mind. No doubt the world has many old fools and dirty old men, but I claim not to be either—I simply derive so much pleasure from observing beauty and grace and being able to say, "Ah yes, I remember it well."

In one of his better moments, R. S. Thomas wrote:

> *She is young, have I the right even to name her?*
> *Child, it is not love I offer your quick limbs, your sparkling eyes; only the*
> *barren homage of an old man who time crucifies.*
> *Take my hand a moment in the dance, ignoring its slight pressure, the dry*
> *ruts of age, and lead me under the boughs of innocence.*
> *Let me smell my youth again in your hair.*

If I needed testimony to support my honourable stance, I found it only three days before my 75th birthday when I attended a late night session at the Hay Festival, chaired by Joan Bakewell. Joan was the same Joan Rowlands of Stockport High School who I dated as a callow youth and she reminded me how long it took for me to venture my first kiss! Where do we get such men? I hadn't seen Joan "in the flesh" for over 50 years, but she is locked in my head as a sassy schoolgirl from Hazel Grove rather than "the thinking man's crumpet" of the 60's or the elegant and incredibly talented lady that she is at threescore years and twelve.

The years may have wrinkled my skin, but not my soul. Enthusiasm still triumphs over worry, doubt, self-distrust and despair. My heart still receives messages of beauty, cheer, courage, grandeur and power from the earth, from my fellow man and from God. So I am 75 years young. This has been my story and I can't say what part of it was fate and how much influence I had over it. I shall find the answer soon enough methinks, but can now only marvel at the things I've seen and done, and the people I have met.

And what I wonder, in a life so rich and varied, so full and fulfilled, might I have missed? Should I be counting as one of God's gifts, the freedom from envy, the comfort of never wishing that I'd been born in another place, at another time into a different family and a different life? Earlier this year I asked myself on seeing yachtswoman Ellen McArthur being fêted for her voyage around the world, whether I would have wanted to be her. Emphatically—No; just as I wouldn't swap places with heroes of mine like Winston Churchill, Douglas Bader, Fred Astaire, Denis Compton, Alex Ferguson—or anyone of any profession or age for that matter. Can you explain why that should be? Why should I not feel envy of those who have been more successful in their professional or sporting lives, made more money, travelled more extensively, earned more respect, moved in more influential circles, made more friends, had more women craving their love and devotion? It's a puzzlement—but I'm happy for it to remain so.

A great deal of rubbish has been acquired carelessly and sticks in my mind for reasons unknown. I invite you to sift what you find useful and to let the rest float with the flotsam and jetsam of your own life. At the outset I queried whether I'd learn anything new about myself or about Life as I backtracked over 70 years. If I draw a conclusion it would be that I'm immensely grateful for having been able to live so full a life, so pleased that I made much of it happen at the right time and in the right place, and thankful that I am not sitting here in old age bemoaning lost opportunities and with passion unspent.

If I say I feel the world turning colder, that may give the impression that one's senses have dulled and that the mind has begun to lose its way and its coherence. But that is not what I am experiencing lately; the problem is that the ways of the world in which I was brought up, what I thought of as civilised behaviour and understood to be the social graces, have changed dramatically. I watch the antics of a fun-seeking crowd in the city at weekends and see a totally different attitude and mood to when I was a young man exploring the bright lights of the day with the attractions of drinking, dancing and of course—the delights of female company.

Now the name of the game is to drink too much, wear too little; be aggressive, objectionable, lewd and disgusting—with the female of the species as bad as the male. An argument over anything to do with cars is sure to become foul-mouthed, confrontational and often violent; a kick up the backside or punch in the mouth has become a bottle in the face or a knife in the ribs. All the benefits of modern education and technology have made the world more brutish instead of civilised. So it's not about it getting colder for us wrinklies, but about simply not being interested in being part of it anymore. Maybe that's what my Dad meant about having "had enough", the day before he died? Perhaps that's the conclusion we're all intended to reach to soften the blow of leaving this wonderful world?

I've also realised, later perhaps than I should have, that there are some advantages to being old. I'm not talking about the physical me; my knees and thighs remind me only too painfully of thousands of hours on a soccer pitch, and my shoulders and back echo the strains of the rugby lineout, too many overs and the marks of a flying career. But I'm not, for instance, expected to be able to work like a dingbat for 16 hours a day; I don't have a boss I must please or crucial deadlines to meet, and I can wear a pair of cords and a sweater instead of a uniform or Saville Row suit. Without pain I can discard ambitions once sacred; philosophically I accept my body cannot do things that I now find I can do without anyway! If I dislike something or somebody I can say so pointedly, tell the truth about a boring speech or a tuneless song, and be outrageous, self-centred and totally unrepentant when I offend or am brutally honest. I'll be labelled eccentric when I criticise the Prime Minister, senile when I deplore the state of English anything, and a nice old chap when I tell a girl wearing next to nothing that she has the most beautiful eyes and should insure her legs. I can get away with almost anything! Maurice Chevalier is not the only mature chap to sing, "I'm glad I'm not young anymore."

I started writing this autobiography in July 2001 on a beautiful summer day on a Cyprus beach. I'm ending it on what has been an equally beautiful summer day in July 2005, sitting in the small garden that Rosemarie and I love, with the chatter and song of the birds around us and the soothing sound of a babbling brook. We were alone then and are alone now, happy and contented with each other's company as we have been since we first set eyes on each other. I squeeze her hand to convey thoughts and emotions that my lips cannot utter for my heart is too full, but she will understand. This tale of this man's life and the people and places in it, would not have been written but for her—my true inspiration, my many-splendoured thing. Thanks Roo-what a wonderful world, to be sure.

FINIS

Repercussions and the odd regret

Assuming you've read this book chronologically, you will have noticed I oft expressed qualms about its content, format and style, and questioned my sanity for writing at all. Indeed over the four years that it evolved, I frequently amended, watered down, accentuated or obliterated the words of wisdom and witticism that flowed from my pen. I was wary of offending and misjudging others, of damning with faint praise and of omitting important events and special folk from the narrative whilst I concentrated on telling a unique story with a personal focus.

So conscious was I of the potential pitfalls that even as my final draft fell into the post box, I was wishing I'd attached a piece of string to retrieve it for further honing. I knew the odd individual would suspect I was writing about them—even though I wasn't—and I expected reactions like "Why is Palmer giving me the bum's rush? and "She didn't tell me she kept a diary!" But even so, I was surprised at the speed of response, the tendency to cry "foul" out of context, and—most remarkably—the extent to which "eye witness" accounts of the same incident could be remembered so differently. Many praised my writings, some to the point of embarrassment, others perhaps humoured me or thought "least said-soonest mended"; but it was the repercussions that had me reaching for my pen and cleaning the spark plugs of a memory engine that I hadn't expected to rev up again.

On Trial

To write a book and allow it to be reviewed is tantamount to putting one's head on a block and inviting the executioner to take swipes at it with his axe. So I always expected that by committing to paper the whole spectrum of my life experiences, I'd certainly not "win 'em all" and could even lose some. But I couldn't be sure who I might offend or from whom I might reap special praise. I should have had some clue because a homespun philosophy of mine is that whenever I've walked into a room—be it a boardroom, dining room, ballroom or crew room—I could expect 20% of the occupants to take an instant dislike to me, 20% to like me, and the other 60% to be up for grabs and for me to influence one way or t'other! We look at the way the light falls on a picture, knowing that for others it falls differently, giving a different message and leaving contrasting impressions. We hear a melody that to some conveys a galleon majestic in full sail on the ocean swell, for others a golden field of waving wheat in a frisky summer breeze, but for us a bittersweet memory of a beguiling girl we loved and lost. We are each unique with a unique set of forces playing on our lives. We play our own instrument in the orchestra of life so the music we make is unique, different and intensely personal.

So what of accusations that much of what is written in an autobiography is fictional rather than factual, perhaps even fraudulent? Many life histories are of course "ghosted" whilst many more are subjected to varying degrees of editing which raises serious doubts about their authenticity. Some sad folk believe all autobiographies to be suspect because writers, in trying to make sense of their lives, fabricate the narrative to protect themselves from that which they don't understand or from painful truths they choose not to face up to, thus going to great lengths in affecting to be something other than they are.

Whatever faults and omissions *A Roving Commission* may have, I defend it from all of the above. There was neither ghosting nor any editing of content—only of my amateurish attempts at page layout and insertion of pictures. Every word was from whatever store life has laid up for me, as was every chapter or paragraph heading, the title and the cover features—if not the design. I told the story of parts of my life just as I remembered it, with no thought of trying to blot out the unpalatable or to exaggerate that which was already good and honourable. It took longer to write than I anticipated, probably because my initial intention was to tell only a love story. What started as merely a good idea on a Cyprus beach in 2000 evolved over four years as I opened up a rusty memory bank and allowed my mind to become more responsive and ultra sensitive to the world about me. In this I was aided by a proven medical fact that the brain performs much like a muscle; it improves by being used rather than its powers of retention and clarity—as I was led to believe—deteriorating with age. Thus I was able to tune in to the frequencies of my youth and look more carefully and analytically at parts of my life that I'd rushed through without noticing because my eyes were more on the future instead of savouring the present. I even asked myself how many messages people have sent me in my life, and how many of them have I missed? A fruitless frustrating exercise in one's advanced years, but oh what flights of fancy it can launch.

The words were mine, and to think them, pen them and type them, I had to be alone and undisturbed. Not for me the mad clatter and chatter of a busy office or house, full of voices, noises and music. Not for me the distraction of TV, mobile telephones or barking dogs; even the kindly cup of tea brought silently by Roo, could upset a train of thought or confuse the new text gathering itself to burst from my eager fingertips. I did not, as one sniper inferred, simply sit down one afternoon and pour the contents off the top of my head into the script. Neither did I gather material by researching what others had done whilst I sat comfortably in my den. If I recounted an experience, I was there, I did it myself, saw it with my own eyes, knew the joy and pain, and felt grateful, disappointed or fulfilled.

I wouldn't presume to claim that every incident happened exactly as described, at the time and in the sequence given, but there is nothing invented. I told my story as it seemed to me and in the words that sprang to my pen. An added bonus from haunting the libraries and secondhand book shops was the realisation of how lucky I was to be an author in 2006 with the technology to hand for writing, amending, copying and printing. I marvelled at how great writers of old ever produced their works when all they had was a dodgy quill, poor quality writing materials and one copy that they must have had to treat like gold dust. I'm surrounded by floppy discs and sexy equipment that I still can't use properly!

Most of my thoughts were mulled over *ad nauseam* over many months; flashes of inspiration that remained unaltered were few. Sometimes to check facts, sometimes to seek encouragement and gauge reactions, I would read a passage to Rosemarie or to my colleagues in the Writers' Circle. But they gave me no words and had no direct impact on what I wrote. I also chatted to hardened writers, both failed and successful, and haunted the libraries to be as sure as I could of not misrepresenting myself. I was happiest writing alone with my own thoughts; writing about my experiences and about what happened in my mind and in my heart. All unique and intensely personal.

I was apt to say when penning accounts that others viewed differently; "This is my version, you have every right to compose your own.". I am what I am, so I wrote and I sang and I painted what I am. I am what my experience, my environment and my heredity have made me, for better or for worse. We are often advised to "find ourselves and be ourselves", and a wise man wrote encouragingly:

> "If you can't be a highway, then just be a trail
> If you can't be the sun, be a star;
> It isn't by size that you win or you fail—
> Be the best of whatever you are."

Would you believe that having played accused, Judge and jury at my own trial, I'm pondering now whether to stick out my neck again to pen a sequel based on repercussions received to *A Roving Commission*? I'm starting with a few ideas, quite sure that if I don't force or rush the process, the messages will gradually and insidiously seep through from all points of the compass for me to suitably frame and present. I can't forecast how this new venture will turn out; how will my thoughts be influenced and which Me will be dominant? It cannot be another, or even a continued, autobiography. I need a new format that might be more fictional than factual. Writers far more experienced than I will attest that an author very quickly becomes a stranger to the book he recently wrote—in the way that a couple once passionately in love may meet in later life and view their tempestuous times calmly from the safe harbour of time and other influences.

So I don't intend to retract that already written, but I have become conscious of many corridors unexplored and many doors unopened in my mansion of life's memories. I propose to take a closer look there just as I promise myself to take a more objective view about my chosen country of residence and its people which, in trying to get across my true thoughts and not wanting to dilute the previous 70 years, I may have misrepresented and undersold. I cannot deny that it's tempting to respond to specific criticisms received and perhaps even to speculate on what could have happened had I taken the right fork in the road instead of the left. However, the latter would not be truly autobiographic and the former might get me in trouble with libel or the Data Protection Act.

Proportionality

I'll settle therefore for responding to those repercussions that surprised or confused me since I've not yet trained myself—as a writer—to be no more affected by censure than by praise. In response, I'm about to call on the word "proportionality" which I'm not even sure is a recognised word. I am however sure that it's one I've learned to distrust, because it is now often used to excuse someone from not being able or willing to meet their obligations. For instance, when that admirable body The Charities Commission call it into play, they mean they do not have sufficient human and financial resources to deal with all the problems that emanate from their thousands of charitable organisations. In practice, that means that if you're a little guy with a small budget living in a backwater, it doesn't matter if your problem is destined to wipe you out; proportionality means you'll be left to sink and those that leave you to do so can rest with a clear conscience, having acted proportionately.

It's also a word the Courts use when meting out punishment, which so often results in a burglar getting a few hours Community Service having "only stolen £50 your honour", whilst his aged victim has been reduced to a nervous wreck who hides behind locked doors and lives in constant fear of a repetition. "Proportionate" does away with "justice", and is another word for "tick-in-box"; giving the illusion of action without actually doing anything. However, as the advice goes, "If you can't beat 'em, join 'em."

So I'm about to employ "proportionality" to defend against the odd inference that I may have used a touch of embroidery in the telling of my life story. For everyone who doubted my UFO experiences, believed my Mau Mau account a fabrication, my midnight swim off Aden an Arabian tale, and my ghostly encounters mere hallucination; there were a dozen who told me of similar experiences, suspected I was actually holding back from telling all, wished they'd been there, and suggested I be more dramatic in the telling. For each sly dig that I'd over-egged my prowess on the sports field, converted something ordinary to extraordinary, and was mistaken or had even lied about who said what, to whom and when; there were many who reminded me of lurid detail that I'd omitted, teased me for being too modest, and suggested I should have been more brutal about the conduct of others. "Proportionately"—the doubters and cynics jot up to about 5% of those who commented. I can live with those proportions.

My children

I was blessed and enormously privileged to have four wonderful children; their opinions of their Dad and what he'd written, clearly meant more to me than whatever anyone else had to say. One or more of them expressed concerns when they saw the book on the net before I'd warned of its imminent release. I stated in the preface that I'd no ambitions of going to print, and later as the book took shape, merely believed it might have merit posthumously. Even so, I vowed not to discuss my previous marriage as to do so might cause pain by opening up wounds slow to heal after prolonged divorce proceedings. Defending myself without legal aid, I had found some of those proceedings difficult to follow as a team of professional experts concocted a fantasy. A phantom is much harder to kill than a reality, and if I as a key player couldn't unravel the tangled web, what chance would anyone not intimately involved have of being able to pierce the mysteries of a marriage, visualise the pain that painted its lines on the faces of the antagonists, and then judge fairly and pardon with love?

The concern of my offsprings was not that I was critical of my ex-wife *per se*, but by telling how my life was led I could cause her more pain. I appreciated where they were coming from and applauded their loyalty, but my wife would tell you—as she told many others—exactly what she believed I had done and was doing. For many years my children had heard her side of the story, but not mine; neither were they at the numerous Court hearings .I've paid my dues for that biased and jaundiced portrayal by being partially ostracized and losing touch with most of my grandchildren. I don't want more pain so I'll stick to my vow not to discuss this further in this book. There is another book just for Cherrie, Kel, Chris and Lori Sue when I'm not around from which they'll know—as they should have since the days they were born—that no father ever loved his children more than this one did and does. Regret for the things we do is tempered by time; regret for the things we did not do, is inconsolable.

RAF Colleagues

RAF folk being what they are, I anticipated many comments with some corrections of fact and some good-natured ribbing. Most were very complimentary, but a few had me scratching my head and inwardly blaspheming. The first, from an ex-Buccaneer pilot, astonished me as I'd forgotten his name, having only flown with him once when converting to that aircraft at Honington. Having said he enjoyed the book, he felt it his duty to remind me (in 2006) that his assessment of my performance (in 1975) on a high/low navigation/bombing exercise, included: "He [me] was so unsure of where we were, that he asked me to bank the aircraft to get a visual fix." He hadn't raised that criticism at our debriefing, and I only saw his report months later. What he couldn't know was that Rosemarie and I, as an item, were then very much a secret. But had he been open in his critique I could have explained that before take-off I'd made an assignation, by phoning Rosemarie then living in Grimsby, to say that at precisely twelve noon, I'd pass directly over her garden and "waggle my wings".

In truth, my navigation and airmanship skills that day were so "poor" that we took off from Honington, climbed for transit before descending into the Welsh low level routes, out over the Irish sea, into the Scottish low level circuit down in the weeds, via two bombing runs at Tain Range in the Moray Firth, back through the east coast clag until climbing to 10K around Flamborough Head, to arrive after a hectic 1 hour and 52 minutes flying over Roo's back garden at precisely twelve noon! Doubtless he raised many a chuckle recounting his story about a doddering old Wing Commander losing his bearings, but it shows how easily we can all be led into reaching the wrong conclusions. Or maybe for 31 years he had harboured another reason to take a swipe at me?

My second "blast from the past" was also unexpected because I thought the writer was dead! I recall the tale being told midst hoots of laughter in a Singapore bar that the gentleman concerned had parachuted during a Jungle Survival course—and landed on his head. He'd somehow got his legs caught up in his rigging (he was notorious for leg overs) and had hit *terra firma* upside down at a high rate of knots. Still much alive, however, he corrected my account of a 23 Squadron party in Malta in 1963, first by revealing the name of a lady to whom I'd given a pseudonym, and then claiming that it was he who mixed the volatile Red Eagle cocktail that memorable evening. I was only too pleased to give him the credit, but reminded him that whilst I had kept a discrete silence over that episode for 43 years, he came back to the bar from Valetta to reveal his outrageous stories concerning his female conquests that night. Ones that stick in the mind include his sly use of foaming alka seltzer tablets in lieu of contraceptive pellets, and his nasty habit of passing on his embarrassing itch to his unsuspecting ladies of the night. I have to give him some credit however. Young unattached officers in those days played a cruel game called "grimmers". Participants assembled in the bar and set out to pick up female partners that they then brought back to the Mess. The officer with the grimmest/ugliest partner won whatever prize was on offer. Our uncouth teller of crude rude tales invariably won the "Grimmers" prize!

Next, the one comment to which I was forced to deliver a stinging response. An unpopular stratospherically-senior ex-officer phoned to object to my mention of a doomed RAF project believing I was criticising him in some way. I wasn't—he wasn't involved as I recall—but he banged on so arrogantly and caustically that I was obliged to point out that had I wanted to mention him in my book it would have been the night I came across him in the Billiards Room of a darkened Officers Mess, playing a pivotal role without a cue with a strange lady wearing little more than a smile! For every page that was printed, another hundred ended on the cutting room floor. It might be fun to resurrect some one day—but as I keep repeating; this is not a revenge trip or an ego trip—just an account of my life as best I can tell it.

I got it wrong

In 2006, I was obliged to do a spot of heart searching after I attended a Squadron reunion that included both old guys and current squadron members. I tentatively accepted the offer to mention my book at the AGM, which drew considerable interest from my generation and veterans, but was coolly received by the 1980's onwards blokes and ignored by the present squadron members. Allowing for the "not invented here" grounds that bedevil many initiatives, I was disappointed that today's airmen were so engrossed in *the now* that they couldn't spare a few moments for *the then*. But as the wine flowed at our splendid dinner, and talk centred on the antics of those who flew Mosquitoes and the early Vampires, Venoms, and Meteors, I realised how little I thought at the time of my predecessors and how critical we young bloods were of some of the wartime guys who became our bosses. They'd come through a war, suffered all the dangers and family trauma, and were trying to adapt in their late 30s /early 40s to a very different air force with new technical challenges—when what they really needed was a rest.

With anguish I remembered how I thought of one Wing Commander as a wimp who hated flying at night, a Squadron Leader who seldom led his squadron in the air but travelled to detachment bases in the transport aircraft, and another who was a jovial buffoon whose navigators always seemed to go sick after a couple of trips. Imagine my chagrin when in researching for mine, I came across their names in a book of wartime "aces". I read that my "wimp" was a special mission's pilot for years dropping and picking up agents in Europe in all weathers in a flimsy single-engined piece of plywood. My reluctant "leader" was in the top three for night fighter kills—not for him "the milk runs" I'd imagined; and my "buffoon" boasted many Mosquito kills and had a reputation as a brave and brilliant fighter pilot who outshone many more famous than he. The CO of our Apprentice Wing in 1948 seemed a remote and aloof man who seemed disinterested in what his teenage brats were doing. We knew nothing of his Spitfire exploits and that he'd been terribly burned and spent years recovering. We see things according to our experience and prejudices, for which "we have to be carefully taught". The result is that we don't see things as they are, and we make mistakes when we are not dealing or able to deal with the facts.

"Birds do it; bees do it—even educated fleas do it!"

I also collected the odd bloody nose for my liberal references to the fair sex. That was predictable I suppose, but all the objections came from men and I guarantee that if any of my fair sex "mentions" read the book, not one will feel uncomfortable. I see no harm in recalling a treasured letter that releases the perfume of an old love, calls up the touch of a vanished hand or the lilt of a voice now still. Older men like to talk of past loves, especially those that have caused them no pain. They will speak fondly of lasses that held their attention briefly, caressing their names affectionately to signify there was no residual regret. There are a very few names that I would decline to mention. But others that never glimpsed my soul or left an ache in its inner depths did figure here and there to bring a smile and a memory of a passing infatuation. I can truthfully say nevertheless that, be she a queen or a lady-in-waiting, there never was a girl who stirred my interest whose name and smile I can't recall. I don't know if people today might think of that as honourable and decent, but any man who has walked those fields of gold in love or admiration of a fair lady will surely know the feeling that betters or matches anything else this world has to offer. A sad commentary perhaps of today's *nostalgie de la boue*, is that any mention of a relationship with the opposite sex, assumes that it starts and ends in bed—usually the first night! Gone are admiration, flirting, holding hands, wooing, courting and even kissing. Young men of my time—which I insist *was* a better time—were therefore apt to proclaim that "The chase is better than the kill" whilst chaste young damsels who said No really meant Hell No, and were respected for that—and frequently married for that!

Civil War

The only part of my book about which I felt uncomfortable concerned Wales. In a misguided impulse to mention my transition to retirement, a few burning resentments and passionate dislikes led me to disregard so much that is good about The Principality. Most critics did what I expected any proud Welsh person to do—call a spade a bloody shovel; an approach I applaud. But not surprisingly, there was a minor uprising by the lunatic fringe that wear a chip on their shoulders about anything English and that very vociferous minority who are unprincipled scroungers and wasters.

Doubtless it occurs elsewhere in the UK, but it is the first time that I've encountered able-bodied people who do no work, have no intention of working, and who live without guilt or shame on state benefits. They are the same folk who will not observe the rules of our society, do little to help their neighbours or preserve the environment, and who seem content to allow their numerous children to follow in their miserable footsteps. But my dislike goes deeper than the disgust of watching them evade all work and responsibility when they have the gall to ally and compare their chosen way of life with the miners and steel workers that lived in these valleys in the 1800s and 1900s.

I knew mining and heavy industry communities in Lancashire in my youth and I visited the Welsh valleys when they were black, grey and rusty red with visibility measured in yards. Rows of small grey houses stacked up the hillsides and behind them, black slag heaps like obscene boils. Dominating every town were smoking chimney stacks, the huge shaft wheels, blackened rivers and noisy dirty railways. Down the narrow streets straggled groups of men and boys; those sullen and weary as they came off shift barely noticing those clean and pale-faced about to go on shift. I came from the great industrial city of Manchester, where one lived in almost perpetual smog, with rain that seemed to lie in the atmosphere rather then fall from the heavens. But the Valleys environment was something different—a virtual hell on earth.

So my blood boils when I hear these modern wastrels claiming affinity with those miners of old because the Welsh miner might have looked like a savage at times, but in essence was a proud sensitive gentleman, mild mannered and polite, cultured, and with a mental curiosity that led him into all sorts of hobbies and pastimes. I find that perfectly understandable for someone who worked extremely hard for long periods in a dark strange and dangerous world. When he emerged into light, he wanted to use the active mind that had been locked in the dark for hours. So he'd follow the Welsh passion for music, read to improve his mind and his knowledge of a world he'd never seen, or learn a trade such as carpentry or fretwork—or simply make the most of his time in the fresh open air with his pigeons, greyhounds or bird watching pursuits. His home might be sparsely furnished, but there'd always be food on the table, the curtains would be snow white, and the outside step would be "slagged"; or clean and shining with what my mum called "red raddle". There'd be little income, but appearances had to be kept up. Hard work, pride, family values, sacrifice and honesty were the keynotes in the life of a miner's family. How dare the lazy foul-mouthed scroungers of today claim to be of the same fraternity!

The only other "How dare you" response I received stemmed from my criticism of the Judicial system as practiced in South Wales. What really frustrates me about that is that the Public, Local Authorities, Police and Crown Prosecution Service, all work their butts off and spend huge sums of money to put offenders before the Courts—only to be let down by the punishments meted out. OK, that's a complaint all over the UK, but what I object to most vehemently is that whenever the judicial system is criticised we are told that the judges have their hands tied and cannot do more. Who actually ties their hands; who are the "They" that fail to ensure that the ordinary British public are protected from the growing criminal fraternity? More to the point—where does the buck stop in what to most of us is clearly a secret society answerable to no one. There are folk who will tell you that our nation is not run from Westminster or Cardiff, but by "secret societies" from which *hoi polloi* are excluded by an accident of birth and inherited wealth. I've avoided taking that extreme view and yet my experience in the voluntary sector since 2000 has convinced me that we do not truly live in a democracy, but in a benevolent dictatorship. (You might say that—I couldn't possibly comment)

Have grudge, must travel

And finally, the contents of a message that arrived in my mailbox from Texas spitting, twisting and writhing like a rattlesnake caught by the tail. Perplexed, I searched for the originator's name and my memory as to how I might have ruffled her feathers. In a nutshell, Cindy from Waco had homed in on my traveller's tales that spanned the book and said I couldn't possible have visited all those places; *ergo* I must have assembled my knowledge from books and films. She said that since husband Carroll had died, she'd been taking three long ocean cruises every year and was writing a travel book of such scope that I gathered it would make H.V. Morton seem like a recluse, and my experiences little more than the extended use of a penny platform ticket!

My first impulse was to E-mail "Sod off, rude letter follows". But then I realised that my memoirs, instead of informing with interest, had provoked her. When one goes to an exotic place, your friends and colleagues are not only rife with jealousy that you went there, but deeply regret that you came back. So I opted to pour oil on troubled waters and encourage her to spend poor old Carroll's legacy wisely by treating every trip as an adventure, as a journey into the future and a quest for happiness.

Whenever someone shows interest in my travels, my tendency is to leap first to my favourite spots, which are often the most spectacular. But I knew that Cindy and Carroll had "done" most of the world, albeit first class, stateroom and five star. So I got my dig in about not needing an ocean liner or a 747. In this neck of the woods, I boasted, I simply had to point my beat-up old jalopy at the lanes and byways of England, or weave my way twixt the mountains and lakes of Scotland, Ireland and Wales; explore an English river bank, lie in Scottish heather, or gaze up at a Celtic sky or down at the coastline of this jewel set in a silver sea. I can leave the beaten track, discover quaint little villages bypassed by the 21st century, go back into history, explore legends and folklore, talk to the well-heeled and the down-at-heel, or just pat the horses and feed the ducks. Nowhere in this wonderful world can I find more variety, history and captivating consummate beauty than in our British Isles. With Cindy being one of those Texans that would tell you that the highlight of her trip to Venice or Rome was finding a place that served barbecued beef and corny dogs, washed down with "bourbon and branch", I suspect my romantic version of an essentially arcadian Britain probably got lost in mid-Atlantic!

To make Miss Dallas 1959 feel better, I explained that 95% of my travel was done either in the RAF or in the defence industry—so someone else was paying the bills that mattered. Not by any means did I always go where I would have chosen to go; and that of course was part of the fun, some "never again" experiences—but many pleasant surprises. So I asked her why, at her ripe old age, she was about to spread her wings. Was it merely to claim "been there, done that"; seek adventure, absorb different cultures, satisfy an interest in history or archaeology, or be better able to identify her place and importance in the order of things? I doubted if she had anything physically demanding in mind; so perhaps the sole objective could be to get away, to relax, and not challenge her mind or body for a short time. Her response was that she'd waited for the perfect time and did I think this might be it for her?

I questioned whether there is a "perfect time". It's the old story; when young we worry about our spots, then one night the spots disappear—but the next morning your mind's gone fuzzy! I told her that the perfect time is Now; now being any time in one's life when you can make the time to travel and meet the cost. That seemed to match her present circumstances, but still in a helpful mood I asked what was the catalyst for her travel bug? Perhaps her geography teacher once struck a chord inside her wandering mind. More likely, her interest stems from the tinsel world of Hollywood where the hero or heroine has stepped out of the seething surf in Bermuda, clung desperately to the hands of big Ben or skied down the Matterhorn ahead of an avalanche wearing a Saville Row suit or a creation from Dior. One of those remarkable TV wildlife programmes may have her convinced that behind every bush in the bundhu there lies a lion, in every shipwreck there lurks a family of Great Whites, and that all the natives are friendly in Bogotá, Baghdad or Bermondsey.

Or like me, she may just like the sound of a place, associate a city with a song, or a country with an old adventure novel. For instance, my "must see" cities from boyhood were San Francisco, Kathmandu, Casablanca, Rangoon and Constantinople. (I lost interest in the last two when they became Yangon and Istanbul!) Hong Kong I associated with a love story of piercing beauty by Han Suyin and the music of "Love is a many splendoured thing", whilst the dreamy haunting lyrics of "Moon River" were Huckleberry Palmer's passport to the magic of the Mississippi. My appetite to see India was whetted by my Dad's favourite novel "Lives of a Bengal Lancer" whilst the 1939 version of "The Four Feathers" drew me inevitably to the wonders and fascinations of the Nile. The lure of Paris was a bell ringer called Quasimodo and a Phantom prowling under the Opera

House—not forgetting the Moules a L'Escargot from the atmospheric "La Grenouille Roger" next door!

Still trying to work out why she'd fired her broadside I banged on about travel being an intensely personal thing; a lottery, a case of trial and error. I admitted that's why Rosemarie and I now return to the same place every year. We've narrowed down the problems, we understand the climate, we've avoided the bugs, we know where to eat and what to drink, we're familiar with the customs and know what it'll cost us in cash and peace of mind. But—I urged her—if you've not been to those special places, not yet fulfilled your dreams, the message is don't delay, do it now. Go see whether all those places are all you thought they'd be, and if they disappoint—as many will—what the hell? You'll die happy and fulfilled knowing you followed your particular star and can be sure that if one place disappoints, there'll be another to surprise and delight you. The beauty of travel is that the experience that prints itself indelibly on your mind is more likely to come like a thief in the night rather than the outcome of any master plan. Be an optimistic traveller, not a pessimistic couch potato.

I can't be sure that my discourse had any impact, but her short sharp retort of "Travel plans on ice, breaking in new stallion" probably means that Cindy has changed her priorities to a fifth husband rather than circumventing the globe on horseback! And I thought the days of human sacrifice were over!

Quitting while I'm ahead

I suspected when I came to add this chapter on Repercussions, that I'd be as uncertain of things as I was when I wrote the first page on a Cyprus beach in 2000.I wasn't wrong. Indeed, as I've peeled the onion of my life I've become increasingly and disconcertingly aware that even in a life as full and interesting as mine, I've barely scratched the surface in understanding what it's all about. How does my version of the times I've lived through tally with those of others, and how can I verify what constitutes my memory of events? The repercussions received so far only serve to confuse me more; a few obvious hurts, some sucking of teeth, and some originating from people I barely recall and who made little impression on me. Fact or fiction, wishful thinking, artist's license—call it what you will; I have not sheltered behind any artificial fictitious character or my *alter ego. T*his is how I saw it. Everyone else has the right to pen their version—and good luck to them. In the words of the haunting melody:

> I've looked at life from both sides now
> From up and down, and still somehow

It's life's illusions I recall
I really don't know life at all.

I've travelled through the years and tried to make this a lively book that you
will have read easily and with lively interest, leaving pleasant and living recollections. Being an absolute novice as a writer, my mood since going to print has
swung between that just-before-dawn anguish of wishing I'd never revealed a
word to anyone, and enthusing later about adding some missing episodes and
clearing up possible misunderstandings. But where would that end and what
would it achieve? I do not have the time or, I admit, the interest to revise old
work and ensure that every fact and reference tallies. I'm conscious that time for
me is telescoping and where once anticipation and ambition urged it to hurry by,
I'm now pleading for it to slow down. Writing this book has helped to keep
things in perspective; in opening up the memory chest I've relived so many good
and happy times and been able to take a second and more educated look at both
friends and enemies. Perhaps in writing what I wanted to write I've left you
scratching your head, examining your own memory—and castigating mine! If so,
I'm sorry—but this is all there is.

When I've admitted to "twitching qualms of conscience", there's always been
someone to quip that if a book isn't controversial it won't have appeal. But whatever responses I've received or are still lurking in wait, I've got no scores to settle,
no grudges still festering, no secrets crying out to be laid bare, no residual bitterness. One day, I may open up more doors in my memory mansion and dig a bit
deeper into the life I led and understand why I led it as I did. If I do discover that
I've misjudged or misinterpreted, then I'll come clean and make amends. Why do
I hear alarm bells warning me that however well-intentioned that might be, I'm
likely merely to move out of the frying pan into the fire? I've learned that you can
do an awful lot of good in this world if you don't mind who gets the credit for it.
By and large, I'm content with my contribution. Thanks for listening.

"When the great scorer comes to write your name
He'll not ask whether you won or lost
But how you played the game."

About the Author

Kel Palmer is a proud Mancunian now retired and living in Wales with second wife Rosemarie. He joined the RAF straight from Grammar School, spurning the attractions of a sporting career for a technical apprenticeship leading to commissioning and flying training. Before retirement in the rank of Group Captain in 1983, he spent 17 years flying operationally in mainly the night/all-weather fighter and low level strike/attack roles, and 20 years in Staff and Flying Training tours including seven years in Operational Requirements posts in Whitehall that led directly to his second career in the Defence Industry in 1983. He has lived in all four home countries, also in the USA, Germany, Cyprus and Belgium, and has travelled to over 110 countries worldwide. He has been an accomplished and versatile sportsman, playing his last game of club rugby at 46 and of soccer at 61; an enthusiastic dancer, he is also a great lover of music and of furry friends. Since retirement from Industry in 2000, he has become intensely involved in Community affairs and youth clubs, averaging over 50 hours per week for which he received The Queen's Award for Voluntary Service in 2004.

More information at www.diadembooks.com/palmer.htm

978-0-595-39189-9
0-595-39189-3

Printed in the United Kingdom
by Lightning Source UK Ltd.
116057UKS00001B/50